LEARNING RESOURCES CTR/NEW ENGLAND TECH.
GEN   BF698.S615 1971
Personality : readings in

3 0147 0000 0582 0

NEW ENGLAND INSTITUTE
OF TECHNOLOGY
LEARNING RESOURCES CENTER

BF698
S615
1971

6B86MSJ
Southwell, Eugene

P9-DGX-850

DATE DUE

Personality: Readings in Theory and Research

Second Edition

OF TECHNOLOGY
LEARNING RESOURCES CENTER

Personality: Readings in Theory and Research

Second Edition

Edited by

Eugene A. Southwell
Indiana University, Gary

Michael Merbaum
Adelphi University

Brooks/Cole
Publishing Company
Belmont, California | A Division of Wadsworth Publishing Company, Inc.

To Kim, Dirk, Bill, Tal, and Marc

© 1971 by Wadsworth Publishing Company, Inc., Belmont, California 94002. All rights reserved. No part of this book may be reproduced, stored in a retrieval system, or transcribed, in any form or by any means, electronic, mechanical, photocopying, recording, or otherwise, without the prior written permission of the publisher: Brooks/Cole Publishing Company, a division of Wadsworth Publishing Company, Inc.

ISBN-0-8185-0003-4
L.C. Cat. Card No: 70-137501
Printed in the United States of America

1 2 3 4 5 6 7 8 9 10−75 74 73 72 71

Preface to First Edition

In bringing together this collection of ideas, observations, and facts representing what is broadly defined as the psychology of personality, we have been guided by the conviction that any serious study of this topic must include an exposure to original writing—theoretical, research, and critical. Therefore, in this volume, each personality theory is represented by three papers: first, a theoretical statement by the theorist himself; second, a research paper that either tests a hypothesis generated by the theoretical statement or illustrates a type of research that is close to the tenor of the theoretical paper; and third, a critique of the theoretical position, an alternative explanation of the research results, or a criticism of the research methodology employed.

In each chapter, our aim has been to present significant contributions to psychological thought in a format that forms a compact, internally consistent unit. Thus, we hope that the reader will gain a familiarity not only with the particular theoretical position but also with the research strategies and the inevitable dissenting opinions that enliver the scientific enterprise.

Textbooks in the field of personality theory are generally limited to discussions and interpretations of and commentary upon the various personality theorists. But because of the lack of agreement among personality theorists about the common core of facts—and because of the inherent complexity of the subject matter itself—popular theories tend to be unique creations that reflect the theorist's particular viewpoint, as well as his personal convictions regarding science and the nature of human behavior. Thus, only by reading original theoretical works can the student obtain a full appreciation of the individuality of the ideas, the particular logic, and the nuances of language that are the signature of a particular personality theorist.

In order for a theory to remain a useful member of the scientific community, it must bring order and meaning to a realm of observational data; and it should also generate hypotheses amenable to testing. This latter feature enables theories to be self-corrective in the light of new evidence, and it makes them potentially useful tools for the discovery of additional knowledge. But what is the most useful strategy in testing hypotheses is open to debate. Some theorists feel that only through rigorous statistical and experimental controls can theoretical statements be supported or enhanced, whereas others maintain that thorough observation of the organism in its social milieu is the most useful means of evaluating and elaborating a particular theoretical view. Although these positions are by no means mutually exclusive, our own bias is firmly toward the former approach, and the research papers we have included here reflect that bias.

Theory construction and research design are by no means straightforward processes. Consequently, ideas, observations, and interpretations of data are frequently open to alternative explanations. In many instances, these alternatives generate lively controversies that sharpen the alertness of the scientific community to relevant issues. Therefore, in order to highlight this facet of science, we have included critical commentaries that bear either upon the particular theory or upon its subsequent research.

It would be impossible to include in a single volume the writings of all those psychologists who have made impressive contributions to the psychology of personality. Therefore, we offer a sample of the theoretical positions that currently exert a strong influence in the constantly developing study of personality.

This book is the result of the cooperation and assistance of many people. We especially wish to thank the authors and publishers who have permitted us to use their material. Although we have modified the titles of some articles to fit the theory-research-critique format of the book, appropriate credit appears in the footnote at the beginning of each selection. We owe a special debt of gratitude to Alicia Blumenthal for her expert handling of correspondence with publishers and authors, and to Helen Vagnone for her assistance in assembling the final manuscript.

Eugene A. Southwell
Michael Merbaum

Preface to Second Edition

In the six years since publication of the first edition of this book we have attempted to evaluate its contribution to the teaching of the psychology of personality. Some of the "feedback" we have received from instructors and students has been positive; some has been negative; all of it has been constructive.

We have received favorable comment on the *theory-research-critique* format of the book. So far as we know, ours was the first readings book to make use of this format, which we have retained in the present edition.

On the negative side, we have learned that students find the research reports, which are sometimes highly statistical, difficult to comprehend. Therefore, in this second edition we have expanded our introductory material and, in particular, we have added detailed explanations of the research methodology employed.

This edition is a major revision and expansion of the 1964 volume; it reflects the changes we have observed in the field of personality theory. We have added new theorists, deleted some, and have selected research papers which will expose the student to the various kinds of research conducted in the field. The first edition contained a total of twenty-seven articles in nine chapters. This edition contains thirty-three articles in eleven chapters. We have deleted one chapter (Murphy) and have replaced the Dollard and Miller chapter with two behavior theory chapters: Joseph Wolpe and B. F. Skinner. In addition, we have added two chapters which did not appear in the first edition: Abraham Maslow and David C. McClelland. Only three chapters have remained intact, Lewin, Kelly, and Festinger, and even for these chapters the introductory material has been substantially expanded.

We hope this new edition will make a worthy contribution to the teaching of the psychology of personality. We are indebted to the authors and publishers who kindly allowed us to use their material. As in the first edition, although we have modified the titles of some articles to fit the theory-research-critique format of the book, appropriate credit is footnoted at the beginning of each selection. We are particularly grateful for the secretarial assistance of Amy Cardaras and Helen Vagnone.

Eugene A. Southwell
Michael Merbaum

Contents

Part Four: Humanistic Theory

Part Five: Cognitive Theory

Part Six: Achievement Motivation Theory

Part One

Psychoanalytic
Theory

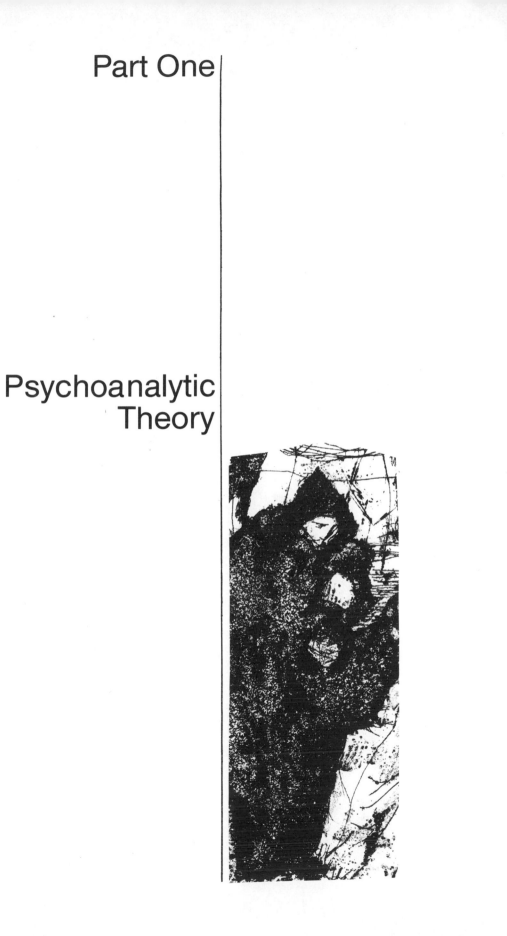

1 Sigmund Freud

Sigmund Freud (1856-1939) has so influenced the development of contemporary personality theory that one could hardly engage in a study of the topic of personality without first becoming aware of the contributions of this remarkable man. His theory, the most comprehensive yet developed, comprises a network of structural and dynamic concepts so elaborate that no single paper can fully represent it.

The first selection in this chapter is as representative of Freud as any that can be found in his voluminous writings. The paper, "Analysis of a Phobia in a Five-Year-Old Boy" (also known as "The Case of Little Hans") was first published in 1909 and occupies 147 pages in the standard edition of Freud's collected works. We have reprinted here only the "Discussion" portion of the paper, roughly the last third of it. The first two thirds of the paper, not reprinted here, consist of some introductory theoretical remarks and a detailed account of the development of Hans' fear (phobia) of horses. Serious students should read the entire paper.

The case of Little Hans was very significant because it confirmed for Freud (and his followers) the validity of the Oedipus complex and castration anxiety in the development of psychoneuroses. Freud's earlier writings about infantile sexuality were based on the psychoanalysis of adults, not children. Following his publication of "Three Essays on the Theory of Sexuality" in 1905, he asked colleagues to make available to him their observations on the sexual lives of children—an attempt, actually, to test the hypotheses set forth in the 1905 paper. Little Hans' father, a physician and close friend of Freud, began sending reports to Freud when Hans was about three years of age. At this time, Hans was expressing a strong interest in his penis ("widdler")—the relative sizes of widdlers, their function, who possesses a widdler, masturbation, and procreation (Hans' mother was at the time pregnant with Hans' sister). These reports continued at frequent intervals and were quite detailed in their descriptions of Hans' dialogues with his mother and father (especially with his father). Although the case-history portion of the original paper cannot be presented here because of its length, the reader will find an excellent summary of it in the third paper of this chapter. It is suggested that these pages be read before reading Freud's article.

The second paper, by Calvin Hall and Robert L. Van de Castle, presents an experimental test of a hypothesis generated from Freud's theory on the castration complex. The theory follows directly from Freud's earlier writings about infantile sexuality and the Oedipus complex and represents an elaboration on his "Three Essays" and "Little Hans" papers. According to the theory, males develop a fear of losing their penis (castration anxiety) while females develop a desire for a penis (penis envy) and want to deprive the male of his penis (castration wish). According to Freud, these anxieties and wishes are rarely (if ever) expressed directly in the adult, and we must discover their existence in indirect ways, such as the analysis of dreams. The Hall and Van de Castle paper presents an attempt to empirically verify the existence of castration anxiety, penis envy, and castration wishes in the dreams of male and female adults. This paper is an example of how one can go about objectively testing psychoanalytic concepts in a much different way than Freud employed when he used the Little Hans case to test his theory of infantile sexuality. The Little Hans paper could be described as a *clinical* test of Freudian theory while the Hall and Van de Castle article represents an *experimental* test. As you will see when you read the third (critique) paper in this chapter, from an objective scientific point of view the case of Little Hans leaves much to be desired as "proof" of psychoanalytic theory.

It is important, when studying the Hall and Van de Castle paper to compare its *methodology* with that of the Little Hans article. After summarizing several previous studies on the content of dreams as a function of the castration complex, the experimenters present two hypotheses to be tested in their study. Note that the hypotheses are stated in such a way that they are amenable to empirical test. That is, they are worded so that the mere operation of counting the frequency of occurrence of dream contents will provide information allowing for the confirmation or rejection of the hypotheses. Stated differently, the theory predicts that the dreams of

males and females will differ and that this difference will be spelled out with respect to the contents of the dreams. One can then go about collecting dreams, sorting the dreams into three categories (castration anxiety, penis envy, castration wish), and *quantitatively* assessing the truth or falsity of the hypotheses.

The design of the experiment is straightforward. Hall and Van de Castle asked a large number of male and female college students to record, on a standard report form, their own dreams. The instructions for reporting dreams were *standardized* for all the subjects. In research done prior to the study reported here, the experimenters had developed a dream-scoring manual. Part of that research involved determining that different scorers, following the rules for scoring provided by the manual, had a high degree of agreement in their classification of dream contents. Thus, the dream-scoring system was highly *reliable*, and Hall and Van de Castle could be confident that the assignment of dreams to categories would not be a haphazard occurrence. In other words, they could be reasonably sure that if one scorer called a dream a "castration anxiety" dream, then other scorers would do the same.

Once the dreams had been classified according to sex and content, the experimenters were ready to apply statistical tests to their *data*. These data consisted of *how many* male and female dreamers fell into the three categories of dreams. Thus, the data are in the form of numbers representing the counting of various events. The statistical test applied to these numbers (the Chi-square test) evaluated mathematically the *probability* (likelihood) that the various combination categories (e.g., males having castration dreams, females having castration dreams, etc.) would contain the amounts they contained *on a chance basis*. That is, on a random basis one would expect the same number of males as females to have castration anxiety dreams. This is the *null hypothesis*—that there is no statistical difference between males and females in terms of the contents of their dreams. The statistical test (Chi-square) is designed to test this null hypothesis, and if the null hypothesis of no difference is *rejected* (as was the case in this study), then the experimenters are obliged to accept the alternative, that there is a difference between males and females in terms of the contents of their dreams. All that remains then is for the experimenters to observe the direction of the difference between male and female dreamers and, if this is in line with their hypothesis, they can accept their results as support of the hypothesis.

As you study the "Discussion" portion of the Hall and Van de Castle article, note how the authors consider other ways of analyzing their data and how they consider alternative theories that would also predict the results of their experiment. While no experiment is an end in itself, the research paper presented here is an excellent example of the interplay among theory, research, and critique—a process that is the hallmark of the scientific method.

To explain a phenomenon in specific theoretical terms is often to invite criticism and alternative explanation. Freud's psychoanalytic theory is no exception, as is evident from the third selection of this chapter. Joseph Wolpe and Stanley Rachman attack Freud's interpretation of the case of Little Hans and present a trenchant criticism of his theoretical analysis from the standpoint of what they term "scientific objectivism." The authors are especially critical of the *method* of data collection utilized by Freud—the anecdotal reports by Hans' father (this could be called the clinical method)—and they question the scientific value of the data collected in this fashion. They question the *reliability* of the father's reports as well as Hans' testimony. In this regard it would be useful for the reader to compare Freud's method of data collection with the method described in the Hall and Van de Castle study. Recall that Hall and Van de Castle were careful to assess the reliability of the "testimony" of their dream scorers—in the Little Hans case there was *only* the father reporting his observations of Little Hans, and thus there is no way to evaluate the reliability of the father's reports. Further, in Wolpe and Rachman's analysis of the reports by Hans' father, they note that many of Hans' statements were suggested by the father; and, on two occasions, the father presented his own interpretation of Hans' behavior as "fact," thereby substantiating the assertion made by many of Freud's critics that psychoanalytic theory is "self-validating" because patients learn to report events which confirm the theory's predictions.

Following their critical appraisal of Freud's method of hypothesis testing and their conclusion that Freud's acceptance of the data as confirmation of his theory of phobia development is not warranted by the evidence, they go on to present an alternative explanation of the development of Hans' phobia, using the principles of classical (Pavlovian) conditioning.

Suggestions for Further Reading

For the student interested in Freud's life and work, the three-volume biography *The Life and Work of Sigmund Freud* (Basic Books, 1953-1957) by Ernest Jones is highly recommended. There is also a one-volume abridged edition available, published in 1961 by Doubleday, abridged by Lionel L. Trilling and Steven Marcus. An excellent paperback presentation of psychoanalytic theory is the small book by G. S. Blum, *Psychodynamics: The Science of Unconscious Mental Forces,* published by Brooks/Cole in 1966.

For Freud's works in translation, *The Standard Edition of the Complete Psychological Works,* edited by James Strachey and published by Hogarth Press, should be consulted. Students who read German should consult the *Gesammelte Werke, Chronologisch Geordnet,* edited by Anna Freud and published by the Imago Publishing Company.

The Psychoanalytic Theory of Neurosis by Otto Fenichel, published by Norton, is difficult reading but worth the effort for the student who is seriously interested in the psychoanalytic technique of psychotherapy.

The now old but still worthwhile monograph by Robert Sears, *Survey of Objective Studies of Psychoanalytic Concepts* (published in 1943 by the Social Science Research Council) is well worth reading for a picture of how some American psychologists have attempted to test Freudian theory.

Critical Essays on Psychoanalysis, edited by Stanley Rachman and published by Pergamon Press, presents some provocative articles critical of psychoanalysis.

The Case of Little Hans

Sigmund Freud

I shall now proceed to examine this observation of the development and resolution of a phobia in a boy under five years of age, and I shall have to do so from three points of view. In the first place I shall consider how far it supports the assertions which I put forward in my *Three Essays on the Theory of Sexuality* (1905). Secondly, I shall consider to what extent it can contribute towards our understanding of this very frequent form of disorder. And thirdly, I shall consider whether it can be made to shed any light upon the mental life of children or to afford any criticism of our educational aims.

(I)

My impression is that the picture of a child's sexual life presented in this observation of little Hans agrees very well with the account I gave of it (basing my views upon psycho-analytic examinations of adults) in my *Three Essays*. But before going into the details of this agreement I must deal with two objections which will be raised against my making use of the present analysis for this purpose. The first objection is to the effect that Hans was not a normal child, but (as events—the illness itself, in fact—showed) had a predisposition to neurosis, and was a young "degenerate"; it would be illegitimate, therefore, to apply to other, normal children conclusions which might perhaps be true of him. I shall postpone consideration of this objection, since it only limits the value of the observation, and does not completely nullify it. According to the second and more uncompromising objection, an analysis of a child conducted by his father, who went to work

From Sigmund Freud, *The Standard Edition of the Complete Psychological Works*, ed. J. Strachey, 24 vols. (London: Hogarth Press, 1953-66), vol. 10, pp. 101-147; also in *The Collected Papers of Sigmund Freud*, ed. E. Jones, 5 vols. (New York: Basic Books, 1959), vol. 3, pp. 243-287. Reprinted by permission of the publishers.

instilled with *my* theoretical views and infected with *my* prejudices, must be entirely devoid of any objective worth. A child, it will be said, is necessarily highly suggestible, and in regard to no one, perhaps, more than to his own father; he will allow anything to be forced upon him, out of gratitude to his father for taking so much notice of him; none of his assertions can have any evidential value, and everything he produces in the way of associations, phantasies, and dreams will naturally take the direction into which they are being urged by every possible means. Once more, in short, the whole thing is simply "suggestion" —the only difference being that in the case of a child it can be unmasked much more easily than in that of an adult.

A singular thing. I can remember, when I first began to meddle in the conflict of scientific opinions twenty-two years ago, with what derision the older generation of neurologists and psychiatrists of those days received assertions about suggestion and its effects. Since then the situation has fundamentally changed. The former aversion has been converted into an only too ready acceptance; and this has happened not only as a consequence of the impression which the work of Liébeault and Bernheim and their pupils could not fail to create in the course of these two decades, but also because it has since been discovered how great an economy of thought can be effected by the use of the catchword "suggestion." Nobody knows and nobody cares what suggestion is, where it comes from, or when it arises,—it is enough that everything awkward in the region of psychology can be labelled "suggestion." I do not share the view which is at present fashionable that assertions made by children are invariably arbitrary and untrustworthy. The arbitrary has no existence in mental life. The untrustworthiness of the assertions of children is due to the predominance of their imagination, just as the untrustworthiness of the assertions of grown-up people is due to the predominance of their prejudices. For the rest, even children do not lie without a reason, and on the whole they are more inclined to a love of truth than are their elders. If we were to reject little Hans's statements root and branch we should certainly be doing him a grave injustice. On the contrary, we can quite clearly distinguish from one another the occasions on which he was falsifying the facts or keeping them back under the compelling force of a resistance, the occasions on which, being undecided himself, he agreed with his father (so that what he said must not be taken as evidence), and the occasions on which, freed from every pressure, he burst into a flood of information about what was really going on inside him and about things which until then no one but himself had known. Statements made by adults offer no greater certainty. It is a regrettable fact that no account of a psycho-analysis can reproduce the impressions received by the analyst as he conducts it, and that a final sense of conviction can never be obtained from reading about it but only from directly experiencing it. But this disability attaches in an equal degree to analyses of adults.

Little Hans is described by his parents as a cheerful, straightforward child, and so he should have been, considering the education given him by his parents, which consisted essentially in the omission of our usual educational sins. So long as he was able to carry on his researches in a state of happy *naïveté*, without a suspicion of the conflicts which were soon to arise out of them, he kept nothing back; and the observations made during the period before the phobia admit of no doubt or demur. It was with the outbreak of the illness and during the analysis that discrepancies began to make their appearance between what he said and what he thought; and this was partly because unconscious material, which he was unable to master all at once, was forcing itself upon him, and partly because the content of his thoughts provoked reservations on account of his relation to his parents. It is my unbiassed opinion that these

difficulties, too, turned out no greater than in many analyses of adults.

It is true that during the analysis Hans had to be told many things that he could not say himself, that he had to be presented with thoughts which he had so far shown no signs of possessing, and that his attention had to be turned in the direction from which his father was expecting something to come. This detracts from the evidential value of the analysis; but the procedure is the same in every case. For a psycho-analysis is not an impartial scientific investigation, but a therapeutic measure. Its essence is not to prove anything, but merely to alter something. In a psycho-analysis the physician always gives his patient (sometimes to a greater and sometimes to a less extent) the conscious anticipatory ideas by the help of which he is put in a position to recognize and to grasp the unconscious material. For there are some patients who need more of such assistance and some who need less; but there are none who get through without some of it. Slight disorders may perhaps be brought to an end by the subject's unaided efforts, but never a neurosis—a thing which has set itself up against the ego as an element alien to it. To get the better of such an element another person must be brought in, and in so far as that other person can be of assistance the neurosis will be curable. If it is in the very nature of any neurosis to turn away from the "other person"—and this seems to be one of the characteristics of the states grouped together under the name of dementia praecox —then for that very reason such a state will be incurable by any efforts of ours. It is true that a child, on account of the small development of his intellectual systems, requires especially energetic assistance. But, after all, the information which the physician gives his patient is itself derived in its turn from analytical experience; and indeed it is sufficiently convincing if, at the cost of this intervention by the physician, we are enabled to discover the structure of the pathogenic material and simultaneously to dissipate it.

And yet, even during the analysis, the small patient gave evidence of enough independence to acquit him upon the charge of "suggestion." Like all other children, he applied his childish sexual theories to the material before him without having received any encouragement to do so. These theories are extremely remote from the adult mind. Indeed, in this instance I actually omitted to warn Hans's father that the boy would be bound to approach the subject of childbirth by way of the excretory complex. This negligence on my part, though it led to an obscure phase in the analysis, was nevertheless the means of producing a good piece of evidence of the genuineness and independence of Hans's mental processes. He suddenly became occupied with "lumf," without his father, who is supposed to have been practising suggestion upon him, having the least idea how he had arrived at that subject or what was going to come of it. Nor can his father be saddled with any responsibility for the production of the two plumber phantasies, which arose out of Hans's early acquired "castration complex." And I must here confess that, out of theoretical interest, I entirely concealed from Hans's father my expectation that there would turn out to be some such connection, so as not to interfere with the value of a piece of evidence such as does not often come within one's grasp.

If I went more deeply into the details of the analysis I could produce plenty more evidence of Hans's independence of "suggestion"; but I shall break off the discussion of this preliminary objection at this point. I am aware that even with this analysis I shall not succeed in convincing any one who will not let himself be convinced, and I shall proceed with my discussion of the case for the benefit of those readers who are already convinced of the objective reality of unconscious pathogenic material. And I do this with the agreeable assurance that the number of such readers is steadily increasing.

The first trait in little Hans which can be regarded as part of his sexual life was a quite peculiar lively interest in his "widdler"—an organ deriving its name from that one of its two functions which, scarcely the less important of the two, is not to be eluded in the nursery. This interest aroused in him the spirit of enquiry, and he thus discovered that the presence or absence of a widdler made it possible to differentiate between animate and inanimate objects. He assumed that all animate objects were like himself, and possessed this important bodily organ; he observed that it was present in the larger animals, suspected that this was so too in both his parents, and was not deterred by the evidence of his own eyes from authenticating the fact in his newborn sister. One might almost say that it would have been too shattering a blow to his "*Weltanschauung*" if he had had to make up his mind to forgo the presence of this organ in a being similar to him; it would have been as though it were being torn away from himself. It was probably on this account that a threat of his mother's, which was concerned precisely with the loss of his widdler, was hastily dismissed from his thoughts and only succeeded in making its effects apparent at a later period. The reason for his mother's intervention had been that he used to like giving himself feelings of pleasure by touching his member: the little boy had begun to practise the commonest—and most normal—form of auto-erotic sexual activity.

The pleasure which a person takes in his own sexual organ may become associated with scopophilia (or sexual pleasure in looking) in its active and passive forms, in a manner which has been very aptly described by Alfred Adler as "confluence of instincts." So little Hans began to try to get a sight of other people's widdlers; his sexual curiosity developed, and at the same time he liked to exhibit his own widdler. One of his dreams, dating from the beginning of his period of repression, expressed a wish that one of his little girl friends should assist him in widdling, that is, that she should share the spectacle. The dream shows, therefore, that up till then this wish had subsisted unrepressed, and later information confirmed the fact that he had been in the habit of gratifying it. The active side of his sexual scopophilia soon became associated in him with a definite theme. He repeatedly expressed both to his father and his mother his regret that he had never yet seen their widdlers; and it was probably the need *for making a comparison* which impelled him to do this. The ego is always the standard by which one measures the external world; one learns to understand it by means of a constant comparison with oneself. Hans had observed that large animals had widdlers that were correspondingly larger than his; he consequently suspected that the same was true of his parents, and was anxious to make sure of this. His mother, he thought, must certainly have a widdler "like a horse." He was then prepared with the comforting reflection that his widdler would grow with him. It was as though the child's wish to be bigger had been concentrated on his genitals.

Thus in little Hans's sexual constitution the genital zone was from the outset the one among his erotogenic zones which afforded him the most intense pleasure. The only other similar pleasure of which he gave evidence was excretory pleasure, the pleasure attached to the orifices through which micturition and evacuation of the bowels are effected. In his final phantasy of bliss, with which his illness was overcome, he imagined he had children, whom he took to the W.C., whom he made to widdle, whose behinds he wiped—for whom, in short, he did "everything one can do with children"; it therefore seems impossible to avoid the assumption that during the period when he himself had been looked after as an infant these same performances had been the source of pleasurable sensations for him. He had obtained this pleasure from his erotogenic zones with the help of the person who had looked after him—his mother, in fact; and thus the pleasure already pointed the way to object-choice. But it is just possible that at a still earlier date he had been in the habit of giving himself this pleasure auto-erotically—that he had been one of those children who like retaining their excreta till they can derive a voluptuous sensation from their evacuation. I say no more than that it is possible, because the matter was not cleared up in the analysis; the "making a row with the legs" (kicking about), of which he was so much frightened later on, points in that direction. But in any case these sources of pleasure had no particularly striking importance with Hans, as they

so often have with other children. He early became clean in his habits, and neither bed-wetting nor diurnal incontinence played any part during his first years; no trace was observed in him of any inclination to play with his excrement, a propensity which is so revolting in adults, and which commonly makes its reappearance at the termination of processes of psychical involution.

At this juncture it is as well to emphasize at once the fact that during his phobia there was an unmistakable repression of these two well-developed components of his sexual activity. He was ashamed of micturating before other people, accused himself of putting his finger to his widdler, made efforts to give up masturbating, and showed disgust at "lumf" and "widdle" and everything that reminded him of them. In his phantasy of looking after his children he undid this latter repression.

A sexual constitution like that of little Hans does not appear to carry with it a predisposition to the development either of perversions or of their negative (we will limit ourselves to a consideration of hysteria). As far as my experience goes (and there is still a real need for speaking with caution on this point) the innate constitution of hysterics—that this is also true of perverts is almost self-evident—is marked by the genital zone being relatively less prominent than the other erotogenic zones. But we must expressly except from this rule one particular "aberration" of sexual life. In those who later become homosexuals we meet with the same predominance in infancy of the genital zone (and especially of the penis) as in normal persons.[1] Indeed it is the high esteem felt by the homosexual for the male organ which decides his fate. In his childhood he chooses women as his sexual object, so long as he assumes that they too possess what in his eyes is an indispensable part of the body; when he becomes convinced that women have deceived him in this particular, they cease to be acceptable to him as a sexual object. He cannot forgo a penis in any one who is to attract him to sexual inter-

[1]As my expectations led me to suppose, and as Sadger's observations have shown, all such people pass through an amphigenic phase in childhood.

course; and if circumstances are favourable he will fix his libido upon the "woman with a penis," a youth of feminine appearance. Homosexuals, then, are persons who, owing to the erotogenic importance of their own genitals, cannot do without a similar feature in their sexual object. In the course of their development from auto-erotism to object-love, they have remained at a point of fixation between the two.

There is absolutely no justification for distinguishing a special homosexual instinct. What constitutes a homosexual is a peculiarity not in his instinctual life but in his choice of an object. Let me recall what I have said in my *Three Essays* to the effect that we have mistakenly imagined the bond between instinct and object in sexual life as being more intimate than it really is. A homosexual may have normal instincts, but he is unable to disengage them from a class of objects defined by a particular determinant. And in his childhood, since at that period this determinant is taken for granted as being of universal application, he is able to behave like little Hans, who showed his affection to little boys and girls indiscriminately, and once described his friend Fritzl as "the girl he was fondest of." Hans was a homosexual (as all children may very well be), quite consistently with the fact, which must always be kept in mind, that *he was acquainted with only one kind of genital organ*—a genital organ like his own.[2]

In his subsequent development, however, it was not to homosexuality that our young libertine proceeded, but to an energetic masculinity with traits of polygamy; he knew how to vary his behaviour, too, with his varying feminine objects—audaciously aggressive in one case, languishing and bashful in another. His affection had moved from his mother on to other objects of love, but at a time when there was a scarcity of these it returned to her, only to break down in a neurosis. It was

[2] (*Footnote added* 1923:) I have subsequently (1923) drawn attention to the fact that the period of sexual development which our little patient was passing through is universally characterized by acquaintance with only *one* sort of genital organ, namely, the male one. In contrast to the later period of maturity, this period is marked not by a *genital* primacy but by a primacy of the *phallus*.

not until this happened that it became evident to what a pitch of intensity his love for his mother had developed and through what vicissitudes it had passed. The sexual aim which he pursued with his girl playmates, of sleeping with them, had originated in relation to his mother. It was expressed in words which might be retained in maturity, though they would then bear a richer connotation. The boy had found his way to object-love in the usual manner from the care he had received when he was an infant; and a new pleasure had now become the most important for him—that of sleeping beside his mother. I should like to emphasize the importance of pleasure derived from cutaneous contact as a component in this new aim of Hans's, which, according to the nomenclature (artificial to my mind) of Moll, would have to be described as satisfaction of the instinct of contrectation.

In his attitude towards his father and mother Hans confirms in the most concrete and uncompromising manner what I have said in my *Interpretation of Dreams* (1900) and in my *Three Essays* (1905) with regard to the sexual relations of a child to his parents. Hans really was a little Oedipus who wanted to have his father "out of the way," to get rid of him, so that he might be alone with his beautiful mother and sleep with her. This wish had originated during his summer holidays, when the alternating presence and absence of his father had drawn Hans's attention to the condition upon which depended the intimacy with his mother which he longed for. At that time the form taken by the wish had been merely that his father should "go away"; and at a later stage it became possible for his fear of being bitten by a white horse to attach itself directly on to this form of the wish, owing to a chance impression which he received at the moment of some one else's departure. But subsequently (probably not until they had moved back to Vienna, where his father's absences were no longer to be reckoned on) the wish had taken the form that his father should be *permanently* away— that he should be "dead." The fear which sprang from this death-wish against his father, and which may thus be said to have had a normal motive, formed the chief obstacle to the analysis until it was removed during the conversation in my consulting-room.[3]

But Hans was not by any means a bad character; he was not even one of those children who at his age still give free play to the propensity towards cruelty and violence which is a constituent of human nature. On the contrary, he had an unusually kind-hearted and affectionate disposition; his father reported that the transformation of aggressive tendencies into feelings of pity took place in him at a very early age. Long before the phobia he had become uneasy when he saw the horses in a merry-go-round being beaten; and he was never unmoved if any one wept in his presence. At one stage in the analysis a piece of suppressed sadism made its appearance in a particular context:[4] but it was *suppressed* sadism, and we shall presently have to discover from the context what it stood for and what it was meant to replace. And Hans deeply loved the father against whom he cherished these death-wishes; and while his intellect demurred to such a contradiction, he could not help demonstrating the fact of its existence, by hitting his father and immediately afterwards kissing the place he had hit. We ourselves, too, must guard against making a difficulty of such a contradiction. The emotional life of a man is in general made up of pairs of contraries such as these.[5] Indeed, if it were not so, repressions and neuroses would perhaps never come about. In the adult these pairs of contrary emotions do not as a rule become simultaneously conscious except at the climaxes of passionate love; at other times they usually go on suppressing each other until

one of them succeeds in keeping the other altogether out of sight. But in children they can exist peaceably side by side for quite a considerable time.

The most important influence upon the course of Hans's psycho-sexual development was the birth of a baby sister when he was three and a half years old. That event accentuated his relations to his parents and gave him some insoluble problems to think about; and later, as he watched the way in which the infant was looked after, the memory-traces of his own earliest experiences of pleasure were revived in him. This influence, too, is a typical one: in an unexpectedly large number of life-histories, normal as well as pathological, we find ourselves obliged to take as our starting-point an outburst of sexual pleasure and sexual curiosity connected, like this one, with the birth of the next child. Hans's behaviour towards the new arrival was just what I have described in *The Interpretation of Dreams* (1900). In his fever a few days later he betrayed how little he liked the addition to the family. Affection for his sister might come later, but his first attitude was hostility. From that time forward fear that yet another baby might arrive found a place among his conscious thoughts. In the neurosis, his hostility, already suppressed, was represented by a special fear—a fear of the bath. In the analysis he gave undisguised expression to his death-wish against his sister, and was not content with allusions which required supplementing by his father. His inner conscience did not consider this wish so wicked as the analogous one against his father; but it is clear that in his unconscious he treated both persons in the same way, because they both took his mummy away from him, and interfered with his being alone with her.

Moreover, this event and the feelings that were revived by it gave a new direction to his wishes: In his triumphant final phantasy he summed up all of his erotic wishes, both those derived from his auto-erotic phase and those connected with his object-love. In that phantasy he was married to his beautiful mother and had innumerable children whom he could look after in his own way.

[3]It is quite certain that Hans's two associations, "raspberry syrup" and "a gun for shooting people dead with," must have had more than one set of determinants. They probably had just as much to do with his hatred of his father as with his constipation complex. His father, who himself guessed the latter connection, also suggested that "raspberry syrup" might be related to "blood."

[4]His wanting to beat and tease horses.

[5]Das heisst, ich bin kein ausgeklügelt Buch.
Ich bin ein Mensch mit seinem Widerspruch.
C. F. Meyer, *Huttens letzte Tage*.
(In fact, I am no clever work of fiction;
I am a man, with all his contradiction.)

(II)

One day while Hans was in the street he was seized with an attack of anxiety. He could not yet say what it was he was afraid of; but at the very beginning of this anxiety-state he betrayed to his father his motive for being ill, the advantage he derived from it. He wanted to stay with his mother and to coax with her; his recollection that he had also been separated from her at the time of the baby's birth may also, as his father suggests, have contributed to his longing. It soon became evident that his anxiety was no longer reconvertible into longing; he was afraid even when his mother went with him. In the meantime indications appeared of what it was to which his libido (now changed into anxiety) had become attached. He gave expression to the quite specific fear that a white horse would bite him.

Disorders of this kind are called "phobias," and we might classify Hans's case as an agoraphobia if it were not for the fact that it is a characteristic of that complaint that the locomotion of which the patient is otherwise incapable can always be easily performed when he is accompanied by some specially selected person—in the last resort, by the physician. Hans's phobia did not fulfil this condition; it soon ceased having any relation to the question of locomotion and became more and more clearly concentrated upon horses. In the early days of his illness, when the anxiety was at its highest pitch, he expressed a fear that "the horse'll come into the room," and it was this that helped me so much towards understanding his condition.

In the classificatory system of the neuroses no definite position has hitherto been assigned to "phobias." It seems certain that they should only be regarded as syndromes which may form part of various neuroses and that we need not rank them as an independent pathological process. For phobias of the kind to which little Hans's belongs, and which are in fact the most common, the name of "anxiety-hysteria" seems to me not inappropriate; I suggested the term to Dr. W. Stekel when he was undertaking a description of neurotic anxiety-states, and I hope it will

come into general use. It finds its justification in the similarity between the psychological structure of these phobias and that of hysteria —a similarity which is complete except upon a single point. That point, however, is a decisive one and well adapted for purposes of differentiation. For in anxiety-hysteria the libido which has been liberated from the pathogenic material by repression is not *converted* (that is, diverted from the mental sphere into a somatic innervation), but is set free in the shape of *anxiety*. In the clinical cases that we meet with, this "anxiety-hysteria" may be combined with "conversion-hysteria" in any proportion. There exist cases of pure conversion-hysteria without any trace of anxiety, just as there are cases of simple anxiety-hysteria, which exhibit feelings of anxiety and phobias, but have no admixture of conversion. The case of little Hans is one of the latter sort.

Anxiety-hysterias are the most common of all psychoneurotic disorders. But, above all, they are those which make their appearance earliest in life; they are *par excellence* the neuroses of childhood. When a mother uses such phrases as that her child's "nerves" are in a bad state, we can be certain that in nine cases out of ten the child is suffering from some kind of anxiety or from many kinds at once. Unfortunately the finer mechanism of these highly significant disorders has not yet been sufficiently studied. It has not yet been established whether anxiety-hysteria is determined, in contradistinction to conversion-hysteria and other neuroses, solely by constitutional factors or solely by accidental experiences, or by what combination of the two.[6] It seems to me that of all neurotic disorders it is the least dependent upon a special constitutional predisposition and that it is consequently the most easily acquired at any time of life.

One essential characteristic of anxiety-

[6](*Footnote added* 1923:) The question which is raised here has not been pursued further. But there is no reason to suppose that anxiety-hysteria is an exception to the rule that both predisposition and experience must cooperate in the aetiology of a neurosis. Rank's view of the effects of the trauma of birth seems to throw special light upon the predisposition to anxiety-hysteria which is so strong in childhood.

hysterias is very easily pointed out. An anxiety-hysteria tends to develop more and more into a "phobia." In the end the patient may have got rid of all his anxiety, but only at the price of subjecting himself to all kinds of inhibitions and restrictions. From the outset in anxiety-hysteria the mind is constantly at work in the direction of once more psychically binding the anxiety which has become liberated; but this work can neither bring about a retransformation of the anxiety into libido, nor can it establish any contact with the complexes which were the source of the libido. Nothing is left for it but to cut off access to every possible occasion that might lead to the development of anxiety, by erecting mental barriers in the nature of precautions, inhibitions, or prohibitions; and it is these defensive structures that appear to us in the form of phobias and that constitute to our eyes the essence of the disease.

The treatment of anxiety-hysteria may be said hitherto to have been a purely negative one. Experience has shown that it is impossible to effect the cure of a phobia (and even in certain circumstances dangerous to attempt to do so) by violent means, that is, by first depriving the patient of his defences and then putting him in a situation in which he cannot escape the liberation of his anxiety. Consequently, nothing can be done but to leave the patient to look for protection wherever he thinks he may find it; and he is merely regarded with a not very helpful contempt for his "incomprehensible cowardice."

Little Hans's parents were determined from the very beginning of his illness that he was neither to be laughed at nor bullied, but that access must be obtained to his repressed wishes by means of psycho-analysis. The extraordinary pains taken by Hans's father were rewarded by success, and his reports will give us an opportunity of penetrating into the fabric of this type of phobia and of following the course of its analysis.

I think it is not unlikely that the extensive and detailed character of the analysis may have made it somewhat obscure to the reader. I shall therefore begin by giving a brief résumé of it, in which I shall omit all distracting side-issues and shall draw attention to the results as they came to light one after the other.

The first thing we learn is that the outbreak of the anxiety-state was by no means so sudden as appeared at first sight. A few days earlier the child had woken from an anxiety-dream to the effect that his mother had gone away, and that now he had no mother to coax with. This dream alone points to the presence of a repressive process of ominous intensity. We cannot explain it, as we can so many other anxiety-dreams, by supposing that the child had in his dream felt anxiety arising from some somatic cause and had made use of the anxiety for the purpose of fulfilling an unconscious wish which would otherwise have been deeply repressed.[7] We must regard it rather as a genuine punishment and repression dream, and, moreover, as a dream which failed in its function, since the child woke from his sleep in a state of anxiety. We can easily reconstruct what actually occurred in the unconscious. The child dreamt of exchanging endearments with his mother and of sleeping with her; but all the pleasure was transformed into anxiety, and all the ideational content into its opposite. Repression had defeated the purpose of the mechanism of dreaming.

But the beginnings of this psychological situation go back further still. During the preceding summer Hans had had similar moods of mingled longing and apprehension, in which he had said similar things; and at that time they had secured him the advantage of being taken by his mother into her bed. We may assume that since then Hans had been in a state of intensified sexual excitement, the object of which was his mother. The intensity of this excitement was shown by his two attempts at seducing his mother (the second of which occurred just before the outbreak of his anxiety); and he found an incidental channel of discharge for it by masturbating every evening and in that way obtaining gratification. Whether the sudden change-over of this excitement into anxiety took place sponta-

---

[7]See my *Interpretation of Dreams* (1900).

neously, or as a result of his mother's rejection of his advances, or owing to the accidental revival of earlier impressions by the "precipitating cause" of his illness (about which we shall hear presently)—this we cannot decide; and, indeed, it is a matter of indifference, for these three alternative possibilities cannot be regarded as mutually incompatible. The fact remains that his sexual excitement suddenly changed into anxiety.

We have already described the child's behaviour at the beginning of his anxiety, as well as the first content which he assigned to it, namely, that a horse would bite him. It was at this point that the first piece of therapy was interposed. His parents represented to him that his anxiety was the result of masturbation, and encouraged him to break himself of the habit. I took care that when they spoke to him great stress was laid upon his affection for his mother, for that was what he was trying to replace by his fear of horses. This first intervention brought a slight improvement, but the ground was soon lost again during a period of physical illness. Hans's condition remained unchanged. Soon afterwards he traced back his fear of being bitten by a horse to an impression he had received at Gmunden. A father had addressed his child on her departure with these words of warning: "Don't put your finger to the horse; if you do, it'll bite you." The words, "don't put your finger to," which Hans used in reporting this warning, resembled the form of words in which the warning against masturbation had been framed. It seemed at first, therefore, as though Hans's parents were right in supposing that what he was frightened of was his own masturbatory indulgence. But the whole nexus remained loose, and it seemed to be merely by chance that horses had become his bugbear.

I had expressed a suspicion that Hans's repressed wish might now be that he wanted at all costs to see his mother's widdler. As his behaviour to a new maid fitted in with this hypothesis, his father gave him his first piece of enlightenment, namely, that women have no widdlers. He reacted to this first effort at helping him by producing a phantasy that he

had seen his mother showing her widdler.[8] This phantasy and a remark made by him in conversation, to the effect that his widdler was "fixed in, of course," allow us our first glimpse into the patient's unconscious mental processes. The fact was that the threat of castration made to him by his mother some fifteen months earlier was now having a deferred effect upon him. For his phantasy that his mother was doing the same as he had done (the familiar *tu quoque* repartee of inculpated children) was intended to serve as a piece of self-justification; it was a protective or defensive phantasy. At the same time we must remark that it was Hans's parents who had extracted from the pathogenic material operating in him the particular theme of his interest in widdlers. Hans followed their lead in this matter, but he had not yet taken any line of his own in the analysis. And no therapeutic success was to be observed. The analysis had passed far away from the subject of horses; and the information that women have no widdlers was calculated, if anything, to increase his concern for the preservation of his own.

Therapeutic success, however, is not our primary aim; we endeavour rather to enable the patient to obtain a conscious grasp of his unconscious wishes. And this we can achieve by working upon the basis of the hints he throws out, and so, with the help of our interpretative technique, presenting the unconscious complex to his consciousness *in our own words*. There will be a certain degree of similarity between that which he hears from us and that which he is looking for, and which, in spite of all resistances, is trying to force its way through to consciousness; and it is this similarity that will enable him to discover the unconscious material. The physician is a step in front of him in knowledge; and the patient follows along his own road, until the two meet at the appointed goal. Beginners in psycho-analysis are apt to assimilate these two events, and to suppose that the moment at which one of the patient's uncon-

---

[8]The context enables us to add: "and touching it." After all, he himself could not show his widdler without touching it.

scious complexes has become known to *them* is also the moment at which the patient himself recognizes it. They are expecting too much when they think that they will cure the patient by informing him of this piece of knowledge; for he can do no more with the information than make use of it to help himself in discovering the unconscious complex *where it is anchored* in his unconscious. A first success of this sort had now been achieved with Hans. Having partly mastered his castration complex, he was now able to communicate his wishes in regard to his mother. He did so, in what was still a distorted form, by means of the *phantasy of the two giraffes,* one of which was calling out in vain because Hans had taken possession of the other. He represented the "taking possession of" pictorially as "sitting down on." His father recognized the phantasy as a reproduction of a bedroom scene which used to take place in the morning between the boy and his parents; and he quickly stripped the underlying wish of the disguise which it still wore. The boy's father and mother were the two giraffes. The reason for the choice of a giraffe-phantasy for the purposes of disguise was fully explained by a visit that the boy had paid to those same large beasts at Schönbrunn a few days earlier, by the giraffe-drawing, belonging to an earlier period, which had been preserved by his father, and also, perhaps, by an unconscious comparison based upon the giraffe's long, stiff neck.[9] It may be remarked that the giraffe, as being a large animal and interesting on account of its widdler, was a possible competitor with the horse for the role of bugbear; moreover, the fact that both his father and his mother appeared as giraffes offered a hint which had not yet been followed up, as regards the interpretation of the anxiety-horses.

Immediately after the giraffe story Hans produced two minor phantasies: one of his forcing his way into a forbidden space at Schönbrunn, and the other of his smashing a railway-carriage window on the Stadtbahn. In each case the punishable nature of the action was emphasized, and in each his father appeared as an accomplice. Unluckily his father failed to interpret either of these phantasies, so that Hans himself gained nothing from telling them. In an analysis, however, a thing which has not been understood inevitably reappears; like an unlaid ghost, it cannot rest until the mystery has been solved and the spell broken.

There are no difficulties in the way of our understanding these two criminal phantasies. They belonged to Hans's complex of taking possession of his mother. Some kind of vague notion was struggling in the child's mind of something that he might do with his mother by means of which his taking possession of her would be consummated; for this elusive thought he found certain pictorial representations, which had in common the qualities of being violent and forbidden, and the content of which strikes us as fitting in most remarkably well with the hidden truth. We can only say that they were symbolic phantasies of intercourse, and it was no irrelevant detail that his father was represented as sharing in his actions: "I should like," he seems to have been saying, "to be doing something with my mother, something forbidden; I do not know what it is, but I do know that you are doing it too."

The giraffe phantasy strengthened a conviction which had already begun to form in my mind when Hans expressed his fear that "the horse'll come into the room"; and I thought the right moment had now arrived for informing him that he was afraid of his father because he himself nourished jealous and hostile wishes against him—for it was essential to postulate this much with regard to his unconscious impulses. In telling him this, I had partly interpreted his fear of horses for him: the horse must be his father—whom he had good internal reasons for fearing. Certain details of which Hans had shown he was afraid, the black on horses' mouths and the things in front of their eyes (the moustaches and eyeglasses which are the privilege of a grown-up man), seemed to me to have been directly transposed from his father on to the horses.

[9]Hans's admiration of his father's neck later on would fit in with this.

By enlightening Hans on this subject I had cleared away his most powerful resistance against allowing his unconscious thoughts to be made conscious; for his father was himself acting as his physician. The worst of the attack was now over; there was a plentiful flow of material; the little patient summoned up courage to describe the details of his phobia, and soon began to take an active share in the conduct of the analysis.[10]

It was only then that we learnt what the objects and impressions were of which Hans was afraid. He was not only afraid of horses biting him—he was soon silent upon that point—but also of carts, of furniture-vans, and of buses (their common quality being, as presently became clear, that they were all heavily loaded), of horses that started moving, of horses that looked big and heavy, and of horses that drove quickly. The meaning of these specifications was explained by Hans himself: he was afraid of horses *falling down,* and consequently incorporated in his phobia everything that seemed likely to facilitate their falling down.

It not at all infrequently happens that it is only after doing a certain amount of psycho-analytic work with a patient that an analyst can succeed in learning the actual content of a phobia, the precise form of words of an obsessional impulse, and so on. Repression has not only descended upon the unconscious complexes, but it is continually attacking their derivatives as well, and even prevents the patient from becoming aware of the products of the disease itself. The analyst thus finds himself in the position, curious for a doctor, of coming to the help of a disease, and of procuring it its due of attention. But only those who entirely misunderstand the nature of psycho-analysis will lay stress upon this phase of the work and suppose that on its account harm is likely to be done by analysis.

The fact is that you must catch your thief before you can hang him, and that it requires some expenditure of labour to get securely hold of the pathological structures at the destruction of which the treatment is aimed.

I have already remarked in the course of my running commentary on the case history that it is most instructive to plunge in this way into the details of a phobia, and thus arrive at a conviction of the secondary nature of the relation between the anxiety and its objects. It is this that accounts for phobias being at once so curiously diffuse and so strictly conditioned. It is evident that the material for the particular disguises which Hans's fear adopted was collected from the impressions to which he was all day long exposed owing to the Head Customs House being situated on the opposite side of the street. In this connection, too, he showed signs of an impulse—though it was now inhibited by his anxiety—to play with the loads on the carts, with the packages, casks and boxes, like the street-boys.

It was at this stage of the analysis that he recalled the event, insignificant in itself, which immediately preceded the outbreak of the illness and may no doubt be regarded as the precipitating cause of its outbreak. He went for a walk with his mother, and saw a bus-horse fall down and kick about with its feet. This made a great impression on him. He was terrified, and thought the horse was dead; and from that time on he thought that all horses would fall down. His father pointed out to him that when he saw the horse fall down he must have thought of him, his father, and have wished that he might fall down in the same way and be dead. Hans did not dispute this interpretation; and a little while later he played a game consisting of biting his father, and so showed that he accepted the theory of his having identified his father with the horse he was afraid of. From that time forward his behaviour to his father was unconstrained and fearless, and in fact a trifle overbearing. Nevertheless his fear of horses persisted; nor was it yet clear through what chain of associations the horse's falling down had stirred up his unconscious wishes.

---

[10]Even in analyses in which the physician and the patient are strangers, fear of the father plays one of the most important parts as a resistance against the reproduction of the unconscious pathogenic material. Resistances are sometimes in the nature of "motifs." But sometimes, as in the present instance, one piece of the unconscious material is capable from its actual *content* of operating as an inhibition against the reproduction of another piece.

Let me summarize the results that had so far been reached. Behind the fear to which Hans first gave expression, the fear of a horse biting him, we had discovered a more deeply seated fear, the fear of horses falling down; and both kinds of horses, the biting horse and the falling horse, had been shown to represent his father, who was going to punish him for the evil wishes he was nourishing against him. Meanwhile the analysis had moved away from the subject of his mother.

Quite unexpectedly, and certainly without any prompting from his father, Hans now began to be occupied with the "lumf" complex, and to show disgust at things that reminded him of evacuating his bowels. His father, who was reluctant to go with him along that line, pushed on with the analysis through thick and thin in the direction in which he wanted to go. He elicited from Hans the recollection of an event at Gmunden, the impression of which lay concealed behind that of the falling bus-horse. While they were playing at horses, Fritzl, the playmate of whom he was so fond, but at the same time, perhaps, his rival with his many girl friends, had hit his foot against a stone and had fallen down, and his foot had bled. Seeing the bus-horse fall had reminded him of this accident. It deserves to be noticed that Hans, who was at the moment concerned with other things, began by denying that Fritzl had fallen down (though this was the event which formed the connection between the two scenes) and only admitted it at a later stage of the analysis. It is especially interesting, however, to observe the way in which the transformation of Hans's libido into anxiety was projected on to the principal object of his phobia, on to horses. Horses interested him the most of all the large animals; playing at horses was his favourite game with the other children. I had a suspicion—and this was confirmed by Hans's father when I asked him—that the first person who had served Hans as a horse must have been his father; and it was this that had enabled him to regard Fritzl as a substitute for his father when the accident happened at Gmunden. When repression had set in and brought a revulsion of feeling along

with it, horses, which had till then been associated with so much pleasure, were necessarily turned into objects of fear.

But, as we have already said, it was owing to the intervention of Hans's father that this last important discovery was made of the way in which the precipitating cause of the illness had operated. Hans himself was occupied with his lumf interests, and thither at last we must follow him. We learn that formerly Hans had been in the habit of insisting upon accompanying his mother to the W.C., and that he had revived this custom with his friend Berta at a time when she was filling his mother's place, until the fact became known and he was forbidden to do so. Pleasure taken in looking on while some one one loves performs the natural functions is once more a "confluence of instincts," of which we have already noticed an instance in Hans. In the end his father went into the lumf symbolism, and recognized that there was an analogy between a heavily loaded cart and a body loaded with faeces, between the way in which a cart drives out through a gateway and the way in which faeces leave the body, and so on.

By this time, however, the position occupied by Hans in the analysis had become very different from what it had been at an earlier stage. Previously, his father had been able to tell him in advance what was coming, while Hans had merely followed his lead and come trotting after; but now it was Hans who was forging ahead, so rapidly and steadily that his father found it difficult to keep up with him. Without any warning, as it were, Hans produced a new phantasy: the plumber unscrewed the bath in which Hans was, and then stuck him in the stomach with his big borer. Henceforward the material brought up in the analysis far outstripped our powers of understanding it. It was not until later that it was possible to guess that this was a remoulding of a *phantasy of procreation,* distorted by anxiety. The big bath of water, in which Hans imagined himself, was his mother's womb; the "borer," which his father had from the first recognized as a penis, owed its mention to its connection with "being born." The interpretation that we are obliged to give to the phantasy will of course sound very curious. "With your big penis you 'bored' me" (i.e., "gave birth to me") "and put me in my mother's womb." For the moment, however, the phantasy eluded interpretation, and merely served Hans as a starting-point from which to continue giving information.

Hans showed fear of being given a bath in the big bath; and this fear was once more a composite one. One part of it escaped us as yet, but the other part could at once be elucidated in connection with his baby sister having her bath. Hans confessed to having wished that his mother might drop the child while she was being given her bath, so that she should die. His own anxiety while he was having his bath was a fear of retribution for this evil wish and of being punished by the same thing happening to him. Hans now left the subject of lumf and passed on directly to that of his baby sister. We may well imagine what this juxtaposition signified: nothing less, in fact, than that little Hanna was a lumf herself—that all babies were lumfs and were born like lumfs. We can now recognize that all furniture-vans and drays and buses were only stork-box carts, and were only of interest to Hans as being symbolic representations of pregnancy; and that when a heavy or heavily loaded horse fell down he can have seen in it only one thing—a childbirth, a delivery. Thus the falling horse was not only his dying father but also his mother in childbirth.

And at this point Hans gave us a surprise, for which we were not in the very least prepared. He had noticed his mother's pregnancy, which had ended with the birth of his little sister when he was three and a half years old, and had, at any rate after the confinement, pieced the facts of the case together—without telling any one, it is true, and perhaps without being able to tell any one. All that could be seen at the time was that immediately after the delivery he had taken up an extremely sceptical attitude towards everything that might be supposed to point to the presence of the stork. *But that—in complete contradiction to his official speeches—he knew in his unconscious where the baby came from and where it had been before,* is proved beyond a shadow of doubt by the present analysis; indeed, this is perhaps its most unassailable feature.

The most cogent evidence of this is furnished by the phantasy (which he persisted in with so much obstinacy, and embellished with such a wealth of detail) of how Hanna had been with them at Gmunden the summer before her birth, of how she had travelled there with them, and of how she had been able to do far more then than she had a year later, after she had been born. The effrontery with which Hans related this phantasy and the countless extravagant lies with which he interwove it were anything but meaningless. All of this was intended as a revenge upon his father, against whom he harboured a grudge for having misled him with the stork fable. It was just as though he had meant to say: "If you really thought I was as stupid as all that, and expected me to believe that the stork brought Hanna, then in return I expect *you* to accept *my* inventions as the truth." This act of revenge on the part of our young enquirer upon his father was succeeded by the clearly correlated phantasy of teasing and beating horses. This phantasy, again, had two constituents. On the one hand, it was based upon the teasing to which he had submitted his father just before; and, on the other hand, it reproduced the obscure sadistic desires directed towards his mother, which had already found expression (though they had not at first been understood) in his phantasies of doing something forbidden. Hans even confessed consciously to a desire to beat his mother.

There are not many more mysteries ahead of us now. An obscure phantasy of missing a train seems to have been a forerunner of the later notion of handing over Hans's father to his grandmother at Lainz, for the phantasy dealt with a visit to Lainz, and his grandmother appeared in it. Another phantasy, in which a boy gave the guard 50,000 florins to let him ride on the truck, almost sounds like a plan of buying his mother from his father, part of whose power, of course, lay in his wealth. At about this time, too, he confessed, with a degree of openness which he had never before reached, that he wished to get rid of his father, and that the reason he wished it was that his father interfered with his own intimacy with his mother. We must not be surprised to find the same wishes constantly reappearing in the course of an analysis. The monotony only attaches to the analyst's interpretations of these wishes. For Hans they were not mere repetitions, but steps in a progressive development from timid hinting to fully conscious, undistorted perspicuity.

What remains are just such confirmations on Hans's part of analytical conclusions which our interpretations had already established. In an entirely unequivocal symptomatic act, which he disguised slightly from the maid but not at all from his father, he showed how he imagined a birth took place; but if we look into it more closely we can see that he showed something else, that he was hinting at something which was not alluded to again in the analysis. He pushed a small penknife which belonged to his mother in through a round hole in the body of an india-rubber doll, and then let it drop out again by tearing apart the doll's legs. The enlightenment which he received from his parents soon afterwards, to the effect that children do in fact grow inside their mother's body and are pushed out of it like a lumf, came too late; it could tell him nothing new. Another symptomatic act, happening as though by accident, involved a confession that he had wished his father dead; for, just at the moment his father was talking of this death-wish, Hans let a horse that he was playing with fall down— knocked it over in fact. Further, he confirmed in so many words the hypothesis that heavily loaded carts represented his mother's pregnancy to him, and the horse's falling down was like having a baby. The most delightful piece of confirmation in this connection—a proof that, in his view, children were "lumfs" —was his inventing the name of "Lodi" for his favourite child. There was some delay in reporting this fact, for it then appeared that he had been playing with this sausage child of his for a long time past.[11]

We have already considered Hans's two concluding phantasies, with which his recovery was rounded off. One of them, that of the plumber giving him a new and, as his father guessed, a bigger widdler, was not merely a repetition of the earlier phantasy concerning the plumber and the bath. The new one was a triumphant, wishful phantasy, and with it he overcame his fear of castration. His other phantasy, which confessed to the wish to be married to his mother and to have many children by her, did not merely exhaust the content of the unconscious complexes which had been stirred up by the sight of the falling horse and which had generated his anxiety. It also corrected that portion of those thoughts which was entirely unacceptable; for, instead of killing his father, it made him innocuous by promoting him to a marriage with Hans's grandmother. With this phantasy both the illness and the analysis came to an appropriate end.

While the analysis of a case is in progress it is impossible to obtain any clear impression of the structure and development of the neurosis. That is the business of a synthetic process which must be performed subsequently. In attempting to carry out such a synthesis of little Hans's phobia we shall take as our basis the account of his mental constitution, of his governing sexual wishes, and of his experiences up to the time of his sister's birth, which we have given in an earlier part of this paper.

The arrival of his sister brought into Hans's life many new elements, which from that time on gave him no rest. In the first place he was obliged to submit to a certain degree of privation: to begin with, a temporary separation from his mother, and later a permanent diminution in the amount of care and attention which he had received from her and which thenceforward he had to grow accustomed to sharing with his sister. In the second place, he experienced a revival of the pleasures he had enjoyed when he was looked

depicted the fate of the pork-butcher's child, who fell into the sausage machine, and then, in the shape of a small sausage, was mourned over by his parents, received the Church's blessing, and flew up to Heaven. The artist's idea seems a puzzling one at first, but the Lodi episode in this analysis enables us to trace it back to its infantile root.

---

[11] I remember a set of drawings by T. T. Heine in a copy of *Simplicissimus*, in which that brilliant illustrator

after as an infant; for they were called up by all that he saw his mother doing for the baby. As a result of these two influences his erotic needs became intensified, while at the same time they began to obtain insufficient satisfaction. He made up for the loss which his sister's arrival had entailed on him by imagining that he had children of his own; and so long as he was at Gmunden—on his second visit there—and could really play with these children, he found a sufficient outlet for his affections. But after his return to Vienna he was once more alone, and set all his hopes upon his mother. He had meanwhile suffered another privation, having been exiled from his parents' bedroom at the age of four and a half. His intensified erotic excitability now found expression in phantasies, by which in his loneliness he conjured up his playmates of the past summer, and in regular auto-erotic satisfaction obtained by a masturbatory stimulation of his genitals.

But in the third place his sister's birth stimulated him to an effort of thought which, on the one hand, it was impossible to bring to a conclusion, and which, on the other hand, involved him in emotional conflicts. He was faced with the great riddle of where babies come from, which is perhaps the first problem to engage a child's mental powers, and of which the riddle of the Theban Sphinx is probably no more than a distorted version. He rejected the proffered solution of the stork having brought Hanna. For he had noticed that months before the baby's birth his mother's body had grown big, and then she had gone to bed, and had groaned while the birth was taking place, and that when she got up she was thin again. He therefore inferred that Hanna had been inside his mother's body, and had then come out like a "lumf." He was able to imagine the act of giving birth as a pleasurable one by relating it to his own first feelings of pleasure in passing stool; and he was thus able to find a double motive for wishing to have children of his own: the pleasure of giving birth to them and the pleasure (the compensatory pleasure, as it were) of looking after them. There was nothing in all of this that could have led him into doubts or conflicts.

But there was something else, which could not fail to make him uneasy. His father must have had something to do with little Hanna's birth, for he had declared that Hanna and Hans himself were his children. Yet it was certainly not his father who had brought them into the world, but his mother. This father of his came between him and his mother. When he was there Hans could not sleep with his mother, and when his mother wanted to take Hans into bed with her, his father used to call out. Hans had learnt from experience how well-off he could be in his father's absence, and it was only justifiable that he should wish to get rid of him. And then Hans's hostility had received a fresh reinforcement. His father had told him the lie about the stork and so made it impossible for him to ask for enlightenment upon these things. He not only prevented his being in bed with his mother, but also kept from him the knowledge he was thirsting for. He was putting Hans at a disadvantage in both directions, and was obviously doing so for his own benefit.

But his father, whom he could not help hating as a rival, was the same father whom he had always loved and was bound to go on loving, who had been his model, had been his first playmate, and had looked after him from his earliest infancy: and this it was that gave rise to the first conflict. Nor could this conflict find an immediate solution. For Hans's nature had so developed that for the moment his love could not but keep the upper hand and suppress his hate—though it could not kill it, for his hate was perpetually kept alive by his love for his mother.

But his father not only knew where children came from, he actually performed it—the thing that Hans could only obscurely divine. The widdler must have something to do with it, for his own grew excited whenever he thought of these things—and it must be a big widdler too, bigger than Hans's own. If he listened to these premonitory sensations he could only suppose that it was a question of some act of violence performed upon his mother, of smashing something, of making an opening into something, of forcing a way into an enclosed space—such were the impulses that he felt stirring within him. But although the sensations of his penis had put him on the road to postulating a vagina, yet he could not solve the problem, for within his experience no such thing existed as his widdler required. On the contrary, his conviction that his mother possessed a penis just as he did stood in the way of any solution. His attempt at discovering what it was that had to be done with his mother in order that she might have children sank down into his unconscious; and his two active impulses—the hostile one towards his father and the sadistic-tender one towards his mother—could be put to no use, the first because of the love that existed side by side with the hatred, and the second because of the perplexity in which his infantile sexual theories left him.

This is how, basing my conclusions upon the findings of the analysis, I am obliged to reconstruct the unconscious complexes and wishes, the repression and reawakening of which produced little Hans's phobia. I am aware that in so doing I am attributing a great deal to the mental capacity of a child between four and five years of age; but I have let myself be guided by what we have recently learned, and I do not consider myself bound by the prejudices of our ignorance. It might perhaps have been possible to make use of Hans's fear of the "making a row with the legs" for filling up a few more gaps in our adjudication upon the evidence. Hans, it is true, declared that it reminded him of his kicking about with his legs when he was compelled to leave off playing so as to do lumf; so that this element of the neurosis becomes connected with the problem whether his mother liked having children or was compelled to have them. But I have an impression that this is not the whole explanation of the "making a row with the legs." Hans's father was unable to confirm my suspicion that there was some recollection stirring in the child's mind of having observed a scene of sexual intercourse between his parents in their bedroom. So let us be content with what we have discovered.

It is hard to say what the influence was which, in the situation we have just sketched, led to the sudden change in Hans and to the transformation of his libidinal longing into anxiety—to say from what direction it was the repression set in. The question could probably only be decided by making a comparison between this analysis and a number of similar ones. Whether the scales were turned by the child's *intellectual* inability to solve the difficult problem of the begetting of children and to cope with the aggressive impulses that were liberated by his approaching its solution, or whether the effect was produced by a *somatic* incapacity, a constitutional intolerance of the masturbatory gratification in which he regularly indulged (whether, that is, the mere persistence of sexual excitement at such a high pitch of intensity was bound to bring about a revulsion)—this question must be left open until fresh experience can come to our assistance.

Chronological considerations make it impossible for us to attach any great importance to the actual precipitating cause of the outbreak of Hans's illness, for he had shown signs of apprehensiveness long before he saw the bus-horse fall down in the street.

Nevertheless, the neurosis took its start directly from this chance event and preserved a trace of it in the circumstance of the horse being exalted into the object of his anxiety. In itself the impression of the accident which he happened to witness carried no "traumatic force"; it acquired its great effectiveness only from the fact that horses had formerly been of importance to him as objects of his predilection and interest, from the fact that he associated the event in his mind with an earlier event at Gmunden which had more claim to be regarded as traumatic, namely with Fritzl's falling down while he was playing at horses, and lastly from the fact that there was an easy path of association from Fritzl to his father. Indeed, even these connections would probably not have been sufficient if it had not been that, thanks to the pliability and ambiguity of associative chains, the same event showed itself capable of stirring the second of the complexes that lurked in Hans's unconscious, the complex of his pregnant mother's confinement. From that moment the way was clear for the return of the repressed; and it returned in such a manner that *the pathogenic material was remodelled and transposed on to the horse-complex, while the accompanying effects were uniformly turned into anxiety.*

It deserves to be noticed that the ideational content of Hans's phobia as it then stood had to be submitted to one further process of distortion and substitution before his consciousness took cognizance of it. Hans's first formulation of his anxiety was: "the horse will bite me"; and this was derived from another episode at Gmunden, which was on the one hand related to his hostile wishes towards his father and on the other hand was reminiscent of the warning he had been given against masturbation. Some interfering influence, emanating from his parents perhaps, had made itself felt. I am not certain whether the reports upon Hans were at that time drawn up with sufficient care to enable us to decide whether he expressed his anxiety in this form *before* or not until *after* his mother had taken him to task on the subject of masturbating. I should be inclined to suspect that it was not until afterwards, though this would contradict the account given in the case history. At any rate, it is evident that at every point Hans's hostile complex against his father screened his lustful one about his mother, just as it was the first to be disclosed and dealt with in the analysis.

In other cases of this kind there would be a great deal more to be said upon the structure, the development, and the diffusion of the neurosis. But the history of little Hans's attack was very short; almost as soon as it had begun, its place was taken by the history of its treatment. And although during the treatment the phobia appeared to develop further and to extend over new objects and to lay down new conditions, his father, since he was himself treating the case, naturally had sufficient penetration to see that it was merely a question of the emergence of material that was already in existence, and not of fresh productions for which the treatment might be held responsible. In the treatment of other cases it would not always be possible to count upon so much penetration.

Before I can regard this synthesis as completed I must turn to yet another aspect of the case, which will take us into the very heart of the difficulties that lie in the way of our understanding of neurotic states. We have seen how our little patient was overtaken by a great wave of repression and that it caught precisely those of his sexual components that were dominant.[12] He gave up masturbation, and turned away in disgust from everything that reminded him of excrement and of looking on at other people performing their natural functions. But these were not the components which were stirred up by the precipitating cause of the illness (his seeing the horse fall down) or which provided the material for the symptoms, that is, the content of the phobia.

This allows us, therefore, to make a radical distinction. We shall probably come to understand the case more deeply if we turn to those other components which *do* fulfil the two conditions that have just been mentioned. These other components were tendencies in Hans which had already been suppressed and which, so far as we can tell, had never been able to find uninhibited expression: hostile and jealous feelings towards his father, and sadistic impulses (premonitions, as it were, of copulation) towards his mother. These early suppressions may perhaps have gone to form the predisposition for his subsequent illness. These aggressive propensities of Hans's found no outlet, and as soon as there came a time of privation and of intensified sexual excitement, they tried to break their way out with reinforced strength. It was then that the battle which we call his "phobia" burst out. During the course of it a part of the repressed ideas, in a distorted form and transposed on to another complex, forced their way into consciousness as the content of the phobia. But it was a decidedly paltry success. Victory lay with the forces of repression; *and they made use of the opportunity to extend their dominion over components other than*

[12]Hans's father even observed that simultaneously with this repression a certain amount of sublimation set in. From the time of the beginning of his anxiety Hans began to show an increased interest in music and to develop his inherited musical gift.

those that had rebelled. This last circumstance, however, does not in the least alter the fact that the essence of Hans's illness was entirely dependent upon the nature of the instinctual components that had to be repulsed. The content of his phobia was such as to impose a very great measure of restriction upon his freedom of movement, and that was its purpose. It was therefore a powerful reaction against the obscure impulses to movement which were especially directed against his mother. For Hans horses had always typified pleasure in movement ("I'm a young horse," he had said as he jumped about); but since this pleasure in movement included the impulse to copulate, the neurosis imposed a restriction on it and exalted the horse into an emblem of terror. Thus it would seem as though all that the repressed instincts got from the neurosis was the honour of providing pretexts for the appearance of the anxiety in consciousness. But however clear may have been the victory in Hans's phobia of the forces that were opposed to sexuality, nevertheless, since such an illness is in its very nature a compromise, this cannot have been all that the repressed instincts obtained. After all, Hans's phobia of horses was an obstacle to his going into the street, and could serve as a means of allowing him to stay at home with his beloved mother. In this way, therefore, his affection for his mother triumphantly achieved its aim. In consequence of his phobia, the lover clung to the object of his love— though, to be sure, steps had been taken to make him innocuous. The true character of a neurotic disorder is exhibited in this twofold result.

Alfred Adler, in a suggestive paper,[13] has recently developed the view that anxiety arises from the suppression of what he calls the "aggressive instinct," and by a very sweeping synthetic process he ascribes to that instinct the chief part in human events, "in real life and in the neuroses." As we have come to the conclusion that in our present case of phobia

the anxiety is to be explained as being due to the repression of Hans's aggressive propensities (the hostile ones against his father and the sadistic ones against his mother), we seem to have produced a most striking piece of confirmation of Adler's view. I am nevertheless unable to assent to it, and indeed I regard it as a misleading generalization. I cannot bring myself to assume the existence of a special aggressive instinct alongside of the familiar instincts of self-preservation and of sex, and on an equal footing with them.[14] It appears to me that Adler has mistakenly promoted into a special and self-subsisting instinct what is in reality a universal and indispensable attribute of *all* instincts—their instinctual [*triebhaft*] and "pressing" character, what might be described as their capacity for initiating movement. Nothing would then remain of the other instincts but their relation to an aim, for their relation to the means of reaching that aim would have been taken over from them by the "aggressive instinct." In spite of all the uncertainty and obscurity of our theory of instincts I should prefer for the present to adhere to the usual view, which leaves each instinct its own power of becoming aggressive; and I should be inclined to recognize the two instincts which became repressed in Hans as familiar components of the sexual libido.

(III)

I shall now proceed to what I hope will be a brief discussion of how far little Hans's phobia offers any contribution of general importance to our views upon the life and upbringing of children. But before doing so I must return to the objection which has so long been held over, and according to which Hans was a

---

[13]"Der Aggressionsbetrieb im Leben und in der Neurose," 1908. This is the same paper from which I have borrowed the term "confluence of instincts." (See above, p. 12)

[14](*Footnote added* 1923:) The above passage was written at a time when Adler seemed still to be taking his stand upon the ground of psycho-analysis, and before he had put forward the masculine protest and disavowed repression. Since then I have myself been obliged to assert the existence of an "aggressive instinct," but it is different from Adler's. I prefer to call it the "destructive" or "death instinct." See *Beyond the Pleasure Principle* (1920) and *The Ego and the Id* (1923). Its opposition to the libidinal instincts finds an expression in the familiar polarity of love and hate. My disagreement with Adler's view, which results in a universal characteristic of instincts in general being reduced to be the property of a single one of them, remains unaltered.

neurotic, a "degenerate" with a bad heredity, and not a normal child, knowledge about whom could be applied to other children. I have for some time been thinking with pain of the way in which the adherents of "the normal person" will fall upon poor little Hans as soon as they are told that he can in fact be shown to have had a hereditary taint. His beautiful mother fell ill with a neurosis as a result of a conflict during her girlhood. I was able to be of assistance to her at the time, and this had in fact been the beginning of my connection with Hans's parents. It is only with the greatest diffidence that I venture to bring forward one or two considerations in his favour.

In the first place Hans was not what one would understand, strictly speaking, by a degenerate child, condemned by his heredity to be a neurotic. On the contrary, he was well formed physically, and was a cheerful, amiable, active-minded young fellow who might give pleasure to more people than his own father. There can be no question, of course, as to his sexual precocity; but on that point there is very little material upon which a fair comparison can be based. I gather, for instance, from a piece of collective research conducted in America, that it is by no means such a rare thing to find object-choice and feelings of love in boys at a similarly early age; and the same may be learnt from studying the records of the childhood of men who have later come to be recognized as "great." I should therefore be inclined to believe that sexual precocity is a correlate, which is seldom absent, of intellectual precocity, and that it is therefore to be met with in gifted children more often than might be expected.

Furthermore, let me say in Hans's favour (and I frankly admit my partisan attitude) that he is not the only child who has been overtaken by a phobia at some time or other in his childhood. Troubles of that kind are well known to be quite extraordinarily frequent, even in children the strictness of whose upbringing has left nothing to be desired. In later life these children either become neurotic or remain healthy. Their phobias are shouted down in the nursery because they are inaccessible to treatment and are decidedly inconvenient. In the course of months or years they diminish, and the child seems to recover; but no one can tell what psychological changes are necessitated by such a recovery, or what alterations in character are involved in it. When, however, an adult neurotic patient comes to us for psycho-analytic treatment (and let us assume that his illness has only become manifest after he has reached maturity), we find regularly that his neurosis has as its point of departure an infantile anxiety such as we have been discussing, and is in fact a continuation of it; so that, as it were, a continuous and undisturbed threat of psychical activity, taking its start from the conflicts of his childhood, has been spun through his life—irrespective of whether the first symptom of those conflicts has persisted or has retreated under the pressure of circumstances. I think, therefore, that Hans's illness may perhaps have been no more serious than that of many other children who are not branded as "degenerates"; but since he was brought up without being intimidated, and with as much consideration and as little coercion as possible, his anxiety dared to show itself more boldly. With him there was no place for such motives as a bad conscience or a fear of punishment, which with other children must no doubt contribute to making the anxiety less. It seems to me that we concentrate too much upon symptoms and concern ourselves too little with their causes. In bringing up children we aim only at being left in peace and having no difficulties, in short, at training up a model child, and we pay very little attention to whether such a course of development is for the child's good as well. I can therefore quite imagine that it may have been to Hans's advantage to have produced this phobia. For it directed his parents' attention to the unavoidable difficulties by which a child is confronted when in the course of his cultural training he is called upon to overcome the innate instinctual components of his mind; and his trouble brought his father to his assistance. It may be that Hans now enjoys an advantage over other children, in that he no longer carries within him that seed in the shape of repressed complexes which must always be of some significance for a child's later life, and which undoubtedly brings with it a certain degree of deformity of character if not a predisposition to a subsequent neurosis. I am inclined to think that this is so, but I do not know if many others will share my opinion; nor do I know whether experience will prove me right.

But I must now enquire what harm was done to Hans by dragging to light in him complexes such as are not only repressed by children but dreaded by their parents. Did the little boy proceed to take some serious action as regards what he wanted from his mother? or did his evil intentions against his father give place to evil deeds? Such misgivings will no doubt have occurred to many doctors, who misunderstand the nature of psychoanalysis and think that wicked instincts are strengthened by being made conscious. Wise men like these are being no more than consistent when they implore us for heaven's sake not to meddle with the evil things that lurk behind a neurosis. In so doing they forget, it is true, that they are physicians, and their words bear a fatal resemblance to Dogberry's, when he advised the Watch to avoid all contact with any thieves they might happen to meet: "for such kind of men, the less you meddle or make with them, why, the more is for your honesty."[15]

On the contrary, the only results of the analysis were that Hans recovered, that he ceased to be afraid of horses, and that he got on to rather familiar terms with his father, as the latter reported with some amusement. But whatever his father may have lost in the boy's respect he won back in his confidence: "I thought," said Hans, "you knew everything, as you knew that about the horse." For analysis does not undo the *effects* of repression. The instincts which were formerly suppressed remain suppressed; but the same effect is produced in a different way. Analysis replaces the process of repression, which is an automatic and excessive one, by a temperate and purposeful control on the part of the highest agencies of the mind. In a word, *analysis replaces repression by condemnation.* This seems to bring us the long-looked-for evidence that consciousness has a biological function, and that with its entrance upon the scene an important advantage is secured.[16]

If matters had lain entirely in my hands, I should have ventured to give the child the one remaining piece of enlightenment which his parents withheld from him. I should have confirmed his instinctive premonitions, by telling him of the existence of the vagina and of copulation; thus I should have still further diminished his unsolved residue, and put an end to his stream of questions. I am convinced that this new piece of enlightenment would have made him lose neither his love for his mother nor his own childish nature, and that he would have understood that his preoccupation with these important, these momentous things must rest for the present—until his wish to be big had been fulfilled. But the educational experiment was not carried so far.

That no sharp line can be drawn between "neurotic" and "normal" people—whether children or adults—that our conception of "disease" is a purely practical one and a question of summation, that predisposition and the eventualities of life must combine before the threshold of this summation is overstepped, and that consequently a number of individuals are constantly passing from the class of healthy people into that of neurotic patients, while a far smaller number also make the journey in the opposite direction,—

---

[15][*Much Ado about Nothing*, III, 3.] At this point I cannot keep back an astonished question. Where do my opponents obtain their knowledge, which they produce with so much confidence, on the question whether the repressed sexual instincts play a part, and if so what part, in the aetiology of the neuroses, if they shut their patients' mouths as soon as they begin to talk about their complexes or their derivatives? For the only alternative source of knowledge remaining open to them are my own writings and those of my adherents.

[16](*Footnote added* 1923:) I am here using the word "consciousness" in a sense which I later avoided, namely, to describe our normal processes of thought—such, that is, as are capable of consciousness. We know that thought processes of this kind may also take place *preconsciously;* and it is wiser to regard their actual "consciousness" from a purely phenomenological standpoint. By this I do not, of course, mean to contradict the expectation that consciousness in this more limited sense of the word must also fulfil some biological function.

all of these are things which have been said so often and have met with so much agreement that I am certainly not alone in maintaining their truth. It is, to say the least of it, extremely probable that a child's upbringing can exercise a powerful influence for good or for evil upon the predisposition which we have just mentioned as one of the factors in the occurrence of "disease"; but what that upbringing is to aim at and at what point it is to be brought to bear seem at present to be very doubtful questions. Hitherto education has only set itself the task of controlling, or, it would often be more proper to say, of suppressing, the instincts. The results have been by no means gratifying, and where the process has succeeded it has only been to the advantage of a small number of favoured individuals who have not been required to suppress their instincts. Nor has any one inquired by what means and at what cost the suppression of the inconvenient instincts has been achieved. Supposing now that we substitute another task for this one, and aim instead at making the individual capable of becoming a civilized and useful member of society with the least possible sacrifice of his own activity; in that case the information gained by psycho-analysis, upon the origin of pathogenic complexes and upon the nucleus of every nervous affection, can claim with justice that it deserves to be regarded by educators as an invaluable guide in their conduct towards children. What practical conclusions may follow from this, and how far experience may justify the application of those conclusions within our present social system, are matters which I leave to the examination and decision of others.

I cannot take leave of our small patient's phobia without giving expression to a notion which has made its analysis, leading as it did to a recovery, seem of especial value to me. Strictly speaking, I learnt nothing new from this analysis, nothing that I had not already been able to discover (though often less distinctly and more indirectly) from other patients analysed at a more advanced age. But the neuroses of these other patients could in every instance be traced back to the same infantile complexes that were revealed behind Hans's phobia. I am therefore tempted to claim for this neurosis of childhood the significance of being a type and a model, and to suppose that the multiplicity of the phenomena of repression exhibited by neuroses and the abundance of their pathogenic material do not prevent their being derived from a very limited number of processes concerned with identical ideational complexes.

References

Freud, S. The interpretation of dreams. 1900, **4-5**.

Freud, S. Three essays on the theory of sexuality. 1905, **7**, 125.

Freud, S. Beyond the pleasure principle. 1920, **18**.

Freud, S. The ego and the id. 1923a, **19**.

Freud, S. The infantile genital organization of the libido. 1923b, **19**.

Freud, S. The origins of psycho-analysis. 1950, **1**.

All in S. Freud, *The standard edition of the complete psychological works*, J. Strachey (Ed.). London: Hogarth Press, 1953-66.

An Empirical Investigation of the Castration Complex in Dreams

Calvin Hall and Robert L. Van de Castle

According to the classical theory of the castration complex as it was formulated by Freud (1925; 1931; 1933), the male is afraid of losing his penis (castration anxiety) and the female envies the male for having a penis (penis envy). One consequence of this envy is that she wants to deprive the male of his organ (castration wish).

The empirical work investigating this topic has generally produced results consistent with Freud's formulation. Hattendorf (1932) indicated that the second most frequent question asked of mothers by children in the two- to five-year-old group concerned the physical differences between the sexes. Horney (1932) reported that when a clinic doctor tried to induce boys and girls to insert a finger in a ball that had developed a split, significantly more boys than girls hesitated or refused to accede to this request. Using a doll-play interview, Conn (1940) noted that two-thirds of children who reported that they had seen the genitals of the opposite sex could not recall their attitude or feelings about the initial discovery and over one third who could recall their attitude definitely felt something was wrong. On the basis of these results the author concludes (Conn, 1940, p. 754), "It appears that the large majority of boys and girls responded to the first sight of genital differences with tranquil, unperturbed acceptance." This conclusion was criticized by Levy (1940) who carried out repeated doll-play interviews with children and concluded (p. 762), "The typical response of the child in our culture, when he becomes aware of the primary

difference in sex anatomy, confirms the psychoanalyst's finding, namely, that castration anxiety is aroused in boys and a feeling of envy with destructive impulse. toward the penis in girls." In a widely quoted review of psychoanalytic studies by Sears (1943) a few years later he summed up the castration studies with the statement (p. 36), "Freud seriously overestimated the frequency of the castration complex." In a study of problem children, Huschka (1944) reported that 73 per cent of parents dealt with masturbation problems destructively and that the most common threat was that of genital injury. The normal children used by Friedman (1952) completed stories involving castration situations and the author interpreted his data as offering support for the commonness of castration anxiety, particularly in the case of boys.

The remaining studies used college students as *S*s. Blum (1949) found significantly more responses to the Blacky Test indicative of castration anxiety among males than females. A method of scoring castration anxiety from TAT scores was developed by Schwartz (1955) who found (1956) that male homosexuals displayed significantly more castration anxiety than normal males and that males obtained higher castration-anxiety scores than females. Using a multiple-choice question about the castration card of the Blacky, Sarnoff and Corwin (1959) reported that males with high castration scores showed a significantly greater increase in fear of death than low-castration males did after being exposed to sexually arousing stimuli.

The foregoing studies indicate that techniques designed to elicit unconscious material are generally successful in demonstrating the

From C. Hall and R. L. Van de Castle, "An Empirical Investigation of the Castration Complex in Dreams," *Journal of Personality*, 1965, **33**, 20-29. Reprinted by permission of the Duke University Press.

manifestations of the castration complex that would be predictable from Freudian theory. It should follow, then, that since dreams have been characterized as "the royal road to the unconscious," manifestations of the castration complex would be clearly discernible in dreams. The present study was undertaken to investigate whether differences in dream contents, presumably related to castration reactions, would appear between adult male and female dreamers.

The specific hypothesis tested in this investigation is that male dreamers will report more dreams expressive of castration anxiety than they will dreams involving castration wishes and penis envy while the pattern will be reversed for females, i.e., they will report more dreams containing expressions of castration wishes and penis envy than they will dreams containing castration anxiety.

Method

Subjects

A total of 120 college students divided into three groups of 20 males and 20 females each served as Ss. Groups 1 and 2 were students in Hall's undergraduate class in personality at Western Reserve University during 1947 and 1948. The recording of nocturnal dreams was described to the students as a class project for which they would be given extra credit if they participated but would not be penalized for not doing so. They were given opportunities to earn extra credit in other ways than recording dreams. Dreams were reported on a standard report form. These dreams have been published in *Primary Records in Psychology* (Barker & Kaplan, 1963) and Groups 1 and 2 consist of the first 40 of the 43 female series and the first 40 of the 44 male series reported therein.

Group 3 were students in Van de Castle's class in abnormal psychology at the University of Denver during 1962 and 1963. They were required to hand in an average of two dreams a week. Standard instructions similar to those on Hall's form were given. Students were allowed to turn in daydreams if they could recall no nocturnal dreams, but only nocturnal dreams were scored in this study.

Scoring for Castration Complex Indicators in Dreams

A scoring manual which sets forth the criteria for castration anxiety (CA), castration wish (CW), and penis envy (PE) in reported dreams was devised. These criteria were selected because either they reflect concern over castration directly or they represent displacements from one part of the body, i.e., the genitals, to another part of the body, e.g., the hand, or they make use of commonly recognized symbols for the male genitals, e.g., guns, knives, and pens. Copies of a revised version of the original manual (Institute of Dream Research, 1964) are available on request to the authors. A summary of the criteria follows.

Criteria for Castration Anxiety

1. Actual or threatened loss, removal, injury to, or pain in a specific part of the dreamer's body; actual or threatened cutting, clawing, biting, or stabbing of the dreamer's body as a whole or to any part of the dreamer's body; defect of a specified part of the dreamer's body; some part of the dreamer's body is infantile, juvenile, or undersized.

2. Actual or threatened injury or damage to, loss of, or defect in an object or animal belonging to the dreamer or one that is in his possession in the dream.

3. Inability or difficulty of the dreamer in using his penis or an object that has phallic characteristics; inability or difficulty of the dreamer in placing an object in a receptacle.

4. A male dreams that he is a woman or changes into a woman, or has or acquires female secondary sex characteristics, or is wearing woman's clothes or accessories.

Criteria for Castration Wish

The criteria for castration wish are the same as those for castration anxiety except that they do not occur to the dreamer but to another person in his dream.

Criteria for Penis Envy

1. Acquisition *within* the dream by the dreamer of an object that has phallic characteristics; acquisition of a better penis or an impressive phallic object.

2. The dreamer envies or admires a man's physical characteristics or performance or possession that has phallic characteristics.

3. A female dreams that she is a man or changes into a man, or has acquired male secondary sex characteristics, or is wearing men's clothing or accessories which are not customarily worn by women.

Each dream was read and scored for each of these criteria. The maximum score was one point for each condition, even if several independent instances of the same condition occurred within the dream. It was possible, however, for the same dream to be scored for more than one condition, e.g., a dream could be given one point for CA and one point for PE.

After the writers had acquired practice in the use of the manual, a reliability study was made. The 119 dreams of eight males and 123 dreams of eight females were scored independently by the writers. The scores were then compared. An agreement was counted if both judges scored the same condition, e.g., castration anxiety, in the same dream or both judges did not score a condition, e.g., penis envy, in the same dream. A disagreement was counted if one judge scored for a condition and the other judge did not score for the same condition in the same dream. The results are presented in Table 1.

Table 1. Percentage of agreement between two scores.

Number dreamers	*Number dreams*	*CA*	*CW*	*PE*
8 males	119	87	94	96
8 females	123	89	94	93
16	242	88	94	94

Results

The number of dreams containing scorable elements for the three groups of *S*s is shown in Table 2. It will be noted that in every group the number of male dreams exceeds the number of female dreams for castration anxiety, while in every group the number of female dreams is higher than male dreams for both the castration-wish and the penis-envy categories.

Since the distribution of scores for any category was markedly skewed with zero scores predominating for many individual dreamers, it was felt that the assumptions for any parametric statistic such as *t* could not be met. Statistical evaluation of the hypothesis was therefore made by use of the chi-square technique. The unit of analysis was the *individual dreamer*. The analysis consisted of determining the number of male and female dreamers whose CA score exceeded the combined total of their CW and PE scores and the number of male and female dreamers whose combined CW and PE scores exceeded their CA score. Ties (10 male and 19 female) were evenly divided between these two groupings. The resulting 2 X 2 table is shown in Table 3.

The majority of male dreamers had higher CA scores while the majority of female dreamers had higher CW and PE scores. The hypothesis of this study was thus supported at a high level of statistical significance (*p* < .001).

Do each of the conditions, CW and PE, contribute substantially to the obtained difference? Table 2 reveals that each of these conditions appears in approximately twice as many female dreams as male dreams. To make sure that such a difference was not produced by a few atypical dreamers, a count was made of the number of women whose scores for each of these separate conditions exceeded that of their CA score. It was found that 20 women had CW scores higher than CA scores, whereas only 5 males scored in this direction, and that 12 women had PE scores higher than their CA scores whereas the same was true for only 1 male. The answer to the question raised earlier is that both CW and PE contribute substantially to the obtained difference.

To look at the sex differences from another viewpoint let us examine the relative freedom from castration anxiety in male and female

Table 2. Number of dreams showing CA, CW, and PE among college students.

Group*	Number of dreams analyzed		Number of dreams containing					
			CA		CW		PE	
	M	F	M	F	M	F	M	F
1	308	305	40	7	5	8	2	5
2	327	328	54	15	11	21	5	13
3	318	323	57	35	21	32	9	14
Total	953	956	151	57	37	61	16	32
Range (per dreamer)	7-24	10-21	0-8	0-4	0-4	0-6	0-2	0-3

*N = 20 male and 20 female dreamers for each group.

Table 3. Number of male and female dreamers with CA scores higher and lower than CW and PE scores.

	CA more than CW and PE	CW and PE more than CA	
Number of male dreamers	48	12	60
Number of female dreamers	21.5	38.5	60
	69.5	50.5	120

chi-square = 23.96

dreamers. Exactly 50 per cent ($N = 30$) of women in the present sample had zero CA scores whereas only 13 per cent ($N = 8$) of males received zero CA scores. These additional analyses concur in supporting the hypothesis of this investigation, namely that manifestations of castration anxiety in dreams is more typical of males and manifestations of both castration wishes and penis envy are more typical of females.

Discussion

Although the differences are clearcut in favor of the hypothesis, nonetheless there are many manifestations of castration wish and penis envy in men's dreams and many manifestations of castration anxiety in women. The male's wish to castrate others and his envy and admiration of another man's physical and sexual equipment are not difficult to understand. In view of the great amount of physical aggression that is expressed in men's dreams (Hall & Domhoff, 1963), and the amount of competition that men engage in during their waking life, perhaps it is not surprising that their dreams should contain cas-

tration wishes and penis envy. Moreover, there may be, as psychoanalytic theory claims, an archaic wish in the male to castrate the father which manifests itself in displaced ways in their dreams. But castration anxiety still takes precedence over these other themes in male dreams.

The amount of castration anxiety in female dreams is less easy, perhaps, to comprehend. Why should there be anxiety over losing something they do not have and never have had? The psychoanalytic explanation is that females unconsciously feel they once had the same genital organs as the male and that they were taken from them. The menses are a constant reminder of this fantasied event. Accordingly, we would expect to find in their dreams expressions of this fantasied castration. Men dream of what might happen whereas women dream of what they think has happened. The fact that anxiety is usually stronger for an anticipated future event than for a realized past one would explain why men have more castration anxiety than women do.

It will be observed (Table 2) that more castration anxiety is expressed in the dreams of males (151 occurrences) than castration wish plus penis envy is in the dreams of females (93 occurrences). The explanation for this may be that the female displaces her penis envy in other ways than that of wishing to castrate others. Freud (1917) mentions two such displacements. He writes: "In girls, the discovery of the penis gives rise to envy for it, which later changes into the wish for a man as the possessor of a penis. Even before this the wish for a penis has changed into a wish for a baby" (p. 132).

This suggested to us another testable hypothesis, namely, that more dreams of babies and of getting married should be reported by women than by men. Accordingly, we went through the 1,909 dreams and scored them for the presence of weddings and babies. Females had 60 dreams in which weddings or preparations for weddings occurred; males had only 9 such dreams. Females had 85 dreams in which babies or very young children figured; males had 32 such dreams. These findings appear to confirm the hypothesis, although, of course, other explanations for women dreaming more than men do of weddings and babies may occur to the reader.

The *S*s of this investigation were for the most part in their late teens and early twenties. What happens to manifestations of the castration complex in dreams with age? Relative to this question we would like to mention the findings obtained from analyzing 600 dreams collected from a man between the ages of 37 and 54. The 600 dreams were divided into six sets of 100 dreams each. Each dream was scored for castration anxiety, castration wish, and penis envy. The results are presented in Table 4. The incidence for each of the three categories does not vary to any

great extent over the 17 years, nor do the averages differ noticeably from the averages for college men. In this one case, at least, castration anxiety appears to express itself at the same rate in dreams into the fifties.

In an earlier investigation by one of the writers (Hall, 1955), it was concluded that the dream of being attacked is not a manifestation of castration anxiety as suggested by the findings of Harris (1948) but represents the feminine attitudes of weakness, passivity, inferiority, and masochism as formulated by Freud. The findings of the present study do not conflict with the earlier one because the criteria used for scoring castration anxiety were different than the criterion used for identifying the dream of being attacked. The dream of being attacked consists, for the most part, of attacks on or threats to the dreamer's *whole* body. In the present study, attacks upon the whole body are categorically excluded except for a small number of cases where the threat is one of cutting, clawing, biting, or stabbing. The damage or threat must be to a *specific part* of the body in order for it to be scored as castration anxiety. Moreover, the criteria used in the present investigation are much more extensive. They include damage to a possession of the dreamer, his difficulty in using phallic objects, and by a male becoming feminized.

Although the hypothesis of this investigation was derived from Freudian theory, and its confirmation therefore supports the theory, the results may be accounted for by other theoretical positions. For example, the greater incidence of injuries and accidents in male dreams may merely reflect the nature of the activities in which they engage in waking life as compared with the activities of women. It

Table 4. Manifestations of the castration complex in the dreams of a middle-aged man.

	Incidence per 100 dreams						Average	Average for College men
	I	*II*	*III*	*IV*	*V*	*VI*		
CA	14	18	13	15	10	17	14.5	15.8
CW	4	3	2	5	8	5	4.5	3.9
PE	2	1	2	0	1	2	1.3	1.7

is believed that men engage in more dangerous activities and take more risks than women do. If this is the case it might be expected that their dreams would be in accord with their waking life experiences. On the other hand, if they do in fact take more chances and risk physical harm, this raises the question of why they do. It does not suffice, we feel, to say that they have adopted the role which "society" has fashioned for them. Why has "society" created such a role and why do boys acquiesce in being shaped to the role? *Ad hoc* explanations of findings, in any event, are not very satisfying.

Summary

This study was undertaken to investigate whether sex differences would be found in the incidence of manifestations of castration anxiety (CA), castration wish (CW), and penis envy (PE) in dreams. Criteria for each of these three components of the castration complex were formulated, on the basis of which a scoring manual was written.

It was hypothesized that male dreamers will report more dreams expressive of CA than they will dreams involving CW and PE whereas the pattern will be reversed for females, i.e., they will report more dreams containing expressions of CW and PE than they will dreams containing CA. The hypothesis was supported for three different groups of college students evenly divided as to sex, and the combined results for the 120 students were significant beyond the .001 level.

Additional data were also presented to show that many more women than men dream about babies and weddings and that the relative incidence of the various castration components remains quite stable throughout a long dream series spanning 17 years.

Although the results are congruent with Freudian theory, and to that extent add to the construct validity of the castration complex, it was recognized that alternative theoretical positions could be invoked to account for the findings of this investigation.

References

Barker, R., & Kaplan, B. (Eds.) *Primary records in psychology.* Publ. No. 2. Lawrence, Kansas: Univer. of Kansas Publ., 1963.

Blum, G. S. A study of the psychoanalytic theory of psychosexual development. *Genet. psychol. Monogr.*, 1949, **39**, 3-99.

Conn, J. H. Children's reactions to the discovery of genital differences. *Amer. J. Orthopsychiat.,* 1940, **10**, 747-754.

Freud, S. (1917) On transformations of instinct as exemplified in anal erotism. In *The standard edition.* London: Hogarth Press, 1955. Vol. 17, pp. 127-133.

Freud, S. (1925) Some psychical consequences of the anatomical distinction between the sexes. In *The standard edition.* London: Hogarth Press, 1961. Vol. 19, pp. 248-258.

Freud, S. (1931) Female sexuality. In *The standard edition.* London: Hogarth Press, 1961. Vol. 21, pp. 225-243.

Freud, S. (1933) *A new series of introductory lectures on psychoanalysis.* New York: Norton, 1933. Chap. 5, pp. 153-185.

Friedman, S. M. An empirical study of the castration and Oedipus complexes. *Genet. psychol. Monogr.*, 1952, **46**, 61-130.

Hall, C. S. The significance of the dream of being attacked. *J. Pers.*, 1955, **24**, 168-180.

Hall, C., & Domhoff, B. Aggression in dreams. *Internat. J. Soc. Psychiat.*, 1963, **9**, 259-267.

Harris, I. Observations concerning typical anxiety dreams. *Psychiat.*, 1948, **11**, 301-309.

Hattendorf, K. W. A study of the questions of young children concerning sex. *J. Soc. Psychol.*, 1932, **3**, 37-65.

Horney, Karen. The dread of woman. *Internat. J. Psychoanal.*, 1932, **13**, 348-360.

Huschka, Mabel. The incidence and character of masturbation threats in a group of problem children. In S. S. Tomkins (Ed.), *Contemporary psychopathology.* Cambridge: Harvard Univer. Press, 1944.

Institute of Dream Research. A manual for scoring castration anxiety, castration wishes, and penis envy in dreams. Miami, 1964.

Levy, D. M. "Control-situation" studies of children's responses to the differences in genitalia. *Amer. J. Orthopsychiat.,* 1940, **10**, 755-762.

Sarnoff, I., & Corwin, S. B. Castration anxiety and the fear of death. *J. Pers.*, 1959, **27**, 374-385.

Schwartz, B. J. Measurement of castration anxiety and anxiety over loss of love. *J. Pers.*, 1955, **24**, 204-219.

Schwartz, B. J. An empirical test of two Freudian hypotheses concerning castration anxiety. *J. Pers.*, 1956, **24**, 318-327.

Sears, R. Survey of objective studies of psychoanalytic concepts. *Soc. Sci. Res. Coun.*, 1943, Bull. 51.

A Critique of Freud's Case of Little Hans

Joseph Wolpe and Stanley Rachman

Beginning with Wohlgemuth's trenchant monograph (1923), the factual and logical bases of psychoanalytic theory have been the subject of a considerable number of criticisms. These have generally been dismissed by psychoanalysts, at least partly on the ground that the critics are oblivious of the "wealth of detail" provided by the individual case. One way to examine the soundness of the analysts' position is to study fully-reported cases that they themselves regard as having contributed significantly to their theories. We have undertaken to do this, and have chosen as our subject matter one of Freud's most famous cases, given in such detail that the events of a few months occupy 140 pages of the *Collected Papers*.

In 1909, Freud published "The Analysis of a Phobia in a Five-year-old Boy" (1950). This case is commonly referred to as "The case of Little Hans." Ernest Jones, in his biography of Freud, points out that it was "the first published account of a child analysis" (1955, p. 289), and states that "the brilliant success of child analysis" since then was "indeed inaugurated by the study of this very case" (1955, p. 292). The case also has special significance in the development of psychoanalytic theory because Freud believed himself to have found in it "a more direct and less round-about proof" of some fundamental psychoanalytic theorems (1950, p. 150). In particular, he thought that it provided a direct demonstration of the essential role of sexual urges in the development of phobias. He felt his position to have been greatly

From J. Wolpe and S. Rachman, "Psychoanalytic 'Evidence': A Critique Based on Freud's Case of Little Hans," *Journal of Nervous and Mental Disease*, 1960, **130**, 135-148. Copyright 1960 by The Williams & Wilkins Co., Baltimore, Md., U. S. A. Reprinted by permission of the publisher and the authors.

strengthened by this case and two generations of analysts have referred to the evidence of Little Hans as a basic substantiation of psychoanalytic theories (e.g., Fenichel, 1945; Glover, 1956; Hendrick, 1939). As an example, Glover (1956, p. 76) may be quoted.

In its time the analysis of Little Hans was a remarkable achievement and the story of the analysis constitutes one of the most valued records in psychoanalytical archives. Our concepts of phobia formation, of the positive Oedipus complex, of ambivalence, castration anxiety and repression, to mention but a few, were greatly reinforced and amplified as the result of this analysis.

In this paper we shall re-examine this case history and assess the evidence presented. We shall show that although there are manifestations of sexual behavior on the part of Hans, there is no scientifically acceptable evidence showing any connection between this behavior and the child's phobia for horses; that the assertion of such connection is pure assumption; that the elaborate discussions that follow from it are pure speculation; and that the case affords no factual support for any of the concepts listed by Glover above. Our examination of this case exposes in considerable detail patterns of thinking and attitudes to evidence that are well-nigh universal among psychoanalysts. It suggests the need for more careful scrutiny of the bases of psychoanalytic "discoveries" than has been customary; and we hope it will prompt psychologists to make similar critical examinations of basic psychoanalytic writings.

The case material on which Freud's analysis is based was collected by Little Hans's father, who kept Freud informed of developments by regular written reports. The father also had several consultations with Freud concerning Little Hans's phobia. During the analysis, Freud himself saw the little boy only once.

The following are the most relevant facts noted of Hans's earlier life. At the age of three, he showed "a quite peculiarly lively interest in that portion of his body which he used to describe as his widdler." When he was three and a half, his mother found him with his hand to his penis. She threatened him in these words, "If you do that, I shall send for Dr. A. to cut off your widdler. And then what will you widdle with?" Hans replied, "With my bottom." Numerous further remarks concerning widdlers in animals and humans were made by Hans between the ages of three and four, including questions directed at his mother and father asking them if they also had widdlers. Freud attaches importance to the following exchange between Hans and his mother. Hans was "looking on intently while his mother undressed."

Mother: "What are you staring like that for?"
Hans: "I was only looking to see if you'd got a widdler, too."
Mother: "Of course. Didn't you know that?"
Hans: "No, I thought you were so big you'd have a widdler like a horse."

When Hans was three and a half his sister was born. The baby was delivered at home and Hans heard his mother "coughing," observed the appearance of the doctor and was called into the bedroom after the birth. Hans was initially "very jealous of the new arrival" but within six months his jealousy faded and was replaced by "brotherly affection." When Hans was four he discovered a seven-year-old girl in the neighborhood and spent many hours awaiting her return from school. The father commented that "the violence with which this 'long-range love' came over him was to be explained by his having no play-fellows of either sex." At this period also, "he was constantly putting his arms round" his visiting boy cousin, aged five, and was once heard saying, "I *am* so fond of you" when giving his cousin "one of these tender embraces." Freud speaks of this as the "first trace of homosexuality."

At the age of four and a half, Hans went with his parents to Gmunden for the summer holidays. On holiday Hans had numerous playmates including Mariedl, a fourteen-year-old girl. One evening Hans said, "I want Mariedl to sleep with me." Freud says that Hans's wish was an expression of his desire to have Mariedl as part of his family. Hans's parents occasionally took him into their bed and Freud claims that, "there can be no doubt that lying beside them had aroused erotic feelings in him;[1] so that his wish to sleep with Mariedl had an erotic sense as well."

Another incident during the summer holidays is given considerable importance by Freud, who refers to it as Hans's attempt to seduce his mother. It must be quoted here in full.

Hans, four and a quarter.[2] This morning Hans was given his usual daily bath by his mother and afterwards dried and powdered. As his mother was powdering round his penis and taking care not to touch it, Hans said, "Why don't you put your finger there?"
Mother: "Because that'd be piggish."
Hans: "What's that? Piggish? Why?"
Mother: "Because it's not proper."
Hans (laughing): "But it's great fun."

Another occurrence prior to the onset of his phobia was that when Hans, aged four and a half, laughed while watching his sister being bathed and was asked why he was laughing, he replied, "I'm laughing at Hanna's widdler." "Why?" "Because her widdler's so lovely." The father's comment is, "Of course his answer was a disingenuous one. In reality her widdler seemed to him funny. Moreover, this is the first time he has recognized in this way the distinction between male and female genitals instead of denying it."

In early January, 1908, the father wrote to Freud that Hans had developed "a nervous disorder." The symptoms he reported were:

---

[1]This is nothing but surmise—yet Freud asserts "there can be no doubt" about it.

[2]Earlier his age during the summer holidays is given as four and a half. Unfortunately, there is no direct statement as to the length of the holiday.

fear of going into the streets; depression in the evening; and a fear that a horse would bite him in the street. Hans's father suggested that "the ground was prepared by sexual over-excitation due to his mother's tenderness" and that the fear of the horse "seems somehow to be connected with his having been frightened by a large penis." The first signs appeared on January 7th, when Hans was being taken to the park by his nursemaid as usual. He started crying and said he wanted to "coax" (caress) with his mother. At home "he was asked why he had refused to go any further and had cried, but he would not say." The following day, after hesitation and crying, he went out with his mother. Returning home Hans said ("after much internal struggling"), "*I was afraid a horse would bite me*" (original italics). As on the previous day, Hans showed fear in the evening and asked to be "coaxed." He is also reported as saying, "I know I shall have to go for a walk again tomorrow," and "The horse'll come into the room." On the same day he was asked by his mother if he put his hand to his widdler. He replied in the affirmative. The following day his mother warned him to refrain from doing this.

At this point in the narrative, Freud provided an interpretation of Hans's behavior and consequently arranged with the boy's father "that he should tell the boy that all this nonsense about horses was a piece of nonsense and nothing more. The truth was, his father was to say, that he was very fond of his mother and wanted to be taken into her bed. The reason he was afraid of horses now was that he had taken so much interest in their widdlers." Freud also suggested giving Hans some sexual enlightenment and telling him that females "had no widdler at all."[3]

"After Hans had been enlightened there followed a fairly quiet period." After an attack of influenza which kept him in bed for two weeks, the phobia got worse. He then had his tonsils out and was indoors for a fur-

ther week. The phobia became "very much worse."

During March, 1908, after his physical illness had been cured, Hans apparently had many talks with his father about the phobia. On March 1, his father again told Hans that horses do not bite. Hans replied that white horses bite and related that while at Gmunden he had heard and seen Lizzi (a playmate) being warned by her father to avoid a white horse lest it bite. The father said to Lizzi, "*Don't put your finger to the white horse*" (original italics). Hans's father's reply to this account given by his son was, "I say, it strikes me it isn't a horse you mean, but a widdler, that one mustn't put one's hand to." Hans answered, "But a widdler doesn't bite." The father: "Perhaps it does, though." Hans then "went on eagerly to try to prove to me that it was a white horse." The following day, in answer to a remark of his father's, Hans said that his phobia was "so bad because I still put my hand to my widdler every night." Freud remarks here that, "Doctor and patient, father and son, were therefore at one in ascribing the chief share in the pathogenesis of Hans's present condition to his habit of onanism." He implies that this unanimity is significant, quite disregarding the father's indoctrination of Hans the previous day.[4]

On March 13, the father told Hans that his fear would disappear if he stopped putting his hand to his widdler. Hans replied, "But I don't put my hand to my widdler any more." Father: "But you still want to." Hans agreed, "Yes, I do." His father suggested that he should sleep in a sack to prevent him from wanting to touch his widdler. Hans accepted this view and on the following day was much less afraid of horses.

Two days later the father again told Hans that girls and women have no widdlers. "Mummy has none, Hanna has none and so on." Hans asked how they managed to wid-

---

[3]Incidentally contradicting what Hans's mother had told him earlier.

[4]The mere fact that Hans repeats an interpretation he has heard from his father is regarded by Freud as demonstrating the accuracy of the interpretation; even though the child's spontaneous responses noted earlier in the paragraph point clearly in the opposite direction.

dle and was told "They don't have widdlers like yours. Haven't you noticed already when Hanna was being given her bath." On March 17 Hans reported a phantasy in which he saw his mother naked. On the basis of this phantasy and the conversation related above, Freud concluded that Hans had not accepted the enlightenment given by his father. Freud says, "He regretted that it should be so, and stuck to his former view in phantasy. He may also perhaps have had his reasons for refusing to believe his father at first." Discussing this matter subsequently, Freud says that the "enlightenment" given a short time before to the effect that women really do not possess a widdler was bound to have a shattering effect upon his self-confidence and to have aroused his castration complex. For this reason he resisted the information, and for this reason it had no therapeutic effect.[5]

For reasons of space we shall recount the subsequent events in very brief form. On a visit to the Zoo Hans expressed fear of the giraffe, elephant and all large animals. Hans's father said to him, "Do you know why you're afraid of big animals? Big animals have big widdlers and you're really afraid of big widdlers." This was denied by the boy.

The next event of prominence was a dream (or phantasy) reported by Hans. "In the night there was a big giraffe in the room and a crumpled one; and the big one called out because I took the crumpled one away from it. Then it stopped calling out; and then I sat down on the top of the crumpled one."

After talking to the boy the father reported to Freud that this dream was "a matrimonial scene transposed into giraffe life. He was seized in the night with a longing for his mother, for her caresses, for her genital organ, and came into the room for that reason. The whole thing is a continuation of his fear of horses." The father infers that the dream is related to Hans's habit of occasionally getting into his parents' bed in the face of his father's disapproval. Freud's addition to "the father's penetrating observation" is that sitting down on the crumpled giraffe means taking possession of his mother. Confirmation of this dream interpretation is claimed by reference to an incident which occurred the next day. The father wrote that on leaving the house with Hans he said to his wife, "Goodbye, big giraffe." "Why giraffe?" asked Hans. "Mummy's the big giraffe," replied the father. "Oh, yes," said Hans, "and Hanna's[6] the crumpled giraffe, isn't she?" The father's account continues, "In the train I explained the giraffe phantasy to him, upon which he said 'Yes, that's right.' And when I said to him that I was the big giraffe and that its long neck reminded him of a widdler, he said 'Mummy has a neck like a giraffe too. I saw when she was washing her white neck.'"

On March 30, the boy had a short consultation with Freud who reports that despite all the enlightenment given to Hans, the fear of horses continued undiminished. Hans explained that he was especially bothered "by what horses wear in front of their eyes and the black round their mouths." This latter detail Freud interpreted as meaning a moustache. "I asked him whether he meant a moustache," and then, "disclosed to him that he was afraid of his father precisely because he was so fond of his mother." Freud pointed out that this was a groundless fear. On April 2, the father was able to report "the first real improvement." The next day Hans, in answer to his father's inquiry, explained that he came into his father's bed when he was frightened. In the next few days further details of Hans's fear were elaborated. He told his father that he was most scared of horses with "a thing on their mouths," that he was scared lest the horses fall, and that he was most scared of horse-drawn buses.

---

[5]It is pertinent at this point to suggest that Hans "resisted" this enlightenment because his mother had told him quite the opposite and his observations of his sister's widdler had not been contradicted. When he was four, Hans had observed that his sister's widdler was "still quite small." When he was four and a half, again while watching his sister being bathed, he observed that she had "a lovely widdler." On neither occasion was he contradicted.

[6]Hans's baby sister, *not* his mother. Again, the more spontaneous response directly contradicts Freud's interpretation. Thus Freud's subsequent comment that Hans only confirmed the interpretation of the two giraffes as his father and mother and not the sexual symbolism, transgresses the facts.

Hans: "I'm most afraid too when a bus comes along."
Father: "Why? Because it's so big?"
Hans: "No. Because once a horse in a bus fell."
Father: "When?"

Hans then recounted such an incident. This was later confirmed by his mother.

Father: "What did you think when the horse fell down?"
Hans: "Now it will always be like this. All horses in buses'll fall down."
Father: "In all buses?"
Hans: "Yes. And in furniture vans too. Not often in furniture vans."
Father: "You had your nonsense already at that time?"
Hans: "*No* (italics added). I only got it then. When the horse in the bus fell down, it gave me such a fright really: That was when I got the nonsense."

The father adds that, "all of this was confirmed by my wife, as well as the fact that *the anxiety broke out immediately afterwards*" (italics added).

Hans's father continued probing for a meaning of the black thing around the horses' mouths. Hans said it looked like a muzzle but his father had never seen such a horse "although Hans asseverates that such horses do exist."[7] He continues, "I suspect that some part of the horse's bridle really reminded him of a moustache and that after I alluded to this the fear disappeared." A day later Hans observing his father stripped to the waist said, "Daddy you are lovely! You're so white."

Father: "Yes. Like a white horse."
Hans: "The only black thing's your moustache. Or perhaps it's a black muzzle."[8]

Further details about the horse that fell were also elicited from Hans. He said there were actually two horses pulling the bus and that they were both black and "very big and fat." Hans's father again asked about the boy's thoughts when the horse fell.

Father: "When the horse fell down, did you think of your daddy?"[9]

[7]Six days later the father reports, "I was at last able to establish the fact that it was a horse with a leather muzzle."
[8]A good example of the success of indoctrination.

Hans: "Perhaps. Yes. It's possible."

For several days after these talks about horses Hans's interests, as indicated by the father's reports, "centered upon lumf (feces) and widdle, but we cannot tell why." Freud comments that at this point "the analysis began to be obscure and uncertain."

On April 11 Hans related this phantasy.

"I was in the bath[10] and then the plumber came and unscrewed it.[11] Then he took a big borer and stuck it into my stomach." Hans's father translated this phantasy as follows: "I was in bed with Mamma. Then Pappa came and drove me away. With his big penis he pushed me out of my place by Mamma."

The remainder of the case history material, until Hans's recovery from the phobia early in May, is concerned with the lumf theme and Hans's feelings towards his parents and sister. It can be stated immediately that as corroboration for Freud's theories all of this remaining material is unsatisfactory. For the most part it consists of the father expounding theories to a boy who occasionally agrees and occasionally disagrees. The following two examples illustrate the nature of most of this latter information.

Hans and his father were discussing the boy's slight fear of falling when in the big bath.

Father: "But Mamma bathes you in it. Are you afraid of Mamma dropping you in the water?"
Hans: "I am afraid of her letting go and my head going in."
Father: "But you know Mummy's fond of you and won't let you go."
Hans: "I only just thought it."
Father: "Why?"
Hans: "I don't know at all."

[9]One of many leading questions, the positive answer to which of course proves nothing. It is worth noticing how the same question, differently phrased, elicits contrasting answers from Hans. When asked earlier what he thought of when the horse fell, Hans replied that he thought it would always happen in future.
[10]"Hans's mother gives him his bath" (Father's note).
[11]"To take it away to be repaired" (Father's note).

Father: "Perhaps it was because you'd been naughty and thought she didn't love you any more?"[12]
Hans: "Yes."
Father: "When you were watching Mummy giving Hanna her bath perhaps you wished she would let go of her so that Hanna should fall in?"[12]
Hans: "Yes."

On the following day the father asks, "Are you fond of Hanna?"

Hans: "Oh, yes, very fond."
Father: "Would you rather that Hanna weren't alive or that she were?"
Hans: "I'd rather she weren't alive."

In response to close, direct questioning Hans voiced several complaints about his sister. Then his father proceeded again:

Father: "If you'd rather she weren't alive, you can't be fond of her, at all."
Hans: (assenting[13]) "Hm, well."
Father: "That's why you thought when Mummy was giving her her bath if only she'd let go, Hanna would fall in the water. . . ."
Hans: (taking me up) ". . . and die."
Father: "and then you'd be alone with Mummy. A good boy doesn't wish that sort of thing, though."

On April 24, the following conversation was recorded.

Father: "It seems to me that, all the same, you do wish Mummy would have a baby."
Hans: "But I don't want it to happen."
Father: "But you wish for it?"
Hans: "Oh, yes, *wish*."[14]
Father: "Do you know why you wish for it? It's because you'd like to be Daddy."
Hans: "Yes. How does it work?"
Father: "You'd like to be Daddy and married to Mummy; you'd like to be as big as me and have a moustache; and you'd like Mummy to have a baby."
Hans: "And Daddy, when I'm married I'll have only one if I want to, when I'm married to Mummy, and if I don't want a baby,

[12]Leading question.
[13]A very questionable affirmation.
[14]Original italics suggest a significance that is unwarranted, for the child has been maneuvered into giving an answer contradicting his original one. Note the induced "evidence" as the conversation continues.

God won't want it either when I'm married."
Father: "Would you like to be married to Mummy?"
Hans: "Oh yes."

The Value of the Evidence

Before proceeding to Freud's interpretation of the case, let us examine the value of the evidence presented. First, there is the matter of selection of the material. The greatest attention is naturally paid to material related to psychoanalytic theory and there is a tendency to ignore other facts. The father and mother, we are told by Freud, "were both among my closest adherents." Hans himself was constantly encouraged, directly and indirectly, to relate material of relevance to the psychoanalytic doctrine.

Second, we must assess the value to be placed on the testimony of the father and of Hans. The father's account of Hans's behavior is in several instances suspect. For example, he twice presents his own interpretations of Hans's remarks as observed facts. This is the father's report of a conversation with Hans about the birth of his sister Hanna.

Father: "What did Hanna look like?"
Hans: (hypocritically): "All white and lovely. So pretty."

On another occasion, despite several clear statements by Hans of his affection for his sister (and also the voicing of complaints about her screaming), the father said to Hans, "If you'd rather she weren't alive, you can't be fond of her at all." Hans (assenting): "Hm, well." (See above.)

The comment in parenthesis in each of these two extracts is presented as observed fact. A third example has also been quoted above. When Hans observes that Hanna's widdler is "so lovely" the father states that this is a "disingenuous" reply and that "in reality her widdler seemed to him funny." Distortions of this kind are common in the father's reports.

Hans's testimony is for many reasons unreliable. Apart from the numerous lies which he told in the last few weeks of his phobia, Hans gave many inconsistent and occasionally conflicting reports. Most important of all, much of what purports to be Hans's views and feelings is simply the father speaking. Freud himself admits this but attempts to gloss over it. He says, "It is true that during the analysis Hans had to be told many things which he could not say himself, that he had to be presented with thoughts which he had so far shown no signs of possessing and that his attention had to be turned in the direction from which his father was expecting something to come. This detracts from the evidential value of the analysis but the procedure is the same in every case. For a psychoanalysis is not an impartial scientific investigation but a therapeutic measure."[15] To sum this matter up, Hans's testimony is subject not only to "mere suggestion" but contains much material that is not his testimony at all!

From the above discussion it is clear that the "facts of the case" need to be treated with considerable caution and in our own interpretation of Hans's behavior we will attempt to make use only of the testimony of direct observation.

Freud's Interpretation

Freud's interpretation of Hans's phobia is that the boy's oedipal conflicts formed the basis of the illness which "burst out" when he underwent "a time of privation and the intensified sexual excitement." Freud says, "These were tendencies in Hans which had already been suppressed and which, so far as we can tell, had never been able to find uninhibited expression: hostile and jealous feelings against his father, and sadistic impulses (premonitions, as it were, of copulation) towards his mother. These early suppressions may perhaps have gone to form the predisposition for his subsequent illness. These aggressive propensities of Hans's found no out-

let, and as soon as there came a time of privation and of intensified sexual excitement, they tried to break their way out with reinforced strength. It was then that the battle which we call his 'phobia' burst out."

This is the familiar oedipal theory, according to which Hans wished to replace his father "whom he could not help rating as a rival" and then complete the act by "taking possession of his mother." Freud refers for confirmation to the following. "Another symptomatic act, happening as though by accident, involved a confession that he had wished his father dead; for, just at the moment that his father was talking of his death-wish Hans let a horse that he was playing with fall down—knocked it over, in fact." Freud claims that, "Hans was really a little Oedipus who wanted to have his father 'out of the way' to get rid of him, so that he might be alone with his handsome mother and sleep with her." The predisposition to illness provided by the oedipal conflicts is supposed to have formed the basis for "the transformation of his libidinal longing into anxiety." During the summer prior to the onset of the phobia, Hans had experienced "moods of mingled longing and apprehension" and had also been taken into his mother's bed on occasions. Freud says, "We may assume that since then Hans had been in a state of intensified sexual excitement, the object of which was his mother. The intensity of this excitement was shown by his two attempts at seducing his mother (the second of which occurred just before the outbreak of his anxiety); and he found an incidental channel of discharge for it by masturbating . . . . Whether the sudden exchange of this excitement into anxiety took place spontaneously, or as a result of his mother's rejection of his advances, or owing to the accidental revival of earlier impressions by the 'exciting cause' of his illness . . . this we cannot decide. The fact remains that his sexual excitement suddenly changed into anxiety."[16]

---

[15]Nevertheless, both the theory and practice of psychoanalysis are built on these "not . . . impartial scientific investigations." For Freud to admit this weakness has some merit, but the admission is neither a substitute for evidence nor a good reason for accepting conclusions without evidence.

[16]Thus a theoretical statement, beginning with "We may assume" ends up as a "fact." The only fact is that the assumed sexual excitement is assumed to have changed into anxiety.

Hans, we are told, "transposed from his father on to the horses." At his sole interview with Hans, Freud told him "that he was afraid of his father because he himself nourished jealous and hostile wishes against him." Freud says of this, "In telling him this, I had partly interpreted his fear of horses for him: the horse must be his father—whom he had good internal reasons for fearing." Freud claims that Hans's fear of the black things on the horses' mouths and the things in front of their eyes was based on moustaches and eyeglasses and had been "directly transposed from his father on to the horses."[17] The horses "had been shown to represent his father."

Freud interprets the agoraphobic element of Hans's phobia thus. "The content of his phobia was such as to impose a very great measure of restriction upon his freedom of movement, and that was its purpose.... After all, Hans's phobia of horses was an obstacle to his going into the street, and could serve as a means of allowing him to stay at home with his beloved mother.[18] In this way, therefore, his affection for his mother triumphantly achieved its aim."

Freud interprets the disappearance of the phobia as being due to the resolution by Hans of his oedipal conflicts by "promoting him (the father) to a marriage with Hans's grandmother ... instead of killing him." This final interpretation is based on the following conversation between Hans and his father.

On April 30, Hans was playing with his imaginary children.

Father: "Hullo, are your children still alive? You know quite well a boy can't have any children."
Hans: "I know. I was their Mummy before, *now I'm their Daddy*" (original italics).
Father: "And who's the children's Mummy?"
Hans: "Why, Mummy, and you're their *Grandaddy*" (original italics).
Father: "So then you'd like to be as big as me, and be married to Mummy, and then you'd like her to have children."

[17]But in fact the child was thinking of a muzzle (see above).
[18]It should be noted, however, that Hans's horse-phobia and general agoraphobia were present even when he went out with his mother.

Hans: "Yes, that's what I'd like, and then my Lainz Grandmamma" (paternal side) "will be their Grannie."

Critique of Freud's Conclusions

It is our contention that Freud's view of this case is not supported by the data, either in its particulars or as a whole. The major points that he regards as demonstrated are these: (1) Hans had a sexual desire for his mother, (2) he hated and feared his father and wished to kill him, (3) his sexual excitement and desire for his mother were transformed into anxiety, (4) his fear of horses was symbolic of his fear of his father, (5) the purpose of the illness was to keep near his mother and finally (6) his phobia disappeared because he resolved his oedipus complex.

Let us examine each of these points.

(1) That Hans derived satisfaction from his mother and enjoyed her presence we will not even attempt to dispute. But nowhere is there any evidence of his wish to copulate with her. Yet Freud says that, "if matters had lain entirely in my hands ... I should have confirmed his instinctive premonitions, by telling him of the existence of the vagina and of copulation." The "instinctive premonitions" are referred to as though a matter of fact, though no evidence of their existence is given.

The only seduction incident described (see above) indicates that on *that particular occasion* Hans desired contact of a sexual nature with his mother, albeit a sexual contact of a simple, primitive type. This is not adequate evidence on which to base the claim that Hans had an Oedipus complex which implies a sexual desire for the other, a wish to possess her and to replace the father. The most that can be claimed for this "attempted seduction" is that it provides a small degree of support for the assumption that Hans had a desire for sexual stimulation by some other person (it will be recalled that he often masturbated). Even if it is assumed that stimulation provided by his mother was especially desired, the two other features of an Oedipus complex (a wish to possess the mother and replace the father) are not demonstrated by the facts of the case.

(2) Never having expressed either fear or hatred of his father, Hans was told by Freud that he possessed these emotions. On subsequent occasions Hans denied the existence of these feelings when questioned by his father. Eventually, he said "Yes" to a statement of this kind by his father. This simple affirmative obtained after considerable pressure on the part of the father and Freud is accepted as the true state of affairs and all Hans's denials are ignored. The "symptomatic act" of knocking over the toy horse is taken as further evidence of Hans's aggression towards his father. There are three assumptions underlying this "interpreted fact"—first, that the horse represents Hans's father; second, that the knocking over of the horse is not accidental; and third, that this act indicates a wish for the removal of whatever the horse symbolized.

Hans consistently denied the relationship between the horse and his father. He was, he said, afraid of horses. The mysterious black around the horses' mouths and the things on their eyes were later discovered by the father to be the horses' muzzles and blinkers. This discovery undermines the suggestion (made by Freud) that they were transposed moustaches and eye-glasses. There is no other evidence that the horses represented Hans's father. The assumption that the knocking over of the toy horse was meaningful in that it was prompted by an unconscious motive is, like most similar examples, a moot point. Freud himself (1938) does not state that *all* errors are provoked by unconscious motives and in this sense "deliberate." This is understandable for it is easy to compile numerous instances of errors which can be accounted for in other, simpler terms[19] without recourse to unconscious motivation or indeed motivation of any kind. Despite an examination of the literature we are unable to find a categorical statement regarding the frequency of "deliberate errors." Furthermore, we do not

know how to recognize them when they do occur. In the absence of positive criteria the decision that Hans's knocking over of the toy horse was a "deliberate error" is arbitrary.

As there is nothing to sustain the first two assumptions made by Freud in interpreting this "symptomatic act," the third assumption (that this act indicated a wish for his father's death) is untenable; and it must be reiterated that there is no independent evidence that the boy feared or hated his father.

(3) Freud's third claim is that Hans's sexual excitement and desire for his mother were transformed into anxiety. This claim is based on the assertion that "theoretical considerations require that what is today the object of a phobia must at one time in the past have been the source of a high degree of pleasure." Certainly such a transformation is not displayed by the facts presented. As stated above, there is no evidence that Hans sexually desired his mother. There is also no evidence of any change in his attitude to her before the onset of the phobia. Even though there is some evidence that horses were to some extent previously a source of pleasure, in general the view that phobic objects must have been the source of former pleasures is amply contradicted by experimental evidence. Apart from the numerous experiments on phobias in animals which disprove this contention (Gantt, 1944; Liddell, 1944; Woodward, 1959), the demonstrations of Watson and Rayner (1920) and Jones (1924) have clearly shown how phobias may be induced in children by a simple conditioning process. The rat and rabbit used as the conditioned stimuli in these demonstrations can hardly be regarded as sources of "a high degree of pleasure," and the same applies to the generalized stimulus of cotton wool.

(4) The assertion that Hans's horse phobia symbolized a fear of his father has already been criticized. The assumed relationship between the father and the horse is unsupported and appears to have arisen as a result of the father's strange failure to believe that by the "black around their mouths" Hans meant the horses' muzzles.

[19]See for example the experiments on learning and habit interference (McGeoch and Irion, 1952; Woodworth and Schlosberg, 1955).

(5) The fifth claim is that the purpose of Hans's phobia was to keep him near his mother. Aside from the questionable view that neurotic disturbances occur for a purpose, this interpretation fails to account for the fact that Hans experienced anxiety even when he was out walking *with his mother.*

(6) Finally, we are told that the phobia disappeared as a result of Hans's resolution of his oedipal conflicts. As we have attempted to show, there is no adequate evidence that Hans had an Oedipus complex. In addition, the claim that this assumed complex was resolved is based on a single conversation between Hans and his father (see above). This conversation is a blatant example of what Freud himself refers to as Hans having to "be told many things he could not say himself, that he had to be presented with thoughts which he had so far *shown* no signs of possessing, and that his attention had to be turned in the direction that his father was expecting something to come."

There is also no satisfactory evidence that the "insights" that were incessantly brought to the boy's attention had any therapeutic value. Reference to the facts of the case shows only occasional coincidences between interpretations and changes in the child's phobic reactions. For example, "a quiet period" early followed the father's statement that the fear of horses was a "piece of nonsense" and that Hans really wanted to be taken into his mother's bed. But soon afterwards, when Hans became ill, the phobia was worse than ever. Later, having had many talks without effect, the father notes that on March 13 Hans, after agreeing that he still *wanted* to play with his widdler, was "much less afraid of horses." On March 15, however, he was frightened of horses, after the information that females have no widdlers (though he had previously been told the opposite by his mother). Freud asserts that Hans resisted this piece of enlightenment because it aroused castration fears, and therefore no therapeutic success was to be observed. The "first real improvement" of April 2 is attributed to the "moustache enlightenment" of March 30 (later proved erroneous), the boy having been

told that he was "afraid of his father precisely because he was so fond of his mother." On April 7, though Hans was constantly improving, Freud commented that the situation was "decidedly obscure" and that "the analysis was making little progress."[20]

Such sparse and tenuous data do not begin to justify the attribution of Hans's recovery to the bringing to consciousness of various unacceptable unconscious repressed wishes. In fact, Freud bases his conclusions entirely on deductions from his theory. Hans's later improvement appears to have been smooth and gradual and unaffected by the interpretations. In general, Freud infers relationships in a scientifically inadmissible manner: if the enlightenments or interpretations given to Hans are followed by behavioral improvements, then they are automatically accepted as valid. If they are not followed by improvement we are told the patient has not accepted them, and not that they are invalid. Discussing the failure of these early enlightenments, Freud says that in any event therapeutic success is not the primary aim of the analysis,[21] thus sidetracking the issue; and he is not deflected from claiming an improvement to be due to an interpretation even when the latter is erroneous, *e.g.,* the moustache interpretation.

No systematic follow-up of the case is provided. However, fourteen years after the completion of the analysis, Freud interviewed Hans, who "declared that he was perfectly well and suffered from no troubles or inhibitions" (!). He also said that he had successfully undergone the ordeal of his parents' divorce. Hans reported that he could not remember anything about his childhood phobia. Freud remarks that this is "particularly remarkable." The analysis itself "had been overtaken by amnesia!"

An Alternative View of Hans's Phobia

In case it should be argued that, unsatisfactory as it is, Freud's explanation is the only

[20]By Freud's admission Hans was improving despite the absence of progress in the analysis.
[21]But elsewhere he says that a psychoanalysis is a therapeutic measure and not a scientific investigation!

available one, we shall show how Hans's phobia can be understood in terms of learning theory, in the theoretical framework provided by Wolpe (1958). This approach is largely Hullian in character and the clinical applications are based on experimental findings.

In brief, phobias are regarded as conditioned anxiety (fear) reactions. Any "neutral" stimulus, simple or complex, that happens to make an impact on an individual at about the time that a fear reaction is evoked acquires the ability to evoke fear subsequently. If the fear at the original conditioning situation is of high intensity or if the conditioning is many times repeated, the conditioned fear will show the persistence that is characteristic of *neurotic* fear; and there will be generalization of fear reactions to stimuli resembling the conditioned stimulus.

Hans, we are told, was a sensitive child who "was never unmoved if someone wept in his presence" and long before the phobia developed became "uneasy on seeing the horses in the merry-go-round being beaten." It is our contention that the incident to which Freud refers as merely the exciting cause of Hans's phobia was in fact the cause of the entire disorder. Hans actually says, "No. I only got it [the phobia] then. When the horse in the bus fell down, it gave me such a fright, really! That was when I got the nonsense." The father says, "All of this was confirmed by my wife, as well as the fact that the anxiety broke out immediately afterwards." The evidence obtained in studies on experimental neuroses in animals (*e.g.,* Wolpe, 1958) and the studies by Watson and Rayner (1920), Jones (1924) and Woodward (1959) on phobias in children indicate that it is quite possible for one experience to induce a phobia.

In addition, the father was able to report two other unpleasant incidents which Hans had experienced with horses prior to the onset of the phobia. It is likely that these experiences had sensitized Hans to horses or, in other words, he had already been partially conditioned to fear horses. These incidents both occurred at Gmunden. The first was the warning given by the father of Hans's friend to avoid the horse lest it bite, and the second

when another of Hans's friends injured himself (and bled) while they were playing horses.

Just as the little boy Albert (in Watson's classic demonstration, 1920) reacted with anxiety not only to the original conditioned stimulus, the white rat, but to other similar stimuli such as furry objects, cotton wool and so on, Hans reacted anxiously to horses, horse-drawn buses, vans and features of horses, such as their blinkers and muzzles. In fact he showed fear of a wide range of generalized stimuli. The accident which provoked the phobia involved two horses drawing a bus and Hans stated that he was more afraid of large carts, vans or buses than small carts. As one would expect, the less close a phobic stimulus was to that of the original incident the less disturbing Hans found it. Furthermore, the last aspect of the phobia to disappear was Hans's fear of large vans or buses. There is ample experimental evidence that when responses to generalized stimuli undergo extinction, responses to other stimuli in the continuum are the less diminished the more closely they resemble the original conditional stimulus.

Hans's recovery from the phobia may be explained on conditioning principles in a number of possible ways, but the actual mechanism that operated cannot be identified, since the child's father was not concerned with the kind of information that would be of interest to us. It is well known that especially in children many phobias decline and disappear over a few weeks or months. The reason for this appears to be that in the ordinary course of life generalized phobic stimuli may evoke anxiety responses weak enough to be inhibited by other emotional responses simultaneously aroused in the individual. Perhaps this process was the true source of Little Hans's recovery. The interpretations may have been irrelevant, or may even have retarded recovery by adding new threats and new fears to those already present. But since Hans does not seem to have been greatly upset by the interpretations, it is perhaps more likely that the therapy was actively helpful, for phobic stimuli were again and again presented to the child in a variety of emotional contexts that may have inhibited the anxiety and in consequence diminished its habit strength. The *gradualness* of Hans's recovery is consonant with an explanation of this kind (Wolpe, 1958).

Conclusions

The chief conclusion to be derived from our survey of the case of Little Hans is that it does not provide anything resembling direct proof of psychoanalytic theorems. We have combed Freud's account for evidence that would be acceptable in the court of science, and have found none. In attempting to give a balanced summary of the case we have excluded a vast number of interpretations but have tried not to omit any material facts. Such facts, and they alone, could have supported Freud's theories. For example, if it had been observed after Gmunden that Hans had become fearful of his father, and that upon the development of the horse phobia the fear of the father had disappeared, this could reasonably have been regarded as presumptive of a displacement of fear from father to horse. This is quite different from observing a horse phobia and then asserting that it must be a displaced father-fear without ever having obtained any direct evidence of the latter; for then that which needs to be demonstrated is presupposed. To say that the father-fear was repressed is equally no substitute for evidence of it.

Freud fully believed that he had obtained in Little Hans a direct confirmation of his theories, for he speaks towards the end of "the infantile complexes that were revealed behind Hans's phobia." It seems clear that although he wanted to be scientific Freud was surprisingly naive regarding the requirements of scientific evidence. Infantile complexes were not *revealed* (demonstrated) behind Hans's phobia: they were merely hypothesized.

It is remarkable that countless psychoanalysts have paid homage to the case of Little Hans, without being offended by its glaring inadequacies. We shall not here attempt to explain this, except to point to one probable major influence—a tacit belief among analysts that Freud possessed a kind of unerring insight that absolved him from the obligation to obey rules applicable to ordinary men. For example, Glover (1952), speaking of other analysts who arrogate to themselves the right Freud claimed to subject his material to "a touch of revision," says, "No doubt when someone of Freud's calibre appears in our midst he will be freely accorded ... this privilege." To accord such a privilege to anyone is to violate the spirit of science.

It may of course be argued that some of the conclusions of Little Hans are no longer held and that there is now other evidence for other of the conclusions; but there is no evidence that in general psychoanalytic conclusions are based on any better logic than that used by Freud in respect of Little Hans. Certainly no analyst has ever pointed to the failings of this account or disowned its reasoning, and it has continued to be regarded as one of the foundation stones on which psychoanalytic theory was built.

Summary

The main facts of the case of Little Hans are presented and it is shown that Freud's claim of "a more direct and less roundabout proof" of certain of his theories is not justified by the evidence presented. No confirmation by direct observation is obtained for any psychoanalytic theorem, though psychoanalysts have believed the contrary for 50 years. The demonstrations claimed are really interpretations that are treated as facts. This is a common practice and should be checked, for it has been a great encumbrance to the development of a science of psychiatry.

References

Fenichel, O. *The psychoanalytical theory of neurosis.* New York: Norton, 1945.

Freud, S. *Collected papers.* London: Hogarth Press, 1950. Vol. 3.

Freud, S. *Psychopathology of everyday life.* Baltimore: Pelican Books, 1938.

Gantt, W. H. *Experimental basis for neurotic behavior.* New York: Hoeber, 1944.

Glover, E. *On the early development of mind.* New York: International Universities Press, 1956.

Glover, E. Research methods in psychoanalysis. *Int. J. Psychoanal.,* 1952, **33**, 403-409.

Hendrick, I. *Facts and theories of psychoanalysis.* New York: Knopf, 1939.

Jones, E. *Sigmund Freud: Life and work.* London: Hogarth Press, 1955. Vol. 2.

Jones, M. C. Elimination of children's fears. *J. exp. Psychol.,* 1924, **7**, 382-390.

Liddell, H. S. Conditioned reflex method and experimental neurosis. In J. McV. Hunt (Ed.), *Personality and the behavior disorders.* New York: Ronald, 1944.

McGeoch, J., and Irion, A. *The psychology of human learning.* New York: Longmans, 1952.

Watson, J. B., and Rayner, P. Conditioned emotional reactions. *J. exp. Psychol.,* 1920, **3**, 1-14.

Wohlgemuth, A. *A critical examination of psychoanalysis.* London: Allen and Unwin, 1923.

Wolpe, J. *Psychotherapy by reciprocal inhibition.* Stanford, Calif.: Stanford Univ. Press, 1958.

Woodward, J. Emotional disturbances of burned children. *Brit. med. J.,* 1959, **1**, 1009-1013.

Woodworth, R., and Schlosberg, H. *Experimental psychology.* London: Methuen, 1955.

2   Harry Stack Sullivan

Of the important psychoanalytic theorists, Harry Stack Sullivan (1892-1949) stands out as a product of the fusion of psychoanalysis with contemporary social theories of behavior. Although the roots of Sullivan's thinking are embedded in psychoanalytic tradition, he distinctively offers a dynamic, social-psychological conception of man that emphasizes *culture* and *the individual's interpersonal experience* as the principal agents in the growth and maturation of the personality. Sullivan does not abandon intrapsychic dynamics, but delicately devises a rapprochement between the psyche and the social context in which man flourishes. Man does not exist in isolation; and for Sullivan, the interpersonal relation constitutes the human condition.

Most of Sullivan's work was published posthumously and remains unformalized in any cohesive, refined, or testable set of theoretical statements. Perhaps for this reason, his work has not generated extensive research. Indirectly, however, research into the centrality of anxiety, interpersonal perception, and interpersonal sensitivity, and studies of thought disorder in schizophrenia all in some way owe a debt to Sullivan's thinking. It would not be an exaggeration to

say that Sullivan's observations are ingrained in the fabric of current psychology and psychiatry.

One of Sullivan's most important contributions is his theoretical and observational analysis of anxiety as an interpersonal phenomenon. In "Beginnings of the Self-System," Sullivan examines the relationship between anxiety and the psychic mechanisms that all individuals devise to evade anxiety-producing experiences. The self-system is formulated as an internal organization of controls evolved from man's constant and inescapable contact with cultural and interpersonal sources of anxiety. The self-system functions solely for the purpose of avoiding anxiety and, because it seeks such an important goal, it eventually develops into a stable, self-perpetuating, and independent aspect of the personality. As a consequence, the self-system is extremely resistant to change and can provide a potent barrier to further interpersonal maturity.

An obvious way to apply Sullivan's interpersonal theory is through an analysis of the marriage interaction. In the paper by Robert L. Romano we find such an application based upon a method of "interpersonal diagnosis" developed by Timothy Leary (*Interpersonal diagnosis of personality,* New York, Ronald Press, 1957). This diagnostic system is designed so that personality data from different levels of psychological functioning can be identified and compared. In this way a much more meaningful description of interpersonal behaviors can be articulated—and in such a way as to be more scientifically and clinically useful. *Interpersonal variables* can be quantified at three different levels of description: Level I data represent how others see the person's interpersonal behavior; Level II data reflect the individual's description of his own interpersonal behavior; and Level III data reflect the individual's perception of his own interpersonal behavior at the private, or fantasy, level. Level I and II behaviors are defined operationally in terms of an "Interpersonal Check List" made up of 96 adjectives selected so that the individual can be described in terms of his relative strength on 16 interpersonal variables. Level III behavior is defined in terms of Thematic Apperception Test (TAT) stories. The TAT is a projective personality test consisting of a number of pictures of people doing various things. The subject is instructed to make up stories about the various pictures, and it is assumed that these stories represent a projection of the person's own inner needs and wishes. Thus, the TAT stories represent the private world of the person. A scoring system has been devised so that the individual can be described in terms of the same 16 interpersonal variables at this level of personality as at Levels I and II. In this way, interpersonal behavior at different levels of personality functioning can be compared. There is a certain resemblance between this system of personality description and the *Q*-sort technique utilized by Rogers (see Chapter 6).

It should be obvious from the above that this method of personality description lends itself perfectly to the analysis of marriage relationships. Spouses can rate themselves and each other on the Interpersonal Check List (Levels I and II), and then comparisons between levels both within and between marriage partners can be made. In this way marital discord (interpersonal maladjustment) can be easily and accurately assessed, a necessary first step in marriage counseling. The usefulness of this approach is demonstrated by Romano's application of the system to two discordant marriages.

The critique paper by Jule Nydes is indicative of the gulf that exists between the classical psychoanalytic view and the school of thought that was given impetus and direction by Sullivan's ideas. Nydes' arguments are sharply leveled at what he considers the superficiality of the Sullivanians' formulations. In his opinion, the compelling and vital quality of intrapsychic dynamics elucidated by Freud become, in the hands of the Sullivanians, mere bland and colorless reproductions of a deeply moving picture of human existence.

Suggestions for Further Reading

Sullivan published only one book, *Conceptions of Modern Psychiatry,* published by the William Alanson White Foundation in 1947. Two other books are collections of his papers and lectures: *The Interpersonal Theory of Psychiatry,* published by Norton in 1953, and *The Psychiatric Interview,* also published by Norton (1954). All three books are excellent sources for the serious student of Sullivan's point of view.

An excellent book about Sullivan is the one by Dorothy Blitsten, *The Social Theories of Harry Stack Sullivan,* published by the William-Frederick Press, 1953.

Two books by Patrick Mullahy, published by Hermitage House, are strongly recommended: *Oedipus: Myth and Complex* (1948) and *The Contributions of Harry Stack Sullivan* (1952).

Beginnings of the Self-System

Harry Stack Sullivan

Three Aspects of Interpersonal Cooperation

We have got our human animal as far, in the process of becoming a person, as the latter part of infancy, and we find him being subjected more and more to the social responsibilities of the parent. As the infant comes to be recognized as educable, capable of learning, the mothering one modifies more and more the exhibition of tenderness, or the giving of tenderness, to the infant. The earlier feeling that the infant must have unqualified cooperation is now modified to the feeling that the infant should be learning certain things, and this implies a restriction, on the part of the mothering one, of her tender cooperation under certain circumstances.

Successful training of the functional activity of the anal zone of interaction accentuates a new aspect of tenderness—namely, the additive role of tenderness as a sequel to what the mothering one regards as good behavior. Now this is, in effect—however it may be prehended by the infant—a *reward*, which, once the approved social ritual connected with defecating has worked out well, is added to the satisfaction of the anal zone. Here is tenderness taking on the attribute of a reward for having learned something, or for behaving right.

Thus the mother, or the parent responsible for acculturation or socialization, now adds tenderness to her increasingly neutral behavior in a way that can be called rewarding. I think that very, very often the parent does this with no thought of rewarding the infant.

Very often the rewarding tenderness merely arises from the pleasure of the mothering one in the skill which the infant has learned—the success which has attended a venture on the toilet chair, or something of that kind. But since tenderness in general is becoming more restricted by the parental necessity to train, these incidents of straightforward tenderness, following the satisfaction of a need like that to defecate, are really an addition—a case of getting something extra for good behavior— and this is, in its generic pattern, a reward. This type of learning can take place when the training procedure has been well adjusted to the learning capacity of the infant. The friendly response, the pleasure which the other takes in something having worked out well, comes more and more to be something special in the very last months of infancy, whereas earlier, tenderness was universal when the mothering one was around, if she was a comfortable mothering one. Thus, to a certain extent, this type of learning can be called learning under the influence of reward —the reward being nothing more or less than tender behavior on the part of the acculturating or socializing mothering one.

Training in the functional activity of the oral-manual behavior—that is, conveying things by the hand to the mouth and so on— begins to accentuate the differentiation of anxiety-colored situations in contrast to approved situations. The training in this particular field is probably, in almost all cases, the area in which *grades of anxiety* first become of great importance in learning; as I have already stressed, behavior of a certain unsatisfactory type provokes increasing anxiety, and the infant learns to keep a distance from, or to veer away from, activities which are attended by increasing anxiety, just as the amoebae avoid high temperatures.

From Harry Stack Sullivan, *The Interpersonal Theory of Psychiatry*, pp. 158 171. Copyright 1953 by The William Alanson White Psychiatric Foundation. Reprinted by permission of W. W. Norton & Company, Inc., New York, and Tavistock Publications Ltd., London.

This is the great way of learning in infancy, and later in childhood—by the grading of anxiety, so that the infant learns to chart his course by mild forbidding gestures, or by mild states of worry, concern, or disapproval mixed with some degree of anxiety on the part of the mothering one. The infant plays, one might say, the old game of getting hotter or colder, in charting a selection of behavioral units which are not attended by an increase in anxiety. Anxiety in its most severe form is a rare experience after infancy, in the more fortunate courses of personality development, and anxiety as it is a function in chronologically adult life, in a highly civilized community confronted by no particular crisis, is never very severe for most people. And yet it is necessary to appreciate that it is anxiety which is responsible for a great part of the inadequate, inefficient, unduly rigid, or otherwise unfortunate performances of people; that anxiety is responsible in a basic sense for a great deal of what comes to a psychiatrist for attention. Only when this is understood, can one realize that this business of whether one is getting more or less anxious is in a large sense the basic influence which determines interpersonal relations—that is, it is not the motor, it does not call interpersonal relations into being, but it more or less directs the course of their development. And even in late infancy there is a good deal of learning by the anxiety gradient, particularly where there is a mothering one who is untroubled, but still intensely interested in producing the right kind of child; and this learning is apt to first manifest itself when the baby is discouraged from putting the wrong things in the mouth, and the like. This kind of learning applies over a vast area of behavior. But in this discussion I am looking for where things are apt to start.

Training of the manual-exploratory function—which I have discussed in connection with the infant's getting his hands near the anus, or into the feces, or, perhaps, in contact with the external genitals—almost always begins the discrimination of situations which are marked by what we shall later discuss as *uncanny emotion*. This uncanny feeling can be described as the abrupt supervention of *severe anxiety,* with the arrest of anything like the learning process, and with only gradual informative recall of the noted circumstances which preceded the extremely unpleasant incident.

Early in infancy, when situations approach the "all-or-nothing" character, the induction of anxiety is apt to be the sudden translation from a condition of moderate euphoria to one of very severe anxiety. And this severe anxiety, as I have said before, has a little bit the effect of a blow on the head, in that later one is not clear at all as to just what was going on at the time anxiety became intense. The educative effect is not by any means as simple and useful as is the educative effect in the other two situations which we have discussed, because the sudden occurrence of severe anxiety practically prohibits any clear prehension, or understanding, of the immediate situation. It does not, however, preclude recall, and as recall develops sufficiently so that one recalls what was about to occur when severe anxiety intervened—in other words, when one has a sense of what one's action was addressed to at the time when everything was disorganized by severe anxiety—then there come to be in all of us certain areas of "uncanny taboo," which I think is a perfectly good way of characterizing those things which one stops doing, once one has caught himself doing them. This type of training is much less immediately useful, and, shall I say, is productive of much less healthy acquaintance with reality, than are the other two.

Good-Me, Bad-Me, and Not-Me

Now here I have set up three aspects of interpersonal cooperation which are necessary for the infant's survival, and which dictate learning. That is, these aspects of interpersonal cooperation require acculturation or socialization of the infant. Infants are customarily exposed to all of these before the era of infancy is finished. From experience of these three sorts—with rewards, with the anxiety gradient, and with practically obliterative sudden severe anxiety—there comes an initial personification of three phases of what presently will be *me*, that which is invariably connected with the sentience of *my body*—and you will remember that *my body* as an organization of experience has come to be distinguished from everything else by its self-sentient character. These beginning personifications of three different kinds, which have in common elements of the prehended body, are organized in about mid-infancy—I can't say exactly when. I have already spoken of the infant's very early double personification of the actual mothering one as the good mother and the bad mother. Now, at this time, the beginning personifications of *me* are *good-me, bad-me*, and *not-me*. So far as I can see, in practically every instance of being trained for life, in this or another culture, it is rather inevitable that there shall be this tripartite cleavage in personifications, which have as their central tie—the thing that binds them ultimately into one, that always keeps them in very close relation—their relatedness to the growing conception of "my body."

Good-me is the beginning personification which organizes experience in which satisfactions have been enhanced by rewarding increments of tenderness, which come to the infant because the mothering one is pleased with the way things are going; therefore, and to that extent, she is free, and moves toward expressing tender appreciation of the infant. Good-me, as it ultimately develops, is the ordinary topic of discussion about "I."

Bad-me, on the other hand, is the beginning personification which organizes experience in which increasing degrees of anxiety are associated with behavior involving the mothering one in its more-or-less clearly prehended interpersonal setting. That is to say, bad-me is based on this increasing gradient of anxiety and that, in turn, is dependent, at this stage of life, on the observation, if misinterpretation, of the infant's behavior by someone who can induce anxiety.[1] The frequent coincidence of certain behavior on the part of

the infant with increasing tenseness and increasingly evident forbidding on the part of the mother is the source of the type of experience which is organized as a rudimentary personification to which we may apply the term bad-me.

So far, the two personifications I have mentioned may sound like a sort of reality. However, these personifications are a part of the communicated thinking of the child, a year or so later, and therefore it is not an unwarranted use of inference to presume that they exist at this earlier stage. When we come to the third of these beginning personifications, *not-me*, we are in a different field—one which we know about only through certain very special circumstances. And these special circumstances are not outside the experience of any of us. The personification of not-me is most conspicuously encountered by most of us in an occasional dream while we are asleep; but it is very emphatically encountered by people who are having a severe schizophrenic episode, in aspects that are to them most spectacularly real. As a matter of fact, it is always manifest—not every minute, but every day, in every life—in certain peculiar absences of phenomena where there should be phenomena; and in a good many people—I know not what proportion—it is very striking in its indirect manifestations (dissociated behavior), in which people do and say things of which they do not and could not have knowledge, things which may be quite meaningful to other people but are unknown to them. The special circumstances which we encounter in grave mental disorders may be, so far as you know, outside your experience; but they were not once upon a time. It is from the evidence of these special circumstances—including both those encountered in everybody and those encountered in grave disturbances of personality, all of which we shall presently touch upon—that I choose to set up this third beginning personification which is tangled up with the growing acquaintance of "my body," the personification

[1]Incidentally, for all I know, anybody can induce anxiety in an infant, but there is no use cluttering up our thought by considering that, because frequency of events is of very considerable significance in all learning processes; and at this stage of life, when the infant is perhaps nine or ten months old, it is likely to be the mother who is frequently involved in interpersonal situations with the infant.

of *not-me*. This is a very gradually evolving personification of an always relatively primitive character—that is, organized in unusually simple signs in the parataxic mode of experience, and made up of poorly grasped aspects of living which will presently be regarded as "dreadful," and which still later will be differentiated into incidents which are attended by awe, horror, loathing, or dread.

This rudimentary personification of not-me evolves very gradually, since it comes from the experience of intense anxiety—a very poor method of education. Such a complex and relatively inefficient method of getting acquainted with reality would naturally lead to relatively slow evolution of an organization of experiences; furthermore, these experiences are largely truncated, so that what they are really about is not clearly known. Thus organizations of these experiences marked by uncanny emotion—which means experiences which, when observed, have led to intense forbidding gestures on the part of the mother, and induced intense anxiety in the infant—are not nearly as clear and useful guides to anything as the other two types of organizations have been. Because experiences marked by uncanny emotion, which are organized in the personification of not-me, cannot be clearly connected with cause and effect—cannot be dealt with in all the impressive ways by which we explain our referential processes later—they persist throughout life as relatively primitive, unelaborated, parataxic symbols. Now that does not mean that the not-me component in adults is infantile; but it does mean that the not-me component is, in all essential respects, practically beyond discussion in communicative terms. Not-me is part of the very "private mode" of living. But, as I have said, it manifests itself at various times in the life of everyone after childhood—or of nearly everyone, I can't swear to the statistics—by the eruption of certain exceedingly unpleasant emotions in what are called nightmares.

These three rudimentary personifications of *me* are, I believe, just as distinct as the two personifications of the objectively same mother were earlier. But while the personifications of me are getting under way, there is some change going on with respect to the personification of mother. In the latter part of infancy, there is some evidence that the rudimentary personality, as it were, is already fusing the previously disparate personifications of the good and the bad mother; and within a year and a half after the end of infancy we find evidence of this duplex personification of the mothering one as the good mother and the bad mother clearly manifested only in relatively obscure mental processes, such as these dreamings while asleep. But, as I have suggested, when we come to consider the question of the peculiarly inefficient and inappropriate interpersonal relations which constitute problems of mental disorder, there again we discover that the trend in organizing experience which began with this duplex affair has not in any sense utterly disappeared.

The Dynamism of the Self-System

From the essential desirability of being good-me, and from the increasing ability to be warned by slight increases of anxiety—that is, slight diminutions in euphoria—in situations involving the increasingly significant other person, there comes into being the start of an exceedingly important, as it were, secondary dynamism, which is purely the product of interpersonal experience arising from anxiety encountered in the pursuit of the satisfaction of general and zonal needs. This secondary dynamism I call the *self-system*. As a dynamism it is secondary in that it does not have any particular zones of interaction, any particular physiological apparatus, behind it; but it literally uses all zones of interaction and all physiological apparatus which is integrative and meaningful from the interpersonal standpoint. And we ordinarily find its ramifications spreading throughout interpersonal relations in every area where there is any chance that anxiety may be encountered.

The essential desirability of being good-me is just another way of commenting on the essential undesirability of being anxious. Since the beginning personification of good-me is based on experience in which satisfactions are enhanced by tenderness, then naturally there is an essential desirability of living good-me. And since sensory and other abilities of the infant are well matured by now—perhaps even space perception, one of the slowest to come along, is a little in evidence—it is only natural that along with this essential desirability there goes increasing ability to be warned by slight forbidding—in other words, by slight anxiety. Both these situations, for the purpose now under discussion, are situations involving another person—the mothering one, or the congeries of mothering ones—and she is becoming increasingly significant because, as I have already said, the manifestation of tender cooperation by her is now complicated by her attempting to teach, to socialize the infant; and this makes the relationship more complex, so that it requires better, more effective differentiation by the infant of forbidding gestures, and so on. For all these reasons, there comes into being in late infancy an organization of experience which will ultimately be of nothing less than stupendous importance in personality, and which comes entirely from the interpersonal relations in which the infant is now involved —and these interpersonal relations have their motives (or their motors, to use a less troublesome word) in the infant's general and zonal needs for satisfaction. But out of the social responsibility of the mothering one, which gets involved in the satisfaction of the infant's needs, there comes the organization in the infant of what might be said to be a dynamism directed at how to live with this significant other person. The self-system thus is an organization of educative experience called into being by the necessity to avoid or to minimize incidents of anxiety.[2] The functional activity of the self-system—I am now

[2]Since *minimize* in this sense can be ambiguous, I should make it clear that I refer, by minimizing, to moving, in behavior, in the direction which is marked by diminishing anxiety. I do not mean, by minimize, to "make little of," because so far as I know, human ingenuity cannot make little of anxiety.

speaking of it from the general standpoint of a dynamism—is primarily directed to avoiding and minimizing this disjunctive tension of anxiety, and thus indirectly to protecting the infant from this evil eventuality in connection with the pursuit of satisfactions—the relief of general or of zonal tensions.

Thus we may expect, at least until well along in life, that the components of the self-system will exist and manifest functional activity in relation to every general need that a person has, and to every zonal need that the excess supply of energy to the various zones of interaction gives rise to. How conspicuous the "sector" of the self-system connected with any particular general need or zonal need will be, or how frequent its manifestations, is purely a function of the past experience of the person concerned.

I have said that the self-system begins in the organizing of experience with the mothering one's forbidding gestures, and that these forbidding gestures are refinements in the personification of the bad mother; this might seem to suggest that the self-system comes into being by the *incorporation* or *introjection* of the bad mother, or simply by the introjection of the mother. These terms, incorporation or introjection, have been used in this way, not in speaking of the self-system, but in speaking of the psychoanalytic superego, which is quite different from my conception of the self-system. But, if I have been at all adequate in discussing even what I have presented thus far, it will be clear that the use of such terms in connection with the development of the self-system is a rather reckless oversimplification, if not also a great magic verbal gesture the meaning of which cannot be made explicit. I have said that the self-system comes into being because the pursuit of general and zonal needs for satisfaction is increasingly interfered with by the good offices of the mothering one in attempting to train the young. And so the self-system, far from being anything like a function of or an identity with the mothering one, is an organization of experience for avoiding increasing degrees of anxiety which are connected with the educative process. But these degrees of anxiety cannot conceivably, in late infancy (and the situation is similar in most instances at any time in life), mean to the infant what the mothering one, the socializing person, believes she means, or what she actually represents, from the standpoint of the culture being inculcated in the infant. This idea that one can, in some way, take in another person to become a part of one's personality is one of the evils that comes from overlooking the fact that between a doubtless real "external object" and a doubtless real "my mind" there is a group of processes—the act of perceiving, understanding, and what not—which is intercalated, which is highly subject to past experience and increasingly subject to foresight of the neighboring future. Therefore, it would in fact be one of the great miracles of all time if our perception of another person were, in any greatly significant number of respects, accurate or exact. Thus I take some pains at this point to urge you to keep your mind free from the notion that I am dealing with something like the taking over of standards of value and the like from another person. Instead, I am talking about the organization of experience connected with relatively successful education in becoming a human being, which begins to be manifest late in infancy.

When I talk about the self-system, I want it clearly understood that I am talking about a *dynamism* which comes to be enormously important in understanding interpersonal relations. This dynamism is an explanatory conception; it is not a thing, a region, or what not, such as superegos, egos, ids, and so on.[3] Among the things this conception explains is something that can be described as a quasi-entity, the personification of the self. The personification of the self is what you are talking

about when you talk about yourself as "I," and what you are often, if not invariably, referring to when you talk about "me" and "my." But I would like to make it forever clear that *the relation of personifications to that which is personified is always complex and sometimes multiple;* and that *personifications are not adequate descriptions of that which is personified.* In my effort to make that clear, I have gradually been compelled, in my teaching, to push the beginnings of things further and further back in the history of the development of the person, to try to reach the point where the critical deviations from convenient ideas become more apparent. Thus I am now discussing the beginning of the terrifically important self-dynamism as the time when—far from there being a personification of the self—there are only rudimentary personifications of good-me and bad-me, and the much more rudimentary personification of not-me. These rudimentary personifications constitute anything but a personification of the self such as you all believe you manifest, and which you believe serves its purpose, when you talk about yourselves one to another in adult life.

The Necessary and Unfortunate Aspects of the Self-System

The origin of the self-system can be said to rest on the irrational character of culture or, more specifically, society. Were it not for the fact that a great many prescribed ways of doing things have to be lived up to, in order that one shall maintain workable, profitable, satisfactory relations with his fellows; or, were the prescriptions for the types of behavior in carrying on relations with one's fellows perfectly rational—then, for all I know, there would not be evolved, in the course of becoming a person, anything like the sort of self-system that we always encounter. If the cultural prescriptions which characterize any particular society were better adapted to human life, the notions that have grown up about incorporating or introjecting a punitive, critical person would not have arisen.

[3]Please do not bog down unnecessarily on the problem of whether my self-system ought to be called the superego or the ego. I surmise that there is some noticeable relationship, perhaps in the realm of cousins or closer, between what I describe as the personification of the self and what is often considered to be the psychoanalytic ego. But if you are wise, you will dismiss that as facetious, because I am not at all sure of it; it has been so many years since I found anything but headaches in trying to discover parallels between various theoretical systems that I have left that for the diligent and scholarly, neither of which includes me.

But even at that, I believe that a human being without a self-system is beyond imagination. It is highly probable that the type of education which we have discussed, even probably the inclusion of certain uncanny experience that tends to organize in the personification of not-me, would be inevitable in the process of the human animal's becoming a human being. I say this because the enormous capacity of the human animal which underlies human personality is bound to lead to exceedingly intricate specializations—differentiations of living, function, and one thing and another; to maintain a workable, profitable, appropriate, and adequate type of relationship among the great numbers of people that can become involved in a growing society, the young have to be taught a vast amount before they begin to be significantly involved in society outside the home group. Therefore, the special secondary elaboration of the sundry types of learning—which I call the self-system—would, I believe, be a ubiquitous aspect of all really human beings in any case. But in an ideal culture, which has never been approximated and at the present moment looks as if it never will be, the proper function of the self-system would be conspicuously different from its actual function in the denizens of our civilization. In our civilization, no parental group actually reflects the essence of the social organization for which the young are being trained in living; and after childhood, when the family influence in acculturation and socialization begins to be attenuated and augmented by other influences, the discrete excerpts, you might say, of the culture which each family has produced as its children come into collision with other discrete excerpts of the culture—all of them more or less belonging to the same cultural system, but having very different accents and importances mixed up in them. As a result of this, the self-system in its actual functioning in life in civilized societies, as they now exist, is often very unfortunate. But do not overlook the fact that the self-system comes into being because of, and can be said to have as its goal, the securing of necessary satisfaction without incurring much anxiety. And however unfortunate the manifestations of the self-system in many contexts may seem, always keep in mind that, if one had no protection against very severe anxiety, one would do practically nothing—or, if one still had to do something, it would take an intolerably long time to get it done.

So you see, however truly the self-system is the principal stumbling block to favorable changes in personality—a point which I shall develop later on—that does not alter the fact that it is also the principal influence that stands in the way of unfavorable changes in personality. And while the psychiatrist is skillful, in large measure, in his ability to formulate the self-system of another person with whom he is integrated, and to, shall I say, "intuit" the self-system aspects of his patient which tend to perpetuate the type of morbid living that the patient is showing, that still, in no sense, makes the self-system something merely to be regretted. In any event, it is always before us, whether we regret or praise it. This idea of the self-system is simply tremendously important in understanding the vicissitudes of interpersonal relations from here on. If we understand how the self-system begins, then perhaps we will be able to follow even the most difficult idea connected with its function.

The self-system is a product of educative experience, part of which is of the character of reward, and a very important part of which has the graded anxiety element that we have spoken of. But quite early in life, anxiety is also a very conspicuous aspect of the self-dynamism *function*. This is another way of saying that experience functions in both recall and foresight. Since troublesome experience, organized in the self-system, has been experience connected with increasing grades of anxiety, it is not astounding that this element of recall, functioning on a broad scale, makes the intervention of the self-dynamism in living tantamount to the warning, or foresight, of anxiety. And warning of anxiety means noticeable anxiety, really a warning that anxiety will get worse.

There are two things which I would like to mention briefly at this point. One is the infant's discovery of the unobtainable, his discovery of situations in which he is powerless, regardless of all the cooperation of the mothering one. The infant's crying for the full moon is an illustration of this. Now even before the end of infancy, it is observable that these unattainable objects gradually come to be treated *as if* they did not exist; that is, they do not call out the expression of zonal needs. This is possibly the simplest example of a very important process manifested in living which I call *selective inattention.*

The other thing I would like to mention is this: Where the parental influence is peculiarly incongruous to the actual possibilities and needs of the infant—before speech has become anything except a source of marvel in the family, before it has any communicative function whatever, before alleged words have any meaning—there can be inculcated in this growing personification of bad-me and not-me disastrous distortions which will manifest themselves, barring very fortunate experience, in the whole subsequent development of personality. I shall soon discuss some typical distortions, one of the most vicious of which occurs in late infancy as the outcome of the mothering one's conviction that infants have *wills* which have to be guided, governed, broken, or shaped. And when, finally, we come to discuss concepts of mental disorders we will have to pick up the manifestations of a few particularly typical distortions, in each subsequent stage from the time that they first occur.

Interpersonal Diagnosis in Marital Counseling

Robert L. Romano

Marital counseling has been described as a special kind of psychotherapy in terms of the aims of the treatment endeavor, and the focus given the marriage interaction during the counseling sessions (Bychowski and Despert, 1952; Gamberg, 1956; Mudd and Kirch, 1957). Most often in practice, both husband and wife are counseled, so that each can be helped to recognize his own perceptual distortions of and inappropriate response to the other. While each marital participant needs to be considered individually from the psychodynamic standpoint, marriage counseling throws special emphasis upon the relationship between husband and wife.

Ailing marriages are most often the result of a mutual failure in "consensual validation." That is to say, husband and wife fail to agree on the interpersonal intent of their own and their spouse's marital behavior. A dependent husband, for example, may seek comfort and support from a wife whom he perceives as nurturant. She, on the other hand, may be in conflict over her own dependency needs and may then view her spouse's request for support as demandingly hostile. She may despise this evidence of his weakness and long for someone whom she, herself, can lean on. However, when the husband attempts to supply her with emotional props and controls, his wife misinterprets his behavior as autocratic and humiliating. A mutual conflict of errors in interpretation ensues.

The psychologist who counsels the "neurotic" marital relationship must be able to define the discrepancies that occur in the way each of the partners perceives himself and the

From R. L. Romano, "The Use of the Interpersonal System of Diagnosis in Marital Counseling," *Journal of Counseling Psychology,* 1960, 7, no. 1, pp. 10-18. Reprinted by permission of the American Psychological Association.

other at various levels of awareness as a preliminary to the correction of these interpretive errors. It might be said that a definition of these discrepancies in perception constitutes a diagnosis of the disturbed marriage relationship.

The Interpersonal System of Diagnosis

The interpersonal methodology described at length by Leary (1957) and others (Freedman, Leary, Ossorio, and Coffey, 1951; Romano, 1954) provides a theory of interpersonal behavior and a set of methods and tools especially suited to the analysis of an ongoing interaction between human beings. It is impossible to give a full description of the system in this paper, so that only those aspects immediately relevant to the topic will be discussed.

The interpersonal theory of personality, derived from the work of Sullivan (1940), emphasizes the psychological processes occurring between individuals. In this frame of reference, behavior is viewed as functional and purposive, motivated by the need to gratify wishes, perhaps only imperfectly understood, and to avoid anxiety.

The variables of the diagnostic method have systematic interpersonal reference, and permit classification of personality data derived from different sources or "levels." For example, the observed interpersonal *behavior* occurring between individuals may differ widely from the participant's *self-report* of his behavior. These levels of observations are different still from the manner in which a person may define the interpersonal role of a hero in a Thematic Apperception story. This last, the projective test response, is considered to reflect one's *private* or *preconscious* interpersonal perceptions. In each case, however, these data can be classified in terms of the same system of variables.

The schema of classification for these personality data can be conceptualized as a two-dimensional field (see Figure 1), where the

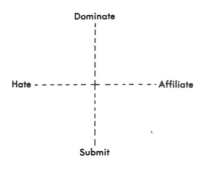

Figure 1. The two-dimensional field comprised by the intersection of the status and affect continua. It should be noted that the verbs designating the ends of the continua are sample terms employed for the sake of clarity.

vertical axis is a status continuum of dominance and submission, while the horizontal axis is an affect continuum of hostility and affiliation. The field readily divides itself into eight sectors which represent the extreme points of the continua, and four blends of these nodal points. (See figures.) Techniques for the reliable measurement and rating of behavior and the personality productions of individuals have been devised (Leary, 1957).

The ratings are then classified around this system of variables, yielding distributions of interpersonal data which can be relegated to the three different levels mentioned above (observed behavior which is termed Level I, conscious report which is Level II, and preconscious projection or Level III data).

In this paper Level I data will not be considered. Level II data, conscious *self* and significant *other* descriptions, were obtained by the use of the Interpersonal Check List.[1] Level III, or private perceptual data, are ob-

tained by rating Thematic Apperception stories in terms of the system of variables.

Scores from the Interpersonal Check List and the TAT can be converted by a trigonometric formula and normative data to a single point on the two-dimensional field or "grid" represented schematically in Figure 1, and in the other figures. This single point represents a summation of the various vectors or "pulls" operating in the interpersonal field (Leary, 1957, pp. 68-69).

The marital partners to be discussed below were chosen to illustrate the diagnostic use of interpersonal data. The case of Mr. and Mrs. George presents for study a conscious view of themselves and each other. Mr. and Mrs. Frank, in addition, present their conscious views of the significant others in their lives (mother and father). In the final case, Mr. and Mrs. Tom, the Level II conscious perceptions are compared with the subject's projective (private, Level III) perceptions as derived from his characterization of the hero and interacting other in TAT stories. Studying the personality data for the marital partners simultaneously provides insight into the marital interaction and its failures.

The Diagnostic Procedure

Following an initial interview held separately with husband and wife, each partner is given a battery of psychological tests, including the Interpersonal Check List described above, and ten cards of the TAT that are used to obtain the Level III ratings.[2]

Both husband and wife are asked to apply the check list to themselves, and to their spouse, mother, and father or any other significant figure in their life.

The special test material is then scored and summarized on the diagnostic grid.

[1]The Interpersonal Check List is an inventory of descriptive phrases or "traits" which locate themselves in the eight sectors of the two-dimensional field of Figure 1. The subject uses the items to characterize himself and various other people. The construction, reliability, and validity of the check list is discussed at length in Leary (1957, pp. 455-463).

[2]These TAT cards are: 1, 2, 3BM, 4, 6BM, 6GF, 7BM, 12M, 13MF, 18BM for men, and: 1, 2, 3GF, 4, 6BM, 6GF, 7GF, 12M, 13MF, 18GF for women. The reliability and validity of this special use of the TAT is discussed at length in Leary (1957, pp. 464-479).

Interpretive
Analysis of the Data

The method described briefly above provides a source of clinical information relevant to the personality of the individual in his social role at large, and in particular in relation to his spouse. His self-regard (Level II) can be compared with his conscious views of his parents and his wife, yielding similarities and discrepancies that reflect upon his capacity to understand or sympathize with the "other." Similarity between his self-regard and his view of the other can be termed *identification* while lack of similarity in scores may reflect *disidentification* or antagonism.

The discrepancy between his Level II self score, and his Level III hero score, throws light upon the internal processes at work. Level III data may represent warded off impulses that result in self-defeating behavior. Sometimes a marital partner may perceive accurately the warded off Level III characteristics of his spouse, and, in fact respond to the spouse, not on the basis of the spouse's conscious view of himself but more accurately in terms of the spouse's warded off traits which creep into his behavior without his awareness. Sometimes mutual deception is unwittingly played, as in the case of Mr. and Mrs. Tom, the third case discussed.

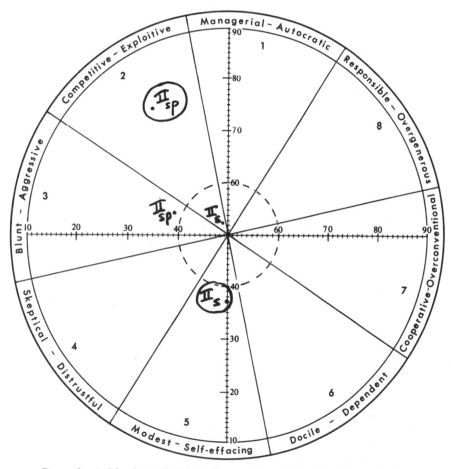

Figure 2. A Marriage of Mutual Frustration and Hostility: Mr. and Mrs. George. The two-dimensional field in the form of a circular grid. (From Leary, 1957) The grid shows how the field is divided into eight sectors. The summary points shown are for Level II ratings. IIs is the summary of the subject's view of himself. IIsp is the summary of the subject's view of his spouse. The circled points are the wife's; the uncircled are the husband's.

A Marriage of Mutual Frustration and Hostility: Mr. and Mrs. George

Figure 2 presents the two-dimensional field in the form of a circular grid.[3]

On the circular grid are summarized a husband and wife's Level II ratings of themselves and each other. It will be noted that there is considerable discrepancy between the way each spouse perceives himself and is perceived *by* his spouse. The wife consciously views herself as a strongly submissive and self-effacing person (her scores total and fall more than one sigma from the mean in the submissive "modest self-effacing" sector of the field) while her husband perceives her as a hostile aggressive person.

She, on the other hand, views *him* as an extremely narcissistic exploitive man, demanding, rejecting and selfish, while he views himself as only mildly competitive; (his score for himself falls so close to the mean as to imply that he actually feels himself to be a well-rounded and flexible individual).

It will readily be seen that such a constellation of scores implies considerable frustration and hostility in this marriage, which, in fact, was the main complaint of each partner. In the interviews each partner expressed the feeling of being victimized and despised by the other. Further, each partner felt that he or she had done nothing to provoke such behavior towards him. The wife felt herself to be a passive docile woman while the husband felt himself to be only "normally" ascendant and aggressive as "a man should be."

Dependency and Rejection: Mr. and Mrs. Frank

Figure 3 presents the Level II scores for a husband and wife and their respective parents.

While considerable mutual misperception of each other is apparent, the data also portray a dependency conflict. The wife perceives

[3]The point of intersection of the two axes is the mean of dominant-submissive and affiliative-hostile scores for the normative population. The inner broken circle is located at one sigma from the mean. (From Leary, 1957.)

herself as an independent and managerial young woman. The significant people in her life, her mother and father, are viewed as more dominating and more exploitive than herself. But she perceives her husband as covertly hostile and weak. In the interview she verbalizes considerable respect for both her parents, but a complete lack of respect for her husband.

The husband views himself as a docile dependent individual, living in a world where the significant others are strong and generous (his mother), dominantly autocratic (his father) and extremely aggressive (his wife). In the interviews, the husband complains of his inability to live up to the expectations set for him, of his failure at a business career for which he knew he was unsuited, and his wife's constant striving.

The wife, on the other hand, continually compares her husband's "failure" to her successful father and comes to the conclusion that her husband is "just obstinate," intentionally depriving her of love and material things. Consciously, she wants her husband to be more like her father, failing to recognize his picture of himself as a dependent individual in need of succorance and support.

The Case of Mr. and Mrs. Tom

This young couple came referred by their family physician who was aware of the marital discord in their lives. Mr. Tom, a 32 year old man presenting a rather hostile and wary facade, complained bitterly against his wife who, he was convinced, had betrayed him with another man. He felt that he was justly hostile since she was by no means a "loving" wife to him.

Mrs. Tom, on the other hand, a somewhat immature 27 year old woman, insisted that she was faithful, although admitting that she had fantasied an escapade with a male acquaintance. She explained that this other man was tender and affectionate in contrast to her harsh punitive husband. Although there was constant marital clash, she denied giving Mr. Tom any provocation for his hos-

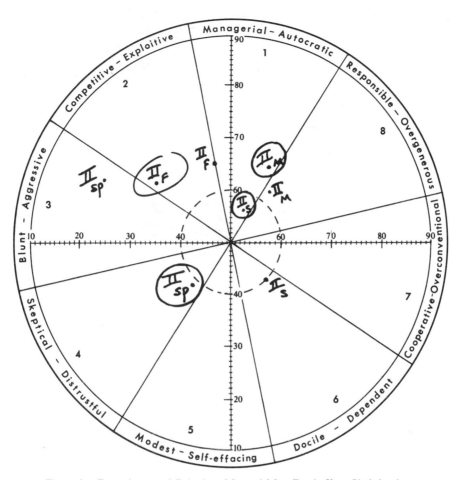

Figure 3. Dependency and Rejection: Mr. and Mrs. Frank. Key: Circled points are the wife's; uncircled points are the husband's. IIs are summary points of conscious self regard; IIsp are points of conscious perceptions of the spouse; IIm are perceptions of the mother; IIf are perceptions of the father.

tility, stating that her aspect of the marital discord was "self defense" or, at the worst, retaliative.

Mrs. Tom:
Interactional Personality Data

Figure 4 presents the interpersonal findings on Mrs. Tom.

Mrs. Tom consciously describes her husband (IIsp) as an extremely competitive and exploitive individual who is selfish and inconsiderate. She describes her own father (IIf) in much the same way, although perceiving him as having these characteristics to a lesser degree. This immediately implies that she tends to identify consciously her husband with her father, and raises the question as to how

much she is responding to Mr. Tom on the basis of the father-daughter relationship.

Her mother (IIm) she characterizes as a responsible and giving individual, slightly more dominant than herself (IIs). She tends to perceive herself and her own actions as cooperative and affiliative, and not deviating very far from the mean. There is a fair correspondence between her own scores and those of her mother, implying a moderate conscious identification.

However, the TAT stories Mrs. Tom creates depict heroes who are aggressive hostile people, reacting violently to their environment and toward those with whom they interact. Mrs. Tom *says* she is kind, cooperative, and affiliative. But her TAT heroes, reflecting

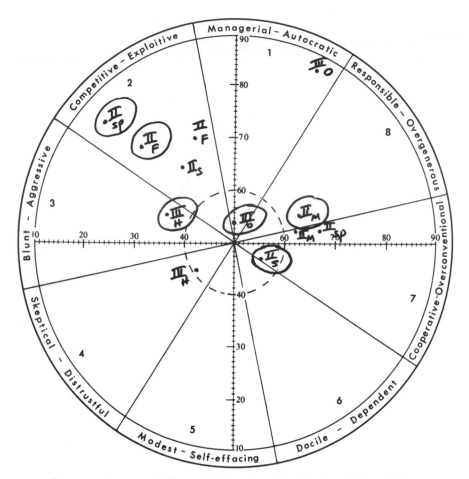

Figure 4. Interpersonal Personality Data from Two Levels on Mr. and Mrs. Tom. Key: Circled points are for Mrs. Tom; uncircled points are for Mr. Tom. IIs is the conscious view of self; IIsp is the conscious view of spouse; IIm is the conscious view of mother; IIf is the conscious view of father; IIIh is the preconscious hero (TAT stories); IIIo is the preconscious "other" (TAT stories).

tendencies within herself only imperfectly perceived, behave in aggressive violent ways. The discrepancy between these two summary points (Level IIs and Level IIIh) is a measure of the amount and type of "repression" and "denial" going on within her personality.

The hostility ratings for her TAT heroes (IIIh) are all the more significant since her TAT "other" figures are not particularly autocratic people. The score for the "other" figures in the TAT stories (IIIo) deviates less than one sigma from the mean in the dominant sector of the grid.

Mr. Tom:
Interactional Personality Data

Consulting the diagnostic grid for Mr. Tom (Figure 4) it will be seen that he con-

sciously ascribes exploitive competitive traits to himself. He sees himself (consciously) in much the same way that his wife views him. He tells us he is very much like his father, pointing up the strength of his conscious paternal identification.

When we examine the nature of his TAT heroes, we get an inkling of considerable turmoil within him. His TAT heroes are weak, distrustful, wary people who need to be constantly on guard against the powerful dominating environment (IIIo). He is striving to "be like father," competitive, self-seeking, and rivalrous, but he needs to hold in abeyance his private perception of his own weakness. This, of course, has considerable implication in regard to his jealousy and doubt regarding his wife.

In spite of his complaints against Mrs. Tom, he continues to characterize and consciously identify her with his mother, as an affiliative and cooperative woman. Apparently, to him this is "femininity" just as his own behavior is viewed as "masculine." An Oedipal coloring to his jealousy of his wife is suggested by the conscious identifications Mr. Tom makes.

Marital Dynamics

Each partner views himself at Level II in a way very similar to his spouse's view of him. At the same time, each partner wards off (Level III) aspects of himself which are incompatible with his conscious self-picture. In the husband's case, these are submissive and covertly resistive traits; in the wife's case, they are hostile, directly aggressive characteristics.

It seems clear that this self deception is maintained not only intrapsychically, but that the disturbed marriage relationship helps to enhance it. That is, by perceiving her husband as an ascendant competitive person, Mrs. Tom helps him to maintain this attitude toward himself, thereby insuring that his fear of weakness remains warded off. Similarly, Mr. Tom "helps" his wife to maintain the illusion that she is a "feminine" woman without aggressive impulses or needs. This is strong evidence for the interpretation that the "neurotic" marital interaction is, in one sense, needed by each of the marital partners to avoid the collapse of their own intrapsychic defense system.

But, as with all neurotic compromise, full satisfaction is impossible. Mr. Tom expresses to the psychologist dissatisfaction with his wife's depriving attitude which he interprets as a reflection on his manhood (i.e., "she prefers another man!"), thereby obscuring his own dependency needs experienced unconsciously. And Mrs. Tom longs for affection and tenderness from her husband, failing to recognize that she threatens and goads him into punitive action.

Prognosis for Counseling

Mr. Tom's marital behavior accords closely with his conscious view of himself and with his wife's description of him, test wise (Level II) and in the interviews. But Mr. Tom consciously identifies with his father (i.e., "I am like father, and father is manly"). Counseling with him will therefore probably be difficult, since he will be threatened by an attempt to help him understand how he contributes to the marital discord. This will be interpreted as an attempt to intervene in his identification with his father. Further, helping him to revise his definition of his wife will add more threat to his burden. These processes will tend to reactivate and bring into consciousness those aspects of himself and the Level IIIo autocratic world which he must ward off (father).

Mrs. Tom can come to an acceptance of her hostile impulses more readily because, according to her definition of the significant others (husband and father), she has justification. She consciously describes these two men as exploitive people who may take advantage of her if she lets them. Mr. Tom, on the other hand, does not have justification for his feelings of weakness and suspicion unless he is willing to perceive his father as a rival with whom he must compete.

On these grounds, the aims of the counseling process will be modified for Mr. Tom. He will be helped to strengthen his positive perceptions of himself, at the same time encouraged to relax his harsh grip on his wife. Mrs. Tom can tolerate a more uncovering approach to her hidden hostility.

Summary

A theoretical approach emphasizing the interpersonal aspects of personality, and a methodology for the analysis of personality in interactional terms was presented. It is believed that the method has particular relevance in the marriage counseling situation where the focus of the treatment endeavor is on the interaction between husband and wife. Marital dynamics are a function of the psychodynamics of the marital participants, since in the final analysis, any structured human interaction has its psychological origins in the intrapsychic processes of the individuals involved. This does not deny the reality of external considerations but insists that the interpretation of these factors depends upon the person's unique internal organization. The diagnostic methodology described here deals systematically with this *intrapersonal* aspect of the marriage partners also.

It is believed that the methodology will be useful in evaluating the effects of marriage counseling, and further work of this sort is in process.

References

Bychowski, G., & Despert, Louise. (Eds.) *Specialized techniques in psychotherapy.* New York: Basic Books, 1952.

Freedman, M., Leary, T., Ossorio, A., & Coffey, H. The interpersonal dimensions of personality. *J. Person.,* 1951, **20**, 143.

Gomberg, M. Present status of treatment program. In V. Eisenstein (Ed.), *Neurotic interaction in marriage.* New York: Basic Books, 1956.

Leary, T. *Interpersonal diagnosis of personality.* New York: Ronald Press, 1957.

Mudd, Emily, & Kirch, A. (Eds.) *Man and Wife: A source book of family attitudes, sexual behavior, and marriage counseling.* New York: Norton, 1957.

Romano, R. A quantification of the psychotherapeutic process. Unpublished doctoral dissertation, Washington Univer., 1954.

Sullivan, H. *Conceptions of modern psychiatry.* Washington, D. C.: W. A. White Psychiatric Foundation, 1940.

Interpersonal Relations: A Critique

Jule Nydes

In the preface to her book (1950) on the evolution and development of psychoanalysis, Dr. Clara Thompson, who is the director of the William Alanson White Institute of Psychiatry in New York City, acknowledges that being human she must have "blind spots"; and that these for the most part are the products of her "cultural and interpersonal" psychoanalytic orientation. This acknowledgement helps us to recognize that her book is less than her title implies and more a history of the various trends which have culminated in the theoretical and therapeutic approach of the psychoanalytic group led by the late Harry Stack Sullivan and generally identified as the "Washington School." As such it serves to highlight, in a lucid and well organized presentation, the underlying premises that have guided the work of Sullivan and his adherents.

Dr. Thompson's writing, aided as it has been by the collaboration of Patrick Mullahy, shares a singular quality with that of Sullivan and quite a few others of his school. A quality that is hard at first to identify, possibly because it makes itself known only in a feeling that something is missing. A feeling one may get perhaps while viewing an exhibit of a model home. We are impressed that the furnishings are well constructed, in good taste and pleasantly arranged; but all the while it remains somehow dreary—because nobody lives there.

Sullivan, according to Dr. Thompson, is "the first person since Freud to offer a systematic theory of personality development," based on an analysis of the relationship that

From J. Nydes, "Interpersonal Relations: Personal and Depersonalized," *Psychoanalysis,* 1952, **1**, no. 1. Reprinted through the courtesy of the editors of the *Psychoanalytic Review,* and of the publisher, the National Psychological Association for Psychoanalysis, Inc.

obtains between the person and the significant people in his environment as he progresses from one phase of growth and maturation to the next. Throughout his life "the human being is concerned with two inclusive goals, the pursuit of satisfaction and the pursuit of security." Sullivan believes that "most psychological problems arise from difficulties encountered in security operations" and that "the avoidance of anxiety, which is at first evoked by disapproval, is the most potent force" in the formation of character structure or the self-system. Within its general framework, however, the self-system may be modified by the impact of different personalities. Built up as it has been by the need to avoid anxiety, the self-system "may endow people falsely with characteristics taken from significant people in one's past," or from imaginary people. This tendency Sullivan terms parataxic distortion, and Dr. Thompson writes, "One of the important purposes of therapy is to make the patient aware of what is going on between him and others based on distorted identifications." Dr. Thompson sums it up in the following passage:

Whatever theory in the long run proves to be most adequate, one thing has been accomplished to date. By establishing the idea that habitual attitudes provide the resistance to cure, a new era in treatment has begun. No longer is the drive to unearth the past paramount in therapy. The way a person defends himself in his daily relations with people has become the main object of study, although his past history is also examined in order to provide insight as to how he got to be the sort of person he is.

Such a brief summary of Sullivan's approach as I have paraphrased it from Dr. Thompson's book, does not of course do him justice. His therapeutic recommendations for meeting the problems presented by the security operations of rigidly defended personalities and his understanding of the genesis of defense in early relationships are masterful, and reflect his keen interest in the schizophrenic and the obsessional for whom the need to avoid anxiety is a consideration overriding all others.

The Problem of Anxiety which Freud in his book of that title (1936) recognizes as "the central problem of neurosis" is the central issue with which Sullivan is preoccupied throughout his work. Freud, after careful scrutiny and modification of a previous hypothesis, identifies anxiety as an affect of the ego which the ego struggles to ward off. He points out that the ego avoids anxiety through the development of inhibitions and symptoms, and that anxiety results when the ego's defenses fail to operate. It is within the limits of Freud's conception of the relationship that obtains between anxiety and symptoms that the main features of Sullivan's "systematic theory of personality development" are encompassed (1949a). Within such limits Sullivan's contribution is profound. It is what lies beyond those limits, however, that leaves a vacuum in the theories of the "cultural interpersonal school."

Not Sullivan alone, but all followers of the "cultural approach," despite differences among themselves, unite in rejecting Freud's instinct theory. Horney (1939) especially in *New Ways in Psychoanalysis* shows how the unfounded biological premises of the instinct theory have distorted the great conceptions of Freud's pioneering work. But in their subsequent work, all fail either overtly or implicitly to appreciate that, closely associated with Freud's emphasis on biological drives, is his profound recognition of the processes of *active* human motivation. They have discarded not simply the instinct theory but have turned their backs as well on the "pursuit of satisfaction" (which Freud terms the pleasure principle) as a vital factor in the human career. For the purposes of this discussion it is irrelevant to attempt to examine the validity of Freudian biology. But it is important to discern the ways in which the rejection of the Freudian biology has been accompanied by the development of a negative psychology which stresses, almost to the exclusion of all other considerations, the importance of the pursuit of security and of defensively motivated habitual attitudes.

If we ignore its biological premises (as Freud does for the most part in his *Psychopathology of Everyday Life*) an instinct is a wish, a desire, a motive, a positive goal. The desire for safety, for self-preservation, is, to be sure, fundamental to the survival of the individual and the species. But a psychology which relies for its understanding almost exclusively on the need for self-preservation, for safety, for security, necessarily must describe life in extremely colorless and uncreative terms. Such a psychology, in so far as it ignores active motivation and directs attention to habitual attitudes, becomes a psychology of patterns, of kinds of relatedness, a psychology of how a person defends himself rather than of how he asserts himself. It strips psychoanalysis of its essential richness and vitality.

The psychology of active motivation (wish fulfillment) and the psychology of attitudes merge at many points and are at times indistinguishable. Motives are reflected in attitudes, and attitudes in turn provide the basis for further motives. It is more a matter of accent or emphasis than rigid classification. An awareness of attitudes helps to define the characteristic structure of a relationship; and understanding of motives tends to clarify the forces that govern a relationship within and beyond the limits of its typical structure. In military terms the study of habitual attitudes would be more like the study of the Maginot Line. Here it is formidable, there it is weak. The builder has a deep investment in the integrity of his fortifications even when he is well aware that no attack is threatening. The study of the psychology involved in the pursuit of satisfaction, on the other hand, is more like the study of an active campaign—of skirmishes, advances, retreats, collaboration with allies, and expenditure of resources. The former is primarily concerned with structure; the latter with interaction and movement.

The former involves an investment of power; the latter an active power operation. When Sullivan writes of security operations, for the most part he seems to be defining a structure in which power has been invested rather than an actual operation. In like vein his reference to "interpersonal relations" may be more accurately understood as interpersonal *attitudes*.

The dissociation of the psychology involved in the pursuit of satisfaction has affected the approach to almost every major topic broached (or evaded) by the theories of the Washington School. Such topics include, among others, Sullivan's definitions of satisfaction and security, and the concepts of transference, guilt, shame, and hysteria.

According to Sullivan (1949a) all satisfactions are strictly biological and relatively unimportant in the development of personality. Concerning sex, which he terms "lust," he writes, ". . . the fully developed feeling of lust comes so very late in biological maturation that it is scarcely a good source for conditioning." (Curiously enough, in one of his last papers (1949b), he complains that his analysts in training almost never discuss sex with him.)

If we accept Sullivan's definitions we are obliged to conclude that the need for self-preservation, which we share biologically with all living creatures, must be classified not under the need for security but rather under the heading of the pursuit of satisfaction. All satisfactions, on the other hand, as they undergo cultural conditioning, are, to the extent of such conditioning, transformed into "security operations." But how would Sullivan classify the deep sense of fulfillment in creative work; or the enjoyment of genuine friendship, of play, and of love? Are all of these satisfactions really a pursuit of security? Surely Sullivan would be the last to classify them strictly as biological.

Sullivan's insistence that the need for satisfaction plays only a minor role in personality development and in the genesis of psychological problems is reflected in the fact that the Washington School has made almost no significant contributions on the subject of sexual perversion. Male homosexuality, to be sure, is regarded as a relationship in which women are dissociated, but little light is shed on the dynamics of the kind of satisfaction of which perversions are an expression. Not only the psychology of satisfaction, but more important for the purpose of therapy, the pathology of satisfaction is also missing in Sullivan's approach.

The vital energy with which we are all endowed, in spite of our fears and defenses, seeks its own fulfillment and expression through whatever avenues are open. As an actuality it manifests itself in activity; and, as a potentiality, in the form of desires, aspirations, and wishes. The sense of self—the immediacy of personal identification, is inseparable from the full recognition by an individual of what it is he wishes. With such recognition he also becomes aware of conflicts in his wishes, of the irrationality and the validity of many of his wishes, and (most important of all) of the discrepancy between what he wishes and the life he leads. To conceive, therefore, of interpersonal relations primarily in terms of defensive integration is, to that extent, to focus on their depersonalized characteristics rather than on their personal interaction.

Whether attitude, motive, or both are interpreted in the actual therapeutic relationship will vary depending on how close to awareness the person's wishes actually are. The emphasis of the Washington School, however, is that "most psychological problems arise from difficulties encountered in security operations" as manifested in habitual attitudes. Sullivan's concept of parataxic distortion and Horney's concept of externalization reflect this emphasis. Both terms tend to generalize the more specific Freudian concepts of transference and projection. Both Sullivan's and Horney's concepts are valid, but it is invalid to attempt to substitute them for the more specific motive-oriented ideas of Freud.

The distinctions mentioned above may be further clarified by the following example:

A young woman, Marie, took advantage of the opportunity to share an apartment with another girl, Stella, whom she had met only recently, and whom she found amiable and cooperative. Marie discovered no good reason to change her opinion of Stella when she moved in. In spite of this she found herself compulsively engaged in numberless needless household chores and, without any basis in Stella's attitude, anxiously expected Stella's criticism whenever they were at home together. She felt she was an inconvenience to Stella, that Stella resented her and wished that Marie had never moved in. Also with no basis, she felt inferior and unattractive in relation to Stella. She realized that she was relating to Stella as if Stella were her mother and recalled numerous times when she was criticized and coldly punished by her mother. This helped her to realize that her apprehension concerning Stella was unjustified, but she was not relieved until the therapist remarked, "You really wish that you had the apartment all to yourself." She smiled and answered, "No, what I really wish is that I were married and living in the apartment with my husband instead of with Stella."

Marie's attitude toward Stella was a *parataxic distortion* in that it was typical of her way of relating to anyone upon whom she looked as an authority. It was *transference* in that she related to Stella specifically as if she were her mother. It was *externalization* in that she was sensitive to Stella's possible discomfort rather than her own. It was *projection,* however, in that *she wished* to be rid of Stella rather than the reverse. Her compulsive housecleaning was, to be sure, her way of warding off anxiety in connection with possible disapproval. But her need for Stella's approval was in reality a need to be acquitted of her guilt for her underlying wish to be married and living in the apartment with her husband instead of with Stella. She was able to assert this freely when the therapist recognized her wish to have the apartment for herself. With her assertion, her feelings of unattractiveness diminished. Her inferiority feelings apparently served the defensive function of withdrawing from competition with Stella (and other women) as if to say to her, "You are the one who is worthy of having a husband, not I. You have nothing to fear from me." Her fear of openly avowing her wish even to herself is, of course, in itself an aspect of her relatedness to others, a relatedness which would manifest itself with her husband

as well if she had one; but the acceptance of her wish in the context of that relatedness tends in itself to modify the need for that kind of relatedness.

The above interpretation is, to be sure, an oversimplification and represents only a small step toward the relief of Marie's difficulties. It is cited only as an example of the dynamic relationship obtaining among different levels of interpretation and to demonstrate the different emphases involved in the recognition of habitual attitudes and the recognition of active motives. *The attitude oriented therapist would tend to stress Marie's defensive self-abnegating relatedness to those whose disapproval she fears. The motive oriented therapist would tend to direct attention to the guilt laden wish against which typical defenses are erected.*

The two orientations, to be sure, are not mutually exclusive. The same therapist may find one more applicable to one patient than to another. An habitually submissive person, for example, who has rarely if ever been conscious of a clear positive wish for himself, hopefully in the course of therapy will find himself fuming with resentment. Such resentment in all probability can most relevantly be related to the personal humiliation involved in his habitually submissive attitude. Another person, however, who also might be characterized as submissive but whose wishes are closer to the surface, may become conscious of hostile feelings, not as a reaction against his submissiveness, but because he expects to be attacked for motives which the submissiveness is designed to conceal. He seeks approval through compliance not because he dissociates his own needs but because he must be reassured that his guilt laden wishes have not been discovered and condemned. The quality and meaning of his hostility, when it emerges, is likely to be quite different from that of one for whom complete reliance on authority has become a way of life.

We sometimes come across a person in whom the pathology of security operations and the pathology of the pursuit of satisfaction are fairly clear cut and distinct. Not long ago, in a seminar, I submitted for discussion the case of a young man. In the opinion of some members of the seminar he was clearly a perfectionistic obsessive-compulsive character. In the opinion of others he was just as clearly a sado-masochistic personality. Both opinions were correct. He related to others with the most extreme propriety, rarely expressed his feelings, was orderly, clean, punctual, and tight. In fantasy, however, and, at times, in practice, he derived great satisfaction out of being beaten as well as inflicting physical pain on women. Any failure in his obsessional defenses would bring on feelings of anxiety, from which he would obtain relief through sado-masochistic fantasies. But these, in turn, would be followed by feelings of guilt and shame and by resolutions to be even more meticulous on his job and in his dealings with others. And so he lived in a perpetual cycle of model behaviour, anxiety, guilt, shame, and more model behaviour.

An understanding of the young man's habitual attitudes tells us a great deal about how he manages to feel safe in a world which he experiences as hostile to his emotional self-realization. But his attitudes tell us little about how his vitality seeks to assert itself. We may know that his fantasies give him some relief from anxiety, but we cannot know *why* his fantasies take the form that they do unless we appreciate the psychological function of guilt and punishment, and the way in which guilt, shame, and anxiety are related to each other.

Except for the writing of Erich Fromm, Sullivan and others in the Washington School reject the phenomenon of guilt as having either no existence or little significance in human psychology. Guilt, to be sure, is a concept concerning which there has been a great deal of confusion but no more so than the concept of anxiety. Its omission from the theories of the Washington School provides the main clue to what I believe is the depersonalization of their approach to interpersonal relations, and reflects their preoccupation with the problems of the emotionally detached. It is a significant omission because it

is primarily in relation to unacceptable wishes and unconscious motives that feelings of guilt and all that follows in their train (the provocation of attack, penance, resentment, defiance, feeling of responsibility, etc.) come to the fore. It is undoubtedly because Freud's first interest was in hysteria (in which the defenses are fluid rather than rigid) that his attention was drawn first to the dynamics involved in the pursuit of satisfaction and in guilt rather than to the problems of anxiety and its defenses. While the frustration of sexual feelings was a big issue in his day, the frustration of other types of satisfactions is no less an issue now. Moreover, unlike hunger, the satisfaction of sexual wishes continues to involve interpersonal relations on their most intimate and revealing level.

The conversion of anxiety to guilt is a crucial aspect of psychoanalytic therapy concerning which there has been little discussion. It is a topic which demands thorough discussion, and certainly the limits of this paper do not permit even an effective introduction to it. But Sullivan's rejection of guilt (which he says is not different from shame) as a distinct and profound factor in human psychology cannot be evaluated unless an attempt at least is made to indicate certain distinctions.

Without intending to do so, Dr. Frieda Fromm-Reichmann in her sensitive book on psychotherapy (1950) provides an observation from which far reaching implications concerning the distinction between shame and guilt may be drawn. In an effort to explain rebellious behaviour she writes, "It is more bearable to be hated for what one *does* than for what one *is*." This statement may very plausibly be taken to mean that when one feels hatred for what he is, he feels ashamed, but that he is more likely to feel guilty if he feels hatred for what he does or (consciously or otherwise) wishes to do or believes himself to have done. Shame seems to be more closely related to a failure to exercise one's powers effectively. It is associated with a feeling of inadequacy, of being held in contempt, of being ignored or disdained and rejected. The foibles of immaturity, soiling oneself, social clumsiness, the naive exposure of oneself to ridicule are experienced as shameful, and deeply threatening to any secure feeling that one can rely on the good will and approval of others. Guilt, on the other hand, appears to be more closely associated with the defiant use of power or with an unconscious will toward the deviant fulfillment of one's wishes. It implies not inadequacy but dangerous effectiveness and a feeling of responsibility. It provokes, either in reality or in one's imagination, not contempt but anger, not disdain but pursuit, not scornful rejection but active punishment. Often it inspires grudging admiration. Consider if you will the difference in attitude toward the helplessness of the innocuous timid soul, and the daring exploits of the legendary Jesse James.

The fact that most frequently people experience a mixture of shame and guilt does not imply that the feelings are identical. Rather, in terms of the above hypotheses, the two feelings are in a dynamic compensatory relationship. The feeling of guilt provides an unhappy and at times only temporary way of dealing with the sense of shame.

In the sense of this discussion, shame is closely allied with anxiety which, according to both Freud and Sullivan, is generated by disapproval or by the fear of losing a source of security. Guilt then would constitute an alternative to a rigid defense structure as a way of dealing with anxiety. The young man mentioned above felt anxious when he failed to measure up to rigid standards, *guilty* about his sadistic fantasy when, freed of his need for approval, he exercised vindictive power; and ashamed when his fantasy subsided because his power was only an illusion and he came face to face with his real sense of inadequacy which he sought again to resolve in reality by trying to live up to impossible standards (Nydes, 1950). But the conversion of anxiety to guilt, even though it appears to involve the substitution of one evil for another, represents a constructive move if guilt can be appreciated as closely related to a defiant, even if distorted, surge of vitality and self-expression. Its constructive element involves the

conversion of the sense of helplessness into, at least, an implied sense of power.

Sullivan's dissociation of the importance of guilt in his theoretical and therapeutic approach is clearly manifest when he writes about the hysteric in whom guilt constitutes such a powerful dynamic. He characterizes the hysteric as self-absorbed, fantastic, melodramatic, wounded, disappointed, etc., and constantly in search of the "good mother." By attempting to describe the hysteric mostly in terms of his manifest character attributes, he succeeds in depicting a fairly trivial personality—a kind of pathetic shadow of a broken down obsessional. In this he ignores the fact that the hysteria has an unstable rather than a rigid character structure, is pervaded by a sense of guilt for which he is continually seeking forgiveness—and punishment against which, in turn, he is continually rebelling. His wishes, and his demands for their satisfaction are too close to the surface to endure the paralyzing constraint of rigid defenses. He is perhaps the clearest example of Freud's observation (1950) "that in analysis we never discover a 'No' in the unconscious. . . ."

Dr. Fromm-Reichmann believes that the problems of the neurotic and the psychotic are substantially similar; that the differences between them are more differences of degree than of kind (1946). This belief may serve most clearly to explain why the pursuit of satisfaction has been played down in the therapeutic approach of the Washington School. For seriously disturbed persons, whose hold on reality is tenuous, almost all psychoanalytic writers agree that the main therapeutic task is one of ego building. Their unconscious drives are all too conscious, too overwhelming. It is the operation of the reality principle rather than the pleasure principle which must be strengthened in the therapeutic relationship. The classical psychoanalytic procedure on the other hand is designed in almost all of its features to expose the role of unconscious forces in the patient's life. The problems of the neurotic and the psychotic are, to be sure, different in degree, but extreme differences in degree lead in turn to differences in kind. It is just as fallacious to apply to mildly disturbed persons the techniques designed for psychotics, as it would be to use classical psychoanalytic methods in dealing with schizophrenics. Many principles are, of course, equally applicable, but the Washington School, in ignoring the essential distinctions, has reared a psychology which, in its total impact, seems more to strengthen inhibition than to release vitality. Preoccupation with the study of inadequate defenses and unhappy kinds of relatedness has led more and more to definitions of ideal kinds of relatedness (Sullivan, Fromm) or, if you will, ideal defenses.

In both the classical approach and in the approach of the Washington School the pleasure principle and the reality principle are placed implicitly in artificial opposition. One step toward their integration would involve a clearer recognition of the fact that satisfaction and security may not be consigned respectively to biology and culture. Both are intimately (perhaps inseparably) related to each other. Just as the old dichotomy of mind and body is yielding to the concept of a psycho-physical unity, so the concept of a bio-cultural unity must synthesize and supersede both Freud's instinct theory and the "security operations" of Harry Stack Sullivan.

Freud's instinct theory, pessimistic though it is for the outlook of the human race, nevertheless contains within it a kindly acceptance of people. His theory may, but his therapy does not, necessarily involve more and more repression of man's inborn aggression. Rather it involves an acceptance of aggression as a natural impulse, one which can be controlled (suppressed), and concerning which one need feel no guilt as long as it remains only a feeling. The acceptance of aggressive feelings without guilt is at least one step (even if the biological premise is mistaken) toward keeping them within bounds; since guilt concerning them serves only to generate more defensive aggression. High expectations for mankind, while fully justified, too often involve, on the part of limited people, self-righteous contempt for man's limitations.

The Washington School seems to respond positively, with understanding and appreciation, to two broad categories of people: those who, having been highly threatened, are rigidly defended; and people (mostly imaginary) who appear to be ideally motivated by love (according to Sullivan's definition) and the rational goals outlined by Erich Fromm. Others, however, who actively struggle with their wishes and defenses, who enter into lively though distorted emotional exchange with others; who may get angry when they feel affection, or who may smile with transparently constrained cordiality when they feel a mixture of superiority and fear; who in destructive, self-damaging, irrational ways, impatient of their own anxiety and guilt, strive to establish some claim on life: these others discover little understanding in the writing of the Washington School. Rather they are characterized, in terms of their manifest relatedness, as being overly ambitious, aggressively exploitative, opportunistic and ingratiating. The Washington School seems out of touch with the deeper sources of such problems; with the complicated dynamics and motivation involved in the peculiar, active, and conflicted pursuit of *both* satisfaction and security. It would be hard to imagine where Dostoevsky's characters, for example, could find room in Dr. Thompson's psychological universe. She might, with some distinction, discern the patterns cast by their shadows, their habitual attitudes; but it is doubtful that she could admit them in the flesh.

References

Freud, Sigmund. Negation. In *Collected papers.* London: Hogarth Press, 1950. Vol. 5, p. 185.

Freud, Sigmund. *The problem of anxiety.* New York: Norton, 1936.

Fromm-Reichmann, Frieda. Remarks on the philosophy of mental disorder. *Psychiatry,* 1946, **9,** 293-308.

Fromm-Reichmann, Frieda. *Principles of intensive psychotherapy.* Chicago: Univ. of Chicago Press, 1950.

Horney, Karen. *New ways in psychoanalysis.* New York: Norton, 1939.

Nydes, Jule. The magical experience of the masturbation fantasy. *Am. J. Psychother.,* 1950, **4,** 303-310.

Sullivan, Harry Stack. *Conceptions of modern psychiatry.* Washington, D.C.: William Alanson White Psychiatric Foundation, 1949a.

Sullivan, Harry Stack. The study of psychiatry. *Psychiatry,* 1949b, **12,** 332-333.

Thompson, Clara, with the collaboration of Mullahy, Patrick. *Psychoanalysis: Evolution and development.* New York: Heritage House, 1950.

Part Two

Behavior Theory

Part Two

3   Joseph Wolpe

In recent years the extension of principles of learning to the understanding of personality and to the practical treatment of psychopathology has become vigorous and widespread. The reasons for this extension are contained largely in a substantial body of theory and experimental research associated with the works of Pavlov, Hull, Skinner, and other learning theorists. To many people, however, the image of learning in general, and of conditioning in particular, conjures up pictures of rats in mazes, pigeons pecking, and dogs in harnesses. Thus, learning theory is often not considered particularly relevant to the study of human personality. However, a good example of the importance of conditioning theory for the understanding of human behavior is found in the work of Ivan Pavlov and of a contemporary re-interpreter of Pavlov, Joseph Wolpe.

Late in his life Pavlov advanced a theory of personality types and speculated on the appropriate treatment for various mental disorders. For this reason it is useful to distinguish between Pavlov's theories of the conditional reflex and the experimental method of classical conditioning. Most students are familiar with the dog strapped into a harness and salivating to the sound of a metronome. In brief, a conditional stimulus (sound) is presented slightly before the unconditional stimulus (meat powder), and through the continual pairing of these two stimuli the conditional stimulus (sound) eventually elicits the conditional response (salivation) which previously, as unconditional response (salivation), could only be evoked by the unconditional stimulus (meat powder). The actual occurrences are far more complicated than the simple paradigm described here because of the many variables involved in the reliable elicitation of the conditioned reflex, but this description should suffice for our purposes. Pavlov's theory, however, is concerned less with the conditioned response *per se* than with the physiological systems that underlie the process of classical conditioning. It is in the brain, the central organizing structure of the body, that the necessary biological adjustments for survival and for higher order mental processes are made. Every person is surrounded by an environment which constantly impinges on his senses. In order to make the environment comprehensible, the brain must organize these signals into some sort of order. According to Pavlov, we learn by making the necessary survival associations between "neutral" stimuli (labeled conditional stimuli) and unconditional stimuli, which already have an intrinsic activating potential. The brain analyzes these incoming signals, makes the physiological associations, and creates the conditions for the formation of the conditional reflexes. Theoretically, what we call personality is, for Pavlov, the result of different characteristics of brain response to incoming stimuli.

Joseph Wolpe is a contemporary theorist

and clinician who has incorporated principles of Pavlovian theory. Wolpe has developed a theory of *reciprocal inhibition* and a therapeutic technique of *systematic desensitization* for the purpose of treating neurotic conditions. As a guiding assumption, Wolpe believes that neurosis can be best described as a persistent learned habit of anxiety response to situations in which there is no actual danger. Furthermore, if neurosis can be learned, it can conceivably be unlearned as well. Following a contiguity assumption of learning, Wolpe conjectures that all human neuroses are produced as a result of the learned association between high intensities of anxiety and neutral stimulus events which have occurred in close temporal relationship. Wolpe reasons that neurotic anxiety, basically a physiological state, can be counter-conditioned through the creation of other behavior that is physiologically antagonistic to anxiety. His major means of producing this counter-conditioning effect is called *systematic desensitization*. In the therapy technique of systematic desensitization, the client is trained in relaxation, which is presumably incompatible with anxiety, and he is eventually exposed to a list of anxiety-arousing items that are imagined by him while he is in a relaxed state. Once the skill of relaxation has been acquired, it serves the purpose of reciprocally inhibiting the client's anxiety. However, in order for relaxation to be a significant agent in counter-conditioning, the anxiety-arousing cues must be presented in a carefully arranged order, from low to high intensity, or else the process will become diluted. The paper by Wolpe describes in detail the treatment methods he has devised, along with his clinical observations regarding the success of his therapeutic program.

The study by Grossberg and Wilson examines the assumption by Wolpe that the imagining of scenes selected as being anxiety-loaded does indeed produce a greater physiological reaction than the visualizing of scenes that have a neutral content. The experimental procedures applied to test this hypothesis required the recording of various physiological measures made at the same time that the experimenter was suggesting imaginary

scenes to the subject. In this study, the independent variables were the neutral scenes and the fear scenes; the dependent variables were the physiological measures and the subject's responses to a questionnaire concerning the clarity with which the subject could imagine each scene. In reading this study, the student should note the complex statistical treatment of these data—this is due partly to the nature of the variables examined. Physiological data is notoriously unstable across subjects because each person has a rate of physiological activity that is uniquely his own. Consequently, in order to control for inter-individual variability a counterbalanced presentation of neutral and fear scenes was arranged so that each subject served as his own control. Then, in order to compare subjects with one another, a difference score was obtained between a resting level of physiological activity (the base level) and the level of activity measured during the experimental treatments. The results of this study generally support a vital assumption of Wolpe's: that physiological arousal tends to show a greater increase with the imagination of scenes of fearful content than with scenes of neutral content.

The critique paper by the eminent learning theorist O. Hobart Mowrer compares the theoretical assumptions of Wolpe, Freud, and Dollard and Miller, and then advances Mowrer's own reformulations. Mowrer argues that Wolpe and Freud offer almost identical explanations for the origins of neurotic fears and that both views suffer from similar misapprehensions. The main thrust of Mowrer's argument is that neurotic anxiety is the consequence of real social danger. This position is in sharp contrast to the position of Wolpe and Freud, who consider neurotic anxiety as having little tangible basis in reality. To bolster his departure from these theorists, Mowrer remarks that there is little experimental evidence for the maintenance of fears when no objective danger is present. Eventually these fears disappear as a result of "reality testing." If, however, neurotics actually design their lives to perpetuate guilt and its attending anxiety, then this style of living is continually reinforced and the fears will be maintained. Thus, in order to extinguish this neurotic pattern the person must renounce genuine defects in his conscience and assume a more moral course of action.

Suggestions for Further Reading

Wolpe's first book, *Psychotherapy by Reciprocal Inhibition*, was published by the Stanford University Press in 1958. His most recent work, *The Practice of Behavior Therapy,* published by Pergamon Press, 1969, deals exclusively with the therapy techniques that can be applied in clinical practice. For a recent comprehensive presentation of behavior therapy consult Albert Bandura's *Principles of Behavior Modification,* published by Holt, Rinehart and Winston, 1969.

The Systematic Desensitization of Neurosis

Joseph Wolpe

Some years ago, studies on the induction and elimination of experimental neuroses in animals (23) showed that these conditions were persistent habits of unadaptive behavior acquired by learning (conditioning); and that their therapy was a matter of unlearning. The central constituent of the neurotic behavior was anxiety, and the most effective way of procuring unlearning was repeatedly to feed the animal while it was responding with a weak degree of anxiety to a "weak" conditioned stimulus. The effect of this was to diminish progressively the strength of the anxiety response to the particular stimulus so that it eventually declined to zero. Increasingly "strong" stimulus situations were successively dealt with in the same way; and finally, the animal showed no anxiety to any of the situations to which anxiety had been conditioned. The basis of the gradual elimination of the anxiety response habit appeared to be an example, at a more complex level, of the phenomenon of *reciprocal inhibition* described originally by Sherrington (17). Each time the animal fed, the anxiety response was to some extent inhibited; and each occasion of inhibition weakened somewhat the strength of the anxiety habit. The experiments suggested the general proposition that *if a response inhibitory to anxiety can be made to occur in the presence of anxiety-evoking stimuli so that it is accompanied by a complete or partial suppression of the anxiety response, the bond between these stimuli and the anxiety response will be weakened.*

I have argued elsewhere (24, 27, 28) that human neuroses are quite parallel to experimental neuroses. On this premise and during the past twelve years, the writer has applied the reciprocal inhibition principle to the treatment of a large number of clinical cases of neurosis, employing a variety of other responses to inhibit anxiety or other neurotic responses. In a recent book (27) an analysis has been given of the results in 210 patients, of whom 89 per cent either recovered or were much improved, apparently lastingly, after a mean of about 30 interviews.

In the case of neurotic responses conditioned to situations involving direct interpersonal relations, the essence of reciprocal inhibition therapy has been to instigate in the situations concerned new patterns of behavior of an anxiety-inhibiting kind whose repeated exercise gradually weakens the anxiety response habit (16, 19, 20, 25, 27, 28). Neurotic responses conditioned to stimuli other than those arising from direct interpersonal relations do not lend themselves, as a rule, to behavioral treatment in the life situation of the patient; and consulting-room applications of the reciprocal inhibition principle have been necessary. The most straightforward examples of neurotic responses requiring such measures have been the phobias. Relatively "simple" though they are, they have hitherto constituted a difficult therapeutic problem. For example, Curran and Partridge (2) state, "Phobic symptoms are notoriously resistant to treatment and their complete removal is rarely achieved." A very different picture is in prospect with the use of conditioning methods (1, 4, 10-12, 14, 15), which are no less effective when used for much more subtle neurotic constellations. Examples will be found below.

In the office treatment of neuroses by reciprocal inhibition, any response inhibitory of anxiety may in theory be used. The almost

From J. Wolpe, "The Systematic Desensitization Treatment of Neuroses," *Journal of Nervous and Mental Disease*, 1961, **132**, 189-202. Copyright 1961 by The Williams & Wilkins Co., Baltimore, Md., U. S. A. Reprinted by permission of the publisher and the author.

forgotten earliest example of therapy of this kind (7) involved inhibiting the anxiety of phobic children by feeding (just as in the animal experiments mentioned above). Conditioned motor responses have occasionally served the same end (27, p. 173); and Meyer (14) and Freeman and Kendrick (4) have made use of ordinary "pleasant" emotions of daily life (see also 27, p. 198). But the behavioral response that has had the widest application is deep muscle relaxation, whose anxiety-inhibiting effects were first pointed out by Jacobson (5, 6). It has been the basis of the technique known as *systematic desensitization* which, because of its convenience, has been most widely adopted (1, 9, 11, 12).

Though several descriptions of the technique of systematic desensitization have been published (*e.g.,* 26, 27) it is now clear that more details are needed to enable practitioners to apply it without assistance. It is the aim of this paper to present a more adequate account, and also for the first time to give a separate statistical analysis of results obtained with this treatment.

The Technique of Systematic Desensitization

It is necessary to emphasize that the desensitization technique is carried out *only after a careful assessment of the therapeutic requirements of the patient.* A detailed history is taken of every symptom and of every aspect of life in which the patient experiences undue difficulty. A systematic account is then obtained of his life history with special attention in intrafamilial relationships. His attitudes to people in educational institutions and to learning and play are investigated. A history of his work life is taken, noting both his experiences with people and those related to work itself. He is questioned about his sexual experiences from first awareness of sexual feelings up to the present. Careful scrutiny is made of his current major personal relationships. Finally, he is asked to describe all kinds of "nervousness" that may have afflicted him at any time and to narrate any distressing experiences he can remember.

The problems posed by the case are now carefully considered; and if there are neurotic reactions in connection with direct interpersonal relations, appropriate new behavior based on the reciprocal inhibition principle is instigated in the patient's life situation (19, 20, 25, 27, 28). Most commonly, it is assertive behavior that is instigated. When systematic desensitization is also indicated, it is conducted as soon as possible, and may be in parallel with measures aimed at other sources of neurotic anxiety.

Systematic desensitization is used not only for the treatment of classical phobias involving anxiety responses to nonpersonal stimulus constellations (like enclosed spaces or harmless animals), but also for numerous less obvious and often complex sources of neurotic disturbance. These may involve ideas, bodily sensations, or extrinsic situations. Examples of each are to be found in Table 1. The most common extrinsic sources of anxiety relate to people in contexts that make irrelevant the use of direct action, such as assertion, on the part of the patient. As examples, one patient reacts with anxiety to the mere presence of particular persons, another to definable categories of people, a third to being the center of attention, a fourth to people in groups, a fifth to inferred criticism or rejection, and so forth. In all instances, *anxiety has been conditioned to situations in which, objectively, there is no danger.*

In brief, the desensitization method consists of presenting to the imagination of the deeply relaxed patient the feeblest item in a list of anxiety-evoking stimuli—repeatedly, until no more anxiety is evoked. The next item of the list is then presented, and so on, until eventually, even the strongest of the anxiety-evoking stimuli fails to evoke any stir of anxiety in the patient. It has consistently been found that at every stage a stimulus that evokes no anxiety when imagined in a state of relaxation will also evoke no anxiety when encountered in reality.

The method involves three separate sets of operations: 1) training in deep muscle relaxation; 2) the construction of anxiety hierarchies; and 3) counterposing relaxation and anxiety-evoking stimuli from the hierarchies.

Table 1. Basic case data.

Patient Sex, Age	No. of Sessions	Hierarchy Theme	Outcome	Comments
1. F,50	62	a) Claustrophobia	+ + + +	See case data.
		b) Illness and hospitals	+ + + +	
		c) Death and its trappings	+ + + +	
		d) Storms	+ + +	
		e) Quarrels	+ + + +	
2. M,40	6	a) Guilt	+ + + +	See case data.
		b) Devaluation	+ + + +	
3. F,24	17	a) Examinations	+ + + +	
		b) Being scrutinized	+ + + +	
		c) Devaluation	+ + + +	
		d) Discord between others	+ + + +	
4. M,24	5	a) Snakelike shapes	+ + + +	
5. M,21	24	a) Being watched	+ + + +	
		b) Suffering of others	+ + + +	
		c) "Jealousy" reaction	+ + + +	
		d) Disapproval	+ + + +	
6. M,28	5	Crowds	+ + +	
7. F,21	5	Criticism	+ + + +	
8. F,52	21	a) Being center of attention	0	No disturbance during scenes. Was in fact not imagining self in situation.
		b) Superstitions	0	
9. F,25	9	Suffering and death of others	+ + +	
10. M,22	17	Tissue damage in others	+ + + +	
11. M,37	13	Actual or implied criticism	+ + + +	
12. F,31	15	Being watched working	+ + +	
13. F,40	16	a) Suffering and eeriness	+ + + +	This case has been reported in detail (26).
		b) Being devalued	+ + + +	
		c) Failing to come up to expectations	+ + + +	
14. M,36	10	a) Bright light	+ + + +	
		b) Palpitations	+ + + +	
15. M,43	9	Wounds and corpses	+ + +	
16. M,27	51	a) Being watched, especially at work	+ + +	No anxiety while being watched at work. Anxious at times while watched playing cards.
		b) Being criticized	+ + + +	
17. M,33	8	Being watched at golf	+ + +	
18. M,13	8	Talking before audience (Stutterer	0	No imagined scene was ever disturbing.
19. M,40	7	Authority figures	+ + + +	
20. M,23	4	Claustrophobia	+ + + +	
21. F,23	6	a) Agoraphobia	0	Later successfully treated by conditioned motor response method (27).
		b) Fear of falling	0	
22. M,46	19	a) Being in limelight	+ + +	
		b) Blood and death	+ + + +	
23. F,40	20	Social embarrassment	+ + + +	
24. F,28	9	Agoraphobia	0	
25. F,48	7	Rejection	+ + +	
26. M,28	13	a) Disapproval	+ + +	
		b) Rejection	+ + + +	
27. M,11	6	Authority figures	+ + + +	
28. M,26	217	a) Claustrophobia	+ + + +	⎫ Finally overcome completely by use of Malleson's method (13).
		b) Criticism (numerous aspects)	+ + +	⎬
		c) Trappings of death	+ + +	⎭
29. F,20	5	Agoraphobia	+ + + +	
30. M,68	23	a) Agoraphobia	+ + + +	
		b) Masturbation	+ + + +	
31. F,36	5	Being in the limelight	+ + + +	
32. M,26	17	a) Illness and death	+ + +	
		b) Own symptoms	+ + +	
33. F,44	9	a) Being watched	+ + + +	
		b) Elevators	+ + + +	
34. F,47	17	Intromission into vagina	+ + +	After 15th session gradual in vivo operation with objects became possible, and subsequently, coitus with husband.
35. M,37	5	a) Disapproval	+ + + +	
		b) Rejection	+ + + +	
36. F,32	25	Sexual stimuli	+ + + +	

Patient Sex, Age	No. of Sessions	Hierarchy Theme		Outcome	Comments
37. M,36	21	a)	Agoraphobia	+ + + +	
		b)	Disapproval	+ + + +	
		c)	Being watched	+ + + +	
38. M,18	6	a)	Disapproval	+ + +	
		b)	Sexual stimuli	+ + + +	Instrumental in overcoming impotence
39. F,48	20	a)	Rejection	+ + + +	Stutter markedly improved as anxiety diminished, partly as result of desensitization, and partly due to assertive behavior in relevant situations.
		b)	Crudeness of others	+ + + +	

Training in Relaxation

The method of relaxation taught is essentially that of Jacobson (5) but the training takes up only about half of each of about six interviews—far less time than Jacobson devotes. The patient is also asked to practice at home for a half-hour each day.

The first lesson begins with the therapist telling the patient that he is to learn relaxation because of its beneficial emotional effects. He is then directed to grip the arm of his chair with one hand to see whether he can distinguish any qualitative difference between the sensations produced in his forearm and those in his hand. Usually he can, and he is asked to take note of the forearm sensation as being characteristic of muscle tension. He is also enjoined to remember the location of the flexors and extensors of the forearm. Next, the therapist grips the patient's wrist and asks him to pull, making him aware of the tension in his biceps; and then, instructing him to push in the opposite direction, draws his attention to the extensor muscles of the arm.

The therapist now again grips the patient's wrist and makes him tense the biceps and then relax it as much as possible, letting go gradually as the patient's hand comes down. The patient is then told to "keep trying to go further and further in the negative direction" and to "try to go beyond what seems to you to be the furthest point." He may report sensations like tingling and numbness which often accompany relaxation. When it appears that the patient has understood how to go about relaxing he is made to relax simultaneously all the muscles of both arms and forearms.

At the second lesson in relaxation, the patient is told that from the emotional point of view the most important muscles in the body are situated in and around the head, and that we shall therefore go on to these next. The muscles of the face are the first to be dealt with, beginning with the forehead. This location lends itself to demonstrating to the patient the step-like manner in which tension is decreased; and I do this by contracting the eyebrow-raising and the frowning groups of muscles in my own forehead very intensely simultaneously, and then relaxing by degrees. The patient is then made aware of his own forehead muscles and given about ten minutes to relax them as far as possible. Patients frequently report spontaneously the occurrence of unusual sensations in their foreheads, such as numbness, tingling, or "a feeling of thickness, as though my skin were made of leather." These sensations are characteristic of the attainment of a degree of relaxation beyond the normal level of muscle tone. At this session attention is drawn also to the muscles in the region of the nose (by asking the patient to wrinkle his nose) and to the muscles around the mouth (by making him purse his lips and then smile). After a few minutes he is asked to bite on his teeth, thus tensing his masseters and temporales. The position of the lips is an important indicator of successful relaxation of the muscles of mastication. When these are relaxed, the lips are parted by a few millimeters. The masseters cannot be relaxed if the mouth is kept resolutely closed.

At the third lesson, attention is drawn to the muscles of the tongue, which may be felt contracting in the floor of the mouth when the patient presses the tip of his tongue firmly against the back of his bottom incisor teeth. Thereafter, with active jaw-opening, infrahyoid tensions are pointed out. All these muscles are then relaxed. At the same session, the tensions produced in the eye muscles and those of the neck are noted and time given for their relaxation.

The fourth lesson deals with the muscles of the shoulder girdle, the fifth with those of the back, thorax and abdomen, and the sixth with those of the thighs and legs. A procedure that many patients find helpful is to coordinate relaxation of various other muscles with the automatic relaxation of the respiratory muscles that takes place with normal exhalation.

Construction of Anxiety Hierarchies

This is the most difficult and taxing procedure in the desensitization technique. Investigation of any case of anxiety neurosis reveals that the stimuli to anxiety fall into definable groups or *themes*. The themes may be obvious ones, like fear of heights, or less apparent ones, like fear of rejection.

Hierarchy construction usually begins at about the same time as relaxation training, but alterations or additions can be made at any time. It is important to note that the gathering of data and its subsequent organizing are done in an ordinary conversational way and *not under relaxation,* since the patient's *ordinary* responses to stimuli are under scrutiny.

The raw data from which the hierarchies are constructed have three main sources: 1) the patient's history; 2) responses to the Willoughby Questionnaire (22); and 3) special probings about situations in which the patient feels anxiety though there is no objective threat. Abundant material is often obtained by setting the patient the homework task of listing all situations that he finds disturbing, fearful, embarrassing, or in any way distressing.

When all identified sources of neurotic disturbance have been listed, the therapist classifies them into groups if there is more than one theme. The items of each thematic group are then rewritten to make separate lists and the patient is asked to rank the items of each list, placing the item he imagines would be most disturbing at the top and the least disturbing at the bottom of the list.

In many instances, the construction of a hierarchy is a very straightforward matter. This is true of most cases of such fears, as of heights (where the greater the height the greater the fear), or enclosed spaces, or, to take a somewhat more complex instance, fears aroused by the sight of illness in others. In such instances as the last, exemplified in Case 1 below, although the items have only a general thematic linkage and do not belong to a stimulus continuum (as do, for example, the items of a height hierarchy), all that has to be done is to obtain a list of situations embodying illnesses in others and then to ask the patient to rank the items according to the amount of anxiety each one arouses.

In other cases, hierarchy construction is more difficult because the sources of anxiety are not immediately revealed by the patient's listing of what he avoids. For example, it may become clear that he reacts to social occasions with anxiety, and that different kinds of social occasions (*e.g.* weddings, parties, and musical evenings) are associated with decreasing degrees of anxiety. There may then be a temptation to arrange a hierarchy based on these types of social occasions, with weddings at the top of the list and musical evenings at the bottom. Usually, little effective therapy would follow an attempt at desensitization based on such a hierarchy, and more careful probing would almost certainly reveal some facet of social occasions that is the real source of anxiety. Frequently, fear and avoidance of social occasions turns out to be based on fear of criticism or of rejection; or the fear may be a function of the mere physical presence of people, varying with the number of them to whom the patient is exposed. The writer once had a patient whose fear of social situations was really a conditioned anxiety response to the smell of food in public places. A good example of the importance of correct identification of relevant sources of anxiety is to be found in a previously reported case (27, p. 152) where a man's impotence was found to be due to anxiety related not to aspects of the sexual situation as such, but to the idea of trauma, which in certain contexts, especially defloration, enters into the sexual act.

It is not necessary for the patient actually to have experienced each situation that is to be included in a hierarchy. The question before him is of the order that, "If you were today confronted by such and such a situation, *would you expect* to be anxious?" To answer this question he must *imagine* the situation concerned, and it is usually not much more difficult to imagine a merely possible event than one that has at some time occurred. The temporal setting of an imagined stimulus configuration scarcely affects the responses to it. A man with a phobia for dogs has about as much anxiety to the idea of meeting a bulldog on the way home this evening as to recalling an encounter with this breed of dog a year previously.

A small minority of patients do not experience anxiety when they imagine situations that in reality are disturbing. In some of these, anxiety is evoked when they *describe* (verbalize) the scene they have been asked to imagine. As in other patients, the various scenes can then be ranked according to the degree of anxiety they evoke.

To a therapist inexperienced in the construction of anxiety hierarchies, the most common difficulty to be encountered is to find that even the weakest item in a hierarchy produces more anxiety than can be counteracted by the patient's relaxation. In many cases, it is obvious where weaker items may be sought. For example, in a patient who had an anxiety hierarchy on the theme of loneliness, the weakest item in the original hierarchy—being at home accompanied only by her daughter—was found to evoke more anxiety than was manageable. To obtain a weaker starting point all that was needed was to add items in which she had two or more companions. But it is not always so easy, and the therapist may be hard put to find manipulable dimensions. For example, following an

accident three years previously, a patient had developed serious anxiety reactions to the sight of approaching automobiles. At first it seemed that anxiety was just noticeable when an automobile was two blocks away, gradually increasing until a distance of half a block and then much more steeply increasing as the distance grew less. This, of course, promised plain sailing, but at the first desensitization session even at two blocks the imaginary car aroused anxiety much too great to be mastered: and it was revealed that the patient experienced anxiety at the very prospect of even the shortest journey by car, since the whole range of possibilities was already present the moment a journey became imminent. To obtain manageable levels of anxiety, an imaginary enclosed field two blocks square was postulated. The patient's car was "placed" in one corner of the field and the early items of the hierarchy involved a trusted person driving his car up to a stated point towards the patient's car, and of bringing this point ever closer as the patient progressed. Another case in whom weak anxiety stimuli were not easily found was a patient with a death phobia, whose items ranged in descending order from human corpses through such scenes as funeral processions to dead dogs. But even the last produced marked anxiety, when they were imagined even at distances of two or three hundred yards. A solution was found in retreating along a temporal instead of a spatial dimension, beginning with the (historically inaccurate) sentence, "William the Conqueror was killed at the Battle of Hastings in 1066."

Desensitization Procedure

When the hierarchies have been constructed and relaxation training has proceeded to a degree judged sufficient, desensitization can then begin. First "weak" and later progressively "strong" anxiety-arousing stimulus situations will be presented to the imagination of the deeply relaxed patient, as described below.

When relaxation is poor, it may be enhanced by the use of meprobamate, chlorpromazine, or codeine given an hour before the interview. Which drug to use is decided by trial. When pervasive ("free-floating") anxiety impedes relaxation, the use of carbon dioxide-oxygen mixtures by La Verne's (8) single inhalation technique has been found to be of the greatest value (27, p. 166) and with some patients this method comes to be used before every desensitization session. In a few patients who cannot relax but who are not anxious either, attempts at desensitization sometimes succeed, presumably because interview-induced emotional responses inhibit the anxiety aroused by the imagined stimuli (27).

It is the usual practice for sessions to be conducted under hypnosis with the patient sitting on a comfortable armchair. He may or may not have been hypnotized in an exploratory way on one or more occasions during earlier interviews. With patients who cannot be hypnotized, and in those who for any reason object to it, hypnosis is omitted and instructions are given merely to close the eyes and relax according to instructions. (There is a general impression that these patients make slower progress.)

The patient having been hypnotized, the therapist proceeds to bring about as deep as possible a state of calm by verbal suggestions to the patient to give individual attention to relaxing each group of muscles in the way he has learned.

The presentation of scenes at the first session is to some extent exploratory. The first scene presented is always a neutral one—to which a patient is not expected to have any anxiety reaction whatsoever. This is followed by a small number of presentations of the mildest items from one or two of the patient's hierarchies. To illustrate this, we shall make use of a verbatim account of the first session of Case 2, whose hierarchies are given below. After hypnotizing and relaxing the patient, the therapist went on as follows.

"You will now imagine a number of scenes very clearly and calmly. The scenes may not at all disturb your state of relaxation. If by any chance, however, you feel disturbed, you will be able to indicate this to me by raising your left index finger an inch or so. (*Pause of about 10 seconds*) First, I want you to imagine that you are standing at a busy street corner. You notice the traffic passing—cars, trucks, bicycles, and people. You see them all very clearly and you notice the sounds that accompany them. (*Pause of about 15 seconds*) Now, stop imagining that scene and again turn your attention to your muscles. (*Pause of about 20 seconds*) Now, imagine that it is a work day. It is 11 A.M. and you are lying in bed with an attack of influenza and a temperature of 103°. (*Pause of about 10 seconds*) Stop imagining the scene and again relax. (*Pause of 15 seconds*) Now, imagine exactly the same situation again. (*Pause of 10 seconds*) Stop imagining the scene and relax. (*Pause of about 20 seconds*) Now, I want you to imagine that you are at the post office and you have just sent off a manuscript to a journal. (*Pause of 15 seconds*) Stop imagining the scene and only relax. (*Pause of about five seconds*) In a few moments, I will be counting up to five and you will wake up feeling very calm and refreshed. (*Pause of about five seconds*) One, two, three, four, five." (*The patient opened his eyes looking somewhat dazed.*)

On being brought out of the trance, the patient is asked how he feels and how he felt during the trance, since it is important to know if a calm basal emotional state was achieved by the relaxation. He is then asked to indicate whether the scenes were clear or not. (It is essential for visualizing to be at least moderately clear.) Finally, the therapist inquires whether or not any of the scenes produced any disturbance in the patient, and if they did, how much. It is not common for a patient to report a reaction to the neutral control scene. It is worth remarking that even though the patient has a signal at his disposal with which to indicate disturbance, the fact that he has not done so during a scene by no means proves that it has not disturbed him at all, for it is a rare patient who makes use of the signal if only mildly disturbed. But the provision of a signal must never be omitted, for the patient will use it if he has a strong emotional reaction, which may not be otherwise manifest. *Exposure, and prolonged exposure in particular, to a very disturbing scene can greatly increase sensitivity.* With less marked disturbance there may be perseveration of anxiety, which makes continuance of the session futile.

At subsequent sessions, the same basic procedure is followed. If at the previous session there was a scene whose repeated presentations evoked anxiety that diminished but was not entirely extinguished, that scene is usually the first to be presented. If at the previous session the final scenes from a hierarchy ceased to arouse any anxiety the scene next higher is now presented, except in a few patients who, despite having had no anxiety at all to a final scene at a previous session, again show a small measure of anxiety to this scene at a subsequent session. It must again be presented several times until all anxiety is eliminated before going on to the next scene.

In order to gauge progress, the following procedure is adopted after two to four presentations of a particular scene. The therapist says, "If you had even the slightest disturbance to the last presentation of this scene, raise your left index finger now. If you had no disturbance, do nothing." If the finger is not raised, the therapist goes on to the next higher scene in the hierarchy. If the finger is raised, the therapist says, "If the amount of anxiety has been decreasing from one presentation to the next, do nothing. If it has not been decreasing, raise your finger again." If the finger is now not raised, this is an indication for further presentations of the scene, since further decrements in anxiety evocation may be confidently expected; but if it is raised, it is clear that the scene is producing more anxiety than the patient's relaxation can overcome, and it is therefore necessary to devise and interpose a scene midway in "strength" between this scene and the last one successfully mastered.

There is great variation in how many themes, how many scenes from each, and how many presentations are given at a session. Generally, up to four hierarchies are drawn upon in an individual session, and not many patients have more than four. Three or

four presentations of a scene are usual, but ten or more may be needed. The total number of scenes presented is limited mainly by availability of time and by the endurance of the patient. On the whole, both of these quantities increase as therapy goes on, and eventually almost the whole interview may be devoted to desensitization, so that whereas at an early stage eight or ten presentations are the total given at a session, at an advanced stage the number may rise to 30 or even 50.

The *duration* of a scene is usually of the order of five seconds, but it may be varied according to several circumstances. It is quickly terminated if the patient signals anxiety by spontaneously raising his finger or if he shows any sharp reaction. Whenever the therapist has a special reason to suspect that a scene may evoke a strong reaction he presents it with cautious brevity—for one or two seconds. By and large, early presentations of scenes are briefer, later ones longer. A certain number of patients require fifteen or more seconds to arrive at a clear image of a scene.

The *interval* between scenes is usually between ten and twenty seconds, but if the patient has been more than slightly disturbed by the preceding scene, it may be extended to a minute or more, and during that time the patient may be given repeated suggestions to be calm.

The *number* of desensitizing sessions required varies according to the number and the intensity of the anxiety areas, and the degree of generalization (involvement of related stimuli) in the case of each area. One patient may recover in as few as a half-dozen sessions; another may require a hundred or more. The patient with a death phobia, mentioned above, on whom a temporal dimension had to be used, also had two other phobias and required a total of about a hundred sessions. To remove the death phobia alone, a total of about 2,000 scene presentations were needed.

The *spacing* of sessions does not seem to be of great importance. Two or three sessions a week are characteristic, but the meetings may be separated by many weeks or take place daily. Occasional patients, visiting from afar, have had two sessions in a single day. Whether sessions are massed or widely dispersed, there is almost always a close relation between the extent to which desensitization has been accomplished and the degree of diminution of anxiety responses to real stimuli. Except when therapy is nearly finished, and only a few loose ends of neurotic reactions are left (that may be overcome through emotions arising spontaneously in the ordinary course of living (27)), very little change occurs, as a rule, between sessions. This was strikingly demonstrated by Case 1 (below) in whom the marked improvement of a severe claustrophobia achieved by a first series of sessions remained almost stationary during a three and one-half year interval, after which further sessions overcame the phobia apparently completely.

Examples of Hierarchies from Actual Cases

Single or multiple anxiety hierarchies occur with about equal frequency. Each of the following two cases had multiple hierarchies. (*The most disturbing item, as always, is at the top of each list with the others ranked below it.*)

Case 1

Mrs. A. was a 50-year-old housewife, whose main complaint was of very disabling fears on the general theme of claustrophobia. The fears had begun about 25 years previously, following a terrifying experience with general anesthesia, and had subsequently spread in a series of steps, each associated with a particular experience, to a wide range of situations. The patient also had other phobias, the most important of which, concerning illness and death, had its origin during childhood. In 46 desensitization sessions between March and July, 1956, all phobias were overcome except the most severe of the claustrophobic possibilities indicated in the first three items of the hierarchy given below, and with item 4 still incompletely conquered therapy

was terminated when the writer went overseas for a year. The patient returned to treatment in October, 1959, having maintained her recovery in all areas, but having made very little additional progress. During the next two months, 16 additional sessions were devoted to desensitizing to numerous scenes relevant to the "top" of the claustrophobia hierarchy. She was eventually able to accept, in the session, being confined for two hours in an imagined room four feet square, and reported complete freedom from fear in tunnels and only slight anxiety in "extreme" elevator situations.

Hierarchies
A. *Claustrophobic Series*
1) Being stuck in an elevator. (The longer the time, the more disturbing.)
2) Being locked in a room. (The smaller the room and the longer the time, the more disturbing.)
3) Passing through a tunnel in a railway train. (The longer the tunnel, the more disturbing.)
4) Traveling in an elevator alone. (The greater the distance, the more disturbing.)
5) Traveling in an elevator with an operator. (The longer the distance, the more disturbing.)
6) On a journey by train. (The longer the journey, the more disturbing.)
7) Stuck in a dress with a stuck zipper.
8) Having a tight ring on her finger.
9) Visiting and unable to leave at will (for example, if engaged in a card game).
10) Being told of somebody in jail.
11) Having polish on her fingernails and no access to remover.
12) Reading of miners trapped underground.
B. *Death Series*
1) Being at a burial.
2) Being at a house of mourning.
3) The word *death*.
4) Seeing a funeral procession. (The nearer, the more disturbing.)

5) The sight of a dead animal, *e.g.,* a cat.

6) Driving past a cemetery. (The nearer, the more disturbing.)

C. *Illness Series*

1) Hearing that an acquaintance has cancer.

2) The word *cancer.*

3) Witnessing a convulsive seizure.

4) Discussions of operations. (The more prolonged the discussion, the more disturbing.)

5) Seeing a person receive an injection.

6) Seeing someone faint.

7) The word *operation.*

8) Considerable bleeding from another person.

9) A friend points to a stranger, saying, "This man has tuberculosis."

10) The sight of a blood-stained bandage.

11) The smell of ether.

12) The sight of a friend sick in bed. (The more sick looking, the more disturbing.)

13) The smell of methylated spirits.

14) Driving past a hospital.

Case 2

Dr. B. was a 41-year-old gynecological resident who had felt anxious and insecure for as long as he could remember. Five years earlier, when anxieties were intensified by divorce proceedings, he had consulted a follower of Harry Stack Sullivan, who had tided him over the immediate situation but left him with attitudes of "acceptance" which had resulted in his becoming more anxious than before. After a few weeks' assertive training, he felt considerably better, but was left with the anxious sensitivities ranked in the hierarchies below. After six desensitization sessions he was completely free from anxiety responses to any actual situations similar to those contained in the hierarchies.

Hierarchies

A. *Guilt Series*

1) "Jackson (Dean of the Medical School) wants to see you."

2) Thinks "I only did ten minutes work today."

3) Thinks "I only did an hour's work today."

4) Thinks "I only did six hours' work today."

5) Sitting at the movies.

6) Reading an enjoyable novel.

7) Going on a casual stroll.

8) Staying in bed during the day (even though ill).

B. *Devaluation Series*

1) A woman doesn't respond to his advances.

2) An acquaintance says, "I saw you in Jefferson Street with a woman." (This kind of activity had locally acquired a disreputable flavor.)

3) Having a piece of writing rejected.

4) Awareness that his skill at a particular surgical operation left something to be desired. (Anxiety in terms of "Will I ever be able to do it?")

5) Overhearing adverse remarks about a lecture he delivered that he knows was not good.

6) Overhearing, "Dr. B. fancies himself as a surgeon."

7) Hearing anyone praised, *e.g.,* "Dr. K. is a fine surgeon."

8) Having submitted a piece of writing for publication.

Results

Table 1 presents basic details of 39 cases treated by desensitization. These patients, comprising about one-third of the total number so treated up to December, 1959, were randomly selected (by a casual visitor) from the alphabetical files of all patients treated. They are considered to be a representative sample of the total treated patient population. Rather than to summarize results from nearly 150 cases, it was felt desirable to present some details about a more limited series.

Many of the patients had other neurotic response habits as well, that were treated by methods appropriate to them. Interspersed among the 39 cases reported were six others eligible for desensitization who had between two and six sessions, but who are excluded from the series because they terminated treatment for various reasons (even though usually showing some evidence of progress). It is felt proper to exclude these, as in evaluating the therapeutic efficacy of an antibiotic it would be proper to omit cases that had received only one or two doses. Also excluded are two cases that turned out to be schizophrenic. Psychotic patients do not respond to this treatment and of course receive it only if misdiagnosed as neurotic. On the other hand, every presenting neurotic case is accepted for treatment.

Outcome of treatment is judged on the basis of several sources of information. In addition to the patient's report of his reactions to stimuli from the hierarchies during sessions, there frequently is observable evidence of diminished anxious responding, inasmuch as many patients display, when disturbed, characteristic muscle tensions (such as grimaces or finger movements). The greatest importance is attached to the patient's reports of changed responses, in real life, to previously fearful situations. I have not regularly checked these reports by direct observation, but in several cases in whom I have made such checks the patient's account of his improved reaction has invariably been confirmed. In general, there is reason to accept the credibility of patients who report *gradual* improvement. A patient who wished to use an allegation of recovery in order to get out of an unsuccessful course of treatment, would be likely to report recovery rather suddenly, rather than to continue in treatment to substantiate a claim of gradual recovery.

Degree of change is rated on a 5-point scale ranging from 4-plus to zero. A 4-plus rating indicates complete, or almost complete, freedom from phobic reactions to all situations on the theme of the phobia; 3-plus means an improvement of response such that the phobia is judged by the patient to retain not more than 20 per cent of its original strength, 2-plus means 30-70 per cent, and 1-plus indicates that more than 70 per cent of the origi-

nal strength of the phobia is judged retained. A zero rating indicates that there is no discernible change. (It will be noted that only 4-plus, 3-plus and zero ratings have been applicable to the patients in this series.)

Table 2 summarizes the data given in Table 1. There were 68 phobias and neurotic anxiety response habits related to more complex situations among the 39 patients, of whom 19 had multiple hierarchies. The treatment was judged effective in 35 of the patients. Forty-five of the phobic and other anxiety habits were apparently eliminated (4-plus rating) and 17 more were markedly ameliorated (3-plus rating). (It is entirely possible that most of the latter would have reached a 4-plus level if additional sessions could have been given; in cases 16 and 29, progress had become very slow when sessions were discontinued, but this was not so in the other cases.)

Table 2. Summary of data of Table 1.

Patients	39	
Number of patients responding to desensitization treatment	35	
Number of hierarchies	68	
Hierarchies overcome	45 }	91%
Hierarchies markedly improved	17	
Hierarchies unimproved	6	9%
Total number of desensitization sessions	762	
Mean session expenditure per hierarchy	11.2	
Mean session expenditure per successfully treated hierarchy	12.3	
Median number of sessions per patient	10.0	

Among the failures, cases 8 and 18 were unable to imagine themselves within situations; case 22 could not confine her imagining to the stated scene and therefore had excessive anxiety, but was later treated with complete success by means of another conditioning method (27, p. 174); case 25 had interpersonal anxiety reactions that led to erratic responses and, having experienced no benefit, sought therapy elsewhere.

The 39 patients had a total of 762 desensitization sessions, including in each case the first exploratory session although in many instances scenes from the hierarchies were not presented at that session. The mean number of sessions per hierarchy was 11.2;

the median number of sessions given to patients 10.0. It should be noted that a desensitization session usually takes up only part of a three-quarter hour interview period, and in cases that also have neurotic problems requiring direct action in the life situation there may be many interviews in which a session is not included.

At times varying between six months and four years after the end of treatment, follow-up reports were obtained from 20 of the 35 patients who responded to desensitization. There was no reported instance of relapse or the appearance of new phobias or other neurotic symptoms. I have never observed resurgence of neurotic anxiety when desensitization has been complete or virtually so.

Discussion

The general idea of overcoming phobias or other neurotic habits by means of systematic "gradual approaches" is not new. It has long been known that increasing measures of exposure to a feared object may lead to a gradual disappearance of the fear. This knowledge has sometimes (21), but unfortunately not very often, contributed to the armamentarium of psychiatrists in dealing with phobias. What is new in the present contribution is 1) the provision of a theoretical explanation for the success of such gradual approaches and 2) the description of a method in which the therapist has complete control of the degree of approach that the patient makes to the feared object at any particular time. The situations, being imaginary, are constructed and varied at will in the consulting room.

The excellent results obtained by this method of treatment are naturally viewed with skepticism by those who in the psychoanalytic tradition regard phobias and other neurotic anxiety response habits as merely the superficial manifestations of deeper unconscious conflicts. Some attempt to clarify the issue must be made. In the majority of cases a phobia is found to have begun at a particular time and in relation to a particular traumatic event. Before that time, presumably the patient already had his assumed unconscious conflicts, but did not feel any need for treatment. At the very least, then, it must surely be admitted that if through desensitization the patient is restored to the state in which he was before the traumatic event, something important has been gained from the point of view of his suffering. The reply could, of course, be made that unless the unconscious conflicts are brought to light and resolved, the patient will relapse or develop other symptoms; but in keeping with follow-up studies on the results of non-analytic psychotherapy in neurotic cases in general my experience has been that relapse or the appearance of new reactions is rare, unless a major group of stimuli in a desensitized area has been neglected.

At the same time, it is indisputable that only a minority of individuals exposed to a given traumatic event develop a phobia; some predisposing condition or conditions must determine which individuals do. The psychoanalysts are undoubtedly right in insisting on this point. But we are not therefore compelled to accept their version of the nature of the predisposing conditions, especially as the factual foundations of that version are far from satisfactory (30). Objective behavior theory can also point to factors that may predispose an individual to particularly severe conditioning of anxiety. First, some people are apparently endowed with much more active autonomic nervous systems than others (*e.g.*, 18). Second, previous experience with similar stimulus constellations may have induced low degrees of anxiety conditioning which would sensitize a person to the traumatic experience. Third, there may be circumstances in the moment of trauma that may bring about an unusually high degree of focusing upon certain stimulus constellations. The second of these suggested factors is probably the most important, for patients do frequently tell of minor sensitivity having pre-existed the precipitating event. In the course of desensitization, these original sensitivities also come to be removed, along with whatever has been more recently conditioned.

Critics of the conditioned response approach to therapy of the neuroses frequently assert that when the desensitization method leads to recovery, it is not the method as such that is responsible, but the "transference" established between patient and therapist. If these critics were right—if desensitization were incidental to rather than causal of recovery—it would be expected that improvement would affect all areas more or less uniformly, and not be confined to those to which desensitization had been applied. The facts are directly contrary to this expectation, for practically invariably it is found that *unless different hierarchies have unmistakable common features desensitization to one hierarchy does not in the least diminish the reactivity to another (untreated) hierarchy.* For example, a recent patient had both a widespread agoraphobic constellation, and a fear of airplanes, extending to the sight and sound of them. Having constructed hierarchies to both series, the writer proceeded to desensitize the patient to the agoraphobia, but ignored the airplane phobia until the agoraphobia had been almost completely overcome. At this stage, re-assessment of the airplane phobia revealed not the slightest evidence of diminution. This is in accord with observations made in connection with experimental neuroses, in which eliminating anxiety conditioned to visual stimuli does not affect the anxiety-evoking potential of auditory stimuli that were conditioned at the same time as the visual stimuli (23, 27).

From the point of view of the scientific investigator the desensitization method has a number of advantages that are unusual in the field of psychotherapy: 1) the aim of therapy can be clearly stated in every case; 2) sources of neurotic anxiety can be defined and delimited; 3) change of reaction to a scene is determined during sessions (and accordingly could be measured by psychophysiological means); 4) there is no objection to conducting therapy before an unconcealed audience (for this has been done without apparent effect on the course of therapy); and 5) therapists can be interchanged if desired.

Summary

The desensitization method of therapy is a particular application of the reciprocal inhibition principle to the elimination of neurotic habits. The experimental background and some theoretical implications of this principle are discussed.

A detailed account is given of the technique of desensitization and an analysis of its effects when applied to 68 phobias and allied neurotic anxiety response habits in 39 patients. In a mean of 11.2 sessions, 45 of the neurotic habits were overcome and 17 more very markedly improved. Six month to four year follow-up reports from 20 of the 35 successfully treated patients did not reveal an instance of relapse or the emergence of new symptoms.

References

1. Bond, I. K. and Hutchison, H. C. Application of reciprocal inhibition therapy to exhibitionism. Canad. Med. Assoc. J., **83**: 23-25, 1960.
2. Curran, D. and Partridge, M. *Psychological Medicine.* Livingstone, Edinburgh, 1955.
3. Eysenck, H. J. *Behavior Therapy and the Neuroses.* Pergamon Press, New York, 1960.
4. Freeman, H. L. and Kendrick, D. C. A case of cat phobia. Brit. Med. J., **2**: 497-502, 1960.
5. Jacobson, E. *Progressive Relaxation.* Univ. of Chicago Press, Chicago, 1938.
6. Jacobson, E. Variation of blood pressure with skeletal muscle tension and relaxation. Ann. Int. Med., **13**: 1619-1625, 1940.
7. Jones, M. C. The elimination of children's fears. J. Exp. Psychol., **7**: 382-390, 1924.
8. LaVerne, A. A. Rapid coma technique of carbon dioxide inhalation therapy. Dis. Nerv. Syst., **14**: 141-144, 1953.
9. Lazarus, A. A. The elimination of children's phobias by deconditioning. Med. Proc., **5**: 261, 1959.
10. Lazarus, A. A. *New group techniques in the treatment of phobic conditions.* Ph.D. dissertation. Univ. of the Witwatersrand, 1959.
11. Lazarus, A. A. and Rachman, S. The use of systematic desensitization in psychotherapy. S. Afr. Med. J., **31**: 934-937, 1957.
12. Lazovik, A. D. and Lang, P. J. A laboratory demonstration of systematic desensitization psychotherapy. J. Psychol. Stud., **11**: 238, 1960.
13. Malleson, N. Panic and phobia. Lancet, **1**: 225-227, 1959.
14. Meyer, V. The treatment of two phobic patients on the basis of learning principles. J. Abnorm. Soc. Psychol., **55**: 261-266, 1957.
15. Rachman, S. The treatment of anxiety and phobic reactions by systematic desensitization psychotherapy. J. Abnorm. Soc. Psychol., **58**: 259-263, 1959.

16. Salter, A. *Conditioned Reflex Therapy.* Creative Age Press, New York, 1950.

17. Sherrington, C. S. *Integrative Action of the Nervous System.* Yale Univ. Press, New Haven, 1906.

18. Shirley, M. *The First Two Years.* Univ. of Minnesota Press, Minneapolis, 1933.

19. Stevenson, I. Direct instigation of behavioral changes in psychotherapy. A. M. A. Arch. Gen. Psychiat., **1**: 99-107, 1959.

20. Stevenson, I. and Wolpe, J. Recovery from sexual deviations through overcoming nonsexual neurotic responses. Amer. J. Psychiat., **116**: 737-742, 1960.

21. Terhune, W. S. The phobic syndrome. Arch. Neurol. Psychiat., **62**: 162-172, 1949.

22. Willoughby, R. R. Some properties of the Thurstone Personality Schedule and a suggested revision. J. Soc. Psychol., **3**: 401-424, 1932.

23. Wolpe, J. Experimental neuroses as learned behavior. Brit. J. Psychol., **43**: 243-268, 1952.

24. Wolpe, J. Learning versus lesions as the basis of neurotic behavior. Amer. J. Psychiat., **112**: 923-927, 1956.

25. Wolpe, J. Objective psychotherapy of the neuroses. S. Afr. Med. J., **26**: 825-829, 1952.

26. Wolpe, J. Psychotherapy based on the principles of reciprocal inhibition. In Burton, A., ed. *Case Studies in Counseling and Psychotherapy,* pp. 353-381. Prentice-Hall, Englewood Cliffs, N. J., 1959.

27. Wolpe, J. *Psychotherapy by Reciprocal Inhibition.* Stanford Univ. Press, Stanford, 1958.

28. Wolpe, J. Reciprocal inhibition as the main basis of psychotherapeutic effects. A. M. A. Arch. Neurol. Psychiat., **72**: 205-226, 1954.

29. Wolpe, J. Recoveries from neuroses without psychoanalysis: Their prognosis and its implications. Amer. J. Psychiat. In press.

30. Wolpe, J. and Rachman, S. Psychoanalytic "evidence": A critique based on Freud's case of Little Hans. J. Nerv. Ment. Dis., **131**: 135-148, 1960.

Physiological Changes Accompanying the Visualization of Fearful and Neutral Situations

John M. Grossberg and Helen K. Wilson

To test an assumption of Wolpe's systematic desensitization therapy that imagining fearful scenes produces physiological arousal, 18 high-anxiety and 18 low-anxiety girls were 1st read and then told to imagine a fearful and neutral scene 4 times. Heart rate (HR), skin conductance (SC), and forehead EMG were recorded during reading and imagining. For HR and SC (a) there were no significant differences between high-anxiety and low-anxiety Ss, (b) during reading there were no significant differences between fearful and neutral scenes, (c) during imagining fearful scenes produced significantly more arousal, (d) both measures declined significantly over trials. EMG failed to differentiate fearful and neutral scenes, but low-anxiety Ss showed significantly more EMG than high-anxiety Ss. To assess possible bias in scene presentation, 10 matched control Ss, neutral to both fearful and neutral scenes, were presented tapes of the experimental group's procedure. Persistence of significant HR and SC differences for fearful vs. neutral scenes suggested a confounding of extraneous factors with self-rated fear in producing greater arousal during fearful scenes.

Although a number of recent experiments have supported the clinical evidence that Wolpe's systematic desensitization technique is indeed effective in alleviating handicapping human fear reactions (Rachman, 1967), some basic features of the procedure need to be examined. This is essential insofar as various elements of the treatment technique are intimately related to Wolpe's reciprocal inhibition theory of maladaptive response elimination (Wolpe, 1958; Wolpe & Lazarus, 1966). The reciprocal inhibition hypothesis assumes that fear responses can be eliminated by the simultaneous evocation of some other re-

From J. M. Grossberg and H. K. Wilson, "Physiological Changes Accompanying the Visualization of Fearful and Neutral Situations," *Journal of Personality and Social Psychology*, 1968, **10**, 124-133. Reprinted by permission of the American Psychological Association.

sponse presumed to be antagonistic to fear. A widely used clinical procedure derived from this hypothesis is called systematic desensitization with relaxation, and uses muscle relaxation as the presumed fear antagonist. After a ranked list of fear-evoking situations has been composed by the therapist and patient, the patient is trained to relax and then is told to imagine vividly the mildest fear item on the list. When he reports that this no longer provokes disturbance, the next fear item is visualized, and so on through the hierarchy. When the visualized fear situation is weak and relaxation deep, the incompatible relaxation pattern should predominate and relaxation responses should then come to be attached to visualized stimulus situations which previously elicited fear.

According to Wolpe, fear responses are eliminated not only for all the visualized situations but also for their real life counterparts. Visualizing fearful situations is assumed to arouse fear responses similar to those evoked by the real life situation but displaced far enough from the real situation on the fear generalization gradient so as to produce a less intense response. This low-intensity fear pattern then is assumed to be inhibited by the stronger antagonistic muscle relaxation pattern. However, if visualizing fear situations did not produce more initial tension than visualizing neutral situations, it would be difficult to maintain that something was being inhibited, replaced, or extinguished with repeated visualizations.

During the peripheralist-centralist controversy in the 1930s regarding the role of body structure in thinking, a number of studies demonstrated that instructions to imagine specific acts led to increases in activity in the muscles involved (Shaw, 1939). Rowland (1936) studied the effects of imagining stimuli graded according to their rated excitability upon heart rate, GSR, and respiration. He devised a hierarchy of 12 scenes, varying from gazing at a flock of sheep (mild) to being attacked by a leopard (intense). The four best hypnotic subjects from a group of 32 undergraduates were hypnotized and told to imagine each scene once a day for 10 days. Rowland found that the more exciting scenes produced larger changes on all three physiological measures, and that the changes were roughly proportional to the scene's excitability. However, the selection method, small sample size, and hypnotic procedure limit the generality of these findings.

McCurdy (1950) reviewed older studies of the relationship between GSR and subjects' subjective estimates of the intensity of various thoughts and feelings. He found consistently high correlations reported between GSR magnitude and estimates of the intensity of experience. Miller (1951, pp. 464-465) gave subjects electric shock when the letter "T" was presented, but no shock for the number "4." After a discrimination had been established, as measured by a larger GSR to T than to 4, they were given a series of dots, and told to say "4" to the first, "T" to the second, "4" to the third, etc. Next they were told to *think* 4 and T in conjunction with the dots, instead of saying them aloud. Miller found that subjects continued to give larger GSRs to those dots associated with T, even though they were now thinking rather than uttering T to the appropriate dot. Barber and Hahn (1964) compared the physiological effects (forehead muscle activity, heart rate, and GSR) of real versus imagined cold stressor pain. They found that instructions to imagine pain produced physiological changes similar to those produced by real pain. However, they suggested that further research include a control for imagining neutral stimuli, since imagining per se could have been activating.

The present experiment measured physiological changes when two groups of subjects previously rated as high or low in anxiety were told to imagine two situations, one they had indicated was fearful, and one which was neutral. A matched control group received a tape recording of the experimental group's procedure. However, the control-group subjects had previously indicated no fear of either of the situations which had been presented to their experimental counterparts. The control group was run to assess the possibility that the experimenter's voice as he presented fear situations might have been arousing, or that the content of these situations was inherently more exciting than neutral situations. After completing imagination trials, all subjects answered two questions concerning the vividness of their imagery, to examine the relationship between self-reports and physiological measures. Changes in heart rate (HR), skin conductance (SC), and forehead muscle activity (EMG) were used because they are generally accepted indicants of anxiety or tension (Duffy, 1962; Goldstein, 1964).

Method

Subjects

The samples were drawn from a pool of 302 female introductory psychology students who had completed the Wolpe-Lang Fear Survey Schedule (Grossberg & Wilson, 1965; Wolpe & Lang, 1964). This test is a self-administered 5-point category scale with 72 items covering the most common sources of fear (e.g., crawling insects, high places). The Fear Survey Schedule (FSS) was scored by assigning a value of 1 to the lowest point of the scale ("not at all disturbing"), a value of 2 to the adjacent category, up to a value of 5 for the highest point on the scale ("very much disturbing"). Each subject's fear score was the sum for all 72 items.

To obtain 18 high- and 18 low-anxiety subjects for the experimental groups the authors began with the highest and lowest scorers and offered payment for participation. Allowing for those who declined to participate, the high-anxiety sample was drawn from the 20 highest scorers, and the low-anxiety sample was drawn from the lowest 31 scorers. The 10 subjects in the matched control group were recruited from among the next consecutive 7 lowest and 12 highest scorers, and consisted of 6 low-anxiety and 4 high-anxiety subjects.

Instructions and Scene Construction

Each subject was run individually. Before the subject's arrival, the experimenter randomly selected from her FSS protocol one item she had checked as "not at all disturbing" (neutral), and one item she had checked "very much disturbing" (fearful). Then he read the following instructions:

> This project is a study of imagination and how different kinds of imagining are related to bodily reactions. On your questionnaire last fall you were asked to indicate on a checklist just how disturbing to you different kinds of situations, objects, or activities were. I've selected two typical situations from among your answers [gives name of the two]. Now you and I will make up a word picture of each of these two situations, and I'll write down the two scenes. Then we'll go to another room where I will tell you to imagine each scene in turn while we record your heart rate, skin resistance, and forehead muscle activity.
>
> Six tiny pickups will be taped to your arm, leg, and forehead with adhesive tape, and you'll be asked to lie down while your responses are recorded. The screened enclosure with the door is to keep out electrical interference from the lights and any other electrical gadgets in the building which could interfere with our measurements. You will not be given any electrical shocks or subjected to any dangerous electricity at all. We're only interested in recording on our polygraph your physiological reactions during active imagination. Any questions?
>
> I won't be asking you to imagine the scenes for the first 10 minutes or so, it takes this long for the equipment to warm up. No conversation or questions will be allowed once we begin recording, so if you have any questions, please ask them now or save them for the end of the session.

The experimenter and subject then jointly composed a scene of approximately 50 words involving the neutral item and another such scene for the fear item. In composing scenes, the authors avoided words suggesting excitement or arousal in favor of terms describing the situation. The following is an example of a fear scene for a subject disturbed by injections:

> You are at Health Services to receive an injection. You can smell the medical odors. You reach the head of the line, then sit down. The nurse rolls up your sleeve and as you watch, she dabs your arm with cold cotton and picks up a needle. She grasps your arm, pushes the needle in, then pulls it out.

After completing the scenes, the subject was taken to the laboratory, which was air conditioned and sound shielded. In the center of the room, a free-standing electrostatic shield made of two independent layers of copper screening enclosed the subject's couch. The experimenters, polygraph, and tape recorder were screened from view by two hinged 4 X 8-foot Masonite panels. Pen-writing noise was effectively masked by noise from the polygraph fan and room air conditioner. Illumination was furnished by two shaded 10-watt lamps.

Apparatus[1]

Physiological data was continuously recorded on a Grass Model 5D six-channel polygraph, with paper speed set at 2.5 millimeters per second.

EMG recording. To lower skin resistance in the contact area, the subject's forehead was scrubbed with Lava soap and then Redux conductive jelly, following which the two electrode placement areas were scratched with a sterile needle. For all subjects, this procedure reduced skin resistance to less than 10,000 ohms. Then bipolar silver surface electrodes (Grass electrode ElB) filled with Redux were taped to the forehead near the hairline, with a 2-inch separation between electrodes. Forehead electrical activity was fed into the Grass 5P5 EEG preamplifier and the raw data integrated with a photoelectronic integrator (Eason & White, 1959).

HR recording. After the subject's skin on the inner surface of her left calf and right forearm had been scrubbed with Lava soap and Redux, Grass ElB electrodes embedded in Plexiglas discs were taped in place. HR in terms of beats per minute (number of R-wave

---

[1]Professor Robert Eason provided invaluable instruction and advice during all phases of electrophysiological measurement.

peaks) was obtained from standard Lead II of the Grass 5P4 EKG preamplifier.

SC recording. After the subject scrubbed her hands with Lava soap, the volar surfaces of the first and third fingers of her left hand were cleaned with alcohol. Then dry silver-silver chloride discs 18 millimeters in diameter were taped to the fingers, and skin resistance obtained from the Grass 5P1 DC preamplifier. Resistance readings were converted to log conductances prior to data analysis.

Procedure

Every subject's neutral and fear scenes were presented four times each in a balanced mirror-image order (e.g., NFFNNFFN), so each subject served as her own control. Since there are six such orders possible, with 18 subjects in each of the two experimental groups, 3 subjects in each group received the same one of the six orders. Subjects were run in three squads of 12, with 6 high- and 6 low-anxiety subjects in each squad.

A control group was run to examine the possibility that the experimenter's voice as he read fear scenes might have been arousing, or that the scenes themselves were inherently more exciting than neutral scenes. The authors tape-recorded the procedure for the last 10 experimental subjects, and then played the tapes to 10 additional subjects who were matched as closely as possible on total FSS score. However, the control group was restricted to those who had indicated on the FSS that they were not at all disturbed by either of the items which had been presented to their experimental counterparts. For example, if the experimental subject was disturbed by injections but neutral toward high places, she would be matched with a control subject who had indicated no disturbance for injections *or* high places. Instructions to the matched control group were similar to those given the experimental groups, except that they were told that the experimenter had already composed two scenes, which were then read to them.

Following electrode attachment, the subject reclined in the shielded enclosure for a 10-minute adaptation period to establish physiological base levels. After 7 minutes, the experimenter announced, "Three more minutes," so that the sensitivity of the skin conductance preamplifier could be adjusted to the individual subject's reactivity level. After adaptation, the experimenter said the following:

All right, [subject's name], close your eyes. Now I want you to picture this scene vividly and clearly. I want you to project yourself right into the scene. In other words, I want you to imagine that you are not here in this room, but in the very scenes themselves. I want you to see them vividly and clearly and realistically. Keep the scene in mind until I tell you to stop picturing it.

After the first scene was read, the experimenter said, "All right, picture that scene."

A 25-second silent visualization interval was introduced immediately. At the end of the interval the experimenter said, "All right, switch it off now, keep your eyes closed, and wait until I tell you to visualize the next scene."

Following a 3-minute silent intertrial interval, the experimenter began the second trial by saying, "Now picture this next scene as clearly and vividly as possible. Project yourself right into the scene, and keep the scene in mind until I tell you to stop picturing it."

After reading the scene, the experimenter introduced and terminated the visualization interval with the same instructions used for the first scene. The remaining six scenes were presented at 3-minute intervals using the same instructions.

After scene presentations were completed, experimental group subjects answered two questions about their imagery by checking a category on a 5-point scale. The questions were:

1. How vivid and clear were the scenes that you were told to imagine?
   Realistically vivid
   Very clear
   Moderately clear
   Dim image
   Little or no picture
2. How well were you able to picture yourself actually being in the imagined scene, rather than here in this room?

Scene felt very real
Occasionally felt real
I felt like a spectator

Results

For statistical treatment, a 25-second time interval 5 seconds prior to the experimenter's reading of each scene was selected as the base level. Then the amount of change was calculated from this base level to a 25-second interval during the reading of the scene, and lastly, the amount of change from reading level to that during the 25-second imagining interval. For each subject, change from base to reading was expressed as the ratio of the amount of change to the base level, and change from reading to imagining as the ratio of the amount of change to the reading level. HR was measured by counting the number of R-wave peaks during the 25-second intervals. To obtain skin conductance measures, the magnitude of deflection of the polygraph pen was sampled at three equidistant points within each 25-second interval. The mean of the three measurements constituted the resistance reading for that interval. Means were then converted to log conductance values. For EMG measurement, the muscle tracings within each scoring interval were converted to arbitrary numerical values directly proportional to the amount of muscle activity by means of a photoelectronic integrator.

Product-moment correlations between base level and change from base were computed to assess any initial values effect (Wilder, 1957). The *r* values were —.13 for HR, +.15 for SC, and —.77 for EMG. Although EMG base showed a high negative correlation with change scores, the theoretical and mathematical implications of data transformations such as Lacey's (1956) Autonomic Lability Score have been worked out almost exclusively for autonomic variables (Johnson & Lubin, 1967, pp. 49-50). Therefore, rather than introduce a different scoring method and statistical analysis for EMG data, the simple change/base ratio scoring method and analyses of variance were used for all three measures.

Analyses of variance indicated no significant differences in base levels between high- and low-anxiety subjects for HR, SC, or EMG. Changes in the three independent variables, high versus low anxiety, fearful versus neutral scene, and trials (scene repetitions) were then tested by analysis of variance (three factors with repeated measures, Winer, 1962, pp. 319-330). Table 1 summarizes the results of the analyses.

The changes from base to reading, and from reading to imagining, are shown in Figures 1, 2, and 3.

For the HR and SC variables, although there were marked increases from base to reading level, the increases were not significantly different for fear versus neutral scenes. In other words, the experimenter's reading a fear scene was no more activating than his reading a neutral scene. However, in going from reading to the imagining interval following, for HR and SC there were significantly greater increases for fear scenes as compared with neutral scenes (HR, $F = 16.50$, $df = 1/34$, $p < .01$; SC, $F = 8.19$, $df = 1/34$, $p < .01$). Thus instructions to imagine fear scenes produced significantly more arousal than instructions to imagine neutral scenes. Table 1 also indicates significant HR and SC decreases over trials, with repeated reading and imagining of scenes. Change measures from base to reading showed such systematic decreases (HR, $F = 4.28$, $df = 3/102$, $p < .01$; SC, $F = 4.66$, $df = 3/102$, $p < 01$), suggesting an adaptation or extinction effect, and for SC this effect was also significant in the change from reading to imagining ($F = 4.21$, $df = 3/102$, $p < .01$). Thus, even without specific relaxation training repeated presentations of scenes produced reliable decreases in their arousal potential.

The forehead EMG data did not show the regularity evident in the two autonomic measures. In the base to reading comparison, low-anxiety subjects showed significantly greater EMG change than high-anxiety subjects ($F = 5.33$, $df = 1/34$, $p < .05$). This difference was the only significant EMG finding, and is difficult to interpret, since activation theory would predict that if differences occurred they should be larger for high-anxi-

Table 1. *F* values obtained from analyses of variance of high and low anxiety groups.

Source	Base to reading			Reading to imagining		
	HR	SC	EMG	HR	SC	EMG
High vs. low anxiety (A)	< 1	< 1	5.33*	1.37	3.07	< 1
Fear vs. neutral scene (B)	3.53	1.15	2.54	16.50**	8.19**	1.88
Trials (C)	4.28**	4.66**	< 1	1.89	4.21**	< 1
A × B	< 1	< 1	3.43	< 1	1.36	1.73
A × C	< 1	1.31	< 1	< 1	1.31	< 1
B × C	< 1	< 1	< 1	1.91	1.05	1.37
A × B × C	1.20	< 1	< 1	< 1	< 1	1.10

*p < .05.
**p < .01.

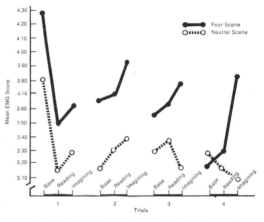

Figure 3. Mean EMG score for combined high- and low-anxiety subjects during successive fear and neutral scenes.

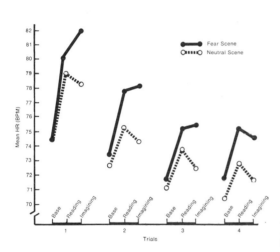

Figure 1. Mean HR for combined high- and low-anxiety subjects during successive fear and neutral scenes.

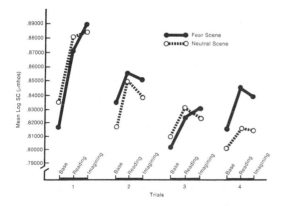

Figure 2. Mean log SC for combined high- and low-anxiety subjects during successive fear and neutral scenes.

ety subjects. Figure 3 shows that fear scenes generally produced more EMG activity than neutral scenes, but there was great variability within groups. In contrast to the HR and SC data, on Trial 1 forehead EMG showed a sharp decrease from base level when the first scene was read.

The amount of change results were corroborated by analyzing the *number* of increases in physiological response for each subject. It is possible that intersubject variability could have been large enough so that differences among treatments in overall amounts of reactivity would be small. Therefore the authors calculated how many of the 36 subjects showed an increase in physiological activity from base to reading, and reading to imagining, regardless of the amount of such increase (Figure 4). To test the number of physiological increases for fear versus neutral scenes, cell frequencies were too small for X^2, so an exact probability test corresponding to McNemar's X^2 for the significance of changes was applied (McNemar, 1962, pp. 224-228). Table 2 shows the *p* values for base to reading and reading to imagining comparisons. There were significantly more increases in SC when fear scenes were read, and significantly more increases in HR when subjects imagined fear scenes. Although the other fear versus neutral comparisons did not reach a .05 level criterion of significance, Figure 4 shows that fear scenes generally produced more activity, especially during the imagining condition.

Analyses of variance indicated no significant differences in base levels between the 10 experimental subjects and their matched controls for HR, SC, or EMG. The results of further analyses of variance comparing the groups' change scores are shown in Table 3. Ideally the authors expected to find significant Group X Scene interactions; that is, experimental subjects should have shown significantly more arousal during fear than neutral scenes, while control subjects should not, since they were theoretically neutral to both. However, only HR change in the base to reading condition showed this effect ($F = 6.20$, $df = 1/18$, $p < .05$). In the base to reading condition there was also a significant trials effect for HR ($F = 4.00$, $df = 3/54$, $p < .05$) and for SC ($F = 3.61$, $df = 3/54$, $p < .05$), reflecting the systematic decline in both autonomic measures, but not EMG, with repeated readings of scenes.

For HR, the significant Group X Trials interaction ($F = 2.95$, $df = 3/54$, $p < .05$) was produced by the experimental group's regular decline in HR over trials, while the control group's HR stayed at the same level. Within the experimental groups, HR during fear scenes declined with repeated readings, while during neutral scenes it did not. In the control group, HR showed little decline with repeated readings of fear or neutral scenes. Thus HR for the experimental group as a

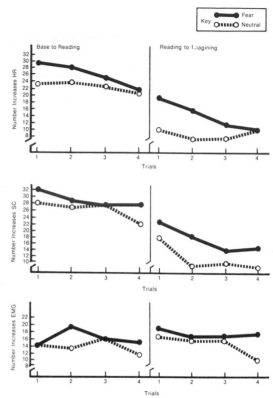

Figure 4. Number of increases in physiological response for combined high- and low-anxiety subjects during reading and imagining.

whole declined over trials relative to the control group.

For SC, the significant Scene X Trials interaction ($F = 3.77$, $df = 3/54$, $p < .05$) appears to contradict the HR data. This interaction resulted from a marked SC decline during repeated readings of neutral scenes, and little SC decline during repeated readings of fear scenes. Considering HR and SC interactions together, it is possible that HR during fear-arousing scenes extinguished more rapidly than SC, which stayed at its initial high

Table 2. p values obtained from X^2 tests of differences in number of response increases.

Measure	Base to reading	Reading to imagining
HR	.15	.01
SC	.02	.07
EMG	.13	.11

Table 3. *F* values obtained from analyses of variance of experimental and matched control groups.

Source	Base to reading			Reading to imagining		
	HR	SC	EMG	HR	SC	EMG
Experimental vs. control (A)	1.28	<1	3.49	<1	3.52	14.14**
Fear vs. neutral scene (B)	1.64	<1	<1	6.26*	5.48*	1.07
Trials (C)	4.00*	3.61*	2.36	<1	2.58	1.38
A × B	6.20*	1.58	<1	2.06	1.66	<1
A × C	2.95*	<1	1.88	1.34	1.27	<1
B × C	<1	3.77*	<1	<1	1.47	2.58
A × B × C	<1	<1	<1	<1	<1	1.55

*p < .05.
**p < .01.

level. However, this interpretation does not explain why HR during neutral scenes remained unchanged, while SC during neutral scenes declined markedly.

In the reading to imagining comparison, both HR and SC showed significantly greater increases for fear than for neutral scenes (HR, $F = 6.26$, $df = 1/18$, $p < .05$; SC, $F = 5.48$, $df = 1/18$, $p < .05$), even though the two types of scenes should have been equivalent for the matched control subjects. This suggests that the content or mode of presentation of fear scenes could have produced the differential arousal, and was confounded with subjects' prior estimates of the fearfulness of the scenes. The EMG results during imagining once again did not conform to the pattern for HR and SC. The matched control group showed significantly greater increases in EMG than the experimental group ($F = 14.14$, $df = 1/18$, $p < .01$), but there were no other significant EMG differences. It is possible that the control group's higher level of EMG activity reflected their relative unfamiliarity with the scenes. Experimental group subjects composed their own scenes, which often embodied surroundings and situations familiar to them. For control group subjects, these same scenes were novel, and it may have required more effort to try and imagine them.

Table 4 shows tetrachoric correlations between physiological changes and subjects' estimates of the vividness of their imagery.

Only HR increases from reading to imagining were significantly correlated with subjects' reports of their success in visualizing scenes ($r = .60, p < .05$).

Table 4. Tetrachoric correlations between vividness of imagery and physiological change.

Item	Base to reading			Reading to imagining		
	HR	SC	EMG	HR	SC	EMG
Question 1	-.30	-.38	-.40	.60*	0	.21
Question 2	0	-.18	-.18	.50	.45	-.18

*p<.05.

Discussion

The results for the autonomic variables, HR and SC, support an essential requirement of Wolpe's systematic desensitization procedure, the activating potential of instructions to imagine disturbing situations. As shown in Table 1 and Figures 1 and 2, although there were marked increases from base level in both HR and SC when fear and neutral scenes were read to subjects, the change during the experimenter's reading a fear scene was not significantly different from the change during his reading a neutral scene. However, in comparing change from reading to the imagining interval following, HR and SC showed significantly greater increases for fear than for neutral scenes. Therefore it would seem that self-produced stimulation such as that involved in following instructions to imagine fear scenes produced more tension or arousal than the externally presented stimulation of the experimenter's reading the scene. Analysis of each subject's *number* of increases in HR and SC (Table 2, Figure 4) confirmed the finding that fear scenes generated more tension. On all but one trial more subjects showed increases during fear scenes, and these differences were significant for the SC variable during the reading interval, and for HR during the imagining interval. A recent experiment by Folkins, Lawson, Opton, and Lazarus (1968) provides independent support of our results. They studied the effectiveness of systematic desensitization with relaxation in reducing stress, and reported SC increases when subjects imagined accident scenes prior to a threat film, but no increases when they imagined pleasant scenes.

In the present experiment, it was found that successive reading trials produced significantly decreasing amounts of arousal for the HR and SC measures, and this effect was also evident for SC during successive imagining trials. The number of HR and SC increases over trials (Figure 4) showed a similar decline. This adaptation or extinction effect occurred without deliberate relaxation training, and raises the question of the role of relaxation training in Wolpe's desensitization procedure. However, this is a complex issue which requires research specifically designed to examine the role of a variety of factors in the fear-reduction process (Cooke, 1966; Davison, 1968; Folkins et al., 1968; Lomont & Edwards, 1967; Rachman, 1967; Wolpin & Raines, 1966).

Although the EMG data did not contradict the autonomic response results, they did not show the same regularity (Figures 3 and 4). While there was a consistent tendency for fear scenes to produce more muscle activity than neutral scenes, the differences were not statistically significant. The sharp decrease in EMG from base level with the first reading of a fear or neutral scene was contrary to the HR and SC reactions, representing an apparent decrease rather than increase in arousal. This effect could have resulted from anticipa-

tory muscle tension. Davis (1959), in studying physiological responses during minimal stimulation (lying on a cot in a dark, sound-proofed room), found increased muscular activity with time, and suggested that this tension pattern could be characteristic of anticipation. In the present experiment, the preliminary 3-minute warning could have augmented any such effect, and reading the first scene might have served to relieve tension from the higher anticipatory level.

The EMG response showed great variability from subject to subject. Although electrodes were placed near the hairline, the frontalis muscle tracings still reflected substantial eye movement activity. It is quite possible that different people interpret instructions to imagine in various ways, so that one subject might wrinkle her brow, another roll her eyes, etc. Autonomic responses are less subject to such intentional effects, and would therefore show more consistency.

With the exception of the EMG base to reading comparison (Table 1), there were no significant differences attributable to the high- versus low-anxiety variable. This is not surprising, however, in view of the fact that studies of the relationship between self-report anxiety test scores and physiological measures have consistently failed to demonstrate strong relationships (Duffy, 1962; Martin, 1961).

In the matched control group analysis (Table 3), the persistence of significant fear-neutral scene differences in HR and SC during imagining suggests a confounding of subjects' self-reported fear estimates (from which fear scenes were selected) and other factors. Otherwise, we should have found significant fear-neutral scene differences for the experimental subjects, no differences for the control subjects who had indicated "neutral" for both scenes, with a resulting significant interaction effect. Some extraneous factors which could have contributed to the differential arousal were the content of the scenes themselves, bias in the experimenter's voice as he read fear and neutral scenes, or the manner of presenting instructions, which may have suggested that we expected different reactions to the scenes. In any case, although the source of the effect is unclear, a conservative conclusion is that psychological manipulation was effective in producing differential physiological reactivity, as required by Wolpe's theory.

The questionnaire concerning the quality of imagery was included because some practitioners have observed that desensitization treatment was difficult with patients who said they were unable to imagine realistically (Wolpe & Lazarus, 1966, pp. 95-96). Table 4 shows tetrachoric correlations between subjects' reports of the vividness of their imagery and physiological reactivity. Of the 12 correlations, only HR change during imagining was significantly related to responses on Question 1 ("How vivid and clear were the scenes you were told to imagine?"). This does not strongly support the assumption that reports of imagining are accurate appraisals of physiological reactivity during imagining.

In summary, despite some inconsistencies, particularly with respect to the EMG variable, these studies sustain the conclusion that visualization or imagining is a specifiable operation which has measurable effects on subjects. Further, the data support those aspects of Wolpe's theory and procedure which require that instructions to imagine fearful situations actually evoke physiological tension or excitation. The results are more impressive in view of the fact that we randomly selected each subject's fear situation, rather than selecting her most feared one. In addition, the subjects were students who were probably not phobic with respect to their fear situations. It is likely that genuine phobics would show considerably more differential arousal in a design such as the present one.

References

Barber, T. X., & Hahn, K. W. Experimental studies in "hypnotic" behavior: Physiologic and subjective effects of imagined pain. *Journal of Nervous and Mental Disease,* 1964, **139**, 416-425.

Cooke, G. *Identification of the efficacious components of reciprocal inhibition therapy.* (Doctoral dissertation, University of Iowa) Ann Arbor, Mich.: University Microfilms, 1966. No. 66-11, 651.

Davis, R. C. Somatic activity under reduced stimulation. *Journal of Comparative and Physiological Psychology,* 1959, **52**, 309-314.

Davison, G. C. Systematic desensitization as a counterconditioning process. *Journal of Abnormal Psychology,* 1968, **73**, 91-99.

Duffy, E. *Activation and behavior.* New York: Wiley, 1962.

Eason, R. G., & White, C. T. A photoelectric method for integrating muscle action potentials. *American Journal of Psychology,* 1959, **72**, 125-126.

Folkins, C. H., Lawson, K. D., Opton, E. M., & Lazarus, R. S. Desensitization and the experimental reduction of threat. *Journal of Abnormal Psychology,* 1968, **73**, 100-113.

Goldstein, I. B. Role of muscle tension in personality theory. *Psychological Bulletin,* 1964, **61**, 413-425.

Grossberg, J. M., & Wilson, H. K. A correlational comparison of the Wolpe-Lang Fear Survey Schedule and Taylor Manifest Anxiety Scale. *Behaviour Research and Therapy,* 1965, **3**, 125-128.

Johnson, L., & Lubin, A. On planning psychophysiological experiments: Design, measurement, and analysis. Technical Report No. 67-19, 1967, Navy Medical Neuropsychiatric Research Unit, San Diego, California, Research Task MR006.02-0001, Bureau of Medicine and Surgery, Department of the Navy.

Lacey, J. I. The evaluation of autonomic responses: Toward a general solution. *Annals of the New York Academy of Science,* 1956, **67**, 123-164.

Lomont, J. F., & Edwards, J. E. The role of relaxation in systematic desensitization. *Behaviour Research and Therapy,* 1967, **5**, 11-25.

Martin, B. The assessment of anxiety by physiological behavioural measures. *Psychological Bulletin,* 1961, **58**, 234-255.

McCurdy, H. G. Consciousness and the galvanometer. *Psychological Review,* 1950, **57**, 322-327.

McNemar, Q. *Psychological statistics.* (3rd ed.) New York: Wiley, 1962.

Miller, N. E. Learnable drives and rewards. In S. S. Stevens (Ed.), *Handbook of experimental psychology,* New York: Wiley, 1951.

Rachman, S. Systematic desensitization. *Psychological Bulletin,* 1967, **67**, 93-103.

Rowland, L. W The somatic effects of stimuli graded in respect to their exciting character. *Journal of Experimental Psychology,* 1936, **19**, 547-560.

Shaw, W. A. The distribution of muscular action potentials during imaging. *Psychological Record*, 1938, **2**, 195-216.

Wilder, J. The law of initial values in neurology and psychiatry: Facts and problems. *Journal of Nervous and Mental Disease,* 1957, **125**, 73-86.

Winer, B. J. *Statistical principles in experimental design.* New York: McGraw-Hill, 1962.

Wolpe, J. *Psychotherapy by reciprocal inhibition.* Stanford, Calif.: Stanford University Press, 1958.

Wolpe, J., & Lang, P. J. A fear survey schedule for use in behaviour therapy. *Behaviour Research and Therapy*, 1964, **2**, 27-30.

Wolpe, J., & Lazarus, A. A. *Behavior therapy techniques*, New York: Pergamon Press, 1966.

Wolpin, M., & Raines, J. Visual imagery, expected roles and extinction as possible factors in reducing fear and avoidance behavior. *Behaviour Research and Therapy*, 1966, **4**, 25-37.

Freudianism, Behaviour Therapy, and "Self-Disclosure"

O. Hobart Mowrer

The editors of this journal have graciously invited me to write "a comparative revaluation of the works of Wolpe and of Dollard and Miller on the subject of psychotherapy." I am happy to accept this assignment but wish to extend it by also placing these works in juxtaposition to another, very different approach and point of view which I believe involves a much more realistic conception of neurosis and holds far greater promise of effective treatment and prevention.

1

Dr. Wolpe is at pains, in the volume which we shall take as the principal basis for our discussion, to give the reader, quickly and clearly, the essence of his argument. He has prepared a concise introductory statement for this purpose; and I shall largely confine myself, as far as Wolpe's views are concerned, to what is said therein.

At the outset Dr. Wolpe contrasts his concepts and procedures with those of Freudian psychoanalysis. The latter is protracted and only minimally effective, whereas his methods work swiftly and surely. Psychoanalysis is predicated on the assumption that repression is the "primal pathogenic act" and its reversal is regarded as the essence of cure. Dr. Wolpe says he is presenting "a new theory of psychotherapy" (p. ix) which is based "on modern learning theory" and is, purportedly, very different. Its central thesis: "Since neurotic behaviour demonstrably originates in learning, it is only to be expected that its elimination will be a matter of unlearning"

From O. H. Mowrer, "Freudianism, Behaviour Therapy, and 'Self-Disclosure,'" *Behaviour Research and Therapy*, 1964, **1**, 321-337. Reprinted by permission of Pergamon Press.

(p. ix): "most neuroses are basically unadaptive conditioned anxiety reactions" (p. xi).

At a high level of generality, this thesis would, I suppose, be acceptable to most psychologists and probably to many psychiatrists. The difficulty arises when the argument is more specifically interpreted by Wolpe as follows. Neurosis, he believes, originates when a human being (or laboratory animal) is arbitrarily punished for behaviour which is motivated by hunger, sex, or some other bodily need or drive. The result is that the subject, when the pertinent need recurs, experiences "anxiety" and is unable to act in a manner appropriate to the need, i.e. is inhibited. Therapy, for Wolpe, therefore involves what he calls "reciprocal inhibition" which, in practice, turns out to be either "experimental extinction" or "counter-conditioning." In other words, it consists of enticing the subject (in fantasy or fact) to perform the previously punished act and then either showing that this act is not really dangerous or else arranging so that it will be followed by reward of some sort. The negative expectancies previously associated with the performance (or mere contemplation) of the fact are thus progressively weakened and the attendant inhibitions eliminated.

Although the language is different, this conception of neurosis and its treatment is deeply—one can almost say "classically"—psychoanalytic. In what has come to be known as his first theory of neurotic anxiety, Freud held that sexual energy ("libido") which is arbitrarily denied expression and satisfaction becomes directly "transformed" into anxiety. But Freud soon moved on to the view (his second theory) that anxiety is, to use Pavlovian terms, simply a fear that has become conditioned to an impulse as a result of that impulse having previously eventuated in behaviour which was punished. Thus, when this impulse subsequently starts to re-emerge into consciousness and to instigate consummatory behaviour, the subject experiences the associated fear without recognizing the instigating impulse. Such a conditioned fear or "anxiety" was seen by Freud as the primary energy of the superego (or archaic, infantile conscience); and the goal of therapy, in the "transference relationship," was to extinguish or counter-condition this fear ("soften" the super-ego) so that inhibition would be replaced by freedom of choice and "spontaneous" action. Stripped of terminological peculiarities and converted into the same standard notation (such as that of symbolic logic), this conception of neurosis and its management differs, it seems, in no significant particular from the "new" interpretation put forward by Dr. Wolpe.

Dr. Wolpe says that psychoanalysis and related therapies are successful in only 50 per cent of the cases (which is no better than can be expected on the basis of spontaneous remission), whereas his own methods, he claims, are 90 per cent successful. It is to be hoped that this high level of effectiveness is substantiated and maintained; but there are reasons for scepticism. Since theory and technique seem basically so similar in both psychoanalysis and Behaviour Therapy, it is not immediately clear why one procedure should work so poorly and the other so well. Both approaches involve a long-recognized enigma; in the laboratory and in ordinary life it has been found that fears which are not reinforced, at least occasionally, "spontaneously" extinguish. Both psychoanalysis and Behaviour Therapy are predicated on the contrary assumption of the essential permanence of some (why not all?) fears unless they are subjected to special "treatment" procedures.

Freud recognized this enigma and tried to resolve it by such *ad hoc* conceptions as the "repetition compulsion," the "death instinct," and the "timelessness of the unconscious" (cf. Mowrer, 1948). Neither Freud nor his followers seem to have regarded any of these speculative constructs as particularly satisfactory or plausible; but this has not prevented them from continuing to operate—however ineffectively, even destructively—on the assumption that certain totally unrealistic fears do not spontaneously extinguish. The simple and obvious alternative view that so-called neurotic fears are persistent precisely because the associated danger is real and persistent (see Section 4) seems to have escaped them.

In the animal laboratory, from the time of Bekhterev and Pavlov on, the extinction of unreinforced fears ("defence reactions," "avoidance responses") has been a well established and dependable phenomenon. Extinction is the rule, not the exception. Miller (1948) has shown that rats which have been trained in a simple, easy avoidance response may continue to display this type of behaviour for many (perhaps 500 or 600) trials after the electric shock which served initially to set up the habit has been withdrawn from the situation. But eventually the subjects do "reality test"; and, finding the "punishment" (for not responding) is no longer present, they stop responding.

Solomon, Kamin and Wynne (1953) have found that if dogs have been subjected to extremely painful ("traumatic") intensities of electric shock in a shuttle box, they will continue to respond for as many as 1200 or 1500 trials before extinguishing. But they do extinguish eventually, without any special "treatment." And I have recently conjectured (Mowrer, 1960a) that in the case of laboratory dogs, the "commands" which are given and reinforced outside the experimental situation generalize back into that situation and thus prolong the "obedience" exhibited there. Moreover, in neither the Miller nor the Solomon study was there any counter-drive or "temptation" (e.g. sex or hunger) such as is often present in instances of so-called neurotic inhibition. When, in the laboratory, we deal with fears which are part of an active conflict, we find that extinction occurs much more rapidly than it does in situations in which the only source of conflict is the effort involved in performing a simple avoidance response.

It is true that Whiteis (1956) and Brown (1962) have been able to design a situation in which rats display a form of "functional autonomy" (cf. Allport, 1937) or "perpetual motion." But here the failure of extinction occurs because the subjects, in escaping from a danger situation, do so in such a way that they subject themselves to a brief shock, which serves to keep the fear alive. The situation is thus one which involves, not a failure extinction, but continuous, self-administered reinforcement.

Wolpe and certain other writers have advanced the unlikely suggestion that fears are preserved by the very success of the habits of defence (avoidance) associated therewith. In other words, the notion is that the relief or reward which the avoidance response provides reinforces the underlying fear. Where, we may ask, is the evidence that fears are either established or perpetuated by means of rewards? Habits, as overt, voluntary behaviour, are reinforced in this way. But fears, which are mediated by the autonomic nervous system (and are involuntary), are established and perpetuated by means of punishment (drive increment), not by means of reward (drive decrement). The notion that fears are reinforced by reward is thus not a legitimate application of "learning theory" but a perversion thereof.

How foolish and abortive "nature" would have been to evolve living organisms with nervous systems which functioned as Freud, Wolpe and others have postulated! In discussing what he called "the dilemma of the conditioned defense reaction," Hull (1929) has long since pointed out that it would be the epitomy of biological inefficiency and maladaption if animals were so constituted that fears were learned without provision, in the natural course of events, for their extinction when the attendant danger no longer exists. Thus, both empirically and theoretically, we have excellent reason for questioning the assumption, which is basic to the thought of both Freud and Wolpe, that unextinguished fears (which are totally unrealistic) are the cause of "neurotic inhibition."

Even more remarkably, Dr. Wolpe regards his approach as "new"—"nobody else tries to treat patients on the reciprocal inhibition principle" (p. xi). At least 10 years ago I recall having heard the Canadian psychiatrist, Dr. Ewen Cameron, in a lecture at the V. A. Hospital at North Little Rock, Arkansas, speak of using the method of "desensitization" (a term which Dr. Wolpe also applies to his approach). A nurse presented herself with complaints of acute anxiety. Inquiry revealed a masturbatory conflict. By means of reassurance and suggestion, the conflict was "desensitized," i.e. the fears associated with the masturbatory behaviour were extinguished and the patient was purportedly cured. When I was a graduate student, more than 30 years ago at Johns Hopkins University where Knight Dunlap was Departmental Head, I was exposed to his concept of "negative practice," which is essentially an extinctive technique (cf. Dunlap, 1932); and Burnham published a book on mental hygiene, in 1924, which reflects similar thinking—he even spoke of "inhibition of the inhibitions" (pp. 388 ff.). Manifestly, the Wolpian approach is neither "different" nor "new," and it goes contrary to some well established principles in the very field from which it purports to draw its main scientific justification. Yet it is enjoying considerable popularity and exciting widespread interest.

The record of therapeutic effectiveness claimed by Wolpe and many of his associates (cf. Eysenck, 1962) is admittedly impressive; and in the light of the foregoing considerations, it is presently difficult to know quite how to evaluate such claims. Time alone will tell the whole story, but there are at least some hints as to what the situation may actually be. Let us consider the following case history, first reported by Wolpe in 1954.

Mr. S., a 40-year-old accountant, was sent to me for the treatment of impotence by a psychoanalyst whom he had told that he could not wait the two years estimated to be necessary for psychoanalytic treatment. He said that his relationship with the woman he loved "could not be kept on ice for so long."

About a year before coming for treatment Mr. S. had fallen progressively more deeply in love with a girl of 24 called May who worked in his office. She was responsive to him and one day, despite ejaculating prematurely, he managed to deflorate her. Finding that he had made a good impression in this act he used all sorts of excuses to avoid further intercourse. After 6 months, when May was about to go on holiday, he felt obliged to make another attempt but ejaculated before entry. During May's absence, Mr. S. tried to seduce two other women but was thwarted by failure of erection. He then saw a psychiatrist who gave him massive injections of testosterone (i.e. male hormone). He was still receiving the hormone when May returned but his performance was worse than ever, for he could not even muster an erection. May began to show signs of coolness towards Mr. S. when later coital attempts were also unsuccessful. It was for this reason that Mr. S. was anxious to find a quick resolution of his sexual difficulties.

The simplicity of the treatment described will be surprising to many.... At the fourteenth interview Mr. S. stated that he had twice had successful intercourse—slightly premature on the first occasion but very prolonged on the second. He was much encouraged—to the extent that he had married May by special licence! Two days later he reported that they had had simultaneous orgasms on two successive nights" (pp. 110-111).

It is not inconceivable that a major reason for improvement in this situation was that Mr. S. married May, thus legitimizing their relationship and assuaging the guilt which might very well have been a factor in his prior sexual incapacity. But Mr. S., it could be pointed out, had been impotent in a previous marriage, which had ended in divorce, so this interpretation, without further information, is not entirely persuasive. Or it may be that here was a man with only a fragment of conscience in the sexual area—not enough to induce him to observe the conventions but enough to impair his sexual abilities—a man who, by means of psychotherapy, was divested of what little inner constrain he had previously had and thus "freed" in the way that a sociopath is free. Can it be that when Dr. Wolpe and his followers report therapeutic successes they are speaking of the disappearance of specific "symptoms" at the price of a general corrosion of character? Stekel (1938) reports the case of a travelling salesman who was impotent with all women except his wife. Would removal of this "symptom" have been counted a great therapeutic

and moral victory? On the assumption that symptoms are the very legitimate protests by conscience against an odious life style, can we be certain that mere symptom removal is either a social or an individual service? Moral as well as "purely medical" (biological) considerations are manifestly involved in situations of this kind and need to be taken into account in judging therapeutic effectiveness.

2

That the underlying assumptions of Dollard and Miller are very similar and also somewhat anterior to those of Wolpe is indicated by the following excerpts from their 1950 book, *Personality and Psychotherapy:* "If neurotic behaviour is learned, it should be unlearned by some combination of the same principles by which it was taught" (p. 7). "Neurotic habits are forced upon an individual by peculiar conditions of life..." (p. 12). "From the patient's standpoint, the novelty of the therapeutic situation lies in its permissiveness.... The therapist is understanding and friendly. He is willing, so far as he can, to look at matters from the patient's side and make the best case for the patient's view of things" (p. 243). "The fears evoked by free communication are gradually extinguished through lack of punishment" (p. 244). "Like any other habit, talking while anxious must be rewarded strongly enough so that the net balance of reward is in favour of talking, else the patient will remain silent or will hit upon lines of sentences which do not produce anxiety" (p. 245).

At first blush it may appear that Dollard and Miller are concerned with symbolic operations whereas Wolpe is more "direct" in his approach. But this difference is more apparent than real. It is true that Dollard and Miller ask their patients (in the traditional psychoanalytic manner) to talk about anxiety-arousing impulses and activities. But Wolpe asks his patients to fantasy or think about such matters, in a context of safety and reward: e.g. "At the twelfth interview Mr. S. was made to relax as deeply as possible under hypnosis and then asked to imagine himself in a bedroom with May" (p. 111). The intent, in both instances, is manifestly to extinguish or counter-condition fear which has become associated with impulses or actions with which punishment has presumably been contiguous. Dollard and Miller regard their approach as simply a learning-theory transliteration of Freudian psychoanalysis; whereas Wolpe, remarkably enough, regards his approach as deriving directly and exclusively from learning theory and as radically different from psychoanalysis.

Dollard and Miller and Wolpe are in agreement in not holding their patients in any way responsible for their neurotic anxiety; it is rather an expression of what has happened, or been done, to them. "The therapist takes the view that what is past had to happen. The patient understands this acceptance as forgiveness which, in a sense, it is. . . . If the recital is followed by condemnation and punishment we would not expect the effect of the confession to be therapeutic" (pp. 245-246). "The therapist showed no alarm or shock at these disclosures and did not condemn Mrs. A." (p. 251).

It was soon evident that (in the first few interviews) she had really been testing the therapist for she shortly found something much more important to say. A few minutes after the end of the session, Mrs. A. came back to the psychiatrist's office and made an important confession. She said, "I have something to tell you. Should I tell you now or wait 'til the next hour?" The therapist encouraged her to say it then and there. Mrs. A. continued: "Well, this is very difficult—my brother took advantage of me when I was a child. I never told anyone—not even my husband. You won't tell anyone, will you?" The therapist assured her that he could not tell anyone since he was expected as a professional man to protect the confidences of his patients (p. 251).

Let us note the extent to which both the patient and the therapist here share the same assumptions:

(1) The therapist was Freudian so would presumably have accepted the view that "neurotic habits are forced upon an individual" and that "what is past had to happen." The patient says: "My brother took advantage of me." This is one of the hallmarks of neuroti-

cism, to take the position that, in the words of Anna Russell, "Everything I do that's wrong is someone else's fault." Mrs. A. presumably had a part in the sexual activities with her brother, yet she holds him responsible. And the fact that analysts are so permissive and accepting, so dedicated to the view that "what is past had to happen" has probably encouraged far more people to move into morally compromised situations than it has helped get out of such situations. In other words, it would appear that this philosophy has been more destructive than therapeutic.

(2) Even if we grant that Mrs. A. could not have avoided (which seems unlikely) whatever it was that her brother did to her, she certainly did not have to keep it a secret subsequently, particularly if she was innocent in the situation. The fact of continued secrecy strongly supports the presumption of original complicity; and the brother could hardly, in any event, have had it within his power to keep his sister silent through all the ensuing years. Yet the analyst shares the patient's assumption that she could not, should not have confessed this behaviour to anyone else and, further, that now telling it just to him will be therapeutically sufficient. This is one of the reasons why psychoanalytic and neoanalytic therapies are so protracted and yet so uncertain in their final outcome: they assume that such problems can be solved by talking to a specialist, rather than to the significant others in one's life. This is perhaps a good way to start a lucrative new profession, but it has not made a strong and happy people.

(3) Note the ambiguity in the case of Mrs. A. as it is presented and interpreted by Dollard and Miller. They, Wolpe, and Freudians in general assume that, basically, the neurotic's trouble is that he is inhibited, that it isn't what he's done and regrets (i.e. fears having known) that matters but rather what he'd like to do but doesn't dare, because of quite unrealistic scruples and moral constraints. However, in the case of Mrs. A. (and every other neurotic, I conjecture, when all the facts are known), we see that her "inhibitions," i.e. her present symptoms and inca-

pacities, are really the result of prior uninhibited action, which has made her guilty, destroyed her self-regard and her confidence in the social and moral sense. At the very least, Mrs. A. was a hypocrite and liar, of long standing, and had on her conscience, it so happened, not only the incident with her brother but also a more recent history of infidelity to her husband.

(4) Dollard and Miller, along with Freudians in general, make the assumption that the patient is sick because of past "condemnation and punishment." An excellent case can be made for quite the reverse supposition, namely, that he is sick because of the absence of these experiences. That is what Mrs. A. has been trying to avoid, "condemnation and punishment"; and if she had earlier faced the consequences of her own conduct, she would have been liberated, freed, and would not have subsequently needed the attentions of a psychiatrist. A neurosis, it seems, is nothing but a state of guilt that has been neither admitted nor atoned for, and the notion that a person needs some special kind of professional treatment to deliver him from such a condition is surely one of the great illusions of modern times. It is most unfortunate that we have so few investigators in this field who are able to dissociate themselves from professional vested interests and think in terms of common human need.

(5) Freud took the position that repression, i.e. the exclusion from consciousness of instinctual impulses whose gratification has previously been harshly punished, was, as he put it, "the primal pathogenic act." It now appears much more probable that the "primal pathogenic act" is suppression, suppression from others of the whole truth about oneself. The analysts have put great emphasis upon what may be called intra-psychic conflict, dissociation, and splitting within the personality. But it now seems that it is interpersonal dissociation, separation, splitting, alienation that's basic here. And this is something that is much more likely to be under the individual's own volition and control than is access to the hypothetically repressed material which has presumably been pushed into the

unconscious and thus made inaccessible, except by the special techniques which psychoanalysis supposedly can provide. It's surely no accident that psychoanalysts have so often told their patients not to discuss their problems with other persons, on the grounds that it "will weaken the transference," "hurt other persons terribly," or heaven knows what. Here, in honest self-revelation and authentication, is the royal road to psychological freedom and personal wholeness, and our attempts to prevent others from traversing it has been sheer professional chauvinism.

(6) It will perhaps not be entirely clear to some what the difference, implied above, is between "neurotic anxiety," in the Freudian manner, and "real guilt." In both instances a form of fear is manifestly present, and this fear is presumably related, in some way, to past punishment, either direct or vicarious. The Freudian conception of unrealistic, false, neurotic anxiety is, as we have seen, readily translatable into conventional learning terms. What, in this frame of reference is guilt—not mere guilt feelings, but real guilt? I have attempted to answer this question in some detail elsewhere (Mowrer, 1960b); but here let it suffice to note that guilt is the fear a person feels after having committed an act which is disapproved by the significant others in his life, before that act is detected or confessed. Guilt, in short, is the fear of being found out and punished (see also the following paragraph and paragraphs 8 and 9 of Section 4). And it persists (i.e. doesn't extinguish) for precisely the reason that in human society the mere passage of time does not reduce culpability. Under the circumstances specified, the original act is, moreover, compounded by deception, which becomes an on-going "sin" which was not merely committed then but is still being practiced and perpetuated, here and now. According to the Freudian conception, Mrs. A. would be neurotically anxious only if and when, for example, the impulse to interact sexually with her brother returned; by contrast, guilt can exist and persist even though there is never again a temptation to perform the same culpable action.

(7) The definition of guilt as fear of a so-

cially realistic danger is necessary but, as far as the condition we call neurosis is concerned, not sufficient. Even the so-called psychopath or, more accurately, sociopath can experience guilt in this sense, i.e. he can be afraid of being caught and punished. But the neurotic, we all agree, is a more highly evolved type of individual, so we must ask what he has which the sociopath lacks. The answer, clearly, is conscience, i.e. the capacity for self-condemnation and self-punishment, even though his "crime" still be unknown, socially and legally speaking. Anton Boisen (1936) has referred to mental hospitals as the abode of the self-condemned, in contrast to those places of socially enforced penance which we call prisons. The neurotic is a person who has behaved improperly but who, unlike the sociopath (who has only society to fear—and not even that so long as his misdeeds are undetected), is doomed in that although he may deceive the public, he cannot keep knowledge of improper action from his conscience. "Neurosis," it seems, is therefore the "trouble" which conscience causes when a person of basically good character in some way compromises himself and persistently refuses to do anything about it. In this frame of reference, symptoms are therefore the tell-tale signs of the struggle which the individual is having with his conscience. Conscience is saying, "Confess and change" (cf. Reik's book, *The Compulsion to Confess*), whereas ego is saying, in effect, "No, I won't." Although, in a struggle of this kind, others may not know the precise nature of the individual's difficulty, they know that something "is wrong." The Freudians and neo-Freudians have said that the trouble lies in a conscience which is unrealistic and tyrannical. The alternative here suggested is that the problem originates, rather, in palpably deviant conduct.

Both of these approaches agree that neurosis involves a moral struggle; but one holds that this struggle is spurious and wasteful and thus to be "analysed" away, whereas the other holds that the struggle is valid and worthwhile and, if properly understood and responded to, capable of leading to better

things. The Freudian approach, although probably wrong, is at least not superficial. The Wolpian approach stands in danger of turning out to be both wrong and superficial. It purportedly has no interest in the moral aspects of neurosis and is concerned only with "symptoms"—and their elimination. If symptoms are the way an otherwise throttled conscience has of calling for help in saving an individual from a deviant, antisocial (sociopathic) life style, do we really wish to eliminate them? Or should we rather try to help the afflicted individual see that conscience is a great and good friend, striving to reverse his trend toward social alienation and psychological "death" and to restore him to a fuller humanity?

(8) But if the neurotic's conscience is adequate, why then, one may ask, does he "sin," in the first place? The sociopath's conscience is, by definition, insufficiently developed; so we are not in the least surprised when he misbehaves. But what about the neurotic? Freud took the position that the neurotic individual hasn't really done anything wrong but has such a turgid conscience that it makes its possessor feel bad quite falsely and unjustifiably. We, on the contrary, are assuming that the neurotic's conscience is quite normal, neither too strong nor too weak, and that the difficulty has arisen because of a course of action which the individual has resolved upon and conscience was unable, at the moment, to block. Later, conscience calls for confession and restitution; and when they are not forthcoming, it begins to pressure ("torment") the individual in ways which produce the "compromise formations" which we call symptoms.

Let us suppose, for the sake of a simple illustration, that there is a rule which says that human beings, in going from A to C, ought to do so by moving along the two perpendicular sides of a right-angle triangle, ABC. But "intelligent" people can see that there is a quicker, easier way to make this trip, namely to proceed directly from A to C, along the hypotenuse of the triangle. Like misconduct or "sin" in general, this is a short-cut and not, in and of itself, a bad idea. But, it so happens, that there are certain undesirable later consequences (or "side-effects") for persons who go directly from A to C which do not arise if they proceed from A to B to C. Thus ABC becomes the socially approved, moral way to behave and AC is the immoral, disapproved way.

Why do we human beings sometimes, then, act immorally, sinfully? Not because we are necessarily stupid or inherently evil but because we are personally inexperienced and unwilling to "take the word" of others. I do not believe in Original Sin, in the formal theological sense; but I do believe that man is originally a sinner, in the sense that by their very nature rules invite violation; and everyone has to do a certain amount of rule-violating before he "grows up" enough to see the "wisdom of the ages." Some "reality testing" of this kind is undoubtedly a good thing, in that it keeps us from persevering in practices which may no longer be functional. But we are never going to do away with rules entirely (that would be anarchy!); and as long as rules exist, people are going to violate them occasionally, and some people are going to then get themselves into further difficulty by trying to deny and hide their folly. This, as we have seen, is not a practical strategy for persons of good character—and "neurosis" is the price they pay. The problem of therapy is therefore to help these people understand their true predicament and to inspire them to take the course of action which will most surely lead to their deliverance.

3

Some psychotherapists are today beginning to think along lines very different from those suggested by Freud and such neo-Freudians as Dollard and Miller, and Wolpe, and much more in accord with the immediately preceding discussion. Here I shall give only one of many possible examples of this new trend. Dr. Sidney S. Jourard will shortly publish a book entitled *The Transparent Self: Openness, Effectiveness, and Health,* from which the following excerpts (taken from various parts of Dr. Jourard's manuscript) are reproduced, with permission:

I have little doubt that self-disclosure is a crucial variable in the broad field of interpersonal relationships, which all of us are seeking the better to understand. In the history of our discipline, there has been only incidental attention paid to self-disclosure, with no direct study of this behaviour as a research variable in its own right.

Would it be too arbitrary an assumption to propose that people become clients because they do not disclose themselves in some optimal degree to the people in their life? I have come to believe that it is not communication *per se* which is fouled up in the mentally ill. Rather it is a foul-up in the process of knowing others, and of becoming known by others.

Every maladjusted person is a person who has not made himself known to another human being, and in consequence does not know himself. Nor can he be himself. More than that, he struggles actively to avoid becoming known by another human being. He works at it ceaselessly, 24 hours daily, and it is work! The fact that resisting becoming known is work offers us a research opening, incidentally. I believe that in the effort to avoid becoming known, a person provides for himself a cancerous kind of stress which is subtle and unrecognized, but none the less effective in producing, not only the assorted patterns of unhealthy personality which psychiatry talks about, but also the wide array of physical ills that have come to be recognized as the stock in trade of psychosomatic medicine. Stated another way, I believe that other people come to be stressors to an individual in direct proportion to his degree of self alienation.

If I am struggling to avoid becoming known by other persons then, of course, I must construct a false public self. The greater the discrepancy between my unexpurgated real self, and the version of myself that I present to others, then the more dangerous will other people be for me. If becoming known by another person is threatening, then the very presence of another person can serve as a stimulus to evoke anxiety, heightened muscle tension, and all the assorted visceral changes which occur when a person is under stress.

When a man does not acknowledge to himself who, what and how he is, he is out of touch with reality, and he will sicken and die; and no one can help him without access to the facts. And it seems to be another empirical fact that no man can acknowledge his real self to himself (that is, know himself) except as an outcome of disclosing himself to another person. This is the lesson we have learned in the field of psychotherapy. When a person has been able to disclose himself utterly to another person, he learns how to increase his contact with his real self, and may then be better able to direct his destiny on the basis of his real-self knowledge.

Self-alienation is a sickness which is so widely shared that no one recognizes it. It means that an individual is estranged from his real self. His real self becomes a stranger, a feared and distrusted stranger. Estrangement, alienation from one's self is at the root of the neurotic personality of our time.

I have gradually come to see therapy, not as a setting in which one person, the therapist, does things to a patient, . . . but rather as a relationship . . . in which growth of both parties is an outcome.

I believe that self-disclosure is the obverse of repression and self-alienation. Alienated man is not known by his fellows, he does not know himself, and he doesn't know his fellows. Self-disclosure appears to be the one means, perhaps the most direct, by which self-alienation is transformed into self-realization. Man hides much of his real self—his experience—behind an iron curtain. Our evidence shows that this iron curtain melts like wax when it is exposed to the warm breath of love.

It is because of the pains arising from real self-being that most of us hide our real selves, even from loved ones, behind the mask of our roles, behind the camouflage of our personage, our public self-being. The price we pay for safety from the penalties of being and being known is steep. It includes loneliness, it includes growing self-alienation, or loss of contact and awareness of our real selves; it includes proneness to mental and physical disease. It includes emptiness and meaninglessness in existence.

Self-disclosure, then, entails courage—the kind of courage that Paul Tillich had in mind in writing his book *The Courage to Be.* I would paraphrase that title to read, *The Courage to Be Known,* since Being always occurs in a social context. Since I seem to be in a paraphrasing frame of mind, let me massacre a couple of other well-known sayings. Not really massacre; I'd say revise them in the light of what we are learning to be antecedent-consequent sequences. The Delphic Oracle advised, "Know Thyself"; I'd say "Make Thyself Known, and then you will Know Yourself." Shakespeare is the source of, "And this above all, to thine own self be true, and thou cans't not be false to any man." Let me re-state it, "And this above all, to other men be true, and thou cans't not then be false to thyself."

If I seem repetitious, enthusiastic, or both, I'm like the guitar player who, daily, for 20 years, sat with a one-string guitar, holding the same fret, making the same sound. One day, his wife said, with surprise, "Dear, I noticed on TV today that a man was playing a guitar, but it had six strings, and the man kept moving his hands around, and making lots of different sounds—not like you." Her husband said, "Don't worry about him dear. He's still huntin' the right note, and I already found it."

4

Here, in the thought of Jourard, is an interpretation of psychopathology and its remediation which contrasts sharply with that of Wolpe, Dollard and Miller, and Freudians and neo-Freudians. In the present, final section of this paper we shall explore a few of the many practical, as well as theoretical, implications which flow from these two very different approaches:

(1) The main thrust of what Jourard is saying is crystal clear: he is saying that the stress, the strain, the danger that characterizes psychopathology is not that the ego will be overwhelmed, as Freud and his followers have thought, by an eruption of repressed instinctual forces (notably those of sex and aggression); it is instead the danger that one's own deviant secrets will become known to others, thus exposing him to criticisms and negative sanctions which he has been intent upon avoiding. In short, Jourard is saying that in neurosis and the functional psychoses the basic problem is social, not instinctual. Freud's interpretation makes of neurosis essentially a biological problem, a disruption of what he called "the stream of life." And who could better deal with this type of difficulty than the physician, with his training in the biological sciences? But it now appears that in psychopathology we are dealing not so much with biology as with sociology, a realm in which physicians are essentially laymen. Who, then, will lead us, heal us if this is the nature of the problem? Social workers, clinical psychologists, and even clergymen have, in the main, patterned their efforts in this area after those of psychiatrists. In psychiatry itself there is today a growing emphasis on "social psychiatry," but this enterprise is still poorly defined and essentially foreign to medical ideology. In the meantime, as I have recently pointed out in a book entitled *The*

New Group Therapy, laymen are taking matters into their own hands and are, themselves, developing therapeutic self-help groups, in which self-disclosure and social re-integration are explicit goals. Here, there is reason to believe, healing follows more swiftly and surely than is likely when we view neurosis as an illness or disease and try to deal with it along Freudian lines, in a strictly professional context. A revolution seems quietly to be in progress here.

(2) The position of Dollard and Miller, as it has been re-examined in this paper, is in certain respects intermediate between the polarities posed by Wolpe and by Jourard. Dollard and Miller speak, for example, of Mrs. A's "confessing" to improper sexual behaviour with her brother, and this "self-disclosure" is seen as beneficial and desirable. Is this because such a communication was a step in the direction of re-establishing the community, the openness, the interpersonal relatedness which had long been lost? Or was it useful only in letting the therapist know what the patient's "problem" was, in order that it could then be "treated"? Wolpe would presumably say that "confession," as such, is irrelevant, since he seems not to be in the least interested in those self-damaging, socially alienating things which people do and call "sin." Guilt, as a consequence of such actions, seems not to exist for him. He is interested only in people's "inhibitions," or "symptoms," and their removal, without much reference to the person who is involved. The possibility that one's present "inhibitions" are due to a prior lack of inhibition, in the sense of proper self-control, evidently has no place in his thinking. He seems (as a physician) to see "patients" primarily as bodies, as mere biological units, and hardly at all as social creatures, as individuals functioning in a social system, in which we "live, move and have our being"—and wherein we find or, by sin and duplicity, destroy our identity, our very selfhood. Jourard is keenly sensitive to this dimension of the problem (cf. Mead, 1934), which Wolpe ignores almost completely and Dollard and Miller treat only obliquely.

(3) Dr. Jourard would, I believe, readily agree—with Wolpe, Dollard and Miller, and others—that "neurosis" is indeed learned (rather than being a "disease" which one catches or inherits); but his conception of what neurosis is and how it can be successfully unlearned is obviously and importantly different. Jourard is saying, first of all, that the so-called neurotic individual is suffering, not from an unrealistic dread of what he might be tempted to do in the future, but from a very realistic and well justified fear of the social consequences of things he has already done, in the past. Thus, "therapy" cannot be predicted on any such simple programme as extinction or counter-conditioning. Instead, the desideratum, as Jourard properly notes, is that of courage, the courage to be known. This aspect of the problem can be illustrated by the following diagram:

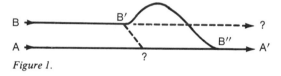

Figure 1.

Let the baseline of this figure (A-A', with time moving from left to right) represent the normal level of human confidence and comfort (i.e. "security"). (This function will, of course, in real life fluctuate considerably in response to varying circumstances; but for our purposes we can consider it as essentially stable.) Now let us represent "neurosis"—as a more or less chronically elevated state of mobilization, vigilance, apprehension, tension (i.e. "insecurity")—by the line B-B'. The very natural and altogether understandable desire of a person experiencing such a state of "anxiety" is to move, directly and rapidly, from this state of tension down to the more "normal" baseline of relaxation (B'-?). Intoxicants and tranquilizers, suggestion and reassurance, and electro-convulsive shock treatments enable people to accomplish this end temporarily; but, typically, "the effect doesn't last." Jourard's conception of neurosis implies that the procedure of choice is for the individual to make a detour, as shown by the line B'-B'', which will take him through a period of temporarily heightened discomfort but will permit an eventual, and permanent, return to the baseline. Professional therapists, it seems, have long been "in business" offering, one way or another, a cure which does not make this demand on the suffering, alienated person (Mowrer, 1963a). Psychoanalysts do not, to be sure, promise quick relief—and very few patients have ever been, in this respect, surprised. But analysts do promise an ultimate cure "in analysis," without the painful but radically healing self-disclosure which Jourard proposes. Sometimes analysts say, cryptically, "Patients don't get well in analysis. They get well in life." But they rarely develop this thought in any very explicit way, and go right on keeping their patients in analysis for very long periods of time and discouraging them against the kinds of interaction with other persons in their ongoing life situation which would make continued analysis (including the so-called "transference" relationship; cf. Mowrer, 1963b) unnecessary.

(4) What, more specifically, then is "therapy" or "help" in the foregoing frame of reference? If one accepts the Freudian notion that neurosis represents either over-socialization or, its equivalent, traumatic accidental inhibition, then some form of treatment, which presumably undoes the mistreatment to which the individual has previously been subjected, is indicated. If, however, we are dealing with guilt as it has been previously described in this paper, then self-disclosure, with its ensuing pressure upon the individual to change, is the right procedure. Here much greater responsibility is put upon the individual himself, both for the causation and the correction of his difficulties—a move, incidentally, which both patients and practitioners have a tendency to oppose, for it, so to say, "disenfranchizes" them. That is, it leaves the practitioner without a speciality, and patients are bereft of the comforting thought that someone else is going to "do it for them," i.e. treat and cure them. However, the disillusionment with professional therapy is today widespread and growing—witness the vitality of the therapeutic self-help group

movement. Here, in these self-help groups, help comes mainly from the example and testimony of other erstwhile sufferers, who have themselves made the "detour" and found wholeness and strength, and who are now willing to "walk" with others through this ordeal. Professional therapists have long presented a pedagogical anomaly: namely, failure to demonstrate the very accomplishments which they urge upon their patients. It is hardly surprising if "closed" therapists have singularly failed to produce genuinely "open" patients (cf. Rogers, 1962). "Do as I say, not as I do" might be said to have been their motto.

Jourard recognizes the resistance which a philosophy of mutual sharing and openness in the healing relationship is bound to excite in some quarters:

There is another phenomenon that arises in the therapist, just as surely as it arises in the patient. I am referring now to what may be called resistance to being in the therapist. Just as a patient will pick and choose his utterances for their intended effect on the therapist (a violation of Freud's fundamental rule), so will a therapist often pick and choose his behaviour for its supposed effect on the patient. This I now see as a violation of what may become a fundamental rule for the therapist ... that he should be spontaneously open in response to the patient. Resistance to being, to being oneself with the patient seems to be quite as characteristic of beginning therapists and of more experienced "technicians" of therapy as it is of patients and often for similar reasons: i.e. latent fear of how one will seem to the other as well as how one will seem to oneself, or dread of what will happen if one "lets go" one's tight self-control.

Saying that one needs courage to make the self-disclosing, personally transforming detour is equivalent to saying that one needs faith; and the best way I know for the faint-hearted and hesitant to get that faith and courage is for them to hear the testimony of others who have themselves made this journey and are willing to "stay with" the neophyte while he does so. This is a conception of "psychotherapy" which is today much more in evidence in lay, self-help groups than in strictly professional circles.

(5) Dr. Jourard is not, however, entirely consistent, or at least not fully explicit, con-

cerning the direction and extent of therapeutic self-disclosure. In one place he speaks of disclosing oneself "to the people in one's life," but on other occasions he implies that the disclosure need be to only one other person, "to a physician, psychotherapist, minister or friend." Or, even more narrowly, he says: "Psychotherapy is a paid-for experience at being and becoming oneself, with a professional expert who is unafraid of your unfolding being and of his own." But if self-disclosure on the part of a "patient" is the essence of "therapy," and if openness and personal transparency on the part of the helping other is the best way of encouraging such a step, then anyone who himself has been in this sense "born again" can be a "therapist," without being, by any means, a "professional expert." He may, admittedly, become something of an expert in his own right, but not "professional," in the sense of having academic degrees and being financially dependent on "fees." The genius of the self-help group movement is that it is made up of amateurs, laymen—who, out of gratitude for their own reconciliation and redemption, are willing to be of assistance to others, freely and gladly. (Here, incidentally, is the Protestant doctrine of "the priesthood of all believers" in action, in a way it is seldom found in more formally religious groups, i.e. our churches!)

The clergyman, traditionally, functions in a somewhat intermediate way. He says that "salvation" is free, in the sense that he does not make a direct charge for his services; but he too, in terms of the diagram previously presented offers something of a "short-cut." "You do not," he tells us, "have to confess your sins and to do penance before men. Bring your sins to me (as God's vicar) or take them directly to God (under my guidance) and if you are properly repentant, you will be forgiven." This procedure is rationalized on the grounds that God is a sort of Generalized Other (cf. Mead, 1934); so that if one has confessed to Him one has in effect made his peace with all mankind as well. Theologically and metaphysically, this type of procedure may, for all I know, be just what is needed; but psycho-socially, as the record abundantly shows, it has not been sufficient for many persons (cf. Mowrer, 1961, 1964). In both the Old and the New Testament there is ample precept as well as precedent for a ministry of human reconciliation (rather than mere divine forgiveness); and it is here, in the realm of disturbed and restored human relations, that psychology and religion have, I believe, their brightest chances for genuine collaboration.

(6) One of the most strenuous, and commonest, objections that is raised against extension of one's openness from a specialized therapist to "others" (or to by-passing the professional healer altogether and beginning with others) is that this is so "dangerous." Jourard recognizes this thinking, and such reality as it represents, when he says: "Why, then, do we conceal instead of disclose? Loving is a scary business, because when you permit yourself to be known, you expose yourself, not only to a lover's balm, but also to a hater's bombs! He knows just where to plant them for maximum effect, when he knows you." The possibility that being open will expose one to malicious persecution cannot, of course, be denied; it simply has to be faced as a calculated risk. But the worst that is at all likely to happen along these lines is much less serious than what is almost certain to happen if concealment continues. To this point Jourard says:

> We are so accustomed to presenting a facade, a mask to others that the idea of letting another person [persons?] really know us can be frightening beyond measure. We are afraid that if others know us as we really are, if they know what we have already done in the past, what we really think, feel, plan, want, and seek at the present, then we would be in much trouble. . . . We suppress and hide any characteristics of ourselves that would endanger our purposes of the moment. . . .
>
> Research and clinical experience as a psychotherapist have shown me, and many of my colleagues in the field, that when such pretense, such attempts to hide one's actual self proceed over a period of years, that the person gradually loses direct contact with his actual self. We may say that the person has become increasingly self-alienated.

Moreover, some punishment (or, at the very least, a willingness to make restitution) may be proper and in order. We have, it seems, gone badly astray in our thinking about punishment. Punishment is not basically a "rejecting" act, as is commonly assumed. It is rather, in its most legitimate form, a way of restoring the person to full status and fellowship, making him again acceptable and worthy of our co-operation and trust. Or, as Jourard prefers to put it, "It is only from the fully felt consequences of being that one truly learns, that is, grows." Is not the brief pain of punishment therefore a small price to pay for such a boon? Recently in a professional audience a man asked me: "But isn't there a danger that openness to non-professional persons will result in your being punished?" In reply I asked: If we do socially forbidden and reprehensible things, and then compound our guilt by keeping these acts concealed, should we expect to get off easier than the person who is "caught in the act"? My questioner laughed in an uneasy way, and did not pursue the matter.

Moreover, is it true, when we seek the services of a professionally trained therapist that we really get off without "punishment"? He may be "warm, accepting, understanding, and nonjudgmental," and in this sense non-punishing; but what about the fee we continue to pay him? In this way do not those of us who can afford it do penance? (This is indeed suggested, for example, by the observation of Dollard and Miller, previously quoted, to the effect that "The patient understands this acceptance as forgiveness which, in a sense, it is.") In the study reported a few years ago by Hollingshead and Redlich (1958), it appears that the kind of psychiatric attention which patients typically receive is a function of their socio-economic status: those who cannot afford psychotherapy are typically sent to state hospitals where they receive inexpensive "shock treatment"—inexpensive, that is, to others but hardly to the patient himself.

(7) Recently a nurse who had just started her training on a psychiatric ward said to me: "But I have seen other patients be very cruel and not at all understanding when a fellow patient tried being open with them." "Open about what?" I asked. "Well, about sex," she said. "This person was getting psychotherapy and was just beginning to be somewhat less inhibited in this area." Here is a very common misconception about the true meaning of openness. Because professional therapists typically think that people are emotionally disturbed because of repressed sexuality or hostility, it is certainly easy for their patients to get the impression that being "expressive" in these areas, not only with the therapist but with others as well, will be helpful. And much professionally directed group therapy is explicitly predicated on this supposition. Our assumption is, rather, that what the neurotic or functionally psychotic person needs to be "expressive" about is his guilt. It has been my observation that others have to be very "crazy" indeed to take exception to this kind of openness and honesty. In fact, in my experience with group therapy in a state hospital, I have noted that other patients have a great deal of intuitive good judgment and compassion in this respect and, with a little encouragement, can be extremely "therapeutic" in their reactions. There are, we must remember, two ways of being "honest" with others: honest about them, and honest about ourselves. When we begin giving other people unsolicited opinions about how "sexy" they are or how much they annoy us, we should not be surprised if we get counter-aggression. But when we invite others who have any sort of meaningful relationship with us to be the vehicle of our redemption and social re-integration, we are almost certain to be surprised by their capacity for being deeply helpful and "loving."

(8) To some it may appear that there is an inconsistency in our previous discussion. We have spoken of the legitimacy and, on occasion, the necessity of punishment; but we have also spoken of the love which one typically receives from others when one properly goes about the task of confessing, i.e. re-establishing contact with the significant others in one's life and also making new friends. The

difficulty has, in some measure, already been resolved by noting that punishment, at the right time and place, is not unloving. Rather, it is an obligation on the part of the one who does the punishment and a favour to the one who receives it. The common error in this connexion is to view punishment as coercive and restrictive, i.e. as an unwarranted interference with and limitation of the other person's rights. But let us consider the homely example of a little boy who disregards his mother's warnings and carelessly runs into a busy street. If the mother spanks the child for such behaviour, she is, to be sure, limiting his "freedom," in the immediate, short-term sense. But note that this is done, not malevolently or restrictively in the long-term sense. The spanking is only a token of what it is like to be hit by a truck and is designed to preserve the child's freedom, capacity for later choices, and general potentiality. If the child is crippled or killed, his total capacity for choice and the free exercise of his powers are far more seriously impaired than they are by the mother's symbolic "punishment." Essentially the same analysis applies, it seems, to many other situations in which parents properly feel called upon to exercise "discipline" over their children. Even when punishment is imposed ostensibly to protect the rights of others, this too is a favour to the individual concerned; for, in the long run, the disregard of other persons' interests is also self-defeating.

(9) But, over and beyond the foregoing considerations, it should be noted that in the situations which one counters "clinically," social (i.e. interpersonal) punishment is often unnecessary. This is the case (a) when the erstwhile offender has already "done penance" in the form of the suffering inherent in "mental" dis-ease and (b) when such a person further resolves to "make up" in some way, in the future, for the negative, destructive things he has done in the past. This is probably what we really mean, or ought to mean, when we speak of "forgiveness." The suffering which the neurotic has, in one way or another, already experienced surely earns him some "credit"; and we ought also to be will-

ing to give him the benefit of the doubt (at least a time or two) by agreeing to let him "work out" his own salvation, if he wishes to, instead of having it occur entirely on a retributory basis.

Thus, forgiveness in this sense involves both giving credit for the self-inflicted punishment which is always a feature of neurosis and functional psychosis and giving the individual a "second chance" to be co-operative, helpful, constructive, good. Therapy, incidentally, may now be defined as the act of helping another individual to make this "conversion," this change-over or transition, from compulsive, "neurotic," conscience-inflicted suffering to the deliberate, voluntary service, co-operation, and loyalty which are the hallmarks of normality. As long as an individual is defiant and unrepentant, his conscience continues to "hurt" him; when he comes to terms with conscience, and with the external community which it represents, the hurting stops and life's zest and meaning return.

(10) To some it may seem remarkable that a "learning theorist" who has himself been identified with past efforts to articulate learning principles with the domain of psychopathology should now be writing as I have written in the preceding pages. For six years I enjoyed close and cordial working relations with John Dollard and Neal Miller at Yale's Institute of Human Relations; Dr. Wolpe has made generous reference to my earlier work in the learning area; a method of "treating" enuresis along conditioning lines by my wife and myself (Mowrer and Mowrer, 1938) is frequently cited in the Behaviour Therapy literature (Eysenck, 1960); and one writer (Metzner, 1961) has gone so far as to suggest that the version of "two-factor" learning theory which I espoused 10 or 15 years ago (Mowrer, 1950; but cf. also Mowrer, 1960a, 1960b) provides the most satisfactory conceptual framework for the operations presently subsumed under the rubric of Behaviour Therapy.

The situation, as I presently see it, is reminiscent of the status of the University of Pittsburgh's skyscraper Cathedral of Learning several years ago, during a rather protracted period in its construction. For some reason, after the steel framework had been completed, the first four or five stories were bricked-in, as was the upper half of the building; but three or four intervening floors remained completely "open." A similar hiatus, it seems to me now exists between "learning theory," as it has evolved as a result of animal studies, and psychopathology as it manifests itself at the distinctively human level. I assume that there is a continuity (i.e., a basic "structural" connexion) here; but I am not willing, at this time, either to over-extend what we today know about learning or to over-simplify the facts of psychopathology just for the sake of closing this "gap" in our knowledge. As already indicated in this paper, I have made some tentative suggestions (Mowrer, 1960b) as to how the concept of guilt may be used as a connecting link between these two domains; but in this paper we have seen, also, that there are certain considerations which suggest that guilt, as we know it at the human level, exists in lower animals, if at all, only in the most primordial way.

One hopeful sign is that psychologists and others are today beginning to ask, not how can conscience be weakened (in the manner of psychoanalysis), but rather: how is conscience acquired, and what are its on-going functions in the life of an individual, and in the social group of which he is a member? Winifred F. Hill's 1960 article on "Learning Theory and the Acquisition of Values" is paradigmatic in this connexion; and we can confidently predict that many similar works will follow in the years ahead. I assume that such complex social and ethical considerations as have been alluded to in the foregoing pages can, and will, be translated into learning-theory terms (when that body of knowledge becomes sufficiently mature). But any interpretation of "neurosis" and "therapy" in currently available learning concepts which fails to do justice to the total reality of the situation is of very limited, perhaps even negative, value. Let us continue to try to articulate and "interpret" the two universes of discourse but not, hopefully, at the cost of distorting or misperceiving either of them.

References

Allport, G. W. (1937) *Personality: A Psychological Interpretation.* Henry Holt, New York.

Boisen, A. T. (1936) *Explorations of the Inner World.* Harper, New York.

Brown, J. S. (1962) Unpublished research.

Burnham, W. H. (1924) *The Normal Mind.* D. Appleton, New York.

Dollard, J. and Miller, N. E. (1950) *Personality and Psychotherapy.* McGraw-Hill, New York.

Dunlap, K. (1932) *Habits, Their Making and Unmaking.* Liveright, New York.

Eysenck, H. J. (Ed.) (1960) *Behaviour Therapy and the Neuroses.* Pergamon Press, New York.

Hill, W. F. (1960) Learning theory and the acquisition of values. *Psychol. Rev.* **67**, 317-331.

Hollingshead, A. and Redlich, F. (1958) *Social Class and Mental Illness.* John Wiley, New York.

Hull, C. L. (1929) A functional interpretation of the conditioned reflex. *Psychol. Rev.* **36**, 498-511.

Jourard, S. M. (1964) *The Transparent Self.* Van Nostrand, Princeton, N.J. In press.

Mead, G. H. (1934) *Mind, Self and Society* (Ed. C. H. Morris). University of Chicago Press, Chicago.

Metzner, R. (1961) Learning theory and the therapy of neurosis. *Brit. J. Psychol. Monogr. Suppl.* No. 33, p. 29.

Miller, N. E. (1948) Studies of fear as an acquirable drive—I. Fear as motivation and fear reduction as reinforcement in the learning of new responses. *J. Exp. Psychol.* **38**, 89-101.

Mowrer, O. H. (1948) Learning theory and the neurotic paradox. *Amer. J. Orthopsychiat.* **18**, 571-610.

Mowrer, O. H. (1950) *Learning Theory and Personality Dynamics.* Ronald Press, New York.

Mowrer, O. H. (1960a) *Learning Theory and Behavior.* John Wiley, New York.

Mowrer, O. H. (1960b) *Learning Theory and the Symbolic Processes.* John Wiley, New York.

Mowrer, O. H. (1961) *The Crisis in Psychiatry and Religion.* Van Nostrand, Princeton, N. J.

Mowrer, O. H. (1962) Payment or repayment?—The problem of private practice. *Amer. Psychol.* **18**, 577-580.

Mowrer, O. H. (1963b) Transference and scrupulosity. *J. Religion and Health.* **2**, 313-343.

Mowrer, O. H. (1964) *The New Group Therapy.* Van Nostrand, Princeton, N. J.

Mowrer, O. H. and Mowrer, Willie Mae (1938) Enuresis—A method for its study and treatment. *Amer. J. Orthopsychiatry* **8**, 436-459.

Reik, T. (1925, republished 1959) *The Compulsion to Confess.* Grove Press, New York.

Rogers, C. R. (1961) *Becoming a Person.* Riverside Press, Cambridge.

Solomon, R. L., Kamin, L. J. and Wynne, L. C. (1953) Traumatic avoidance learning: The outcomes of several extinction procedures with dogs. *J. abnorm. (soc.) Psychol.* **48**, 291-302.

Stekel, W. (1938) *Technique of Analytic Psychotherapy.* Liveright, New York.

Whiteis, U. E. (1956) Punishment's influence on fear and avoidance. *Harv. Educ. Rev.* **26**, 360-373.

Wolpe, J. (1954) Reciprocal inhibition as the main basis of psychotherapeutic effects. *A.M.A. Arch. Neurol. Psychiat.* **72**, 205-226.

Wolpe, J. (1958) *Psychotherapy by Reciprocal Inhibition.* Stanford University Press, Stanford, Calif.

4 B. F. Skinner

In contrast to the typical personality theorist, who observes man in natural, therapeutic, and (sometimes) laboratory settings and who then creates his theory from these data, the learning theorist has traditionally used animals as the subjects of his experimental investigations. Eventually, as the learning theorist acquires more and more data, he feels an urge to extrapolate from the apparent regularities in animal behavior to the realm of human behavior. Such is the case with B. F. Skinner (1904-) one of our most important contemporary learning theorists. His work provides a theoretical and applied science of behavior which attempts to account not only for animal behavior but also for the intricate patterns of human behavior.

Skinner's interest is in the identification and manipulation of the environmental variables that create the conditions for the development, maintenance, and change in overt behavior. He is widely known for his theory and research in *operant conditioning*. An *operant* is, according to Skinner's definition, any behavior that is controlled by its environmental consequences or reinforcements. A major empirical principle that guides his theoretical and experimental work is that *behavior which is reinforced tends to recur,* whereas behavior which has no positive environmental consequence has a low probability of recurrence. It should be mentioned that operant behavior consists of all the "voluntary" and "purposive" actions of the organism. Operant conditioning is, therefore, intended to modify behavior that already exists in the organism's behavioral repertoire.

Insofar as the concept of personality is concerned, Skinner generally dismisses the popular theoretical approaches on the grounds that they perpetuate a vague and unscientific attitude toward the study of human behavior. Mentalistic concepts such as "the ego" and "the id" hold no appeal for Skinner because they are seldom tied to any observable behavior. The proper goal of a behavioral analysis, Skinner says, is to establish the connections between behavior and the environmental context in which it is emitted and then to use this understanding to further behavioral control. Skinner argues that, in order for the study of human behavior to be a science, its data must be capable of being observed, measured, and reproduced. Yet despite his scientific rigor and commitment to experimental evidence, Skinner is not reluctant to boldly extend the principles of his system to the establishment of a utopian com-

121

munity as in his novel, *Walden Two*. He has also speculated on social behavior, language, psychotherapy, and other complex human functions in his book *Science and Human Behavior.*

The theory paper by Skinner on the process of self-control analyzes the variables that influence the way a person will go about regulating his own behavior. The learning principles used in this analysis are really no different from those that are manipulated in other situations in which control of some sort is required. However, in this instance, the person is controlling his own behavior by arranging for the manipulation of variables of which his own behavior is a function.

The research paper by Kanfer and Goldfoot examines the varieties of self-control methods that subjects use in order to better tolerate pain. The authors start with the assumption that people do try to control themselves in stressful situations. Their research goal was to determine which of the several experimental self-control options presented to their subjects was the most successful. Subjects were randomly assigned in equal numbers to five experimental groups. Each group was instructed to cope with the pain stimuli (the *independent variable*) in a special way. The *dependent variable*—that is, the subject's response to the effects of the independent variable—was the amount of time that the subject tolerated the pain stimuli. The subjects were also asked to rate the efficiency of the self-control mechanisms used to deal with the unpleasant experience. In analyzing these data Kanfer and Goldfoot discovered that the use of external stimulation (such as watching picture slides or a clock) as a distraction was significantly more effective than self-control mechanisms generated without external stimulation. Two important points illustrated by this research are (1) that all people naturally employ previously learned self-control devices and (2) that self-control can be enhanced through the mediation of relevant training procedures.

Rogers' critique paper is a vigorous commentary on the social and philosophical implications of Skinner's position on the control of human behavior. Skinner argues that be-

havioral control is a historical reality and that in the course of history this control has been used improperly, exploitatively, and unproductively. However, Skinner says, with advances in our knowledge the behavioral scientist has within his grasp the ability to design, create, and control the social conditions which would be instrumental in creating an ideal environment for man to live in. This strategy emphasizes the use of positive reinforcement, in contrast to the use of punishment and aversive methods that are frequently employed in the attempt to control behavior.

Rogers and Skinner agree that the behavioral sciences are acquiring an enormous potential for behavioral control and that the dangers inherent in this potential ought not to be underestimated or ignored. But, to Rogers, Skinner's idea of a good society created by means of a benevolent science is especially unappetizing. Unlike Skinner, Rogers feels that if science begins with a predetermined set of goals which cannot be modified along the way, then science becomes locked into its own rigid design. If science is seen in this light, then values, subjective choice and individual freedom become mere appendages of science. For Rogers, however, free choice and humanistic values are the foundations of a humane science.

Suggestions for Further Reading

The most comprehensive view of Skinner's thinking on personality, psychotherapy, and social institutions is found in *Science and Human Behavior,* published by the Macmillan Company in 1953. Skinner's *Walden Two* is a visionary utopian fantasy which has aroused tremendous controversy since its publication by the Macmillan Company in 1948. Since that time, various Walden communities have sprung up around the country that are based to a large extent upon Skinner's behavioral principles. An article titled "Walden Two, Three, Many More" in the New York Times Magazine, March 15, 1970, provides an in-depth picture of some of these communities.

Self-Control

B. F. Skinner

The "Self-Determination" of Conduct

Implicit in a functional analysis is the notion of control. When we discover an independent variable which can be controlled, we discover a means of controlling the behavior which is a function of it. This fact is important for theoretical purposes. Proving the validity of a functional relation by an actual demonstration of the effect of one variable upon another is the heart of experimental science. The practice enables us to dispense with many troublesome statistical techniques in testing the importance of variables.

The practical implications are probably even greater. An analysis of the techniques through which behavior may be manipulated shows the kind of technology which is emerging as the science advances, and it points up the considerable degree of control which is currently exerted. The problems raised by the control of human behavior obviously can no longer be avoided by refusing to recognize the possibility of control. Later sections of this book will consider these practical implications in more detail. In Section IV, for example, in an analysis of what is generally called social behavior, we shall see how one organism utilizes the basic processes of behavior to control another. The result is particularly impressive when the individual is under the concerted control of a group. Our basic processes are responsible for the procedures through which the ethical group controls the behavior of each of its members. An even more effective control is exerted by such well-defined agencies as government, religion, psychotherapy, economics, and education; certain key questions concerning such control will be considered in Section V. The general

Reprinted with permission of The Macmillan Company from B. F. Skinner, *Science and Human Behavior*, pp. 227-241. Copyright 1953 by The Macmillan Company.

issue of control in human affairs will be summarized in Section VI.

First, however, we must consider the possibility that the individual may control his own behavior. A common objection to a picture of the behaving organism such as we have so far presented runs somewhat as follows. In emphasizing the controlling power of external variables, we have left the organism itself in a peculiarly helpless position. Its behavior appears to be simply a "repertoire"—a vocabulary of action, each item of which becomes more or less probable as the environment changes. It is true that variables may be arranged in complex patterns; but this fact does not appreciably modify the picture, for the emphasis is still upon behavior, not upon the behaver. Yet to a considerable extent an individual does appear to shape his own destiny. He is often able to do something about the variables affecting him. Some degree of "self-determination" of conduct is usually recognized in the creative behavior of the artist and scientist, in the self-exploratory behavior of the writer, and in the self-discipline of the ascetic. Humbler versions of self-determination are more familiar. The individual "chooses" between alternative courses of action, "thinks through" a problem while isolated from the relevant environment and guards his health or his position in society through the exercise of "self-control."

Any comprehensive account of human behavior must, of course, embrace the facts referred to in statements of this sort. But we can achieve this without abandoning our program. When a man controls himself, chooses a course of action, thinks out the solution to a problem, or strives toward an increase in self-knowledge, he is *behaving*. He controls himself precisely as he would control the behavior of anyone else—through the manipulation of variables of which behavior is a function. His behavior in so doing is a proper object of analysis, and eventually it must be accounted for with variables lying outside the individual himself.

It is the purpose of Section III to analyze how the individual acts to alter the variables of which other parts of his behavior are functions, to distinguish among the various cases which arise in terms of the processes involved, and to account for the behavior which achieves control just as we account for behavior of any other kind. The present chapter concerns the processes involved in *self-control*, taking that term in close to its traditional sense, while Chapter XVI concerns behavior which would traditionally be described as *creative thinking*. The two sets of techniques are different because in self-control the individual can identify the behavior to be controlled while in creative thinking he cannot. The variables which the individual utilizes in manipulating his behavior in this way are not always accessible to others, and this has led to great misunderstanding. It has often been concluded, for example, that self-discipline and thinking take place in a nonphysical inner world and that neither activity is properly described as behavior at all. We may simplify the analysis by considering examples of self-control and thinking in which the individual manipulates *external* variables, but we shall need to complete the picture by discussing the status of private events in a science of behavior (Chapter XVII). A purely private event would have no place in a study of behavior, or perhaps in any science; but events which are, for the moment at least, accessible only to the individual himself often occur as links in chains of otherwise public events and they must then be considered. In self-control and creative thinking, where the individual is largely engaged in manipulating his own behavior, this is likely to be the case.

When we say that a man controls himself, we must specify who is controlling whom. When we say that he knows himself, we must also distinguish between the subject and object of the verb. Evidently selves are multiple and hence not to be identified with the biological organism. But if this is so, what are they? What are their dimensions in a science of behavior? To what extent is a self an integrated personality or organism? How can one self act upon another? The interlocking systems of responses which account for self-control and thinking make it possible to answer questions of this sort satisfactorily, as we shall see in Chapter XVIII. We can do this more conveniently, however, when the principal data are at hand. Meanwhile, the term "self" will be used in a less rigorous way.

"Self-Control"

The individual often comes to control part of his own behavior when a response has conflicting consequences—when it leads to both positive and negative reinforcement. Drinking alcoholic beverages, for example, is often followed by a condition of unusual confidence in which one is more successful socially and in which one forgets responsibilities, anxieties, and other troubles. Since this is positively reinforcing, it increases the likelihood that drinking will take place on future occasions. But there are other consequences—the physical illness of the "hang-over" and the possibly disastrous effects of over-confident or irresponsible behavior—which are negatively reinforcing and, when contingent upon behavior, represent a form of punishment. If punishment were simply the reverse of reinforcement, the two might combine to produce an intermediate tendency to drink, but we have seen that this is not the case. When a similar occasion arises, the same or an increased tendency to drink will prevail; but the occasion as well as the early stages of drinking will generate conditioned aversive stimuli and emotional responses to them which we speak of as shame or guilt. The emotional responses may have some deterrent effect in weakening behavior—as by "spoiling the mood." A more important effect, however, is that any behavior which weakens the behavior of drinking is automatically reinforced by the resulting reduction in aversive stimulation. We have discussed the behavior of simply "doing something else," which is reinforced because it displaces punishable behavior, but there are other possibilities. The organism may make the punished response less probable by altering the variables of which it is a function. Any behavior which succeeds in doing this will automatically be reinforced. We call such behavior self-control.

The positive and negative consequences generate two responses which are related to each other in a special way: one response, the *controlling response,* affects variables in such a way as to change the probability of the other, the *controlled response.* The controlling response may manipulate any of the variables of which the controlled response is a function; hence there are a good many different forms of self-control. In general it is possible to point to parallels in which the same techniques are employed in controlling the behavior of others. A fairly exhaustive survey at this point will illustrate the process of self-control and at the same time serve to summarize the kind of control to be emphasized in the chapters which follow.

Techniques of Control

Physical restraint and physical aid

We commonly control behavior through physical restraint. With locked doors, fences, and jails, we limit the space in which people move. With strait-jackets, gags, and arm braces, we limit the movement of parts of their bodies. The individual controls his own behavior in the same way. He claps his hand over his mouth to keep himself from laughing or coughing or to stifle a verbal response which is seen at the last moment to be a "bad break." A child psychologist has suggested that a mother who wishes to keep from nagging her child should seal her own lips with adhesive tape. The individual may jam his hands into his pockets to prevent fidgeting or nail-biting or hold his nose to keep from breathing when under water. He may present himself at the door of an institution for incarceration to control his own criminal or psychotic behavior. He may cut his right hand off lest it offend him.

In each of these examples we identify a controlling response, which imposes some degree of physical restraint upon a response to be controlled. To explain the existence and strength of the controlling behavior we point to the reinforcing circumstances which arise when the response has been controlled. Clapping the hand over the mouth is reinforced and will occur again under similar circumstances because it reduces the aversive stimulation generated by the cough or the incipient bad break. In the sense of Chapter XII, the controlling response *avoids* the negatively reinforcing consequences of the controlled response. The aversive consequences of a bad break are supplied by a social environment; the aversive consequences of breathing under water do not require the mediation of others.

Another form of control through physical restraint is simply to move out of the situation in which the behavior to be controlled may take place. The parent avoids trouble by taking an aggressive child away from other children, and the adult controls himself in the same way. Unable to control his anger, he simply walks away. This may not control the whole emotional pattern, but it does restrain those features which are likely to have serious consequences.

Suicide is another form of self-control. Obviously a man does not kill himself because he has previously escaped from an aversive situation by doing so. As we have already seen, suicide is not a form of behavior to which the notion of frequency of response can be applied. If it occurs, the components of the behavior must have been strengthened separately. Unless this happens under circumstances in which frequency is an available datum, we cannot say meaningfully that a man is "likely or unlikely to kill himself"— nor can the individual say this of himself (Chapter XVII). Some instances of suicide, but by no means all, follow the pattern of cutting off one's right hand that it may not offend one; the military agent taken by the enemy may use this method to keep himself from divulging secrets of state.

A variation on this mode of control consists of removing the situation, so to speak, rather than the individual. A government stops inflationary spending by heavy taxation

—by removing the money or credit which is a condition for the purchase of goods. A man arranges to control the behavior of his spendthrift heir by setting up a trust fund. Non-coeducational institutions attempt to control certain kinds of sexual behavior by making the opposite sex inaccessible. The individual may use the same techniques in controlling himself. He may leave most of his pocket money at home to avoid spending it, or he may drop coins into a piggy bank from which it is difficult to withdraw them. He may put his own money in trust for himself. H. G. Wells's Mr. Polly used a similar procedure to distribute his funds over a walking trip. He would mail all but a pound note to himself at a village some distance along his route. Arriving at the village, he would call at the post office, remove a pound note, and readdress the balance to himself at a later point.

In a converse technique we increase the probability of a desirable form of behavior by supplying physical *aid*. We facilitate human behavior, make it possible, or expand and amplify its consequences with various sorts of equipment, tools, and machines. When the problem of self-control is to generate a given response, we alter our own behavior in the same way by obtaining favorable equipment, making funds readily available, and so on.

Changing the stimulus

Insofar as the preceding techniques operate through physical aid or restraint, they are not based upon a behavioral process. There are associated processes, however, which may be analyzed more accurately in terms of stimulation. Aside from making a response possible or impossible, we may create or eliminate the occasion for it. To do so, we manipulate either an eliciting or a discriminative stimulus. When a drug manufacturer reduces the probability that a nauseous medicine will be regurgitated by enclosing it in tasteless capsules—or by "sugar-coating the pill"—he is simply removing a stimulus which elicits unwanted responses. The same procedure is available in the control of one's own reflexes. We swallow a medicine quickly and "chase" it with a glass of water to reduce comparable stimuli.

We remove *discriminative* stimuli when we turn away from a stimulus which induces aversive action. We may forcibly look away from a wallpaper design which evokes the compulsive behavior of tracing geometrical patterns. We may close doors or draw curtains to eliminate distracting stimuli or achieve the same effect by closing our eyes or putting our fingers in our ears. We may put a box of candy out of sight to avoid overeating. This sort of self-control is described as "avoiding temptation," especially when the aversive consequences have been arranged by society. It is the principle of "Get thee behind me, Satan."

We also *present* stimuli because of the responses they elicit or make more probable in our own behavior. We rid ourselves of poisonous or indigestible food with an emetic—a substance which generates stimuli which elicit vomiting. We facilitate stimulation when we wear eyeglasses or hearing aids. We arrange a discriminative stimulus to encourage our own behavior at a later date when we tie a string on our finger or make an entry in a date book to serve as the occasion for action at an appropriate time. Sometimes we present stimuli because the resulting behavior displaces behavior to be controlled—we "distract" ourselves just as we distract others from a situation which generates undesirable behavior. We amplify stimuli generated by our own behavior when we use a mirror to acquire good carriage or to master a difficult dance step, or study moving pictures of our own behavior to improve our skill in a sport, or listen to phonograph recordings of our own speech to improve pronunciation or delivery.

Conditioning and extinction provide other ways of changing the effectiveness of stimuli. We arrange for the future effect of a stimulus upon ourselves by pairing it with other stimuli, and we extinguish reflexes by exposing ourselves to conditioned stimuli when they are not accompanied by reinforcement. If we blush, sweat, or exhibit some other emotional response under certain circumstances because of an unfortunate episode, we may expose ourselves to these circumstances under more favorable conditions in order that extinction may take place.

Depriving and satiating

An impecunious person may make the most of an invitation to dinner by skipping lunch and thus creating a high state of deprivation in which he will eat a great deal. Conversely, he may partially satiate himself with a light lunch before going to dinner in order to make the strength of his ingestive behavior less conspicuous. When a guest prepares himself for an assiduous host by drinking a large amount of water before going to a cocktail party, he uses self-satiation as a measure of control.

Another use is less obvious. In *Women in Love,* D. H. Lawrence describes a practice of self-control as follows:

> A very great doctor ... told me that to cure oneself of a bad habit, one should force oneself to do it, when one would not do it;—make oneself do it—and then the habit would disappear. ... If you bite your nails, for example, then when you don't want to bite your nails, bite them, make yourself bite them. And you would find the habit was broken.

This practice falls within the present class if we regard the behavior of "deliberately" biting one's finger nails, or biting a piece of celluloid or similar material, as automatically satiating. The practice obviously extends beyond what are usually called "bad habits." For example, if we are unable to work at our desk because of a conflicting tendency to go for a walk, a brisk walk may solve the problem—through satiation.

A variation on this practice is to satiate one form of behavior by engaging in a somewhat similar form. Heavy exercise is often recommended in the control of sexual behavior on the assumption that exercise has enough in common with sexual behavior to produce a sort of transferred satiation. (The effect is presumed to be due to topographical overlap rather than sheer exhaustion.) A similar overlap may account for a sort of transferred deprivation. The practice of leaving the table while still hungry has been recom-

mended as a way of generating good work habits. Presumably for the same reason the vegetarian may be especially alert and highly efficient because he is, in a sense, always hungry. Self-deprivation in the field of sex has been asserted to have valuable consequences in distantly related fields—for example, in encouraging literary or artistic achievements. Possibly the evidence is weak; if the effect does not occur, we have so much the less to explain.

Manipulating emotional conditions

We induce emotional changes in ourselves for purposes of control. Sometimes this means simply presenting or removing stimuli. For example, we reduce or eliminate unwanted emotional reactions by going away for a "change of scene"—that is, by removing stimuli which have acquired the power to evoke emotional reactions because of events which have occurred in connection with them. We sometimes prevent emotional behavior by eliciting incompatible responses with appropriate stimuli, as when we bite our tongue to keep from laughing on a solemn occasion.

We also control the *predispositions* which must be distinguished from emotional *responses* (Chapter X). A master of ceremonies on a television program predisposes his studio audience toward laughter before going on the air—possibly by telling jokes which are not permissible on the air. The same procedure is available in self-control. We get ourselves into a "good mood" before a dull or trying appointment to increase the probability that we shall behave in a socially acceptable fashion. Before asking the boss for a raise, we screw our courage to the sticking place by rehearsing a history of injustice. We reread an insulting letter just before answering it in order to generate the emotional behavior which will make the answer more easily written and more effective. We also engender strong emotional states in which undesirable behavior is unlikely or impossible. A case in point is the practice described vulgarly as "scaring the hell out of someone." This refers almost literally to a method of controlling strongly punished behavior by reinstating stimuli which have accompanied punishment. We use the same technique when we suppress our own behavior by rehearsing past punishments or by repeating proverbs which warn of the wages of sin.

We reduce the extent of an emotional reaction by delaying it—for example, by "counting ten" before acting in anger. We get the same effect through the process of adaptation, described in Chapter X, when we gradually bring ourselves into contact with disturbing stimuli. We may learn to handle snakes without fear by beginning with dead or drugged snakes of the least disturbing sort and gradually moving on to livelier and more frightening kinds.

Using aversive stimulation

When we set an alarm clock, we arrange for a strongly aversive stimulus from which we can escape only by arousing ourselves. By putting the clock across the room, we make certain that the behavior of escape will fully awaken us. We *condition* aversive reactions in ourselves by pairing stimuli in appropriate ways—for example, by using the "cures" for the tobacco and alcohol habits already described. We also control ourselves by creating verbal stimuli which have an effect upon us because of past aversive consequences paired with them by other people. A simple command is an aversive stimulus—a threat—specifying the action which will bring escape. In getting out of bed on a cold morning, the simple repetition of the command "Get up" may, surprisingly, lead to action. The verbal response is easier than getting up and easily takes precedence over it, but the reinforcing contingencies established by the verbal community may prevail. In a sense the individual "obeys himself." Continued use of this tendency may lead to a finer discrimination between commands issued by oneself and by others, which may interfere with the result.

We prepare aversive stimuli which will control our own future behavior when we make a resolution. This is essentially a prediction concerning our own behavior. By making it in the presence of people who supply aversive stimulation when a prediction is not fulfilled, we arrange consequences which are likely to strengthen the behavior resolved upon. Only by behaving as predicted can we escape the aversive consequences of breaking our resolution. As we shall see later, the aversive stimulation which leads us to keep the resolution may eventually be supplied automatically by our own behavior. The resolution may then be effective even in the absence of other people.

Drugs

We use drugs which simulate the effect of other variables in self-control. Through the use of anesthetics, analgesics, and soporifics we reduce painful or distracting stimuli which cannot otherwise be altered easily. Appetizers and aphrodisiacs are sometimes used in the belief that they duplicate the effects of deprivation in the fields of hunger and sex, respectively. Other drugs are used for the opposite effects. The conditioned aversive stimuli in "guilt" are counteracted more or less effectively with alcohol. Typical patterns of euphoric behavior are generated by morphine and related drugs, and to a lesser extent by caffeine and nicotine.

Operant conditioning

The place of operant reinforcement in self-control is not clear. In one sense, all reinforcements are self-administered since a response may be regarded as "producing" its reinforcement, but "reinforcing one's own behavior" is more than this. It is also more than simply generating circumstances under which a given type of behavior is characteristically reinforced—for example, by associating with friends who reinforce only "good" behavior. This is simply a chain of responses, an early member of which (associating with a particular friend) is strong because it leads to the reinforcement of a later member (the "good" behavior).

Self-reinforcement of operant behavior presupposes that the individual has it in his power to obtain reinforcement but does not do so until a particular response has been emitted. This might be the case if a man denied himself all social contacts until he had finished a particular job. Something of this sort unquestionably happens, but is it operant reinforcement? It is certainly roughly parallel to the procedure in conditioning the behavior of another person. But it must be remembered that the individual may at any moment drop the work in hand and obtain the reinforcement. We have to account for his not doing so. It may be that such indulgent behavior has been punished—say, with disapproval—except when a piece of work has just been completed. The indulgent behavior will therefore generate strong aversive stimulation except at such a time. The individual finishes the work in order to indulge himself free of guilt (Chapter XII). The ultimate question is whether the consequence has any strengthening effect upon the behavior which precedes it. Is the individual more likely to do a similar piece of work in the future? It would not be surprising if he were *not,* although we must agree that he has arranged a sequence of events in which certain behavior has been followed by a reinforcing event.

A similar question arises as to whether one can extinguish one's own behavior. Simply emitting a response which is not reinforced is not self-control, nor is behavior which simply brings the individual into circumstances under which a particular form of behavior will go unreinforced. Self-extinction seems to mean that a controlling response must arrange the lack of consequence; the individual must step in to break the connection between response and reinforcement. This appears to be done when, for example, a television set is put out of order so that the response of turning the switch is extinguished. But the extinction here is trivial; the primary effect is the removal of a source of stimulation.

Punishment

Self-punishment raises the same question. An individual may stimulate himself aversively, as in self-flagellation. But punishment is not merely aversive stimulation; it is aversive stimulation which is contingent upon a given response. Can the individual arrange this contingency? It is not self-punishment simply to engage in behavior which is pun-

ished, or to seek out circumstances in which certain behavior is punished. The individual appears to punish himself when, having recently engaged in a given sort of behavior, he injures himself. Behavior of this sort has been said to show a "need for punishment." But we can account for it in another way if in stimulating himself aversively, the individual escapes from an even more aversive condition of guilt (Chapter XII).

There are other variations in the use of aversive self-stimulation. A man concerned with reducing his weight may draw his belt up to a given notch and allow it to stay there in spite of a strong aversive effect. This may directly increase the conditioned and unconditioned aversive stimuli generated in the act of overeating and may provide for an automatic reinforcement for eating with restraint. But we must not overlook the fact that a very simple response—loosening the belt—will bring escape from the same aversive stimulation. If this behavior is not forthcoming, it is because it has been followed by even more aversive consequences arranged by society or by a physician—a sense of guilt or a fear of illness or death. The ultimate question of aversive self-stimulation is whether a practice of this sort shows the effect which would be generated by the same stimulation arranged by others.

"Doing something else"

One technique of self-control which has no parallel in the control of others is based upon the principle of prepotency. The individual may keep himself from engaging in behavior which leads to punishment by energetically engaging in something else. A simple example is avoiding flinching by a violent response of holding still. Holding still is not simply "not-flinching." It is a response which, if executed strongly enough, is prepotent over the flinching response. This is close to the control exercised by others when they generate incompatible behavior. But where another person can do this only by arranging external variables, the individual appears to generate the behavior, so to speak, simply by executing it. A familiar example is talking about something else in order to avoid a particular topic. Escape from the aversive stimulation generated by the topic appears to be responsible for the strength of the verbal behavior which displaces it (Chapter XXIV).

In the field of emotion a more specific form of "doing something else" may be especially effective. Emotions tend to fall into pairs—fear and anger, love and hate—according to the direction of the behavior which is strengthened. We may modify a man's behavior in fear by making him angry. His behavior is not simply doing something else; it is in a sense doing the opposite. The result is not prepotency but algebraic summation. The effect is exemplified in self-control when we alter an emotional predisposition by practicing the opposite emotion—reducing the behavioral pattern in fear by practicing anger or nonchalance, or avoiding the ravages of hatred by "loving our enemies."

The Ultimate Source of Control

A mere survey of the techniques of self-control does not explain why the individual puts them into effect. This shortcoming is all too apparent when we undertake to engender self-control. It is easy to tell an alcoholic that he can keep himself from drinking by throwing away available supplies of alcohol; the principal problem is to get him to do it. We make this controlling behavior more probable by arranging special contingencies of reinforcement. By punishing drinking—perhaps merely with "disapproval"—we arrange for the automatic reinforcement of behavior which controls drinking because such behavior then reduces conditioned aversive stimulation. Some of these additional consequences are supplied by nature, but in general they are arranged by the community. This is indeed the whole point of ethical training (Chapter XXI). It appears, therefore, that society is responsible for the larger part of the behavior of self-control. If this is correct, little ultimate control remains with the individual. A man may spend a great deal of time

designing his own life—he may choose the circumstances in which he is to live with great care, and he may manipulate his daily environment on an extensive scale. Such activity appears to exemplify a high order of self-determination. But it is also behavior, and we account for it in terms of other variables in the environment and history of the individual. It is these variables which provide the ultimate control.

This view is, of course, in conflict with traditional treatments of the subject, which are especially likely to cite self-control as an important example of the operation of personal responsibility. But an analysis which appeals to external variables makes the assumption of an inner originating and determining agent unnecessary. The scientific advantages of such an analysis are many, but the practical advantages may well be even more important. The traditional conception of what is happening when an individual controls himself has never been successful as an educational device. It is of little help to tell a man to use his "will power" or his "self-control." Such an exhortation may make self-control slightly more probable by establishing additional aversive consequences of failure to control, but it does not help anyone to understand the actual processes. An alternative analysis of the *behavior* of control should make it possible to teach relevant techniques as easily as any other technical repertoire. It should also improve the procedures through which society maintains self-controlling behavior in strength. As a science of behavior reveals more clearly the variables of which behavior is a function, these possibilities should be greatly increased.

It must be remembered that formulae expressed in terms of personal responsibility underlie many of our present techniques of control and cannot be abruptly dropped. To arrange a smooth transition is in itself a major problem. But the point has been reached where a sweeping revision of the concept of responsibility is required, not only in a theoretical analysis of behavior, but for its practical consequences as well.

Self-Control and Tolerance of Noxious Stimulation

Frederick H. Kanfer and David A. Goldfoot

Summary.—This study investigated the effects of several behaviors as potential self-controlling devices in the tolerance of a noxious stimulus. In a cold-pressor test, experimental groups were instructed: (1) to expect severe pain; (2) to verbalize aloud their momentary experiences; (3) to use a clock for setting a goal for tolerance; or (4) to view and describe slides, in order to enhance tolerance of the ice water. Duration of tolerance differed significantly, with a descending order of mean tolerance in groups (4), (3), (1), control, (2). Post-test questionnaires revealed varying use of other self-controlling mechanisms in the groups. The utility of Skinner's paradigm for the study of self-control was discussed.

Tolerance of pain can be modified by changing the stimulational input to an *S*, or by physiological and pharmacological agents which change the threshold for the pain stimulus. When continuing exposure to a pain stimulus is under *S*'s *own* control, the event can be classified under the general paradigm provided by Skinner (1953) for the operation of self-controlling mechanisms. Skinner defines self-control as a process in which a person makes a response that alters the probability of the occurrence of another response. The first of these may be called a controlling response and the second the controlled response. The self-control paradigm characteristically involves either of two types of conflict situations. In the first, *S* has available the means for terminating a noxious stimulus at any time, but continuation of exposure to the noxious stimulus is also associated with reinforcement of high magnitude. In the second, *S* can make a response which leads to immediate reinforcement, but the behavior also has ultimate aversive consequences which tend to inhibit the occurrence of the instrumental response, or to strengthen antagonistic responses.[1]

The present study utilized the first type of situation. The purpose of this study was to examine the effectiveness of several different behaviors as self-controlling responses which might alter tolerance of a noxious stimulus.

All *S*s were given the cold-pressor test and asked to keep a hand in ice water as long as possible. For two experimental groups the potential self-controlling responses were verbal and related in content to the noxious stimulus. In a *Negative Set* group, emphasis on the aversive aspects of the stimulus was intended to shorten tolerance by increasing *S*'s attention to the ice water effects and arousing a repertoire of motor responses associated with pain stimuli. In a *Talk* group, the availability of competing verbal responses was intended to facilitate pain tolerance. In the remaining two experimental groups, the self-controlling responses involved *ad lib* use by *S* of environmental objects (a timing clock or a slide projector) not directly related to the pain stimulus. These external stimuli represented potential sources of distraction for *S*.

Method

Subjects

*S*s were 60 female undergraduates in business and psychology courses who volunteered

From F. H. Kanfer and D. A. Goldfoot, "Self-Control and Tolerance of Noxious Stimulation," *Psychological Reports*, 1966, **18**, 79-85. Reprinted by permission of the publisher and the authors.

---

[1]The first of these conflict situations is illustrated by such widely known dilemmas as that of a brave boy's pain endurance in the presence of peers, or the silence of a military prisoner in the face of physical assaults. The second type is encountered in "resistance to temptation" situations, such as those faced by the alcoholic or the obese excessive eater.

and were paid for their participation. Three additional *S*s began the experiment but terminated after discovering the nature of the task. All *S*s were naive about the purpose of the experiment. *S*s were randomly assigned to five equal groups of 12 *S*s.

The Noxious Stimulus

It is known that phasic vasoconstriction and vasodilatation (Lewis effect) occur during the course of hand immersion in ice water (Lewis, 1929). Various *E*s (Carlson, 1962; Krog, *et al.,* 1960; Kunckle, 1949; Teichner, 1965) have demonstrated that this phasic phenomenon is associated with the perception of pain. Kunckle (1949) hypothesizes that cyclic pain is associated with the Lewis effect. Although this hypothesis has not been thoroughly studied, it is apparent that *S*s not manifesting the Lewis effect find the ice water task exceedingly uncomfortable (Teichner, 1965). In addition, Teichner (1965) has shown that the absence of phasic vasodilatation is in part a function of *S*'s emotional state.

Marked individual differences can be expected in this stimulus situation, then, due to both the physiological and psychological state of *S*. Since the majority of *S*s who experience the Lewis effect do so within 4 1/2 min. (Teichner, 1965), and since Kunckle (1949), and Wolff and Hardy (1941) reported an increasing numbness for *S*s between 4 and 7 min., it was decided to expose *S*s for a maximum of 5 min. to ice water kept at a constant temperature of 1° C.

Design and Procedure

The experiment was conducted in a bare, soundproof room, softly illuminated and containing only *S*'s chair and a low table for holding the ice water pan. Precautions were taken to eliminate any distracting visual or auditory stimuli in the room, since pilot work had shown that the amount of environmental stimulation is a relevant variable in the present experimental procedure.

Each *S* was seated in the experimental room and asked to remove her rings, bracelet and watch. These items were collected and kept in the adjoining room from which *E* monitored the experimental procedure. *S*s in all groups were then told: "We are interested in measuring some physical changes that occur in people under various circumstances. For the first part of this experiment I would like you to wear these electrodes around your arm. They will measure the electrical activity in your skin. Now, when I tell you to, please place your hand in this cold water, and keep it there as long as you can." *S*'s dominant hand was placed in the water and a signal button, activated by *S*'s other hand, was used to permit *S* to make a definite decision and to provide a clear-cut response for terminating the task. In order to increase the plausibility of the stated purpose of the study, *E* excused himself at this point "to take a reading in the adjoining room." He then returned and continued with the instructions appropriate for each *S*'s particular group. Since the instructions describe the experimental treatments of the groups, they are reproduced verbatim:

Group I (*Control*).—You might find this experience uncomfortable. Keep your hand in the water as long as you can. Be sure to let me know when you take your hand out of the water by pushing this button.

Group II (*Verbal*, Negative set).—You will find this water very uncomfortable. Most people experience severe pain and cramping, especially in the area of the back of the hand, the palm, and in the joints of the fingers. The pain is quite severe. Keep your hand in the water as long as you can. Be sure to let me know when you take your hand out of the water by pushing this button.

Group III (*Verbal*, Talk).—You might find this experience uncomfortable. To help you keep your hand in the water, please describe aloud your moment-to-moment sensations. Be careful to observe and to verbalize all sensations and thoughts you have pertaining to this situation. This microphone will record what you say. Try to verbalize every thought. Keep your hand in the water as long as you can. Be sure to let me know when you take your hand out of the water by pushing this button.

Group IV (*External distraction*, Clock.)—You might find this experience uncomfortable. To help you keep your hand in the water, you may use this clock. It will be useful for you to know how long you have kept your hand in the water. Most people use the clock to set goals for themselves to continue for another *X* amount of time. Please use the clock to help you keep your hand in the water as long as you can. Be sure to let me know when you take your hand out of the water by pushing this button.

Group V (*External distraction,* Slide).—You might find this experience uncomfortable. To help you keep your hand in the water, you may use this slide projector. Please describe aloud each slide which you look at. Press this button with your (nondominant) hand to change slides. You may change slides as often as you wish. Please use the slide projector to help you keep your hand in the water as long as you can. Be sure to let me know when you take your hand out of the water by pushing this button.

For the *Clock* group only, a large wall clock was mounted at *S*'s eye level. For the *Slide* group, a Sawyer 700 projector with remote control was arranged to project a picture in front of *S* at eye level. The projector was loaded with 100 slides of Europe. Slides varied, containing pictures of landscapes, buildings, landmarks, and people. The slides were arranged in random order and started at different points for each *S*.

The electrodes were non-functional, terminating in wires clearly leading to *E*'s monitoring room. A one-way observation screen permitted *E* to observe *S* in the soundproof room. *S* was asked to submerge her hand into the water up to her wrist, palm down, under the floating ice. *E* determined proper positioning of *S*'s hand, began timing, and left the soundproof room.

Each S was stopped when her hand had been in the ice water for 5 min. After completion of the cold-pressor test, *S* was asked to complete a post-test questionnaire. On this questionnaire, *S* was asked: (1) to rate the discomfort of the water on a scale from 1 (mildly unpleasant) to 8 (absolutely intolerable); (2) to describe what she was thinking about while her hand was in the water; (3) to indicate any mechanisms or tricks which she might have used; (4) to indicate whether she had ever used these tricks before; (5) to predict whether she could have done better if something else were available to help her keep her hand in the water; (6) to indicate whether and how the particular self-controll-

ing response used in her group affected her performance; (7) to rate her everyday sensitivity to pain on a scale from 1 (intolerant) to 5 (very tolerant); (8) to state what made her want to keep her hand in the water; and (9) to estimate the total duration of having kept her hand in the water.

Results

The main measure of the effectiveness of the self-controlling devices was the time *S*s kept their hands in the standard ice water preparation. The mean numbers of seconds for the groups were: *Control,* 174.2; *Negative* set, 178.2; *Talk,* 129.0; *Clock,* 196.5; *Slide,* 271.3. An *F* test for the total number of seconds of toleration (Table 1) indicates a significant difference between groups at $p < .05$. The significant *F* value indicates that the various controlling devices differed in their effectiveness in prolonging pain tolerance. The *Slide* group showed the longest tolerance, with least tolerance by the *Talk* group.

A Neuman-Keuls test was carried out to examine further the differences among groups. The greatest difference, significant at $p < .05$, was obtained between the *Slide* group and the *Talk* group. The order of means suggests the superiority of those groups using environmental distraction responses (*Slide* and *Clock* groups) over those using verbal mechanisms, and over the *Control* group.

Several post-test questionnaire data gave frequency distributions and limited ranges which precluded use of statistical comparisons. Therefore, only descriptive statistics are given. Average water discomfort ratings were as follows: *Control,* 4.3; *Negative,* 5.2; *Talk,* 4.1; *Clock,* 4.7; *Slide,* 4.3. Similarly, when *S*s rated their tolerance of pain in everyday life, their average ratings ranged from 2.8 to 3.5, and appeared to be similar in the groups.

All *S*s were asked whether the self-control mechanism they were instructed to use, affected their tolerance time. Table 2 summarizes the findings. In addition, *S*s were asked to indicate whether any further external aid would have helped them. Fifty percent of the

*S*s in the *Negative, Talk,* and *Clock* groups responded in the affirmative, whereas 58.0% of the *Control* group and only 16.6% of the *Slide* group responded in the affirmative. From these data and from Table 2, it appears that the subjective appraisal of the utility of the self-controlling devices closely paralleled the toleration time data. The *Slide* group indicat-

Table 1. Analysis of variance of toleration time (in sec.) for all groups.

Source	df	MS	F	p
Between	4	32266.0	2.97	.05
Within	55	10869.4		
Total	59			

Table 2. Responses to the question, "Did (the self-control mechanism) affect your performance?"

Response	Negative set	Talk	Clock	Slide
Hindrance	2	3	0	0
Help	4	5	9	12
No effect	6	4	3	0

ed the greatest satisfaction with the provided self-control mechanism and also performed better than the other groups.

*S*s also reported the mechanisms which they actually employed during the task, in addition to those which they were instructed to use. While 9 *S*s in the *Slide* group and 7 *S*s in the *Clock* group reported that they used no additional mechanisms, 10 *S*s in the *Negative* group, and 6 *S*s in *Control* and *Talk* groups used other self-controlling behaviors. The *Negative* group reported the greatest use of motor mechanisms. Eight *S*s said that they tried "squirming," fist clenching, etc., to reduce their discomfort and increase tolerance. The questionnaire replies suggest that, when the self-control mechanism supplied by *E* was effective, no additional mechanisms were employed by *S*.

The results indicate that *S*s in all groups significantly underestimated the length of time they tolerated the ice water. Thirty-five *S*s underestimated this period of time, as opposed to 4 correct estimations and 9 over-estimations. The *Clock* group, for obvious reasons, was not included in this analysis. A product-moment correlation between actual time and estimated time of toleration was computed, with $r = .57$ ($p < .005$, 47 df).

Discussion

The results of this study support the hypothesis that tolerance of an aversive stimulus can be affected by providing *S* with controlling responses which he can utilize at his own discretion, without further intervention by *E*. The findings further suggest that self-control behaviors which provide some external stimulation, e.g., a clock or slides, effect greater facilitation than verbal devices. Particular parameters of the environmental distraction procedure, e.g., modality of presentation, stimulus complexity, *S*s interest in the task, etc., remain to be investigated. Since it appears that those cues which compete with the response-produced cues associated with noxious events may further prolong toleration, it would be of interest to explore further effects of direct reduction of the pain-associated cues by self-controlling devices. For instance, if increased muscle tension or irregular breathing characterized response to the cold-pressor test, then behaviors which result in normal breathing and reduced muscle tension may be effective responses to be utilized in self-control.

The low tolerance in the *Talk* group is of interest because clinicians often ascribe beneficial "cathartic" effects to verbalized reports of subjective experiences. Under the conditions of the present study, it is more plausible to hypothesize that attention to a noxious stimulus and the labelling of its aversive effects enhanced the tendency toward hand withdrawal because, in *S*'s past history, these additional responses have probably been followed by an escape response from the stimuli which are described or experienced as aversive. In the *Negative Set* group the instructions also may have resulted in increased attention to the aversive stimulus. In addition, anticipation of severe pain would be expected to arouse anticipatory motor responses designed to reduce pain. Further, *S*s indicated on the post-experimental questionnaire that the instructions in this group led them to set a tolerance goal toward longer exposure. These conflicting response tendencies produced by the instructions in the *Negative Set* group could have acted to yield the results for this group. Isolation of the contribution of each of these factors would have to be carried out in a separate experiment.

An inherent problem in research on self-control lies in the fact that most *S*s come to the experiment with well-learned self-controlling mechanisms. If a noxious stimulus must be tolerated in an experiment, and no further instructions are given, *S*s use the particular devices which they had found helpful in their past experience. In the *Control* group, for example, *S*s reported the use of many self-controlling devices including thinking of something else, counting, teeth clenching, and others. Consequently, the experimental groups in this study differed from the *Control* group mainly because *E* provided the same method for control of the tolerance response to all *S*s, or because the controlling response involved some external stimulation. With adult *S*s it would be difficult to eliminate completely the occurrence of self-instructed devices in the study of self-control. The results therefore represent only the relative increase in effectiveness of experimental mechanisms as compared to the uncontrolled and variable effects of pre-experimentally learned self-controlling responses.

The behavioral analysis of self-control reveals yet another set of variables which influence the behavioral outcome. Since the controlled response is usually an element in an approach-avoidance conflict situation, conflict theory suggests that manipulations of any of the variables which change the approach or avoidance tendency in *S* could serve as self-controlling devices. Thus, the probability of occurrence of those approach or avoidance responses could be altered by varying responses on which they are contingent. The present study has served mainly the methodological purpose of testing the utility of the Skinnerian self-control paradigm rather than establishment of substantive knowledge about different forms of self-control. The main advantage of the present approach over the traditional concept of self-control as a "voluntary" act lies in its potential for application of training methods for this behavior. It suggests that a person may learn to manipulate and control his own behavior and that the manner in which he does so is subject to learning as a function of the very same variables which affect other behaviors not commonly considered to be under *S*'s "voluntary" control.

References

Carlson, L. D. Temperature. *Annu. Rev. Physiol.*, 1962, **24**, 85-101.

Krog, J., Folkow, B., Fox, R. H., & Andersen, K. L. Hand circulation in the cold of Lapps and North Norwegian fishermen. *J. appl. Physiol.*, 1960, **15**, 654-658.

Kunckle, E. C. Phasic pains induced by cold. *J. appl. Physiol.*, 1949, **1**, 811-824.

Lewis, T. Observations upon the reaction of the vessels of the human skin to cold. *Heart*, 1929, **15**, 177-189.

Skinner, B. F. *Science and human behavior.* New York: Macmillan, 1953.

Teichner, W. H. Delayed cold-induced vasodilation and behavior. *J. exp. Psychol.*, 1965, **69**, 426-432.

Wolff, S., & Hardy, J. D. Studies on pain: observations on pain due to local cooling and factors involved in the cold pressor response. *J. clin. Invest.*, 1941, **20**, 521-533.

The Individual in the New World of the Behavioral Sciences

Carl R. Rogers

In the preceding lecture I endeavored to point out, in a very sketchy manner, the advances of the behavioral sciences in their ability to predict and control behavior. I tried to suggest the new world into which we will be advancing at an evermore headlong pace. Today I want to consider the question of how we —as individuals, as groups, as a culture—will live in, will respond to, will adapt to, this brave new world. What stance will we take in the face of these new developments?

I am going to describe two answers which have been given to this question, and then I wish to suggest some considerations which may lead to a third answer.

Deny and Ignore

One attitude which we can take is to deny that these scientific advances are taking place, and simply take the view that there can be no study of human behavior which is truly scientific. We can hold that the human animal cannot possibly take an objective attitude toward himself, and that therefore no real science of behavior can exist. We can say that man is always a free agent, in some sense that makes scientific study of his behavior impossible. Not long ago, at a conference on the social sciences, curiously enough, I heard a well known economist take just this view. And one of this country's most noted theologians writes, "In any event, no scientific investigation of past behavior can become the basis of predictions of future behavior." (3, p. 47)

The attitude of the general public is some-

what similar. Without necessarily denying the possibility of a behavioral science, the man in the street simply ignores the developments which are taking place. To be sure he becomes excited for a time when he hears it said that the Communists have attempted to change the soldiers they have captured, by means of "brainwashing." He may show a mild reaction of annoyance to the revelations of a book such as Whyte's (13) which shows how heavily, and in what manipulative fashion, the findings of the behavioral sciences are used by modern industrial corporations. But by and large he sees nothing in all this to be concerned about, any more than he did in the first theoretical statements that the atom could be split.

We may, if we wish, join him in ignoring the problem. We may go further, like the older intellectuals I have cited, and looking at the behavioral sciences may declare that "there ain't no such animal." But since these reactions do not seem particularly intelligent I shall leave them to describe a much more sophisticated and much more prevalent point of view.

The Formulation of Human Life in Terms of Science

Among behavioral scientists it seems to be largely taken for granted that the findings of such science will be used in the prediction and control of human behavior. Yet most psychologists and other scientists have given little thought to what this would mean. An exception to this general tendency is Dr. B. F. Skinner of Harvard who has been quite explicit in urging psychologists to use the powers of control which they have in the interest

From C. R. Rogers, *On Becoming a Person*, pp. 384-402. Copyright © 1961 by Carl R. Rogers. Reprinted by permission of the publisher, Houghton Mifflin Company.

of creating a better world. In an attempt to show what he means Dr. Skinner wrote a book some years ago entitled *Walden Two* (12), in which he gives a fictional account of what he regards as a Utopian community in which the learnings of the behavioral sciences are fully utilized in all aspects of life—marriage, child rearing, ethical conduct, work, play, and artistic endeavor. I shall quote from his writings several times.

There are also some writers of fiction who have seen the significance of the coming influence of the behavioral sciences. Aldous Huxley, in his *Brave New World* (1), has given a horrifying picture of saccharine happiness in a scientifically managed world, against which man eventually revolts. George Orwell, in *1984* (5), has drawn a picture of the world created by dictatorial power, in which the behavioral sciences are used as instruments of absolute control of individuals so that not behavior alone but even thought is controlled.

The writers of science fiction have also played a role in visualizing for us some of the possible developments in a world where behavior and personality are as much the subject of science as chemical compounds or electrical impulses.

I should like to try to present, as well as I can, a simplified picture of the cultural pattern which emerges if we endeavor to shape human life in terms of the behavioral sciences.

There is first of all the recognition, almost the assumption, that scientific knowledge is the power to manipulate. Dr. Skinner says: "We must accept the fact that some kind of control of human affairs is inevitable. We cannot use good sense in human affairs unless someone engages in the design and construction of environmental conditions which affect the behavior of men. Environmental changes have always been the condition for the improvement of cultural patterns, and we can hardly use the more effective methods of science without making changes on a grander scale. ... Science has turned up dangerous processes and materials before. To use the facts and techniques of a science of man to the fullest extent without making some mon-

strous mistake will be difficult and obviously perilous. It is no time for self-deception, emotional indulgence, or the assumption of attitudes which are no longer useful." (10, p. 56-57)

The next assumption is that such power to control is to be used. Skinner sees it as being used benevolently, though he recognizes the danger of its being misused. Huxley sees it as being used with benevolent intent, but actually creating a nightmare. Orwell describes the results if such power is used malignantly, to enhance the degree of regulation exercised by a dictatorial government.

Steps in the Process

Let us look at some of the elements which are involved in the concept of the control of human behavior as mediated by the behavioral sciences. What would be the steps in the process by which a society might organize itself so as to formulate human life in terms of the science of man?

First would come the selection of goals. In a recent paper Dr. Skinner suggests that one possible goal to be assigned to the behavioral technology is this: "Let man be happy, informed, skillful, well-behaved, and productive" (10, p. 47). In his *Walden Two,* where he can use the guise of fiction to express his views, he becomes more expansive. His hero says, "Well, what do you say to the design of personalities? Would that interest you? The control of temperament? Give me the specifications, and I'll give you the man! What do you say to the control of motivation, building the interests which will make men most productive and most successful? Does that seem to you fantastic? Yet some of the techniques are available, and more can be worked out experimentally. Think of the possibilities! ... Let us control the lives of our children and see what we can make of them." (12, p. 243)

What Skinner is essentially saying here is that the current knowledge in the behavioral sciences plus that which the future will bring, will enable us to specify, to a degree which today would seem incredible, the kind of behavioral and personality results which we wish to achieve. This is obviously both an opportunity and a very heavy burden.

The second element in this process would be one which is familiar to every scientist who has worked in the field of applied science. Given the purpose, the goal, we proceed by the method of science—by controlled experimentation—to discover the means to these ends. If for example our present knowledge of the conditions which cause men to be productive is limited, further investigation and experimentation would surely lead us to new knowledge in this field. And still further work will provide us with the knowledge of even more effective means. The method of science is self-correcting in thus arriving at increasingly effective ways of achieving the purpose we have selected.

The third element in the control of human behavior through the behavioral sciences involves the question of power. As the conditions or methods are discovered by which to achieve our goal, some person or group obtains the power to establish those conditions or use those methods. There has been too little recognition of the problem involved in this. To hope that the power being made available by the behavioral sciences will be exercised by the scientists, or by a benevolent group, seems to me a hope little supported by either recent or distant history. It seems far more likely that behavioral scientists, holding their present attitudes, will be in the position of the German rocket scientists specializing in guided missiles. First they worked devotedly for Hitler to destroy Russia and the United States. Now depending on who captured them, they work devotedly for Russia in the interest of destroying the United States, or devotedly for the United States in the interest of destroying Russia. If behavioral scientists are concerned solely with advancing their science, it seems most probable that they will serve the purposes of whatever individual or group has the power.

But this is, in a sense a digression. The main point of this view is that some person or group will have and use the power to put into effect the methods which have been discovered for achieving the desired goal.

The fourth step in this process whereby a society might formulate its life in terms of the behavioral sciences is the exposure of individuals to the methods and conditions mentioned. As individuals are exposed to the prescribed conditions this leads, with a high degree of probability, to the behavior which has been desired. Men then become productive, if that has been the goal, or submissive, or whatever it has been decided to make them.

To give something of the flavor of this aspect of the process as seen by one of its advocates, let me again quote the hero of *Walden Two.* "Now that we *know* how positive reinforcement works, and why negative doesn't," he says, commenting on the method he is advocating, "we can be more deliberate and hence more successful, in our cultural design. We can achieve a sort of control under which the controlled, though they are following a code much more scrupulously than was ever the case under the old system, nevertheless *feel free.* They are doing what they want to do, not what they are forced to do. That's the source of the tremendous power of positive reinforcement—there's no restraint and no revolt. By a careful design, we control not the final behavior, but the *inclination* to behave —the motives, the desires, the wishes. The curious thing is that in that case *the question of freedom never arises.*" (12, p. 218)

The Picture and Its Implications

Let me see if I can sum up very briefly the picture of the impact of the behavioral sciences upon the individual and upon society, as this impact is explicitly seen by Dr. Skinner, and implied in the attitudes and work of many, perhaps most, behavioral scientists. Behavioral science is clearly moving forward; the increasing power for control which it gives will be held by some one or some group; such an individual or group will surely choose the purposes or goals to be achieved; and most of us will then be increasingly controlled by means so subtle we will not even be aware of them as controls. Thus whether a council of wise psychologists (if this is not a contradiction in terms) or a Stalin or a Big Brother has the power, and whether the goal is happiness, or productivity, or resolution of the Oedipus complex, or submission, or love of Big Brother, we will inevitably find ourselves moving toward the chosen goal, and probably thinking that we ourselves desire it. Thus if this line of reasoning is correct, it appears that some form of completely controlled society—a *Walden Two* or a *1984*—is coming. The fact that it would surely arrive piecemeal rather than all at once, does not greatly change the fundamental issues. Man and his behavior would become a planned product of a scientific society.

You may well ask, "But what about individual freedom? What about the democratic concepts of the rights of the individual?" Here too Dr. Skinner is quite specific. He says quite bluntly. "The hypothesis that man is not free is essential to the application of scientific method to the study of human behavior. The free inner man who is held responsible for the behavior of the external biological organism is only a pre-scientific substitute for the kinds of causes which are discovered in the course of a scientific analysis. All these alternative causes lie *outside* the individual." (11, p. 447)

In another source he explains this at somewhat more length. "As the use of science increases, we are forced to accept the theoretical structure with which science represents its facts. The difficulty is that this structure is clearly at odds with the traditional democratic conception of man. Every discovery of an event which has a part in shaping a man's behavior seems to leave so much the less to be credited to the man himself; and as such explanations become more and more comprehensive, the contribution which may be claimed by the individual himself appears to approach zero. Man's vaunted creative powers, his original accomplishments in art, science and morals, his capacity to choose and our right to hold him responsible for the consequences of his choice—none of these is conspicuous in this new self-portrait. Man, we once believed, was free to express himself in art, music and literature, to inquire into na-

ture, to seek salvation in his own way. He could initiate action and make spontaneous and capricious changes of course. Under the most extreme duress some sort of choice remained to him. He could resist any effort to control him, though it might cost him his life. But science insists that action is initiated by forces impinging upon the individual, and that caprice is only another name for behavior for which we have not yet found a cause." (10, pp. 52-53)

The democratic philosophy of human nature and of government is seen by Skinner as having served a useful purpose at one time. "In rallying men against tyranny it was necessary that the individual be strengthened, that he be taught that he had rights and could govern himself. To give the common man a new conception of his worth, his dignity, and his power to save himself, both here and hereafter, was often the only resource of the revolutionist." (10, p. 53) He regards this philosophy as being now out of date and indeed an obstacle "if it prevents us from applying to human affairs the science of man." (10, p. 54)

A Personal Reaction

I have endeavored, up to this point, to give an objective picture of some of the developments in the behavioral sciences, and an objective picture of the kind of society which might emerge out of these developments. I do however have strong personal reactions to the kind of world I have been describing, a world which Skinner explicitly (and many other scientists implicitly) expect and hope for in the future. To me this kind of world would destroy the human person as I have come to know him in the deepest moments of psychotherapy. In such moments I am in relationship with a person who is spontaneous, who is responsibly free, that is, aware of this freedom to choose who he will be, and aware also of the consequences of his choice. To believe, as Skinner holds, that all this is an illusion, and that spontaneity, freedom, responsibility, and choice have no real existence, would be impossible for me.

I feel that to the limit of my ability I have played my part in advancing the behavioral sciences, but if the result of my efforts and those of others is that man becomes a robot, created and controlled by a science of his own making, then I am very unhappy indeed. If the good life of the future consists in so conditioning individuals through the control of their environment, and through the control of the rewards they receive, that they will be inexorably productive, well-behaved, happy or whatever, then I want none of it. To me this is a pseudo-form of the good life which includes everything save that which makes it good.

And so I ask myself, is there any flaw in the logic of this development? Is there any alternative view as to what the behavioral sciences might mean to the individual and to society? It seems to me that I perceive such a flaw, and that I can conceive of an alternative view. These I would like to set before you.

Ends and Values in Relation to Science

It seems to me that the view I have presented rests upon a faulty perception of the relationship of goals and values to the enterprise of science. The significance of the *purpose* of a scientific undertaking is, I believe, grossly underestimated. I would like to state a two-pronged thesis which in my estimation deserves consideration. Then I will elaborate the meaning of these two points.

1. In any scientific endeavor—whether "pure" or applied science—there is a prior personal subjective choice of the purpose or value which that scientific work is perceived as serving.

2. This subjective value choice which brings the scientific endeavor into being must always lie outside of that endeavor, and can never become a part of the science involved in that endeavor.

Let me illustrate the first point from Dr. Skinner's writings. When he suggests that the task for the behavioral sciences is to make man "productive," "well-behaved," etc., it is obvious that he is making a choice. He might have chosen to make men submissive, dependent, and gregarious, for example. Yet by his own statement in another context man's "capacity to choose," his freedom to select his course and to initiate action—these powers do not exist in the scientific picture of man. Here is, I believe, the deep-seated contradiction, or paradox. Let me spell it out as clearly as I can.

Science, to be sure, rests on the assumption that behavior is caused—that a specified event is followed by a consequent event. Hence all is determined, nothing is free, choice is impossible. But we must recall that science itself, and each specific scientific endeavor, each change of course in a scientific research, each interpretation of the meaning of a scientific finding and each decision as to how the finding shall be applied, rests upon a personal subjective choice. Thus science in general exists in the same paradoxical situation as does Dr. Skinner. A personal subjective choice made by man sets in motion the operations of science, which in time proclaims that there can be no such thing as a personal subjective choice. I shall make some comments about this continuing paradox at a later point.

I stressed the fact that each of these choices initiating or furthering the scientific venture, is a value choice. The scientist investigates this rather than that, because he feels the first investigation has more value for him. He chooses one method for his study rather than another because he values it more highly. He interprets his findings in one way rather than another because he believes the first way is closer to the truth, or more valid—in other words that it is closer to a criterion which he values. Now these value choices are never a part of the scientific venture itself. The value choices connected with a particular scientific enterprise always and necessarily lie outside of that enterprise.

I wish to make it clear that I am not saying that values cannot be included as a subject of science. It is not true that science deals only with certain classes of "facts" and that these classes do not include values. It is a bit more complex than that, as a simple illustration or two may make clear.

If I value knowledge of the "three R's" as a goal of education, the methods of science can give me increasingly accurate information as to how this goal may be achieved. If I value problem-solving ability as a goal of education, the scientific method can give me the same kind of help.

Now if I wish to determine whether problem-solving ability is "better" than knowledge of the three R's, then scientific method can also study those two values, but *only*—and this is very important—only in terms of some other value which I have subjectively chosen. I may value college success. Then I can determine whether problem-solving ability or knowledge of the three R's is most closely associated with that value. I may value personal integration or vocational success or responsible citizenship. I can determine whether problem-solving ability or knowledge of the three R's is "better" for achieving any one of these values. But the value or purpose which gives meaning to a particular scientific endeavor must always lie outside of that endeavor.

Though our concern in these lectures is largely with applied science what I have been saying seems equally true of so-called pure science. In pure science the usual prior subjective value choice is the discovery of truth. But this is a subjective choice, and science can never say whether it is the best choice, save in the light of some other value. Geneticists in Russia, for example, had to make a subjective choice of whether it was better to pursue truth, or to discover facts which upheld a governmental dogma. Which choice is "better"? We could make a scientific investigation of those alternatives, but only in the light of some other subjectively chosen value. If, for example, we value the survival of a culture then we could begin to investigate with the methods of science the question as to whether pursuit of truth or support of governmental dogma is most closely associated with cultural survival.

My point then is that any scientific endeavor, pure or applied, is carried on in the pursuit of a purpose or value which is subjectively chosen by persons. It is important that this choice be made explicit, since the particular value which is being sought can never be tested or evaluated, confirmed or denied, by the scientific endeavor to which it gives birth and meaning. The initial purpose or value always and necessarily lies outside the scope of the scientific effort which it sets in motion.

Among other things this means that if we choose some particular goal or series of goals for human beings, and then set out on a large scale to control human behavior to the end of achieving those goals, we are locked in the rigidity of our initial choice, because such a scientific endeavor can never transcend itself to select new goals. Only subjective human persons can do that. Thus if we choose as our goal the state of happiness for human beings (a goal deservedly ridiculed by Aldous Huxley in *Brave New World*), and if we involved all of society in a successful scientific program by which people became happy, we would be locked in a colossal rigidity in which no one would be free to question this goal, because our scientific operations could not transcend themselves to question their guiding purposes. And without laboring this point, I would remark that colossal rigidity, whether in dinosaurs or dictatorships, has a very poor record of evolutionary survival.

If, however, a part of our scheme is to set free some "planners" who do not have to be happy, who are not controlled, and who are therefore free to choose other values, this has several meanings. It means that the purpose we have chosen as our goal is not a sufficient and satisfying one for human beings, but must be supplemented. It also means that if it is necessary to set up an elite group which is free, then this shows all too clearly that the great majority are only the slaves—no matter by what high-sounding name we call them—of those who select the goals.

Perhaps, however, the thought is that a continuing scientific endeavor will evolve its own goals; that the initial findings will alter the directions, and subsequent findings will alter them still further and that the science somehow develops its own purpose. This seems to be a view implicitly held by many scientists. It is surely a reasonable description, but it overlooks one element in this continuing development, which is that subjective personal choice enters in at every point at which the direction changes. The findings of a science, the results of an experiment, do not and never can tell us what next scientific purpose to pursue. Even in the purest of science, the scientist must decide what the findings mean, and must subjectively choose what next step will be most profitable in the pursuit of his purpose. And if we are speaking of the application of scientific knowledge, then it is distressingly clear that the increasing scientific knowledge of the structure of the atom carries with it no necessary choice as to the purpose to which this knowledge will be put. This is a subjective personal choice which must be made by many individuals.

Thus I return to the proposition with which I began this section of my remarks—and which I now repeat in different words. Science has its meaning as the objective pursuit of a purpose which has been subjectively chosen by a person or persons. This purpose or value can never be investigated by the particular scientific experiment or investigation to which it has given birth and meaning. Consequently, any discussion of the control of human beings by the behavioral sciences must first and most deeply concern itself with the subjectively chosen purposes which such an application of science is intended to implement.

An Alternative Set of Values

If the line of reasoning I have been presenting is valid, then it opens new doors to us. If we frankly face the fact that science takes off from a subjectively chosen set of values, then we are free to select the values we wish to pursue. We are not limited to such stultifying goals as producing a controlled state of happiness, productivity, and the like. I would like to suggest a radically different alternative.

Suppose we start with a set of ends, values, purposes, quite different from the type of goals we have been considering. Suppose we do this quite openly, setting them forth as a possible value choice to be accepted or rejected. Suppose we select a set of values which

focuses on fluid elements of process, rather than static attributes. We might then value:

Man as a process of becoming; as a process of achieving worth and dignity through the development of his potentialities;

The individual human being as a self-actualizing process, moving on to more challenging and enriching experiences;

The process by which the individual creatively adapts to an ever-new and changing world;

The process by which knowledge transcends itself, as for example the theory of relativity transcended Newtonian physics, itself to be transcended in some future day by a new perception.

If we select values such as these we turn to our science and technology of behavior with a very different set of questions. We will want to know such things as these:

Can science aid us in the discovery of new modes of richly rewarding living? More meaningful and satisfying modes of interpersonal relationships?

Can science inform us as to how the human race can become a more intelligent participant in its own evolution—its physical, psychological and social evolution?

Can science inform us as to ways of releasing the creative capacity of individuals, which seem so necessary if we are to survive in this fantastically expanding atomic age? Dr. Oppenheimer has pointed out (4) that knowledge, which used to double in millenia or centuries now doubles in a generation or a decade. It appears that we will need to discover the utmost in release of creativity if we are to be able to adapt effectively.

In short, can science discover the methods by which man can most readily become a continually developing and self-transcending process in his behavior, his thinking, his knowledge? Can science predict and release an essentially "unpredictable" freedom?

It is one of the virtues of science as a method that it is as able to advance and implement goals and purposes of this sort as it is to serve static values such as states of being well-informed, happy, obedient. Indeed we have some evidence of this.

A Small Example

I will perhaps be forgiven if I document some of the possibilities along this line by turning to psychotherapy, the field I know best.

Psychotherapy, as Meerloo (2) and others have pointed out, can be one of the most subtle tools for the control of one person by another. The therapist can subtly mold individuals in imitation of himself. He can cause an individual to become a submissive and conforming being. When certain therapeutic principles are used in extreme fashion, we call it brainwashing, an instance of the disintegration of the personality and a reformulation of the person along lines desired by the controlling individual. So the principles of therapy can be used as a most effective means of external control of human personality and behavior. Can psychotherapy be anything else?

Here I find the developments going on in client-centered psychotherapy (8) an exciting hint of what a behavioral science can do in achieving the kinds of values I have stated. Quite aside from being a somewhat new orientation in psychotherapy, this development has important implications regarding the relation of a behavioral science to the control of human behavior. Let me describe our experience as it relates to the issues of the present discussion.

In client-centered therapy, we are deeply engaged in the prediction and influencing of behavior. As therapists we institute certain attitudinal conditions, and the client has relatively little voice in the establishment of these conditions. Very briefly we have found that the therapist is most effective if he is: (a) genuine, integrated, transparently real in the relationship; (b) acceptant of the client as a separate, different, person, and acceptant of each fluctuating aspect of the client as it comes to expression; and (c) sensitively empathic in his understanding, seeing the world through the client's eyes. Our research permits us to predict that if these attitudinal conditions are instituted or established, certain behavioral consequences will ensue. Putting it this way sounds as if we are again back in the familiar groove of being able to predict behavior, and hence able to control it. But precisely here exists a sharp difference.

The conditions we have chosen to establish predict such behavioral consequences as these: that the client will become more self-directing, less rigid, more open to the evidence of his senses, better organized and integrated, more similar to the ideal which he has chosen for himself. In other words we have established by external control conditions which we predict will be followed by internal control by the individual, in pursuit of internally chosen goals. We have set the conditions which predict various classes of behaviors—self-directing behaviors, sensitivity to realities within and without, flexible adaptiveness—which are by their very nature *unpredictable* in their specifics. The conditions we have established predict behavior which is essentially "free." Our recent research (9) indicates that our predictions are to a significant degree corroborated, and our commitment to the scientific method causes us to believe that more effective means of achieving these goals may be realized.

Research exists in other fields—industry, education, group dynamics—which seems to support our own findings. I believe it may be conservatively stated that scientific progress has been made in identifying those conditions in an interpersonal relationship which, if they exist in B, are followed in A by greater maturity in behavior, less dependence upon others, an increase in expressiveness as a person, an increase in variability, flexibility and effectiveness of adaptation, an increase in self-responsibility and self-direction. And quite in contrast to the concern expressed by some we do not find that the creatively adaptive behavior which results from such self-directed variability of expression is too chaotic or too fluid. Rather, the individual who is open to his experience, and self-directing, is harmonious, not chaotic, ingenious rather than random, as he orders his responses imaginatively toward the achievement of his own purposes. His creative actions are no more a chaotic accident than was Einstein's development of the theory of relativity.

Thus we find ourselves in fundamental agreement with John Dewey's statement: "Science has made its way by releasing, not by suppressing, the elements of variation, of invention and innovation, of novel creation in individuals." (7, p. 359) We have come to believe that progress in personal life and in group living is made in the same way, by releasing variation, freedom, creativity.

A Possible Concept of the Control of Human Behavior

It is quite clear that the point of view I am expressing is in sharp contrast to the usual conception of the relationship of the behavioral sciences to the control of human behavior, previously mentioned. In order to make this contrast even more blunt, I will state this possibility in a form parallel to the steps which I described before.

1. It is possible for us to choose to value man as a self-actualizing process of becoming; to value creativity, and the process by which knowledge becomes self-transcending.

2. We can proceed, by the methods of science, to discover the conditions which necessarily precede these processes, and through continuing experimentation, to discover better means of achieving these purposes.

3. It is possible for individuals or groups to set these conditions, with a minimum of power or control. According to present knowledge, the only authority necessary is the authority to establish certain qualities of interpersonal relationship.

4. Exposed to these conditions, present knowledge suggests that individuals become more self-responsible, make progress in self-actualization, become more flexible, more unique and varied, more creatively adaptive.

5. Thus such an initial choice would inaugurate the beginnings of a social system or subsystem in which values, knowledge, adaptive skills, and even the concept of science would be continually changing and self-transcending. The emphasis would be upon man as a process of becoming.

I believe it is clear that such a view as I have been describing does not lead to any definable Utopia. It would be impossible to predict its final outcome. It involves a step by step development, based upon a continuing subjective choice of purposes, which are implemented by the behavioral sciences. It is in the direction of the "open society," as that term has been defined by Popper (6), where individuals carry responsibility for personal decisions. It is at the opposite pole from his concept of the closed society, of which *Walden Two* would be an example.

I trust it is also evident that the whole emphasis is upon process, not upon end states of being. I am suggesting that it is by choosing to value certain qualitative elements of the process of becoming, that we can find a pathway toward the open society.

The Choice

It is my hope that I have helped to clarify the range of choice which will lie before us and our children in regard to the behavioral sciences. We can choose to use our growing knowledge to enslave people in ways never dreamed of before, depersonalizing them, controlling them by means so carefully selected that they will perhaps never be aware of their loss of personhood. We can choose to utilize our scientific knowledge to make men necessarily happy, well-behaved, and productive, as Dr. Skinner suggests. We can, if we wish, choose to make men submissive, conforming, docile. Or at the other end of the spectrum of choice we can choose to use the behavioral sciences in ways which will free, not control; which will bring about constructive variability, not conformity; which will develop creativity, not contentment; which will facilitate each person in his self-directed process of becoming; which will aid individuals, groups, and even the concept of science, to become self-transcending in freshly adaptive ways of meeting life and its problems. The choice is up to us, and the human race being what it is, we are likely to stumble about, making at times some nearly disastrous value choices, and at other times highly constructive ones.

If we choose to utilize our scientific knowledge to free men, then it will demand that we live openly and frankly with the great paradox of the behavioral sciences. We will recognize that behavior, when examined scientifically, is surely best understood as determined by prior causation. This is the great fact of science. But responsible personal choice, which is the most essential element in being a person, which is the core experience in psychotherapy, which exists prior to any scientific endeavor, is an equally prominent fact in our lives. We will have to live with the realization that to deny the reality of the experience of responsible personal choice is as stultifying, as closed-minded, as to deny the possibility of a behavioral science. That these two important elements of our experience appear to be in contradiction has perhaps the same significance as the contradiction between the wave theory and the corpuscular theory of light, both of which can be shown to be true, even though incompatible. We cannot profitably deny our subjective life, any more than we can deny the objective description of that life.

In conclusion then, it is my contention that science cannot come into being without a personal choice of the values we wish to achieve. And these values we choose to implement will forever lie outside of the science which implements them; the goals we select, the purposes we wish to follow, must always be outside of the science which achieves them. To me this has the encouraging meaning that the human person, with his capacity of subjective choice, can and will always exist, separate from and prior to any of his scientific undertakings. Unless as individuals and groups we choose to relinquish our capacity of subjective choice, we will always remain free persons, not simply pawns of a self-created behavioral science.

References

1. Huxley, A. *Brave New World.* New York and London: Harper and Bros., 1946.
2. Meerloo, J. A. M. Medication into submission: the danger of therapeutic coercion. *J. Nerv. Ment. Dis.*, 1955, **122**, 353-360.
3. Niebuhr, R. *The Self and the Dramas of History.* New York: Scribner, 1955.
4. Oppenheimer, R. Science and our times. *Roosevelt University Occasional Papers.* 1956, **2**, Chicago, Illinois.
5. Orwell, G. *1984.* New York: Harcourt, Brace, 1949; New American Library, 1953.
6. Popper, K. R. *The Open Society and Its Enemies.* London: Routledge and Kegan Paul, 1945.
7. Ratner, J. (Ed.). *Intelligence in the Modern World: John Dewey's Philosophy.* New York: Modern Library, 1939.
8. Rogers, C. R. *Client-Centered Therapy.* Boston: Houghton Mifflin, 1951.
9. Rogers, C. R. and Rosalind Dymond (Eds.). *Psychotherapy and Personality Change.* University of Chicago Press, 1954.
10. Skinner, B. F. Freedom and the control of men. *Amer. Scholar*, Winter, 1955-56, **25**, 47-65.
11. Skinner, B. F. *Science and Human Behavior.* New York: Macmillan, 1953. Quotation by permission of The Macmillan Co.
12. Skinner, B. F. *Walden Two.* New York: Macmillan, 1948. Quotations by permission of The Macmillan Co.
13. Whyte, W. H. *The Organization Man.* New York: Simon & Schuster, 1956.

Part Three

Phenomenological Theory

5　Kurt Lewin

Kurt Lewin's (1890-1947) contribution to psychology was extensive. Though some aspects of his contribution—such as his attempts to develop a mathematical field theory of human behavior—have been severely criticized, in most respects his originality as a psychologist stands unchallenged. Lewin saw clearly the necessity for a rapprochement between the clinical and experimental bodies of psychological knowledge. To this end he contributed his superb skill for analyzing and translating complex clinical concepts into experimentally manageable propositions. Throughout his career, Lewin devoted his creative talents to attempts to understand the vital aspects of man's behavior by using experimental methodology. He brought under experimental attack problems that had long remained in the province of the psychotherapist or the social worker. In so doing he broke the ground for experimental investigation in such virgin territories as regression, conflict behavior, and group dynamics. Examples of Lewin's work as a theoretical analyst and an experimental scientist are presented in the first two papers of this chapter.

Any personality theory that attempts to explain the phenomena of development must face the fact that development seldom follows a smooth, steady progression from old to new behavior patterns. Even in normal, healthy individuals the process of development will frequently reverse. Psychologists refer to these reversions as "regressions." In his theoretical paper, "Regression, Retrogression, and Development," Lewin attempts to differentiate the various meanings of regression and to indicate the kinds of phenomena that should be included in the concept. However, before the concept of regression can be of use to the science of psychology, we must have some notion about what constitutes normal development. Consequently, Lewin is also led to examine the directions which we may expect development to take.

The paper by Roger G. Barker, Tamara Dembo, and Kurt Lewin attempts to demonstrate experimentally that one of the possible antecedents of regression is frustration. It also attempts to determine what kinds of regression are produced by this variable. The experimental procedure is ingenious and represents Lewin's penchant for testing hypotheses in settings that are as natural and lifelike as possible. It is important to note how the Barker, Dembo, and Lewin definition of "regression" follows from Lewin's theory of personality development, which is articulated in the first selection of this chapter. For them, regression seems a "primitivization" of behavior, a regression in the *maturity* of performance rather than a return to *specific* immature behaviors. Child and Waterhouse, in their critique paper, call this a lowering of "quality of performance" and they argue that conceptualizing regression in this way is more theoretically and empirically useful since it allows one to take into account the possible progressive effects of frustration as well as the regressive effects. Thus, what Barker, Dembo, and Lewin attempted to measure in their experiment is the general level of *organization of behavior* before and after the introduction of frustration conditions. Frustration is operationally defined as preventing a person from doing something he wants to do; regression is operationally defined in terms of the "constructiveness (quality) of play" of the person's behavior.

Barker, Dembo, and Lewin used preschool-age children as their subjects. The children's behavior (playing with toys) is recorded by two observers under two different conditions: a nonfrustration condition and a frustration condition. The behaviors of the children in these two conditions are then compared to test the hypothesis that their play activity will be less constructive (more primitive) after frustration than before frustration.

In order to make quantitative comparisons of the subjects' behavior before and after frustration, Barker, Dembo, and Lewin had to develop a "constructiveness of play" scale, a kind of psychological yardstick. This was done by taking the behavior observations collected during the experiment, ordering these observations into "play units" according to certain criteria, and then having three judges rate these play units on a scale from 2 to 8, representing a continuum from low constructiveness (2) to high constructiveness (8). Each child's record was then scored according to this scale, and a formula was derived so that a "mean constructiveness score" could be computed for each subject. The final step in the development of the scale involved assessing the scale's *reliability* and *validity*. The *re-*

liability of the scale was evaluated by determining how *consistently* the scale classified play behavior. If a scale can be determined to be highly reliable, then one can place confidence in its ability to measure whatever it is measuring when it is applied in an experiment. The "whatever it is measuring" phrase in the preceding sentence relates to the scale's *validity*. In other words, is the scale measuring what it is supposed to measure? In this instance, it was supposed to be measuring the constructiveness of play, which had been related operationally to the theoretical construct of regression. According to the theory, the older the child, the more constructive his play. Thus, the play of older children should be rated as more constructive than the play of younger children. The statistical technique used here is the computation of the correlation between the ages of the children and their constructiveness-of-play scores, the prediction being that this correlation will be high and positive.

Following the demonstration that their scale is both reliable and valid, Barker, Dembo, and Lewin then go on to use this scale in testing their hypothesis that frustration leads to regression.

The critique paper by Irvin L. Child and Ian K. Waterhouse attacks on logical and empirical grounds the conclusions of Barker, Dembo, and Lewin regarding not only the causal connection between frustration and regression but also the nature of the "regression" observed in the experiment. In a detailed reanalysis of the data and ideas of the experiment, they question the validity of the theory and the inferences drawn from the data. They then show that the data of the experiment actually generate a conclusion (namely, that frustration leads to a lowered quality of performance) that is more significant than the general conclusion of Barker, Dembo, and Lewin.

Suggestions for Further Reading

For the student who wishes to read Lewin in depth, his two books, *A Dynamic Theory of Personality* (1935) and *Principles of Topo-*

logical Psychology (1936), both published by McGraw-Hill and now in paperback editions, are highly recommended. Lewin's later interest in group dynamics is well represented in his 1948 Harper publication, *Resolving Social Conflicts: Selected Papers on Group Dynamics.*

Short biographies of Lewin can be found in articles by Gordon Allport and Edward Tolman, two psychologists who were influenced by Lewin. The article by Allport, "The Genius of Kurt Lewin," is in the *Journal of Personality,* 1947, volume 16, pages 1-10. Tolman's article, "Kurt Lewin, 1890-1947," is

published in *Psychological Review,* 1948, volume 55, pages 1-4. An excellent recently published biography that should be read by any student interested in his theory of personality is *Kurt Lewin: The Practical Theorist* (1969) by Alfred J. Marrow, published by Basic Books.

The excellent book by F. H. Allport (Gordon's younger brother), *Theories of Perception and the Concept of Structure,* published in 1955 by Wiley, contains a searching analysis and critique of Lewin's theory as phenomenology.

Regression, Retrogression, and Development

Kurt Lewin

Kinds of Regression

Regression of Behavior and of the Person: Pseudo-Regression

A girl of two years stands before a mirror making herself small and tries to find out how she would look if she really were small. The situation in which this behavior occurs is as follows. The girl has a baby brother of whom she is envious. She is obviously trying to make up her mind whether she should try to grow up or grow smaller. Numerous cases exist in which children in such a situation try to imitate their younger siblings and begin to show babylike behavior in their table manners, in their way of crying, or in being naughty, etc.

Is this regression? If we refer only to the face value of this behavior we may have to speak of regression in line with the definition given above. The style of behavior has been lowered from a pattern typical of a three-year level to that of a two-year level. Nevertheless, one hesitates to identify such a change with regression resulting from sickness or acute emotional tension. The girl, showing the behavior of her younger brother, may actually "play a role," although that of a younger child. This role may be played with the skill of a good actor, although not as a play but in earnest. It would probably be fairer to call it refined rather than primitive behavior.

If the child keeps up such a role for a long time she actually may become primitive. She may lose, at least to some degree, her ability to act more mature. Until such a state is reached we may speak of a "pseudo-regres-

sion of behavior" without a "regression of the person." In other words, regression of behavior may or may not be a symptom of regression of the person.

Similarities of behavior are not necessarily indications of similarities of the underlying state of the person. That the same state of the person can manifest itself in rather different symptoms has been shown in detail in regard to anger (Dembo, 1931) and holds for all fields of psychology. It follows from the basic formula that the behavior (B) is a function of the person (P) and the environment (E), i.e., $B = F (P, E)$. This makes it necessary to distinguish the directly observable "symptoms" (B) from the underlying "state of the person" (P) which methodologically always has the position of a "construct."

In connection with developmental states it means that the maturity level of a person may actually be higher or lower than that indicated by his behavior. The girl mentioned above is an example of the former case. An example of the latter is found in the child who sticks to certain imposed rules in a way which is typical of a greater "maturity of aspiration" and shows in consequence in many respects a more adultlike behavior as a result of firm pressure from the outside; he will behave on a lower maturity level as soon as the pressure is released.

The distinction between regression of behavior and regression of the person is closely related to the necessity of referring to comparable situations if one wishes to use differences of behavior as symptoms for differences in the state of the person.

Temporary and Permanent Regression

Regression may last only a few minutes, for instance in a case of a slight shock, dis-

From K. Lewin, *Field Theory in Social Science*, ed. D. Cartwright, pp. 96-113. Copyright 1951 by Harper & Brothers. Reprinted by permission of Harper & Row, Publishers, Inc., New York, and Tavistock Publications Ltd., London.

turbance, or emotion, or it may last many years, for example as a result of sickness. Regression may be a slow sinking or a sudden drop. The individual may stay regressed, he may slowly or suddenly regain his previous level, or he may return to an intermediate level.

Situational and Established Regression

Under emotional stress both the behavior and the person may regress to a more primitive level. In such circumstances the individual is actually unable to behave on a higher level. Yet even in this case the primitivation may be confined to a particular situation, such as "being in prison" or "being severely frustrated." As soon as the person leaves this particular situation he may regain his previous level. In other cases the person may regress in such a way that he will not show his previous higher level even in a most favorable situation. The former case we will call *situational* regression, the latter *established* regression. There exist, of course, transitional cases.

It is important not to identify this difference with the distinction between temporary and permanent regression. A permanent regression may result from the fact that the individual is kept permanently within one specific situation; a regression may be relatively permament and still situational. The terms situational and established regression do not refer to duration. In case of situational regression the developmental level fluctuates greatly with changes in the situation, whereas the established regression is more independent of such changes. This distinction is of practical importance for the diagnosis and treatment of cases, such as in social-psychiatric work with children. It is clear that experiments with human beings have to be limited to creating situational regression.

Partial and General Regression

Regression may affect more or less restricted areas of a person. For example, regression may affect only the motor functions, or the emotional life of a person, without much change in his intellectual capacities. Psychopathology gives many examples of different patterns of regression of specific areas of the person as well as general deterioration. Of course any regression of specific areas does, to some degree, affect all behavior of the individual.

Main Differences in Behavior at Different Age Levels

In order to understand the situations which lead to regression, it will be necessary to develop definite concepts which characterize the behavior and state of the person corresponding to different developmental levels. This should be done in such a way as to permit a logical derivation of statements in regard to forces which change a person from the state corresponding to a higher level to the state corresponding to a lower level. If this task were fulfilled one would have a full theory of regression which would permit predictions about the amount and the kind of regression of a given person under various circumstances.

It is evident that such a goal can be reached only very gradually. We will try first of all to give a survey of what one might call the main aspects of behavior differences at the different age levels. We will then proceed to discuss certain kinds of constructs which may make possible the conceptual representation of the state of the person in such a way that at least some of the behavior differences may be understood and some conditions of regression derived.

The differences of behavior at different age levels may be classed under the following five aspects: variety of behavior, organization of behavior, extension of areas of activity, interdependence of behavior, and degree of realism.

Variety of Behavior

One speaks of the increasing variety of the behavior of a child as he grows older. (This holds true despite the fact that certain types of behavior drop out during development.) The increasing variety of behavior is noticeable in many ways.

a. The *behavior* of the newborn is more or less confined to sleeping, crying, drinking, eliminating, and lying awake. The behavior of the growing child includes increasingly more types of activities: talking, walking, reading, etc. The undifferentiated behavior becomes differentiated by a branching out into a variety of species of action. For instance, an approach to a goal is at first always a direct approach. Later on, indirect ways of approach arise by means of roundabout routes and the use of physical and social tools. In addition, the direct approach shows more variety, for instance, in the degree of activeness, the amount of real or gesturelike behavior, etc. The indirect approach becomes differentiated in regard to the kind of physical and social tools used. Similar differentiation can be observed in practically all fields of activities (Irwin, 1932). The language of the individual increases in regard to the number of words used (McCarthy, 1930; Smith, 1926), the types of words used, and the grammatical construction. If one regards the activities as possibilities that the individual has, one speaks of an increase in the variety of "skills."

b. A similarly increasing variety can be observed in the field of *emotions* (Bridges, 1931; Goodenough, 1931). Again, primitive undifferentiated emotional expressions branch out into distinct varieties. At first joy may be difficult to distinguish from a grimace caused by stomach trouble. Later, smiling is something rather distinct in character and unmistakable. Step by step more types of smiles arise, such as friendly open smiles, happy smiles, arrogant smiles, defiant smiles, and so on.

c. A similar differentiation can be observed in the field of *needs,* interests, and goals. Step by step the few needs of the infant branch out into a greater variety. This increase is very noticeable during childhood. In addition, there occurs a shift in the dominance of certain needs.

d. The process of differentiation into a great variety is particularly clear in the field of *knowledge.* The comparatively undifferentiated psychological world of the infant widens and structures itself in a process which can be described as differentiation (Koffka, 1935). The change in knowledge includes many cognitive changes which are restructurization rather than an increase in varieties of areas. However, one of the predominant characteristics of the change of knowledge with age, both in regard to learning and insight, is its increased differentiation, its greater richness.

e. The *social behavior* and the social relations show an increasing variety. The number of persons with whom social relations exist increases as do the types of social interrelations. The relations to different individuals become more and more articulated as to specific kinds of friendship, dependence or leadership. A clearer distinction is made between superficial and deeper attachments.

On the whole then, we may say that the variety of behavior increases during childhood with normal development. This may be expressed by the formula:

$$(1) \; var \; (B^{Ch}) \; < \; var \; (B^{Ad})$$

where *var* means variety; B^{Ch} behavior of the child; B^{Ad} behavior of the adult. To simplify our formulistic representation and to indicate that we merely wish to characterize the main trends of development, we will refer in the formulas to two levels only, indicated as *Ch* and *Ad*.

Organization of Behavior

If development in behavior led merely to an increased variety of behavior, one might expect the conduct of an individual to become more and more chaotic or at least more and more unconnected. This is obviously not the case. Parallel to the increasing differentiation goes a development according to which an increasingly greater variety of parts is included in *one* unit of action. There are a number of ways in which different actions may become parts of a larger unit of action. Frequently the unity of a behavior which is carried through a certain period of time and containing a number of more or less different subparts is characterized by one leading idea which guides and controls the parts. This leading idea may be a governing purpose or the reaching of a goal. The subparts may be certain preparations, followed by actions which carry the individual to the goal, and finally certain consummatory actions. In this case, some of the subparts of the action have the relation of means to an end. The guiding purpose may be a precise goal, such as scaling a fence, or a more general idea, like playing house. In other cases, for instance in many recreational or play activities, such as reading a book, the various parts have mainly the character of coordinated subunits.

In connection with all types of unity in behavior that are due to the guidance or steering of a governing purpose or a leading idea we will speak of the organization of behavior.[1] In these cases one can distinguish at least two levels: the guiding idea and the guided manipulation.

In development one can distinguish three aspects of the organization of behavior.

Complexity of Units. One can say that the maximum number of subparts and the variety of subparts contained in one unit of action increases with development. Instead of handling two building blocks at a time the child as he grows older uses an increasingly greater number of building blocks in making a primitive pattern. One symptom of the greater complexity is the increasing maximum duration of continuous play with increasing age (Bühler, 1935).

Hierarchical Organization. Aside from the increasing number of manipulations which may be kept together by a guiding idea, the type of organization itself seems to become more and more complicated: a goal which steers a series of manipulations may become the subgoal of a more inclusive goal.

The subgoals seem to be governed by the higher goals in much the same fashion as the actual manipulation is governed by the subgoal. For instance, the main idea of playing house may contain a number of subideas; father goes to work, mother dresses the children, does the washing, etc.—all established in a certain sequence guided by the main idea. A subgoal such as dressing the children may contain dressing Mary and dressing George. In other words, a more inclusive unit of behavior may contain a number of hierarchical levels, each of which is ruled by the next higher level. Referring to the number of levels we will speak of different "degrees of hierarchical organization" of a behavioral unit.

The maximal degree of hierarchical organization seems to increase with age, i.e., one unit can contain more levels in older than in younger children.

Complicated Organization. An activity guided by one idea may not be carried through as a continuous action but may be interrupted by other activities and later taken up again. To carry through successfully an activity which is to be repeatedly interrupted obviously requires a relatively complicated organization. A second kind of complicated organization exists in overlapping behavior, when simultaneously two or more activities which are guided by practically unrelated ideas are carried on. An example of such behavior is secondary play, i.e., play which occurs simultaneously with other activities, such as a conversation with a second person about matters unrelated to the play. Closely related to this is the organization of behavior which has two levels of meaning. Lying, joking, showing overfriendly behavior out of hate or similar "perverted expressions" are actions on two levels which may be said to be more or less contradictory. The more overt level frequently serves to cover up the contrary meaning of the deeper level, and indicates a somewhat complicated organization of the action. Obviously, the problem of self-control is closely related to this type of organization.

Lies and jokes are rather early achievements. However, the lying of the two-year-old child is relatively overt and primitive. The

[1]Frequently the term "integration" is used in this connection. We prefer to speak of organization because, mathematically, integration is the reverse of differentiation. However, it has been rightly emphasized that psychological "integration" does not mean dedifferentiation. It may be better to replace this term by the term "organization." This use of the term "organization" seems to be well in line with its use in embryology and also in sociology.

ability to exhibit this type of complicated organization seems to increase with age.

It cannot be said that every action of an older child is more highly organized than every action of a younger child. The behavior of an older child frequently includes units which are less complicated than those of younger children. However, the maximum degree of organization of behavioral units seems to increase with age; in other words, we can say:

$$(2) \ hier \ org^{max} \ (B^{Ch}) < hier \ org^{max} \ (B^{Ad})$$

where *hier org^{max}* stands for the maximum degree of hierarchical organization; B^{Ch} for the behavioral unit of a child; B^{Ad} for the behavioral unit of an adult.

Extension of the Area of Activities and Interests

The psychological world which affects the behavior of the child seems to extend with age both in regard to the areas and the time span which are taken into consideration.

Scope of the Field. The three-month-old child living in a crib knows few geographical areas around him, and the areas of possible activities are comparatively few. The child of one year is familiar with a much wider geographical area and a wider field of activities. He is likely to know a number of rooms in the house, the garden, and certain streets. Some of these areas are accessible to him, others are not. He may be able to crawl under the table or the couch, but he may not be able to climb on a certain chair although he would like to do so. Such areas of his life space lie outside his space of free movement (Lewin, 1938), which is limited partly by his own ability and partly by social taboos. The child may, for instance, like to tear books. In this case, tearing books is an area in his life space and may influence his behavior considerably. This is true even though the "no" of the mother keeps the child outside this area of activity. The discrepancy between the attractive areas of the life space and the space of free movement is one of the dominant factors

determining the level of aspiration of an individual.

During development, both the space of free movement and the life space usually increase. The area of activity accessible to the growing child is extended because his own ability increases, and it is probable that social restrictions are removed more rapidly than they are erected as age increases, at least beyond the infant period. Certain events, like the arrival of a younger sibling, may well reverse the balance of change at a given period. However, even at times when the space of free movement is not increasing, the life space usually extends with age into new, partly accessible, partly inaccessible regions. The widening of the scope of the life space occurs sometimes gradually, sometimes in rather abrupt steps. The latter is characteristic for so-called crises in development. This process continues well into adulthood (Bühler, 1935).

Time Perspective. A similar extension of the life space during development occurs in what may be called the "psychological time dimension." During development, the scope of the psychological time dimension of the life space increases from hours to days, months, and years. In other words, the young child lives in the immediate present; with increasing age an increasingly more distant psychological past and future affect present behavior.

It may be possible to interpret the increasing extension of the life space merely as the combination of an increasing variety of behavior and of different types of organization of behavior. However, we prefer to express this change in a separate statement:

$$(3) \ L \ Sp \ (Ch) < L \ Sp \ (Ad)$$

where $L \ Sp \ (Ch)$ means the size of the life space of the child and $L \ Sp \ (Ad)$ the size of the life space of the adult.

Also, for the space of free movement (i.e., the totality of accessible regions within the life space) it holds on the average that:

$$(4) \ SFM \ (Ch) < SFM \ (Ad)$$

where *SFM* (*Ch*) means the size of the space of free movement of the child and *SFM* (*Ad*) the size of the space of free movement of the adult. However, the space of free movement may be narrowed down during certain developmental periods, such as when a child is subjected to a rigid regime.

Interdependence of Behavior

The statement that the individual becomes increasingly differentiated can have two meanings. It can mean that the variety of behavior increases, i.e., that the totality of behavior observable at a given age becomes less homogeneous. In this case, the term differentiation refers to relations of similarity and dissimilarity; it means "specialization" or "individualization." On the other hand, the term differentiation can refer to relations of dependence and independence between parts of a dynamic whole. In this case, increasing differentiation means that the number of parts of the person which can function relatively independently increases; i.e., that their degree of independence increases.[2] As we have already discussed the increasing variety of behavior, we will now turn to the questions of dependence and independence.

The statement that the child shows a greater unity than the adult has been emphasized in psychology relatively recently. Previously, it was customary to consider that the adult exhibited the greater unity, because in childhood different needs and different areas of activity may develop more or less independently. The adult, on the other hand, is more likely to have these different areas of activity integrated.

Today it is generally acknowledged that the development of the child includes an increase both in differentiation and in integration. Development seems to increase the number of relatively independent subparts of

the person and their degree of independence, thus decreasing the degree of unity of the individual. On the other hand, development involves integration which increases the unity of the person. As both of these processes advance at the same time, obviously, integration cannot be a process which is actually the reversal of differentiation. It does not eliminate differentiation, and it is not dedifferentiation. But, integration presupposes differentiation. To avoid misunderstandings we prefer, therefore, to use the term "organization" instead of integration.

The kind of functional interdependence which underlies the degree of organizational unity of a person must be different obviously from that kind of interdependence which underlies the degree of his differentiation. Concepts dealing with interdependence are on the level of constructs, and any attempt to determine more precisely the different types of interdependence presupposes a discussion of a number of constructs. We will approach them after surveying the empirical data referring to the individual's increasing differentiation on the one hand and his increasing organization on the other.

Decrease of Simple Interdependence. We start with those facts which indicate the increasing differentiation of the person.

Differentiation of the Motor Systems. The so-called mass action of the fetus and infant is a characteristic example of the undifferentiated reaction of the individual with his whole body rather than with certain limbs. The development of the child is characterized by an increasing differentiation of the motor functions, indicated by the increasing extent to which the different parts exhibit relatively independent actions. The development of grasping, for example (Halverson, 1931), starts with a tendency to approach the object simultaneously with eyes, legs, arms, mouth. Gradually, the other activities drop out and the child comes to use first his arms and his hands as relatively undifferentiated units and finally his fingers independently. It is probably fair to say that a young child shows a tendency to do everything with his whole

---

[2] In morphology the term "differentiation" is limited to cases where the parts become not only more independent but also different from each other. It would be advisable to use two different terms for the two concepts of differentiation. We shall speak of "specification" or "individualization" in case of increasing dissimilarity, of "differentiation" in referring to increasing independence.

body to a greater degree than an older child. The gradual decrease of the so-called involuntary accompanying movements is but another expression of the same fact. In a child, the increase of tonus in one part of the muscular system is more likely to be accompanied by tonus in other parts than in an adult. In other words, the motor system shows an increasing differentiation as regards muscular tension.

Interdependence of Inner Personal and Motor Regions. A similar decrease in degree of interdependence can be observed in the way needs or emotions express themselves. The amount of muscular activity in the infant is a direct function of its hunger (Irwin, 1932). It is probably true that for older children and adults a similar relation exists between hunger and amount of restlessness, fighting and other emotional expressions. However, this dependence is less direct. The satiated infant is whole-heartedly satiated; he is drunk; his body expresses his state in every aspect, and he is helpless against its expression. The older child is more self-controlled. His motor system does not show as openly his needs and his emotional state. In other words, with increasing age there is less direct interdependence between the motor systems and the "inner personal systems," i.e., those regions of the person which are related to his needs.

The decrease in direct dependence between these two sections of the person is apparent, also, in the effect which the state of the motor system has upon the inner personal region. With the younger child, the mood and practically every sector of behavior depends more directly on bodily state, e.g., fatigue, hunger, upset stomach, etc., than with older children.

Interdependence within the Inner Personal Regions. Certain facts indicate that the various needs may become less directly interdependent also. The cosatiation of one need through the satiation of another decreases with age (Kounin, 1941). Experiments on substitute value (Sliosberg, 1934) indicate that the satisfaction of one need is more likely to bring about a general state of satisfaction in younger than in older children. For older individuals the state of tension of the various needs is independent to a higher degree.

Interdependence of Person and Environment. The very young child is helplessly exposed to the stimuli of the momentary situation. The older child can more easily place himself above the situation. This difference has been found to be essential for the conduct of infants and older children in a conflict situation. It is partly the result of the change in time perspective, but it indicates also a greater "functional distance" between the "ego" and the psychological environment. Spencer (1872, p. 316) and more recently Piaget (1937, p. 360) have discussed this greater remoteness or greater "distance" between the central ego of the person and the environment. The growing child becomes differentiated into an increasing number of more central and more peripheral layers. It is also true that the "superficial" aspects of things and events in the perceived environment become increasingly distinguished from their "deeper" meaning.

The greater distance between the central layer of the ego and the psychological environment involves a greater independence, or at least a less direct interdependence between those areas of the life space, namely the psychological person and the psychological environment. It makes the child less helpless against the immediate influences of his environment, and makes the perceived environment less dependent on the mood and the momentary state of the needs of the child. We know that the adult will perceive a given physical setting as a different psychological environment if his needs, fears, wishes, etc., change. However, the dependence of the perceived environment on the needs and fears of the individual is probably more complete and more immediate in the child. Fantasy and reality, lies and truths, seem to be more interwoven in the child than in the adult and more so in a younger child than in an older one.

On the whole, then, there are a great number of facts which indicate that development brings about a differentiation within the life space of an individual so that certain parts of it become less directly interdependent. This decrease in direct interdependence is observable within the motor system of the individual, within his inner personal regions, in the relation between the inner personal and the motor regions, and finally in the relation between the inner psychological regions and the psychological environment. We may express this observation by the formula:

$$(5) \; si \; uni \; (Ch) \; > \; si \; uni \; (Ad)$$

where *si uni* (*Ch*) means the degree of unity of the child as indicated by the degree of simple interdependence of certain subparts of the child's life space and *si uni* (*Ad*) means the degree of unity of the adult.

In addition we can state:

$$(5a) \; dif \; (Ch) \; < \; dif \; (Ad)$$

where *dif* (*Ch*) and *dif* (*Ad*) mean the degree of differentiation of the child and of the adult.

Change in Organizational Interdependence. The increasing differentiation of the life space into relatively separated subparts is somehow counteracted by the increasing organization of the life space. There is a wealth of material which indicates this increasing organization with age. It refers to the increasing scope of coexisting parts of the life space which can be organized as a unit and the increasingly larger sequence of actions which are unitedly governed. The latter point has already been discussed.

Organization of the Motor Systems. Psychologists have collected a great number of data which reveal the increasing organization of the motor functions in development. For example, the child's postural control of his head, and his learning to sit and to stand; the stages of the development of locomotion, such as creeping, walking, climbing, running, jumping; the development of speech; and the control of elimination can all be viewed as examples of the increasing organization of the various parts of the motor system for unified action. The organization of different muscular systems into constellations and of the constellations into sequences of constellations both show an increase to more and more complicated types. The precision of motor organization is indicated by the increasing accuracy of voluntary movements (Wellman, 1925). Talking presupposes the

organization of highly complicated sequences of muscular constellations.

Organization of the Motor System by the Inner Personal Regions. The relation between the inner personal and the motor regions acquires increasingly the character of an organization in which the motor functions take the place of a tool. The following example illustrates this change. A young child who wishes to perform a manipulation, such as threading a needle, is likely to get muscularly more tense the more eager he is to succeed, even if the task is of such a nature that the muscles have to be relatively relaxed if the task is to be carried out. In other words, in a young child a greater inner personal need tension is likely to lead to a higher muscular tonus. This is in line with the direct, simple interdependence of the inner personal and motor systems discussed previously.

If the unorganized "spreading of tension" from the inner personal to the motor regions becomes too dominant, it necessarily blocks any orderly purposeful muscular action. In the "organized" dependence of the motor functions upon the inner personal regions there is not a general increase in tonus, but rather sequences of relaxation and tonus in certain groups of muscles occur and are steered in such a way that the pattern of action and the intensity of tonus is adequate for reaching the objective in the given setting. This presupposes that the pattern and intensity of muscular tonus is independent of the intensity of the tension corresponding to the need behind the action. For threading a needle, the muscles have to be relatively relaxed, even if the person is most eager to hurry; for carrying a heavy load the tonus has to be high, even if the need for doing this work is small. With increasing age the organized interdependence seems to gain in strength relative to the simple interdependence; and the position of the motoric system as a tool becomes more firmly established.

Organization of the Inner Personal Regions. In discussing the increasing differentiation of inner personal regions, we dealt with the simple interdependence of needs, i.e., the spreading of tension. The effect of the tension within one need system upon the general tension level of the need systems of an individual (Birenbaum, 1930) can be understood as such a spreading. The process of cosatiation of one need by the satiation of another need (Karsten, 1928) seems also to have the characteristics of spreading.

It seems, however, that a second type of interdependence between inner personal regions exists which has the characteristics of an organizational interdependence: one system may hold the position of a governing need, the other the position of a governed need. An individual may, for instance, show a great desire to join an art school. This need may be derived from and be governed by the need for doing art work. The need to enter the art school may in turn create and regulate a need for fulfilling certain requirements, such as preparing for an entrance examination; and this, in turn, the *quasi* need to buy a certain book in a certain store. In other words, there may exist a hierarchy of needs so that a more dominant need rules one or more subordinate needs which in turn dominate subordinate needs at the next lower level.

Frequently the dominated need is set up by a combination of more than one governing need. For instance, the need to enter art school may have its historical source in the need for doing art work and in the additional need to earn a living for which the school work seems to be a preparation. The derived need to enter art school may become more or less autonomous, that is, more or less independent of the needs to which it can be traced. We wish to stress here that the attempt to secure the satisfaction of one or more source needs in a given environmental situation may give rise to a dependent need. This type of dependence does not involve spreading of tension, but here one need is governed by another, one need is a tool of another. In other words, this is an organizational dependence similar to that between the motor systems and the inner personal regions. The hierarchy of organizational interdependence between needs seems to increase during development.

Organization of the Psychological Environment. The increasing organization of the psychological environment by the individual does not need much illustration. Simple examples of such an organization are the use of some parts of the environment as tools. The growing child becomes increasingly more able to organize parts of his physical and of his social environment in this way, and this organization becomes increasingly complicated, particularly in the social field. The approach to a goal by way of roundabout routes, instead of by direct action, also exemplifies the ability of the child to organize intelligently his actions in relation to an increasingly greater scope of his psychological environment. Such organization presupposes a decrease in the simple dependence of the person upon his immediate surroundings. For satisfying his needs the infant depends mainly on the circumstances which arise. Actually, he would die if these occasions were not provided by a grownup. The growing child tries increasingly to organize his environment so that the satisfaction of his needs is not left to chance. In other words, the life space containing the psychological person and his environment tends to become a more highly organized unit. Such an organization is frequently facilitated by certain ideologies and rationalizations which bring certain otherwise contradictory facts and needs into psychological harmony with each other.

On the whole, then, the hierarchical organization of the life space increases with age. Such an increase can be observed within the motor system, within the inner psychological regions, in the relation of the motor to the inner psychological regions, and in the relation of the psychological environment to the inner personal regions. We can express this change through the formula:

$$(6)\ hier\ org\ (Ch) < hier\ org\ (Ad)$$

where *hier org* (*Ch*) means the degree of hierarchical organization of parts of the child's life space, and (*Ad*) refers to the life space of the adult. Formula (6) is closely related to (2). The latter refers to the hierarchical organization of the single unit of behavior, the former to the hierarchical organization of the individual as a whole.

That the number of hierarchical strata increases during development does not necessarily mean a steady increase in the unity of he person. The older child does not always show a more harmonious personality or a personality more strictly governed by one center. One has, rather, to expect ups and downs in the degree of unity of the person, whereby differentiation tends to decrease the unity from time to time and organization to reestablish or to increase the unity on consecutively higher levels. The degree of organizational unity (*org uni*) at a later developmental level can therefore be either greater or smaller than that of an earlier level. We can express this through the formula:

$$(7)\ org\ uni\ (Ch) \lesseqgtr org\ uni\ (Ad)$$

There seem to be great individual differences in regard to the degree of organizational unity of the grownup.

Finally, one can probably make the following statement in regard to organization. The importance of processes of organization (interdependence of the organizational type) seems to increase during development relative to the importance of simple interdependence (of the type of spreading tension):

(8)
$$\frac{weight\ (org\ interdep)}{weight\ (simple\ interdep)}\ (Ch) < \frac{weight\ (org\ interdep)}{weight\ (simple\ interdep)}\ (Ad)$$

In summarizing the symptoms for the change of dependence of the different parts of the person (life space) during development, we present the schematic Figure 1. There are definite indications of a decreasing unity on the basis of "simple interdependence" of certain parts of the life space and of the life space as a whole, resulting from an increasing differentiation. At the same time, the degree of hierarchical organization of these parts of the life space and of the life space as a whole increases. The degree of unity of the person based on "organizational interdependence" fluctuates.

Degree of Realism

We have mentioned that during development the perceived environment seems to

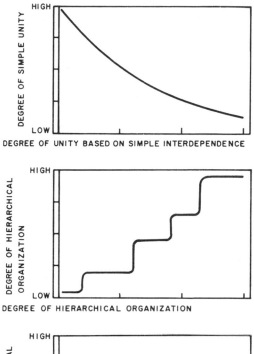

DEGREE OF UNITY BASED ON SIMPLE INTERDEPENDENCE

DEGREE OF HIERARCHICAL ORGANIZATION

DEGREE OF UNITY BASED ON ORGANIZATIONAL INTER-DEPENDENCE

Figure 1. Schematic representation of certain changes during development. The degree of unity based on simple interdependence decreases with age; the degree of hierarchical organization increases stepwise; the degree of organizational unity varies.

become less "subjectively colored." What is perceived is less directly dependent on the changing moods and the needs of the individual. This increasing realism of perception is particularly noticeable in the perception of social relations. In other words, reality and fantasy are more clearly distinguished. One might view this development merely as an expression of the increased differentiation of the life space, the increasing hierarchical organization. However, we probably have to deal here with a somewhat different dimension of change, namely, an increasing crystallization of an objective world within the life space and an increasing tendency to be realistic. The world of an insane person may be as highly differentiated and organized as that of a normal person but may lack the realism of the latter.

Piaget (1937) has discussed in detail the growing realism of the child's world as shown in his various stages of thinking. A somewhat parallel process in the field of action shows one of the outstanding differences between a child's and an adult's behavior to be that the child does not "economize" his action to the same degree. To be efficient, striving to obtain a maximum result with a minimum effort, is an attitude typical of the older individual. We have to deal here with a specific organization in reference to the properties of the objective world.

One can express this change by the formula:

$$(9) \ real \ (Ch) < real \ (Ad)$$

where *real (Ch)* means the degree of realism of the child and *real (Ad)* the degree of realism of the adult. However, we are aware that children are frequently more realistic than adults in some respects; for instance, they may be less blinded by ideologies. The statement (9) therefore is made very tentatively, with the intention mainly of pointing to an important aspect of development.

As main differences in the behavior of the child of different age levels, we have mentioned changes in the variety of behavior, in the organization of behavior, in the extension of the life space, in the unity of the person, and in the degree of realism. We do not, however, mean to suggest that these are the only behavioral changes typical of development.

References

Allport, Gordon W. *Personality: A psychological interpretation.* New York: Holt, 1937.

Birenbaum, Gita. Das Vergessen einer Vornahme. *Psychol. Forsch.,* 1930, **13**, 218-284.

Bridges, K. M. *The social and emotional development of the preschool child.* London: Kegan, Paul, Trench, Trubmer, 1931.

Bühler, Charlotte. *From birth to maturity: An outline of the psychological development of the child.* London: Kegan, Paul, 1935.

Dembo, Tamara. Der Ärger als dynamisches Problem. *Psychol. Forsch.,* 1931, **15**, 1-144.

Goodenough, Florence L. *Anger in young children.* Univ. of Minnesota, Monogr. Series, No. 9, 1931.

Halverson, H. M. An experimental study of prehension in infants by means of systematic cinema records. *Genet. psychol. Monogr.,* 1931, **10**, 107-286.

Irwin, Orwis C. The amount of motility of seventy-three newborn infants. *J. comp. Psychol.,* 1932, **14**, 415-428.

Irwin, Orwis C. The distribution of amount of motility in young infants between two nursing periods. *J. comp. Psychol.,* 1932, **14**, 429-445.

Karsten, Anitra. Psychische Sättigung. *Psychol. Forsch.,* 1928, **10**, 142-254.

Koffka, Kurt. *The growth of the mind: An introduction to child psychology.* Trans. by Robert Morris Ogden. 2nd ed. New York: Harcourt, Brace & Co., 1935.

Kounin, Jacob S. Experimental studies in rigidity. *Char. & Pers.,* 1941, **9**, 251-282.

Lewin, Kurt. The conceptual representation and the measurement of psychological forces. *Contrib. to Psychol. Theory,* 1938, **1**, No. 4.

McCarthy, Dorothea A. *The language development of the preschool child.* University of Minnesota, Institute of Child Welfare Monograph Series, No. 4, 1930.

Piaget, Jean. *La construction du réel chez l'enfant.* Neuchatel:Delachaux, 1937.

Sliosberg, Sarah. Zur Dynamik des Ersatzes in Spiel und Ernstsituationen. *Psychol. Forsch.,* 1934, **19**, 122-181.

Smith, M. E. An investigation of the development of the sentence and the extent of vocabulary in young children. *Univ. Iowa Stud. in Child Welf.,* 1926, **3**, No. 5.

Spencer, Herbert. *The principles of psychology.* London: Williams & Norgate, 1872.

Wellman, Beth L. The development of motor coordination in young children: An experimental study in the control of hand and arm movements, *Univ. Iowa Stud. in Child Welf.,* 1925, **3**, No. 4.

Frustration and Regression

*Roger G. Barker,
Tamara Dembo, and
Kurt Lewin*

Introduction

In psychology the term "regression" refers to a primitivization of behavior, a "going back" to a less mature way of behaving which the individual has "outgrown." A temporary regression frequently occurs in intense emotional situations with normal adults and children, particularly if these situations are unpleasant. Extreme joy, too, may lead to certain primitive actions. Fatigue, oversatiation, and sickness often cause transient regression. A more or less permanent type of regression can be observed in certain cases of senility, in a great variety of neuroses, and in functional and organic psychoses. Regression, therefore, has to be considered a common phenomenon which is related to many situations and problems and which concerns the total behavior of the person rather fundamentally.

The relation between regression and development is of special interest and significance. Knowledge of psychological development has increased considerably during the last decade. An impressive variety of developmental processes has been revealed. However, our knowledge of the factors determining development is extremely meager. Regression can be viewed as a negative development. The experimental study of regression seems to be technically somewhat easier than that of development as it is ordinarily conceived. Therefore, the indirect way of studying the dynamics of development by studying regression may prove to be fruitful for the whole problem of development.

From R. G. Barker, J. S. Kounin, and H. F. Wright (Eds.), *Child Behavior and Development*, pp. 441-458. Copyright 1943 by McGraw-Hill, Inc. Reprinted by permission of the McGraw-Hill Book Company.

Our first step was to describe in conceptual terms the behavior and state of the person corresponding to different developmental levels. It was our hope that, since regression involves a reversal of the direction of these changes, such conceptualization might provide some basis for hypotheses as to the conditions which should lead to regression.

Developmental Stages

Degree of Differentiation

There is much evidence to indicate that during development the degree of differentiation of the person and of his behavior increases greatly. This is shown by the increasing variety in all aspects of the growing child's behavior, and the shift from generalized mass activity in the fetus and neonate to highly specialized actions in the child and adult. The change of the arm and hand, for example, from a highly unitary and inflexible reaching and prehensile organ in the infant to a highly differentiated instrument capable of many complicated and specialized actions in the child and adult is a case in point.

Type of Organization

The type of organization changes as the child develops. In the fetus and infant, organization of the parts is to a great extent in the nature of simple dependence of one part upon contiguous parts. Changes in state and function result from the diffuse spreading of influences to neighboring parts. With the increasing differentiation of the organism, however, a stratified or hierarchical type of organization becomes increasingly important. In this type of organization there is a series of levels of control. It is exemplified in such diverse fields as motor behavior, language, and play. In each of these the occurrence of increasing numbers of behavior possibilities—e.g., independent movements of digits, new words and parts of speech, new ideas—does not result in more chaotic behavior, as would be expected if the simple diffusion-of-influence type of organization persisted. Activities are extended to longer and longer episodes in which small units of action are guided and organized by larger intentions. The independent fingers become tools under the dominance of higher centers that can enforce upon them many kinds of organized unity, whereas with the undifferentiated hand but one form of unity is possible. The larger vocabulary does not result in more profuse babbling, but in sentences organized to express controlling ideas.

Scope

The scope of the child's life space increases with age. In the present connection we are particularly interested in the lengthening of time perspective (Frank, 1939). The infant lives in the present, but behavior becomes increasingly controlled by goals and expectations that are temporally more and more remote as development proceeds.

Reality and Phantasy

During development the perceived environment seems to become less subjectively colored. What is perceived becomes less directly dependent on the changing moods and needs of the individual. In other words, reality and phantasy become more clearly distinguished, yet not completely separated (Lewin, 1935; Piaget, 1929). Creative activity seems to depend upon the maintenance of a particular relation between reality and phantasy. The too realistic person who does not have the imagination to "see" possibilities of changing the existing real situation cannot be creative; on the other hand, the dreamer who phantasies with no regard for the exigencies of reality is also unproductive.

There are, of course, many other characteristics of development, but these appear to be rather fundamental, and we assume that any influences that operate to change the child in directions that are opposed to them should lead to primitive behavior, i.e., lead to regression.

Conditions for Regression

This study reports an attempt to create regression in children by frustration. It can be viewed from two angles. (a) It is an attempt to clarify the nature of regression and the conditions leading to it by testing certain theoretical assumptions about regression. (b) It can be viewed as a contribution to the study of frustration.

Theoretical considerations suggest that one of the conditions which may lead to regression is a situation in which the person is in a state of blocked tension. From the description of developmental stages it follows that a state of high tension should lead to a regression in at least three respects. (a) If the state of tension in some parts is maintained at a high level, the variety of patterns of states of the person which can be realized will be greatly diminished (Barker et al., 1941, pp. 40, 247). (b) If the tension is so great that it spreads beyond the parts immediately involved and extends to the whole organism or to large parts of it, an obliteration of the divisions between weakly differentiated parts will result. In both of these cases a condition of high tension produces a dedifferentiation of the person. This, as we have seen, is a change in a direction opposite to that occurring in development, and it should show itself in a regression of behavior (Baker et al., 1941, p. 241). (c) In states of high tension the hierarchical organization is likely to be affected. The direct spreading of tension will be greater when the tension is high than when it is low; hence organization processes of the type of simple diffusion of tension will increase in importance relatively to hierarchical organizing processes. This, too, is a change opposite to developmental changes and should lead to regression (Barker et al., 1941, pp. 41, 257).

The experiments which we are going to report are not intended primarily to give proof that in a state of high tension the action toward an obstructed goal regresses to a primitive level. They are an attempt to go one step further. If the assumption is correct that a sufficiently high tension leads to regression of the individual, this condition should reveal itself not only in action toward the inaccessible goal, but also in behavior that is not related to this goal. Presenting a frustrating situation, i.e., one in which an individual is prevented from reaching a desired goal, is one way of creating tension.

Procedures

In the investigation we have studied the effects of frustration upon behavior by comparing the behavior of children in a nonfrustrating or free-play situation with their behavior in a frustrating situation. We have used as a major criterion of these effects the productivity or creativity of play behavior. We choose to use constructiveness of play as one of the main indicators of the effects of frustration for the following reasons. (a) It was assumed that the constructiveness of play would vary according to the developmental stage of the child. (b) It seemed probable that, in a free-play situation, where there is very little outside pressure, behavior would reveal with particular sensitivity the inner state of the child. (c) Constructiveness of play appeared to be closely related to many aspects of the child's life space, particularly

to reality and phantasy, to scope, and to degree of differentiation.

In addition to the constructiveness of play, emotional expression has been analyzed, also.

Every child was observed on two occasions. First, the child was placed in a standardized playroom and allowed to play without restriction. On a second occasion, he was placed in the same room and with the same toys. However, on this second occasion there were also in the room a number of highly attractive, *but inaccessible*, toys. The latter arrangement was provided by replacing a temporary wall of the original room with a wire-net partition through which the subject could easily see the fine toys but through which locomotion was impossible.

The subjects in the experiment were children who attended the preschool laboratories of the Iowa Child Welfare Research Station. The experiment was conducted during the academic year 1935-1936. Data concerning chronological and mental ages and I.Q.'s are given in Table 1. The Kuhlmann-Binet was used with the 10 younger subjects, the Stanford-Binet with the 20 older subjects.

Free-Play Situation

On the floor of the room there were three squares of paper, each 24 by 24 in. A set of standardized play materials was placed on each square. On one square there were the following things: a little chair on which a Teddy bear and a doll were seated, a cup, a small truck and trailer, a saucer, a teapot without a lid, an ironing board and an iron

Table 1. Chronological and mental age data for subjects.

	Chronological age, months	Mental age, months	I.Q.
10 Younger subjects:			
Range	25-40	30-44	100-141
Mean	32.3	36.9	114.8
20 Older subjects:			
Range	42-61	49-82	110-157
Mean	51.7	64.6	125.5
Total group, mean	45.2	55.4	121.9

(but nothing to iron), and a telephone receiver which squeaked when shaken. On another square were placed a box of crayons and two pieces of writing paper 8 1/2 by 11 in. On the third square there were a small wooden motorboat, a sailboat, a celluloid duck and frog, and a fishing pole with a line and a magnet for a hook.

After entering the experimental room with the child, the experimenter approached Square 1, and picking up each toy said, "Look, here are some things to play with. Here is a Teddy bear and a doll. Here is an iron to iron with," etc. In proceeding this way, the experimenter named and demonstrated every toy on all three squares. Then he said, "You can play with everything. You can do whatever you like with the toys, and I'll sit down here and do my lesson." The experimenter then sat on the chair at the table.

The child was left to play alone for a 30-min. period. During this time the experimenter, as if occupied with his own work, sat at his table in the corner and took notes on the child's behavior.

Frustration Situation

Prefrustration Period

Three parts of the frustration experiment can be distinguished in the temporal order of their occurrence: (a) the prefrustration period, (b) the frustration period, and (c) the postfrustration period. The partition dividing the room was lifted so that the room was twice the size it had been in the free-play situation.

The squares were in their places, but all toys except the crayons and paper had been incorporated into an elaborate and attractive set of toys in the part of the room that had been behind the partition.

In one corner there was a big dollhouse (3 by 3 ft.). It was brightly decorated and large enough to admit the child. Inside there was a bed upon which the doll was lying, a chair in which the Teddy bear sat, a stove with cook-

ing utensils, and a cupboard. The ironing board with the iron on it stood against one wall, and the telephone, this time on its base with a dial and bell, was in a corner. The house had electric lights, curtains, and a carpet.

Outside the house there was a laundry line on which the doll's clothes hung. A rubber rabbit sat near the entrance to the house, and behind it was a small truck and trailer used in the preceding experiment. Near by there was a child's table prepared for a luncheon party. On the table there were cups, saucers, dishes, spoons, forks, knives, a small empty teapot, and a large teapot with water in it.

In the other corner of the new part of the room there was a toy lake (3 by 3 ft.) filled with real water. It contained an island with a lighthouse, a wharf, a ferryboat, small boats, fishes, ducks, and frogs. The lake had sand beaches.

In all cases the children showed great interest in the new toys and at once started to investigate them. Each child was left entirely free to explore and play as he wished. During this time, the experimenter did his "lesson."

If, after several minutes, the child had played with only a limited number of objects, the experimenter approached and demonstrated the other toys; e.g., he dialed the telephone or showed the child how to get the water from the spout of the teapot. In general, the experimenter tried to call the child's attention to every toy he had overlooked. Then he returned to his place and waited until the child had become thoroughly involved in play; this took from 5 to 15 min.

The prefrustration period was designed to develop for the child a highly desirable goal which he could later be prevented from reaching. This was a prerequisite of creating frustration.

The transition from prefrustration to frustration was made in the following way. The experimenter collected in a basket all the play materials which had been used in the free-play experiment and distributed them, as before, on the squares of paper. He then approached the child and said, "And now let's play at the other end," pointing to the "old" part of the room. The child went or was led to the other end and the experimenter lowered the wire partition and fastened it by means of a large padlock. The part of the room containing the new toys was now physically inaccessible but visible through the wire netting.

Frustration Period

With the lowering of the partition, the frustration period began. This part of the experiment was conducted exactly as the free-play experiment. The experimenter wrote at his table, leaving the child completely free to play or not as he desired. The child's questions were answered, but the experimenter remained aloof from the situation in as natural a manner as possible.

Thirty minutes after the lowering of the partition, the experimenter suggested that the child leave.

Postfrustration Situation

After the experimenter had made sure that the child wanted to leave, the partition was lifted. Usually the child was pleasantly surprised and, forgetting his desire to leave, joyfully hurried over to the fine toys. If the child did not return spontaneously, the experimenter suggested his doing so, and a second suggestion was never necessary. The lifting of the partition at the end of the frustration period was not done with an experimental purpose, but to satisfy the desire of the child to play with the toys and to obviate any undesirable aftereffects. The child was allowed to play with the house, lake, etc., until he was ready to leave.

Results

The raw data consisted of two synchronized running accounts of the course of events, one made by an observer behind a one-way vision screen, the other by the experimenter. These separate records were combined into a single, more complete, account. This was desirable since it allowed the observers to concentrate their attention upon the different aspects of the behavior that they

could best observe. An observer behind a screen necessarily misses much: the verbalizations of the child are often incomprehensible, and facial expressions and gestures lose much of their significance. However, he can observe the larger aspects of the behavior adequately. On the other hand, the very wealth of detail which the experimenter within the room is able to observe causes him sometimes to miss the sequence of activities and their larger significance.

Both the free-play situation and the frustration situation produce two general kinds of behavior: (a) occupation with accessible goals, and (b) activities in the direction of inaccessible goals. We shall call the first "free activities" and the second "barrier and escape behavior." Playing with the available toys and turning on the light are examples of free activities; trying to leave the experimental situation or attempting to reach the inaccessible toys behind the barrier are examples of barriers and escape behavior. Within each of these categories it is useful to differentiate further.

Types of Behavior

Free Activities

The free activity includes play with the accessible toys and diversions with nontoy objects.

Diversions, i.e., occupation with nontoy objects, include the following: (a) *Activities with the experimenter* (other than those which are social attempts to reach the inaccessible toys or to escape from the experimental situation). This behavior takes the form of conversation with the experimenter, helping him with his "lessons," and playing with him. It has been mentioned before that every effort was made not to encourage these contacts. (b) *Activities at the window*: climbing upon the sill and looking out. (c) *"Island" behavior*: despite our continual vigilance in excluding any but standardized objects from the room, the children were forever finding additional material—e.g., a nail or a piece of string—or selecting for special attention some indifferent object in the room, as the light switch or a crack in the floor. Such objects not infrequently appeared to have the significance of a foreign object to the child, i.e., one not naturally connected with the rest of the situation, and as such to provide a refuge or an island of escape within the situation. (d) *Looking and wandering about.* (e) *Disturbances*: reactions to outside noises, lights failing, etc.

Barrier and Escape Behavior

Both attempts to gain access to the toys behind the barrier and attempts to leave the experimental situation may entail (a) actual physical approaches to the inaccessible regions, such as trying to lift or climb over the barrier or kicking the door; (b) social attempts by means of requests, pleadings, coaxing, threats, etc., to get the experimenter to raise the barrier or open the door; or (c) passive, directed actions such as looking at or talking about the inaccessible toys or the outside regions.

Overlapping Activities

A subject can be involved in more than one activity simultaneously; e.g., he may ask to have the barrier raised while swinging the fish line; in these cases we speak about "overlapping regions of activity." A type of overlapping behavior of special importance to us exists when play and nonplay activities overlap. We will call this "secondary play." Primary play, on the other hand, occurs when the subject gives the play his complete attention.

Substitute Behavior

Passive barrier and escape behavior frequently seemed to be in the nature of a substitute for playing with the inaccessible toys or for leaving the experimental situation. This was particularly true of conversation about the inaccessible objects. Active barrier and escape behavior also seemed sometimes to be a substitution; e.g., "fishing" through the barrier, throwing the accessible toys into the inaccessible region, playing that the

accessible portion of the room was a part of the inaccessible part, etc.

Emotional Behavior

Two sorts of emotional expression occurred: (a) "pure" emotional actions, e.g., whimpering, whining, restless actions, and (b) strong "emotional component" to barrier and escape behavior, play, etc.

Topology and Dynamics of the Frustration Situation

The simplest way to approach the situation of frustration is probably to treat it as a particular case of a limited space of free movement (Lewin, 1936). The space of free movement, i.e., the totality of accessible regions, may be limited by either an "inner" or an "outer" barrier or by both. In the first case, a goal region (G, Fig. 1a), a region with positive valence, is surrounded by a barrier region (B) separating it from the individual (P), who is otherwise free. In the second case, the individual is surrounded by a barrier, the goal being outside (Fig. 1b).

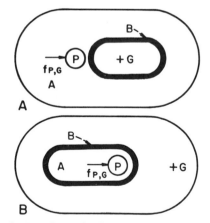

Figure 1. Topology of a frustration situation. P, person; G, goal; B, barrier; A, space of free movement; fP,G, force toward the goal. (a) The barrier surrounds the goal; otherwise the person is free. (b) The barrier surrounds the person.

For most of our subjects, Figure 1a seems to be an adequate representation for the early periods of the frustration situation, i.e., the subject sees himself separated from the fine toys without otherwise feeling himself to be in a prisonlike situation. Later, the situation usually changes to that represented in Figure 1b; he becomes imprisoned.

The barrier has for the child either the character of an "objective" physical obstacle or the character of an obstacle which is created and kept in place by the experimenter, i.e, a social barrier. Frequently it is a combination of both. This is why the action toward the inaccessible toys often takes the form of both a physical attack on the barrier and a social approach to the experimenter.

Sample Record

A part of a record will be given to acquaint the reader with the sequence and content of the course of events occurring during the experiment. This is the type of material with which we have had to work.

Child 22 is a girl fifty-three months old. Her I.Q. is 122.

Each unit of action is numbered consecutively. At the end of each unit the length of the unit in seconds is given and the constructiveness rating of the play. (Constructiveness ratings are discussed in the section immediately following.)

(*Free-Play Situation*)

1. *S:* "Here," to *E*, "you make me something from this clay."[1] She takes clay to Square 1 and asks, "Where are the other things?" (Referring to the toys present in another experiment.) "I want you to play with me." The experimenter continues recording. Constructiveness 2; 45 sec.

2. *S* throws clay onto Square 2. "This is an elephant." Then finding a small peg on the floor, "Look what I found. I'll put it at his eye." Looks at it. Makes elephant sit up. Constructiveness 6; 70 sec.

3. *S* starts to draw. "I'm going to draw a picture. Do you know what I'm going to draw? That will be a house. That is where you go in." Constructiveness 7; 45 sec.

4. Someone moves in another room. *S:* "Who is that?" 10 sec.

5. *S* goes to Square 1, shakes phone, and examines it. Manipulates phone, pretends conversation, but does not use words. ("How do . . ." are the

[1]In a few experiences a piece of modeling clay was included on the square with the crayons and paper.

only words that *E* can distinguish.) Constructiveness 5; 30 sec.

6. *S* sits down on chair and looks around. "I guess I'll sit here and iron." Repeats, then says gaily, "See me iron." Constructiveness 5; 45 sec.

(*Frustration Situation*)

1. *S* watches *E* lower the partition. She asks, "I will not play on the other side again?" *E* answers, "You can play here now." *S* faces the experimenter for about 15 sec. with hands behind her neck. 25 sec.

2. *S* looks around. 5 sec.

3. *S* goes to Square 3 and examines sailboat and fish pole. Constructiveness 2; 15 sec.

4. *S* stands at Square 3 and looks at barrier. 5 sec.

5. Turning to the play material on Square 3, *S* takes the fish line and dangles it about sailboat. Constructiveness 2; 20 sec.

6. *S* goes to the barrier and reaches through the meshes of the screen. 5 sec.

7. *S* turns around, looks at the experimenter, laughs as she does so. 15 sec.

8. *S* goes to Square 3, takes the fish pole, and returns to the barrier. She asks, "When are we going to play on that side?" Experimenter does not answer. Then, in putting the fish pole through the barrier, *S* says, "I guess I'll just put this clear back." She laughs and says, "Out it comes!" taking pole out again. Constructiveness 2; 35 sec.

9. *S* walks to experimenter's table. 10 sec.

10. *S* goes to Square 2 and manipulates clay. Constructiveness 2; 10 sec.

11. From Square 2 she looks at the objects behind the barrier and says, "I do not like the balloon," and then she asks, "Who put that house there?" *E* answers, "Some of my friends." She asks again, "Who put that over there?" 35 sec.

Constructiveness of Play

From this sample, the reader will gain an impression of the richness of the play which occurred. It is possible to use such manifold material for many purposes. In the present connection, we have been most interested in phases of the play that are related to the creative aspects of the child's behavior.

Constructiveness Scale

For this purpose we have made an analysis of the play activities on the basis of their constructiveness. One can distinguish variations in the type of play on a continuum ranging from rather primitive, simple, little-structured activities to elaborate, imaginative, highly developed play. We speak in the former case of low constructiveness; in the latter, of high constructiveness. In our experiment, constructiveness was rated on a seven-point scale (2 to 8) devised to be applicable to occupations with all the toys.

To demonstrate the use of this scale, we present a few examples of various constructiveness levels with the same toy, the truck and trailer. Our remarks are not definitions of the various constructiveness levels. They are intended merely to point to some characteristics of these specific examples.

Constructiveness 2. The toys are examined superficially. Example: Sits on floor and takes truck and trailer in hand. 10 sec.

Constructiveness 3. The truck is moved to a definite place or from one place to another. Example: Phone, truck and trailer, manipulated and carried to window sill. 25 sec.

Constructiveness 4. This is a somewhat more complicated manipulation of the truck. Example: Truck and trailer back under chair. 15 sec.

Constructiveness 5. This is definitely a more complicated and elaborated manipulation of the truck. Example: Truck and trailer unloaded, detached; pulled in circles, reattached, detached, reattached; pulled in circles. 45 sec.

Constructiveness 6. The truck is used as a means to haul other things. Example: Takes truck and trailer. "More things are going to be hauled." Puts cup, saucer, teapot on trailer. Talks to self. "Ride along, mister." To Square 3. 60 sec.

Constructiveness 7. The meaning of the play is an extensive "trip" or another elaborated story in which the handling of the truck is merely a part of a larger setting. Example: "Here's a car truck, and it's going out fishing, so we have to take the trailer off. First, we have to go to the gas station. Toot! Toot! Now, he's going to the gas station. Ding, ding, ding." Gets gas. Now back for the trailer and the fish pole: child has truck and takes the motor boat. Attaches it to truck and trailer. "Hmmmm! Here he goes." Behind Square 2 to 1. "Quack! Quack! Mr. Ducky come" (places on truck and trailer). Goes to Square 3. "Here's the sailboat." 225 sec.

Constructiveness 8. Play showing more than usual originality is placed here. Example: To Square 1. Truck and trailer reattached. "I'll bring them here." Detaches truck, has it coast down trailer as an incline, reattaches. 30 sec.

The scale was constructed in the following way: The play units were transcribed serially upon cards which were grouped according to the toy or group of toys involved. Three persons working in conference arranged the play units for each toy in order of their increasing constructiveness. No attempt at independent ranking was made. The resultant order represented the consensus of opinion of the raters after discussion, disagreement, and compromise. It became evident that, irrespective of particular theories of "constructiveness," it was possible to agree upon the relative ranking of different play with the same toys.

The play units were briefly characterized and the characterizations set down in tabular form. Each rank order was assigned a numerical weight which in the final scale ranged from 2 to 8. This original table constituted the first constructiveness scale. The items were brief characterizations of very specific kinds of behavior; general categories were omitted. A record was then scored by assigning a numerical value to each consecutive play unit in the record in accordance with the rating given in the scale and weighted for the duration of the unit by multiplying by the time. The mean constructiveness of each child's play was determined by summing these values for the whole record and dividing by the total duration of play, i.e.,

$$\text{mean constructiveness} = \frac{\Sigma [\text{Cons.} (u) \times \text{Dur} (u)]}{\Sigma [\text{Dur} (u)]}$$

where Cons. (u) = constructiveness rating of a play unit
Dur (u) = duration of a play unit
$\Sigma [\text{Dur}(u)]$ = total duration of play

Reliability

We have two sources of evidence as to the reliability of the ratings of constructiveness. One is the correlation between the constructiveness of play in different parts of the experimental period. For this purpose we have computed the mean constructiveness of play in each consecutive third of each experimental record in free play. The product-moment correlations between the mean constructiveness of play in the various thirds of the period are as follows:

Third of period	Correlation
1st and 2d	.72 $\pm$ .06

| 1st and 3d | .39 ± .10 |
| 2d and 3d | .48 ± .10 |

It will be pointed out later that the psychological situation was not stable throughout the experimental sessions and that it was necessary to take into consideration the changes which occurred. The above correlations are indications not primarily of the reliability of the ratings, but of the stability of the function involved. The correlation between constructiveness in the first and second third, i.e., .72, indicates, however, even if the reduction from 1.00 results entirely from unreliability of the constructive ratings, that they have a reliability sufficient for the group comparisons here involved.

Another source of evidence of reliability of the constructiveness ratings involves the use of a method which approximates the so-called "split-half" procedure used in questionnaire studies. There the score obtained by using the odd-numbered items is correlated with that obtained when the even-numbered items are used. In the present case play units of different lengths are scattered at random throughout the records. We have taken advantage of this to secure two independent estimates of constructiveness based on different lengths of play units. First we computed the mean constructiveness of each child's play based only on play units of the following lengths in seconds: 1 to 15, 31 to 45, 61 to 90, and 121 to 180. We then determined the mean constructiveness of each child's play on the basis of play units of alternative lengths, i.e., 16 to 30, 46 to 60, 91 to 120, and 181 sec. long or more. The correlation between these two independent estimates of mean constructiveness of play is .79 ± .05. The estimated reliability of constructiveness based upon all the play units is .88.

Validity

If one intends to use constructiveness of play as an indication of the developmental level of a child and as an instrument for measuring the effects of regression, it must be demonstrated that, in normal children under comparable conditions, constructiveness increases with age. In other words, constructiveness of play, as determined by the constructiveness scale, should show a high correlation with age in a free situation. On the other hand, constructiveness is a characteristic of behavior which one would expect to show considerable variation from individual to individual of the same age. This means that constructiveness would be technically best fitted for our purpose if the correlation with age were high but sufficiently below 1.00 to allow for individual differences.

The product-moment correlations between mean constructiveness of primary play in the free-play situation and mental age is .73 ± .05. With chronological age the correlation is .79 ± .05. We have also calculated these correlations, omitting the data for four subjects who showed marked dissatisfaction in free play as indicated by a great amount of escape behavior. This dissatisfaction was taken to mean that these subjects were more or less frustrated in the free-play situation. Inasmuch as it was our intention to obtain the best possible estimate of the relation with constructiveness of *nonfrustrated, satisfied* play, it was necessary to eliminate the subjects who did not satisfy these requirements. When they are eliminated the correlation with both mental and chronological age is raised to .81 ± .05. The mathematical regression of mean constructiveness of play upon mental age (months) in the free-play situation is linear; b=.06.

These correlations are important insofar as they establish the fact that constructiveness of play varies positively with age between two and one-half and five years (thirty to eighty-two months mental age). Although the constructiveness scale is a first attempt and may be greatly improved technically, the degree of correlation with chronological age is not far from the value which would appear to be optimal for our purposes.

The first requisite for using constructiveness of play for studying regression seems therefore to be sufficiently met, and the constructiveness scale is valid at least in the degree to which it measures something related to changes in age levels.

Frequency of Various Activities in Free-Play and Frustration Situations

Although the same types of behavior occurred in both experimental situations, their frequency of occurrence changed greatly from free play to frustration. The amount of time occupied with different activities is shown in Table 2.

constructiveness points, corresponding to a regression of approximately 9.6 months mental age, and in the latter case it is 1.29 points, equivalent to 21.5 months mental age. Proportionately, the per cent of decrease in functional level (as measured by constructiveness or mental-age equivalents) seems to be quite similar in the younger and the older group.

Table 2. Average time in seconds occupied by different activities in free play and in frustration.

Activity	Mean time		Difference	Difference
	Free play	*Frustration*	*Difference*	σ *diff.*
Barrier behavior	19.50	510.50	+491.00*	11.47
Primary play	1144.17	569.83	−574.34	8.88
Secondary play	33.12	128.16	+95.04	4.00
Escape behavior	49.67	112.67	+63.00	2.68
Diversions	177.17	204.17	+27.00	†

* + indicates increase in frustration; − indicates decrease in frustration.
† Not computed.

Average Constructiveness of Play in Free Play and Frustration

The mean constructiveness of the play of each child in free play and in frustration is shown in the correlation chart, Figure 2. These data include all play, both primary and secondary. The mean constructiveness of play in free play is 4.99 constructiveness points and in frustration, 3.94 points. The mean regression is 1.05 constructiveness points with a standard error of .24; i.e., the mean regression is 4.39 times its standard error. Stated in terms of mental-age equivalents, i.e., in terms of the regression of constructiveness upon mental age, the mean regression amounts to 17.3 months of mental age. Twenty-two of the subjects regressed in the constructiveness of their play, three did not change, and five increased.

Analysis of the results for primary play alone indicates that the mean regression in constructiveness, although less in amount, is statistically significant.

For the 10 younger subjects, twenty-eight to forty months of age, the regression is smaller than for the 20 older subjects, aged forty-two to sixty-one months. In the former case, the mean regression is 0.58

These data establish rather definitely the fact that a frustrating situation of the kind considered here reduces, on the average, the constructiveness of play below the level upon which it normally occurs in a nonfrustrating, free-play situation. Before considering how this reduction in constructiveness is effected it may be well to stress the fact that these crude results are of significance.

The results show that frustration not only affects actions related to the inaccessible goal, such as attempts to find round-about routes or aggression against the physical or social obstacles, but that it may affect behavior in other regions of activity as well. The main expectation of the experiment has been fulfilled. More specifically, the findings show the importance of the total situation for promoting or hindering a child's creative achievement.

Measurement of Strength of Frustration

The technical arrangements were planned to provide frustration and free play. Inevitably, these effects were not secured in all cases, inasmuch as we had control over only the immediate, experimental situation and not over the expectations, anxieties, and various

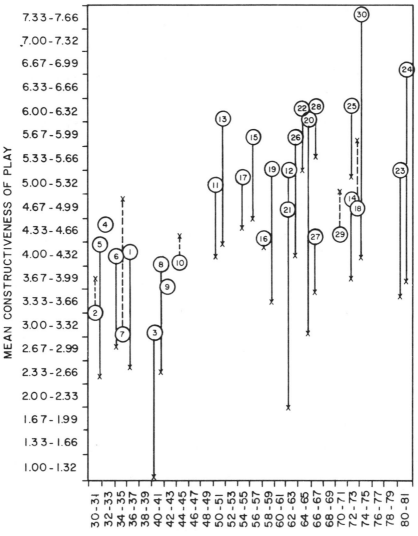

Figure 2. The relation between mean constructiveness of play and mental age and the change of constructiveness in the frustration situation. (1) The mean constructiveness of (primary plus secondary) play in the free-play situation is indicated for each child by a circle. The number given is that of the subject. (2) The mean constructiveness of play in the frustration situation is indicated by a cross. (3) Change in constructiveness from the free-play to the frustration situation is designated by a solid line when constructiveness decreases in frustration, by a broken line when constructiveness increases. The absence of a cross indicates no change in mean constructiveness for that child.

attitudes which the child brought to the experiment. In some instances frustration occurred in the free-play situation and in others there was no frustration in the frustration situation. In addition, all degrees of strength of frustration occurred. Thus far in the analysis we have proceeded as if the technical arrangements had functioned as intended with all subjects. The data have been classified according to the intention of the experi-

menters rather than according to the realities of the situation for the subject. We turn now to the analysis of some quantitative differences in the dynamical properties of the existing psychological situations. We propose to make use of certain measures of the strength of frustration in order to refine our data further.

We have been faced here with the necessity of determining the amount of frustration in the experimental situations. When such general aspects of situations are important, one notes a tendency to handle them in terms of nonpsychological concepts, i.e., in terms of economic, social, geographic, and physical categories rather than in psychological terms. We have attempted to avoid this error and to describe and measure in psychological, behavioral terms.

In doing this we are faced with two problems: (a) to determine the strength of the frustration which is created by prohibiting the subjects from reaching the inaccessible toys; (b) to determine the extent to which this background of frustration is of importance for the play activity of the children. Obviously, these factors are not independent of each other.

The problem of how the background of a situation influences behavior in an immediate situation is a general problem of prime importance. It is particularly significant for what is frequently called the larger life situation which plays such an important role in problems of personality and development.

An attempt to solve this problem touches rather basic theoretical and methodological problems. The regions of the life space which constitute the background are not a part of the activity regions in which the individual is involved at the time. They are not overlapping with the immediate situation in the same way as the two situations in secondary play, for example. Frequently the subject will be so fully occupied with his immediate situation that he will not be aware of the background. On the other hand, the background still influences the behavior in some way. It cannot be omitted from the life space, if one is to account for the actual behavior.

It seems possible to clear up this conceptual difficulty by considering the implications of the concept of contemporaneity (Lewin, 1936). In an empirical science the concept of a field existing at a given moment actually does not refer to a section without any duration through the flow of events. Even in physics it is impossible to describe such essential properties of a situation as the velocity of a point without treating the momentary situa-

tion as a segment which has a certain duration. Here it may suffice to say that in psychology, too, the situation existing at a given moment cannot be described without referring to a certain time depth. There seems to exist in psychology a definite relation between what one might call the "size" of the situation and the minimum extent of time which has to be taken into account in describing the "momentary" situation. To describe the state of the immediate situation a shorter period can usually be taken into account than if one has to describe the state of a larger situation.

These considerations open up a technical way to treat problems of background without resorting to new concepts. We merely have to realize that statements concerning overlapping situations should always be related to a situation of definite size. An individual may be involved in two overlapping activities within the immediate situation, as in secondary play (e.g., play with the truck while talking about the nursery school). However, it is possible that the immediate situation does not have the character of an overlapping situation(e.g., complete attention to truck play), while at the same time the more inclusive life situation does have this character (e.g., "games" with the experimenter overlaps with nursery-school situation). It seems to be conceptually permissible and, as we shall see, technically fruitful to treat the effect of the background upon behavior as an inclusive overlapping situation, involving the immediate situation and the background. Thus, the concept of relative potency (Lewin, 1938) can be used to characterize the influence of the background and of the immediate situation on behavior.

The problem of determining the amount of frustration becomes, in terms of these concepts, one of measuring the potency of the overlapping frustrating and nonfrustrating regions. We have taken as a symptom of the potency of an overlapping region, in the case of successive rather than simultaneous actions, the relative proportion of the total time occupied by the behavior to which the situation in question is coordinated. In the present case, this means that we have assumed that the potency of the frustration region is indicated by the proportion of the total experimental period occupied by frustrated behavior (barrier and escape behavior). It should be mentioned again that the inaccessible toys are not the only source of frustration. Frustration arises also when the child is prevented from leaving the experimental room, and it occurs even in the free-play situation. However, there is some indication that much of the escape behavior in the frustration situation derives from the separation from the inaccessible toys. Whatever the source of the need to leave the room, it, in its turn, leads to frustration and must be included in the total estimate. The estimate of the potency of frustration is therefore based upon the sum of both barrier and escape behavior.

Inasmuch as we are here concerned with the *change* in potency of frustration from the free-play situation to the frustration situation, we have limited ourselves to a consideration of the *difference* in the amount of time occupied with frustrated actions in the two settings. The 10 children for whom the increment of potency of frustration from the free-play situation to the frustration situation is least, i.e., those for whom the increment in duration of frustrated behavior is less than 450 sec., are considered together as the "weak" frustration group. The 20 subjects for whom this increment is greater are dealt with together as the "strong" frustration group.

Constructiveness of Play in Strong and Weak Frustration

There is a highly significant reduction in the constructiveness of play in the frustration situation in the strong frustration group, amounting to $1.46 \pm .15$ constructiveness points for primary and secondary play and $1.11 \pm .15$ constructiveness points for primary play. The first is equivalent to a regression of twenty-four months' mental age, the latter to a regression of nineteen months' mental age. With the weak frustration group, on the other hand, there is a small and not significant reduction in constructiveness, amounting to 0.23 constructiveness points for primary and secondary play and 0.12 points for primary play. When we consider both primary and secondary play, every child of the strong frustration group shows a decrease in average constructiveness during the frustration situation. The cases showing increase all fall in the weak frustration group. When only the primary play is considered, five of the seven exceptional cases fall in the weak group and only two in the strong group. These results suggest that most of the exceptions are due to differences in the dynamics of the situation, i.e., to differences in the potency of frustration.

Any doubt that real frustration, such as occurs with the strong group, leads to a significant reduction in constructiveness is dispelled by these data. It should be kept in mind, in this connection, that the selection of the strong and weak frustration groups was made on the basis of the time spent in barrier and escape behavior, a criterion which had no direct relation to level of constructiveness. The strength of frustration and the amount of regression are measured independently. Perhaps it should be emphasized, too, that these groups were not made until after the experiments were made, the records completed, and the mean constructiveness determined. Both groups were treated in all respects the same.

When the analysis is carried further and episodes of strong and weak frustration within the experimental sessions are treated separately, the magnitude of the effects of strong and weak frustration is increased.

Emotion and Regression

Pari passu with the shift in constructiveness of play there occurs a change in emotional expression. In frustration there is a decrease in freedom of expression, i.e., in the self-revealing actions. This is revealed by a decrease in play monologue and friendly conversation with the experimenter and by the frequent occurrence of masking or tactical, social behavior. There is a decrease in the happiness of the mood in the frustration situation; happy emotional expressions decrease in frequency and unhappy expressions increase. In frustration there is an increase in motor restlessness and hypertension as revealed by loud singing and talking, restless actions, stuttering, and thumb sucking. There is an increase in aggressiveness in frustration; hitting, kicking, breaking, and destroying all increase in frequency.

Theoretical Considerations

Theory in science has two main functions: (a) to open the way to new knowledge, and (b) to organize that which is known. The first, and probably most essential function, determines the fruitfulness of a theory. This function is fulfilled in the following way: the theory, which at first is stated in the form of an hypothesis, envisions unrevealed facts or relations or denies certain relations which are believed to hold; in other words, the theory predicts certain facts or relations of facts. This prediction is tested, usually through experiments. It is found to be valid or invalid. However, even if it has been found valid, the new data need not be treated in terms of the theory.

It is an essential characteristic of a fruitful empirical theory that it gives birth, as it were, to new knowledge, which is then independent of its theoretical ancestry. In an empirical science new data, although discovered by theory, are something in themselves which anyone is free to interpret theoretically in his own way or to accept as mere facts. In other words, the fruitful empirical theory is instrumental in establishing new scientific data which should be able to outlive the theory.

The main results which have been presented here have actually been predicted on the basis of a theory or group of theories. The experiment was set up to test the theoretical predictions.

Originally, our experiment was designed to test the prediction that tension in strong frustration leads to a dedifferentiation of the person and therefore to regression. This regression has been found. However, the

experiments have shown that, aside from dedifferentiation, other factors may enter. In other words, there are several possibilities of explaining the observed regression in a situation such as the one studied here. We shall leave it open which factor or which constellation of factors has caused the results. Probably, different factors were important for different subjects.

One of the best symptoms for the increasing differentiation of the life space (including the person and the psychological environment) during development is the increasing variety of behavior. In the frustration situation the richness and complexity of the play activity definitely decreases. This regression may be caused by dedifferentiation of the individual, in which case the spreading of tension is probably important. It can be shown that the degree of differentiation of a whole is inversely related to the strength of the pressure of tension when this pressure passes certain limits that are determined by the strength of the boundaries of the natural parts of the whole. Constructiveness in play decreases with the strength of the frustration because frustration causes tension.

A decrease in the variety of behavior must also occur if a part of the whole is kept in a fixed state. This follows from certain properties of a dynamic whole. The amount of decrease depends upon the extent of the fixed areas, their degree of centrality, and their divergency from the normal level. Frustration involving a particular goal keeps a certain part of the person in a state of more or less permanent tension, and the variety of all behavior should therefore decrease.

Change in organization can be derived from the overlapping between play and barrier behavior. To be governed by two strong goals is equivalent to the existence of two conflicting controlling heads within the organism. This should lead to a decrease in degree of hierarchical organization. Also, a certain disorganization should result from the fact that the cognitive-motor system loses to some degree its character of a good medium because of these conflicting heads. It ceases to be in a state of near equilibrium: the forces under the control of one head have to counteract the forces of the other before they are effective.

The extension of the life space, particularly in the psychological time dimension, is one of the essential characteristics of development. Planning presupposes time perspective. In the frustration experiment, the experimenter interrupted the elaborate play with the beautiful toys and caused the child to move to the other side of the partition. In the previous free-play situation the child had not been interrupted and may have become confident that his play would not be interrupted. With this security he was able to make relatively long-range plans. The interference at the end of the prefrustration period may have shattered the security and stability of the play situation. If the possibility existed that a superior power, such as the experimenter, might interfere at any moment, it might not seem worth while to develop a long-range plan. This should lead to a weakening of the connection between the reality and phantasy levels and to a narrowing of the life space with respect to its extension into the psychological future. It is possible to attribute regression in the frustration situation at least partly to this lack of security.

References

Barker, Roger G., Dembo, Tamara, and Lewin, Kurt. Frustration and regression: An experiment with young children. *Univ. Ia. Stud. Child Welf., 1941,* **18**, No. 1, xv + 314.

Frank, L. K. Time perspective. *J. soc. Phil.,* 1939, **4**, 293-312.

Lewin, Kurt. *A dynamic theory of personality.* New York: McGraw-Hill, 1935. Pp. ix + 286.

Lewin, Kurt. *Principles of topological psychology.* New York: McGraw-Hill, 1936. Pp. xv + 231.

Lewin, Kurt. The conceptual representation and measurement of psychological force. *Duke Univ. Series Contr. psychol. Theory,* 1938, **1**, No. 4, 247.

Piaget, J. *The child's conception of the world.* New York: Harcourt, 1929. Pp. ix + 397.

A Critique of the Barker - Dembo - Lewin Experiment

Irvin L. Child and Ian K. Waterhouse

Introduction

The Freudian concept of regression has given rise to varied research and theoretical work. In particular, it has on at least two occasions given rise to an attempt to bring the concept and the phenomena of regression within the scope of another theoretical system than that of psychoanalysis. In each case the attempt to do this is characterized by a redefinition of the concept of regression and by an account of the dynamics responsible for regression, as interpreted in relation to the particular theoretical system.

One of these attempts is that of Mowrer (5) and later Sears (8), relating regression to behavioristic theory of learning. They define regression, in effect, as the reappearance of behavior which earlier characterized the person, when more recently acquired behavior disappears under frustration. The account of the underlying dynamics is as follows. A particular situation will have some tendency to evoke a number of different response-sequences in an individual. The response-sequence for which this tendency is strongest will always be the one which is actually evoked; this will quite commonly be the most recently learned sequence. If frustration occurs, the strength of the tendency for evocation of this particular sequence will be diminished through the process known as extinction. When it is diminished below the strength of the tendency for evocation of the response-sequence of second greatest strength, this latter sequence will be evoked. This sequence will often be an earlier learned one. Thus does frustration lead to regression. Mowrer ap-

pears to feel that the variety of phenomena which have been termed "regression" by Freud fit adequately this definition and explanation.

The other attempt, relating regression to the Lewinian system, is that of Barker, Dembo and Lewin (2).[1] They define regression, in effect, as the primitivation of behavior, as a shift from more mature behavior to less mature behavior. The account of the underlying dynamics is roughly as follows. Under frustration (or at least strong frustration) the person becomes less highly or less adequately organized, and his behavior is therefore more like that of a less mature person than it was before frustration. Actually several different dynamic sequences are suggested by BDL as possibly responsible in various cases, but the previous sentence seems to be a fair summary of them. These several sequences have in common that what becomes less mature is the *general* degree of organization of behavior, rather than *specific* acts or response-sequences, and that resemblance of any kind to *earlier* behavior is not an essential part of the concept.

These two redefinitions of "regression" clearly involve very different concepts—one, the reappearance of specific response-sequences which were learned earlier than the frustrated sequence; the other, a change in the organizational properties of behavior and its internal determinants. In our opinion, neither of the concepts corresponds very closely to the total meaning of "regression" as used in psychoanalytic writing, though each seems to correspond to part of the psychoanalytic meaning. Our opinion on this point appears to have been shared by Sears (8, pp. 96-98) and by BDL (2, pp. 2-7).

From I. L. Child and I. K. Waterhouse, "Frustration and the Quality of Performance: I. A Critique of the Barker, Dembo, and Lewin Experiment," *Psychological Review*, 1952, **59**, 351-362. Reprinted by permission of the American Psychological Association.

[1]Hereafter referred to as BDL.

In this series of papers, we are concerned with essentially the same concept for which BDL have employed the term "regression." But because of the great variation in the meaning of this term, and because the psychoanalytic usage seems to be the most widely accepted, we feel that to continue to use the same term would be confusing.

In our choice of a term to substitute for "regression" we are guided by the fact that we are concerned not only with this phenomenon but also with its opposite. We are interested not only in what leads behavior to be less organized but also in what leads behavior to be more organized. A term would be useful which would call attention to the possibility of variation in either direction. The term we have adopted is "quality of performance." We shall be concerned, then, with the opposite effects that frustration may have on quality of performance—the raising and the lowering of quality of performance.

This term is, we admit, somewhat general and vague. In the case of clearly defined intellectual tasks such as are used in intelligence tests, quality of performance may readily be given meaning through highly reliable judgments of correctness of solution, speed, and the like. In the case of systematic observations of a category of behavior, such as BDL's observations of children's play in a standardized situation, criteria can be worked out for obtaining reliable judgments of an aspect of the behavior that could be called "quality of performance"; BDL have done just this, though they have used the narrower term "constructiveness." In applying our concept to everyday behavior, there would often be difficulty in evaluating the quality of performance. None the less, we believe that even here the concept would have a sufficiently common meaning to justify our devoting attention primarily to the factors influencing quality of performance, rather than to the development of a more refined set of concepts which might ultimately replace this general one.

Of experiments concerned with the effects of frustration on quality of performance, that by BDL is perhaps the most ambitious and the best known. The great wealth of data and ideas contained in their lengthy report of the experiment, unfortunately, do not seem to be nearly as well known as a general conclusion drawn from their report—the general conclusion that frustration leads to a lowered quality of performance. When the data and ideas presented by BDL are looked at in detail, other inferences may be drawn that are much more significant than this general conclusion—more significant for an understanding of their study, and more significant for the orienting of future research. Hence we feel that a critique of this major piece of scientific work is fully justified.

The Barker, Dembo, and Lewin Experiment

A critique of the BDL experiment must begin, for those who are not familiar with it, with a brief account of the experiment itself. The subjects were children between the ages of 25 months and 61 months. The experiment was conducted in a room which could be divided by a screen into two parts, which we shall call parts A and B. For the first session with each child the two parts of the room were separated by a completely opaque screen. The child was brought into part A and allowed to play with a set of play materials which we shall call set A; this session is referred to as the free-play situation. On a later day the child was brought back into the room after two changes had been made in preparation; the barrier had been removed, so that the child had free access to the entire room; and in part B there were a number of much more attractive toys, which we shall call set B, with which set A had also been integrated. When the child had become fully involved in play in this situation, the frustration situation was introduced in the following way: The toys of set A were withdrawn from those of set B and placed in their original position in part A of the room; the child and experimenter withdrew into part A, and the experimenter lowered a transparent screen (of wire netting) between the two parts of the room and padlocked it. The child was then objectively in the same physical situation as in the free-play situation of the first day, except for the visibility of the more desirable toys, those of set B. The child's play with the toys of set A was rated on a scale of constructiveness,[2] both in this frustration situation and in the free-play situation of the first day.

Most of the children showed a lower constructiveness of play in the frustration situation than in the free-play situation.[3] This finding appears to us to be capable of a very simple and very illuminating interpretation. It is that frustration of one activity will produce lowered quality of performance in the second activity to the extent that it leads to the making of responses that are incompatible with or interfere with the responses of the second activity. This may be called an interference interpretation of the findings. It will be considered at somewhat greater length in the next section of this article. Meanwhile, we wish to consider its relation to BDL's interpretation of their findings.[4]

This interpretation we are offering is not entirely new. In a short paper published by Barker alone (1) in advance of the full report of the experiment, essentially this interpretation is presented, and it is the sole interpretation offered there for the lowered constructiveness found in the experiment.[5] Essentially

the same interpretation is offered in the full report by BDL, in a section entitled "A Simplified Quantitative Theory of Constructiveness" (pp. 212-216)[6] and elsewhere. But at the same time these authors argue against this interpretation. In a briefer report of the experiment later prepared for inclusion in a textbook (3), the same authors relegate this interpretation to an even more subordinate and inconspicuous position.

Let us consider, then, the justice of the denial or minimization of this interpretation in the reports of BDL. There are two separate arguments to consider. The first is the minimization of this interpretation by giving it equal status with a number of other alternative interpretations. The second consists of specific arguments against the supposition that an interpretation in terms of interference might adequately explain the whole of the findings.

BDL minimize the role of interference in explaining lowered constructiveness by presenting it as one of four possible sequences of internal events which are given equal explanatory status. We shall comment below on the other three of these sequences, reserving for the next section of this paper extended discussion of the interference interpretation.

(1) It is suggested (pp. 44-45, 217) that frustration produces a dedifferentiation of the person, probably because frustration causes tension and tension causes dedifferentiation, and that this dedifferentiation of the person leads to lowered constructiveness of play. This hypothesis cannot be altogether rejected. But its application to explaining the results of the experiment involves circular reasoning, since no criterion of dedifferentiation is used other than the lowered constructiveness of the play. Moreover, if variety of total behavior were used as the criterion for degree of differentiation, it seems quite

---

[2]To ensure faithfulness to the statements by BDL, we shall continue to use the term "constructiveness" in discussing their experiment. In our opinion, their scale of constructiveness is an instance of a scale of what we are calling "quality of performance."

[3]Some children showed instead a heightened constructiveness. The problems to which these exceptions give rise will be discussed in a later paper (4).

[4]BDL's experiment is, unhappily, subject to still another and quite different interpretation. This is that the lowered constructiveness of play with the toys of set A was due entirely to satiation with respect to them. The experiment was so designed that there is no control for the influence of satiation. BDL argue that this interpretation may be rejected because the more frustrated individuals showed a greater lowering of constructiveness than did the less frustrated individuals and hence frustration must have been responsible. This argument is not conclusive, since the measure which is called a measure of degree of frustration could with equal justice have been called a meaaure of degree of satiation. We are influenced, however, by the qualitative reports of behavior, as BDL must have been by their observation of the behavior, to believe that frustration probably had *something* to do with the lowered constructiveness; how much, in relation to the influence of satiation, there is no way of guessing from the data of the experiment.

[5]In saying, "essentially this interpretation," we are, of course, making a sort of translation between Lewinian constructs and behavioristic constructs. We believe the

translation is a reasonable one in this case, and that the arguments which apply to our interpretation apply equally to the analogous interpretation as stated by these Lewinian authors. Hence, we have felt justified in referring, in the rest of this paper, to an interference interpretation even when we are discussing these other authors' statements about an interpretation which they describe in very different terms.

[6]This and subsequent page references are to the BDL monograph (2).

certain that frustration would be found to have led to increased differentiation instead of the opposite, for the total behavior in the frustration period appears to have been much more varied than in the free-play situation, even though the play itself was less varied.

(2) It is suggested (p. 217) that frustration leads to keeping a part of the whole person in a fixed state, and that this leads to a decrease in the variety of behavior and hence to lowered constructiveness. The same objections apply here as in the former case. With respect to a part of the person being kept in a fixed state, there is no operation suggested for determining whether this has happened and no evidence that it would be true if a suitable operation were used. With respect to the consequent lowered variety of behavior, we would raise the same doubts as in the previous paragraph as to whether the facts were not directly contrary to what is suggested.[7]

(3) It is suggested (p. 218) that in the free-play situation the child was free to make long-range plans for play because he had no reason to expect to be interrupted, whereas in the frustration situation he had just experienced an interruption of his play by the experimenter, might have expected another interruption and hence "it might not seem worth while to start a long-range plan." This lack of security is then supposed to lead to a lowered constructiveness of play. This hypothesis is clearly meaningful and tenable. It may account for some or all of the lowered constructiveness of play. The experiment was not designed in a way that would permit certainty on this point. Yet, as in the case of the interpretation in terms of satiation which has been discussed above in footnote 4, we are swayed by certain relevant evidence. Evidence that the children's play was being interfered with by other behavioral tendencies

is simply overwhelming, as will be shown later. Evidence that the children expected to be interrupted is lacking; that the authors suggest this interpretation but do not cite any evidence to support it tends to suggest that there was not evidence of its being very important.

Against all three of these alternative interpretations there is an argument to be made from the evidence of the experiment which is rather persuasive though not conclusive. All three of these interpretations refer to rather general, pervasive states of the person during the frustration period which might be expected to influence the constructiveness of various categories of his play activity. Each separate incident of play was in fact classified by the investigators into one of two categories, primary play and secondary play. Primary play is play in which the child was, so far as could be judged from watching him, entirely absorbed. Secondary play is play in which the child was simultaneously doing something else, such as talking to the experimenter or looking at the more desirable toys. The constructiveness of primary play is markedly different in free play and in frustration. The constructiveness of secondary play shows no consistent difference between free play and frustration.[8] When the child's play is suffering from interference in a way that is clearly visible to an observer, then none of the factors mentioned in these three alternative interpretations, supposedly present in the frustration period more than in the free-play period, is sufficient to produce any additional decrement in constructiveness.

There is, on the other hand, considerable evidence in favor of the interference interpretation which we shall review later in this paper. We conclude, therefore, that BDL misplace emphasis in giving equal weight to it and to these three other interpretations. The experiment itself is not decisive with respect to the several interpretations, but it can provide qualitative evidence about their relative plausibility and compellingness as major explanations.

[7] We find the meaning of this second interpretation especially difficult to grasp, and would suggest the possibility that upon further clarification "keeping a part of the whole in a fixed state" might turn out to mean only that there was a continuing system of responses which would tend to interfere with any subsequent responses. In this case, this second interpretation is actually identical with the one we are supporting, but the mention of variety of behavior should be omitted from it.

[8] This fact is not mentioned by BDL but may be read from their Table 6 (p. 119).

A reason for the lack of emphasis by BDL on the interference interpretation is probably to be found in the fact that they believe they have definite evidence against its tenability as a sole explanation of their findings. To this second point we now turn.

There are three lines of evidence which BDL quite explicitly apply against the interference interpretation, and a fourth which they seem to apply also. Let us consider each of them.

(1) It is argued (pp. 131-134) that because the lowered constructiveness in frustration cannot be accounted for entirely by an increase in the proportion of secondary play (i.e., play which is accompanied by the child's simultaneously making other overt responses) and is still found when a comparison is made between primary play in the free-play and the frustration situations, the interference interpretation cannot be the sole explanation. This argument appears to involve the assumption that primary play (i.e., play in which the child was not obviously and overtly doing something else at the same time) had the same meaning in both free-play and frustration; that is, that in both situations, it involved no internal conflict, no preoccupation with competing interests. This assumption seems to us altogether unlikely from a commonsense analysis of what had been done to the children in the two situations and of what their probable reactions would be, and from other statements by BDL (pp. 78-81). It involves a naive objectivism of a degree which would be rather surprising in a behaviorist, and in these authors is quite astonishing.

(2) It is argued (pp. 147-152) that because the most strongly frustrated children showed a greater lowering of constructiveness than did the less strongly frustrated children, frustration rather than conflict (or satiation) must be the explanation. But here it is necessary to note the particular measure which was used in gauging the strength of frustration in each child. It was the proportion of the total experimental period which he devoted to barrier and escape behavior. But this is at the same time a measure of the extent to which certain behavior tendencies were

strong enough to win complete dominance, for periods of time, over the tendency to play with the available toys of set A.[9] Surely a measure of strength of competing tendencies based on the proportion of time in which they are dominant may be expected to provide an index also of their strength during the periods in which they are not dominant! Hence what the investigators have chosen to consider a measure of degree of frustration could with equal cogency be called a measure of strength of competing tendencies. We can for this reason see no merit at all in this particular argument by BDL.

(3) Another argument is based on the fact that the maximum of constructiveness reached at any time during the frustration period is typically lower than the maximum of constructiveness reached at any time during the free-play period. This argument is expressed very concisely by Barker, Dembo and Lewin:

. . . these results . . . suggest that even with play of highest constructiveness, where the probability is smallest that overlapping regions of play and nonplay are involved, there is a tendency for constructiveness of play to be reduced under the influence of frustration. This is further evidence, therefore, that division of the person between two simultaneous actions is not the only cause of the reduction of constructiveness in the frustration situation. (Pp. 135-136)

We cannot see the cogency of this argument either. If the interference interpretation is correct, then the facts referred to here do indicate that the competing tendencies to get through the barrier, to escape, etc., were characteristically present throughout the frustration period. But there is nothing farfetched about the supposition that these competing tendencies were present more or less continuously. In fact, the whole experimental procedure was planned in an effort to make this supposition correct, and BDL seem else-

[9]This measure is, of course, only of the *relative* strength of the competing tendencies; it is possible that the variations arise from differences in the absolute strength of the tendency to play with the available toys rather than from differences in the absolute strength of the competing tendencies. (See footnote 4 above.)

where in their report to assume that it is correct (pp. 58-59, 71-82).

(4) It seems also to be argued that the fact that lowered constructiveness is found even when units of play of equal length only are compared contributes some evidence against the interference interpretation (p.152). Again, we cannot agree with this argument, if we are correct in believing it to be implied. The fact cited here is important as showing that the effect of interference on constructiveness is not produced solely by shortening the duration of each unit of play. But there is nothing about the interference interpretation, either as we understand it or as it is presented by BDL, that would require that interference be supposed to produce an effect in only this one way.

We would conclude, therefore, that the arguments adduced by BDL against the interference interpretation of their results are not valid.

Evidence for the Interference Interpretation

We offer the hypothesis that frustration of one activity effects a lowering of quality of performance in a second activity to the extent that it gives rise to competing responses which interfere with the responses involved in the second activity. The interfering responses may usefully be divided into two sorts:

(1) Responses made in continuation, or attempted continuation, of the frustrated activity. These are what Rosenzweig (7) terms need-persistive responses to the frustration. Frustration implies that the individual has not reached, or has not completed his enjoyment of, his goal; and frustration hence may be followed by continued attempts to reach the goal or by substitutive goal-responses such as fantasies about enjoying the goal or striving for the goal. All these responses, made with reference to the goal of the frustrated activity, may interfere with the responses required for high-quality performance in a second activity.

(2) Responses evoked more specifically by the fact of frustration itself. These include

what Rosenzweig calls *ego-defensive* responses to frustration, and also some of the internal drive-producing responses which occasion the defense. They include, for example, the internal responses which constitute anxiety and anger, aggressive responses made to these conditions, attempts at self-justification, attempts to escape from the unpleasant situation, and the like. Such responses, evoked by frustration in one activity, may interfere with high-quality performance in a second activity.

We suggest that the lowered constructiveness of play found in the BDL experiment is adequately explained by the interference of responses of these two sorts with the responses of playing with the available toys of set A during the frustration period. We feel also that some of the best experimental evidence at present available for this general hypothesis is provided by the BDL experiment. It is appropriate, therefore, to review that experiment from the point of view of the positive evidence supporting this interpretation of its findings. This evidence is presented below under four main headings.

I. An Analysis of the Situation

An analysis of the situation with which children were confronted in BDL's experiment makes it extremely likely that the children's play in the frustration period would be subjected to a great deal of interference; that is, that there would be evoked strong tendencies toward behavior which would compete with the responses of playing with the available toys of set A. The salient points in such an analysis appear to be the following:

A. The children were interrupted at a point of thorough involvement in play with the combined toys of sets A and B. From the results of experiments on resumption of interrupted tasks (6), it would be expected that this would lead to definite persisting tendencies to resume the interrupted activity. Since, moreover, the interrupted activity in this case appears to have been much more desirable than the ones which have been generally used in those experiments, one might expect the persisting tendencies to be very strong indeed.

B. The more desirable toys of set B remained clearly in sight, likely to evoke tendencies to respond to them and attempts to secure the opportunity of continuing to play with them.

C. There was a special circumstance in the social situation which seems likely to have strengthened the tendency to get across the barrier, to play with the toys of set B. There was no definite statement to the child that the frustration would be permanent or would last for any given time; the situation might for this reason appear to the child as similar to everyday situations in which some behavior on his part could lead to the removal of a socially imposed barrier.

D. If he played with the available toys of set A, he was playing with toys which had just previously been integrated with the more desirable toys of set B, and might therefore remind him repeatedly of his unfinished play with set B.

E. There was no special urging that the child play with the toys of set A. No motives of conformity or achievement were thus evoked by social stimulation. The tendency to play with these toys must have arisen from the general desire for play or for occupying oneself. Since these toys were so much less satisfying than those the child had just been playing with, the tendency to play with them, unsupported by adult urging, might be expected to be relatively weak and hence to require not very strong competing tendencies for effective interference.

F. The situation was one in which the alternative of escape was likely to be a relatively attractive one, as the child evidently knew that when he could get away from this situation he would be returned to his accustomed and presumably enjoyed activities in nursery school. Hence a tendency to escape might be expected as a relatively important component in the conflicts created by the experimental situation.

II. Evidence of Increased Interference in the Frustration Situation

The investigators' observations of the children's behavior, and their analysis of it, provide evidence that play with the toys of set A was in fact interfered with by other overt behavior, more during the frustration period than during the free-play period. It seems a reasonable inference that what was true of overt interference was also true of covert interference. Two lines of evidence are pertinent here.

A. Time Devoted to Play and to Other Activities. During all of the free-play and frustration periods, the toys of set A were available for the child to play with. To what extent in each period was play interfered with by other overt activity? A simple answer is provided by the amount of time devoted to play and to other activities. This information may be calculated from data in two of BDL's tables (pp. 85-86). The average amount of time devoted to primary play in the frustration period was just half what it was in the free-play period—570 seconds against 1144 seconds. The amount of time devoted to all other recorded activities was more than three times as great in the frustration period as in the free-play period—827 seconds against 246 seconds.

B. Proportion of Play Which Was "Secondary." There is a second way of answering the question, to what extent was play interfered with, in each period, by other overt activity? This second answer is provided by BDL's observations on the amount of what they call "secondary play." In the free-play period the child was simultaneously playing with the toys and doing something else 2.3 per cent of the time, on the average; for the frustration period the corresponding figure is 8.9 per cent (p. 87). In view of the fact that there was only half as much primary play in the frustration period, it appears that the proportion of playing time in which other behavior was visibly intruding on the play was about 7 or 8 times as great in the frustration period as in the free-play period.

It is perfectly clear, then, that other behavioral tendencies which might interfere with play were very much stronger, relative to tendencies to play, during the frustration period than during the free-play period. It is natural to suppose that this fact is pertinent to explaining the difference between the two periods in constructiveness of play, or quality of performance.

III. Evidence of Correlation between Interference and Quality of Performance, in the Frustration Period

We have just seen that the difference in quality of performance between the free-play period and the frustration period may well be explained in terms of interference, inasmuch as there is ample evidence that interfering activities were present to a much greater degree during the frustration period than during the free-play period. We may now turn to another line of evidence which may be drawn from the BDL monograph to support the same interpretation. It is evidence deriving from the data of the frustration period alone, evidence indicating that within that period alone variations in quality of performance are correlated with variations in the extent to which interfering responses are being made. This evidence comes from three specific sources.

A. Comparison between Primary and Secondary Play. For children's play during the frustration period, the ratings of constructiveness were higher for "primary play" than for "secondary play"; this finding is highly significant statistically (t = 4.72, d.f. =19, as computed from data in Table 6, p. 119). Since the difference between primary and secondary play is a matter of whether response tendencies which might compete with play are present in sufficient strength to have some directly observable effect, this finding provides direct evidence of a correlation between interference and quality of performance.

B. Individual Differences. BDL divide their subjects, for purposes of analysis, into two groups—10 weakly frustrated subjects and 20 strongly frustrated subjects. They provide some evidence of lower constructiveness of play, and of more lowering of constructiveness in comparison with the free-play period, in the strongly frustrated subjects than in the weakly frustrated subjects. They call attention to this latter evidence, and place more stress on it than is justified by their analysis since the differences are not statistically significant (as may be determined by calculations based on their Tables 11 and 12, pp. 148-149). But the differences are certainly in this direction.

The important point here is that, as we have mentioned earlier, the "strongly frustrated" subjects could just as well have been called the subjects "with strong interfering tendencies," and the "weakly frustrated" subjects could just as well have been called the subjects "with weak interfering tendencies." The measure of frustration was the time spent by a subject in barrier and escape behavior (actually, the measure used was the increase in time so spent between free-play and frustration periods, but the division into two groups of subjects is exactly the same as though time so spent in the frustration period were the measure—see Table 9, p. 142). Barrier and escape behavior is behavior which is competing, in this situation, with the behavior of playing with the available toys. Moreover, this division of subjects into two groups also divides them into groups differing consistently, on the average, in every other form of competing behavior itemized by BDL. The "strongly frustrated" subjects exceed the "weakly frustrated" subjects in amount of time spent in play with the experimenter, in "island behavior," in activity at the window, and in looking and wandering about (p. 145). It is a reasonable inference that subjects in whom these various other responses are dominant in more of their overt behavior will also have their play interfered with more by tendencies toward making these responses. But if this is doubted, then specific evidence may be offered: the proportion of play during which the subject is visibly making other responses simultaneously is more than twice as great in the "strongly frustrated" group as in the "weakly frustrated" group (p. 145).

Now that we have presented this interpretation of what BDL's analysis of individual differences means, let us return to the evidence. The question arises, could their differences be lacking in statistical significance simply because of the considerable variability introduced in their data by the age range of the subjects, since constructiveness of play is closely related to age? This question can readily be dealt with if we turn from an analysis of group differences to an analysis of correlations. The correlation between constructiveness of play and time spent in barrier and escape behavior, during the frustration period is – 0.33. When the effects of chronological age and mental age are partialed out, this correlation rises to – 0.72) a highly significant relationship in the predicted direction.[10] We do have clear and dependable evidence from individual differences, then, to indicate that the equality of performance in play is correlated with an index of amount of interference from competing behavioral tendencies.

From our general hypothesis it might be predicted that a similar relationship would be found between constructiveness and amount of time spent in other activities than barrier and escape behavior—in play with the experimenter, "island behavior," activity at the window, and looking and wandering about. We tested this and found that the raw correlation is almost zero. One might be tempted to conclude that barrier and escape behavior has some unique predictive power; in section IV, however, we shall present evidence which argues against this conclusion.

C. Comparison of Episodes. BDL apply to specific episodes of play an analysis similar to that used for individual differences. For each episode the constructiveness of play is rated and a measure of degree of frustration is obtained. Here the measure of "frustration" is slightly different. It is the proportion of time devoted by the subject, during the episode, to all the other responses which were recorded; barrier behavior, escape behavior, activities with the experimenter, "island behavior," activities at the window, and looking and wandering about (p. 156). There is very marked and consistent evidence that the constructiveness of play, for specific episodes, varies inversely with the proportion of time devoted to all these other activities (pp. 164-170). This finding provides strong and direct evidence of a relationship between strength of interfering tendencies and quality of performance.

IV. Evidence of Correlation between Interference and Quality of Performance in the Free-Play Period

The simple notion that frustration produces regression does not lead to predictions about the behavior of subjects during the free-play period (unless it can be established that frustration occurred there too). Our interpretation is a more general hypothesis, *viz.*, that quality of performance is lowered to the extent that interfering response tendencies are present; this more general hypothesis leads directly to predictions about the behavior of subjects during the free-play period as well. Fortunately, BDL present the data of their study in such detail that it is possible to test some of these predictions by new calculations made from certain of their tables.

A. Comparison between Primary and Secondary Play. Our interpretation would lead to a prediction that "primary play" should be more constructive than "secondary play" in the free-play period, just as it was in the frustration period. This prediction is very strongly confirmed by the data, and the difference is highly significant (t = 5.03, d.f. = 12, data from Table 6, p. 119). Here is further confir-

[10]These calculations are based on data presented by BDL on pp. 48, 85, and 123.

mation of the relation between interference and quality of performance.

B. Individual Differences. Individual differences during the free-play period may be analyzed in the same way as individual differences during the frustration period. Our hypothesis leads to a prediction that here too the constructiveness of play should be related inversely to the strength of interfering tendencies. We have used the correlation technique again, since it permits statistical control of the influences of age. For purposes of comparison with the frustration period we have again dealt separately with two measures of interfering tendencies—time spent in barrier and escape behavior, and time spent in the other four categories of activity which were recorded.

For the free-play period the correlation between constructiveness and amount of time spent in barrier and escape behavior is only − .06. The correlation between constructiveness and time spent in the other four categories of activity, however, is − .25; when the effects of chronological age and mental age are partialed out, this correlation rises to − .83, a highly significant value. Once again, then, for one of the two measures of strength of interfering tendencies we obtain strong confirmation of a relationship between strength of interfering tendencies and quality of performance. This time our hypothesis is confirmed in a setting in which there appears to be no convincing reason to suppose that the concept of frustration is pertinent.

Putting together these findings and our parallel analysis for the frustration period, we may ask why different measures of interfering tendencies are significantly related to quality of performance. A partial answer may be provided by noting that in the free-play period much more time is spent in the other four activities than in barrier and escape behavior, while the reverse is true for the frustration period, and that these differences in mean time are accompanied by differences in variability among subjects. For the frustration period, barrier and escape behavior has the higher standard deviation by a ratio of 1.4 to

1; for the free-play period, the other activities have the higher standard deviation by a ratio of 2.1 to 1. In each situation, the types of interfering activity which are the major locus of individual differences have the greater predictive power. It may still remain true that in the frustration period barrier and escape behavior has a predictive advantage not entirely accounted for in this way; but it clearly does not have a unique predictive power.

Conclusion

We have interpreted BDL's study of "regression" as pertinent to the following hypothesis: that frustration of one activity will produce lowered quality of performance in a second activity to the extent that it leads to the making of responses which interfere with the responses of the second activity. An interpretation which appears to be essentially the same as this was suggested by BDL but rejected by them as a sole explanation of their results. We have shown that their arguments against this hypothesis are not convincing. Various aspects of their analysis specifically support this hypothesis. We have analysed other aspects of their data which are not relevant to frustration; these too are confirmed by new analyses. We conclude that BDL's experiment provides highly significant evidence in favor of the hypothesis we are advancing; and that when viewed in this light their experiment is a contribution to psychological knowledge even more important than it is already justly recognized to be.

References

1. Barker, R. G. Frustration as an experimental problem. V. The effect of frustration upon cognitive ability. *Charact. & Pers.*, 1938, **7**, 145-150.
2. Barker, R. G., Dembo, T., & Lewin, K. Frustration and regression: An experiment with young children. *Univ. Ia. Stud. Child Welf.*, 1941, **18**, 1-314.
3. ──────. Frustration and regression. In Barker, R. G., Kounin, J. S., and Wright, H. F. (eds.),

Child behavior and development. New York: McGraw-Hill, 1943, pp. 441-458.

4. Child, I. L., & Waterhouse, I. K. Frustration and the quality of performance. II. A theoretical statement.

5. Mowrer, O. H. An experimental analogue of "regression" with incidental observations on "reaction formation." *J. abnorm. soc. Psychol.*, 1940, **35**, 56-87.

6. Ovsiankina, Maria. Die Wiederaufnahme unterbrochener Handlungen. *Psychol. Forsch.*, 1928, **11**, 302-379.

7. Rosenzweig, S. An outline of frustration theory. In Hunt, J. McV. (ed.), *Personality and the behavior disorders.* New York: Ronald, 1944, pp. 379-388.

8. Sears, R. Survey of objective studies of psychoanalytic concepts. *Soc. Sci. Res. Coun. Bull.*, 1943, No. 51.

6   Carl R. Rogers

Carl R. Rogers (1902-) is perhaps best known for his development of a psychotherapeutic approach—client-centered therapy—which is rivaled in popularity only by psychoanalysis. Rogers' interest, however, has never been limited to the problems of abnormal psychology; he has, throughout his career, been a champion of the view that the psychotherapeutic situation offers psychology a valuable laboratory for the development and testing of hypotheses that are relevant to the more general area of personality theory. In this role, he has been concerned mainly with personality change and growth and with the factors that bring about these phenomena. Perhaps Rogers' unique contribution to the psychology of personality and psychotherapy has been his success in subjecting a psychology of inner experience to the rigors of scientific objectivism. His humanism and deep respect for the value of the person have certainly influenced Rogers' basic assumptions about the nature of man while, at the same time, his insistence on using the scientific method and empirical research to test hypotheses has placed Rogerian theory squarely in the arena of psychological science.

The first of the following papers is illustrative of Rogers' ability to study man in an objective scientific way without stripping him of his humanness. By assuming a *phenomenological* stance Rogers is able to achieve this. For the phenomenologist all behavior is determined by immediate, individual perceptual events (experience); accordingly the focus of psychological study should be on these perceptual events. Note in this paper how Rogers, using his own phenomenal experience, attempts to abstract from it certain theoretical principles that can be subjected to scientific scrutiny. (Nevertheless, the phenomenological approach is still controversial within the psychological community. The M. Brewster Smith article in Chapter 7, although friendly toward phenomenology, could be read as a criticism of Rogers' phenomenological approach.)

Rogers first presents his theoretical principles as "conditions." Though these conditions are initially stated in brief (and untestable) form, Rogers, in his characteristic style, refines these statements by focusing on the experiential aspects of human interaction. Even in so doing, it is possible for him to maintain his scientific perspective and to *operationally define* each of these conditions in such a way that he is able to generate hypotheses amenable to empirical test.

The research paper by Walker, Rablen, and Rogers illustrates how the Rogerians operationalize their concepts. In this instance their goal is the construction of a scale that will reliably and validly measure psychotherapeutic movement (progress). They begin with the concepts of the theory and restate these in terms of observable experimental operations. That is to say, the theory makes certain conceptual statements relating to various degrees of therapeutic movement; but, in order to test the theory, these conceptual statements (which are not observable) must be translated into empirical terms. In this way the theory becomes connected with observational data and the theoretical concepts become operationally defined.

After extensive study of actual recordings of psychotherapeutic interviews, Rogers postulated a certain identifiable and orderly scale of movement in the process of constructive personality change. He suggested that the client, during the course of successful therapy, progresses through several stages; and he described the characteristics of these stages in terms of excerpts taken from therapy recordings. These excerpts constitute the observational data (the observation language) which define the various stages along the (conceptualized) therapeutic process continuum (the theory language). The purpose of the Walker et al. study was to determine experimentally if the excerpts from therapy recordings (observational data) truly represented the postulated stages of the therapeutic process continuum. Thus the study is an attempt to validate an objective measure of therapeutic movement by asking the question "Does the scale as presented in observational terms really measure therapeutic progress as defined in Rogers' theory?"

In the final article in this chapter we have the very desirable (from a scientific point of view) opportunity to collate, in a single experiment, two opposing theoretical positions. Charles B. Truax designed an experiment which allowed him to test a prediction generated by Rogers' theory against an alternative prediction derived from the theory of B. F. Skinner. This type of research is a rarity in the area of personality theory, where much of the research is designed only to confirm or reject hypotheses generated by a single theory.

The primary difference between Rogers and Skinner on what is central to psychotherapeutic personality change stems from their basic philosophical positions on the issue of *control* (see Chapter 4). Rogers' contention is that it is the therapist's non-controlling attitude in the therapeutic relationship that results in successful psychotherapy. This non-directive attitude is reflected in the therapist's non-selective responding to the client; the therapist neither approves nor disapproves of what the client says or does. Skinner, on the other hand, insists that behavior is controlled by its consequences and that therefore the successful therapist modifies the client's behavior by the systematic, selective use of reinforcement techniques.

Using the transcript of a successful therapy case in which Rogers was the therapist, Truax is able to analyze his data so that the results will support only one of the alternative predictions. Thus, if the results show that the therapist responds to the client in an unsystematic, non-selective manner, Rogers' theory would be supported. If, however, it is demonstrated that there is a systematic relationship between the therapist's behavior and that of the client, and if it is also evident that client behaviors followed by therapist responses significantly increase during therapy while client behaviors not followed by therapist responses show no change during therapy, then the results of the experiment would support Skinner's position.

The results are overwhelmingly in support of the Skinnerian position.

Suggestions for Further Reading

The historical development of Rogers' thinking can be discerned in three books published from 1942 through 1961. The 1942 book, *Counseling and Psychotherapy*, presents Rogers' first systematic statement of what he then called "non-directive therapy." In 1951, while at the University of Chicago, he published *Client-Centered Therapy*. A book called *On Becoming a Person* was published in 1961; it is a collection of his most recent papers. All three books are published by Houghton Mifflin Company and are highly readable.

For a formalized recent statement of Rogers' theory, the student is advised to read Rogers' chapter in volume 3 of *Psychology: A Study of a Science*, a seven-volume treatment of contemporary psychology edited by Sigmund Koch and published by McGraw-Hill. This chapter is entitled "A Theory of Therapy, Personality, and Interpersonal Relationships, As Developed in the Client-Centered Framework."

Rogers' autobiography appears in volume 5 of *A History of Psychology in Autobiography*, published by Appleton-Century-Crofts in 1967.

For a thorough presentation of Rogers' research on client-centered therapy, the volume edited by him and Rosalind F. Dymond entitled *Psychotherapy and Personality Change*, published by the University of Chicago Press in 1954, should be consulted. A critique of Rogers and Dymond's book is contained in a book edited by Hans J. Eysenck entitled *Handbook of Abnormal Psychology*. This critique by Eysenck has also been reprinted as a little book called *The Effects of Psychotherapy*, published by The International Science Press in 1966.

The Necessary and Sufficient Conditions of Therapeutic Personality Change

Carl R. Rogers

For many years I have been engaged in psychotherapy with individuals in distress. In recent years I have found myself increasingly concerned with the process of abstracting from that experience the general principles which appear to be involved in it. I have endeavored to discover any orderliness, any unity which seems to inhere in the subtle, complex tissue of interpersonal relationship in which I have so constantly been immersed in therapeutic work. One of the current products of this concern is an attempt to state, in formal terms, a theory of psychotherapy, of personality, and of interpersonal relationships which will encompass and contain the phenomena of my experience. What I wish to do in this paper is to take one very small segment of that theory, spell it out more completely, and explore its meaning and usefulness.

The Problem

The question to which I wish to address myself is this: Is it possible to state, in terms which are clearly definable and measurable, the psychological conditions which are both necessary and sufficient to bring about constructive personality change? Do we, in other words, know with any precision those elements which are essential if psychotherapeutic change is to ensue?

Before proceeding to the major task let me dispose very briefly of the second portion of the question. What is meant by such phrases as "psychotherapeutic change," "constructive personality change"? This problem also deserves deep and serious consideration, but for the moment let me suggest a common-sense type of meaning upon which we can perhaps agree for purposes of this paper. By these phrases is meant: change in the personality structure of the individual, at both surface and deeper levels, in a direction which clinicians would agree means greater integration, less internal conflict, more energy utilizable for effective living; change in behavior away from behaviors generally regarded as immature and toward behaviors regarded as mature. This brief description may suffice to indicate the kind of change for which we are considering the preconditions. It may also suggest the ways in which this criterion of change may be determined.[1]

The Conditions

As I have considered my own clinical experience and that of my colleagues, together with the pertinent research which is available, I have drawn out several conditions which seem to me to be *necessary* to initiate constructive personality change, and which, taken together, appear to be *sufficient* to inaugurate that process. As I have worked on this problem I have found myself surprised at the simplicity of what has emerged. The statement which follows is not offered with any assurance as to its correctness, but with the

From C. R. Rogers, "The Necessary and Sufficient Conditions of Therapeutic Personality Change," *Journal of Consulting Psychology*, 1957, **21**, 95-103. Reprinted by permission of the American Psychological Association.

[1]That this is a measurable and determinable criterion has been shown in research already completed. See (7), especially chapters 8, 13, and 17.

expectation that it will have the value of any theory, namely that it states or implies a series of hypotheses which are open to proof or disproof, thereby clarifying and extending our knowledge of the field.

Since I am not, in this paper, trying to achieve suspense, I will state at once, in severely rigorous and summarized terms, the six conditions which I have come to feel are basic to the process of personality change. The meaning of a number of the terms is not immediately evident, but will be clarified in the explanatory sections which follow. It is hoped that this brief statement will have much more significance to the reader when he has completed the paper. Without further introduction let me state the basic theoretical position.

For constructive personality change to occur, it is necessary that these conditions exist and continue over a period of time:

1. Two persons are in psychological contact.
2. The first, whom we shall term the client, is in a state of incongruence, being vulnerable or anxious.
3. The second person, whom we shall term the therapist, is congruent or integrated in the relationship.
4. The therapist experiences unconditional positive regard for the client.
5. The therapist experiences an empathic understanding of the client's internal frame of reference and endeavors to communicate this experience to the client.
6. The communication to the client of the therapist's empathic understanding and unconditional positive regard is to a minimal degree achieved.

No other conditions are necessary. If these six conditions exist, and continue over a period of time, this is sufficient. The process of constructive personality change will follow.

A Relationship

The first condition specifies that a minimal relationship, a psychological contact, must exist. I am hypothesizing that significant positive personality change does not occur except in a relationship. This is of course an hypothesis, and it may be disproved.

Conditions 2 through 6 define the characteristics of the relationship which are regarded as essential by defining the necessary characteristics of each person in the relationship. All that is intended by this first condition is to specify that the two people are to some degree in contact, that each makes some perceived difference in the experiential field of the other. Probably it is sufficient if each makes some "subceived" difference, even though the individual may not be consciously aware of this impact. Thus it might be difficult to know whether a catatonic patient perceives a therapist's presence as making a difference to him—a difference of any kind—but it is almost certain that at some organic level he does sense this difference.

Except in such a difficult borderline situation as that just mentioned, it would be relatively easy to define this condition in operational terms and thus determine, from a hardboiled research point of view, whether the condition does, or does not, exist. The simplest method of determination involves simply the awareness of both client and therapist. If each is aware of being in personal or psychological contact with the other, then this condition is met.

This first condition of therapeutic change is such a simple one that perhaps it should be labeled an assumption or a precondition in order to set it apart from those that follow. Without it, however, the remaining items would have no meaning, and that is the reason for including it.

The State of the Client

It was specified that it is necessary that the client be "in a state of incongruence, being vulnerable or anxious." What is the meaning of these terms?

Incongruence is a basic construct in the theory we have been developing. It refers to a discrepancy between the actual experience of the organism and the self picture of the individual insofar as it represents that experience. Thus a student may experience, at a total or organismic level, a fear of the university and of examinations which are given on the third floor of a certain building, since these may demonstrate a fundamental inadequacy in him. Since such a fear of his inadequacy is decidedly at odds with his concept of himself, this experience is represented (distortedly) in his awareness as an unreasonable fear of climbing stairs in this building, or any building, and soon an unreasonable fear of crossing the open campus. Thus there is a fundamental discrepancy between the experienced meaning of the situation as it registers in his organism and the symbolic representation of that experience in awareness in such a way that it does not conflict with the picture he has of himself. In this case to admit a fear of inadequacy would contradict the picture he holds of himself; to admit incomprehensible fears does not contradict his self concept.

Another instance would be the mother who develops vague illnesses whenever her only son makes plans to leave home. The actual desire is to hold on to her only source of satisfaction. To perceive this in awareness would be inconsistent with the picture she holds of herself as a good mother. Illness, however, is consistent with her self concept, and the experience is symbolized in this distorted fashion. Thus again there is a basic incongruence between the self as perceived (in this case as an ill mother needing attention) and the actual experience (in this case the desire to hold on to her son).

When the individual has no awareness of such incongruence in himself, then he is merely vulnerable to the possibility of anxiety and disorganization. Some experience might occur so suddenly or so obviously that the incongruence could not be denied. Therefore, the person is vulnerable to such a possibility.

If the individual dimly perceives such an incongruence in himself, then a tension state occurs which is known as anxiety. The incongruence need not be sharply perceived. It is enough that it is subceived—that is, discriminated as threatening to the self without any awareness of the content of that threat. Such anxiety is often seen in therapy as the individual approaches awareness of some element of his experience which is in sharp contradiction to his self concept.

It is not easy to give precise operational definition to this second of the six conditions, yet to some degree this has been achieved. Several research workers have defined the self concept by means of a *Q* sort by the individual of a list of self-referent items. This gives us an operational picture of the self. The total experiencing of the individual is more difficult to capture. Chodorkoff (2) has defined it as a *Q* sort made by a clinician who sorts the same self-referent items independently, basing his sorting on the picture he has obtained of the individual from projective tests. His sort thus includes unconscious as well as conscious elements of the individual's experience, thus representing (in an admittedly imperfect way) the totality of the client's experience. The correlation between these two sortings gives a crude operational measure of incongruence between self and experience, low or negative correlation representing of course a high degree of incongruence.

The Therapist's Genuineness in the Relationship

The third condition is that the therapist should be, within the confines of this relationship, a congruent, genuine, integrated person. It means that within the relationship he is freely and deeply himself, with his actual experience accurately represented by his awareness of himself. It is the opposite of presenting a facade, either knowingly or unknowingly.

It is not necessary (nor is it possible) that the therapist be a paragon who exhibits this degree of integration, of wholeness, in every aspect of his life. It is sufficient that he is accurately himself in this hour of this relationship, that in this basic sense he is what he actually is, in this moment of time.

It should be clear that this includes being himself even in ways which are not regarded as ideal for psychotherapy. His experience may be "I am afraid of this client" or "My attention is so focused on my own problems that I can scarcely listen to him." If the therapist is not denying these feelings to awareness, but is able freely to be them (as well as being his other feelings), then the condition we have stated is met.

It would take us too far afield to consider the puzzling matter as to the degree to which the therapist overtly communicates this reality in himself to the client. Certainly the aim is not for the therapist to express or talk out his own feelings, but primarily that he should not be deceiving the client as to himself. At times he may need to talk out some of his own feelings (either to the client, or to a colleague or supervisor) if they are standing in the way of the two following conditions.

It is not too difficult to suggest an operational definition for this third condition. We resort again to Q technique. If the therapist sorts a series of items relevant to the relationship (using a list similar to the ones developed by Fiedler [3, 4] and Bown [1]), this will give his perception of his experience in the relationship. If several judges who have observed the interview or listened to a recording of it (or observed a sound movie of it) now sort the same items to represent *their* perception of the relationship, this second sorting should catch those elements of the therapist's behavior and inferred attitudes of which he is unaware, as well as those of which he is aware. Thus a high correlation between the therapist's sort and the observer's sort would represent in crude form an operational definition of the therapist's congruence or integration in the relationship; and a low correlation, the opposite.

Unconditional Positive Regard

To the extent that the therapist finds himself experiencing a warm acceptance of each aspect of the client's experience as being a part of that client, he is experiencing unconditional positive regard. This concept has been developed by Standal (8). It means that there are no *conditions* of acceptance, no feeling of "I like you only *if* you are thus and so." It means a "prizing" of the person, as Dewey has used that term. It is at the opposite pole from a selective evaluating attitude "You are bad in these ways, good in those." It involves as much feeling of acceptance for the

client's expression of negative, "bad," painful, fearful, defensive, abnormal feelings as for his expression of "good," positive, mature, confident, social feelings, as much acceptance of ways in which he is inconsistent as of ways in which he is consistent. It means a caring for the client, but not in a possessive way or in such a way as simply to satisfy the therapist's own needs. It means a caring for the client as a *separate* person, with permission to have his own feelings, his own experiences. One client describes the therapist as "fostering my possession of my own experience . . . that [this] is *my* experience and that I am actually having it: thinking what I think, feeling what I feel, wanting what I want, fearing what I fear: no 'ifs,' 'buts,' or 'not reallys.'" This is the type of acceptance which is hypothesized as being necessary if personality change is to occur.

Like the two previous conditions, this fourth condition is a matter of degree,[2] as immediately becomes apparent if we attempt to define it in terms of specific research operations. One such method of giving it definition would be to consider the Q sort for the relationship as described under Condition 3. To the extent that items expressive of unconditional positive regard are sorted as characteristic of the relationship by both the therapist and the observers, unconditional positive regard might be said to exist. Such items might include statements of this order: "I feel no revulsion at anything the client says"; "I feel neither approval nor disapproval of the client and his statements—simply acceptance"; "I feel warmly toward the client—toward his weaknesses and problems as well as his potentialities"; "I am not inclined to pass judgment on what the client

---

[2]The phrase "unconditional positive regard" may be an unfortunate one, since it sounds like an absolute, an all or nothing dispositional concept. It is probably evident from the description that completely unconditional positive regard would never exist except in theory. From a clinical and experiential point of view I believe the most accurate statement is that the effective therapist experiences unconditional positive regard for the client during many moments of his contact with him, yet from time to time he experiences only a conditional positive regard and perhaps at times a negative regard, though this is not likely in effective therapy. It is in this sense that unconditional positive regard exists as a matter of degree in any relationship.

tells me"; "I like the client." To the extent that both therapist and observers perceive these items as characteristic, or their opposites as uncharacteristic, Condition 4 might be said to be met.

Empathy

The fifth condition is that the therapist is experiencing an accurate, empathic understanding of the client's awareness of his own experience. To sense the client's private world as if it were your own, but without ever losing the "as if" quality—this is empathy, and this seems essential to therapy. To sense the client's anger, fear, or confusion as if it were your own, yet without your own anger, fear, or confusion getting bound up in it, is the condition we are endeavoring to describe. When the client's world is this clear to the therapist, and he moves about in it freely, then he can both communicate his understanding of what is clearly known to the client and can also voice meanings in the client's experience of which the client is scarcely aware. As one client described this second aspect: "Every now and again, with me in a tangle of thought and feeling, screwed up in a web of mutually divergent lines of movement, with impulses from different parts of me, and me feeling the feeling of its being all too much and suchlike—then whomp, just like a sunbeam thrusting its way through cloudbanks and tangles of foliage to spread a circle of light on a tangle of forest paths, came some comment from you. [It was] clarity, even disentanglement, an additional twist to the picture, a putting in place. Then the consequence—the sense of moving on, the relaxation. These were sunbeams." That such penetrating empathy is important for therapy is indicated by Fiedler's research (3) in which items such as the following placed high in the description of relationships created by experienced therapists:

The therapist is well able to understand the patient's feelings.
The therapist is never in any doubt about what the patient means.

The therapist's remarks fit in just right with the patient's mood and content.
The therapist's tone of voice conveys the complete ability to share the patient's feelings.

An operational definition of the therapist's empathy could be provided in different ways. Use might be made of the Q sort described under Condition 3. To the degree that items descriptive of accurate empathy were sorted as characteristic by both the therapist and the observers, this condition would be regarded as existing.

Another way of defining this condition would be for both client and therapist to sort a list of items descriptive of client feelings. Each would sort independently, the task being to represent the feelings which the client had experienced during a just completed interview. If the correlation between client and therapist sortings were high, accurate empathy would be said to exist, a low correlation indicating the opposite conclusion.

Still another way of measuring empathy would be for trained judges to rate the depth and accuracy of the therapist's empathy on the basis of listening to recorded interviews.

The Client's Perception of the Therapist

The final condition as stated is that the client perceives, to a minimal degree, the acceptance and empathy which the therapist experiences for him. Unless some communication of these attitudes has been achieved, then such attitudes do not exist in the relationship as far as the client is concerned, and the therapeutic process could not, by our hypothesis, be initiated.

Since attitudes cannot be directly perceived, it might be somewhat more accurate to state that therapist behaviors and words are perceived by the client as meaning that to some degree the therapist accepts and understands him.

An operational definition of this condition would not be difficult. The client might, after an interview, sort a Q-sort list of items referring to qualities representing the relationship between himself and the therapist. (The same list could be used as for Condition 3.) If several items descriptive of acceptance and empathy are sorted by the client as characteristic of the relationship, then this condition could be regarded as met. In the present state of our knowledge the meaning of "to a minimal degree" would have to be arbitrary.

Some Comments

Up to this point the effort has been made to present, briefly and factually, the conditions which I have come to regard as essential for psychotherapeutic change. I have not tried to give the theoretical context of these conditions nor to explain what seem to me to be the dynamics of their effectiveness. Such explanatory material is available in my chapter in volume 3 of *Psychology: A Study of a Science*, edited by Sigmund Koch and published by McGraw-Hill.

I have, however, given at least one means of defining, in operational terms, each of the conditions mentioned. I have done this in order to stress the fact that I am not speaking of vague qualities which ideally should be present if some other vague result is to occur. I am presenting conditions which are crudely measurable even in the present state of our technology, and have suggested specific operations in each instance even though I am sure that more adequate methods of measurement could be devised by a serious investigator.

My purpose has been to stress the notion that in my opinion we are dealing with an if-then phenomenon in which knowledge of the dynamics is not essential to testing the hypotheses. Thus, to illustrate from another field: if one substance, shown by a series of operations to be the substance known as hydrochloric acid, is mixed with another substance, shown by another series of operations to be sodium hydroxide, then salt and water will be products of this mixture. This is true whether one regards the results as due to magic, or whether one explains it in the most adequate terms of modern chemical theory.

In the same way it is being postulated here that certain definable conditions precede certain definable changes and that this fact exists independently of our efforts to account for it.

The Resulting Hypotheses

The major value of stating any theory in unequivocal terms is that specific hypotheses may be drawn from it which are capable of proof or disproof. Thus, even if the conditions which have been postulated as necessary and sufficient conditions are more incorrect than correct (which I hope they are not), they could still advance science in this field by providing a base of operations from which fact could be winnowed out from error.

The hypotheses which would follow from the theory given would be of this order:

If these six conditions (as operationally defined) exist, then constructive personality change (as defined) will occur in the client.

If one or more of these conditions is not present, constructive personality change will not occur.

These hypotheses hold in any situation whether it is or is not labeled "psychotherapy."

Only Condition 1 is dichotomous (it either is present or is not), and the remaining five occur in varying degree, each on its continuum. Since this is true, another hypothesis follows, and it is likely that this would be the simplest to test:

If all six conditions are present, then the greater the degree to which Conditions 2 to 6 exist, the more marked will be the constructive personality change in the client.

At the present time the above hypothesis can only be stated in this general form—which implies that all of the conditions have equal weight. Empirical studies will no doubt make possible much more refinement of this hypothesis. It may be, for example, that if anxiety is high in the client, then the other conditions are less important. Or if unconditional positive regard is high (as in a mother's love for her child), then perhaps a modest degree of empathy is sufficient. But at the moment we can only speculate on such possibilities.

Some Implications

Significant Omissions

If there is any startling feature in the formulation which has been given as to the necessary conditions for therapy, it probably lies in the elements which are omitted. In present-day clinical practice, therapists operate as though there were many other conditions in addition to those described, which are essential for psychotherapy. To point this up it may be well to mention a few of the conditions which, after thoughtful consideration of our research and our experience, are not included.

For example, it is *not* stated that these conditions apply to one type of client, and that other conditions are necessary to bring about psychotherapeutic change with other types of clients. Probably no idea is so prevalent in clinical work today as that one works with neurotics in one way, with psychotics in another; that certain therapeutic conditions must be provided for compulsives, others for homosexuals, etc. Because of this heavy weight of clinical opinion to the contrary, it is with some "fear and trembling" that I advance the concept that the essential conditions of psychotherapy exist in a single configuration, even though the client or patient may use them very differently.[3]

It is *not* stated that these six conditions are

the essential conditions for client-centered therapy, and that other conditions are essential for other types of psychotherapy. I certainly am heavily influenced by my own experience, and that experience has led me to a viewpoint which is termed "client centered." Nevertheless my aim in stating this theory is to state the conditions which apply to *any* situation in which constructive personality change occurs, whether we are thinking of classical psychoanalysis, or any of its modern offshoots, or Adlerian psychotherapy, or any other. It will be obvious then that in my judgment much of what is considered to be essential would not be found, empirically, to be essential. Testing of some of the stated hypotheses would throw light on this perplexing issue. We may of course find that various therapies produce various types of personality change, and that for each psychotherapy a separate set of conditions is necessary. Until and unless this is demonstrated, I am hypothesizing that effective psychotherapy of any sort produces similar changes in personality and behavior, and that a single set of preconditions is necessary.

It is *not* stated that psychotherapy is a special kind of relationship, different in kind from all others which occur in everyday life. It will be evident instead that for brief moments, at least, many good friendships fulfill the six conditions. Usually this is only momentarily, however, and then empathy falters, the positive regard becomes conditional, or the congruence of the "therapist" friend becomes overlaid by some degree of facade or defensiveness. Thus the therapeutic relationship is seen as a heightening of the constructive qualities which often exist in part in other relationships, and an extension through time of qualities which in other relationships tend at best to be momentary.

It is *not* stated that special intellectual professional knowledge—psychological, psychiatric, medical, or religious—is required of the therapist. Conditions 3, 4, and 5, which apply especially to the therapist, are qualities of experience, not intellectual information. If they are to be acquired, they must, in my opinion, be acquired through an experiential

---

[3]I cling to this statement of my hypothesis even though it is challenged by a just completed study by Kirtner (5). Kirtner has found, in a group of 26 cases from the Counseling Center at the University of Chicago, that there are sharp differences in the client's mode of approach to the resolution of life difficulties, and that these differences are related to success in psychotherapy. Briefly, the client who sees his problem as involving his relationships, and who feels that he contributes to this problem and wants to change it, is likely to be successful. The client who externalizes his problem, feeling little self-responsibility, is much more likely to be a failure. Thus the implication is that some other conditions need to be provided for psychotherapy with this group. For the present, however, I will stand by my hypothesis as given, until Kirtner's study is confirmed, and until we know an alternative hypothesis to take its place.

training—which may be, but usually is not, a part of professional training. It troubles me to hold such a radical point of view, but I can draw no other conclusion from my experience. Intellectual training and the acquiring of information has, I believe, many valuable results—but becoming a therapist is not one of those results.

It is *not* stated that it is necessary for psychotherapy that the therapist have an accurate psychological diagnosis of the client. Here too it troubles me to hold a viewpoint so at variance with my clinical colleagues. When one thinks of the vast proportion of time spent in any psychological, psychiatric, or mental hygiene center on the exhaustive psychological evaluation of the client or patient, it seems as though this *must* serve a useful purpose insofar as psychotherapy is concerned. Yet the more I have observed therapists, and the more closely I have studied research such as that done by Fiedler and others (4), the more I am forced to the conclusion that such diagnostic knowledge is not essential to psychotherapy.[4] It may even be that its defense as a necessary prelude to psychotherapy is simply a protective alternative to the admission that it is, for the most part, a colossal waste of time. There is only one useful purpose I have been able to observe which relates to psychotherapy. Some therapists cannot feel secure in the relationship with the client unless they possess such diagnostic knowledge. Without it they feel fearful of him, unable to be empathic, unable to experience unconditional regard, finding it necessary to put up a pretense in the relationship. If they know in *advance* of suicidal impulses they can somehow be more acceptant of them. Thus, for some therapists, the security they perceive in diagnostic information may be a basis for permitting themselves to be integrated in the relationship, and to experience empathy and full acceptance. In these instances a psychological diagnosis would certainly be justified as adding to the

comfort and hence the effectiveness of the therapist. But even here it does not appear to be a basic precondition for psychotherapy.[5]

Perhaps I have given enough illustrations to indicate that the conditions I have hypothesized as necessary and sufficient for psychotherapy are striking and unusual primarily by virtue of what they omit. If we were to determine, by a survey of the behaviors of therapists, those hypotheses which they appear to regard as necessary to psychotherapy, the list would be a great deal longer and more complex.

Is This Theoretical Formulation Useful?

Aside from the personal satisfaction it gives as a venture in abstraction and generalization, what is the value of a theoretical statement such as has been offered in this paper? I should like to spell out more fully the usefulness which I believe it may have.

In the field of research it may give both direction and impetus to investigation. Since it sees the conditions of constructive personality change as general, it greatly broadens the opportunities for study. Psychotherapy is not the only situation aimed at constructive personality change. Programs of training for leadership in industry and programs of training for military leadership often aim at such change. Educational institutions or programs frequently aim at development of character and personality as well as at intellectual skills. Community agencies aim at personality and behavioral change in delinquents and criminals. Such programs would provide an opportunity for the broad testing of the hypotheses offered. If it is found that constructive personality change occurs in such programs when the hypothesized conditions are not fulfilled, then the theory would have to be revised. If however the hypotheses

[4]There is no intent here to maintain that diagnostic evaluation is useless. We have ourselves made heavy use of such methods in our research studies of change in personality. It is its usefulness as a precondition to psychotherapy which is questioned.

[5]In a facetious moment I have suggested that such therapists might be made equally comfortable by being given the diagnosis of some other individual, not of this patient or client. The fact that the diagnosis proved inaccurate as psychotherapy continued would not be particularly disturbing, because one always expects to find inaccuracies in the diagnosis as one works with the individual.

are upheld, then the results, both for the planning of such programs and for our knowledge of human dynamics, would be significant. In the field of psychotherapy itself, the application of consistent hypotheses to the work of various schools of therapists may prove highly profitable. Again the disproof of the hypotheses offered would be as important as their confirmation, either result adding significantly to our knowledge.

For the practice of psychotherapy the theory also offers significant problems for consideration. One of its implications is that the techniques of the various therapies are relatively unimportant except to the extent that they serve as channels for fulfilling one of the conditions. In client-centered therapy, for example, the technique of "reflecting feelings" has been described and commented on (6, pp. 26-36). In terms of the theory here being presented, this technique is by no means an essential condition of therapy. To the extent, however, that it provides a channel by which the therapist communicates a sensitive empathy and an unconditional positive regard, then it may serve as a technical channel by which the essential conditions of therapy are fulfilled. In the same way, the theory I have presented would see no essential value to therapy of such techniques as interpretation of personality dynamics, free association, analysis of dreams, analysis of the transference, hypnosis, interpretation of life style, suggestion, and the like. Each of these techniques may, however, become a channel for communicating the essential conditions which have been formulated. An interpretation may be given in a way which communicates the unconditional positive regard of the therapist. A stream of free association may be listened to in a way which communicates an empathy which the therapist is experiencing. In the handling of the transference an effective therapist often communicates his own wholeness and congruence in the relationship. Similarly for the other techniques. But just as these techniques *may* communicate the elements which are

essential for therapy, so any one of them may communicate attitudes and experiences sharply contradictory to the hypothesized conditions of therapy. Feeling may be "reflected" in a way which communicates the therapist's lack of empathy. Interpretations may be rendered in a way which indicates the highly conditional regard of the therapist. Any of the techniques may communicate the fact that the therapist is expressing one attitude at a surface level, and another contradictory attitude which is denied to his own awareness. Thus one value of such a theoretical formulation as we have offered is that it may assist therapists to think more critically about those elements of their experience, attitudes, and behaviors which are essential to psychotherapy, and those which are nonessential or even deleterious to psychotherapy.

Finally, in those programs—educational, correctional, military, or industrial—which aim toward constructive changes in the personality structure and behavior of the individual, this formulation may serve as a very tentative criterion against which to measure the program. Until it is much further tested by research, it cannot be thought of as a valid criterion, but, as in the field of psychotherapy, it may help to stimulate critical analysis and the formulation of alternative conditions and alternative hypotheses.

Summary

Drawing from a larger theoretical context, six conditions are postulated as necessary and sufficient conditions for the initiation of a process of constructive personality change. A brief explanation is given of each condition, and suggestions are made as to how each may be operationally defined for research purposes. The implications of this theory for research, for psychotherapy, and for educational and training programs aimed at constructive personality change, are indicated. It is pointed out that many of the conditions which are commonly regarded as necessary to psychotherapy are, in terms of this theory, nonessential.

References

1. Bown, O. H. An investigation of therapeutic relationship in client-centered therapy. Unpublished doctor's dissertation, Univer. of Chicago, 1954.
2. Chodorkoff, B. Self-perception, perceptual defense, and adjustment. *J. abnorm. soc. Psychol.*, 1954, **49**, 508-512.
3. Fiedler, F. E. A comparison of therapeutic relationships in psychoanalytic, non-directive and Adlerian therapy. *J. consult. Psychol.*, 1950, **14**, 436-445.
4. Fiedler, F. E. Quantitative studies on the role of therapists' feelings toward their patients. In O. H. Mowrer (Ed.), *Psychotherapy: Theory and research*. New York: Ronald, 1953.
5. Kirtner, W. L. Success and failure in client-centered therapy as a function of personality variables. Unpublished master's thesis, Univer. of Chicago, 1955.
6. Rogers, C. R. *Client-centered therapy*. Boston: Houghton Mifflin, 1951.
7. Rogers, C. R. & Dymond, Rosalind F. (Eds.) *Psychotherapy and personality change*. Chicago: Univer. of Chicago Press, 1954.
8. Standal, S. The need for positive regard: A contribution to client-centered theory. Unpublished doctor's dissertation, Univer. of Chicago, 1954.

Development of a Scale to Measure Process Changes in Psychotherapy

Alan M. Walker, Richard A. Rablen, and Carl R. Rogers

Introduction

This paper describes the application of a scale for the objective assessment of process or movement in psychotherapy and reports the degree of reliability and validity found in a preliminary investigation. Before proceeding to the study itself, some indication of the way in which it developed is necessary. The scale in its original form was proposed by Rogers (7) after he had undertaken an extended study of recorded interviews for the purpose of discovering commonalities in the process of personality change. He proposed that clients who feel received in therapy tend to move away from a general fixity of functioning and rigidity of structure toward greater openness, fluidity, and changingness, along a continuum from stasis to process. As first presented, the scale was organized into several stages along the general continuum. Short interview excerpts and descriptive comments were provided to illustrate the salient characteristics of each stage.

The present scale represents a refinement of the original scale based upon further analysis and study of additional therapy protocols. A number of separate elements or "strands" were isolated and identified within the more general framework of the stage conception of process. The seven strands constituting the form of the scale used in this study are briefly described below and are presented schematically in Table 1. Fuller descriptions of the characteristics of each strand at each level are available elsewhere (10). The descriptions presented here follow closely those of Rogers' (8) paper to the 1958 APA conference on research, which also included a preliminary report on the present research.

From A. M. Walker, R. A. Rablen, and C. R. Rogers, "Development of a Scale to Measure Process Changes in Psychotherapy," *Journal of Clinical Psychology*, 1960, **16**, 79-85. Reprinted by permission of the publisher and the authors.

Strands of the Process Continuum

The Relationship to Feelings and Personal Meanings. This strand refers to the relationship of the individual to the feelings and personal meanings which exist within himself. The phrase "feeling and personal meaning" refers to an emotionally tinged experience together with its significance to the individual. At the lower end of the continuum feelings and personal meanings are unrecognized by the individual and unexpressed, though feelings are perhaps exhibited. Near the midpoint of the scale they are expressed as owned feelings in the present. At the upper end of the continuum, living in the process of experiencing a continually changing flow of feelings becomes characteristic of the individual.

The Manner of Experiencing. Experiencing is regarded as the directly given, felt datum which is implicitly meaningful (1). It refers to the individual's sense of *having* experience, which is given in the phenomenal field of every person. When the individual asks himself, "What kind of an experiencing is this?" there is always an implicit answer even though no explicit answer has as yet been conceptualized. The manner of experiencing refers to the extent to which the individual finds himself in this subjective experiencing or very remote from it. At one end of the scale the individual may be quite unaware

Table 1. A schematic presentation of the general process continuum. (For simplicity, the salient characteristics of each strand are presented at low, medium, and high points only on the general process continuum. In the study proper, seven stages were discriminated.)

Strands	Process Stages		
	Low (I-II)	Medium (III-V)	High (VI-VII)
Feelings and personal meanings	Unrecognized Unexpressed	Increasing ownership Increasing expression	Living in flow Fully experienced
Experiencing	Remote from experiencing Unaware	Decreasing remoteness Increasing awareness	Lives in process of experiencing Uses as major referent
Incongruence	Unrecognized	Increasing recognition Increasing direct experiencing	Temporary only
Communication of self	Lacking	Increasing self-communication	Rich self-awareness communicated when desired
Construing of experience	Rigid constructions Construction seen as fact	Decreasing rigidity Increasing recognition of own contribution	Tentative constructions Meaning held loosely to be checked against experiencing
Relationship to problems	Unrecognized No desire to change	Increasing responsibility assumed Change often feared	Problem not seen as external object Living in some aspect of problem
Manner of relating	Close relationships avoided as dangerous	Decreasing danger felt	Relates openly and freely on basis of immediate experiencing

of the process of experiencing which he is undergoing and keeps himself distant from its implicit meanings. Gradually the individual moves toward a greater awareness of his inner experiencing. Finally, he becomes able to live freely and acceptantly in a fluid process of experiencing, using it comfortably as the major referent for his behavior.

The Degree of Incongruence. Incongruence has been defined (9) as the discrepancy which exists between what the individual is now experiencing and the representation of this in his awareness or in his communication. Such discrepancy cannot be directly known to the individual himself but may be observed. Its opposite is a congruence between the experiencing of the individual and the symbolization or conceptualization of this in his awareness. The continuum runs from a maximum of incongruence which is quite unknown to the individual, through stages where there is an increasingly sharp recognition of the contradictions and discrepancies existing within himself, to the experiencing of incongruence in the immediate present in a way which dissolves it. At the upper end of the continuum there would never be more than temporary incongruence between experiencing and awareness since the individual would not need to defend himself against the threatening aspects of his experience.

The Communication of Self. This continuum deals with the extent to which and the manner in which the individual is able and willing to communicate himself in a receptive climate. The continuum runs from a complete unwillingness to communicate self to a stage where the self involves a rich and changing awareness of internal experiencing which is readily communicated when the individual desires to do so.

The Manner in which Experience is Construed. This and the two following strands are not as sharply differentiated as the four preceding. Nevertheless, their end points and some of their mid points are recognizable. Experience at one end of the continuum is construed rigidly. These constructions are unrecognized as creations of the individual but are thought of as fixed facts. At the other end of the continuum experience is never given more than a tentative meaning or construction. This meaning is always held loosely to be checked and rechecked against further experiencing.

The Relationship to Problems. This is a strand which endeavors to describe the individual's changing relationship to the problem elements of himself. At one end of the scale, the problems are unrecognized and there is no desire to change. Gradually there is increasing recognition that the individual has contributed to these problems. At the upper end there is a living or experiencing of some aspect of the problem. The individual is responsibly in it subjectively rather than seeing it as a kind of external object.

The Manner of Relating. At one end of the continuum, the individual avoids close relationships which are perceived as being dangerous. At the other end of the continuum, he lives openly and freely in relation to the therapist and to others, guiding his behavior in the relationship on the basis of his immediate experiencing.

Method

Six completely transcribed cases from the University of Chicago Counseling Center provided the source of materials for the initial application of the process scale. It was assumed in all cases that the therapist fulfilled, to an adequate degree, the set of conditions thought (5) to be optimal for facilitating the process of change. These cases were mostly brief ones for which research data on outcomes were available. They were chosen to represent a considerable range of outcome,

with three representing marked progress and three minimal progress. The cases and the order in which they were ranked by the third author as to progress in therapy, using all the available evidence are shown in Table 2.

Sets of four single pages of interview material were chosen systematically from each of the six transcribed cases and recopied without identifying information. The method of sampling provided two pages of material from early interviews and two pages of material from late interviews for each case. Typically, the interviews chosen for the early sets were the second and third and for the late sets, the two immediately preceding the last interview. Thus there were in all 24 pages of interview material, each identified only by a code number. The pages were placed in random order for presentation to the judges.

Two judges, who differed in theoretical orientation and amount of experience in clinical psychology, worked together for a number of hours training themselves on interview material from other cases in order to learn to make the discriminations called for in the scale. After this training, the judges turned to

Editorial Note: Every editor has the duty to simplify presentations as much as possible, to hold to a minimum new theoretical constructs where older ones are still valid, and to relate new developments to existing theory. In particular, we question the value in this article of the introduction of the concept of "strand" as opposed to the older concept of "factor," and the resulting speculative concept of the "strands" converging to form a "stream."

Historically, Adolf Meyers' concept of the stream of life attempted to depict the viscissitudes of component processes in the ongoing process of mental status. It is desirable to attempt to visualize the genetic development of personality factors over the time dimension. The fact that a "factor" may make varying contributions to mental status over a period of time would seem not to necessitate the coining of the new concept of strand."

An alternative explanation is offered by modern integration theory. As a result of therapy resulting in more self-awareness and insight, it is assumed that behavior becomes "integrated" on higher levels which may be objectively identified. The discrete (separable and distinct) nature of the factors at the "fixity" end of the process actually may be an expression of lack of integration, inconsistency or conflict. In therapy the client becomes able to organize formerly discrete behaviors into unified integrations. Simply the process of bringing together formerly discrete or unperceived factors in consciousness is an integrative process which raises the level of functional integration.

The Law of Parsimony requires that every effort should be made to relate the factors measured by the author's scale with known personality factors, and not to introduce speculative new concepts until the possibility of identifying them with established factors is exhausted.

Table 2. Ranking of progress in therapy of cases included in the study of process.

Rank	Code	Total number of interviews	Sample Interviews	Explanation of ranking
1	Vib	9	2, 3, 7, 8	Rated first in 1949 study (2) on objective evidence.
2	Oak	48	2, 3, 46, 47	Showed marked objective progress in 1954 study (4).
3	Sar	4	1, 2, 3, 4	Showed dramatic improvement in four interviews. Judged as a very successful brief case by observers.
4	Bebb	9	2, 3, 7, 8	Showed objective progress in therapy, but decrement during followup period in 1954 study (3).
5	Sim	7	2, 3, 5, 6	Ranked 7.5 out of 10 in progress in 1949 study (2).
6	Sketch	3	1, 2, 2, 3	Ranked 9 out of 10 in progress in 1949 study (2).

the data of this study, considering each page as a unit for their purpose. At all times, the judges attempted to assume a "listening attitude" toward the data, trying to understand the significance of the client's remarks for him rather than to evaluate his comments diagnostically.

Several sortings of the data were made following a pre-planned order designed to avoid contamination or confounding within the sequence of discriminations. Since it was possible that time cues might appear in the materials and provide a basis for judging the relative position in therapy of some protocols, the material was sorted for objective evidence of chronology in therapy. Only one segment was positively identified as to time by the two judges. It was therefore concluded that there were no time cues operating in the sample of interviews which would bias the raters' judgment of the stage of therapy.

The most difficult discrimination attempted was to assign an absolute global stage rating to each of the twenty-four unidentified segments using the seven-stage scale of process. For this purpose, the judges introduced decimals between stages for greater precision, resulting essentially in a seventy-point scale. The segments were also independently rank

ordered as to process, and as a third task were independently divided into equal groups of eight segments judged to be high, medium, and low on the process continuum.

Results

Reliability. On the seventy-point scale, the two judges' independent ratings of the twenty-four segments correlated (Pearson r) .83, significant at the .01 level. On the rank ordering of the segments, a correlation (rho) of .84 was obtained, significant at the .01 level. When judgments as to the eight high, eight medium, and eight low segments were compared, there was 75% exact agreement, 25% one-step disagreement, and 0% two-step disagreement.

Validity. The six cases had been ranked on external criteria as noted above. These rankings were not disclosed to the judges until they had completed their work. An index of change for each case was derived from each rater's judgments by adding together the process ratings for the two late interviews of each case and subtracting from this value the sum of ratings for the two early interviews. Using this index, it was found that the two judges had given identical rankings to the six cases, the order being (1) Vib, (2) Sar, (3) Oak, (4) Bebb, (5) Sketch, (6) Sim. Comparing this order or ranking to that obtained using the external criteria data (Table 2) yielded a rho of .89, significant at the .02 level.

Another way of considering the validity of the ratings is to compare the change on the process scale of the three cases selected as representing marked progress with the change in the three cases selected as representing minimal progress. For the marked progress group the mean changes (based on a process change index derived from pooling the ratings of both judges) were 2.3, 2.0, and 1.5. The overall mean change for the group was 1.93. In the minimal progress group, the changes were 1.2, 0.3, and -0.6. The overall mean for this group was 0.30. It will be noted that there is no overlap between the two groups.

Discussion

It seems apparent that satisfactory inter-judge reliability can be obtained in using the process scale in its present form, and that ratings derived from it bear a meaningful relationship to other measures of successful change in therapy. These results were found despite the use of quite small samples of transcribed material, implying that higher reliability should be obtained with increased sampling and perhaps use of auditory cues as well as verbal ones.

Relationship between Continuum and Strands of Process. In our experience with the strand approach to a continuum of process change, it has seemed to us that the usual model of discrete and parallel continua which can be summed or averaged to obtain an overall stage rating does not fit our data. Rather, the strands seem more separable and distinct at the fixity end of the process continuum, where they can be more independently evaluated and rated. Whether the individual is exhibiting a rigid personal construct, or expressing himself on non-self topics, or describing feelings in a way which shows no di-

rect ownership of them, these are rather clearly discriminable elements. But in the later stages of the process, the individual may be experiencing feelings with immediacy— knowing them and experiencing them being synonymous. These feelings are his expression of himself at the moment. They may represent an immediately experienced change in a personal construct. Here all the previously identifiable strands are fused into one moment, and to separate them is artificial. It therefore appears that the most adequate diagrammatic model is one of converging lines, separable at first, but becoming less and less clearly distinguishable. Rogers (8) has suggested the analogy of a stream, originating in separate frozen rivulets, which under the impact of psychological warmth, gradually begin to trickle. The beginning flow may be frozen or dammed at some further point. If the psychological climate continues to be favorable then these individual rivulets increasingly flow into one another. At the optimal point of flow, they form a unified stream of change in which the contribution of the separate tributaries can no longer be accurately distinguished, although all are present. Evaluation of the adequacy of such an assumed model must await further pattern analysis of the strands.

Implications for Change. A prediction is implicit in the development of this conception of the process of personality change. It hints at the possibility that a brief sample of an individual's expressive behavior, taken in a situation in which he feels fully received, can be analyzed to yield knowledge of where he stands on the continuum of personality development and flow; and that this analysis may be possible without knowledge of the individual's genetic history, social and personal background, personality type, psychological diagnosis, or length of time in therapy. If this implicit prediction is even partly fulfilled, it means that the interaction process in therapy is moving into the realm of objective research.

When a reliable operational meaning can be given to this theory of the process of therapy, it will be feasible to test a variety of hypotheses as to the quality and nature of personality change as it occurs in psychotherapy. For example, with an adequate scale of process in therapy, more precise answers than before should be found to such questions as where an individual starts in therapy, how far he progresses, and the amount of difficulty involved in moving from different stages. It may be necessary to reach certain stages in process for lasting change to occur. If the latter is true, it may help explain the puzzle of apparent progress in therapy which is not evident in a later follow-up.

When we turn to implications for the more general area of personality development and for all helping relationships (6, 9) the process concept suggests several lines of thought. If personality development proceeds in the direction of full experiencing and living in an integrated flow of implicit meaning, then the fully functioning person is one who is a stream of process himself, who has become the process of experiencing through which his development has been moving. The difference between this concept and the more usual one of movement toward a new fixity is great and its meaning needs to be explored. The potential applications of the process concept to all helping relationships—not only therapy but teacher-student relationships, parent-child relationships, industrial consultation, and community development—deserve consideration as well.

Summary

A conception of process change in psychotherapy has been elaborated into an overall scale manifest in various partially separable elements or strands of process. The general direction of change is conceived to be from stasis and fixity to changingness and flow in such areas as one's relations to feelings and personal meanings, his manner of experiencing, degree of incongruence, communication of self, construing of experience, relationship to problems, and manner of relating to others. The strands are thought to be more distinct at the fixity end of the continuum and more unitary at the flow end.

The scale was applied to twenty-four unidentified samples, selected without bias from early and late interviews of six cases, judged to vary in amount of change by external criteria. Two judges, working independently, achieved a high degree of reliability in all comparisons. Two different methods of estimating process change from application of the scale showed high agreement with estimates of progress in therapy as derived from objective evidence and counselor ratings.

These results are interpreted to imply that a significant dimension of personality change is being tapped and that further development of the process concept and scale promises to have important implications for our knowledge of therapy, personality change, and perhaps social change as well.

References

1. Gendlin, E. The function of experiencing in symbolization. Unpublished doctoral dissertation, Univer. of Chicago, 1958.
2. Raskin, N. J. An analysis of six parallel studies of therapeutic process. *J. consult. Psychol.*, 1949, **13**, 206-220.
3. Rogers, C. R. The case of Mr. Bebb: The analysis of a failure case. In C. R. Rogers and Rosalind F. Dymond (Eds.), *Psychotherapy and personality change*. Chicago: Univer. of Chicago Press, 1954, pp. 349-412.
4. Rogers, C. R. The case of Mrs. Oak: A research analysis. In C. R. Rogers and Rosalind F. Dymond (Eds.). *Psychotherapy and personality change*. Chicago: Univer. of Chicago Press, 1954. Pp. 259-348.
5. Rogers, C. R. The necessary and sufficient conditions of therapeutic personality change. *J. consult. Psychol.*, 1957, **21**, 95-103.
6. Rogers, C. R. The characteristics of a helping relationship. *Personnel and Guidance Journal*, 1958, **37**, 6-16.
7. Rogers, C. R. A process conception of psychotherapy. *Amer. Psychologist*, 1958, **13**, 142-149.
8. Rogers, C. R. A tentative scale for the measurement of process in psychotherapy. In E. A. Rubinstein and M. B. Parlof (Eds.), *Research in psychotherapy*. Washington, D. C.: American Psychological Association, 1959. Pp. 96-108.

9. Rogers, C. R. A theory of therapy, personality, and interpersonal relationships, as developed in the client-centered framework. In Koch, S. (Ed.) *Psychology: A study of a science. Vol. 3. Formulations of the person and the social context.* New York: McGraw-Hill, 1959.

10. Rogers, C. R., and Rablen, R. A. A scale of process in psychotherapy. Unpublished manual, Univer. of Wisconsin, 1958.

Reinforcement vs. Nonreinforcement in Client-Centered Psychotherapy

Charles B. Truax

Excerpts from tape recordings of a single, long-term, successful therapy case handled by Rogers were analyzed to evaluate the adequacy of the client-centered view that empathy, warmth, and directiveness are offered throughout therapy in a manner not contingent upon the patient's behavior. Findings indicate that the therapists respond in a significantly differential way to 5 of the 9 patient behavior classes studied. Concomitantly, significant increases in the emission rates of 4 of the 5 behavior classes were noted throughout therapy. Findings thus indicated significant reinforcement effects in the client-centered therapy.

The present study is aimed at exploring the possibility that important reinforcement effects occur within the transactions of nondirective therapy.[1]

Client-centered theorists have specified the "therapeutic conditions" of empathic understanding and acceptance or unconditional positive regard as two main antecedents to constructive behavioral or personality change in the client (Dymond, 1949; Hobbs, 1962; Jourard, 1959; Rogers, 1951, 1957; Rogers & Truax, 1965; Truax, 1961; Truax & Carkhuff, 1963). Rogers, as the leading exponent of this viewpoint, holds that these "conditions" are primarily attitudinal in nature and are offered in a nonselective fashion to the

From C. B. Truax, "Reinforcement and Nonreinforcement in Rogerian Psychotherapy," *Journal of Abnormal Psychology*, 1966, **71**, 1-9. Reprinted by permission of the American Psychological Association.

[1] Appreciation is gratefully extended to Carl R. Rogers for his freely given consent to the use of the completed successful counseling case recorded at the University of Chicago Counseling Center in 1955. This particular case is perhaps of special significance since it was heavily used by Rogers and others in the development of the "process conception of psychotherapy" and the "Process Scale" developed in 1957. Thanks are also due to James C. Baxter and Leon D. Silber for their critical comments. This work was supported in part by a grant from the Vocational Rehabilitation Administration, No. RD-906-PM.

patient: they are specifically not contingent upon the patients' verbalizations or behaviors. This viewpoint, in pure form, is incompatible with the behavioristic view of therapy and was one basis for the Rogers-Skinner debates (1956).

The basic difference between the views exemplified by Rogers and Skinner is that the latter holds that an effective therapist attempts to alter the patient's behavior while Rogers holds otherwise. Differential reinforcement is one of the procedures used in operant research *positions*. Thus, whether or not Rogers as a therapist uses differential reinforcement, thereby altering patient behavior, is a central question in the basic issue of control which philosophically differentiates the two positions.

The growing body of evidence indicates that the therapist's accurate empathy and unconditional positive regard are significant antecedents to therapeutic change (Rogers, 1962; Rogers, Kiesler, Gendlin & Truax, 1965). This evidence has been used both as support of Rogers's view and as an argument against the behavioristic views of psychotherapy typified by such theorists as Krasner (1962), Wolpe (1958), Eysenck (1952, 1960), and Bandura (1961). The evidence does suggest that when patients receive high levels of empathy and warmth there is significantly more constructive personality and behavioral change than when the patients receive relatively lower levels (Barrett-Lennard, 1962; Bergin & Solomon, 1963; Cartwright & Lerner, 1963; Dickenson & Truax, 1965; Halkides, 1958; Lesser, 1961; Rogers, 1962; Strupp, 1960; Truax, 1961a, 1961b, 1963; Truax & Carkhuff, 1964; Truax, Carkhuff &

Kodman, in press; Truax, Wargo, & Silber, 1965; Wargo, 1962; and Whitehorn & Betz, 1954). None of the research just cited, however, *necessarily* argues against a behavioristic view of psychotherapy.

If, in contrast to Rogers's contention, the therapist does respond differentially to different patient behaviors (i.e., more accepting of and empathic to, some patient behaviors but less accepting of and more directive in response to other patient behaviors) then a reinforcement view would not be inconsistent with the findings. It could be argued that if empathic understanding, warmth (and nondirectiveness) are therapeutic, then it may also be argued that these therapeutic conditions are reinforcing, rewarding, or somehow encouraging, and that the types of patient behavior (presumably more adaptive ones) that are followed by high levels of these therapeutic conditions will consequently increase during the course of therapy. For example, it may be that the "high conditions" therapist offers more intense levels of accurate empathy and unconditional warmth or acceptance on both a nonselective random basis at, say, a 40% rate of reinforcement for all behaviors and, say, an 85% rate for exploration of material relevant to the private self. By contrast the "low conditions" therapist may offer less intense levels of empathy and warmth, with only a 20% rate of reinforcement for all behavior emitted and only a 40% rate of reinforcement for the patient's explorations of private material.

Support for the position exemplified by Rogers, viewed from the findings on empathy and warmth, rests upon the assumption that the therapist offers levels of conditions that do not systematically covary with the verbalizations or behavior emitted by the patient. If this were true (if, say, the level of therapist empathy or warmth did not systematically covary with patient response classes) then differential reinforcement could not account for the research findings of relationships between therapist behavior and patient outcome. On the other hand, if the therapist, in this case Rogers, does systematically vary his level of empathy depending on the be-

havior, then Rogers's position would not be supported.

In an attempt to add clarity to this theoretic controversy, an exploratory analysis of a single successful case handled by Rogers was aimed at determining whether or not important reinforcing effects are imbedded in the transactions of client-centered therapy.

Three qualities of the therapist's behavior were studied as potential reinforcers: (*a*) empathic understanding, (*b*) acceptance or unconditional positive regard, and (*c*) directiveness (a negative reinforcer). These therapist behaviors were examined in relation to nine classes of patient behavior in order to determine the presence or absence of differential therapist responding and any consequent changes in the patient behaviors.[2] The patient behaviors studied which might theoretically be of significance were: (*a*) degree of discrimination learnings by the patient, (*b*) ambiguity of patient's statements, (*c*) degree of insight development by the patient, (*d*) degree of similarity of patient's style of expression to that of the therapist, (*e*) problem orientation of the patient, (*f*) degree of patient catharsis, (*g*) degree of patient blocking, (*h*) degree of patient anxiety, and (*i*) degree of patient negative versus positive feeling expression.

Case Analysis Procedure

Five clinical psychologists rated an unbiased sample of 40 typewritten interaction units consisting of (*a*) a therapist statement, (*b*) a succeeding patient statement, (*c*) the succeeding therapist statement. These interaction units (TPT, Therapist-Patient-Therapist) were designated by code numbers prior to the ratings, and were then assigned in random order to the five clinical psychologists who served as judges. Each judge rated separately each of the nine patient scales and the three therapist scales in different order, so as to minimize rating biases. The ratings were then decoded, and the ratings of the three classes of "reinforcers" were simply correlat-

[2]Thanks are due to Israel Goldiamond for critical and helpful questions which served as the stimulus for the analysis of change in patient behaviors over time.

ed separately with the nine classes of patient behavior under examination. The presence of significant correlations would then be positive evidence to indicate systematic, nonrandom use of these reinforcers with particular classes of patient behavior. Thus the question became, for example, "Does the therapist's degree of acceptance significantly covary with the patient's degree of discrimination learning?" If a positive correlation was found, this would indicate that the therapist systematically was most accepting and unconditionally warm when the patient was engaged in discrimination learning, and was least accepting and warm when the patient engaged in very little discrimination learning.

The Interaction Unit Sample. The TPT interaction units were selected from the following interviews out of a total of 85 therapy sessions for the complete case, 1, 3, 5, 7, 10, 15, 20, 25, 30, 35, 40, 45, 50, 55, 60, 65, 70, 75, 80, and 85. Two intersection units were taken from each of the above 20 interviews for a total of 40 interaction units. Interviews from which the samples were drawn, with the exception of Numbers 3 and 7, which were added to give more weight to the earlier stages of therapy, were evenly spaced and should constitute an unbiased sample of interviews throughout the therapy case. The two interaction units from each interview were obtained by starting the playback of the recordings at approximately the end of the first and second one-third of the hour-long tape and then listening until the therapist made a statement. Transcriptions started at the therapist's first words and included the ensuing TPT interaction unit. As a result of this sampling procedure, the length of the therapist and the patient statements varied considerably. When measured to the nearest one-tenth of an 80-character type line the range was from 0.4 to 14.0 lines.

The Clinical Psychologists as Raters. Of the five raters, none was trained in client-centered psychotherapy. One was trained in analytic therapy, while the remaining four clinicians described themselves as eclectic in orientation. All five judges had a minimum of 100 hours of supervised training as therapists, and 1,000 hours of experience as therapists. All post-doctoral clinical psychologists, the judges did not know the hypothesis being investigated. Further, they wrongly assumed that some of the more "nondirective" and "directive" statements could not have come from the same therapist.

The Rating Scales. A set of graphic rating scales was prepared for each of the three therapist behaviors and nine patient behaviors, each having a brief statement of the variable to be rated and horizontal lines 170 millimeters long on which the rating was marked. The rating was made by simply placing an X along the line labeled "most," "very much," to "least," and "very little." The scales for each therapist and patient behavior class stated a bipolarity of the variable. The bipolar definitions for the three reinforcer variables were taken from Rogers's (1951) theoretic descriptions.

Although the actual therapy samples did not contain extreme examples of the scale values, examples from the present case should add meaning to the present study. Two examples of TPT samples, rated high on each of the three reinforcer variables, are presented below.

Therapist Acceptance of Unconditional Positive Regard. The first example illustrates relatively high acceptance of the patient as he is feeling disappointed in the early results of therapy. This sample was rated relatively low on both empathy and directiveness:

T: There is nothing that I can do, but I can and do hope that the person will "lift" or something.
P: Yeh, but, well, for something to happen, or things to change, or me to change . . . inside, or . . . things to change outside, so I can change inside or something. Talking about it . . . doesn't really . . . seem to help, this kind of feeling. I mean, well . . . well, I don't know what I mean. I mean, I guess we're just talking about it. Well I don't know what I'm doing (he has been thumping on something—beating on the desk?—long, long pause) . . . I feel so tremendously self-conscious. I don't know,

maybe it was the therapy session yesterday, and the other thing that happened yesterday, that has just thrown, so much on me, myself again. And dangerous, I don't know, not dangerous but ... I feel so un-free today. So ... Hmm ... (long pause) ... Yeh, boy I really am self-conscious ... sure tensed up inside.

T: I can't get the feel of what you mean by "self-conscious." It's very much aware of yourself? Or something, or generally embarrassed?

The second example illustrates relatively high acceptance of the patient's feelings of inadequacy and dependency. This sample was rated slightly above average on empathy but below average on directiveness:

T: I guess you're saying "I just can't trust those weak, and helpless and inadequate parts of me. I have to have someone to ..."

P: To really be me. (T: Mmm, mmm) Someone else, you know ... that's so absurd ... that would never work. It's the same thing as, as this, uh ... being afraid of people. It ties in with being afraid. It's like ... well, you can use any one of a number of examples. If you really want to be someone genuinely ... or express something genuinely ... then, all you have to do is feel the slightest tinge of fear and you won't be able to—really. And it's like that with myself ... It's kind of ... when I am myself, it kind of echoes on me and makes me afraid. I suddenly hear myself saying that, and then know, "careful" (T: Mmm, mmm) "Hold on here! Lookout!" (T: Mmm, mmm) ... like that. (T: Mmm, mmm) "You won't be allowed to live if you do that." (T: Mmm, mmm) "You won't be allowed to ... *anything*" ... just, "You'll be blown to smithereens if you try that kind of thing."

T: Mmmm, So that if you sense yourself ... being yourself ... then my (P: I become afraid) Gosh! Lookout! You don't know what you're getting into—you'll be destroyed.

Therapist Directiveness. The first example shows the therapist making a direct request to change the topic of discussion. This sample was rated slightly below average in empathy and low in acceptance:

T: Let's talk about something closer to you than that.

P: Or closer to you. I don't understand this at all, because I was really looking forward to this all the time, and now I just don't feel very good ... about having harmed you.

T: You anticipated coming in, and now ... today.

A second example of directiveness involves a more subtle "leading" of the patient. This sample was rated as average in empathy but above average in acceptance or unconditional positive regard:

T: It frightens you to even start to put it into words.

P: I guess I'll have to find it with someone else ... first.

T: You feel that what would be demanded would be ... put it in terms of "me" and, "you" ... uh ... make this the sort of thing you can sort of dimly visualize. I would need to want to really relate to that fine part of you, and find that so personally rewarding that, that in an attempt I would just ... keep after it, or something. (P interjects: Yeh) One, one phrase that I ... I'm bringing in my feelings rather than yours, but ... ever read the poem "The Hound of Heaven"? It's kinda a weird thing, but, uh, the kind of persistent love of God is the whole theme, that, that won't let the person go ... and, and, I think that's sort of what you're talking about.

Therapist Empathy. The first example illustrates an excerpt in which the therapist attempts to verbalize what he senses is the client's uncertainty; this sample received an average rating on acceptance and a slightly above average rating on directiveness:

T: I've been trying to soak up that tone, uh, I'm not sure I'm right, but does it have some meaning like this, "What is it you want with me? I'm possibly willing to, to meet that, but I don't know what you want." Does that kinda describe it?

P: Yes, I'm sympathetic, I'll try and do what I can. "Don't be this, and this, and this way to me." What is it? Yeh, that's it.

T: "So if you want me to get in with whatever it is you expect of me, just let me know."

The second example involves a moment when the therapist attempts to reflect the client's feelings and move one step beyond. This sample was rated average on directiveness and acceptance:

T: Seems as though all the dark things—hurting, and being hurt—and ... decay, and corruption, ugliness, uhmmm, Death. It's all of those that (P: frightening) that you're afraid of.

P: Yeh ... stink and corruption and ... pus, and ... There's just as ... It's something dark that ties them all together (T: Mmm, uhuh). Something putrid and (T: Mmm, mmm) ... there are 10 times the words (T: Mmm, mmm) for it ... (laughs) it scares me.

T: Just to wander into that field verbally, and ... and even name all these things that have to do with it ... this dark side of hurting and rottenness ... that's hurting in itself.

The patient scales measuring the degree of insight developed, the degree of similarity of the patient's style of expression to that of the therapist, the degree of problem orientation, the degree of catharsis, the degree of blocking in thought and feeling, the degree of anxiety present, and the degree of positive- versus negative-feeling expression were defined by the trained clinical psychologists who served as judges. Degree of ambiguity of the patient's statement was defined in terms of its clarity of meaning. The judges were asked to disregard speech disturbances and length of statement in rating ambiguity. Discrimination learning was defined as making new distinctions between old feelings or experiences, and thus included both cognitive and emotional discrimination learning.[3]

Findings and Discussion

Qualitative Aspects

There are three qualitative aspects exemplified in this case which perhaps are worth noting. The first concerns the style of expression by the therapist: it was characteristic of the therapist to express, restate, or interpret what the patient has been saying by "quoting" what the patient *might well have said* in the first person singular—"In a sense I feel...." Out of the 40 sampled interaction units, 23 involved first person singular quotes while an additional five (for a total of 28 out of 40) involved impersonal quotes of the type: "In a sense it's like feeling...." A second characteristic of this particular case was the almost total absence of psychological jargon.

[3]Available from the author.

Few even semitechnical terms such as "anxious" or "hostile" were used by the therapist. Instead, the therapist relied heavily on everyday language that conveys effect. Thus instead of saying "depressed" the therapist says "hopeless badness." The third qualitative characteristic of this case is the tentative character of therapist statements. There is almost universal use of such prefacing remarks as "in a sense," "I guess," and "maybe." This tentative approach might tend to elicit less resistance from the patient so that actual confrontation might sound much like an attempt to agree with the patient.

The Question of Selective Responding

The reliability of each scale, which is given in parentheses under the scale label in Table 1, was estimated by the variance formula presented by Ebel (1951) for the intraclass correlation. As can be seen in Table 1, reliabilities range from .26 to .64 for the classes of patient behavior, and from .48 to .68 for levels of "reinforcement" offered by the therapist.

The low reliabilities obtained on certain classes of patient behavior would make it difficult to detect any but the strongest of relationships. For the present hypothesis of selective reinforcement the absence of particular relationships is not critical. Rather, the *presence* of selective responding (as indicated by some significant relationship between therapist and patient classes of behavior) would be evidence in support of the hypothesis.

The obtained average intercorrelations between the levels of therapist reinforcements and the levels of the selected patient behaviors are presented in Table 1. These average intercorrelations were obtained in the following manner. First a matrix of intercorrelations was generated for each of the five raters separately. The matrices were then inspected separately for correlations which were significant at or beyond the .05 level of significance. Average correlations for the five

Table 1. Interrelationships between the level of therapist reinforcement and levels of patient behaviors.

Classes of patient behavior	Reinforcers		
	Therapist empathy (r = .48)	*Therapist acceptance UPR (r = .59)*	*Therapist directiveness (r = .68)*
Patient learning of discriminations (r = .59)	.47	.37	ns
Patient ambiguity (r = .35)	−.35	−.38	.33
Patient insight (r = .32)	.46	.37	ns
Similarity of patient style of expression to that of the therapist (r = .57)	.48	.32	−.31
Problem orientation (r = .64)	ns	.35	ns
Catharsis (r = .44)	ns	ns	ns
Blocking (r = .54)	ns	ns	ns
Anxiety (r = .26)	ns	ns	ns
Patient negative feeling expression (r = .29)	ns	ns	ns

raters combined were then obtained for those intercorrelations that were significant in three out of five individual rater matrices. All other correlations were recorded as nonsignificant in the present study so that the reported correlations tend to minimize rather than maximize the possibility of obtaining significant relationships.

The significant intercorrelations presented in Table 1 show a quite different pattern than would be expected if therapist responses were not highly selective in client-centered psychotherapy. If there was no systematic selective use of empathy, acceptance, or directiveness, then all correlations would be nonsignificant and would approach zero. Such is not the case. The therapist significantly tended to respond selectively with differential levels of empathy, warmth, or directiveness to high and low levels of the following classes of patient behavior: (*a*) learning of discriminations about self and feelings, (*b*) a lack of patient ambiguity (patient clarity), (*c*) patient expressions of insight, (*d*) patient verbal expressions that were similar in style to the therapist's way of expressing himself, and (*e*) problem orientation of the patient. Thus, when the patient expressed himself in a style similar to that of the therapist, the therapist was more empathic, more warm and accepting, and less directive. When the patient ex-

pressed himself in a style quite different from that of the therapist, the therapist tended to show significantly less empathy, less acceptance or warmth, and more directiveness.

No significant relationships were obtained between the therapist's use of empathy, acceptance, or directiveness, and patient behaviors described as blocking, anxiety, negative- versus positive-feeling expression, or catharsis. While it may be that the absence of these relationships might, in part, be accounted for by the relatively low reliabilities of measurement, it also seems likely that Rogers as a therapist does not tend to respond differentially to these classes of patient behavior. In particular, as a theoretician and therapist, Rogers (1957, 1961) has felt it important for the therapist *not* to respond selectively to negative- versus positive-feeling expression.

The Further Question of Reinforcement

The above findings are consistent with, but not direct evidence for, the view that the therapist, in this case Rogers, is consciously or unconsciously using empathy, acceptance, and directiveness as reinforcers. The basic property of a reinforcer is that its use with specific classes of behavior leads to consequent changes in the probability of occurrence of these classes of behavior.

From Table 1, the nine classes of patient behavior can be ranked according to the degree of contingency between therapist "reinforcer" responses and patient responses. Now, if the therapist's systematic selective responding has the properties of reinforcement it would be predicted that, other things being equal, the five patient classes of behavior that were selectively "reinforced" would show increases over time in therapy, while the four classes of patient behavior not reinforced would show no such increase over time. Thus, for example, one would expect an increase over time in therapy of the "Similarity of the Patient's Style of Expression to that of the Therapist" and of "Patient-Learning Discriminations," and no such increase (or decrease) in patient "Blocking" or "Negative Feeling Expression."

To evaluate this the ratings of the 40 samples for each class of patient behavior were grouped into five blocks across time-in-therapy (five raters for eight samples per block or 40 ratings per block) and the Grant Orthogonal Polynomial Trend Test Analysis of Variance (Grant, 1956) was used to test for the significance of components of trend. Further, *t* tests were used to test for significance of differences between early and late in therapy on all nine patient behavior classes. These data are presented in Table 2.

Of the classes of patient behavior to which the therapist selectively responded (i.e., reinforced), four out of five showed changes in patient behavior over time-in-therapy. Thus the data agree with the predictions in seven out of the nine classes of patient behaviors (78 % correct prediction).

Considering the probability that the therapist also used other types of rewards or reinforcers and also rewarded other related patient behavior classes, considering the unknown differential complexity levels of the patient response classes, and considering the crudity of measurement, the findings strongly suggest that important reinforcement effects do indeed occur even in client-centered therapy.

Toward Evaluating the Validity of the Findings

There are, of course, some difficulties in interpreting the intercorrelation matrix. One might argue that these are simply interrelationships in the "heads" of the raters, as the raters might have known what the "X" value was when they rated a sample on "Y." However, each of the 12 variables was rated separately and they were rated in different orders. One would think it difficult to recall the X value of a given unit when the rating of the other units intervened between the X value and its corresponding Y value (an average of

Table 2. Analysis of changes over time in patient response classes.

Patient response classes	Highest single correlation with therapist "reinforcer"	Grant orthogonal polynomial analysis of variance for trend			t Test between first and all later blocks
		F Linear Trend	F Quadratic Trend	F Cubic Trend	
Similarity of patient style of expression to that of the therapist	.48	7.89***	1.20	.85	2.84***
Patient learning of discriminations	.47	3.10	.79	1.05	2.94***
Patient insight	.46	4.73**	1.70	0.75	2.73***
Patient ambiguity	−.38	3.04	1.50	0.91	1.35
Problem orientation	.35	3.28*	1.61	2.10	1.76**
Catharsis	ns	6.10**	2.13	1.20	2.03**
Blocking	ns	1.50	6.01**	1.50	1.29
Anxiety	ns	2.00	0.98	1.70	0.93
Patient negative-feeling expression	ns	1.17	0.65	0.89	0.75

 * $p \leq .07$ for 1/39 *df* for trend.
 ** $p \leq .05$ for 1/39 *df* for trend or for 38 *df* for *t*.
*** $p \leq .01$ for 1/39 *df* for trend or for 38 *df* for *t*.

240 ratings intervening between corresponding X and Y values). It could be argued that some of this bias is removed by the procedure for averaging the five different raters, since the raters were unaware of the actual hypothesis under study.

Beyond the above considerations, tabulation of one well-known characteristic of the therapist's behavior also suggests selective differential responding. The use of "uh huh" or "Mmm mmm" verbalizations has become, perhaps unfortunately, the hallmark of Rogerian psychotherapy. In the samples used in the present analysis, Mmm mmm's or Uh huh's occurred 23 times in a total of 12 of the 40 samples (in 30% of the samples). The Mmm mmm occurred in 9 of the 12 samples (75% of its occurrence) during high expression of negative feeling by the patient (all above the mean of ratings), while 0% occurred during low "patient negative feeling expression." In the remaining three samples, they occurred during the patient's direct restatement of what the therapist had just said. This tabulation alone suggests conscious or unconscious selective responding by the therapist, and is consistent with the obtained findings based upon relationships between rated therapist and patient classes of behavior.[4]

Finally, and most importantly, the obtained data dealing with changes in patient-in-therapy behavior were consistent with the obtained findings based upon prediction from a reinforcement view. Since the raters had no knowledge of whether a given sample came from early- or late-in-therapy, those findings of a tendency for significant linear increases to occur over time in reinforced patient behaviors and not to occur in nonreinforced patient behaviors, would also argue strongly against the notion that the obtained intercorrelations were simply "in the heads" of the raters.

Implications

The present findings point to the presence of significant differential reinforcement effects imbedded in the transactions of client-centered psychotherapy. Since differential reinforcement is one of the procedures used in operant research to alter (or control) behavior, the findings suggest that the therapist, in this case Rogers, implicitly alters (or controls) the patient's behavior in the therapeutic setting. To this extent, then, the evidence weighs in favor of the view proposed by Skinner rather than that of Rogers. The present findings are not consistent with Rogers' view that relatively *uniform conditions* which are globally "facilitative of personal growth and integration," are offered to patients in a manner not contingent upon the patient's behavior.

The present data, by demonstrating the role of empathy and warmth as positive reinforcers, suggest that the available evidence relating levels of these therapeutic conditions to patient outcome in therapy does not argue against a reinforcement interpretation of psychotherapy. On the contrary, the finding that empathy and warmth act as reinforcers suggests that the evidence relating empathy and warmth to patient outcome is open to a behavioristic interpretation, based in part on the therapist's use of differential reinforcement.

Recent studies have suggested that such humanistic qualities as empathy and warmth are antecedents to patient personality or behavioral change. In attempting to understand *how* such therapist qualities operate in producing therapeutic change, the present data suggest the potential value of studies utilizing behavioristic models. Since the available evidence relating empathy and warmth to patient outcome deals primarily with differences in *intensity levels* contaminated by differences in *rates* between therapists, it seems likely that additional and more precise understanding of the role of empathy (and hence more effective practice) might grow out of studies carried out from a reinforcement frame of reference. Considering only empathy as the type of reinforcer used in psychotherapy, it would be expected that successful and nonsuccessful therapists might differ in: (*a*) the particular patient behaviors chosen for differential reinforcement (say, self-concept

---

[4] It should be noted that the therapist's use of the "Uh huh reinforcer" is relatively ineffective since there is no increase over time in "patient negative feeling expression."

statements versus historical-genetic statements); (*b*) the differential rate of reinforcement (say, 25% versus 75% for a specific class of patient behavior); (*c*) the intensity levels of the reinforcer used (say, the depth of empathy); and even the (*d*) scheduling of reinforcement (say, fixed ratio versus variable ratio).

Research aimed at identifying which patient behaviors, if reinforced at what intensity levels etc., lead to positive therapeutic outcomes would provide more specific knowledge of how such positive human qualities as empathy and warmth operate to produce personality or behavioral change in the patient.

Such an approach aims toward more specific knowledge, but not at all toward more mechanical therapy. As the communication of any "reinforcing machine" qualities would by definition mean a low level of empathy and warmth, the present viewpoint is in full agreement with Schonbar's (1964) statement that "as a therapist I am no more a 'reinforcing machine' than my patient is a 'talking pigeon.'"

References

Bandura, A. Psychotherapy as a learning process. *Psychological Bulletin*, 1961, **58**, 143-159.

Barrett-Lennard, G. T. Dimensions of therapist response as causal factors in therapeutic change. *Psychological Monographs*, 1962, **76**(43, Whole No. 562).

Bergin, A. E., & Solomon, S. Personality and performance correlates of empathic understanding in psychotherapy. Paper read at American Psychological Association, Philadelphia, September 1963.

Cartwright, R. D., & Lerner, B. Empathy: Need to change and improvement with psychotherapy. *Journal of Consulting Psychology*, 1963, **27**, 138-144.

Dickenson, W. A., & Truax, C. B. Group counseling with college underachievers: Comparisons with a control group and relationship to empathy, warmth, and genuineness. University of Kentucky and Kentucky Mental Health Institute, 1965.

Dymond, R. A scale for the measurement of empathic ability. *Journal of Consulting Psychology*, 1949, **13**, 127-133.

Ebel, R. L. Estimation of the reliability of ratings. *Psychometrika*, 1951, **16**, 407-424.

Eysenck, H. J. The effects of psychotherapy: An evaluation. *Journal of Consulting Psychology*, 1952, **16**, 319-324.

Eysenck, H. J. The effects of psychotherapy. In H. J. Eysenck (Ed.), *Handbook of abnormal psychology*. New York: Basic Books, 1960. Pp. 697-725.

Grant, David A. Analysis of variance tests in the analysis and comparison of curves. *Psychological Bulletin*, 1956, **53**, 141-154.

Halkides, G. An investigation of therapeutic success as a function of four variables. Unpublished doctoral dissertation, University of Chicago, 1958.

Hobbs, N. Sources of gain in psychotherapy. *American Psychologist*, 1962, **17**, 741-747.

Jourard, S. I-thou relationship versus manipulation in counseling and psychotherapy. *Journal of Individual Psychology*, 1959, **15**, 174-179.

Krasner, L. The therapist as a social reinforcement machine. In H. H. Strupp & L. Luborsky (Eds.), *Research in psychotherapy*. Vol. II. Washington, D. C.: American Psychological Association, 1962.

Lesser, W. M. The relationship between counseling progress and empathic understanding. *Journal of Counseling Psychology*, 1961, **8**, 330-336.

Rogers, C. R. *Client-centered therapy*. Cambridge, Mass.: Riverside Press, 1951. Pp. 73-74.

Rogers, C. R. The necessary and sufficient conditions of therapeutic personality change. *Journal of Consulting Psychology*, 1957, **21**, 95-103.

Rogers, C. R. *On becoming a person*. Cambridge, Mass.: Riverside Press, 1961.

Rogers, C. R. The interpersonal relationship: The core of guidance. *Harvard Educational Review*, 1962, **32**, 416-429.

Rogers, C. R., Kiesler, D., Gendlin, E. T., & Truax, C. B. *The therapeutic relationship and its impact: A study of psychotherapy with schizophrenics*. Madison: Univer. Wisconsin Press, 1965, in press.

Rogers, C. R., & Skinner, B. F. Some issues concerning the control of human behavior. *Science*, 1956, **124**, 1057-1066.

Rogers, C. R., & Truax, C. B. The therapeutic conditions antecedent to change: A theoretical view. Chapter in, *The therapeutic relationship and its impact: A study of psychotherapy with schizophrenics*. Univer. Wisconsin Press, 1965.

Schonbar, R. A. A practitioner's critique of psychotherapy research. Paper read at American Psychological Association, Los Angeles, September 1964.

Strupp, H. H. Nature of psychotherapists' contribution to the treatment process. *Archives of General Psychiatry*, 1960, **3**, 219-231.

Truax, C. B. Clinical implementation of therapeutic conditions. In Carl R. Rogers (Chm.), Therapeutic and research progress in a program of psychotherapy research with hospitalized schizophrenics. Symposium presented at the American Psychological Association, New York, September 1961. (a)

Truax, C. B. The process of group psychotherapy. *Psychological Monographs*, 1961, **75**(7), Whole No. 511). (b)

Truax, C. B. Effective ingredients in psychotherapy: An approach to unraveling the patient-therapist interaction. *Journal of Counseling Psychology*, 1963, **10**, 256-263.

Truax, C. B., & Carkhuff, R. R. For better or for worse: The process of psychotherapeutic personality change. Chapter in, *Recent advances in the study of behavioral change.* Montreal: McGill Univer. Press, 1963. Pp. 118-163.

Truax, C. B., & Carkhuff, R. R. Significant developments in psychotherapy research. In Abt & Riess (Eds.), *Progress in clinical psychology.* New York: Grune & Stratton, 1964. Pp. 124-155.

Truax, C. B., Carkhuff, R. R., & Kodman, F., Jr. Relationships between therapist-offered conditions and patient change in group psychotherapy. *Journal of Clinical Psychology.*

Truax, C. B., Wargo, D. G., & Silber, L. D. Effects of high conditions group psychotherapy with female juvenile delinquents. University of Kentucky and Kentucky Mental Health Institute, 1965.

Wargo, D. G. The Barron Ego Strength and LH[4] scales as predictors and indicators of change in psychotherapy. *Brief Research Reports*, 1962, **21**. (University of Wisconsin, Wisconsin Psychiatric Institute.)

Whitehorn, J. C., & Betz, B. J. A study of psychotherapeutic relationships between physicians and schizophrenic patients. *American Journal of Psychiatry*, 1954, **3**, 321-331.

Wolpe, J. *Psychotherapy by reciprocal inhibition.* Stanford: Stanford Univer. Press, 1958.

Part Four

Humanistic Theory

7   Abraham H. Maslow

Perhaps the most widely respected personality theorist representing the "third force" in contemporary psychology is Abraham H. Maslow (1908-1970). This movement comprises a variety of psychological and philosophical viewpoints and includes an assortment of Adlerian, Jungian, gestalt, ego psychoanalytic, and existential theorists. Although differing on many substantive issues, the members of this movement are united in a reaction against what they consider to be the sterile provincialism of classical psychoanalytic and experimental behavioristic influences that have dominated twentieth century psychology. Their alternative is a rejection of orthodoxy in science and a redirection of scientific inquiry toward such intimate human concerns as creativity, beauty, love, and value. Maslow's theoretical posture is fully consistent with this attitude.

The theory paper by Maslow is a broad outline of his philosophical and theoretical views on the nature of man. The central core of his position is that man is continually striving toward the realization of his basic biological and psychological potentials. The human organism is motivated by both survival and self-actualization, but once the survival motive has been satisfied, man is free to choose a productive course of psychological growth. This growth can be stunted, however, if the "inner nature" is frustrated by circumstance or by emotional defeats as the person strives toward maturity. Unlike many theorists, Maslow has constructed a model of the person that is essentially optimistic. His contribution to the understanding of psychological health, maturity, and self-fulfillment is a significant achievement.

The intensive study of one individual is a research procedure highly valued by many personality theorists. The paper entitled "Case Study of a Happy Man," by Ricks and Wessman, is an excellent example of the richness of insights that can be gained through the personality analysis of a single case. As you will observe, the study of Winn is a synthesis of a wide variety of psychological tools designed to tap different levels of personality expression. At one level were self-reported autobiographical material and life history interviews which focused on the conscious revelations of Winn. At another level, considerably more indirect, were the Rorschach and Thematic Apperception tests. The Rorschach Test consists of ten cards, each containing an ambiguous inkblot. The subject is instructed to tell what he sees in the card and what it was about the card that suggested his response. He is asked which part of the inkblot comprises his response; for example, if he sees a bat, is it the whole inkblot or a part of it (and which part)? It is felt that the personally unique reactions to this test will add insight into the style and content of the individual's personality dynamics. The Thematic Apperception Test consists of a series of cards with pictures of various scenes, some of them common, others vague and indefinite. Most of the cards, however, have to do with conflictful social situations. The subject's task is to develop a complete story describing the situation, how the participants are thinking and feeling, and how the story will turn out. This procedure may also elicit themes pertinent to the subject's personality organization. The overall aim of the projective test is to reveal aspects of personality functioning that are presumably not directly accessible through conscious mediation. A final source of data was Winn's participation in a study of mood and personality. In this research, Winn filled out daily mood scales and self-description rating devices.

Ricks and Wessman's approach to understanding the unique qualities of Winn is fully consistent with Maslow's phenomenological interests and humanistic values. In addition, this case study is particularly relevant to Maslow because it centers on human qualities that are often ignored by personologists: the qualities of happiness and self-satisfaction. Psychological literature is so replete with descriptions of psychopathology that it is rare to come across a chronicle of personal adjustment and health. Yet it is toward just these qualities that much of Maslow's attention is directed.

The critique paper by M. Brewster Smith, while not a direct evaluation of Maslow's position, nevertheless deals with a basic feature of his work: phenomenology. The phenomenological position asserts that an understanding of the person must comprise, by definition, an awareness of his immediate, individual, perceptual experience. The truth of experience is not a function of how an observer regards someone else's experience but rather of how each person sees the world through his own eyes. Accordingly, phenomenologists say that the focus of psychological study should be on these personal, subjective, perceptual events. Maslow is deeply committed to the phenomenological and existential reality of choice. He holds that human growth is invariably tied up with choice and that choice is a function of each individual's unique experience. Although the critique by M. Brewster Smith takes a friendly position toward phenomenology, it argues against excessive enthusiasm in accepting phenomenology as the sole avenue to psychological knowledge.

Suggestions for Further Reading

An excellent collection of Maslow's papers is in *Toward a Psychology of Being*, an Insight Book, published by the D. Van Nostrand Company in 1962. A recent theoretical paper and a personal interview are both contained in the July, 1968, issue of the magazine *Psychology Today*.

The latest statement by Maslow of his personality theory, completed just prior to his death, is *Motivation and Personality* (2nd ed.), published by Harper and Row in 1970.

Some Basic Propositions of a Growth and Self-Actualization Psychology

Abraham Maslow

When the philosophy of man (his nature, his goals, his potentialities, his fulfillment) changes, than everything changes, not only the philosophy of politics, of economics, of ethics and values, of interpersonal relations and of history itself, but also the philosophy of education, the theory of how to help men become what they can and deeply need to become.

We are now in the middle of such a change in the conception of man's capacities, potentialities and goals. A new vision is emerging of the possibilities of man and of his destiny, and its implications are many, not only for our conceptions of education, but also for science, politics, literature, economics, religion, and even our conceptions of the non-human world.

I think it is now possible to begin to delineate this view of human nature as a total, single, comprehensive system of psychology even though much of it has arisen as a reaction *against* the limitations (as philosophies of human nature) of the two most comprehensive psychologies now available—behaviorism (or associationism) and classical, Freudian psychoanalysis. Finding a single label for it is still a difficult task, perhaps a premature one. In the past I have called it the "holistic-dynamic" psychology to express my conviction about its major roots. Some have called it "organismic" following Goldstein. Sutich and others are calling it the Self-psychology or Humanistic psychology. We shall see. My own guess is that, in a few decades, if it remains suitably eclectic and comprehensive, it will be called simply "psychology."

From A. Maslow, *Toward a Psychology of Being* (Princeton, N. J.: Van Nostrand, 1962), pp. 177-200. Reprinted by permission of Van Nostrand-Reinhold, a division of Litton Industries.

I think I can be of most service by speaking primarily for myself and out of my own work rather than as an "official" delegate of this large group of thinkers, even though I am sure that the areas of agreement among them are very large. . . . Because of the limited space I have, I will present here only some of the major propositions of this point of view, especially those of importance to the educator. I should warn you that at many points I am way out ahead of the data. Some of these propositions are more based on private conviction than on publicly demonstrated facts. However, they are all in principle confirmable or disconfirmable.

1. We have, each one of us, an essential inner nature which is instinctoid, intrinsic, given, "natural," i.e., with an appreciable hereditary determinant, and which tends strongly to persist.

It makes sense to speak here of the hereditary, constitutional and very early acquired roots of the *individual* self, even though this biological determination of self is only partial, and far too complex to describe simply. In any case, this is "raw material" rather than finished product, to be reacted to by the person, by his significant others, by his environment, etc.

I include in this essential inner nature instinctoid basic needs, capacities, talents, anatomical equipment, physiological or temperamental balances, prenatal and natal injuries, and traumata to the neonate. This inner core shows itself as natural inclinations, propensities or inner bent. Whether defense and coping mechanisms, "style of life," and other characterological traits, all shaped in the first few years of life, should be included is still a matter for discussion. This raw material very quickly starts growing into a self as it meets the world outside and begins to have transaction with it.

2. These are potentialities, not final actualizations. Therefore they have a life history and must be seen developmentally. They are actualized, shaped or stifled mostly (but not altogether) by extra-psychic determinants (culture, family, environment, learning, etc.). Very early in life these goalless urges and tendencies become attached to objects ("sentiments") by canalization but also by arbitrarily learned associations.

3. This inner core, even though it is biologically based and "instinctoid," is weak in certain senses rather than strong. It is easily overcome, suppressed or repressed. It may even be killed off permanently. Humans no longer have instincts in the animal sense, powerful, unmistakable inner voices which tell them unequivocally what to do, when, where, how and with whom. All that we have left are instinct-remnants. And furthermore, these are weak, subtle and delicate, very easily drowned out by learning, by cultural expectations, by fear, by disapproval, etc. They are *hard* to know, rather than easy. Authentic selfhood can be defined in part as being able to hear these impulse-voices within oneself, i.e., to know what one really wants or doesn't want, what one is fit for and what one is *not* fit for, etc. It appears that there are wide individual differences in the strength of these impulse-voices.

4. Each person's inner nature has some characteristics which all other selves have (species-wide) and some which are unique to the person (idiosyncratic). The need for love characterizes every human being that is born (although it can disappear later under certain circumstances). Musical genius however is given to very few, and these differ markedly from each other in style, e.g., Mozart and Debussy.

5. It is possible to study this inner nature scientifically and objectively (that is, with the right kind of "science") and to discover what it is like (*discover*—not invent or construct). It is also possible to do this subjectively, by inner search and by psychotherapy, and the two enterprises supplement and support each other.

6. Many aspects of this inner, deeper nature are either (a) actively repressed, as Freud has described, because they are feared or disapproved of or are ego-alien, or (b) "forgotten" (neglected, unused, overlooked, unverbalized or suppressed), as Schachtel has described. Much of the inner, deeper nature is therefore unconscious. This can be true not only for impulses (drives, instincts, needs) as Freud has stressed, but also for capacities, emotions, judgments, attitudes, definitions, perceptions, etc. Active repression takes effort and uses up energy. There are many specific techniques of maintaining active unconsciousness, such as denial, projection, reaction-formation, etc. However, repression does not kill what is repressed. The repressed remains as one active determinant of thought and behavior.

Both active and passive repressions seem to begin early in life, mostly as a response to parental and cultural disapprovals.

However, there is some clinical evidence that repression may arise also from intra-psychic, extra-cultural sources in the young child, or at puberty, i.e., out of fear of being overwhelmed by its own impulses, of becoming disintegrated, of "falling apart," exploding, etc. It is theoretically possible that the child may spontaneously form attitudes of fear and disapproval toward its own impulses and may then defend himself against them in various ways. Society need not be the only repressing force, if this is true. There may also be intra-psychic repressing and controlling forces. These we may call "intrinsic counter-cathexes."

It is best to distinguish unconscious drives and needs from unconscious ways of cognizing because the latter are often easier to bring to consciousness and therefore to modify. Primary process cognition (Freud) or archaic thinking (Jung) is more recoverable by, e.g., creative art education, dance education, and other non-verbal educational techniques.

7. Even though "weak," this inner nature rarely disappears or dies, in the usual person, in the U. S. (such disappearance or dying is possible early in the life history, however). It persists underground, unconsciously, even though denied and repressed. Like the voice

of the intellect (which is part of it), it speaks softly but it *will* be heard, even if in a distorted form. That is, it has a dynamic force of its own, pressing always for open, uninhibited expression. Effort must be used in its suppression or repression from which fatigue can result. This force is one main aspect of the "will to health," the urge to grow, the pressure to self-actualization, the quest for one's identity. It is this that makes psychotherapy, education and self-improvement possible in principle.

8. However, this inner core, or self, grows into adulthood only partly by (objective or subjective) discovery, uncovering, and acceptance of what is "there" beforehand. Partly it is also a creation of the person himself. Life is a continual series of choices for the individual in which a main determinant of choice is the person as he already is (including his goals for himself, his courage or fear, his feeling of responsibility, his ego-strength or "will power," etc.). We can no longer think of the person as "fully determined" where this phase implies "determined only by forces external to the person." The person, insofar as he *is* a real person, is his own main determinant. Every person is, in part, "his own project" and makes himself.

9. If this essential core (inner nature) of the person is frustrated, denied or suppressed, sickness results, sometimes in obvious forms, sometimes in subtle and devious forms, sometimes immediately, sometimes later. These psychological illnesses include many more than those listed by the American Psychiatric Association. For instance, the character disorders and disturbances are now seen as far more important for the fate of the world than the classical neuroses or even the psychoses. From this new point of view, new kinds of illness are most dangerous, e.g., "the diminished or stunted person," i.e., the loss of any of the defining characteristics of humanness, or personhood, the failure to grow to one's potential, valuelessness, etc.

That is, general-illness of the personality is seen as any falling short of growth, or of self-actualization, or of full-humanness. And the main source of illness (although not the only one) is seen as frustrations (of the basic needs, of the B-values, of idiosyncratic potentials, of expression of the self, and of the tendency of the person to grow in his own style and at his own pace) especially in the early years of life. That is, frustration of the basic needs is not the only source of illness or of human diminution.

10. This inner nature, as much as we know of it so far, is definitely not "evil," but is either what we adults in our culture call "good," or else it is neutral. The most accurate way to express this is to say that it is "prior to good and evil." There is little question about this if we speak of the inner nature of the infant and child. The statement is much more complex if we speak of the "infant" as he still exists in the adult. And it gets still more complex if the individual is seen from the point of view of B-psychology rather than D-psychology.

This conclusion is supported by all the truth-revealing and uncovering techniques that have anything to do with human nature: psychotherapy, objective science, subjective science, education and art. For instance, in the long run, uncovering therapy lessens hostility, fear, greed, etc., and increases love, courage, creativeness, kindness, altruism, etc., leading us to the conclusion that the latter are "deeper," more natural, and more basic than the former, i.e., that what we call "bad" behavior is learned or removed by uncovering, while what we call "good" behavior is strengthened and fostered by uncovering.

11. We must differentiate the Freudian type of superego from intrinsic conscience and intrinsic guilt. The former is in principle a taking into the self of the disapprovals and approvals of persons other than the person himself, fathers, mothers, teachers, etc. Guilt then is recognition of disapproval by others.

Intrinsic guilt is the consequence of betrayal of one's own inner nature or self, a turning off the path to self-actualization, and is essentially justified self-disapproval. It is therefore not as culturally relative as is Freudian guilt. It is "true" or "deserved" or "right and just" or "correct" because it is a discrepancy from something profoundly real within the person rather than from accidental, arbitrary or purely relative localisms. Seen in this way it is good, even *necessary*, for a person's development to have intrinsic guilt when he deserves to. It is not just a symptom to be avoided at any cost but is rather an inner guide for growth toward actualization of the real self, and of its potentialities.

12. "Evil" behavior has mostly referred to unwarranted hostility, cruelty, destructiveness, "mean" aggressiveness. This we do not know enough about. To the degree that this quality of hostility is instinctoid, mankind has one kind of future. To the degree that it is reactive (a response to bad treatment), mankind has a very different kind of future. My opinion is that the weight of the evidence so far indicates that indiscriminately *destructive* hostility is reactive, because uncovering therapy reduces it, and changes its quality into "healthy" self-affirmation, forcefulness, selective hostility, self-defense, righteous indignation, etc. In any case, the *ability* to be aggressive and angry is found in all self-actualizing people, who are able to let it flow forth freely when the external situation "calls for" it.

The situation in children is far more complex. At the very least, we know that the healthy child is also able to be justifiably angry, self-protecting and self-affirming, i.e., reactive aggression. Presumably, then, a child should learn not only how to control his anger, but also how and when to express it.

Behavior that our culture calls evil can also come from ignorance and from childish misinterpretations and beliefs (whether in the child or in the repressed or "forgotten" child-in-the-adult). For instance, sibling rivalry is traceable to the child's wish for the exclusive love of his parents. Only as he matures is he in principle capable of learning that his mother's love for a sibling is compatible with her continued love for him. Thus out of a childish version of love, not in itself reprehensible, can come unloving behavior.

The commonly seen hatred or resentment of or jealousy of goodness, truth, beauty, health or intelligence, ("counter-values") is largely (though not altogether) determined by threat of loss of self-esteem, as the liar is

threatened by the honest man, the homely girl by the beautiful girl, or the coward by the hero. Every superior person confronts us with our own shortcomings.

Still deeper than this, however, is the ultimate existential question of the fairness and justice of fate. The person with a disease may be jealous of the healthy man who is more deserving than he.

Evil behaviors seem to most psychologists to be reactive as in these examples, rather than instinctive. This implies that though "bad" behavior is very deeply rooted in human nature and can never be abolished altogether, it may yet be expected to lessen as the personality matures and as the society improves.

13. Many people still think of "the unconscious," of regression, and of primary process cognition as necessarily unhealthy, or dangerous or bad. Psychotherapeutic experience is slowly teaching us otherwise. Our depths can also be good, or beautiful or desirable. This is also becoming clear from the general findings from investigations of the sources of love, creativeness, play, humor, art, etc. Their roots are deep in the inner, deeper self, i.e., in the unconscious. To recover them and to be able to enjoy and use them we must be able to "regress."

14. No psychological health is possible unless this essential core of the person is fundamentally accepted, loved and respected by others and by himself (the converse is not necessarily true, i.e., that if the core is respected, etc., then psychological health must result, since other prerequisite conditions must also be satisfied).

The psychological health of the chronologically immature is called healthy growth. The psychological health of the adult is called variously, self-fulfillment, emotional maturity, individuation, productiveness, self-actualization, authenticity, full-humanness, etc.

Healthy growth is conceptually subordinate, for it is usually defined now as "growth toward self-actualization," etc. Some psychologists speak simply in terms of one overarching goal or end, or tendency of human development, considering all immature growth phenomena to be only steps along the path to self-actualization (Goldstein, Rogers).

Self-actualization is defined in various ways but a solid core of agreement is perceptible. All definitions accept or imply, (a) acceptance and expression of the inner core or self, i.e., actualization of these latent capacities, and potentialities, "full functioning," availability of the human and personal essence. (b) They all imply minimal presence of ill health, neurosis, psychosis, of loss or diminution of the basic human and personal capacities.

15. For all these reasons, it is at this time best to bring out and encourage, or at the very least, to recognize this inner nature, rather than to suppress or repress it. Pure spontaneity consists of free, uninhibited, uncontrolled, trusting, unpremeditated expression of the self, i.e., of the psychic forces, with minimal interference by consciousness. Control, will, caution, self-criticism, measure, deliberateness are the brakes upon this expression made intrinsically necessary by the laws of the social and natural worlds outside the psychic world, and secondarily, made necessary by fear of the psyche itself (intrinsic counter-cathexis). Speaking in a very broad way, controls upon the psyche which come from *fear of the psyche* are largely neurotic or *psychotic*, or not intrinsically or theoretically necessary. (The healthy psyche is not terrible or horrible and therefore doesn't have to be feared, as it has been for thousands of years. Of course, the *unhealthy* psyche is another story.) This kind of control is usually lessened by psychological health, by deep psychotherapy, or by any *deeper* self-knowledge and self-acceptance. There are also, however, controls upon the psyche which do not come out of fear, but out of the necessities for keeping it integrated, organized and unified (intrinsic counter-cathexes). And there are also "controls," probably in another sense, which are necessary as capacities are actualized, and as higher forms of expression are sought for, e.g., acquisition of skills through hard work by the artist, the intellectual, the athlete. But these controls are eventually transcended and become aspects of spontaneity, as they become self.

The balance between spontaneity and control varies, then, as the health of the psyche and the health of the world vary. Pure spontaneity is not long possible because we live in a world which runs by its own, non-psychic laws. It *is* possible in dreams, fantasies, love, imagination, sex, the first stages of creativity, artistic work, intellectual play, free association, etc. Pure control is not permanently possible, for then the psyche dies. Education must be directed then *both* toward cultivation of controls and cultivation of spontaneity and expression. In our culture and at this point in history, it is necessary to redress the balance in favor of spontaneity, the ability to be expressive, passive, unwilled, trusting in processes other than will and control, unpremeditated, creative, etc. But it must be recognized that there have been and will be other cultures and other areas in which the balance was or will be in the other direction.

16. In the normal development of the normal child, it is now known that, *most* of the time, if he is given a really free choice, he will choose what is good for his growth. This he does because it tastes good, feels good, gives pleasure or *delight*. This implies that *he* "knows" better than anyone else what is good for him. A permissive regime means not that adults gratify his needs directly but make it possible for *him* to gratify his needs, and make his own choices, i.e., let him *be*. It is necessary in order for children to grow well that adults have enough trust in them and in the natural processes of growth, i.e., not interfere too much, not *make* them grow, or force them into predetermined designs, but rather *let* them grow and *help* them grow in a Taoistic rather than an authoritarian way.

17. Coordinate with this "acceptance" of the self, of fate, of one's call, is the conclusion that the main path to health and self-fulfillment for the masses is via basic need gratification rather than via frustration. This contrasts with the suppressive regime, the mistrust, the control, the policing that is necessarily implied by the belief in basic, instinctive evil in the human depths. Intrauterine life

is completely gratifying and non-frustrating and it is now generally accepted that the first year or so of life had better also be primarily gratifying and non-frustrating. Asceticism, self-denial, deliberate rejection of the demands of the organism, at least in the West, tend to produce a diminished, stunted or crippled organism, and even in the East, bring self-actualization to only a very few, exceptionally strong individuals.

18. But we know also that the *complete absence* of frustration is dangerous. To be strong, a person must acquire frustration-tolerance, the ability to perceive physical reality as essentially indifferent to human wishes, the ability to love others and to enjoy their need-gratification as well as one's own (not to use other people only as means). The child with a good basis of safety, love and respect-need-gratification, is able to profit from nicely graded frustrations and become stronger thereby. If they are more than he can bear, if they overwhelm him, we call them traumatic, and consider them dangerous rather than profitable.

It is via the frustrating unyieldingness of physical reality and of animals and of other people that we learn about *their* nature, and thereby learn to differentiate wishes from facts (which things wishing makes come true, and which things proceed in complete disregard of our wishes), and are thereby enabled to live in the world and adapt to it as necessary.

We learn also about our own strengths and limits and extend them by overcoming difficulties, by straining ourselves to the utmost, by meeting challenge and hardship, even by failing. There can be great enjoyment in a great struggle and this can displace fear.

Overprotection implies that the child's needs are gratified *for* him by his parents, without effort of his own. This tends to infantilize him, to prevent development of his own strength, will and self-assertion. In one of its forms it may teach him to use other people rather than to respect them. In another form it implies a lack of trust and respect for the child's own powers and choices, i.e., it is essentially condescending and insulting, and can help to make a child feel worthless.

19. To make growth and self-actualization possible, it is necessary to understand that capacities, organs and organ systems press to function and express themselves and to be used and exercised, and that such use is satisfying, and disuse irritating. The muscular person likes to use his muscles, indeed, *has* to use them in order to "feel good" and to achieve the subjective feeling of harmonious, successful, uninhibited functioning (spontaneity) which is so important an aspect of good growth and psychological health. So also for intelligence, for the uterus, the eyes, the capacity to love. Capacities clamor to be used, and cease their clamor only when they *are* well used. That is, capacities are also needs. Not only is it fun to use our capacities, but it is also necessary for growth. The unused skill or capacity or organ can become a disease center or else atrophy or disappear, thus diminishing the person.

20. The psychologist proceeds on the assumption that for his purposes there are two kinds of worlds, two kinds of reality, the natural world and the psychic world, the world of unyielding facts and the world of wishes, hopes, fears, emotions, the world which runs by non-psychic rules and the world which runs by psychic laws. This differentiation is not very clear except at its extremes, where there is no doubt that delusions, dreams and free associations are lawful and yet utterly different from the lawfulness of logic and from the lawfulness of the world which would remain if the human species died out. This assumption does not deny that these worlds are related and may even fuse.

I may say that this assumption is acted upon by *many* or *most* psychologists, even though they are perfectly willing to admit that it is an insoluble philosophical problem. Any therapist *must* assume it or give up his functioning. This is typical of the way in which psychologists bypass philosophical difficulties and act "as if" certain assumptions were true even though unprovable, e.g., the universal assumption of "responsibility," "will power," etc. One aspect of health is the ability to live in both of these worlds.

21. Immaturity can be contrasted with maturity from the motivational point of view,

as the process of gratifying the deficiency-needs in their proper order. Maturity, or self-actualization, from this point of view, means to transcend the deficiency-needs. This state can be described then as metamotivated, or unmotivated (if deficiencies are seen as the only motivations). It can also be described as self-actualizing, Being, expressing, rather than coping. This state of Being, rather than of striving, is suspected to be synonymous with selfhood, with being "authentic," with being a person, with being fully human. The process of growth *is* the process of *becoming* a person. *Being* a person is different.

22. Immaturity can also be differentiated from maturity in terms of the cognitive capacities (and also in terms of the emotional capacities). Immature and mature cognition have been best described by Werner and Piaget. We can now add another differentiation, that between D-cognition and B-cognition (D = Deficiency, B = Being). D-cognition can be defined as the cognitions which are organized from the point of view of basic needs or deficiency-needs and their gratification and frustration. That is, D-cognition could be called selfish cognition, in which the world is organized into gratifiers and frustrators of our own needs, with other characteristics being ignored or slurred. The cognition of the object, in its own right and its own Being, without reference to its need-gratifying or need-frustrating qualities, that is, without primary reference to its value for the observer or its effects upon him, can be called B-cognition (or self-transcending, or unselfish, or objective cognition). The parallel with maturity is by no means perfect (children can also cognize in a selfless way), but in general, it is mostly true that with increasing selfhood or firmness of personal identity (or acceptance of one's own inner nature) B-cognition becomes easier and more frequent. (This is true even though D-cognition remains for *all* human beings, including the mature ones, the main tool for living-in-the-world.)

To the extent that perception is desire-less and fear-less, to that extent is it more veridical, in the sense of perceiving the true, or essential or intrinsic whole nature of the object (without splitting it up by abstraction). Thus the goal of objective and true description of any reality is fostered by psychological health. Neurosis, psychosis, stunting of growth—all are, from this point of view, cognitive diseases as well, contaminating perception, learning, remembering, attending and thinking.

23. A by-product of this aspect of cognition is a better understanding of the higher and lower levels of love. D-love can be differentiated from B-love on approximately the same basis as D-cognition and B-cognition, or D-motivation and B-motivation. No ideally good relation to another human being, especially a child, is possible without B-love. Especially is it necessary for teaching, along with the Taoistic, trusting attitude that it implies. This is also true for our relations with the natural world, i.e., we can treat it in its own right, or we can treat it as if it were there only for our purposes.

24. Though, in principle, self-actualization is easy, in practice it rarely happens (by my criteria, certainly in less than 1% of the adult population). For this, there are many, many reasons at various levels of discourse, including all the determinants of psychopathology that we now know. We have already mentioned one main cultural reason, i.e., the conviction that man's intrinsic nature is evil or dangerous, and one biological determinant for the difficulty of achieving a mature self, namely that humans no longer have strong instincts which tell them unequivocally what to do, when, where and how.

There is a subtle but extremely important difference between regarding psychopathology as blocking or evasion or fear of growth toward self-actualization, and thinking of it in a medical fashion, as skin to invasion from without by tumors, poisons or bacteria, which have no relationship to the personality being invaded. Human diminution (the loss of human potentialities and capacities) is a more useful concept than "illness" for our theoretical purposes.

25. Growth has not only rewards and pleasures but also many intrinsic pains and always will have. Each step forward is a step into the unfamiliar and is possibly dangerous. It also means giving up something familiar

and good and satisfying. It frequently means a parting and a separation, even a kind of death prior to rebirth, with consequent nostalgia, fear, loneliness and mourning. It also often means giving up a simpler and easier and less effortful life, in exchange for a more demanding, more responsible, more difficult life. Growth forward *is in spite* of these losses and therefore requires courage, will, choice, and strength in the individual, as well as protection, permission and encouragement from the environment, especially for the child.

26. It is therefore useful to think of growth or lack of it as the resultant of a dialectic between growth-fostering forces and growth-discouraging forces (regression, fear, pains of growth, ignorance, etc.). Growth has both advantages and disadvantages. Non-growing has not only disadvantages, but also advantages. The future pulls, but so also does the past. There is not only courage but also fear. The total way of growing healthily is, in principle, to enhance all the advantages of forward growth and all the disadvantages of not-growing, and to diminish all the disadvantages of growth forward and all the advantages of not-growing.

Homeostatic tendencies, "need-reduction" tendencies, and Freudian defense mechanisms are not growth-tendencies but are often defensive, pain-reducing postures of the organism. But they are quite necessary and not always pathological. They are generally prepotent over growth-tendencies.

27. All this implies a naturalistic system of values, a by-product of the empirical description of the deepest tendencies of the human species and of specific individuals. The study of the human being by science or by self-search can discover where he is heading, what is his purpose in life, what is good for him and what is bad for him, what will make him feel virtuous and what will make him feel guilty, why choosing the good is often difficult for him, what the attractions of evil are. (Observe that the word "ought" need not be used. Also such knowledge of man is relative to man only and does not purport to be "absolute.")

28. A neurosis is not part of the inner core but rather a defense against or an evasion of it, as well as a distorted expression of it (under the aegis of fear). It is ordinarily a compromise between the effort to seek basic need gratifications in a covert or disguised or self-defeating way, and the fear of these needs, gratifications and motivated behaviors. To express neurotic needs, emotions, attitudes, definitions, action, etc., means *not* to express the inner core or real self fully. If the sadist or exploiter or pervert says, "Why shouldn't *I* express myself?" (e.g., by killing), or, "Why shouldn't *I* actualize myself?" the answer to them is that such expression is a denial of, and not an expression of, instinctoid tendencies (or inner core).

Each neuroticized need, or emotion or action is a *loss of capacity* to the person, something that he cannot do or *dare* not do except in a sneaky and unsatisfying way. In addition, he has usually lost his subjective well-being, his will, and his feeling of self-control, his capacity for pleasure, his self-esteem, etc. He is diminished as a human being.

29. The state of being without a system of values is psychopathogenic, we are learning. The human being needs a framework of values, philosophy of life, a religion or religion-surrogate to live by and understand by, in about the same sense that he needs sunlight, calcium or love. This I have called the "cognitive need to understand." The value-illnesses which result from valuelessness are called variously anhedonia, anomie, apathy, amorality, hopelessness, cynicism, etc., and can become somatic illness as well. Historically, we are in a value interregnum in which all externally given value systems have proven to be failures (political, economic, religious, etc.) e.g., nothing is worth dying for. What man needs but doesn't have, he seeks for unceasingly, and he becomes dangerously ready to jump at *any* hope, good or bad. The cure for this disease is obvious. We need a validated, usable system of human values that we can believe in and devote ourselves to (be willing to die for), because they are true rather than because we are exhorted to "believe and have faith." Such an empirically based Weltanschauung seems now to be a real possibility, at least in theoretical outline.

Much disturbance in children and adolescents can be understood as a consequence of the uncertainty of adults about their values. As a consequence, many youngsters in the United States live not by adult values but by adolescent values, which of course are immature, ignorant and heavily determined by confused adolescent needs. An excellent projection of these adolescent values is the cowboy, "Western" movie, or the delinquent gang.

30. At the level of self-actualizing, many dichotomies become resolved, opposites are seen to be unities and the whole dichotomous way of thinking is recognized to be immature. For self-actualizing people, there is a strong tendency for selfishness and unselfishness to fuse into a higher, superordinate unity. Work tends to be the same as play; vocation and avocation become the same thing. When duty is pleasant and pleasure is fulfillment of duty, then they lose their separateness and oppositeness. The highest maturity is discovered to include a childlike quality, and we discover healthy children to have some of the qualities of mature self-actualization. The inner-outer split, between self and all else, gets fuzzy and much less sharp, and they are seen to be permeable to each other at the highest levels of personality development. Dichotomizing seems now to be characteristic of a lower level of personality development and of psychological functioning; it is both a cause and an effect of psychopathology.

31. One especially important finding in self-actualizing people is that they tend to integrate the Freudian dichotomies and trichotomies, i.e., the conscious, preconscious and the unconscious, (as well as id, ego, superego). The Freudian "instincts" and the defenses are less sharply set off against each other. The impulses are more expressed and less controlled; the controls are less rigid, inflexible, anxiety-determined. The superego is less harsh and punishing and less set off against the ego. The primary and secondary cognitive processes are more equally available and more equally valued (instead of the primary processes being stigmatized as pathological). Indeed, in the "peak-experience" the walls between them tend to fall together.

This is in sharp contrast with the early Freudian position in which these various forces were sharply dichotomized as (a) mutually exclusive, (b) with antagonistic interests, i.e., as antagonistic forces rather than as complementary or collaborating ones, and (c) one "better" than the other.

Again we imply here (sometimes) a healthy unconscious, and desirable regression. Furthermore, we imply also an integration of rationality and irrationality with the consequence that irrationality may, in its place, also be considered healthy, desirable or even necessary.

32. Healthy people are more integrated in another way. In them the conative, the cognitive, the affective and the motor are less separated from each other, and are more synergic, i.e., working collaboratively without conflict to the same ends. The conclusions of rational, careful thinking are apt to come to the same conclusions as those of the blind appetites. What such a person wants and enjoys is apt to be just what is good for him. His spontaneous reactions are as capable, efficient and right as if they had been thought out in advance. His sensory and motor reactions are more closely correlated. His sensory modalities are more connected with each other (physiognomical perception). Furthermore, we have learned the difficulties and dangers of those age-old rationalistic systems in which the capacities were thought to be arranged dichotomously-hierarchically, with rationality at the top, rather than in an integration.

33. This development toward the concept of a healthy unconscious, and of a healthy irrationality, sharpens our awareness of the limitations of purely abstract thinking, of verbal thinking and of analytic thinking. If our hope is to describe the world fully, a place is necessary for preverbal, ineffable, metaphorical, primary process, concrete-experience, intuitive and esthetic types of cognition, for there are certain aspects of reality which can be cognized in no other way. Even in science this is true, now that we know (1) that creativity has its roots in the nonrational, (2) that language is and must

always be inadequate to describe total reality, (3) that any abstract concept leaves out much of reality, and (4) that what we call "knowledge" (which is usually highly abstract and verbal and sharply defined) often serves to blind us to those portions of reality not covered by the abstraction. That is, it makes us more able to see some things, but *less* able to see other things. Abstract knowledge has its dangers as well as its uses.

Science and education, being too exclusively abstract, verbal and bookish, don't have enough place for raw, concrete, esthetic experience, especially of the subjective happenings inside oneself. For instance, organismic psychologists would certainly agree on the desirability of more creative education in perceiving and creating art, in dancing, in (Greek style) athletics and in phenomenological observation.

The ultimate of abstract, analytical thinking, is the greatest simplification possible, i.e., the formula, the diagram, the map, the blueprint, the schema, the cartoon, and certain types of abstract paintings. Our mastery of the world is enhanced thereby, but its richness may be lost as a forfeit, *unless* we learn to value B-cognitions, perception-with-love-and-care, free-floating attention, all of which enrich the experience instead of impoverishing it. There is no reason why "science" should not be expanded to include both kinds of knowing.

34. This ability of healthier people to dip into the unconscious and preconscious, to use and value their primary processes instead of fearing them, to accept their impulses instead of always controlling them, to be able to regress voluntarily without fear, turns out to be one of the main conditions of creativity. We can then understand why psychological health is so closely tied up with certain universal forms of creativeness (aside from special talent), as to lead some writers to make them almost synonymous.

This same tie between health and integration of rational and irrational forces (conscious and unconscious, primary and secondary processes) also permits us to understand why psychologically healthy people

are more able to enjoy, to love, to laugh, to have fun, to be humorous, to be silly, to be whimsical and fantastic, to be pleasantly "crazy," and in general to permit and value and enjoy emotional experiences in general and peak-experiences in particular and to have them more often. And it leads us to the strong suspicion that learning *ad hoc* to be able to do all these things may help the child move toward health.

35. Esthetic perceiving and creating and esthetic peak-experiences are seen to be a central aspect of human life and of psychology and education rather than a peripheral one. This is true for several reasons. (1) All the peak-experiences are (among other characteristics) integrative of the splits within the person, between persons, within the world, and between the person and the world. Since one aspect of health is integration, the peak-experiences are moves toward health and are themselves, momentary healths. (2) These experiences are life-validating, i.e., they make life worth while. These are certainly an important part of the answer to the question, "Why don't we all commit suicide?" (3) They are worth while in themselves, etc.

36. Self-actualization does not mean a transcendence of all human problems. Conflict, anxiety, frustration, sadness, hurt, and guilt can all be found in healthy human beings. In general, the movement, with increasing maturity, is from neurotic pseudo-problems to the real, unavoidable, existential problems, inherent in the nature of man (even at his best) living in a particular kind of world. Even though he is not neurotic he may be troubled by real, desirable and necessary guilt rather than neurotic guilt (which isn't desirable or necessary), by an intrinsic conscience (rather than the Freudian superego). Even though he has transcended the problems of Becoming, there remain the problems of Being. To be untroubled when one *should* be troubled can be a sign of sickness. Sometimes, smug people have to be scared "*into* their wits."

37. Self-actualization is not altogether general. It takes place via femaleness *or* maleness, which are prepotent to general-human-

ness. That is, one must first be a healthy, femaleness-fulfilled woman or maleness-fulfilled man before general-human self-actualization becomes possible.

There is also a little evidence that different constitutional types actualize themselves in somewhat different ways (because they have different inner selves to actualize).

38. Another crucial aspect of healthy growth of selfhood and full-humanness is dropping away the techniques used by the child, in his weakness and smallness for adapting himself to the strong, large, all-powerful, omniscient, godlike adults. He must replace these with the techniques of being strong and independent and of being a parent himself. This involves especially giving up the child's desperate wish for the exclusive, total love of his parents while learning to love others. He must learn to gratify his own needs and wishes, rather than the needs of his parents, and he must learn to gratify them himself, rather than depending upon the parents to do this for him. He must give up being good out of fear and in order to keep their love, and must be good because *he* wishes to be. He must discover his own conscience and give up his internalized parents as a sole ethical guide. All these techniques by which weakness adapts itself to strength are necessary for the child but immature and stunting in the adult. He must replace fear with courage.

39. From this point of view, a society or a culture can be either growth-fostering or growth-inhibiting. The sources of growth and of humanness are essentially within the human person and are not created or invented by society, which can only help or hinder the development of humanness, just as a gardener can help or hinder the growth of a rosebush, but cannot determine that it shall be an oak tree. This is true even though we know that a culture is a *sine qua non* for the actualization of humanness itself, e.g., language, abstract thought, ability to love; but these exist as potentialities in human germ plasm prior to culture.

This makes theoretically possible a comparative sociology, transcending and including cultural relativity. The "better" culture gratifies all basic human needs and permits self-actualization. The "poorer" cultures do not. The same is true for education. To the extent that it fosters growth toward self-actualization, it is "good" education.

As soon as we speak of "good" or "bad" cultures, and take them as means rather than as ends, the concept of "adjustment" comes into question. We must ask, "What kind of culture or subculture is the 'well adjusted' person well adjusted *to?*" Adjustment is, very definitely, *not* necessarily synonymous with psychological health.

40. The achievement of self-actualization (in the sense of autonomy) paradoxically makes *more* possible the transcendence of self, and of self-consciousness and of selfishness. It makes it *easier* for the person to be homonomous, i.e., to merge himself as a part in a larger whole than himself. The condition of the fullest homonomy is full autonomy, and to some extent, vice versa, one can attain to autonomy only via successful homonomous experiences (child dependence, B-love, care for others, etc.). It is necessary to speak of levels of homonomy (more and more mature), and to differentiate a "low homonomy" (of fear, weakness, and regression) from a "high homonomy" (of courage and full, self-confident autonomy), a "low Nirvana" from a "high Nirvana," union downward from union upward.

41. An important existential problem is posed by the fact that self-actualizing persons (and *all* people in their peak-experiences) occasionally live out-of-time and out-of-the-world (atemporal and aspatial) even though mostly they *must* live in the outer world. Living in the inner psychic world (which is ruled by psychic laws and not by the laws of outer-reality), i.e., the world of experience, of emotion, of wishes and fears and hopes, of love, of poetry, art, and fantasy, is different from living in and adapting to the non-psychic reality which runs by laws he never made and which are not essential to his nature even though he has to live by them. (He *could*, after all, live in other kinds of worlds, as any science fiction fan knows.) The person who is

not afraid of this inner, psychic world, can enjoy it to such an extent that it may be called Heaven by contrast with the more effortful, fatiguing, externally responsible world of "reality," of striving and coping, of right and wrong, of truth and falsehood. This is true even though the healthier person can also adapt more easily and enjoyably to the "real" world, and has better "reality testing," i.e., doesn't confuse it with his inner psychic world.

It seems clear now that confusing these inner and outer realities, or having either closed off from experience, is highly pathological. The healthy person is able to integrate them both into his life and therefore has to give up neither, being able to go back and forth voluntarily. The difference is the same as the one between the person who can *visit* the slums and the one who is forced to live there always. (*Either* world is a slum if one can't leave it.) Then, paradoxically, that which was sick and pathological and the "lowest" becomes part of the healthiest and "highest" aspect of human nature. Slipping into "craziness" is frightening only for those who are not fully confident of their sanity. Education must help the person to live in both worlds.

42. The foregoing propositions generate a different understanding of the role of action in psychology. Goal-directed, motivated, coping, striving, purposeful action is an aspect or by-product of the necessary transactions between a psyche and a non-psychic world.

(a) The D-need gratifications come from the world outside the person, not from within. Therefore adaptation to this world is made necessary, e.g., reality-testing, knowing the nature of this world, learning to differentiate this world from the inner world, learning the nature of people and of society, learning to delay gratification, learning to conceal what would be dangerous, learning which portions of the world are gratifying and which dangerous, or useless for need-gratification, learning the approved and permitted cultural paths to gratification and techniques of gratification.

(b) The world is in itself interesting, beautiful and fascinating. Exploring it, manipulating it, playing with it, contemplating it, enjoying it are all motivated kinds of action (cognitive, motor, and esthetic needs).

But there is also action which has little or nothing to do with the world, at any rate at first. Sheer expression of the nature or state or powers (Funktionslust) of the organism is an expression of Being rather than of striving. And the contemplation and enjoyment of the inner life not only is a kind of "action" in itself but is also antithetical to action in the world, i.e., it produces stillness and cessation of muscular activity. The ability to wait is a special case of being able to suspend action.

43. From Freud we learned that the past exists *now* in the person. Now we must learn, from growth theory and self-actualization theory that the future also *now* exists in the person in the form of ideals, hopes, duties, tasks, plans, goals, unrealized potentials, mission, fate, destiny, etc. One for whom no future exists is reduced to the concrete, to hopelessness, to emptiness. For him, time must be endlessly "filled." Striving, the usual organizer of most activity, when lost, leaves the person unorganized and unintegrated.

Of course, being in a state of Being needs no future, because it is already *there.* Then Becoming ceases for the moment and its promissory notes are cashed in the form of the ultimate rewards, i.e., the peak-experiences, in which time disappears and hopes are fulfilled.

Winn: Case Study of a Happy Man

David F. Ricks and Alden E. Wessman

Conditions favorable to happiness and the characteristics of the happy man have always interested thoughtful people. But happiness is not a favored topic in psychology, nor are case studies of even moderately happy men frequent in our literature. Most psychologists with whom we have discussed Winn have been skeptical, cautious, or even pessimistic and cynical about the possibility that we have been able to study a really happy man. But is this pessimism justified? With Aristotle, we might ask if we have to wait until an exemplary man is dead before we can say that he was happy, and whether, while he is still alive, we cannot try to speak the truth about him.

"Winn" was studied for three of his undergraduate years by a team of psychologists directed by Henry A. Murray. Consistent with Murray's belief in consensual validation, Winn was studied by many people using their own special methods, all ultimately related into a consistent case formulation. Winn wrote an autobiography, took over a dozen tests, confronted himself on film, and opened his memory, moods, and fantasies to psychological scrutiny. This report draws on everything we know of Winn, with particular emphasis on a six-week study into the variations and levels of his moods.

Winn was originally picked for study after his self report indicated a higher general level of happiness than other students. His happiness was confirmed by an exceptionally low score on the MMPI Depression scale and by consistently high hedonic levels during the intensive study of moods. Independent observers of his behavior ranked him at the top

From D. F. Ricks and A. E. Wessman, "Winn: A Case Study of a Happy Man," *Journal of Humanistic Psychology*, 1966, **6**, 2-16. Reprinted by permission of the publisher.

of the group on current happiness, while those who studied his life history considered it the happiest of the twenty we investigated. It might be possible to find more happy men, but these data seem sufficient to show that Winn can serve as a model of happiness until they are discovered.

Winn's Beliefs and Character

The language of psychology, like the language of everyday discourse, provides many words for misery and few for happiness. Our description of Winn suffers from this poverty, and we will have to resort too often to words that common use has so weakened and vulgarized that we distrust their communicative power. When we say that Winn had always had the admiration and love of a fine family; that he was satisfied with his background and his accomplishments; that he enjoyed life and expected to go to Heaven; we know that these words fail to convey the full meaning they had for Winn. Some readers will ask themselves, "What was he trying to hide?" We believe that he hid very little, and that what he did hide from himself was partly revealed in our tests and observations.

When we first met him in the fall of his sophomore year Winn impressed us as tall, lean, handsome, and a good natural athlete. Busy with his own activities, he was cooperative with our research project but not overly involved with it. Although he was always friendly, an intrusive question could bring a quick flush of anger to his face and a good-natured but sharp retort. He had the manly ability to know his ground and stand on it.

If Winn created any negative reaction, it was a feeling that he was too good to be true, too assured of his own superiority, or too limited in his perspectives. He was generally tolerant and he detested dogmatism, but he had apparently not given much consideration to ways of others or seriously doubted that his current track in life was the best possible.

Winn had noticed his impact on girls and female teachers since early adolescence, and he was equally confident about his other qualities:

> I would regard my customary attitude as genial and confident. I am sure most people like and respect me. I am likewise sure some people feel me conceited and self-centred, especially if they know me only slightly. My good friends find me understanding and interested in them. Many people have me marked for success.

Well aware of his own good fortune, he felt that "fortunate people should use some energy in making others happy," and hoped to help solve some of the world's problems of hunger, despotism, and poverty. "I would like to make some truly great contribution in the field of science, believing that this will, in the long run, help almost everyone." He esteemed "people engaged in the search for truth and also people who make life happy and good for others." He had tasted strong draughts of success but felt that American society over-stressed competition, since "some people cannot stand the strain." For himself, though, competition was a stimulus: "I have always found that as soon as I attained something I had hoped for something else always attracted my ambition. . . . I have the potentialities to do something really worthwhile." His anticipated future included raising a good family, contributing to knowledge, helping people, and a substantial income.

Success was important to Winn, as was the innate satisfaction of work, but these were not exclusive goals. Although he occasionally felt that he should be more conscientious, he contented himself with a high but not spectacular grade record and reserved time for music, talk with friends, dating, and social life.

Winn had thus far been able to get and to do almost everything he wanted. Like most of the other happy people, he had a strong bent toward sociability, enjoyed his work but was not immersed in it, and was able to relax and enjoy both active play and the passive pleasures of food and rest.

Personal Philosophy

Winn's beliefs, although apparently strongly felt products of personal experience, sounded closer to the well-trodden utilitarian ways of J. S. Mill than to contemporary philosophies of anxiety and despair:

> Central to my philosophy of life is happiness. I think I have the right to be happy and I want to make other people happy. . . . Often the two aspects are concomitant—I am happy when I have made someone else happy. . . . To be fully happy, I need to be loved, and thus I feel marriage is essential to my complete happiness. I want to be loved for what I do, to be sure, but mostly I want to be loved for what I am.
>
> Gratification of the senses, when not immoderate, brings happiness. I do not mean only sexual gratification; pleasant and beautiful sights and sounds are included.
>
> My religion is essentially personal; I need not be a devout member of any religious sect to live a good life. . . . My concept of the after-life does not include a hell . . . because I feel everyone has the same right to heaven. . . . If one has lived a bad, unhappy life on earth, there are too many contributing factors to say he is bad and should be punished. In my after-life I will be happy and I will be with all those I loved while alive.
>
> Also in my after-life, infinite wisdom and knowledge will be available. I love knowledge, or truth; I find it beautiful. . . .
>
> I think the criterion for action is this: do what you will, just so long as you retain your self-respect. . . . This self-respect ties in with my happiness and with the happiness of loved ones, for to respect myself I cannot make them unhappy.
>
> I have the right to my own philosophy and every person has the right to live his own life according to his own philosophy, so long as he does not interfere with my happiness. . . . My philosophy is not one that everyone can live by; it is not a universal one, it is mine. This is important; some people would not live good lives according to my philosophy, I imagine.

Winn was deeply aware that he was "society's child." Since "society has laid down some good rules for the protection of the human race," he did not care to oppose society. The tinge of rebellion in his philosophy, and his assertion of individuality, were mild compared to the philosophies of his peers. Winn was essentially in harmony with his family, his community, and his religion.

The only *passion* Winn strongly expressed was a "thirst" for knowledge. Pure thought provided some of his most intense experiences. He compared mathematics to music, in that each time he worked with a familiar set of equations it was like listening to a symphony that he knew well but in which new things appeared on each new hearing.

Winn's philosophical emphasis on happiness, the possibility that any admission of unhappiness would be an admission of shortcoming, raises a question as to the validity of his conscious descriptions. We believe that his desire to be good may have slightly biased the report of his moods, but careful examination of his life history, and of the deeper levels of his personality, show that Winn's happiness had a solid foundation.

Life History

Until he came to Harvard, Winn lived in "the middle of a middle class area" in a small Middle Western city. According to his autobiography, his parents were both white, Protestant, and valedictorians. Winn's father worked his way through college during the depression, then taught school, served as Sunday School Superintendent, and took an active part in community affairs. When Winn was about ten years old his father, with a growing family, left teaching for more lucrative work in industry, and the family moved into an upper middle class social position. Winn's early life was bounded by his neighborhood and the farm of his mother's parents, but in this little territory Winn was top dog: the boss of younger brothers at home, the most talented student in schools, a leader in every activity. At college he continued near the top, no longer the most brilliant student, but still bright enough to major in physics, graduate with honors, compete for major fellowships, and enjoy college social life and the Harvard band. He might have realized that there were larger worlds to conquer—but

except for science, in which he knew he was a novice, he was not troubled by ambitions beyond his present reach. Like his father, he had "done excellent jobs on all projects he entered," and that was enough.

Winn's family life was conventional—the middle class home, summer trips to Grandpa's farm, and the relatives' pride in his accomplishments could come out of stock fiction—but it was unusual in its happiness. His parents' harmony and affection reflected their continuing affectionate ties with their own families. Both were highly respected in their community. Neither parent had disappointed Winn and both had been "wonderful, kind, and understanding." "Perhaps they do a little too much to see that I have the best in life, but they are firm with me when needs be." In Winn's training "all of the vices and virtues were stressed, truth perhaps more than the others." Winn was punished by a spanking, by either parent, if he "got too far out of line." He attended Sunday School regularly.

Winn began his own life story with his uneventful birth, bottle feeding, and the foods he liked as a child. He was not an exceptionally happy baby—"I did cry a great deal, or so I am told"—but he was soon a self-confident child, "I was not retarded in learning to walk, and I was in general confident on my feet." A dislike for being alone began early and persisted, "solitariness was my one important fear." He did not want to "leave my Mommy" in the first two grades and frequently missed school. He still felt that he was not so adventurous as Billy, his next younger brother, nor so independent as Carl, the youngest. The combination of an exceptional interest in food and a marked dependence on adults, particularly his mother, indicated a lasting theme in Winn's life. Winn was still his family's and his society's child, with a philosophy of life that was "pretty much of a family philosophy" and "not independent of the way my society looks at things." Luckily for Winn's oral optimism, the world was still his oyster, and, as we will see when we reach his Rorschach, his breast of chicken, ice cream, and lemon meringue pie as well.

Another theme began with his first memory, the birth of his brother Billy when he was two and a half years old:

> I was playing outside with a ball and a stick. It was a rather dark, cloudy, November day, and my father came out of the house (Billy was born at home) and told me I had a little brother. This did not "shake me up" at all, and I went inside to see my new brother. I was not impressed and went back outside to play ball.

Given Winn's close tie to his mother, it is likely that he was impressed by this intruder. In Winn's loving but controlled family it is probable that open anger about Billy and his claims on their mother was not encouraged. Minor "accidental" injuries to Billy punctuated the next several years of Winn's history and continued to find reflections in Winn's projective tests.

Winn's tie with his mother might have made trouble later, but the birth of Billy, and later of Carl, seemed to shake him up, in spite of his negation, and to force him to work free. His dependency was overcome and his self-control established early in life. He became quite adept in dealing comfortably with peers and potential rivals. This pattern was long established and by the time he was in high school "I quarreled seldom (usually my word was *law*!) and was not too moody."

An element of over-control, however, ran through Winn's history. His steady girl, for example, accused him of never acting on impulse. His brother Billy, unlike Winn, was a "wild" boy, often hurt in accidents, and his example may have pushed Winn to caution. Also, Winn recalled that he had acted on impulse and hurt himself. Once he fell down stairs and bent his nose. Once he ran into a fence and cut his jaw. Neither of these defects was apparent to the observer, but to Winn, who had few, any defect made a difference.

From childhood on Winn had a varied but not exceptionally intense fantasy life. He was troubled by the quick vividness of his fantasies, so unlike the restrained quality of his everyday thought. For a while he played with a fantasy of being a kind of turtle, possibly in response to feelings of holding himself in check. Until the age of sixteen he occasionally had a dream of being carried off his feet by a tornado, probably a fear of what would happen if his impulses were allowed expression. This dream was always the same, and eventually he feared it enough to permanently refuse sulfa drugs, which seemed to cause it.

Winn's school history was filled with steady achievement, prizes, adulation, and affection from teachers. He was "president of everything," and his best friend was a boy who "usually ran against me for office, and was always very gracious when he lost." Winn had many playmates when he was little. When he entered high school he limited himself to a few intimate friendships, though his activities produced many casual ones. An early admiration for athletes had given way, by junior high school, to a desire to be a professional musician. Although Winn was regarded as a "near-prodigy," he disliked his music teacher and decided by ninth grade to be a scientist, a career that embodied the qualities he most admired—beauty, truth, dignity, and intelligence. A theme in his fantasies became, and continued to be throughout college, somehow combining these goals with making money. At the end of high school these fantasies reached preliminary fruition when Winn won a large Harvard scholarship.

Winn's sexual activities were not unusual —some mutual fondling in pre-adolescence, a bit of sexual display with other boys, spin-the-bottle and post-office in early adolescence, quickly settling to steady dates with a girl whose background was like his own. He received sex instruction from his parents, beginning with his mother's explanation of pregnancy when he was eight and ending with his father's discussion of masturbation when he was thirteen. His sexual fantasies were about girls he knew and involved ordinary sexual play. He had not engaged in intercourse at the time we knew him, and he had never picked up girls. It would be hard to regard either Winn's behavior or his fantasies as wild, yet he reported:

I've got a pretty good imagination and will run hog-wild and crazy sometimes, so that what I do isn't—never is it—well, almost never—a reflection of some of the wild things that go on within.

In his behavior, on the other hand, he felt:

I have been pretty conventional. The first son ... always make your parents proud of you.... Very little rebellion at all really.

His sexual fantasies from thirteen to sixteen concerned romantic conquests and erotic adventures. But from sixteen on he had even stronger, more frequent fantasies of a satisfying, harmonious, and enduring marriage that would produce a large, happy family. His fantasies were almost as monogamous, faithful, and mature as his behavior.

The marriage Winn fantasied for himself was very close to the one that nurtured him. Winn's innocent narcissism might have played some part in this—he was not critical of the family that produced his own character —but more important was love for his parents and identification with his admired father. Winn, as a little boy, listened in wonder to his father's series of bedtime stories about an original mock-heroic character. Later he watched his father become a community leader while remaining a loving parent. In school he was given special attention by teachers who liked his father. The fact that his college age fantasies had already moved beyond adolescent identity turmoil and on to intimacy and family life was probably due to the model provided by his father's exemplary role in his family and community.

Rorschach Test

Four seconds after Winn was handed the first card he reported "Looks like Cupid with wings." His performance throughout followed as quickly, without apparent effort. Within a few minutes he was through, yet his last response, "Looks like some X-rays I've seen of kidney and urinary tracts," suggests that the Rorschach shook Winn. Comparison of the anxiety implicit in his last response with the almost vapid Cupid might suggest that Winn's depths were not completely in harmony with his surface. Though neither the Rorschach nor any other evidence indicted Winn for conscious bad faith, the Rorschach did show a repressive trend that was less definite in other material. Like the TAT, it indicated a need to take flight from strongly emotional situations, to resort to distancing and intellectualization—and so to form and maintain a barrier between the deeper springs of his personality and its calm surface.

Most of the thirty-seven responses Winn produced in his orderly way were unoriginal interpretations of the obvious details of the cards, and many were only revisions and refinements of his first responses. Most of Winn's percepts were mainly determined by form, with other determinants subdued. Winn's intellect was clearly in the saddle, but the effort of keeping it there was apparent in the unimaginative use of his fine mind.

Winn had an unusually sensitive response to those elements of the cards that suggest texture, to "shaggy," "furry," "bushy" dogs, rabbits, and furs. He was open and undefensive about the tenderness these percepts suggested: his dogs were touching noses, the furry mink stole would "go around your neck." He was less at ease with more powerful feelings: "The red parts don't seem to help. I can't seem to get them into anything." Later, in the inquiry, he said that "just their shape" suggested "gun holsters" and "cowboy boots with spurs," both indicative of a "cowboys and Indians" kind of aggression, not enough to frighten most people but enough to make Winn anxious. He saw in Card VI "maybe something nasty to bash someone over the head with—jagged and sharp—those whiskers are what do the damage when you swipe."

Winn's need to abstract himself from angry feelings was indicated by the response that followed this "nasty" percept: "That looks to me like looking down on an atoll in the South Pacific, a coral reef formation." Distance (looking down), intellectualization (an atoll), and rigidification (coral reef formation) are all suggested in this percept. The progressive fading out of a lively response was even more apparent in the sequence of responses to Card

III, with "people playing the piano," an activity in which he himself took part, giving way to "native types dancing," followed by the dehumanization of the dancers into two birds facing each other, "a kind of abstract painting that doesn't really look like birds." Certainly Winn did not have a pathological degree of inhibition, yet even this paragon had his problems, and his defensive ways of handling them.

Winn's oral optimism was mentioned earlier. In addition to lemon meringue pie and banana splits, his Rorschach was filled with lavishly described drumsticks, chicken breasts, a bowl of ice cream, a shrimp cocktail, and a smoking pipe. Though Winn would blush at the association, these percepts might be related to the girls he preferred: "My female partner is usually of the voluptuous type with pleasantly large, well-formed breasts—small petite girls do not appeal to me."

Thematic Apperception Test

Winn's stories dealt with the perils that beset the ways of "nice, average" boys and girls who live in a world of temptations. Johnny struggles between the violin his parents gave him and his love of football; Nancy, who is "just a common girl," is "very sensitive to the wants and needs of other people." Two "level-headed, intelligent, sensible" young people wait for each other, marry, and have nice children. As if to defend a world in which Pandora's box is still unopened, he told one story in which innocence was confronted with suspicion and emerged triumphant. Sin was only allowed around the edges of his fantasy, a warning against the unwary impulse and its potential for destruction: in Card 4 an "average guy" in "a nice neighborhood" began to run around with boys his parents didn't like and then to smoke and drink and keep late hours. In spite of his wife's efforts to reform him he killed a man and ended life in prison. Another man, who was "never much good" because he "didn't care to work," became a hobo and ended as a cadaver on the table of an "up-and-coming" medical student.

In Winn's early stories good was rewarded and evildoing led to grief. The community was omnipresent—even more than parents, the agency through which rewards and punishments were channeled to the hero. The only disturbing element was, not too surprisingly for Winn, injury to someone near to him. Winn's active, self-assertive, confident drive must have involved him often in situations which verged on aggression toward others. In the stories he told, as in the Rorschach, the most usual fate of an aggressive thought was modulated expression, followed by attempts at undoing or minimizing consequences, by attempts to achieve distance, or by active mastery through skill and control. Virtue and community always triumphed over the aggressive individual—a state that changed, however, as Winn moved on to the more "fantastic" last ten pictures in the TAT.

In Winn's story to Card 11 impulse finally won a round. In this story, an apparent symbolic battle over masturbation was concluded when "Beelzebub" knocked the hero "down into a deep gorge, where the fiery river flowed." In another long, involved story a mysterious woman "expressed an interest" in the hero and "seemed to be able to defy the law of gravity" because she "could take an object and make it float around," a situation which fascinated the hero but made him feel in mortal danger. Against powers such as these—sexual impulses, particularly toward fascinating women—Winn fantasied having a "magic charm" which would "stand firm" and protect him against their pagan charms. But the charm failed him (being secretly in league with the enemy power), and he could concede without distress "so Beelzebub won again." If Winn had been less able to relax controls he might have had serious neurotic inhibitions—but while he did keep a firm grip on aggression, he could enjoy his sexual fantasies. Yet sexual activity was dangerous. Sexual misdeeds might be reported home and make everybody "terribly ashamed of what kind of man" one was. And if one relaxed controls too much, got too excited, it might be hard to control *both* sex and aggression.

Thus a story of extra-marital flirtation ended in rape, murder, and execution. In another story a young man turned out to be a vampire who preyed on young girls and had to be eliminated to protect the community. Where sex alone was concerned Winn's private morality did not seem so strong as his fear of damaging his public image. But when sexuality was fused with aggression, or when aggression alone was concerned, he drew back with horror.

The other act punished by drastic retributions was discovering forbidden knowledge. The impulse that frightened him seemed to reflect concern over the origins of his little brothers, a curiosity not completely satisfied by his mother's explanation of pregnancy. One of his stories dealt with an archaeologist who wondered about a "dark, terrible secret" in a pyramid, found a papyrus that told him "the rules of how to get into this room," and made his way in, only to find that the "mummy cases" opened up and held tight to him. As he died he realized that he "had violated a curse and was going to be done away with by supernatural powers."

We have speculated that Winn's mild narcissism and exhibitionism originated in the situation of being displaced by his little brothers and at the same time prohibited from being either too outraged or too curious. Forced to stand on his own two feet, he could still outshine his brothers, and all rivals, by the glory of his achievements. When he gave his fantasy free rein, as he did in a story about the world's fastest rope climber, his fantasied exhibitionistic pleasure was intense:

He got terrific feelings of power in this, because all of those people would stand there and look at him, and marvel at him, and nobody felt that anybody else in the world could be able to do things like that.

This desire for favorable attention and admiration seemed to be successfully diverted and socialized in his school successes and thirst for knowledge, though the story above suggests that secret knowledge, even science, could be dangerous.

The most original of Winn's productions, in any test or situation, was the image he created for the blank TAT card (16):

This scene is on the planet Alpha Centuri ... sort of half desert and half jungle. And the desert part is very rocky and, strangely, the rocks seem to be sculptured into architectural forms. They're square rocks and rectangular rocks and spherical rocks, and then there's a piece of sand stretching as far as the eye can see. . . .

Then, over on the jungle side, there's this lush red-jungle red because chlorophyll is red on this planet. And there are . . . plants there that are kind of like animals. They are able to move in a certain way, and they can fight each other, and if you get near one it'll grab you and eat you up. These plants are grouped together to form a community, and they fight against each other all of the time. The wars of these plants are really something terrible and they have darts that they can shoot off, and secretions that come out of them. And they strangle each other by vines and roots, and dam up water supplies. . . . The way they kill one another is to drag the person, or the plant, to the edge of the jungle and throw him out into the desert. So that, sprinkled along the desert I've described, occasionally you'll see a little ashy crust. . . .

We might speculate that this vivid image portrayed an unconscious feeling of inner division, half dry, abstract, static intellect; the other half an infant jungle of fantasy. Winn had half renounced the capacity to tame fantasy by subjecting it to reality, and to give vitality to conscious thought by feeding it with imagination. Too often, his impulses died in the full light of conscious thought.

Winn's TAT, like his Rorschach, suggested depths at which he was not completely integrated, nor entirely the conventional All-American success story that he appeared on the surface. Was he then not really as happy as he seemed? We believe that at college he was truly happy, though at some later time he might find himself less satisfied with his work, less content with his successes, and more in need of inner refreshment than public adulation. Then even Winn might become unhappy. Yet these hints in his projective tests should not be overemphasized: to deny Winn any weaknesses at all would be to deny him humanity, and he certainly had more than enough strengths to counterbalance his weaknesses.

Data from Mood Study

A. Mood Levels. In a study specifically designed to study characteristic levels and degrees of variability in happiness, anxiety, anger, and other moods, Winn's average hedonic level over a period of forty-two days was at the 7th level of a 10 point scale, "Feeling very good and cheerful." This level placed Winn at the top of the set of college students we studied, with only one other man near him. Only twice did his daily average drop below "Feeling pretty good, O.K.," and then it slid only to "Feeling a little bit low, just so-so." On six of the forty-two days his average mood for the day was "Elated and in high spirits." Only once, during a sudden painful illness, did his lowest mood drop to a really low point—and the next day he was able to report "Still in infirmary but feeling well and in good spirits. Only slight pain and discomfort."

Winn's high hedonic level was matched by equally high means on several other scales. According to these long-term reports, he was consistently confident that people thought well of him, felt that his abilities were sufficient and his prospects good, that he was accepted and liked, and that his life was ample and satisfying. He generally felt that he was open and responsive, pretty close to his own best self, and free within wide limits to act as he wanted. Thus, in the broad area of human interaction and social and moral judgment Winn felt that he was living a highly satisfying life. Winn did not feel quite as well off regarding work, nor was he regularly as energetic or secure as he might have been had his impulse expression been more free. But, taken together, Winn's day-to-day reports indicated that he was a very contented and happy person in the major aspects of his life and remarkably free from emotional distress.

B. Mood Changes and Their Relationships. Besides studying characteristic *levels* of happiness and unhappiness, we investigat-ed the ways in which men *varied* in their moods of happiness and unhappiness, anxiety and ease, openness to the world or withdrawal from it, and so on. The ways in which feelings varied in concert or in opposition were studied by factor analysis of individual patterns of change over six weeks. Winn was slightly toward the stable end of the group. But unlike most of the stable men, who had differentiated kinds of mood perturbations, Winn experienced his ups and downs as general mood swings. One large factor accounted for about two-thirds of the common variance in Winn's emotional changes. Four smaller factors reflected subsidiary feeling variations, each partially independent from Winn's fluctuations in hedonic level.

The major contrast in Winn's emotional life contrasted zestful, extremely happy days with somewhat less happy ones. Although all feelings were related to this major axis of happiness, they differed in the degree to which they were related. Energy, harmony and sociability with others, receptivity toward the world, and loving tenderness, together with feelings of approval by the community, were the main components of Winn's happiest moods. His best times came when he was involved with others, three of his happiest days coming in a series of parties over a football weekend, another set coming during a period of easy work and much socializing around the Thanksgiving weekend. Winn was exhilarated by social events of all kinds, reporting with equal excitement "The Yale weekend has started! Party in room!" and "Thanksgiving Dinner at Professor B's. What a good day!" In every report of happy times the food and liquor consumed played a large part. When Winn was in danger of being put on a restrictive diet to control an illness he discovered during the course of the study he reported in his daily diary, "I'll *die* if I have to give up frappes," and later he wrote, "Thank God! (for ice cream)." Unlike sadder men who had found the world less to their liking, Winn nourished an ardent openness to people, food, and fun. Unlike the more strictly work-oriented men, Winn could have a happy social time without guilt and could get along without over-concern for getting ahead.

The second factor described a contrast between calm, steady days and more excited, adventurous days with high peaks and low troughs. The first, and main, element in Winn's mood changes might be called American Epicureanism, the second Protestant Stoicism. On his less stoic, more excited days Winn hit his worst *troughs* of anxiety and anger, but also achieved his highest *peaks* of impulse expression, work, and thought. These seemed to be the days when some exceptionally powerful inner drive worked its way toward expression and powered both work and thought to new levels. At the end of one week when impulses, work, and thought had all hit high peaks, Winn reported "Have had very vivid dreams all week. Sex and violence."

The other idiosyncratic factors, describing variations on these general themes, will not be described here.

C. Self and Ideal Descriptions in Depression and Elation. Each subject in our mood study twice filled out *Q*-sorts describing his self and his ideal concepts, once when elated and another time when depressed. The consistency of Winn's *Q*-sort self-descriptions in the two moods was about average for this group, his self-description in depression correlating .59 with his self-description in elation.

Winn chose two items as "most characteristic" of himself in both of his extreme moods:

Comfortable in intimate relationships. Sexually aware.

In elation the other items he selected as "most characteristic" were:

Adventuresome. Warm and friendly. Excels in his work. Placid and untroubled. Dynamic. Ambitious. Inventive, delights in finding new solutions to new problems. Accomplishes much, truly productive.

When Winn felt depressed this self-description was replaced by a less lively set of "most characteristic" qualities:

Doesn't apply himself fully. Able to take things as they come. Stands on his own two feet. Preoc-

cupied with himself. Attempts to appear at ease. Quietly goes his own way. Good judge of when to comply and when to assert himself. Tactful in personal relationships.

Study of all the changes suggests that Winn, in his more elated moods, conceived of himself as warm, outgoing, and successful. When his mood lowered he retreated to a cautious position in which autonomy became more important than social participation and self-preoccupation threatened to replace both human relationships and intellectual productivity. But the changes were not great, and Winn remained oriented toward others and satisfied with himself even at his lowest.

Winn's self-description was rather close to his ideal in elation ($r = .75$) and only moderately different in depression ($r = .40$). Both of these figures were well within the top third of the group. The slight differences between his self-conception and his ideal in elation need not be reported here. The somewhat larger gaps in his depressed moods between the self and what Winn would have liked it to be were mainly concerned with work. Winn's super-ego was apparently a standard Protestant Ethic conscience, emphasizing work as temporal salvation. His slight deviations from this conscience carried him toward a more playful, resilient, responsive, and less driven character. We do not want to minimize the healthy significance of Winn's close approximation to his ideals, but it is also clear that Winn as he was had more life than he would have had if he came closer to his ideal.

Case Summary

Every source of data seems to confirm Winn's happiness and to show consistent themes in his character. Other men we studied surpassed Winn in depth and extent of social awareness, in richness of personality, in dedication to particular goals, or in other valued characteristics. But none equalled him in genuine, consistent, zest and happiness.

What generated and sustained Winn's happiness? Part of the explanation seems rooted in his background and his gifts. Favored with a loving family that was respected in its community, fostered growth, and provided worthy and approachable models, possessed of sufficient means and opportunities, and gifted in face, form, intellect, health, and talent, Winn was consistently successful in his enterprises and his relationships. To the degree that the future is his responsibility this success seems likely to continue.

But Winn can also be seen as more than the sum of his background and his talents. His current personality showed a steadfast optimism, supported by a lively, active orientation toward the world, love of human contact, and balanced, mature judgment. We found only minor flaws in his general well-being, the main ones being an overly strong barrier between rationality and impulse and too much fear of community disapproval. But Winn's successes were not crass or calculating, and one of the sources of his happiness was reasonable willingness to accept limitations, to curb any inclinations toward narcissistic insatiability he may have had, and to tread the middle road between excess and deprivation with caution, intelligence, and due regard for his fellow man.

General Characteristics of Happy and Unhappy Men

We noted that Winn was studied as part of a general investigation of mood and personality. The contrasts between the happy and unhappy men suggest some general characteristics of happiness. The happy men possessed self-esteem and confidence. They were successful and satisfied in interpersonal relations. They showed ego-strength and a gratifying sense of identity. Their lives had organization, purpose, and the necessary mastery of themselves to attain their goals. The less happy men were pessimistic in their expectations and lower in self-esteem and self-confidence. More unsuccessful with their interpersonal relations, with evidence of isolation, anxiety, and guilt, they showed little sense of satisfying ego-identity. They felt inferior in their academic performance and their lives lacked continuity and purpose.

No single developmental success or trauma seems to account for happiness or unhappiness. Rather, multiple sources are found in the cumulative series of an individual's long-term life experiences. Important bases for self-esteem had been impaired in the lives of the unhappy men. Their damaged identities hampered their potential for intimacy and satisfying commitment. Unfavorable outcomes of several developmental crises had left the unhappy men prone to self-limitation, frustration, and disappointment. Nor could one source account for the success of the well-adjusted, social extroverts such as Winn. These men were not of a single pattern, but did generally come from warm, supportive home environments that were conducive to growth and responsibility. Though there were exceptions, developmental transitions were generally smooth and residual conflicts subdued. Important needs had not become overly checked by disturbing affect. They were able to make positive identifications with respected, approachable role models and these had in turn favored the establishment of a worthwhile sense of self.

Lest our readers conclude that this is a simple and unqualified paean to happiness, let us make our position clear. We hold that it is desirable that people be happy—it is generally superior to misery. But happiness can also be constricting. There was much to admire and respect in the lives of some of the more complicated and less happy men.

Is Psychology Ready for Happiness?

Can we move on from these empirical descriptions to a systematic formulation of the character of the happy man and of the conditions for happiness? Can psychology add anything not yet said in the long history of the problem? The classic Socratic formula, that the happy man is temperate, just, brave, and pious, seems a remarkably apt summary of Winn's main characteristics. If we add to this

Aristotle's comment that happiness requires, in addition to excellence, the possession of good birth, personal gifts, and external fortune, we have summarized most of Winn's outstanding virtues.

Modern psychology has emphasized other qualities possessed by Winn—pro-action, adjustment, ego-strength, competence, and identity. But these seem, while necessary, not yet sufficient. Since Freud and Abraham, psychoanalysts have also emphasized the oral qualities of the optimistic person. Winn typified these, together with the qualities of good conscience and self-acceptance psychoanalysis posits for the man free from depression. The skeptical analyst might also note that denial might contribute to happiness, or even be necessary if one is to be happy. Identification with suffering can upset complacency. Winn, in the bright sunshine of successful youth, did seem lacking in shadows, perspective, and awareness of tragedy. His happiness perhaps rested on his limitations as well as on his gifts.

We can only note here that Winn's adjustment, while beautifully articulated with current American society, does not offer a transsocietal formula for happiness. Winn, society's child, had both the assets and the limitations of his particular segment of American culture. But a full treatment of this aspect of Winn would take us far afield.

The most tantalizing puzzle offered by Winn arises from his inhibitions and the limited degree to which his personality can be considered spontaneous, self-actualizing, or internally congruent. If a controlled, well-socialized man such as Winn can stand as a model for happiness, then we must consider that civilization must have inherent satisfactions as well as inherent discontents, and that due regard for maturation and refinement of impulses must temper our enthusiasm for the simpler prescriptions of psychological hedonism. The formula that happiness equals the sum of satisfactions minus the sum of dissatisfactions, which is the logical derivative of hedonistic theories, must be tempered by consideration of the quality, age appropriateness, and last value of the satisfactions being considered. We often hope that the study of psychology can increase human insight and awareness, and so increase the range of alternatives available to the lives of its students. To do this psychology must deal with human lives on a scale that boldly comes to grips with problems of quality and value. The study of happy men and women can perhaps be a step in this direction.

Some Remarks on the Humanizing of Psychology

M. Brewster Smith

The "phenomenological approach" has recently come to be something of a rallying cry to a number of psychologists who share the "tender-minded" bias that psychology must, after all, come to terms with human experience, and who go so far as to believe that careful attention to this experience will leave the science of psychology not merely more satisfying to like-minded people, but also better science. Sharing this point of view and agreeing heartily with the program recommended by MacLeod (1947) in his article on "The Phenomenological Approach in Social Psychology," the present writer has been dismayed by some recent publications which, it seems to him, misconstrue the appropriate role of a phenomenological approach in a way that invites the critical to reject a humanized psychology lock, stock, and barrel. Since the writer would regard such an outcome as highly unfortunate, he feels that a clarification of the issues is badly needed, and herewith makes an attempt in this direction.

The position with which he would take particular issue is that of Snygg and Combs (1949; Combs, 1949) whose point of view has also been espoused by Rogers (1947). These authors contrast the objective or external frame of reference in psychology with the phenomenological, or internal frame of reference, and declaring their stand firmly with phenomenology, proceed to muster on their side the names of Lewin, Lecky, Allport, Murphy, and Angyal, among others, even including the seemingly less tractable father-figure of Freud. In essence, their contention is that the locus of psychological causation lies entirely within the phenomenal field of conscious experience, and that it therefore

From M. B. Smith, "The Phenomenological Approach in Personality Theory: Some Critical Remarks," *Journal of Abnormal and Social Psychology*, 1950, **45**, 516-522. Reprinted by permission of the American Psychological Association.

behooves the psychological theorist—and therapist—to formulate his problems and concepts accordingly. Snygg and Combs give much attention to the individual's perceptual-cognitive field, particularly to the *self*, as its most salient feature. Written from this standpoint, psychology comes close to a rapprochement with common sense.

While applauding their emphasis on perception and the self, the present writer proposes that they are confusing phenomenology with what may be termed the subjective frame of reference. Sharply maintained, this distinction further helps to clarify certain persistent ambiguities in the theory of ego and self.

Phenomenology and Common Sense

One of the genuine merits of the phenomenological approach is that it brings psychology somewhat closer to the world of common sense. There is always the danger that psychology, in its concern for rigor and neatness, may divorce itself too completely from this source of problems and partial insights. Focussing scientific attention on the phenomenal world as it is presented to us, the world from which common sense also takes its start, the phenomenological approach can bring into the ken of the psychologist data and problems too often left to common sense by default. Like common sense, and unlike some current varieties of psychological theory, it does deal with experience, and thus presents itself as an attractive alternative to those who find a behavioristic psychology uncongenial.

But phenomenology is not common sense, nor can it rightly be called upon to justify a common-sense psychology. In MacLeod's phrase, the phenomenological approach "involves the adoption of what might be called an attitude of disciplined naïvete" (1947), p. 194). In many respects, its result may run exactly counter to common-sense conclusions. Common sense, with its preconceived categories and stock explanations, neither disciplined nor naïve, is full of pseudo-scientific theory, while phenomenology limits its concern to the unprejudiced *description* of the world of phenomena. To take the phenomenal world presented in conscious experience as completely explanatory of behavior is closer to common sense than to phenomenology or adequate science.

Yet this is essentially what Snygg and Combs have done in their attempt to rewrite psychology in a "phenomenological frame of reference." *"All behavior, without exception,"* they say, *"is completely determined by and pertinent to the phenomenal field of the behaving organism"* (1949, p. 15, italics theirs). And they go on to explain that

by the phenomenal field we mean the entire universe, including himself, as it is experienced by the individual at the instant of action. . . . Unlike the "objective" physical field, the phenomenal field is not an abstraction or an artificial construction. It is simply the universe of naïve experience in which each individual lives, the everyday situation of self and surroundings which each person takes to be reality (1949, p. 15).

While they bow unnecessarily to current prejudice in avoiding the word *consciousness*, their meaning is clear, and their index spells it out: "Consciousness, *see* Phenomenal field."

It is one variant of common sense that consciousness completely explains behavior, but at this juncture, it is hard to see how such a view can be regarded as an acceptable scientific postulate. Quite apart from the metaphysical controversy about the status of consciousness as "real" or respectable, we have behind us Würzburg and we have behind us Freud, to mention but two major sources of evidence that a psychology of experience or consciousness has distinct explanatory limits. Where is the determining tendency represented in the phenomenal field? What of the inac-

ceptable strivings that warp our behavior, what of our defensive techniques of adjustment that so often prove most effective precisely when we are least aware of them? It is no satisfactory solution to speak, as Snygg and Combs do, of a "unified field of figure-ground phenomena of which the individual is more or less conscious . . . [in which] the vague and fuzzy aspects of behavior correspond to and are parts of the vague and incompletely differentiated aspects of the field" (1949, p. 17). The clinical literature abounds with instances of unconsciously determined behavior which, far from being "vague and fuzzy," is on the contrary highly differentiated.

One suspects that such a psychology of consciousness has an element of common-sense appeal not unlike the attraction of allied forms of psychotherapy. It does make sense to the layman: it accords with what he is ready and able to recognize in himself. And it has distinct value within limits that it refuses to recognize. Because it over-states its claims, however, it may tend to promote the state of affairs away from which we have been striving—every man his own psychologist.

But MacLeod has already made the relevant point succinctly: "The phenomenological method, in social psychology as in the psychology of perception [and we would add, psychology generally] can never be more than an approach to a scientific inquiry" (1947, p. 207). It provides certain kinds of data, not *all* the data. It furnishes the basis for certain valuable theoretical constructs; it does not give birth to them in full concreteness. It sets some problems and provides some clues; the psychologist, theorist or clinician, must *infer* the answers.

Subjective Constructs and the Observer's Frame of Reference

Here we reach the crux of the matter. If a psychology of consciousness is necessarily incomplete yet we do not abandon our hope for a psychology that comes to terms with human experience, what is the solution? A discussion of two lesser questions may indicate the nature of the answer. In the first place, does the decision to frame our psychological concepts and theories in terms appropriate to the "private world" of the behaving person commit us to the exclusive use of phenomenal concepts? Secondly, what is the appropriate role of the phenomenological approach in the service of this kind of theory-building?

Lewin, whose psychological life space Snygg and Combs equate to their phenomenal field (1949, p. 15), was entirely clear in maintaining a sharp distinction between the two concepts. He said:

It is likewise doubtful whether one can use consciousness as the sole criterion of what belongs to the psychological life space at a given moment in regard to social facts and relationships. The mother, the father, the brothers and sisters are not to be included as real facts in the psychological situation of the child only when they are immediately present. For example, the little child playing in the garden behaves differently when he knows his mother is at home than when he knows she is out. One cannot assume that this fact is continually in the child's consciousness. Also a prohibition or a goal can play an essential role in the psychological situation without being clearly present in consciousness. . . . Here, as in many other cases it is clear that one must distinguish between "appearance" and the "underlying reality" in a dynamic sense. In other words, the phenomenal properties are to be distinguished from the conditional-genetic characteristics of objects and events, that is, from the properties which determine their causal relationships. . . . As far as the conceptual derivation is concerned, one may use effectiveness as the criterion for existence: *"What is real is what has effects"* (1936, p. 19).

Lewin's life space, then, is *not* merely the phenomenal field. And he adds to our previous considerations cogent reasons for thinking that a psychology of the phenomenal field cannot be adequately explanatory. His life space is not immediately given in the concreteness of experience; it is an abstract, hypothetical construct, inferred by the psychologist-observer to account for the individual's behavior.

It is, however, a construct of a type that differs from constructs of behavioristic psychology. It is formulated in terms of what is behaviorally real to the acting individual, not primarily in terms of what is physically observable to the scientist. Hence it is legitimate to speak of theories like Lewin's as anchored in a *subjective* (not phenomenological) *frame of reference*. Lewin's concepts and many of Freud's are in this sense *subjective constructs*, not because they are built of the stuff of conscious experience, but because they attempt to deal with what is effectively real to the individual, even when it is real to the scientific observer only in this secondary, indirect way.

The subjective frame of reference in theory construction is to be contrasted with the *objective frame of reference*, wherein concepts are chosen so as to be rooted as closely as possible in effective realities shared by any qualified observer. This is the distinction that Snygg and Combs seek, which makes them see both Freud and Lewin as precursors. There is no absolute difference between the two frames of reference; it is rather a question of which criteria are weighted most strongly in the selection of constructs.

Both the subjective and objective frames of reference pertain to the choice of constructs and the theoretical context in which they are embedded. They in no sense conflict with what has been called the *observer's frame of reference*, which, indeed, lies at the foundation of all science. The problem of establishing a bridge between the point of view of the observer and *either* subjective or objective inferential constructs is the familiar one of operational definition. It cannot, in the last analysis, be avoided unless one chooses the alternative of claiming *direct* access to the point of view of the observed. This is the position of intuitionism, which asserts that the observer's and subject's points of view can be merged. But is this science? Not in the sense of a systematic search for understanding that can withstand the equally systematic doubt of the man from Missouri.

Subjective constructs framed in terms of the "private world" of the behaving individual remain constructs, and as such must ultimately be rooted in data accessible to the observer's frame of reference. There is no reason at all why their source should be restricted to the data of communicated conscious experience, in answer to our first question. But the phenomenological approach, or, more generally, any means of access to the experience of the subject, is of course crucial to the formulation of subjective constructs and the investigation of their relationships. Perhaps the point has been labored, but it is an essential one: the phenomenological approach, the clinical interview, the projective protocol, the behavioral observation—none of these yield direct knowledge of psychological constructs, subjective or objective, while all of them can provide the basis for inferring explanatory constructs and their relationships. If the canons of inference can be made sufficiently explicit, they provide the operational definitions that secure the constructs in the scientific home base of the observer's frame of reference.

Methods that get the subject to reveal his private world as he sees it need to be supplemented by others which permit the observer to infer effective factors that are distorted or disguised in the subject's awareness. But the broadly phenomenological methods remain a signally important source of data. Certain important subjective constructs such as the *self*, moreover, are anchored fairly directly in the data of phenomenological report.

Ego, Self, and Phenomenology

Although there is still considerable confusion in usage, a degree of consensus seems to be emerging to employ the term *self* for the phenomenal content of the experience of personal identity. A salient feature of the phenomenal field that has figured largely in personality theory, the self in this sense has the conceptual properties of a phenomenal object. Murphy (1947) and Chein (1944) use it with this meaning. Snygg and Combs agree, writing with somewhat franker circularity:

> Of particular importance in the motivation of behavior will be those parts of the phenomenal field perceived by him to be part or characteristic of himself. To refer to this important aspect of the total field we have used the term *phenomenal self* (1949, p. 111).

Within the phenomenal self, they distinguish as a stable core the *self-concept:* "Those parts of the phenomenal field which the individual had differentiated as definite and fairly stable characteristics of himself" (1949, p. 112).

Sharing with Murphy a strong emphasis on responses to the self as fundamental to motivational theory, Snygg and Combs go so far as to state that the basic human need is "the preservation and enhancement of the phenomenal self" (1949, p. 58). Changes in the perception of the self play a major role in the theory of the therapeutic process that they share with Rogers (1947).

Let us look more closely, however, at how these writers actually use the term. Passages like the following can readily be found:

> ... when the self is free from any threat of attack or likelihood of attack, then it is possible for the self to consider these hitherto rejected perceptions, to make new differentiations, and to reintegrate the self in such a way as to include them (Rogers, 1947, p. 365).
> A self threatened by its perceptions may deny the perception by simply refusing to enter the situation where such a perception is forced upon him (Snygg and Combs, 1949, p. 148).

Can a phenomenal self consider perceptions and reintegrate itself; can a threatened phenomenal self deny perceptions; or is this rather double-talk resulting from the attempt to make one good concept do the work of two? If, as this writer suspects, the latter is the case, what is the nature of the hidden second concept, which evidently is not merely a percept or phenomenal entity? To give it a name he would suggest the conventional term *ego*, realizing that usage in this respect is even more ambiguous than with the term *self.* The important point is that the concept, implicit in the writings of Rogers and of Snygg and Combs, is a subjective construct but does not refer to a phenomenal entity, whereas the self, on the other hand, is a coordinate subjective construct that does. The relation between the two will bear closer examination.

It is not necessary, at this juncture, to propose a definitive theory of the ego, nor to enter into an involved discussion of alternative views about its nature. What is relevant is that starting from an attempt to write a psychology in phenomenal terms, our authors in spite of themselves give implicit recognition to organizing, selective processes in the personality which are somehow guided by the nature and status of the self (among other things) and somehow, in turn, have an influence in its nature and status. So conceived, the relation of ego and self is highly interdependent[1] but by no means an identity. The distinction is that between a dynamic configuration of on-going processes, inferred from many facts of biography and behavior, and a phenomenal entity resulting from these processes and affecting them in turn, inferred primarily (but not exclusively) from phenomenological report.

Approaching the problem on a slightly different tack, we may find it rewarding to consider three of the eight conceptions of the ego listed by Allport (1943, p. 459) in the light of the distinction just made: the ego "as one segregated behavioral system among others," "as knower," and "as object of knowledge." The fundamental conception advanced here is not unlike the first of these senses, if one reads into it a dynamic quality not expressed in Allport's formulation. As an on-going system or organizing and selective processes mediating the individual's intercourse with reality, it includes a variety of processes without being coterminous with the total personality.[2] Among these processes or functions is that of the ego as "knower," which the writer would take in a less metaphysical sense than Allport's to embrace the cognitive-perceptual functions of personality. These have been described with reason in psychoanalytic theory (Freud, 1933, pp. 105-106) as an integral aspect of the ego system. Among the phenomena that the ego "knows" is the *self*, Allport's "ego as object of knowledge." Like any cognitive-perceptual object, the self only imperfectly mirrors the

physical, psychological, and social facts that underlie the perception. And also like similar phenomenal objects it serves as a guide to appropriate behavior. But the relation of self to ego-processes is no more and no less obscure than the relation of cognitive structures to behavior generally.

"Ego-Involvements" and "Ego Defense"

We have sought to reinstate the ego as a subjective but non-phenomenal construct mainly through an examination of the pitfalls encountered by the attempt to avoid such a concept. If the ego-self distinction as outlined above is worth making, however, it should make a difference in the formulation of other knotty problems. Does it? Two such problems—the nature of "ego-involvements" and of the "mechanisms of defense"—will be examined briefly as test cases.

As it emerges in the work of Sherif and Cantril (1947), the concept of ego-involvement lacks clarity and focus. Widely divergent sorts of psychological facts turn out to be embraced by the term, which, like so many in popular psychological currency, rather identifies a disparate group of problems than clarifies them. More often that not, ego-involvement means the involvement of a person's pride and self-esteem in a task; he feels put to the test and ready to be ashamed of a poor performance. In other instances, the term is invoked to cover immersion in a cause, or falling in love—cases in which the person, to be sure, cares as deeply about outcomes as in the first type, but may be engrossed to the point of losing self-awareness.

Now the present self-ego distinction makes excellent sense when applied here. Since the distinctive character of the first sort of examples lies in the fact that the individual's conception of his self and its worth is at stake, these can aptly be described as *self-involvement*. The second type of case can often still be called ego-involvement without inconsistency. The situation in the latter instances touches on the person's central system of on-going psychological processes so closely that

---

[1] The writer doubts that it is advisable to construct the ego as narrowly around the self as do Chein (1944) and Murphy (1947).

[2] How to distinguish within the personality between *ego* and *non-ego* is, of course, an important problem, though it will not be attempted here. The distinction, however, is not the same as the phenomenal one between the *self* and *not-self* (often described, confusingly, as *ego-alien*).

he may lose himself in it. Similar engrossment can, to be sure, result from the involvement of equally imperative non-ego processes: who is to say, without intimate acquaintance with the principals, whether being in love should be called ego-involvement or "id-involvement"! However that may be, note that self-involvement and ego-involvement thus conceived may vary independently. A person may care about a task both because of its intrinsic meaning for him and with afterthought for its bearing on his prestige and self-esteem. Or either or neither may be the case. The behavioral conditions and consequences of ego- and self-involvement should furthermore be quite distinct.

The situation is somewhat different in regard to the theoretical status of the mechanisms of defense. Here the classical formulation by Anna Freud (1946) regards the defense mechanisms as employed by the ego (the term is used essentially in our sense) to protect itself, primarily from disruption by strong unassimilated urges, but also from threats from the external world. As a more or less precariously balanced system mediating between inner strivings and outer reality, the ego, in this view, has recourse to these sometimes drastic techniques in order to preserve its balance, and maintain the course of behavior at a lower level of adjustment if need be rather than run the risk of its catastrophic disruption. Murphy (1947), and later Snygg and Combs (1949), on the other hand, say in effect that it is rather the self that is defended. Under conditions of threat, enhancement and preservation of the self may be achieved by the classical defense mechanisms. Is it necessary to choose between these divergent formulations, or can the conflict be resolved?

The present writer would maintain that the mechanisms of defense can ultimately all be conceived as defenses of the ego, since they serve to bolster up the ego's adjustive compromise. As contributors to this compromise, they can also best be regarded as a part of the activity included in the ego system. But in a more immediate sense, any particular one of an individual's defenses may or may *not* be a *self*-defense mechanism. Since the mainte-nance of a favorable self-image is important to sound ego functioning, though not its only requisite, the end of ego defense can often be served most efficiently by self-defense mechanisms. Certain mechanisms, like identification, may, indeed, always take effect through the defense of the self. There are, however, instances of ego-defense mechanisms which involve the self only indirectly if at all. In regression, for example, one can hardly suppose that the self is enhanced in any way. What is more likely is that by retreating to an earlier, more deeply established, or simpler level of ego organization, the person seeks, perhaps ineptly, to cope with disturbing experiences that, by reason of circumstance, constitution, or previous learning, he has not the strength to meet maturely. In most cases, the relative significance of the self in the defensive process probably cannot be assessed in any simple way, since changes in the self for better or worse may be the *consequence* of the fortunes of the ego and its defenses, as well as the focus of defensive techniques.

A formulation of this sort, which seems to agree with present clinical experience, again suggests the usefulness of a distinction between phenomenal and non-phenomenal (shall we say *functional?*) subjective constructs, with both employed in proper coordination. A purely phenomenological psychology, on the other hand, cannot adequately describe *all* the defensive processes, since neither all the effective threats to the ego nor all the defenses against them are registered accurately in conscious awareness. Indeed, it is largely the consequence of "silent" defensive processes that phenomenological reports must be viewed with so much circumspection in personality research.

Conclusions

Starting from a discussion of Snygg and Combs' proposal of a phenomenological frame of reference for psychology (1949) the writer has sought to establish the following major points:

1. While common sense may favor an explanatory psychology framed entirely in

terms of conscious experience, such a psychological system does violence to currently available knowledge.

2. Phenomenology, as distinct from common sense, is descriptive, not explanatory. It is an approach or method ancillary to the formulation of problems and derivation of constructs, and does not give birth to these constructs full blown.

3. The subjective and objective frames of reference, which denote relatively different alternative contexts within which constructs may be selected, are both entirely compatible with the observer's frame of reference. Subjective constructs to be scientifically admissible must ultimately be anchored in the data of observation.

4. The phenomenological approach provides one method of deriving subjective constructs. But not all subjective constructs need represent phenomenal entities. They may, thus, denote functional entities that are either absent from the phenomenal field or inaccurately presented in it.

5. The coordinate use of phenomenal and non-phenomenal subjective constructs, maintained in clear distinction from one another, serves to clarify the theory of the ego and the self. It is proposed that an adequate theory of personality must distinguish, among other constructs,

a. the *ego*, a *non-phenomenal* subjective construct representing a configuration of ongoing processes, among which is the cognitive-perceptual function. Through exercise of this function, the ego "knows," among other things,

b. the *self*, a *phenomenal* subjective construct.

6. When carried into current problems concerning the nature of "ego-involvement" and of the "mechanisms of defense," the above distinction seems productive.

References

Allport, G. W. The ego in contemporary psychology. *Psychol. Rev.*, 1943, **50**, 451-478.

Chein, I. The awareness of self and the structure of the ego. *Psychol. Rev.*, 1944, **51**, 304-314.

Combs, A. W. A phenomenological approach to adjustment. *J. abnorm. soc. Psychol.*, 1949, **44**, 29-35.

Freud, A. *The ego and the mechanisms of defense.* New York: International Universities Press, 1946.

Freud, S. *New introductory lectures on psychoanalysis.* New York: Norton, 1933.

Lewin, K. *Principles of topological psychology.* New York: McGraw-Hill, 1936.

MacLeod, R. B. The phenomenological approach to social psychology. *Psychol. Rev.*, 1947, **54**, 193-210.

Murphy, G. *Personality: A biosocial approach to origins and structure.* New York: Harper, 1947.

Rogers, C. R. Some observations on the organization of personality. *Amer. Psychologist*, 1947, **2**, 358-368.

Sherif, M., and Cantril, H. *The psychology of ego-involvements.* New York: Wiley, 1947.

Snygg, D., and Combs, A. W. *Individual behavior: A new frame of reference for psychology.* New York: Harper, 1949.

8   Gordon W. Allport

Over the years, Gordon W. Allport (1897-1967) was one of the most compelling of personality theorists. He eloquently championed and elaborated a viewpoint that rested firmly on the foundation of individuality, uniqueness, and the personal experience of the single human organism as the most meaningful subject matter for the exploration of personality. In Allport's view, to minimize these realities violates the integrity of the concept of personality itself and constitutes a scientifically incomplete analysis.

Like most personality theorists, Allport gave considerable attention to the role of motivation in directing human behavior. His treatment of motivation was both provocative and controversial, thus leading to vigorous arguments from many quarters. The major motivational concept that Allport employed was the concept of *functional autonomy*, which, in brief, means that while many adult motives are historically continuous with past experience *they are not necessarily functionally dependent upon the earlier conditions which originated them*. In most instances, therefore, motivation is a contemporary phenomenon. Allport thought that the first stage of motive development was guided by extrinsic and instrumental considerations.

The interest or activity usually began as a means for achieving a particular end. This was its major purpose. However, in pursuing its later course the motive somehow becomes disengaged from its earlier connections and operates as an intrinsic part of the individual's self-image. The motive now exists in and of itself and is an integral part of the personality style.

The first paper in this chapter is a selection from Allport in which the concept of functional autonomy is presented. It is important to note that Allport concedes that it is difficult to know exactly how much of a given motive system is either partially or completely functionally autonomous from its earlier roots. But, despite this concession of sorts, the functionally autonomous motives of Allport's man are active, searching, and not intolerably bound by earlier needs. The mature self-determined man is optimistically in a process of becoming.

One of the most significant areas of study in Allport's research career was the study of intolerance and prejudice. The research paper by Allport and Ross is a penetrating examination of the relationships between extrinsic, intrinsic, and indiscriminate religious orientation and prejudice. For purposes of the research design, Allport and Ross categorized subjects (churchgoers of various Christian denominations from different geographic regions) into the three religious types. For this selection process a *religious orientation scale* was devised. Each subject was also rated on a scale designed to measure direct prejudice against blacks, Jews, and other minority groups.

In addition, an indirect measure of prejudice was also obtained. On the basis of the religious orientation scale, the subjects were divided into three religious orientation groups. The responses of these three orientation groups to the prejudice measures were compared by using various statistical procedures that assessed the degree of relationship between these variables.

Although the term *functional autonomy* is not used in the research paper, the conclusions are clearly related to it. Allport and Ross found that people who are indiscriminately pro-religious and extrinsically religious (defined as persons who use their religious views to provide for social comfort and personal status) are more prone to intolerance than people who are intrinsically religiously oriented. In interpreting their findings, Allport and Ross suggest that the intrinsically oriented religious person has internalized humanistic, religious values such as humility and compassion and is thus less likely to reject other human beings. One might say that for the intrinsically religious person the motive state has become functionally autonomous, whereas the indiscriminately pro-religious person and the extrinsically religious person are still tied to the infantile derivations of their behavior. Of the three groups of religious orientation studied, the indiscriminately pro-religious group was the most prejudiced. Allport and Ross speculate that these individuals lack the ability to make fine discriminations, in the sense that all differences, no matter how small, pose considerable threats to their security. The world must be one way, which is good, or the other way,

which is bad. There is very little in between these poles.

The critique paper by John P. Seward is a searching examination of the concept of functional autonomy; it takes a thorough look at the relevant research evidence. Seward feels that traditional learning theory approaches to motivation, which are generally uncongenial to Allport's position, have failed to account for the acquisition of the social motives that are so important in Allport's concept of functional autonomy. At the same time, Seward feels that the kinds of functionally autonomous motives Allport was talking about are functionally autonomous to begin with. Thus, the theory of functional autonomy becomes "superfluous." Seward's contention is that social motives are not learned in conjunction with primary conditions such as hunger or fear, but are acquired independently and continue unabated as long as the individual experiences the stimulation of other human beings.

Suggestions for Further Reading

Allport's revision of his earlier book on personality theory is a must for the serious student. *Pattern and Growth in Personality*, published by Holt, Rinehart and Winston in 1961, covers the panorama of Allport's thinking.

An article which focuses on a particularly important psychological issue is "The General and the Unique in Psychological Science," in the *Journal of Personality*, 1962, **30**, 405-421. In this paper Allport provocatively expresses his conviction that the most important area of personality study should be the individuality of each person. A scholarly rejoinder to this issue is to be found in a paper by Robert Holt, "Individuality and Generalization in the Psychology of Personality," *Journal of Personality*, 1962, **30**, 377-402. Both papers were also published in the first edition of Southwell and Merbaum, *Personality: Readings in Theory and Research*.

The Concept of Functional Autonomy

Gordon W. Allport

We turn now to one general law of motivation that allows fully for the concrete uniqueness of personal motives, and observes all other criteria for an adequate theory of motivation. It is by no means the only valid principle pertinent to the development of human motives; nor does it explain *all* motivation. It is, however, our attempt to escape the limitations of uniform, rigid, abstract, backward-looking theories, and to recognize the spontaneous, changing, forward-looking, concrete character that much adult motivation surely has.

Functional autonomy regards adult motives as varied, and as self-sustaining, contemporary systems, growing out of antecedent systems, but functionally independent of them. Just as a child gradually outgrows dependence on his parents, becomes self-determining, and outlives his parents, so it is with many motives. The transition may be gradual but it is nonetheless drastic. As the individual (or the motive) matures, the bond with the past is broken. The tie is historical, not functional.

Such a theory is obviously opposed to all conceptions of "unchanging energies." It declines to view the energies of adults as infantile or archaic in nature. Motivation is always contemporary. The life of modern Athens is *continuous* with the life of the ancient city, but in no sense *depends* upon it for its present "go." The life of a tree is continuous with that of its seed, but the seed no longer sustains and nourishes the full-grown tree. Earlier purposes lead into later purposes, but are abandoned in the latter's favor.

Let us take a few commonplace examples.

An ex-sailor has a craving for the sea, a musician longs to return to his instrument after an enforced absence, a miser continues to build up his useless pile. Now the sailor may have first acquired his love for the sea as an incident in his struggle to earn a living. The sea was "secondary reinforcement" for his hunger drive. But now the ex-sailor is perhaps a wealthy banker; the original motive is destroyed, and yet the hunger for the sea persists and even increases in intensity. The musician may first have been stung by a slur on his inferior performance into mastering his instrument; but now he is safely beyond these taunts, and finds that he loves his instrument more than anything else in the world. The miser perhaps learned his habit of thrift in dire necessity, but the miserliness persists and becomes stronger with the years even after the necessity has been relieved.

Workmanship is a good example. A good workman feels compelled to do a clean-cut job even though his income no longer depends on maintaining high standards. In fact, in a day of jerry-building his workmanlike standards may be to his economic disadvantage. Even so he cannot do a slipshod job. Workmanship is not an instinct, but so firm is the hold it may acquire on a man that it is no wonder Veblen mistook it for one.

A businessman, long since secure economically, works himself into ill-health, perhaps even back into poverty, for the sake of carrying on his plans. Hard work, once a means to an end, becomes an end in itself.

Neither necessity nor reason can make a person contented on an isolated country farm after he is adapted to active, energetic city life. Citified habits urge him to a frenzied existence, even though health may demand the simpler life.

The pursuit of literature, the development

From G. W. Allport, *Pattern and Growth in Personality*, pp. 226-244. Copyright 1937, © 1961 by Holt, Rinehart and Winston, Inc. Reprinted by permission of Holt, Rinehart and Winston, Inc.

of good taste in clothes, the use of cosmetics, strolls in the public park, or a winter in Miami may first serve, let us say, the interests of sex. But every one of these "instrumental" activities may become an interest in itself, held for a lifetime, even after they no longer serve the erotic motive.

Some mothers bear their children unwillingly, dismayed at the thought of drudgery in the future. The "parental instinct" is wholly lacking. The mother may be held to her child-tending by fear of what her critical neighbors will say, or by fear of the law, or perhaps by a dim hope that the child will provide security for her in her old age. Gross as these motives may be, they hold her to her work until gradually, through the practice of devotion, her burden becomes a joy. As her love for the child develops, her earlier practical motives are lost. In later years not one of these original motives may operate. The tenacity of the maternal sentiment is proverbial, even when, as in this case, it can be shown to be not an original but an acquired motive.

Let us add one more example. Many boys choose occupations that follow in their fathers' footsteps. Also, most young boys go through a period of passionate "father identification." Joe, let us say, is the son of a famous politician. As a young lad he imitates everything his father does, even perhaps giving "speeches." Years pass and the father dies. Joe is now middle-aged and is deeply absorbed in politics. He runs for office, perhaps the self-same job his father held. What, then, motivates Joe today? Is it his earlier father fixation? Conceivably yes, for Joe may never have outgrown his Oedipal complex (trying to be like Daddy in order to win his mother's affection). If Joe's political activity today is of this neurotic variety we shall probably find him behaving in a compulsive, rigid, even maladaptive manner. The chances, however, are that his interest in politics has outgrown its roots in "father identification." There is historical continuity but no longer any functional continuity. Politics is now his dominant passion; it is his style of life; it is a large part of Joe's personality. The original seed has been discarded.

All our illustrations have one feature in common. The adult interest we describe began as something else. In all cases the activity that later became motivational was at first instrumental to some other end (i.e., to some earlier motive). What was once extrinsic and instrumental becomes intrinsic and impelling. The activity once served a drive or some simple need; it now serves itself, or in a larger sense, serves the self-image (self-ideal) of the person. Childhood is no longer in the saddle; maturity is.

Functional autonomy, then, refers to any acquired system of motivation in which the tensions involved are not of the same kind as the antecedent tensions from which the acquired system developed.[1]

[1] Functional autonomy (without the label) has been acknowledged by many writers. Many years ago F. Brentano called it a "well-known psychological law" that "what at first was desired merely as a means to something else, comes at last from habit to be desired for its own sake." *The origin of the knowledge of right and wrong* (Transl. by C. Hague; London: Constable, 1902), p. 16. E. C. Tolman speaks of "acquired adherences to specific types of means objects" as having the power to set up "in their own right," and acquire "a strangle hold." *Phil. Sci.*, 1935, **2**, 370. Elsewhere Tolman acknowledges "independent tertiary motives" which for all practical purposes must be regarded as functionally autonomous. In T. Parsons and E. A. Shils, *Toward a general theory of action* (Cambridge, Mass.: Harvard Univ. Press, 1951), pp. 321 f.

A more familiar statement is R. S. Woodworth's phrase "mechanisms may become drives." "The fundamental drive towards a certain end may be hunger, sex, pugnacity, or what not, but once the activity is started, the means to the end becomes an object of interest on its own account." *Dynamic psychology* (New York: Columbia Univ. Press, 1918), p. 201. W. Stern makes the same point when he writes that "phenomotives" may turn into "genomotives." *General psychology from the personalistic standpoint* (Transl. by H. Spoerl; New York: Macmillan, 1938). H. Hartmann's concept of "secondary ego autonomy," as we saw in the previous chapter, supports our position.

In spite of this extensive endorsement, many critics have shown marked resistance to the concept. In general, they argue that if instinct theory or drive-reduction theory are extended far enough they will cover all cases of "functional autonomy." Illustrating this critical literature are the following references: P. A. Bertocci, Critique of Gordon W. Allport's theory of motivation, *Psychol. Rev.*, 1940, **47**, 501-532; and O. Oppenheimer, The functional autonomy of motives, *J. soc. Psychol.*, 1947, **25**, 171-179.

Among the critics who believe that stimulus-response psychology remains adequate are D. C. McClelland, Functional autonomy of motives as an extinction phenomenon, *Psychol. Rev.*, 1942, **49**, 272-283; and Dorothy Rethlingshaefer, Experimental evidence of functional autonomy of motives, *Psychol. Rev.*, 1943, **50**, 397-407.

Whether the present exposition of the case for functional autonomy will satisfy these is doubtful. And yet

Two Levels of Autonomy

Examples of functional autonomy could be multiplied endlessly and aimlessly. Better, however to be more systematic about the matter. After giving some years of thought to the problem, I am now inclined to believe that the phenomenon should be inspected on two levels. We shall do well to speak of (1) *perseverative* functional autonomy, and (2) *propriate* functional autonomy. The former level skirts close to what are (or may be assumed to be) simple neurological principles. The latter level, however, frankly depends upon certain philosophical assumptions regarding the nature of human personality— not that these assumptions contradict in any way known neurological fact, but they reach beyond present knowledge of the way the nervous system operates.

Perseverative Functional Autonomy

Let us speak first of certain animal experiments. One scarcely knows how much weight to give them. On the one hand, animals possess the basic neural and emotional rudiments that are also found in man. On the other hand, the higher cortical centers are so poorly developed that the capacities for symbolization, delay, and self-reference are largely or wholly lacking.

1. *Animal evidence.* An experimenter feeds a rat at regular intervals. The rat is most active just prior to the time for feeding. After a while the experimenter starves the rat. But though it is now hungry all the time, the previous rhythm of maximum activity (just prior to the usual feeding time) persists.[2]

Even a mollusc, whose habits of burrowing in the sand and reappearing depend on the movements of the tide, will, when removed from the beach to the laboratory, continue the same rhythm without the tide.[3]

A rat who has learned a maze under the incentive of hunger will, even when fed to repletion, run the maze correctly, not for food, but apparently "for the fun of it."[4]

One investigator applied collodion to the ears of an animal, thus setting up removing and cleaning movements. A month after the beginning of the experiment when the ears of the rats as studied by the microscope showed no further trace of irritation, the number of "cleaning" movements was still very great.[5]

As far as they go these experiments and many like them show what we mean by *perseveration*. A mechanism set in action because of one motive continues at least for a time to "feed" itself. Here we have the most elementary instance of functional autonomy.

As yet it is not possible to designate the underlying neurological basis for perseverative functional autonomy of this type. The phenomena just mentioned, as well as those listed below, indicate the presence of self-sustaining circuits or substructures, no longer geared exclusively to stimulus-control. Neurologists acknowledge the phenomena and speculate concerning the nervous mechanisms involved.[6]

[3]S. C. Crawford, Characteristics of nocturnal animals, *Quart. Rev. Biol.*, 1934, **9**, 201-214.

[4]J. D. Dodson, Relative value of reward and punishment in habit formation, *Psycho-biol.*, 1917, **1**, 231-276.

[5]W. C. Olson, *The Measurement of nervous habits in normal children* (Minneapolis: Univ. of Minnesota Press, 1929), pp. 62-65.

[6]Thus D. O. Hebb believes that "open assemblies of cells in the brain" may allow for some enduring reverberative activity: *The organization of behavior* (New York: Wiley, 1949). Morgan speaks of "central motive states." C. T. Morgan, Physiological psychology (New York: McGraw-Hill, 1943), Chap. 22. J. C. Eccles holds that while old learning is never lost it may be reorganized in such a way that it no longer manifests itself in the behavior-pattern to which it initially "belonged." *The neurophysiological basis of mind* (Oxford: Clarendon, 1953). Olds introduces the concept of self-stimulation to account for "long-run continuities": J. Olds, *The growth and structure of motives* (Glencoe, Ill.: Free Press, 1956).

A related line of speculation is offered by W. S. McCulloch, A hierarchy of values determined by the topology of nervous nets, *Bull. math. Biophysics*, 1945, **7**, 89. This author holds that the nervous system is not organized on a linear basis, but that cortical neurones are ordered in a circle. An impulse does not fire a motor neurone until it has passed continuously around the circle, and has been modified accordingly. In all these specula-

the argument has benefited from their criticism and is, I think, more convincing (when taken in conjunction with Chapters 5 and 9) than the general exposition published in *Personality: a psychological interpretation* (New York: Holt, Rinehart and Winston, 1937), Chap. 7.

[2]C. P. Richter, A behavioristic study of the activity of the rat, *Comp. Psychol. Monogr.*, 1922, **1**, No. 2.

2. *Addictions.* No one will deny that the craving for tobacco, alcohol, or opiates is an acquired appetite, or that the craving may be very intense. An alcoholic under treatment writes:

> Those craving paroxysms occur at regular intervals, three weeks apart, lasting for several days. They are not weak, namby pamby things for scoffers to laugh at. If not assuaged with liquor they become spells of physical and mental illness. My mouth drools saliva, my stomach and intestines seem cramped, and I become bilious, nauseated, and in a shaky nervous funk.[7]

One may say that such physical hunger, artificially induced by drugs, is not a fair example. Yet recent work on addiction indicates that the dynamism involved is largely psychological. Thus, monkeys and medical patients who are injected with opiates become habituated and suffer greatly from "withdrawal"; but once cured they show no desire to use the drug again. True addicts, on the other hand, even after a cure, when all withdrawal symptoms have vanished, still, in a vast majority of cases, return to their addiction. It cannot be because of *physiological* hunger, but because a subsystem of personality has been formed which handles life's frustrations by taking to narcotics. Thus the person who is "hooked" is one who has developed an acquired and autonomous motivational structure.[8]

3. *Circular mechanisms.* Everyone has observed the almost endless repetition of acts by a child. The good-natured parent picks up a spoon repeatedly thrown down by a baby. The parent wearies of the game long before the infant does. The child's babbling, early manipulations, and play show the same self-perpetuation. Each activity seems to "feed back" into the sensory channels, thus maintaining a "circular reflex."[9] Admittedly this example illustrates only a temporary functional autonomy. It is, however, an important example in showing that there is some neural machinery for maintaining activity patterns without our needing to trace every act to a drive motive.

4. *Task perseveration.* Many experiments show that incompleted tasks set up tensions that keep the individual at work until the task is completed—no matter how long it takes. Even a trivial task can become haunting for a considerable time. Ask a subject to spend an hour thinking of, and writing down, all the words he can beginning with the letter *c*. When he leaves the experimental room, even during his sleep, and perhaps into the next day, he will continue to perseverate, and without wishing to do so will recall many new words beginning with *c*.[10] Here, too, the functional autonomy is of short duration, but the point is that no hypothesis of self-assertion, rivalry, or any other basic need is required to explain the self-maintaining dynamic system temporarily in force.

Gestalt psychologists speak of a "closure tendency" (*Gestaltdrang*) which persists until the completion of a task. It is known that the memory for incompleted tasks is better than for completed tasks.[11] There is pressure to continue work on any unfinished assignment.

Woodworth originally spoke of "habits becoming drives." This statement is only partially acceptable. When once learned, most habits seem to become merely instrumental skills. We use our typewriter, our automobile, or our language habits only in the service of active motives. Yet "habits on the make" are highly dynamic. The child who is just learning to talk or to walk seems driven

tions we note the recurrence of the concept of a reverberating cortical circuit. This principle may turn out to provide a neural base for perseverative functional autonomy.

[7] Inmate Ward Eight, *Beyond the door of delusion* (New York: Macmillan, 1932), p. 281.

[8] A. Wikler, *Opiate addiction: physiological and neurophysiological aspects in relation to clinical problems* (Springfield, Ill.: Charles C. Thomas, 1953); A. R. Lindesmith, *Opiate addiction* (Bloomington, Ind.: Principia Press, 1947).

[9] E. B. Holt, *Animal drive and the learning process* (New York: Holt, Rinehart and Winston, 1931), especially Chaps. 7 and 8. On a higher level of speculation. F. H. Allport raises the question whether all "event structures" at the physical, psychological, and social levels do not by their inherent nature have the property of self-maintenance in *Theories of perception and the concept of structure* (New York: Wiley, 1955), especially Chap. 21.

[10] Isabel Kendig, Studies in perseveration, *J. Psychol.*, 1936, **3**, 223-264.

[11] R. Zeigarnik, Über das Behalten von erledigten und unerledigten Handlungen, *Psychol. Forsch.*, 1927, **9**, 1-85.

to perfect these skills. The adolescent is haunted until he completes his skill in skating, dancing, or driving. Of course, some skills are never really perfected. The concert pianist feels driven every day to hours of practice. We may conclude the matter this way: It is not the perfected talent nor the automatic habit that has driving power, but rather the imperfect talent and the habit-in-the-making.

5. *Familiarity and routine.* John Dewey has written:

It is the essence of routine to insist upon its own continuation. Breach of it is a violation of right. Deviation from it is transgression.[12]

Especially in childhood, as we have seen, does repetitiveness have a compelling quality. If you tell a story to a young child he will not let you vary it in the retelling. Familiar playthings, foods, family customs are preferred. Trips away from home, perhaps to a summer camp, often bring acute homesickness. Childhood morality, as Piaget points out, is largely a morality of custom, obedience, and routine.[13]

The reader may object that a familiar setting is only a conditioned assurance that our drives will be met. Thus, our customary bed is associated with refreshing sleep; we like it because it is a "secondary reinforcer" of rest. But this explanation is not satisfactory. The pleasure that comes from a familiar bed is not the pleasure of somnolence but of simple familiarity. A child finds no more gratification of hunger in a familiar food than in a novel one, but he wants the familiar. And what drive does the exact repetition of a story satisfy?

The dynamism of routine may be found where no drives are present—even when they are thwarted. It sometimes happens, for example, that we enter a new city and lose our sense of direction. We think east is north, or that north is south. This condition of being "turned around" is annoying and certainly

satisfies no drives; but it persists. A frame of reference is quickly established that for us becomes routine and almost impossible to correct. We don't want it, but we can't shake it off.

In a series of experiments Maslow has shown that people rapidly develop preferences for works of art and even for foreign names that they have previously encountered. They think a Russian name they have heard once or twice previously more euphonious, and like it better, than a totally novel Russian name.[14]

Suppose that you attend a conference which has morning and afternoon sessions. Do you not find everyone making for the same seat in the afternoon that he occupied in the morning? And if the conference continues over several days the space habit is firmly set. This routinization satisfies no drives unless the desire for sameness (familiarity) is itself a drive.

Gardner Murphy has introduced a concept that partly, but only partly, overlaps functional autonomy. He names it *canalization*.[15] This author points out that the pull of familiarity is often closely tied to the satisfaction of drives.

We want our drives satisfied in a familiar way. Most of us eat three meals a day, not two or five. This mealtime rhythm is not independent of the hunger drive, but does define it and imposes upon it an acquired preference. Some people cannot sleep well unless they have one pillow, two pillows, or sometimes, none at all. Everyone needs oxygen, but some people are fresh-air fiends, and like to have gales of air blowing into their bedrooms; others prefer only to let it filter through cracks. The times, places, and seasons that we select for our eating, drinking, elimination, and sex activity are highly individual, and are profoundly important ingredients in the total motivational pattern.

But, strictly speaking, such acquired attachments are not functionally autonomous,

[12]J. Dewey, *Human nature and conduct* (New York: Holt, Rinehart and Winston, 1922), p. 78.

[13]J. Piaget, *The moral judgment of the child* (New York: Harcourt, Brace, 1932).

[14]A. H. Maslow, The influence of familiarization on preference, *J. exp. Psychol.*, 1937, **21**, 162-180.

[15]G. Murphy, *Human potentialities* (New York: Basic Books, 1958).

for a basic drive motive is always present. At the same time, the drives can sometimes scarcely operate at all unless the highly individual, acquired tastes are fulfilled. And so we conclude that while there is a surface resemblance, the concept of canalization belongs fundamentally among theories of "unchanging energies" and not with functional autonomy.

Propriate Functional Autonomy

Up to now we have fixed our attention on relatively "low-grade" processes that manifest a shift of earlier dynamisms into later dynamisms. The latter derive from the former although they no longer depend on them. In all our illustrations we have assumed that some kind of servo- or feedback mechanism is at work helping to sustain systems at their contemporary level even while these systems undergo internal change.

We shall not, however, succeed in accounting for all adult motives if we stop at this point. For one thing, if we did so, the resulting picture of personality would be like that of a jeweler's repair shop filled with unrelated self-winding watches. Although personality contains many such self-maintaining systems, its principal energies are master systems of motivation that confer more unity on personality than disparate perseverating systems can do. Our account, therefore, cannot be complete until we relate the concept of functional autonomy to the propriate functions of personality (pages 126-128). Let us consider a few examples from this level of functional autonomy.

1. *Ability often turns into interest.* It is an established fact that ordinarily people *like* to do what they can do well (the correlation between abilities and interests is high). Now the original reason for learning a skill may not be interest at all. For example, a student who first undertakes a field of study in college because it is required, because it pleases his parents, or because it comes at a convenient hour may end by finding himself absorbed in the topic, perhaps for life. The original motives may be entirely lost. What was a means to an end becomes an end in itself.

It is true that rewards are often given to an able person for exercising his talents. But does he exercise them merely to get a reward? It seems unlikely. No such motivation accounts for the drive behind genius. For the genius, creative passion itself is the motive. How hollow to think of Pasteur's concern for reward, or for health, food, sleep, or family, as the root of his devotion to his work. For long periods of time he was oblivious of them all, losing himself in the white heat of research. And the same passion is seen in the histories of geniuses who in their lifetimes received little or no reward for their work: Galileo, Mendel, Schubert, van Gogh, and many others.

It is important to note that major life-interests are seldom clearly formed or even indicated in childhood (musical prodigies being an exception).

One study of children between the tenth and twelfth grades showed that the strength of their interests over a three-year period correlated only +.57, whereas the same test showed a stability of interests over a twenty-two-year period following graduation from college to a much higher extent (+.75).[16]

Clearly youthful interests are less stable than adult interests. Further, it seems safe to say that the interests of most children, even into the teens, are very much like those of other children, whereas adults grow in uniqueness (individuation). The ruling passions of adults are exceedingly diverse. One man is absorbed in business and golf; another, in religion and art. An old woman in a home for the aged pivots her life solely on the hope that "some people may remember me kindly."

Whether we shall call these propriate motives *interests, sentiments, values,* or something else, does not for the moment matter. Whatever we call them, they are acquired pre-eminent motives. Since the tensions involved are not of the same kind as the tensions of the seed motives, they are, by our definition, functionally autonomous.

---

[16]L. Canning, *et al.,* Permanence of vocational interests of high school boys, *J. educ. Psychol.,* 1941, **32,** 481-494; E. Strong, Permanence of interest test scores over twenty-two years, *J. appl. Psychol.,* 1951, **51,** 89-91.

2. *Acquired interests and values have selective power.* In the following chapter we shall show that what a person perceives, remembers, and thinks is in large part determined by his own propriate formations. As an interest grows it creates a lasting tensional condition that leads to congruent conduct, and also acts as a silent agent for selecting and directing whatever is related to the interest. Thus people with a strong esthetic interest respond more quickly to words connected with this interest than to words relating to interests they lack.[17] Given a newspaper to scan, they will read more items pertaining to art than will nonesthetic people.[18] The same selective tendency is discovered in all forms of interest that have been tested.

3. *Self-image and life-style are organizing factors.* It would be an error to think of interests as single and separate mainsprings. Together they form a complex self-image or life-style which is also functionally autonomous. It evolves gradually in the course of life, and day by day guides and unifies all, or at least many, of a person's transactions with life.

I am speaking here of the highest levels of organization in personality. Most theories of personality (especially those postulating "unchanging energies") overlook the motivational power of higher-level formations. My position is that, although lower-level self-maintaining (perseverative) systems exist, the more important instance of functional autonomy is found in the complex propriate organization that determines the "total posture" of a mature life-system.

A prominent ingredient of this master dynamism is the sense of responsibility one takes for one's life. The way one defines one's role and duties in life determines much of one's daily conduct. (McDougall calls this level of organization the "self-regarding sentiment"; others call it the "ego-ideal.")

[17]H. Cantril, General and specific attitudes, *Psychol. Monogr.*, 1932, No. 192; N. Jenkin, Affective processes in perception, *Psychol. Bull.*, 1957, **54**, 100-127.
[18]H. Cantril and G. W. Allport, Recent applications of the *Study of Values*, *J. abnorm. soc. Psychol.*, 1933, **28**, 259-273; also W. C. Engstrom and Mary E. Power, A revision of the *Study of Values* for use in magazine readership research, *J. appl. Psychol.*, 1959, **43**, 74-78.

What Processes Are Not Functionally Autonomous?

I have argued that for the most part personality structure is postinstinctive: it is not wholly dominated by innate drives; nor is it dominated normally by early formations of juvenile complexes. Unlike Freud or Adler, I do not hold that the guidelines of personality are ordinarily laid down by the age of three or five.

Yet not all motives are functionally autonomous. Several types are not.

1. *Drives.* From birth to death a human being is subject to biological drives. He must eat, breathe, sleep, and eliminate, and his body must make countless homeostatic adjustments to maintain the delicate balance of life. To be sure, it has been pointed out above that most drives develop canalized styles of expression and seek satisfaction in some preferred manner. But canalization is not true functional autonomy. For our first generalization, then, let us say that if a motive is primarily traceable to drive-tensions it is not an instance of functional autonomy.

2. *Reflex action.* The eye blink, the knee jerk, the digestive process—although they, too, manifest individuality of functioning—are not to be considered functionally autonomous. They are automatic responses, capable of only slight modification, geared to specific stimulation, and doubtfully to be classed as motivational at all.

3. *Constitutional equipment.* Some capacities and formations are best regarded as relatively fixed and unchanged in the course of life. We refer primarily to the "raw materials" of *physique, intelligence, temperament* (Chapter 4). We may add here individual limitations of bodily strength and health. Of the same order are the given constitutional laws of development (such as the maturation of capacities with age, the occurrence of puberty, and so on). Although none of these items directly constitute "motives," it is well to have in mind their limiting effects on the transformation of motives.

4. *Habits.* Although it was argued that "habits-on-the-make" nicely fit into our conception of perseverative functional autono-

my, still it is not wise to hold that habits-in-general are examples of functionally autonomous motivation. Indeed, most habits are not motivational at all. They are instrumental systems brought into play in the service of motives.

5. *Primary reinforcement.* All patterns of conduct that require primary reinforcement fall outside the conception of functional autonomy.

A little neighbor child comes to our door and receives a cooky. He returns again and again. Has he acquired a new (functionally autonomous) motive? To find the answer we shall have to abolish the cooky. If the child stops coming it shows that his motivation was tied wholly to his sweet tooth. He has not formed a new interest *in us.*

If a workman depends upon praise in order to maintain his standards we cannot say that workmanship is for him an acquired motive. Similarly, if he receives a legacy and stops working altogether, we can safely say that for him his occupation was only an extrinsic habit (serving his need to make a living) and not an intrinsic functionally autonomous motive.

I hope that my position on "reinforcement" is now clear. Whenever, as in the above instances, a form of behavior is "extinguished" unless it satisfies an original drive, we cannot speak at all of the transformation of motives. Functional autonomy is not involved. As for "secondary reinforcement" it was shown in Chapters 5 and 9 that this explanation of the transformation of motives is too vague and still too tied to "unchanging energies" to provide a satisfactory theory of the growth of mature interests.

6. *Infantilisms and fixations.* Whenever an older person is acting out an infantile or juvenile conflict, we cannot speak of functional autonomy. He is following an urge that is basically unaltered from early years.

A girl of twelve had a most disconcerting habit of smacking her lips several times a minute. Analysis finally revealed that eight years previously her mother had told her that when she inhaled air it was "good" air, but when she exhaled it the air was "bad." These moralistic terms distressed the four-year-old because she understood from them that she had been naughty in making the air "bad." Deeply perturbed, she tried not to breathe at all. Failing in this heroic effort she invented the ritual of kissing the air she exhaled to "make it well again." The habit persisted, but the whole affair was so distressing that she repressed the memory of the event; but the tic still persisted. It took a psychoanalysis to bring the buried conflict into consciousness and to cure the tic.

In this case conduct at the age of twelve is in reality acting out an unresolved conflict at the age of four.

The astute reader may ask, "Do we not have here a case of *perseverative* functional autonomy? The little girl seems to have suffered from a dissociated, self-maintaining motivational system." The observation is a good one. Compulsions of hand-washing, facial tics, nail-biting, scratching, thumb-sucking do certainly act like self-feeding systems. Scarcely is the compulsive act completed before it seems to set off a repetition of the same compulsive act. We may do well to allow the conception of perseverative functional autonomy a place in the theory of compulsive neuroses.

At the same time there is an essential difference. We note that the little girl was *cured* when her eight-year-old conflict was removed. Her neurotic behavior then was not *primarily* self-sustaining.

7. *Some neuroses.* The problem of neurotic behavior, as our example shows, is complicated from the point of view of functional autonomy. Basically we should like to maintain that neurotic motives are not functionally autonomous, for the present acts of a neurotic person are laden primarily with bygone considerations. Some echo of early life is haunting his conduct. The neurotic seems unable to focus adequately on the present or the future. Freud has taught us that the roots of a neurosis often lie in the first years of life.

But now there is another side to the picture. Any neurosis is a complicated interlocking system of maneuvers designed to maintain life under difficult conditions.[19] It is a learned style of survival, and may be viewed without reference to early unfulfilled needs. It seems possible for a neurotic style of life to be rigidly set, and no longer harbor in any clear sense past conflicts. Especially what is called a "character neurosis" reflects a self-image badly matched to reality but nonetheless persistent and permanently stylistic. Is it not therefore functionally autonomous?

There is at least a theoretical distinction to help us decide. If under psychoanalysis the patient relives the past (as did our twelve-year-old girl), and learns what repressed incidents have been troublesome, and *if this backward tracing effects a cure* (because the patient sees that the troublesome element has no place in his current motivational system), then the neurosis was *not* functionally autonomous. If, on the other hand, a "character neurosis" is so firmly structured that it now constitutes the life-pattern, and if nothing can dislodge it, then we have no choice but to admit that it is an acquired, functionally autonomous, motivational system.

There is a moral here for psychotherapy. It would seem wise for the therapist to determine whether the patient's symptoms are to be relieved by "going to the root of the problem" or whether the most that can be hoped for is to reconcile the patient to his own developed style of life. In the first instance he is assuming that the neurosis is not functionally autonomous. In the latter case it is, and can be handled better by re-education than by reliving.

Psychoses can be looked at from the same point of view. Some psychotic upsets are temporary, reflecting unbalance in the existing systems of motivation. The disturbance is not functionally autonomous. Some mental patients, however, are wholly unable to handle their existence and permanently "go over to another world." Such a patient adopts a delusional pattern and a shrunken range of behavior as his permanent life-style, and for him this new level of existence becomes functionally autonomous. He "gets used" to his malady, and builds his life around it.

Finally, let us glance back at the case of the politician who is following in his father's footsteps. There we raised the question whether his occupational interest as an adult is merely a neurotic "acting out" of his early father-identification. If it is so (as shown by his compulsiveness and rigidity), then this interest is not to be regarded as functionally autonomous. If, however, he has long since worked through his juvenile dependence, and now has an interest in politics for its own sake, the motivation is functionally autonomous. We mention this case here to emphasize the fact that it is necessary to examine each specific instance in order to determine to what extent, and in what way, functional autonomy may be involved.

8. *Sublimation.* Freud's familiar theory holds that all adult motives—even the most socially prized and idealistic —are "transparent sublimation" of the primitive motives of sex and aggression. The physician, the artist, the missionary are displacing their "aim inhibited wishes"; they are finding substitutes for the things they *really* want in life. Undoubtedly "transparent sublimations" do sometimes exist, but that they account for *all* adult motives we emphatically deny.

Critics of functional autonomy cite special cases to prove their point. One student writes:

My own bias is biological, mechanistic, and Freudian. Let me describe a case that fits my bias and seems to deny functional autonomy.

I have a friend who appears to be motivated by a strong esthetic value. Everything he does seems consistent with this well-integrated motivational system. He looks up from his perusal of photographs of armless Aphrodites and sighs, "Ah, if there were only people like these alive today." Every week end he dates a different girl, looking for the perfect one. Returning from one such foray he said, "She's all right but she hasn't any *bust.*" He loves poetry. When he reads it he drops the words out of his mouth like marbles. He quotes Noel Coward. And in many other ways he is an

[19]Cf. A. Angyal, A theoretical model for personality studies. In D. Krech and G. S. Klein (Eds.), *Theoretical models and personality theory* (Durham, N.C.: Duke Univ. Press, 1952), p. 141.

archesthete. Does his love of beauty and of what is charming constitute a functionally autonomous motive? I think not.

Lars is his name. His divorced mother and he are extremely devoted to each other. His "ideal girl" is, after all, his mother. His preoccupation with breasts, his "chewing and sucking" of the beautiful lines of poetry—all show his desire to possess (or return to) his mother. The estheticism of Lars is neurotic—a mere transparent sublimation of his true motives.

If the case is essentially as the student states it, there is no basis for assuming that Lars's esthetic style of life is functionally autonomous. It is not intrinsic to his nature but exists in the service of another stronger, and at best half-conscious, motive.

Here is another case, also written by a student skeptical of functional autonomy.

I am interested in the case of a priest whom I recently met. Many people had told me that he is a man with a single motive in life: to raise money for a convent he hopes to build. Until I met him I could not even imagine the overpowering dominance of this one motive in all his conduct.

For example, my errand with him was to see about renting his school's auditorium for a teenage dance. He asked what percentage of the profits he would receive for his convent project. I tried to discuss the needs of adolescents for some recreational facility; he was not interested. I tried to discuss the interreligious tensions of the community; he tossed them off. To every conversational gambit he replied, "How much do I get for the convent?"

His relations with people in the town are poor, for he hounds them unmercifully for money. In his office is a large picture of the proposed convent, not hung on the wall, but displayed on a conspicuous easel. Even the Archbishop does not seem strongly to favor the priest's project because he is thought to have misappropriated some of his parish funds for this purpose.

Now how can we explain his singleness of purpose? Shall we accept the psychoanalytic interpretation that the celibate is sexually repressed and thus is eager to gather nuns about him? While conceivably valid, I doubt this explanation, for there seems to be no other evidence of sexual interest in his behavior—and he is a very old man. One can scarcely accept the hedonistic explanation, for not only is he unpopular because of his unpleasant persistence; he is actually not making much headway. His behavior is more punished than rewarded.

Perhaps to say that this ruling passion is functionally autonomous is the best statement we can make. But is it not a doctrine of despair? It does not even attempt to explain his central motive!

In this case, as in many others, we simply do not know enough about the life in question to reach a clear decision. On the one hand, the highly obsessive nature of the priest's behavior raises the question whether a compulsive neurosis is involved, displacing some inhibited wish (sexual perhaps). On the other hand, many people, like Faust of old, have found their whole reason for living in some limited project of a similar scope. In this priest's life the project may be merely the concrete focus of a religious motive and style of life. We may have to accept it as the way in which all his complex life-influences, integrating with his evolving needs and interests, have converged into a unique pattern of propriate striving. From this point of view his convent-building motive is functionally autonomous. We cannot actually say in this case whether "sublimation" or functional autonomy is the best fit to this case—simply because we do not know enough about the life in question.

We must add a word concerning the writer's complaint that the doctrine of functional autonomy "does not even attempt to explain this central motive." If the writer means that he would like a historical explanation in terms of the steps in the priest's life that led him to his present ruling passion, there is no objection to his attempting to reconstruct the life-story. But historical explanation is *not* functional explanation. In a very real sense a functionally autonomous motive *is* the personality. We cannot ask for any further reduction. Life itself is the energy and the "explanation." We need not, and cannot, look "deeper"—not if the motive is functionally autonomous.

We may, however, tie any functionally autonomous motive to the total propriate system, and discover its relative importance in the life-style. Functional autonomy is not a "doctrine of despair." Rather, it is a straightforward labeling of one important, and widely neglected, aspect of human motivation.

To sum up: if we are dealing with sublimation, transparent or otherwise, then we do not have a case of functional autonomy. On the other hand, to declare without proof that all adult interests are masquerades for what man really wants (chiefly sex and aggression) is as improbable as gargoyles.

Degrees of Functional Autonomy

Our discussion has made clear that it is not always possible to determine whether a given motive is rooted in drives, in infantile fixation, in sublimations, or in wholly adult formulations of life. For that matter, a motive may reflect a combination of forces: infant and adult, instinctive and intentional, conscious and unconscious, extrinsic and intrinsic. Even drives, as we have seen, by virtue of canalization, acquire new and highly individual tastes. For these reasons we cannot declare that a motive is always *either/or*. We must allow for the possibility that life's motives may show many degrees of purity and impurity in respect to functional autonomy.

Hence, to the question "When is it not so?" there can be no categorical answer. The decision can come only after an intensive study of each individual life. Practically, the decision is often hard to make. In principle, however, we can say that *to the extent that a present motive seeks new goals (i.e., manifests a different kind of tension from the motives from which it developed) it is functionally autonomous.*

An Investigation of Personal Religious Orientation and Prejudice

Gordon W. Allport and J. Michael Ross

Three generalizations seem well established concerning the relationship between subjective religion and ethnic prejudice: (a) On the average churchgoers are more prejudiced than nonchurchgoers; (b) the relationship is curvilinear; (c) people with an extrinsic religious orientation are significantly more prejudiced than people with an intrinsic religious orientation. With the aid of a scale to measure extrinsic and intrinsic orientation this research confirmed previous findings and added a 4th: people who are indiscriminately proreligious are the most prejudiced of all. The interpretations offered are in terms of cognitive style.

Previous psychological and survey research has established three important facts regarding the relationship between prejudiced attitudes and the personal practice of religion.

1. On the average, church attenders are more prejudiced than nonattenders.

2. This overall finding, if taken only by itself, obscures a curvilinear relationship. While it is true that most attenders are *more* prejudiced than nonattenders, a significant minority of them are *less* prejudiced.

3. It is the casual, irregular fringe members who are high in prejudice; their religious motivation is of the extrinsic order. It is the constant, devout, internalized members who are low in prejudice; their religious motivation is of the *intrinsic* order.

The present paper will establish a fourth important finding—although it may properly be regarded as an amplification of the third. *The finding is that a certain cognitive style*

From G. W. Allport and J. M. Ross, "Personal Religious Orientation and Prejudice," *Journal of Personality and Social Psychology*, 1967, 5, 432-443. Reprinted by permission of the American Psychological Association.

permeates the thinking of many people in such a way that they are indiscriminately proreligious and, at the same time, highly prejudiced.

But first let us make clear the types of evidence upon which the first three propositions are based and examine their theoretical significance.

Churchgoers Are More Prejudiced

Beginning the long parade of findings demonstrating that churchgoers are more intolerant of ethnic minorities than nonattenders is a study by Allport and Kramer (1946). These authors discovered that students who claimed no religious affiliation were less likely to be anti-Negro than those who declared themselves to be protestant or Catholic. Furthermore, students reporting a strong religious influence at home were higher in ethnic prejudice than students reporting only slight or no religious influence. Rosenblith (1949) discovered the same trend among students in South Dakota. *The Authoritarian Personality* (Adorno, Frenkel-Brunswik, Levinson, & Sanford, 1950, p. 212) stated that scores on ethnocentrism (as well as on authoritarianism) are significantly higher among church attenders than among nonattenders. Gough's (1951) findings were similar. Kirkpatrick (1949) found religious people in general to be slightly less humanitarian than nonreligious people. For example, they had more punitive attitudes toward criminals, delinquents, prostitutes, homosexuals, and those in need of psychiatric treatment. Working with a student population Rokeach (1960) discovered nonbelievers to be consistently less dogmatic, less authoritarian, and less ethnocentric than believers. Public-opinion polls (as summarized by Stember, 1961) revealed confirmatory evidence across the board.

Going beyond ethnic prejudice, Stouffer (1955) demonstrated that among a representative sample of American church members those who had attended church within the past month were more intolerant of nonconformists (such as socialists, atheists, or communists) than those who had not attended. It seems that on the average religious people show more intolerance in general—not only toward ethnic but also toward ideological groups.

Is this persistent relationship in any way spurious? Can it be due, for example, to the factor of educational level? Many studies show that people with high education tend to be appreciably less prejudiced than people with low education. Perhaps it is the former group that less often goes to church. The reasoning is false. Sociological evidence has shown conclusively that frequent church attendance is associated with high socioeconomic status and with college education (Demerath, 1965). Furthermore, Stouffer's study found that the intolerant tendency among churchgoers existed only when educational level was held constant. Struening (1963), using as subjects only faculty members of a large state university (all highly educated), discovered that nonattenders were on the average less prejudiced than attenders. These studies assure us that the association between churchgoing and prejudice is not merely a spurious product of low education.

Turning to the theoretical implications of these findings, shall we say that religion in and of itself makes for prejudice and intolerance? There are some arguments in favor of such a conclusion, especially when we recall that certain powerful *theological* positions—those emphasizing revelation, election (chosen people), and theocracy (Allport, 1959, 1966)—have throughout history turned one religion against another. And among *sociological* factors in religion we find

many that make for bigotry. One thinks of the narrow composition of many religious groups in terms of ethnic and class membership, of their pressure toward conformity, and of the competition between them (see Demerath, 1965; Lenski, 1961). It does seem that religion as such makes for prejudice.

And yet it is here that we encounter the grand paradox. One may not overlook the teachings of equality and brotherhood, of compassion and humanheartedness, that mark all the great world religions. Nor may one overlook the precept and example of great figures whose labors in behalf of tolerance were and are religiously motivated—such as Christ himself, Tertullian, Pope Gelasius I, St. Ambrose, Cardinal Cusa, Sebastian Castellio, Schwenckfeld, Roger Williams, Mahatma Gandhi, Martin Luther King, and many others, including the recently martyred clergy in our own South. These lives, along with the work of many religious bodies, councils, and service organizations would seem to indicate that religion as such *unmakes prejudice*. A paradox indeed.

The Curvilinear Relationship

If religion as such made *only* for prejudice, we would expect that churchgoers who expose themselves most constantly to its influence would, as a result, be more prejudiced than those who seldom attend. Such is not the case.

Many studies show that frequent attenders are less prejudiced than infrequent attenders and often less prejudiced even than nonattenders. Let us cite one illustrative study by Struening (1963). The curvilinear trend is immediately apparent in Table 1. In this particular study nonattenders had lower prejudice scores than any group, save only those devotees who managed to attend 11 or more times a month. Without employing such fine time intervals other studies have shown the same curvilinear trend. Thus, in *The Authoritarian Personality* (p. 212) we learned that in 12 out of 15 groups "regular" attenders (like nonattenders) were less prejudiced than "seldom" or "often" attenders. Employing a 26-

Table 1. Church attendance and prejudice among faculty members of a midwestern university.

Frequency of attendance (times per mo.)	N	Prejudice score
0	261	14.7
1	143	25.0
2	103	26.0
3	84	23.8
4	157	22.0
5-7	94	19.9
8-10	26	16.3
11 or more	21	11.7

Note.—From Struening (1957).

item Desegregation Scale in three separate studies, Holtzman (1956) found the same trend as shown in Table 2. If more evidence for the curvilinear relationship is needed, it will be found in community studies made in New Jersey (Friedrichs, 1959), North Carolina (Tumin, 1958), New England (Pettigrew, 1959), and Ohio and California (Pinkney, 1961). One could almost say there is a unanimity of findings on this matter. The trend holds regardless of religion, denomination, or target of prejudice (although the case seems less clear for anti-Semitism than for prejudice against other ethnic groups).

Table 2. Church attendance and prejudice among students in the border states.

	1956 study % intolerant	Mean score on D scale	
		1958 study	1960 study
Nonattenders	37	41.3	38.1
Once a mo.	66	48.5	51.4
Twice a mo.	67	50.6	48.4
Once a wk. or oftener	49	44.5	44.3

Note.—Adapted from Holtzman (1956), Kelley, Ferson, and Holtzman (1958), Young, Benson, and Holtzman (1960).

What are the theoretical implications? To find that prejudice is related to frequency of church attendance is scarcely explanatory, since it may reflect only formal behavior, not involvement or commitment to religious values. And yet it seems obvious that the regular attenders who go to church once a week or oftener (and several studies indicate that oftener than once a week is especially significant) are people who receive something of special ideological and experiential meaning. Irregular, casual fringe members, on the other hand, regard their religious contacts as less binding, less absorbing, less integral with their personal lives.

At this point, therefore, we must pass from external behavioral evidence into the realm of experience and motivation. Unless we do so we cannot hope to understand the curvilinear relationship that has been so clearly established.

Extrinsic versus Intrinsic Motivation

Perhaps the briefest way to characterize the two poles of subjective religion is to say that the extrinsically motivated person *uses* his religion, whereas the intrinsically motivated *lives* his religion. As we shall see later, most people, if they profess religion at all, fall upon a continuum between these two poles. Seldom, if ever, does one encounter a "pure" case. And yet to clarify the dimension it is helpful to characterize it in terms of the two ideal types.

Extrinsic Orientation

Persons with this orientation are disposed to use religion for their own ends. The term is borrowed from axiology, to designate an interest that is held because it serves other, more ultimate interests. Extrinsic values are always instrumental and utilitarian. Persons with this orientation may find religion useful in a variety of ways—to provide security and solace, sociability and distraction, status and self-justification. The embraced creed is lightly held or else selectively shaped to fit more primary needs. In theological terms the extrinsic type turns to God, but without turning away from self.

Intrinsic Orientation

Persons with this orientation find their master motive in religion. Other needs, strong as they may be, are regarded as of less ultimate significance, and they are, so far as possible, brought into harmony with the religious beliefs and prescriptions. Having embraced a creed the individual endeavors to internalize it and follow it fully. It is in this sense that he *lives* his religion.

A clergyman was making the same distinction when he said,

Some people come to church to thank God, to acknowledge His glory, and to ask His guidance. . . . Others come for what they can get. Their interest in the church is to run it or exploit it rather than to serve it.

Approximate parallels to these psychological types have been proposed by the sociologists Fichter (1954) and Lenski (1961). The former, in studying Catholic parishioners, classified them into four groups: the dormant, the marginal, the modal, and the nuclear. Omitting the dormant, Fichter estimated in terms of numbers that 20% are marginal, 70% modal, and less than 10% nuclear. It is, of course, the latter group that would most closely correspond to our conception of the "intrinsic." Lenski distinguished between church members whose involvement is "communal" (for the purpose of sociability and status) and those who are "associational" (seeking the deeper values of their faith).

These authors see the significance of their classifications for the study of prejudice. Fichter has found less prejudice among devout (nuclear) Catholics than among others (see Allport, 1954, p. 421). Lenski (1961, p. 173) reported that among Detroit Catholics 59% of those with a predominantly "communal" involvement favored segregated schools, whereas among those with predominantly an "associational" involvement only 27% favored segregation. The same trend held for Detroit Protestants.

The first published study relating the extrinsic-intrinsic dimension directly to ethnic prejudice was that of Wilson (1960). Limiting himself to a 15-item scale measuring an extrinsic (utilitarian-institutional) orientation, Wilson found in 10 religious groups a median correlation of .65 between his scale and anti-Semitism. In general these correlations were higher than he obtained between anti-Semitism and the Religious-Conventionalism

Scale (Levinson, 1954). From this finding Wilson concluded that orthodoxy or fundamentalism is a less important factor than extrinsicness of orientation.

Certain weaknesses may be pointed out in this pioneer study. Wilson did not attempt to measure intrinsicness of orientation, but assumed without warrant that it was equivalent to a low score on the extrinsic measures. Further, since the items were worded in a unidirectional way there may be an error of response set. Again, Wilson dealt only with Jews as a target of prejudice, and so the generality of his finding is not known.

Finally, the factor of educational level plays a part. Wilson used the California Anti-Semitism scale, and we know that high scores on this scale go with low education (Christie, 1954; Pettigrew, 1959; Titus & Hollander, 1957; Williams, 1964). Further, in our own study the extrinsic subscale is negatively correlated with degree of education ($r = -.32$). To an appreciable extent, therefore, Wilson's high correlations may be "ascribed" to educational level.

At this point, however, an important theoretical observation must be made. Low education may indeed predispose a person toward an exclusionist, self-centered, extrinsic, religious orientation and may dispose him to a stereotyped, fearful image of Jews. This fact does not in the least affect the functional relationship between the religious and the prejudiced outlooks. It is a common error for investigators to "control for" demographic factors without considering the danger involved in doing so. In so doing they are often obscuring and not illuminating the functional (i.e., psychological) relationships that obtain (see Allport, 1950).

Following Wilson the task of direct measurement was taken up by Feagin (1964) who used a more developed scale—one designed to measure not only extrinsic orientation but also the intrinsic. His scales are essentially the same as those discussed in a later section of this paper. In his study of Southern Baptists Feagin reached four conclusions: (*a*) Contrary to expectation, extrinsic and intrinsic items did not fall on a unidimensional scale but represented two independent dimensions; (*b*) only the extrinsic orientation was related to intolerance toward Negroes; (*c*) orthodoxy as such was not related to the extrinsic or intrinsic orientation; (*d*) greater orthodoxy (fundamentalism of belief) did, however, relate positively to prejudice.

Taking all these studies together we are justified in assuming that the inner experience of religion (what it means to the individual) is an important causal factor in developing a tolerant or a prejudiced outlook on life.

Yet, additional evidence is always in place, and new insights can be gained by a closer inspection of the rather coarse relationships that have been established up to now.

The Present Study

We wished to employ an improved and broader measure of prejudice than had previously been used. And since direct measures of prejudice (naming the target groups) have become too sensitive for wide use, we wished to try some abbreviated indirect measures. Further, we wished to make use of an improved Extrinsic-Intrinsic scale, one that would give reliable measures of both extrinsic and intrinsic tendencies in a person's religious life. For these reasons the following instruments were adopted.

Social Problems Questionnaire

This scale, devised by Harding and Schuman (unpublished[1]; see also Schuman & Harding, 1963, 1964), is a subtly worded instrument containing 12 anti-Negro, 11 anti-Jewish, and 10 anti-other items (pertaining to Orientals, Mexicans, and Puerto Ricans). The wording is varied so as to avoid an agreement response set.

Indirect Prejudice Measures

Six items were taken from Gilbert and Levinson's (1956) Custodial Mental Illness Ideology Scale (CMI). Example: "We should be sympathetic with mental patients, but we

[1]J. Harding and H. Schuman, "Social Problems Questionnaire," Cornell University.

cannot expect to understand their odd behavior. a) I definitely disagree. b) I tend to disagree. c) I tend to agree. d) I definitely agree."

Four items are related to a "jungle" philosophy of life, suggesting a generalized suspiciousness and distrust. Example: "The world is a hazardous place in which men are basically evil and dangerous. a) I definitely disagree. b) I tend to disagree. c) I tend to agree. d) I definitely agree."

In all cases the most prejudiced response receives a score of 5 and the least prejudiced response, 1. No response was scored 3.

From Table 3 we see that while the indirect measures have a positive correlation with each other and with direct measures the relationship is scarcely high enough to warrant the substitution of the indirect for the direct. The high correlations between prejudice for the three ethnic target groups once again illustrate the well-established fact that ethnic prejudice tends to be a broadly generalized disposition in personality.

Table 3. Intercorrelations between five measures of prejudice.

	Anti-Jewish	Anti-Other	Jungle	CMI
Anti-Negro	.63	.70	.20	.25
Anti-Jewish		.67	.24	.31
Anti-Other			.33	.36
Jungle				.43

Note.—*N* = 309.

Religious Orientation Measure

The full scale, entitled "Religious Orientation," is available from ADI.[2] It separates the intrinsically worded items from the extrinsic, gives score values for each item, and reports on item reliabilities. In all cases a score of 1 indicates the most intrinsic response, a score of 5, the most extrinsic. While it is possible to use all 20 items as one continuous scale, it will soon become apparent that it is often

[2]The full Religious Orientation scale has been deposited with the American Documentation Institute. Order Document No. 9268 from ADI Auxiliary Publications Project, Photoduplication Service, Library of Congress, Washington, D. C. 20540. Remit in advance $1.25 for microfilm or $1.25 for photocopies and make checks payable to: Chief, Photoduplication Service, Library of Congress.

wise to treat the two subscales separately. A sample item from the extrinsic subscale follows: "What religion offers me most is comfort when sorrows and misfortune strike. a) I definitely disagree, 1. b) I tend to disagree, 2. c) I tend to agree, 4. d) I definitely agree, 5." A sample item from the intrinsic subscale: "My religious beliefs are what really lie behind my whole approach to life. a) this is definitely not so, 5. b) probably not so, 4. c) probably so, 2. d) definitely so, 1.

Sample

While our sample of six groups of churchgoers shows some diversity of denomination and region, it is in no sense representative. Graduate-student members of a seminar collected the 309 cases from the following church groups: Group A, 94 Roman Catholic (Massachusetts); Group B, 55 Lutheran (New York State); Group C, 44 Nazarene (South Carolina); Group D, 53 Presbyterian (Pennsylvania); Group E, 35 Methodist (Tennessee); Group F, 28 Baptist (Massachusetts).

We labeled the groups alphabetically since such small subsamples could not possibly lead to valid generalizations concerning denominations as a whole. All subjects knew that they were invited to participate as members of a religious group, and this fact may well have introduced a "proreligious" bias.

Gross Results

If we pool all our cases for the purpose of correlating religious orientation with prejudice, we discover that while the findings are in the expected direction they are much less impressive than those of previous studies, especially Wilson's.

Correlations with Extrinsic Subscale

Since Wilson employed an extrinsic scale similar to ours, we first present in Table 4 our findings using this subscale and the various measures of prejudice. Whereas Wilson found

Table 4. Correlations between extrinsic subscale and prejudice.

Anti-Negro	.26
Anti-Jewish	.21
Anti-Other	.32
Jungle	.29
CMI	.44

Note.—N = 309.

a correlation of .65 between his extrinsic and anti-Semitic measures, our correlation falls to .21. In part the reason no doubt lies in certain features of Wilson's method which we have criticized.

Correlations with Combined Extrinsic-Intrinsic Scale

From the outset it was our intention to broaden Wilson's unidirectional (extrinsic) measure to see whether our hypothesis might hold for the total scale (combined scores for the 11 extrinsic and 9 intrinsic items). As Table 5 shows, matters do not improve but seem to worsen. The logic of combining the two subscales is of course to augment the

Table 5. Correlations between total extrinsic-intrinsic scale and prejudice.

Anti-Negro	.26
Anti-Jewish	.18
Anti-Other	.18
Jungle	.21
CMI	.17

Note.—N = 309.

continuum in length and presumably enhance the reliability of the total measure. It soon became apparent, however, that subjects who endorse extrinsically worded items do not necessarily reject those worded intrinsically, or vice versa. It turns out that there is only a very low correlation in the expected direction between the two subscales ($r = .21$). Obviously at this point some reformulation is badly needed.

Reformulation of the Approach

Examination of the data reveals that some subjects are indeed "consistently intrinsic," having a strong tendency to endorse intrinsically worded items and to reject the extrinsically worded. Correspondingly others are "consistently extrinsic." Yet, unfortunately for our neat typology, many subjects are provokingly inconsistent. They persist in endorsing any or all items that to them seem favorable to religion in any sense. Their responses, therefore, are "indiscriminately proreligious."

The problem is essentially the same as that encountered by the many investigators who have attempted to reverse the wording of items comprising the F scale, in order to escape an unwanted response-set bias. Uniformly the effort has proved to be frustrating, since so many subjects subscribe to both the positive and negative wording of the same question (see Bass, 1955; Chapman & Bock, 1958; Chapman & Campbell, 1959; Christie, 1954; Jackson & Messick, 1957).

An example from our own subscales would be: "My religious beliefs are what really lie behind my whole approach to life" (intrinsic). "Though I believe in my religion, I feel there are many more important things in my life" (extrinsic).

The approach used by Peabody (1961) offers us a model for analyzing our data in a meaningful way. Peabody administered both positive and negative F-scale items to subjects at two different testing sessions. By comparing each individual's responses to the same question stated positively at one time and in reverse at another he was able to separate out those who were consistently pro or anti toward the content of authoritarian items. But he found many who expressed double agreement (or disagreement) with both versions of the same question. Table 6 applies Peabody's paradigm to our data.

In assigning our 309 cases to these categories we employed the following criteria.

Intrinsic type includes individuals who agree with intrinsically worded items on the intrinsic subscale, and who disagree with extrinsically stated items on the extrinsic subscale. By the scoring method employed these individuals fall below the median scores on both subscales.

Table 6. Four patterns of religious orientation.

	Agrees with intrinsic choice	Disagrees with intrinsic choice
Agrees with extrinsic choice	Indiscriminately proreligious	Consistently extrinsic in type
Disagrees with extrinsic choice	Consistently intrinsic in type	Indiscriminately antireligious or nonreligious[a]

[a]Not found in present sample.

Extrinsic type includes individuals who agree with extrinsically stated items on the extrinsic subscale, and who disagree with items on the intrinsic subscale. By our scoring method these individuals all fall above the median scores on both subscales.

Indiscriminately proreligious includes those who on the intrinsic subscale score at least 12 points less than on the extrinsic subscale. (This figure reflects the fact that a subject gives approximately 50 % more intrinsic responses on the intrinsic subscale than we should expect from his extrinsic responses to the extrinsic subscale.)

Indiscriminately antireligious or nonreligious includes those who would show a strong tendency to disagree with items on both subscales. Since nonchurchgoers are excluded from our samples, such cases are not found. (Some pilot work with markedly liberal groups indicates that this type does exist, however, even among members of "religious" organizations.)

Table 7 gives the percentage of the three types.

Results of the Reformulation

The five measures of prejudice were analyzed by a 6 (Groups) X 3 (Religious Types) analysis of variance. Table 8 presents the overall effects for religious types for each of the five measures of prejudice. The multivariate analysis of variance indicates that there is both a significant difference between the three types of religious orientation and between the six subsamples in the level of prejudice.[3] Examination of the means shows two trends: (*a*) The extrinsic type is more prejudiced than the intrinsic type for both direct and indirect measures; (*b*) the indis-

Table 7. Percentage of each religious type in each subsample.

Religious group	N	Consistently intrinsic	Consistently extrinsic	Indiscrim- inately pro- religious
A	(94)	36	34	30
B	(55)	35	36	29
C	(44)	36	39	25
D	(53)	32	30	38
E	(35)	31	29	40
F	(28)	39	39	22

criminate type of religious orientation is more prejudiced than either of the two consistent types. Statistically all these trends are highly significant.

We note especially that the scores of the indiscriminate type are markedly higher on all measures than the scores of the intrinsic type. Corresponding F ratios for paired comparisons range from 8.4 for the jungle scale to 20.4 for the CMI scale. The differences be-

tween the indiscriminate and extrinsic types are smaller. For the anti-Jewish and CMI scales these differences are, however, beyond the .005 level; for the anti-other and jungle scales, at the .05 level. For the anti-Negro the difference falls below significance.

The relationship between the indiscriminately proreligious orientation and prejudice receives support (see Table 9) when we compare subjects who are *moderately* indiscriminate with those who are *extremely* indiscriminate. (In the first group the scores on the intrinsic subscale average 16 points lower than on the extrinsic subscale, whereas the extreme cases average 23 points less on

Table 9. Degrees of indiscriminateness and average prejudice scores.

Target of prejudice	Moderately indiscriminate N = 56	Extremely indiscriminate N = 39	F ratio
Anti-Negro	35.4	37.9	.97
Anti-Jewish	28.0	30.1	.90
Anti-Other	24.9	28.2	3.25*
Jungle	9.5	10.2	1.11
CMI	10.2	14.6	3.99*

* $p > .05$.

Table 8. Prejudice and religious orientation.

Target of prejudice	Mean prejudice score			F ratio
	Intrinsic type N = 108	Extrinsic type N = 106	Inconsistent type N = 95	
Anti-Negro	28.7	33.0	36.0	8.6**
Anti-Jewish	22.6	24.6	28.9	11.1**
Anti-Other	20.4	23.3	26.1	10.9**
Jungle	7.9	8.7	9.6	8.4**
CMI	10.2	11.8	13.4	20.4**

Multivariate analysis of variance

Source of variation	F ratio	df
Religious type (A)	5.96***	10,574
Sample groups (B)	3.19***	25,668
A × B	1.11*	50,1312

* $p > .25$.
** $p > .001$.
*** $p > .0005$.

[3]The multivariate F reported here is Wilk's lambda (Anderson, 1958). Statistical computations are summarized by Bock (1963) and programmed for the IBM 7090 by Hall and Cramer (1962). The univariate tests to be reported are adjusted for unequal Ns to obtain orthogonal estimates according to mathematical procedures described in Hall and Cramer.

the intrinsic than on the extrinsic subscale.)

The discovery that the degree of indiscriminateness tends to relate directly to the degree of prejudice is an important finding. It can only mean that some functional relationship obtains between religious muddleheadedness (for that is what indiscriminate scores imply) and antagonism toward ethnic groups. We shall return to this interpretation in the concluding section of this paper.

Results for Subsamples

It would not be correct to assume that the variance is distributed equally over all the subsamples, for it turns out that the denominational groups differ appreciably in prejudice scores and in religious type, as Tables 10 and 11 indicate.

It is true that when we combine subsamples all the trends are in the expected direction, but troublesome exceptions occur for single groups as indicated by the nearly significant interaction effects. The most troublesome contradictions appear in relation to the anti-Negro measures based on the Harding-Schuman scale. Table 10 discloses certain sore points, even though the average trend over all the subsamples is in the predicted direction.

For Groups A, B, and C we note that the indiscriminate type is slightly less prejudiced than the extrinsic type, and for Groups D and E the extrinsic type seems actually less preju-

Table 10. Anti-Negro prejudice: mean scores on social problems scale.

Religious group	Intrinsic type	Extrinsic type	Indiscriminate type	Group M
A	27.4 (34)	34.8 (32)	32.2 (28)	31.4 (94)
B	27.2 (19)	32.3 (20)	31.9 (16)	30.4 (55)
C	22.4 (16)	36.2 (17)	35.0 (11)	30.9 (44)
D	35.5 (17)	28.7 (16)	42.5 (20)	36.1 (53)
E	40.5 (11)	35.5 (10)	43.0 (14)	40.1 (35)
F	22.6 (11)	27.9 (11)	28.7 (6)	26.0 (28)
Type M	28.7 (108)	33.0 (106)	36.0 (95)	32.5 (309)

Analysis of variance

Source of variation	df	MS	F ratio
Religious type (A)	2	1077.8	8.6**
Religious group (B)	5	952.2	7.6**
A × B	10	251.1	2.0*
Error (w)	291	125.6	

* $p > .10$.
** $p > .001$.

Table 11. Indirect (CMI) measure of prejudice.

Religious group	Intrinsic type	Extrinsic type	Indiscriminate type	Group M
A	11.2 (34)	12.4 (32)	13.6 (28)	12.3 (94)
B	10.1 (19)	10.8 (20)	13.4 (16)	11.3 (55)
C	9.5 (16)	12.2 (17)	12.6 (11)	11.3 (44)
D	10.6 (17)	11.4 (16)	14.8 (20)	12.4 (53)
E	8.6 (11)	12.9 (10)	13.6 (14)	11.8 (35)
F	9.2 (11)	10.7 (11)	9.2 (6)	9.8 (28)
Type M	10.2 (108)	11.8 (106)	13.4 (95)	11.9 (309)

Analysis of variance

Source of variation	df	MS	F ratio
Religious type (A)	2	255.0	20.4**
Religious group (B)	5	36.5	2.9*
A × B	10	15.3	1.2
Error (w)	291	12.5	

* $p > .05$.
** $p > .001$.

diced than the intrinsic. (Groups D and E are consistently more troublesome than other subsamples, perhaps because of some salient racial issue in the local community. It will be noted that both these groups are considerably more anti-Negro than the other subsamples.)

By way of contrast we present in Table 11 the results for the short (five-item) CMI scale. With the exception of the indiscriminate type in Group F, the progression of scores is precisely as expected. Each subsample shows that the intrinsic type is less prejudiced toward the mentally ill than the extrinsic type, and the extrinsic type is less prejudiced than the indiscriminately proreligious.[4]

Returning in a different way to the original question of whether consistent extrinsic and intrinsic orientations make for prejudice and for tolerance, respectively, we shall now examine this matter in each subsample separately. Inspection of the mean scores and variance for the total scale indicates that we are dealing with a relatively narrow range of variation. To minimize the effect of a narrow range of scores and skewed distributions, we used Kendal's (1955) tau as a measure of degree of relationship between prejudice and consistent religious orientation. The results are given in Table 12. While the correlations are not high (14 are significant in the expected direction), only one (in the troublesome Group E) is significant in the reverse direction.

Educational Differences

Computing the actual years of schooling for all groups we find that the indiscriminate type has significantly less formal education than the intrinsic cases ($p > .005, F = 18.29$), and somewhat less than the extrinsic type ($p > .10, F = 2.89$). Comparing extrinsic with intrinsic types we find that the former has finished fewer years of schooling ($p > .10, F = 3.45$). (Oddly enough the groups with highest average education are D and E, which also displayed the highest anti-Negro and anti-Semitic prejudice—perhaps because of particular local conditions.)

In our survey of earlier studies we saw that educational level is often a factor in the various relationships discovered between religion and prejudice. We have also argued that demographic factors of this sort should not be allowed to obscure the functional (psychological) analysis that the data call for. Granted that low education makes for indiscriminate thinking, the mental confusion that results from low education may have its own peculiar effects on religious and ethnic attitudes.

Table 12. Correlations between combined extrinsic-intrinsic religious scores (for consistent subjects) and prejudice (Kendal's tau).

Religious group	Anti-Negro	Anti-Jewish	Anti-Other	Jungle	CMI
A	.31***	.26***	.24***	.14*	.19***
B	.19*	.13	.15	-.05	.03
C	.32***	.17*	.35***	.14*	.28***
D	-.12	.05	-.09	.03	.11
E	-.24*	-.11	-.13	.26*	.46***
F	.39***	.13	.25*	-.01	.24*

  * $p > .10$.
 ** $p > .05$.
*** $p > .01$.

[4]If we apply a more severe test, asking whether *all* differences between groups are significant, we find the following results. In four of the six groups (in both Tables 10 and 11) the extrinsic type is significantly more prejudiced than the intrinsic. Likewise in four out of six groups (Table 10) and five out of six (Table 11), the indiscriminate type is significantly more prejudiced than the intrinsic. However, in only two of the six groups (in both Tables 10 and 11) is the indiscriminate type significantly more prejudiced than the extrinsic.

Summary and Interpretations

At the outset we stated three propositions that seem to be firmly established: (*a*) Churchgoers on the broad average harbor more ethnic prejudice than nonchurchgoers; (*b*) in spite of this broad tendency a curvilinear relationship in fact exists; (*c*) the intrinsically motivated churchgoers are significantly less prejudiced than the extrinsically motivated. Our present research supplies additional strong support for the second and third of these propositions.

To these propositions we add a fourth: *churchgoers who are indiscriminately proreligious are more prejudiced than the consistently extrinsic, and very much more prejudiced than the consistently intrinsic types.*

The psychological tie between the intrinsic orientation and tolerance, and between the extrinsic orientation and prejudice, has been discussed in a series of papers by Allport (1959, 1963, 1966). In brief the argument holds that a person with an extrinsic religious orientation is using his religious views to provide security, comfort, status, or social support for himself—religion is not a value in its own right, it serves other needs, and it is a purely utilitarian formation. Now prejudice too is a "useful" formation: it too provides security, comfort, status, and social support. A life that is dependent on the supports of extrinsic religion is likely to be dependent on the supports of prejudice, hence our positive correlations between the extrinsic orientation and intolerance. Contrariwise, the intrinsic religious orientation is not an instrumental device. It is not a mere mode of conformity, nor a crutch, nor a tranquilizer, nor a bid for status. All needs are subordinated to an overarching religious commitment. In internalizing the total creed of his religion the individual necessarily internalizes its values of humility, compassion, and love of neighbor. In such a life (where religion is an intrinsic and dominant value) there is no place for rejection, contempt, or condescension toward one's fellow man. Such is our explanation for the relationship between extrinsic religion and prejudice, and between intrinsic religion and tolerance.

Our present task is to discover, if we can, some similar functional tie between prejudice (as measured both directly and indirectly) and the indiscriminately proreligious orientation. The common factor seems to be a certain cognitive style. Technically it might be called "undifferentiated thinking," or excessive "category width," as defined by Pettigrew (1958). Rokeach (1960) notes the inability of the "dogmatic" mind to perceive differences; thus, whereas some people distinguish in their thinking and feeling between Communists and Nazis, the undifferentiated dogmatist has a global reaction (cognitive and emotional) toward "Communazis."

We have no right, of course, to expect all our subjects to make discriminations exactly corresponding to our own logic. Nor should we expect them to read and respond to every item on the Extrinsic-Intrinsic scale according to its full meaning as intended by the investigators. Perhaps we should be gratified that two-thirds of our cases can be safely classified as "consistent" (i.e., having about the same strength of disposition toward an extrinsic or intrinsic orientation across most of the items). These consistent cases, as we have seen, support the hypothesis with which we started. It is the remaining (indiscriminate) one-third of the cases which obscure the trend (or diminish its statistical significance).

In responding to the religious items these individuals seem to take a superficial or "hit and run" approach. Their mental set seems to be "all religion is good." "My religious beliefs are what really lie behind my whole life"—Yes! "Although I believe in my religion, I feel there are many more important things in my life"—Yes! "Religion is especially important to me because it answers many questions about the meaning of life"—Yes! "The church is most important as a place to formulate good social relationships"—Yes!

There seems to be one wide category—"religion is OK." From the way in which the scale is constructed this undifferentiated endorsement can be the product of an agreement response set. Our inconsistently proreligious may be "yeasayers" (Couch & Keniston, 1960). But if so, we are still dealing with an undifferentiated cognitive disposition. We recall likewise that the inconsistent cases have a lower level of formal education than the consistent cases. This factor also is relevant to the formation and holding of overwide categories.

But why should such a disposition, whatever its source, be so strongly related to prejudice, in such a way that the *more* undifferentiated, the *more* prejudiced—as Table 9 shows?

The answer is that prejudice itself is a matter of stereotyped overgeneralization, a failure to distinguish members of a minority group as individuals (Allport, 1954, Chaps. 2, 10). It goes without saying that if categories are overwide the accompanying feeling tone will be undifferentiated. Thus, religion as a whole is good; a minority group as a whole is bad.

It seems probable that people with undifferentiated styles of thinking (and feeling) are not entirely secure in a world that for the most part demands fine and accurate distinctions. The resulting diffuse anxiety may well dispose them to grapple onto religion and to distrust strange ethnic groups. The positive correlation between the jungle items and other prejudice scales (Table 3) is evidence for this interpretation.

Our line of reasoning, readers will recognize, is compatible with various previous contributions to the theory of prejudice. One thinks here of Rokeach's concept of dogmatism; of Schuman and Harding's (1964) discovery of a "confused" type in their study of the relation between rational consistency and prejudice; of the same authors' work on sympathetic identification (1963); of studies on the dynamics of scapegoating, the role in insecurity, of authoritarian submission, of intolerance for ambiguity, and of related concepts.

All in all we conclude that prejudice, like tolerance, is often embedded deeply in personality structure and is reflected in a consistent cognitive style. Both states of mind are enmeshed with the individual's religious orientation. One definable style marks the individual who is bigoted in ethnic matters and extrinsic in his religious orientation. Equally apparent is the style of those who are bigoted and at the same time indiscriminately proreligious. A relatively small number of people show an equally consistent cognitive style in their simultaneous commitment to religion as a dominant, intrinsic value and to ethnic tolerance.

One final word: our research argues strongly that social scientists who employ the variable "religion" or "religiosity" in the future will do well to keep in mind the crucial distinction between religious attitudes that are *intrinsic, extrinsic,* and *indiscriminately pro.* To know that a person is in some sense "religious" is not as important as to know the role religion plays in the economy of his life. (The categories of *nonreligious* and *indiscriminately antireligious* will also for some purposes be of central significance, although the present research, confined as it is to churchgoers, does not employ them.)

References

Adorno, T. W., Frenkel-Brunswik, E., Levinson, D. J., & Sanford, R. N. *The authoritarian personality.* New York: Harper, 1950.

Allport, G. W. Review of S. A. Stouffer, E. A. Suchman, L. C. De Vinney, S. A. Star, & R. W. Williams, Jr., *The American soldier.* Vol. 1. *Adjustment during Army life. Journal of Abnormal and Social Psychology,* 1950, **45,** 168-173.

Allport, G. W. *The nature of prejudice.* Reading, Mass.: Addison-Wesley, 1954.

Allport, G. W. Religion and prejudice. *The Crane Review,* 1959, **2,** 1-10.

Allport, G. W. Behavioral science, religion, and mental health. *Journal of Religion and Health,* 1963, **2,** 187-197.

Allport, G. W. Religious context of prejudice. *Journal for the Scientific Study of Religion,* 1966, **5,** 447-457.

Allport, G. W., & Kramer, B. M. Some roots of prejudice. *Journal of Psychology,* 1946, **22,** 9-39.

Anderson, T. W. *An introduction to multivariate statistical analysis.* New York: Wiley, 1958.

Bass, B. M. Authoritarianism or acquiescence. *Journal of Abnormal and Social Psychology,* 1955, **56,** 616-623.

Bock, R. D. Programming univariate and multivariate analysis of variance. *Technometrics,* 1963, **5,** 95-117.

Chapman, L. J., & Bock, R. D. Components of variance due to acquiescence and content in the

F-scale measure of authoritarianism. *Psychological Bulletin*, 1958, **55**, 328-333.

Chapman, L. J., & Campbell, D. T. The effect of acquiescence response-set upon relationships among the F-scale, ethnocentrism, and intelligence. *Sociometry*, 1959, **22**, 153-161.

Christie, R. C. Authoritarianism re-examined. In R. C. Christie & M. Jahoda (Eds.), *Studies in the scope and method of the authoritarian personality*. New York: Free Press of Glencoe, 1954. Pp. 123-196.

Couch, A., & Keniston, K. Yeasayers and naysayers: Agreeing response set as a personality variable. *Journal of Abnormal and Social Psychology*, 1960, **60**, 151-174.

Demerath, N. J., III. *Social class in American Protestantism*. Chicago: Rand McNally, 1965.

Feagin, J. R. Prejudice and religious types: A focused study of southern fundamentalists. *Journal for the Scientific Study of Religion*, 1964, **4**, 3-13.

Fichter, J. H. *Social relations in the urban parish*. Chicago: University of Chicago Press, 1954.

Friedrichs, R. W. Christians and residential exclusion: An empirical study of a northern dilemma. *Journal of Social Issues*, 1959, **15**, 14-23.

Gilbert, D. C., & Levinson, D. J. Ideology, personality, and institutional policy in the mental hospital. *Journal of Abnormal and Social Psychology*, 1956, **53**, 263-271.

Gough, H. G. Studies in social intolerance: IV. *Journal of Social Psychology*, 1951, **33**, 263-269.

Hall, C. E., & Cramer, E. *General purpose program to compute multivariate analysis of variance on an IBM 7090*. Washington, D. C.: George Washington University Biometric Laboratory, 1962.

Holtzman, W. H. Attitudes of college men toward non-segregation in Texas schools. *Public Opinion Quarterly*, 1956, **20**, 559-569.

Jackson, D. H., & Messick, S. J. A note on ethnocentrism and acquiescence response sets. *Journal of Abnormal and Social Psychology*, 1957, **54**, 132-134.

Kelly, J. G., Ferson, J. E., & Holtzman, W. H. The measurement of attitudes toward the Negro in the South. *Journal of Social Psychology*, 1958, **48**, 305-317.

Kendal, M. G. *Rank correlation methods*. (2nd ed.) London: Griffin, 1955.

Kirkpatrick, C. Religion and humanitarianism: A study of institutional implications. *Psychological Monographs*, 1949, **63** (9, Whole No. 304).

Lenski, G. *The religious factor*. Garden City, N. Y.: Doubleday, 1961.

Levinson, D. J. The inter-group workshop: Its psychological aims and effects. *Journal of Psychology*, 1954, **38**, 103-126.

Peabody, D. Attitude content and agreement set in scales of authoritarianism, dogmatism, anti-Semitism, and economic conservatism. *Journal of Abnormal and Social Psychology*, 1961, **63**, 1-11.

Pettigrew, T. F. The measurement and correlates of category width as a cognitive variable. *Journal of Personality*, 1958, **26**, 532-544.

Pettigrew. T. F. Regional differences in anti-Negro prejudice. *Journal of Abnormal and Social Psychology*, 1959, **49**, 28-36.

Pinkney, A. The anatomy of prejudice: Majority group attitudes toward minorities in selected American cities. Unpublished doctoral dissertation, Cornell University, 1961.

Rokeach, M. *The open and closed mind: Investigations into the nature of belief systems and personality systems*. New York: Basic Books, 1960.

Rosenblith, J. F. A replication of "Some roots of prejudice." *Journal of Abnormal and Social Psychology*, 1949, **44**, 470-489.

Schuman, H., & Harding, J. Sympathetic identification with the underdog. *Public Opinion Quarterly*, 1963, **27**, 230-241.

Schuman, H., & Harding. J. Prejudice and the norm of rationality. *Sociometry*, 1964, **27**, 353-371.

Stember, H. C. *Education and attitude change*. New York: Institute of Human Relations Press, 1961.

Stouffer, S. A. *Communism, civil liberties, and conformity*. Garden City, N. Y.: Doubleday, 1955.

Struening, E. L. Antidemocratic attitudes in a Midwest university. In H. H. Remmers (Ed.), *Anti-democratic attitudes in American schools*. Evanston: Northwestern University Press, 1963. Ch. 9.

Titus, H. E., & Hollander, E. P. The California F scale in psychological research: 1950-1955. *Psychological Bulletin*, 1957, **54**, 47-64.

Tumin, M. *Desegregation: Resistance and readiness*. Princeton: Princeton University Press, 1958.

Williams, R. M. *Strangers next door: Ethnic relations in American communities*. Englewood Cliffs, N. J.: Prentice-Hall, 1964.

Wilson, W. C. Extrinsic religious values and prejudice. *Journal of Abnormal and Social Psychology*, 1960, **60**, 286-288.

Young, R. K., Benson, W. M., & Holtzman, W. H. Changes in attitudes toward the Negro in a southern university. *Journal of Abnormal and Social Psychology*, 1960, **60**, 131-133.

A Critique of the Concept of Functional Autonomy

John P. Seward

Like many others, I first turned to psychology with questions about motivation. I remember when it happened. I had just graduated from Cornell, where my only contact with psychology had been a 1-semester course in my sophomore year taught by Karl Dallenbach (Titchener's section was already full). Titchener's textbook left me cold. For me the only spark was struck by Dallenbach's lecture on how magicians deceive audiences.

Having left economics for literature, I hoped, of course, to write. But since I had nothing to say, I would have to write about Life, and since I knew nothing about life it would have to be fiction. And before I could write fiction I would have to find out how my characters would probably act. So I went to the library and found a book by Troland called *The Mystery of Mind*. I divided that summer between beginning Greek and struggling with nociceptors, beneceptors, cortical conductance, and retroflex action—also largely Greek. Troland had a quasi-neurological model of Thorndike's law of effect that tantalized me; at least it did not discourage me from entering the graduate psychology department at Columbia in the fall.

By 1926 instincts had had their day and biological drives were invoked to supply the energy for behavior. But hunger, thirst, and sex, even with the help of fear and rage, could hardly fill the gap left by constructive, destructive, filial, parental, acquisitive, inquisitive, self-assertive, and self-abasing instincts. If not innate, how were these undeniable motives, social or antisocial, to be accounted for? John B. Watson had already suggested the answer that became orthodox. You recall his three primary emotions of fear, rage, and love, and his experiment—perhaps the most famous in psychology—in which the clang of a steel bar probably prevented an 11-months infant from ever becoming a student of rat behavior. The answer, of course, was to be found in the principle of conditioning. But no one was altogether happy with the solution. Why, it was objected, if a mother's face is loved because it was perceived along with mild tactile stimulation, wouldn't a pillow do just as well? At that time, 30 years before Harlow's experiments with terry-cloth "mothers" for orphaned monkeys, the objection carried more weight than it would today.

In 1937 Gordon Allport proposed a new solution: the functional autonomy of motives. In his own words:

> Each motive has a definite point of origin which may possibly lie in instincts, or, more likely, in the organic tensions of infancy ... but as the individual matures the tie is broken. Whatever bond remains is historical, not functional [p. 143].

Allport expressed his idea more clearly by paraphrasing Woodworth's (1918) earlier suggestion that a mechanism might become a drive: "activities and objects that earlier in the game were *means* to an end, now become *ends* in themselves [1937, p. 144]."

The trouble was that although Allport gave many examples of what he meant, he made no attempt to analyze how it worked. So his principle stood as a statement of faith rather than an explanation. Before accepting it,

From J. P. Seward, "The Structure of Functional Autonomy," *American Psychologist*, 1963, **18**, 703-710. Reprinted by permission of the American Psychological Association.

learning theorists (e.g., McClelland, 1942; Rethlingshafer, 1943) insisted on proof that Allport's examples were not simply cases of long-delayed extinction of instrumental acts. But no acceptable form of proof was specified, and since none was forthcoming the principle has lived on in a sort of limbo, never openly acknowledged but never finally renounced.

It is conceivable, of course, that there is no real problem here, that social motives are not autonomous, and that they will be extinguished if not biologically reinforced. A hen low in the pecking order may need an occasional peck to keep her in line. A friendship may not survive many months without an invitation to dinner. Another way to evade the issue would be to draw a Cartesian dichotomy between infrahuman species goaded by bodily needs and Homo sapiens somehow capable of emergent values.

I prefer to resort to neither of these dodges. Without severing kinship with our fellow creatures, let us assume that human adults are not exclusively concerned with eating and sleeping and excreting and fighting and copulating, and that all their remaining activities will not necessarily be extinguished, even if repeated indefinitely. First, I want to make sure that traditional learning theory cannot derive such activities from bodily deficits and disturbances. Second, I shall invite you to consider some recent developments in the study of animal and human motivation. Third, we shall return to the question of functional autonomy and re-examine Allport's notion in the light of newer concepts.

Orthodox Behavior Theory

Behavior theory has invented two constructs to deal with acquired motives: learned drives, and learned rewards or secondary reinforcement. Let us start with the first construct.

A drive is presumably learned by being conditioned to stimuli present when it is aroused. A child badly frightened in a dark room may thereafter insist on keeping the light on when he goes to bed. A rat that has escaped from a shock box by dashing through a door will learn new ways to open the door even after the shock has been turned off (Miller, 1948). Theoretically its efforts will continue as long as they succeed in reducing fear. But what keeps the fear alive? By the laws of classical conditioning, unless it is reinstated from time to time by more shocks, the fear must eventually be extinguished.

On the whole, empirical findings support the theory. Rats and dogs have been known to avoid a nonexistent shock for hundreds of trials, but under most conditions they finally quit (Solomon & Brush, 1956). Solomon and Wynne's (1954) traumatized dogs stand as possible exceptions; to explain their remarkable tenacity the authors finally had to postulate a principle of "partial irreversibility," logically equivalent to functional autonomy itself. But even if the theoretical scene changed and some psychologist invented a nonextinguishable fear, it is doubtful if Allport would consider it adequate to the functions he had in mind.

So much for aversive behavior; what of appetites? If fear can be conditioned, so might hunger and thirst. At first thought, the ubiquitous advertising of foods and drinks would seem to exploit some such tendency. But we must be careful to distinguish between genuine hunger and a desire for sugar-cured ham. For a more definitive test we might half starve an animal repeatedly in a certain closet, always feeding him somewhere else; then see if we could make him hungry just by putting him back in the closet when his stomach was full. Such experiments in one form or another have been tried many times with varying results, but so far they have failed to prove that the so-called homeostatic drives can be "externalized" (Hall, 1961, pp. 45-49).

Secondary reinforcement looks more promising. It has already played a prominent role in bolstering Hull's learning theory, based on the satisfaction of bodily needs. According to this theory a response is learned if it is closely followed by the reduction of a drive; this is known as primary reinforcement. But the response can also be strengthened if it produces a stimulus *associated* with drive reduction, i.e., a *secondary reinforcer*. So a hungry rat at a choice point will learn to choose the path to a food box even if it is prevented from eating by a wire screen (Schlosberg & Pratt, 1956). So, too, a hostess may keep her hungry guests hanging around an extra hour if she lets the aroma of a casserole waft from the kitchen.

Our concern is whether a secondary reinforcer can achieve independence of its origins. That means, first of all, continuing to function in the absence of the original class of drives. The rats I just mentioned dropped to chance scores after they were fed. More experiments are needed, but so far we have no convincing evidence that satiated animals find food signals rewarding (Myers, 1958).

Second, an autonomous secondary reinforcer, unlike ordinary conditioned stimuli, would have to maintain itself indefinitely after the primary satisfier was withdrawn. Serious attempts have been made to render secondary reinforcers immune to extinction. At the empirical level Zimmerman (1959) first trained rats at a starting signal to go down a runway to food on a partial reinforcement schedule. He then removed the food and trained them in the start box on a bar pressing response that occasionally produced the signal and opened the door to the runway. This procedure resulted in thousands of responses over 10 to 14 daily sessions after food rewards had been discontinued. Such persistence, he ventured, "offers a close approximation at the animal level to the 'functional autonomy' ... hypothesized as sometimes characteristic of human behavior [p. 353]."

Further studies of the "Zimmerman effect" (Wike, Platt, & Knowles, 1962; Wike, Platt, & Scott, 1963), however, have cast serious doubt on the role of secondary reinforcement in his results. Untrained control groups given the same partial reinforcement for bar pressing responded as persistently as those that had been previously trained to food. It would seem that release from the box, not a food-associated runway, was the effective reward. I mention these studies in some detail because in a sense they epitomize the thesis to follow shortly.

At the theoretical level Skinner (1953) has proposed another solution, the "generalized reinforcer." *Multiconditioned reinforcer* would be more accurate, since Skinner is talking about a learned reinforcer based on more than a single unlearned one. An obvious example is money; equally pertinent are social favors such as attention, approval, affection, and submissiveness. Such stimuli generally accompany the satisfaction of assorted needs. They remain effective because they can draw on a pool of deprivations; on any given occasion we are likely to have at least one complaint—flu or frustration or fatigue or an itch. But the flaw in this argument is clear: In the long run, after the generalized reinforcer has failed to satisfy all the needs it was based on, it must lose its power. Skinner himself seems aware of the defect and tries to remedy it by fiat. "Eventually," he writes, "generalized reinforcers are effective even though the primary reinforcers on which they are based no longer accompany them.... We get attention or approval for its own sake [p. 81]." Functional autonomy again!

Earlier in his discussion, however, Skinner makes a more cogent conjecture. Speaking of the "sensory feedback" from controlling the environment, he suggests that some of its reinforcing effect may be innate. A baby shaking its rattle is getting all the reinforcement it needs simply from "making the world behave."

I shall try to convince you that Skinner's guess carries more weight today than it did when he made it. Since you are probably already convinced that neither drive conditioning nor secondary reinforcement can transform visceral needs into social motives, I may as well start now.

"New Look" in Motivation Theory

The development I speak of was foreshadowed years ago by Woodworth's (1918) contention that capacity provides its own motivation and by Karl Bühler's (1924) concept of "function pleasure." In the same vein Diamond (1939) pointed out "a neglected aspect of motivation," proposing that the demand for stimulation was a fundamental property of organisms. Woodworth (1947) asserted a "will to perceive" at the same time that Murphy (1947) was making a strong case for adding activity drives and sensory drives to the visceral variety. But it was not until experimenters began to produce supporting evidence that the idea took hold. Today we can work with a broader base of unconditioned motivation. We look to the external rather than the internal milieu for many of the instigators and reinforcers of behavior; it is easier to think of responses as directed outward rather than merely pushed from within. In case you doubt this statement let me run over briefly some of the evidence I have in mind.

Evidence

1. Contact receptors. A number of stimuli not obviously drive reducing have been nominated for the list of primary positive reinforcers. (*a*)Saccharine, a nonnutritive substance, has proved rewarding to rats (Sheffield & Roby, 1950). It would seem that it must taste good. (*b*) Motherless infant monkeys find comfort in clinging to terry-cloth models that have never provided milk (Harlow & Zimmerman, 1959). (*c*) Sexually naive male rats are reinforced by intromission with a female without reducing drive through ejaculation (Whalen, 1961). Aside from the question of secondary reinforcement, however, these stimuli may strike you as too "biological" to carry us far. Tastes and touches are likely to be loaded with affect. So let us look further.

2. Distance receptors. Mounting evidence shows that distance receptors can also supply unconditioned positive reinforcement. A striking example is *imprinting*, most clearly demonstrated in birds. As you all know, newly hatched goslings, ducklings, and chicks are prone to follow the first moving object they see, whether it is their mother or a red cube or Konrad Lorenz. What is more, their following increases for a while in vigor and persistence (Jaynes, 1956), and this implies positive reinforcement. But imprinting is so close to instinct that one tends to put it in a special category. Another example is *sensory reinforcement*. Mice and rats show a marked rise in rate of bar pressing when its only effect is

to turn on a weak light that has never been paired with need reduction (Kish, 1955; Marx, Henderson, & Roberts, 1955). Mice with four platforms to choose from prefer to step on the one that moves and clicks (Kish & Antonitis, 1956).

3. Manipulation and exploration. The rising flood of experiments on inquisitive behavior has been better publicized. Harlow's (1953b) monkeys needed no reward to induce them to pull mechanical puzzles apart. Köhler's genius ape Sultan had great difficulty in joining two sticks *to reach a banana*, but when Schiller (1957) gave adult chimpanzees two sticks *to play with*, 19 out of 20 joined them within 15 minutes. Butler's (1953) monkeys in solitary confinement learned which colored card would let them look out of the window. Nor are primates the only explorers. Since the work of Montgomery (1952) and Glanzer (1953) we know why rats so frequently alternate at a choice point. It is not to exercise a fresh set of muscles but to examine a fresh set of stimuli.

4. "Irrational" fears. Not all stimulus patterns are attractive, however; some appear to be aversive, even though never paired with pain. Rats hesitate to come out of holes into strange places (Welker, 1957). Some of Hebb's (1946) chimpanzees were thrown into a panic by the sight of a clay model of a chimpanzee's head. Melzack's (1952) dogs showed fear of a horse skin, especially if it was draped over a sofa.

5. Stimulus deprivation. Finally let me remind you of the recent studies, starting in Hebb's laboratory, on the effects of severe sensory restriction in human adults (cited by Fiske, 1961). Subjects were required to spend many consecutive hours in isolation, lying on a bed, with external stimulation reduced to a minimum. All bodily needs were provided for. Yet most subjects found the experience extremely unpleasant and some found it so distressing that they asked to be released. Ordinarily we find ways of relieving boredom, like hunger, before it becomes acute. If all outlets are cut off the drive may become almost intolerable.

Theory

Naturally these findings have released a wave of activity on the theoretical front. Harlow (1953a) launched a vigorous attack on the doctrine that traced all motives to metabolic drives. Woodworth (1958) now had fresh ammunition for his "behavior-primacy" theory: "that all behavior is directed primarily toward dealing with the environment [p. 102]." After years of observing primate behavior, Nissen (1954) held that every tissue has a primary drive to perform its function, the eyes to see, the brain to know. More recently White (1959) proposed that much of behavior is motivated solely by its *effectance* in changing the environment. These and other writers urge us to recognize that there are extraorganic needs as basic as those arising from the viscera.

It is interesting to see that behavior theorists are not alone in this movement. White noted a parallel trend in psychoanalytic theory. Freud's idea of a reality-oriented ego subservient to the erotic and aggressive drives of the id could be considered a counterpart of Hull's concept of habits energized by primitive drives. On the other hand, Hartmann's (1958) version of the ego, with its adaptive functions, developing independently of instinctual conflicts, is comparable with Woodworth's emphasis on interaction with the external environment. So, too, is Erikson's (1950) interpretation of the stages of development in childhood: The oral, anal, and phallic zones represent not so much successive outlets of the libido as means of relating to parent figures.

In behavior theory, as in psychoanalysis, the old guard has yielded ground but slowly. For all its defects, Hull's system contained a definite mechanism for the conditioning of drives to new stimuli and of new goals to drives. We cannot afford to discard an inadequate theory unless a more promising one can be found. What does the New Look have to offer? A cluster of theories has appeared; they overlap quite a bit and are more or less rudimentary, but they represent a healthy beginning. This is not the place to review them, especially since they have been treated elsewhere (Fiske & Maddi, 1961; Glanzer, 1958; White, 1959). Instead I should like to give you my present view of this matter, quite informally and without claiming originality or crediting all sources.

As we have seen, many of the activities of organisms appear to be aroused by and directed toward the environment with little help from the viscera. These activities may be grouped along several dimensions, that serve both to order the data and to identify possible mechanisms. They suggest, that is, a number of mediating processes—let us call them *exogenous motives*—each process or motive having a different function in dealing with the environment. The three dimensions I have in mind, with the motives and functions they subsume, are as follows:

1. A *perceptual-motor* dimension. Instead of lumping the exploratory behaviors I suggest that we distinguish between tendencies to explore and to manipulate the environment. An unfamiliar situation may move an organism to inspect it more closely, or novel objects may induce it to lift or squeeze or pound or rearrange them. We may call the first motive *curiosity* and assign it the function of *learning* the environment (Woodworth, 1958). The second motive is what White (1959) called *effectance*, and its function is to *control* the environment.

2. An *affective* dimension. No matter how we try to evade the issue, it is hard to pretend that animals do not find some perceptual experiences preferable to others. What experimental work there is (e.g., Pfaffmann, 1961; Schneirla, 1959; Warren, 1963; Young, 1955) confirms our homemade convictions. There is little doubt that cats prefer soft cushions to hard floors, warm hearths to cold baths, and head rubbing to tail pulling. To make the assumption explicit let us borrow from common usage the terms *attraction* and *aversion*, and assign to them the function of *improving* the environment.

3. A *quantitative* dimension. We have seen that extraordinary stimulus patterns,

such as a head without a body or a body without movement, may disturb a chimpanzee to the point of attack or flight. On the other hand, severely restricted or monotonous stimulation, if prolonged, can be a form of torture. A number of writers (Berlyne, 1963; Fiske & Maddi, 1961; Hebb, 1955; Leuba, 1955) have advocated the principle, more inclusive than drive reduction, of an optimal level of excitation. Such a concept could be a handy tool for explaining why rats turn on lights, monkeys open windows, children play, and adults visit museums—or why so many people read about space flights and so few volunteer.

There are two difficulties with the hypothesis, at least in some versions. For one thing, it implies a positive feedback that engineers tell us could cause serious trouble. For another, if reduced stimulation lowers the drive level below its optimum, whence comes the energy for the subject's increasing complaints? Berlyne (1963) has met these objections by assuming that below some middle value falling stimulation sends the arousal level *up*, not down.

However this question is settled, we may designate two more exogenous motives: *emotional shock*, aroused when stimulation exceeds the organism's tolerance; and *boredom*, produced when it falls below the level required for smooth functioning. Together the two motives serve to regulate the impact of the environment.

The foregoing treatment raises a basic question: Is there some property of stimulation common to the exogenous motives? Students of exploratory behavior attribute it to novelty, which they go on to define in different words. Information theorists would call it uncertainty (Dember & Earl, 1957) and behavior theorists, conflict (Berlyne, 1963), but both would agree that the crucial feature is a discrepancy between what is expected and what is observed. The same property takes care of the quantitative dimension, for if the discrepancy is too great the result is emotional shock, and if it is too little the result is boredom. As to effectance, its essential condition may also be reduced to a discrepancy,

in this case between the situation now and the situation after a response.

That leaves the affective dimension. With so many likes and dislikes to be accounted for, it is not obvious how a common factor of discrepancy could play much part. But the hypothesis is well worth testing. We are reminded of Schneirla's (1959) view that mild stimulation leads to approach and intense stimulation, to withdrawal. Directly pertinent, of course, is McClelland and Clark's (McClelland, Atkinson, Clark, & Lowell, 1953) theory of affect, in which pleasantness and unpleasantness depend on the discrepancy between a sensory quality and the adaptation level of the organism.

To give this picture a biological frame, let us assume that the central nervous system has the primary function of correlating stimuli and integrating appropriate responses. Its business is, as Woodworth (1958) put it, to "learn the environment." In the course of life it does so by interiorizing the external world, both as perceived and as altered by the organism's own reactions. Here I refer to what Bartlett (1932) called a *schema*; call it a life space (Lewin, 1936) if you prefer, or a situation-set (Woodworth, 1937), or a cognitive map (Tolman, 1948), or an image (Miller, Galanter, & Pribram, 1960). By any name, such a construct can be built and maintained only by a continuing transaction with the environment. To do its job the brain must have materials to work with, sensory input to organize, information to process (Glanzer, 1958). It is at critical points in this transaction that exogenous motives arise: when novel stimuli call for revision of the schema, or when radical incongruities threaten its stability, or when a routine conforms too closely to the schema for too long.

Implications for Functional Autonomy

It is time to return to Allport's problem to see if we are now in a better position to solve it. The question is whether exogenous motives have the properties Allport sought to embody in the concept of functional autonomy. Let us look at three such properties with that question in mind.

1. Functional autonomy stressed the importance of social motives; the need for approval, prestige, superiority, belonging, and the like. This is just what the concept of exogenous motives would lead us to expect. The most varied and consequently most exciting stimulation comes from other organisms. As far as we know, this may be true for all species. On the whole, though it is hard to give the statement precise meaning, social interactions probably become more important as we go up the phylogenetic scale. More is probably involved here than varied stimulation, but this factor should be recognized. In the long infancy and childhood of primates, mothers give nourishment, parent figures caress and slap, playmates provide reciprocal response. As the human child approaches maturity and no longer needs parental care, he finds himself no less dependent on other persons in his efforts to predict, to control, and to improve his environment. Backed by vast powers of reward and punishment, small wonder if social agents are the most compelling source of exogenous motivation in his life.

2. "Functionally autonomous motives" were by definition learned. They started as subgoals or instrumental acts and later were supposed to become ultimate objectives in their own right. No such transmutation is imputed to exogenous motives. On the contrary, there is enough evidence of their independence of hunger and fear (Harlow, 1953b; Montgomery, 1953, 1955; Schiller, 1957) to make it extremely unlikely that investigatory behavior was originally a search for food or security. But in another sense curiosity, effectance, and boredom *are* learned, or at least are products of learning. We have assumed that they are evoked, essentially, by some kind or degree of departure from a learned schema. Hebb (1949, 1955) emphasized this point in his discussion of fear, citing the infant chimpanzee frightened by seeing one familiar attendant wearing the equally familiar coat of another. So whenever an individual "builds a new wing" on his schema he sets the stage for a new interest, aversion, or indifference.

3. Functionally autonomous motives, as their name implies, were not subject to extinction. In this respect exogenous motives are fully qualified to take their place. Play is intrinsically rewarding; so is finding a bird's nest or solving an equation. Trips to the candy jar will cease when the jar is empty, but the desire for candy lives on. True, all the exogenous motives except boredom can be satiated to some extent as new learning reduces whatever discrepancy aroused them. So it might seem that we have merely exchanged one frailty for another. But the argument would hold only if we had exhausted the possible varieties of experience, an extremity seldom reached outside of concentration camps and zoos. Most of the earth's human inhabitants, cheerfully ignoring the specter of overpopulation, do not face psychic satiation as an immediate threat. Artists, composers, and advertisers continue to explore their media for fresh combinations to titillate or appall us. Scientists race one another into the unknown. Ordinary people find that even the companion of a lifetime is never completely predictable.

Summary

To summarize, we have seen that traditional drive theory could account for only a fraction of animal and human motivation. Its innate drives were too few and its acquired rewards too transitory. The concept of functional autonomy of motives did little more than stress the inadequacy of established doctrine.

We have noted the increasing acceptance of a class of exogenous motives, long recognized but ignored, concerned with attempts of organisms to predict and control their environments. We have adopted the view that an organism approaches and withdraws, explores and manipulates, as a function of specific differences between the present situation and the expectancies built into his schema of the world. I believe this view deserves consideration as a substitute for Allport's. In a literal sense exogenous motives *are* functionally autonomous; since they began that way, a *theory* of functional autonomy becomes superfluous.

A final word: At first glance terms like curiosity and effectance look like instincts revisited. At second glance I see no cause for alarm in this "return of the repressed." The instincts of old were stigmatized as barriers to research; today's "instincts" have opened up a new and exciting area to investigation. They give me a twinge of hope that we may have, if not a key, then the mold of a key to unlock one mystery of mind: the persistence and individuality of human motives.

References

Allport, G. W. The functional autonomy of motives. *Amer. J. Psychol.*, 1937, **50**, 141-156.

Bartlett, F. C. *Remembering: A study in experimental and social psychology.* New York: Macmillan, 1932.

Berlyne, D. E. Motivational problems raised by exploratory and epistemic behavior. In S. Koch (Ed.), *Psychology: A study of a science.* Vol. 5. New York: McGraw-Hill, 1963. Pp. 284-364.

Bühler, K. *Die geistige Entwicklung des Kindes.* (4th ed.) Jena: Gustav Fischer, 1924.

Butler, R. A. Discrimination learning by rhesus monkeys to visual-exploration motivation. *J. comp. physiol. Psychol.*, 1953, **46**, 95-98.

Dember, W. N., & Earl, R. W. Analysis of exploratory, manipulatory, and curiosity behaviors. *Psychol. Rev.*, 1957, **64**, 91-96.

Diamond, S. A neglected aspect of motivation. *Sociometry*, 1939, **2**, 77-85.

Erikson, E. H. *Childhood and society.* New York: Norton, 1950.

Fiske, D. W. Effects of monotonous and restricted stimulation. In D. W. Fiske & S. R. Maddi (Eds.), *Functions of varied experience.* Homewood, Ill.: Dorsey Press, 1961. Pp. 106-144.

Fiske, D. W., & Maddi, S. R. A conceptual framework. In D. W. Fiske & S. R. Maddi (Eds.), *Functions of varied experience.* Homewood, Ill.: Dorsey Press, 1961. Pp. 11-56.

Glanzer, M. The role of stimulus satiation in spontaneous alternation. *J. exp. Psychol.*, 1953, **45**, 387-393.

Glanzer, M. Curiosity, exploratory drive, and stimulus satiation. *Psychol. Bull.*, 1958, **55**, 302-315.

Hall, J. F. *Psychology of motivation.* Chicago: Lippincott, 1961.

Harlow, H. F. Mice, monkeys, men, and motives. *Psychol. Rev.*, 1953, **60**, 23-32. (a)

Harlow, H. F. Motivation as a factor in the acquisition of new responses. In, *Current theory and research in motivation: A symposium.* Lincoln: Univer. Nebraska Press, 1953. Pp. 24-49. (b)

Harlow, H. F., & Zimmerman, R. R. Affectional responses in the infant monkey. *Science*, 1959, **130**, 421-432.

Hartmann, H. *Ego psychology and the problem of adaptation.* New York: International Universities Press, 1958.

Hebb, D. O. On the nature of fear. *Psychol. Rev.*, 1946, **53**, 259-276.

Hebb, D. O. *The organization of behavior.* New York: Wiley, 1949.

Hebb, D. O. Drives and the C.N.S. (conceptual nervous system). *Psychol. Rev.*, 1955, **62**, 243-254.

Jaynes, J. Imprinting: The interaction of learned and innate behavior. *J. comp. physiol. Psychol.*, 1956, **49**, 201-206.

Kish, G. B. Learning when the onset of illumination is used as reinforcing stimulus. *J. comp. physiol. Psychol.*, 1955, **48**, 261-264.

Kish, G. B., & Antonitis, J. J. Unconditioned operant behavior in two homozygous strains of mice. *J. genet. Psychol.*, 1956, **88**, 121-129.

Leuba, C. Toward some integration of learning theories: The concept of optimal stimulation. *Psychol. Rep.*, 1955, **1**, 27-33.

Lewin, K. *Principles of topological psychology.* New York: McGraw-Hill, 1936.

McClelland, D. C. Functional autonomy of motives as an extinction phenomenon. *Psychol. Rev.*, 1942, **49**, 272-283.

McClelland, D. C., Atkinson, J. W., Clark, R. A., & Lowell, E. L. *The achievement motive.* New York: Appleton-Century, 1953.

Marx, M. H., Henderson, R. L., & Roberts, C. L. Positive reinforcement of the bar-pressing response by a light stimulus following dark operant pretests with no aftereffect. *J. comp. physiol. Psychol.*, 1955, **48**, 73-76.

Melzack, R. Irrational fears in the dog. *Canad. J. Psychol.*, 1952, **6**, 141-147.

Miller, G. A., Galanter, E., & Pribram, K. H. *Plans and the structure of behavior.* New York: Holt, 1960.

Miller, N. E. Studies of fear as an acquirable drive: I. Fear as motivation and fear-reduction as reinforcement in the learning of new responses. *J. exp. Psychol.*, 1948, **38**, 89-101.

Montgomery, K. C. A test of two explanations of spontaneous alternation. *J. comp. physiol. Psychol.*, 1952, **45**, 287-293.

Montgomery, K. C. The effect of the hunger and

thirst drives upon exploratory behavior. *J. comp. physiol. Psychol.*, 1953, **46**, 315-319.

Montgomery, K. C. The relation between fear induced by novel stimulation and exploratory behavior. *J. comp. physiol. Psychol.*, 1955, **48**, 254-260.

Murphy, G. *Personality: A biosocial approach to origins and structure.* New York: Harper, 1947.

Myers, J. L. Secondary reinforcement: A review of recent experimentation. *Psychol. Bull.*, 1958, **55**, 284-301.

Nissen, H. W. The nature of the drive as innate determinant of behavioral organization. In M. R. Jones (Ed.), *Nebraska symposium on motivation: 1954.* Lincoln: Univer. Nebraska Press, 1954. Pp. 281-321.

Pfaffman, C. The sensory and motivating properties of the sense of taste. In M. R. Jones (Ed.), *Nebraska symposium on motivation: 1961.* Lincoln: Univer. Nebraska Press, 1961. Pp. 71-108.

Rethlingshafer, D. Experimental evidence for functional autonomy of motives. *Psychol. Rev.*, 1943, **50**, 397-407.

Schiller, P. H. Innate motor action as a basis of learning. In C. H. Schiller (Ed.), *Instinctive behavior: The development of a modern concept.* New York: International Universities Press, 1957. Pp. 264-287.

Schlosberg, H., & Pratt, C. H. The secondary reward value of inaccessible food for hungry and satiated rats. *J. comp. physiol. Psychol.*, 1956, **49**, 149-152.

Schneirla, T. C. An evolutionary and developmental theory of biphasic processes underlying approach and withdrawal. In M. R. Jones (Ed.), *Nebraska symposium on motivation: 1959.* Lincoln: Univer. Nebraska Press, 1959. Pp. 1-42.

Sheffield, F. S., & Roby, T. B. Reward value of a non-nutritive sweet taste. *J. comp. physiol. Psychol.*, 1950, **43**, 471-481.

Skinner, B. F. *Science and human behavior.* New York: Macmillan, 1953.

Solomon, R. L., & Brush, E. S. Experimentally derived conceptions of anxiety and aversion. In M. R. Jones (Ed.), *Nebraska symposium on motivation: 1956.* Lincoln: Univer. Nebraska Press, 1956. Pp. 212-305.

Solomon, R. L. & Wynne, L. C. Traumatic avoidance learning: The principles of anxiety conservation and partial irreversibility. *Psychol. Rev.*, 1954, **61**, 353-385.

Tolman, E. C. Cognitive maps in rats and men. *Psychol. Rev.*, 1948, **55**, 189-208.

Warren, R. P. Preference aversion in mice to bitter substance. *Science*, 1963, **140**, 808-809.

Welker, W. I. "Free" versus "forced" exploration of a novel situation by rats. *Psychol. Rep.*, 1957, **3**, 95-108.

Whalen, R. E. Effects of mounting without intromission and intromission without ejaculation on sexual behavior and maze learning. *J. comp. physiol. Psychol.*, 1961, **54**, 409-415.

White, R. W. Motivation reconsidered: The concept of competence. *Psychol. Rev.*, 1959, **66**, 297-333.

Wike, E. L., Platt, J. R., & Knowles, J. M. The reward value of getting out of a starting box: Further extensions of Zimmerman's work. *Psychol. Rec.*, 1962, **12**, 397-400.

Wike, E. L., Platt, J. R., & Scott, D. Drive and secondary reinforcement: Further extensions of Zimmerman's work. *Psychol. Rec.*, 1963, **13**, 45-49.

Woodworth. R. S. *Dynamic psychology.* New York: Columbia Univer. Press, 1918.

Woodworth, R. S. Situation-and-goal set. *Amer. J. Psychol.*, 1937, **50**, 130-140.

Woodworth, R. S. Reënforcement of perception. *Amer. J. Psychol.*, 1947, **60**, 119-124.

Woodworth, R. S. *Dynamics of behavior.* New York: Holt, 1958.

Young, P. T. The role of hedonic processes in motivation. In M. R. Jones (Ed.), *Nebraska symposium on motivation: 1955.* Lincoln: Univer. Nebraska Press, 1955. Pp. 193-238.

Zimmerman, D. W. Sustained performance in rats based on secondary reinforcement. *J. comp. physiol. Psychol.*, 1959, **52**, 353-358.

Part Five

Cognitive Theory

9   George A. Kelly

George A. Kelly's (1905-1967) theory of constructive alternativism proposes that we look at man from a radically different angle and view him as "man the scientist" rather than as "man the beast" or "man the object." For Kelly, the most essential characteristic of man is that he *construes* his environment by giving meaning, or interpretation, to the social and physical events that surround him. It is by means of these *cognitive constructions* that he makes predictions about his world, using these predictions as guides to help himself act and move about in his world. Consequently, to understand man's behavior it is not nearly as important to know what pushes and pulls impinge upon him as it is to know what and how he thinks about these pushes and pulls.

In this view the concept of motivation (which is so central to almost all theories of personality) is rejected, and behavior is conceived of as being determined by how the individual *personally constructs* the world around him. The primary function of this personal construct system is to aid man in his attempt to predict and control events in his environment.

In the first of the following three papers Kelly argues against the continued use of the concept of motivation and delivers a short exposition of how "motivational phenomena" are dealt with by the theory of constructive alternativism.

Cognitive complexity represents the kinds of concepts that are central to Kelly's theory —concepts dealing with cognitive styles. This particular concept refers to the degree of differentiation in the system of constructs that is employed by an individual in understanding his world. Does the individual use only a few gross constructs or does he interpret his surroundings in terms of many finely delineated meanings? The research report by James Bieri demonstrates the use of Kelly's *Role Construct Repertory Test* (the "Rep Test"), an instrument devised specifically to measure a person's cognitive complexity-simplicity. The "Rep Test" procedure places more faith in the subject's ability (and willingness) to report the important determinants of his behavior than is usual in most measures of personality, but this faith is totally in keeping with Kelly's view of man as a being governed by thought and perceptions rather than by pushes and pulls of drives and stimuli. Thus, in Kelly's view the person who uses many constructs in describing people on the "Rep Test" is cognitively-complex, while the person who uses only a few constructs is cognitively-simple. It then follows from Kelly's theory that the cognitively-complex person should be more accurate than the cognitively-simple person in predicting the behavior of other people *and* in perceiving the behavior of others as being different from his own. Stated in another way, the cognitively-complex person (as opposed to the cognitively-simple person) is accurate not merely in predicting the behavior of others but also in perceiving the behavior of others as different from his own when in fact it is different.

The subjects of the Bieri experiment were 34 college undergraduates, 22 women and 12 men. The subjects were first administered the "Rep Test" and then, on the basis of their individual scores, were rank ordered along a dimension of cognitive complexity-simplicity. The higher the score, the more cognitively-complex the individual; the lower the score, the more cognitively-simple the individual. Since Kelly's theory predicts that cognitive complexity determines the accuracy of an individual's perceptions and predictions of the behavior of others, hypotheses generated by the theory can be tested by making predictions about the responses of the same individual on a second test. This second test, called the "Situations Questionnaire," describes various social situations which demand a response. Each of Bieri's subjects was instructed to select from various alternatives how he would respond to each situation. The questionnaire was also administered to classmates of each subject, and each of the 34 experimental subjects was asked to predict the responses of two of his classmates to the Situations Questionnaire. Scores on the two tests were then subjected to a correlation analysis. Bieri found that as predicted, cognitive complexity was *positively correlated* with a person's accuracy in predicting the behavior of others. This means that the higher the subject's score on the Rep Test, the more accurate were his predictions of classmates' responses on the Situations Questionnaire. Bieri also found that cognitive complexity

was *negatively correlated* with inaccurate perception. This means that the lower the subject's score on the Rep Test (cognitive simplicity), the less accurate were his predictions on the Situations Questionnaire. Thus, the theory is supported: cognitively-complex individuals are more accurate in predicting the behavior of others, and cognitively-simple persons tend to wrongly perceive similarities between themselves and others (*assimilative projection*).

Critics of Kelly feel that he has placed too great an emphasis upon cognitive variables in his theory. In the third selection of this chapter both Jerome S. Bruner and Carl R. Rogers take Kelly to task because he has ignored man's emotions in an attempt to do full justice to man's intellect. Rogers' criticism addresses itself to the method of psychotherapy that Kelly derives from his personality theory, and he deplores Kelly's inattention to the emotional relationship between therapist and patient. Though Bruner would certainly agree with Rogers' criticism of Kelly's psychotherapeutic approach, he levels his critical remarks at Kelly's personality theory *per se*, namely Kelly's failure to deal with what Bruner considers to be the essence of the human condition—man as an emotional being.

Suggestions for Further Reading

Kelly's definitive work is *The Psychology of Personal Constructs*, published in two volumes by Norton in 1955. Volume 1 presents his theory of personality, and volume 2 deals with his theory of psychotherapy. Both volumes are highly recommended to the serious student.

For consideration of research on Kelly's theory the student should consult the chapter by James Bieri in *Functions of Varied Experience*, edited by S. Maddi and D. W. Fiske (Dorsey Press, 1961), and the chapter by J. C. J. Bonarius in *Progress in Experimental Research*, edited by B. A. Maher (Academic Press, 1965).

Man's Construction of His Alternatives

George A. Kelly

Some twenty years or more ago a group of us were attempting to provide a traveling psychological clinic service to the schools in the State of Kansas. One of the principal sources of referrals was, of course, teachers. A teacher complained about a pupil. This word-bound complaint was taken as prima-facie grounds for kicking the bottle—I mean, examining the pupil. If we kicked the pupil around long enough and hard enough we could usually find some grounds to justify any teacher's complaint. This procedure was called in those days, just as it is still called, "diagnosis." It was in this manner that we conformed to the widely accepted requirements of the scientific method—we matched hypothesis with evidence and thus arrived at objective truth. In due course of time we became quite proficient in making something out of teachers' complaints, and we got so we could adduce some mighty subtle evidence. In short, we began to fancy ourselves as pretty sensitive clinicians.

Now, as every scientist and every clinician knows and is fond of repeating, treatment depends upon diagnosis. First you find out what is wrong—really wrong. Then you treat it. In treatment you have several alternatives; you can cut it out of the person, or you can remove the object toward which the child behaves improperly, or you can remove the child from the object, or you can alter the mechanism he employs to deal with the object, or you can compensate for the child's behavior by taking up a hobby in the basement, or teach the child to compensate

From G. A. Kelly, "Man's Construction of His Alternatives," in G. Lindzey (Ed.), *Assessment of Human Motives*, pp. 33-64. Copyright © 1958 by Gardner Lindzey. Reprinted by permission of Holt, Rinehart and Winston, Inc.

for it, or, if nothing better turns up, you can sympathize with everybody who has to put up with the youngster. But first, always first, you must kick the bottle to make it either confirm or reject your diagnostic hunches. So in Kansas we diagnosed pupils, and having impaled ourselves and our clients with our diagnoses, we cast about more or less frantically for ways of escape.

After perseverating in this classical stupidity—the treatment-depends-on-objective-diagnosis stupidity—for more years than we like to count, we began to suspect that we were being trapped in some pretty fallacious reasoning. We should have liked to blame the teachers for getting us off on the wrong track. But we had verified their complaints, hadn't we? We had even made "differential diagnoses," a way of choosing up sides in the name-calling games commonly played in clinical staff meetings.

Two things became apparent. The first was that the teacher's complaint was not necessarily something to be verified or disproved by the facts in the case, but was, rather, a construction of events in a way that, within the limits and assumptions of her personal construction system, made the most sense to her at the moment. The second was the realization that, in assuming diagnosis to be the independent variable and treatment the dependent variable, we had got the cart before the horse. It would have been better if we had made our diagnoses in the light of changes that do occur in children or that can be made to occur, rather than trying to shape those changes to independent but irrelevant psychometric measurements or biographical descriptions.

What we should like to make clear is that

both these difficulties have the same root—the traditional rationale of science that leads us to look for the locus of meaning of words in their objects of reference rather than in their subjects of origin. We hear a word and look to what is talked about rather than listen to the person who utters it. A teacher often complained that a child was "lazy." We turned to the child to determine whether or not she was right. If we found clear evidence that would support a hypothesis of laziness, then laziness was what it was—nothing else—and diagnosis was complete. Diagnosis having been accomplished, treatment was supposed to ensue. What does one do to cure laziness? While, of course, it was not quite as simple as this, the paradigm is essentially the one we followed.

Later we began to put "laziness" in quotes. We found that a careful appraisal of the teacher's construction system gave us a much better understanding of the meaning of the complaint. This, together with some further inquiry into the child's outlook, often enabled us to arrive at a vantage point from which we could deal with the problem in various ways. It occurred to us that we might, for example, help the teacher reconstrue the child in terms other than "laziness"—terms which gave her more latitude for exercising her own particular creative talents in dealing with him. Again, we might help the child deal with the teacher and in this way alleviate her discomfort. And, of course, there was sometimes the possibility that a broader reorientation of the child toward himself and school matters in general would prove helpful.

We have chosen the complaint of "laziness" as our example for a more special reason. "Laziness" happens to be a popular motivational concept that has widespread currency among adults who try to get others to make something out of themselves. Moreover, our disillusionment with motivational conceptualization in general started with this particular term and arose out of the specific context of school psychological services.

Our present position regarding human motives was approached by stages. First we realized that even when a hypothesis of lazi-

ness was confirmed there was little that could be said or done in consequence of such a finding. While this belief originally appeared to be less true of other motivational constructs, such as appetite or affection, in each instance the key to treatment, or even to differential prediction of outcomes, appeared to reside within the framework of other types of constructs.

Another observation along the way was that the teachers who used the construct of "laziness" were usually those who had widespread difficulties in their classrooms. Soon we reached the point in our practice where we routinely used the complaint of "laziness" as a point of departure for reorienting the teacher. It usually happened that there was more to be done with her than there was to be done with the child. So it was, also, with other complaints cast in motivational terms. In general, then, we found that the most practical approach to so-called motivational problems was to try to reorient the people who thought in such terms. Complaints about motivation told us much more about the complainants than it did about their pupils.

This generalization seems to get more and more support from our clinical experience. When we find a person who is more interested in manipulating people for his own purposes, we usually find him making complaints about their motives. When we find a person who is concerned about motives, he usually turns out to be one who is threatened by his fellow men and wants to put them in their place. There is no doubt that the construct of motives is widely used, but it usually turns out to be a part of the language of complaint about the behavior of other people. When it appears in the language of the client himself, as it does occasionally, it always—literally always—appears in the context of a kind of rationalization apparently designed to appease the therapist, not in the spontaneous utterances of the client who is in good rapport with his therapist.

One technique we came to use was to ask the teacher what the child would do if she did not try to motivate him. Often the teacher would insist that the child would do nothing

—absolutely nothing—just sit! Then we would suggest that she try a nonmotivational approach and let him "just sit." We would ask her to observe how he went about "just sitting." Invariably the teacher would be able to report some extremely interesting goings on. An analysis of what the "lazy" child did while he was being lazy often furnished her with her first glimpse into the child's world and provided her with her first solid grounds for communication with him. Some teachers found that their laziest pupils were those who could produce the most novel ideas; others, that the term "laziness" had been applied to activities that they had simply been unable to understand or appreciate.

It was some time later that we sat down and tried to formulate the general principles that undergirded our clinical experiences with teachers and their pupils. The more we thought about it, the more it seemed that our problems had always resolved themselves into questions of what the child would do if left to his own devices rather than questions about the amount of his motivation. These questions of what the child would do seemed to hinge primarily on what alternatives his personal construction of the situation allowed him to sense. While his construed alternatives were not necessarily couched in language symbols, nor could the child always clearly represent his alternatives, even to himself, they nonetheless set the outside limits on his day-to-day behavior. In brief, whenever we got embroiled in questions of motivation we bogged down, the teachers bogged down, and the children continued to aggravate everybody within earshot. When we forgot about motives and set about understanding the practical alternatives which children felt they were confronted by, the aggravations began to resolve themselves.

What we have said about our experiences with children also turned up in our psychotherapeutic experiences with adults. After months or, in some cases, years of psychotherapy with the same client, it did often prove to be possible to predict his behavior in terms of motives. This, of course, was gratifying; but predictive efficiency is not the only

criterion of a good construction, for one's understanding of a client should also point the way to resolving his difficulties. It was precisely at this point that motivational constructs failed to be of practical service, just as they had failed to be of service in helping children and teachers get along with each other. Always the psychotherapeutic solution turned out to be a reconstruing process, not a mere labeling of the client's motives. To be sure, there were clients who never reduced their reconstructions to precise verbal terms, yet still were able to extricate themselves from vexing circumstances. And there were clients who got along best under conditions of support and reassurance with a minimum of verbal structuring on the part of the therapist. But even in these cases, the solutions were not worked out in terms of anything that could properly be called motives, and the evidence always pointed to some kind of reconstruing process that enabled the client to make his choice between new sets of alternatives not previously open to him in a psychological sense.

Approach to a New Psychological Theory

Now, perhaps, it is time to launch into the third phase of our discussion. We started by making some remarks of a philosophical nature and from there we dropped back to recall some of the practical experiences that first led us to question the construct of motivation. Let us turn now to the formulation of psychological theory and to the part that motivation plays in it.

A half-century ago William McDougall published his little volume *Physiological Psychology* (1905). In the opening pages he called his contemporary psychologists' attention to the fact that the concept of *energy* had been invented by physicists in order to account for movement of objects, and that some psychologists had blandly assumed that they too would have to find a place for it in their systems. While McDougall was to go on in his lifetime to formulate a theoretical system based on instinctual drives and thus, it seems to us, failed to heed his own warning, what he said about the construct of energy still provides us with a springboard for expounding a quite different theoretical position.

The physical world presented itself to preclassical man as a world of solid objects. He saw matter as an essentially inert substance, rather than as a complex of related motion. His axes of reference were spatial dimensions —length, breadth, depth—rather than temporal dimensions. The flow of time was something he could do very little about, and he was inclined to take a passive attitude toward it. Even mass, a dimension which lent itself to more dynamic interpretations, was likely to be construed in terms of size equivalents.

Classical man, as he emerged upon the scene, gradually became aware of motion as something that had eluded his predecessors. But for him motion was still superimposed upon nature's rocks and hills. Inert matter was still the phenomenon, motion was only the epiphenomenon. Action, vitality, and energy were the breath of life that had to be breathed into the inertness of nature's realities. In Classical Greece this thought was magnificently expressed in new forms of architecture and sculpture that made the marble quarried from the Greek islands reach for the open sky, or ripple like a soft garment in the warm Aegean breeze. But motion, though an intrinsic feature of the Greek idiom, was always something superimposed, something added. It belonged to the world of the ideal and not to the hard world of reality.

The Construct of Motivation Implies That Man Is Essentially Inert

Today our modern psychology approaches its study of man from the same vantage point. He is viewed as something static in his natural state, hence something upon which motion, life, and action have to be superimposed. In substance he is still perceived as like the marble out of which the Greeks carved their statues of flowing motion and ethereal grace. He comes alive, according to most of the psychology of our day, only through the application of special enlivening forces. We call these forces by such names as

"motives," "incentives," "needs," and "drives." Thus, just as the physicists had to erect the construct of energy to fill the gap left by their premature assumption of a basically static universe, so psychology has had to burden itself with a construct made necessary by its inadequate assumption about the basic nature of man.

We now arrive at the same point in our theoretical reasoning at which we arrived some years earlier in appraising our clinical experience. In each instance we find that efforts to assess human motives run into practical difficulty because they assume inherently static properties in human nature. It seems appropriate, therefore, at this juncture to reexamine our implied assumptions about human nature. If we then decide to base our thinking upon new assumptions we can next turn to the array of new constructs that may be erected for the proper elaboration of the fresh theoretical position.

In This Theory the Construct of Motivation Is Redundant in Explaining Man's Activity

There are several ways in which we can approach our problem. We could, for example, suggest to ourselves, as we once suggested to certain unperceptive classroom teachers, that we examine what a person does when he is not being motivated. Does he turn into some kind of inert substance? If not— and he won't—should we not follow up our observation with a basic assumption that any person is motivated, motivated for no other reason than that he is alive? Life itself could be defined as a form of process or movement. Thus, in designating man as our object of psychological inquiry, we should be taking it for granted that movement is an essential property of his being, not something that has to be accounted for separately. We should be talking about a form of movement—man— not something that has to be motivated.

Pursuant to this line of reasoning, motivation ceases to be a special topic of psychology. Nor, on the other hand, can it be said that motivation constitutes the whole of psychological substance, although from the standpoint of another theoretical system it might be proper to characterize our position so. *Within our system*, however, the term "motivation" can appear only as a redundancy.

How can we further characterize this stand with respect to motivation? Perhaps this will help: Motivational theories can be divided into two types, push theories and pull theories. Under push theories we find such terms as drive, motive, or even stimulus. Pull theories use such constructs as purpose, value, or need. In terms of a well-known metaphor, these are the pitchfork theories on the one hand and the carrot theories on the other. But our theory is neither of these. Since we prefer to look to the nature of the animal himself, ours is probably best called a jackass theory.

Thus far our reasoning has led us to a point of view from which the construct of "human motives" appears redundant—redundant, that is, as far as accounting for human action is concerned. But traditional motivational theory is not quite so easily dismissed. There is another issue that now comes to the fore. It is the question of what directions human actions can be expected to take.

The Construct of Motivation Is Not Needed to Explain Directionality of Movement

We must recognize that the construct of "motive" has been traditionally used for two purposes; to account for the fact that the person is active rather than inert, and also for the fact that he chooses to move in some directions rather than in others. It is not surprising that, in the past, a single construct has been used to cover both issues; for if we take the view that the human organism is set in motion only by the impact of special forces, it is reasonable to assume also that those forces must give it direction as well as impetus. But now, if we accept the view that the organism is already in motion simply by virtue of its being alive, then we have to ask ourselves if we do not still require the services of "motives" to explain the directionality of the

movement. Our answer to this question is "No." Let us see why.

Here, as before, we turn first to our experiences as a clinician to find the earliest inklings of a new theoretical position. Specifically, we turn to experiences in psychotherapy.

Clinical Experience. When a psychologist undertakes psychotherapy with a client he can approach his task from any one of a number of viewpoints. He can, as many do, devote most of his attention to a kind of running criticism of the mistakes the client makes, his fallacies, his irrationalities, his misperceptions, his resistances, his primitive mechanisms. Or, as others do, he can keep measuring his client; so much progress today, so much loss yesterday, gains in this respect, relapses in that. If he prefers, he can keep his attention upon his own role, or the relation between himself and his client, with the thought that it is not actually given to him ever to know how the client's mind works, nor is it his responsibility to make sure that it works correctly, but only that he should provide the kind of warm and responsive human setting in which the client can best solve his own problems.

Any one of these approaches may prove helpful to the client. But there is still another approach that, from our personal experience, can prove most helpful to the client and to the psychotherapist. Instead of assuming, on the one hand, that the therapist is obliged to bring the client's thinking into line, or, on the other, that the client will mysteriously bring his own thinking into line once he has been given the proper setting, we can take the stand that client and therapist are conjoining in an exploratory venture. The therapist assumes neither the position of judge nor that of the sympathetic bystander. He is sincere about this; he is willing to learn along with his client. He is the client's fellow researcher who seeks first to understand, then to examine, and finally to assist the client in subjecting alternatives to experimental test and revision.

The psychologist who goes at psychotherapy this way says to himself, "I am about to have the rare opportunity of examining the inner workings of that most intricate creation in all of nature, a human personality. While many scholars have written about the complexity of this human personality, I am now about to see for myself how one particular personality functions. Moreover, I am about to have an experienced colleague join me in this venture, the very person whose personality is to be examined. He will help me as best he can, but there will be times when he cannot help, when he will be as puzzled and confused as I am."

When psychotherapy is carried out in this vein the therapist, instead of asking himself continually whether his client is right or not, or whether he himself is behaving properly, peers intently into the intimate psychological processes which the unusual relation permits him to see. He inquires rather than condemns. He explores rather than rejects or approves. How does this creature, man, actually think? How does he make choices that seem to be outside the conventionalized modes of thought? What is the nature of his logic—quite apart from how logicians define logic? How does he solve his problems? What ideas does he express for which he has no words?

Conventional Psychological Concepts. Out of this kind of experience with psychotherapy we found ourselves becoming increasingly impatient with certain standard psychotherapeutic concepts. "Insight" was one of the first to have a hollow sound. It soon became apparent that, in any single case, there was any number of different possible insights that could be used to structure the same facts, all of them more or less true. As one acquires a variety of psychotherapeutic experience he begins to be amazed by how sick or deviant some clients can be and still surmount their difficulties, and how well or insightful others can be and yet fall apart at every turn. Certainly the therapist who approaches his task primarily as a scientist is soon compelled to concede that unconventional insights often work as well or better than the standardized

insights prescribed by some current psychological theory.

Another popular psychotherapeutic concept that made less and less sense was "resistance." To most therapists resistance is a kind of perverse stubbornness in the client. Most therapists are annoyed by it. Some accuse the client of resisting whenever their therapeutic efforts begin to bog down. But our own experiences with resistance were a good deal like our experiences with laziness—they bespoke more of the therapist's perplexity than of the client's rebellion. If we had been dependent entirely on psychotherapeutic experiences with our own clients we might have missed this point; it would have been too easy for us, like the others, to blame our difficulties on the motives of the client. But we were fortunate enough to have opportunities also for supervising therapists, and here, because we were not ourselves quite so intimately involved, it was possible to see resistance in terms of the therapist's naïveté.

When the so-called resistance was finally broken through—to use a psychotherapist's idiom—it seemed proper, instead of congratulating ourselves on our victory over a stubborn client, to ask ourselves and our client just what had happened. There were, of course, the usual kinds of reply, "I just couldn't say that to you then," or "I knew I was being evasive, but I just didn't know what to do about it," etc.

But was this stubbornness? Some clients went further and expressed it this way, "To have said then what I have said today would not have meant the same thing." This may seem like a peculiar remark, but from the standpoint of personal construct theory it makes perfectly good sense. A client can express himself only within the framework of his construct system. Words alone do not convey meaning. What this client appears to be saying is this: When he has the constructs for expressing himself, the words that he uses ally themselves with those constructs and they make sense when he utters them. To force him to utter words which do not parallel his constructs, or to mention events which are precariously construed, is to plunge him into a chaos of personal nonsense, however much it may clarify matters for the therapist. In short, our experience with psychotherapy led us to believe that it was not orneriness that made the client hold out so-called important therapeutic material, but a genuine inability to express himself in terms that would not appear, from his point of view, to be utterly misconstrued.

Perhaps these brief recollections of therapeutic experiences will suffice to show how we began to be as skeptical of motives as direction-finding devices as we were skeptical of them as action-producing forces. Over and over again, it appeared that our clients were making their choices, not in terms of the alternatives we saw open to them, but in terms of the alternatives they saw open to them. It was their network of constructions that made up the daily mazes that they ran, not the pure realities that appeared to us to surround them. To try to explain a temper tantrum or an acute schizophrenic episode in terms of motives only was to miss the whole point of the client's system of personal dilemmas. The child's temper tantrum is, for him, one of the few remaining choices left to him. So for the psychotic, with his pathways structured the way they are in his mind, he has simply chosen from a particular limited set of alternatives. How else can he behave? His other alternatives are even less acceptable.

We have not yet fully answered the question of explaining directionality. We have described only the extent to which our therapeutic experiences led us to question the value of motives. But, after all, we have not yet found, from our experience, that clients do what they do because there is nothing else they can do. We have observed only that they do what they do because their choice systems are definitely limited. But even by this line of reasoning, they do have choices, often bad ones, to be sure, but still choices. So our question of directionality of behavior is narrowed down by the realization that a person's behavior must take place within the limited dimensions of his personal construct system.

Yet, as long as his system does have dimensions, it must provide him with some sets of alternatives. And so long as he has some alternatives of his own making we must seek to explain why he chooses some of them in preference to others.

"Neurotic Paradox." Before we leave off talking about clinical experience and take up the next and most difficult phase of our discussion, it will do no harm to digress for a few moments and talk about the so-called neurotic paradox. O. H. Mowrer has described this as "the paradox of behavior which is at one and the same time self-perpetuating and self-defeating" (1950, p. 486). We can state the paradox in the form of a question, "Why does a person sometimes persist in unrewarding behavior?" Reinforcement theory finds this an embarrassing question, while contiguity theory, to which some psychologists have turned in their embarrassment, finds the converse question equally embarrassing, "Why does a person sometimes not persist in unrewarding behavior?"

From the standpoint of the psychology of personal constructs, however, there is no neurotic paradox. Or, to be more correct, the paradox is the jam which certain learning theorists get themselves into rather than the jam their clients get themselves into. Not that clients stay out of jams, but they have their own ingenious ways of getting into them and they need no assistance from us psychologists. To say it another way, the behavior of a so-called neurotic client does not seem paradoxical to him until he tries to rationalize it in terms his therapist can understand. It is when he tries to use his therapist's construction system that the paradox appears. Within the client's own limited construction system he may be faced with a dilemma but not with a paradox.

Perhaps this little digression into the neurotic paradox will help prepare the ground for the next phase of our discussion. Certainly it will help if it makes clear that the criteria by which a person chooses between the alternatives, in terms of which he has structured his world, are themselves cast in terms of constructions. Not only do men construe their alternatives, but they construe also criteria for choosing between them. For us psychologists who try to understand what is going on in the minds of our clients it is not as simple as saying that the client will persist in rewarding behavior, or even that he will vacillate between immediate and remote rewards. We have to know what this person construes to be a reward, or, still better, we can bypass such motivational terms as "reward," which ought to be redefined for each new client and on each new occasion, and abstract from human behavior some psychological principle that will transcend the tedious varieties of personalized motives.

If we succeed in this achievement we may be able to escape that common pitfall of so-called objective thinking, the tendency to reify our constructs and treat them as if they were not constructs at all, but actually all the things that they were originally only intended to construe. Such a formulation may even make it safer for us to write operational definitions for purposes of research, without becoming lost in the subject-predicate fallacy. In clinical language it may enable us to avoid concretistic thinking—the so-called brain-injured type of thinking—which is what we call operationalism when we happen to find it in a client who is frantically holding on to his mental faculties.

Now we have been procrastinating long enough. Let us get on to the most difficult part of our discussion. We have talked about experiences with clients who, because they hoped we might be of help to them, honored us with invitations to the rare intimacies of their personal lives and ventured to show us the shadowy processes by which their worlds were ordered. We turned aside briefly in our discussion to talk about the neurotic paradox, hoping that what we could point to there would help the listener anticipate what needed to come next. Now we turn again to a more theoretical form of discourse.

Man Links the Past with the Future—Anticipation

If man, as the psychologist is to see him,

exists primarily in the dimensions of time, and only secondarily in the dimensions of space, then the terms which we erect for understanding him ought to take primary account of this view. If we want to know why man does what he does, then the terms of our whys should extend themselves in time rather than in space; they should be events rather than things; they should be mileposts rather than destinations. Clearly, man lives in the present. He stands firmly astride the chasm that separates the past from the future. He is the only connecting link between these two universes. He, and he only, can bring them into harmony with each other. To be sure, there are other forms of existence that have belonged to the past and, presumably, will also belong to the future. A rock that has rested firm for ages may well exist in the future also, but it does not link the past with the future. In its mute way it links only past with past. It does not anticipate; it does not reach out both ways to snatch handfuls from each of the two worlds in order to bring them together and subject them to the same stern laws. Only man does that.

If this is the picture of man, as the psychologist envisons him—man, a form of movement; man, always quick enough, as long as he is alive, to stay astride the darting present —then we cannot expect to explain him either entirely in terms of the past or entirely in terms of the future. We can explain him, psychologically, only as a link between the two. Let us, therefore, formulate our basic postulate for a psychological theory in the light of this conjunctive vision of man. We can say it this way: *A person's processes are psychologically channelized by the ways in which he anticipates events.*

The Nature of Personal Constructs

Taking this proposition as a point of departure, we can quickly begin to sketch a theoretical structure for psychology that will, undoubtedly, turn out to be novel in many unexpected ways. We can say next that man develops his way of anticipating events by construing, by scratching out his channels of thought. Thus he builds his own maze. His runways are the constructs he forms, each a two-way street, each essentially a pair of alternatives between which he can choose.

Another person, attempting to enter this labyrinth, soon gets lost. Even a therapist has to be led patiently back and forth through the system, sometimes for months on end, before he can find his way without the client's help, or tell to what overt behavior each passageway will lead. Many of the runways are conveniently posted with word signs, but most of them are dark, cryptically labeled, or without any word signs at all. Some are rarely traveled. Some the client is reluctant to disclose to his guest. Often therapists lose patience and prematurely start trying to blast shortcuts in which both they and their clients soon become trapped. But worst of all, there are therapists who refuse to believe that they are in the strangely structured world of man; they insist only that the meanderings in which they are led are merely the play of whimsical motives upon their blind and helpless client.

Our figure of speech should not be taken too literally. The labyrinth is conceived as a network of constructs, each of which is essentially an abstraction and, as such, can be picked up and laid down over many different events in order to bring them into focus and clothe them with personal meaning. Moreover, the constructs are subject to continual revision, although the complex interdependent relation between constructs in the system often makes it precarious for the person to revise one construct without taking into account the disruptive effect upon major segments of the system.

In our efforts to communicate the notion of a personal construct system we repeatedly run into difficulty because listeners identify personal constructs with the classic view of a concept. Concepts have long been known as units of logic and are treated as if they existed independently of any particular person's psychological processes. But when we use the notion of "construct" we have nothing of this sort in mind; we are talking about a psychological process in a living person. Such a construct has, for us, no existence independent of the person whose thinking it characterizes. The question of whether it is logical or not

has no bearing on its existence, for it is wholly a psychological rather than a logical affair. Furthermore, since it is a psychological affair, it has no necessary allegiance to the verbal forms in which classical concepts have been traditionally cast. The personal construct we talk about bears no essential relation to grammatical structure, syntax, words, language, or even communication; nor does it imply consciousness. It is simply a psychologically construed unit for understanding human processes.

We must confess that we often run into another kind of difficulty. In an effort to understand what we are talking about, a listener often asks if the personal construct is an intellectual affair. We find that, willy-nilly, we invite this kind of question because of our use of such terms as thought and thinking. Moreover, we are speaking in the terms of a language system whose words stand for traditional divisions of mental life, such as "intellectual."

Let us answer this way. A construct owes no special allegiance to the intellect, as against the will or the emotions. In fact, we do not find it either necessary or desirable to make that classic trichotomous division of mental life. After all, there is so much that is "emotional" in those behaviors commonly called "intellectual," and there is so much "intellectualized" contamination in typical "emotional" upheavals that the distinction becomes merely a burdensome nuisance. For some time now we have been quite happy to chuck all these notions of intellect, will, and emotion; so far, we cannot say we have experienced any serious loss.

Now we are at the point in our discourse where we hope our listeners are ready to assume, either from conviction or for the sake of argument, that man, from a psychological viewpoint, makes of himself a bridge between past and future in a manner that is unique among creatures, that, again from a psychological viewpoint, his processes are channelized by the personal constructs he erects in order to perform this function, and, finally, that he organizes his constructs into a personal system that is no more conscious than it is unconscious and no more intellectual than it is emotional. This personal construct system provides him with both freedom of decision and limitation of action—freedom, because it permits him to deal with the meanings of events rather than forces him to be helplessly pushed about by them, and limitation, because he can never make choices outside the world of alternatives he has erected for himself.

The Choice Corollary

We have left to the last the question of what determines man's behavioral choices between his self-construed alternatives. Each choice that he makes has implications for his future. Each turn of the road he chooses to travel brings him to a fresh vantage point from which he can judge the validity of his past choices and elaborate his present pattern of alternatives for choices yet to be made. Always the future beckons him and always he reaches out in tremulous anticipation to touch it. He lives in anticipation; we mean this literally; *he lives in anticipation!* His behavior is governed, not simply by *what* he anticipates—whether good or bad, pleasant or unpleasant, self-vindicating or self-confounding—but by *where* he believes his choices will place him in respect to the remaining turns in the road. If he chooses this fork in the road, will it lead to a better vantage point from which to see the road beyond or will it be the one that abruptly brings him face-to-face with a blank wall?

What we are saying about the criteria of man's choices is not a second theoretical assumption, added to our basic postulate to take the place of the traditional beliefs in separate motives, but is a natural outgrowth of that postulate—a corollary to it. Let us state it so. *A person chooses for himself that alternative in a dichotomized construct through which he anticipates the greater possibility for extension and definition of his system.*

Such a corollary appears to us to be implicit in our postulate that a person's processes are psychologically channelized by the ways in which he anticipates events. For the sake of simplification we have skipped over the formal statement of some of the interven-

ing corollaries of personal construct theory: the corollary that deals with construing, the corollary that deals with the construct system, and the corollary that deals with the dichotomous nature of constructs. But we have probably covered these intervening ideas well enough in the course of our exposition.

What we are saying in this crucial *Choice Corollary* gives us the final ground for dismissing motivation as a necessary psychological construct. It is that if a person's processes are channelized by the ways in which he anticipates events he will make his choices in such a way that he apparently defines or extends his system of channels, for this must necessarily be his comprehensive way of anticipating events.

At the risk of being tedious, let us recapitulate again. We shall be brief. Perhaps we can condense the argument into three sentences. First we saw no need for a closet full of motives to explain the fact that man was active rather than inert; there was no sense in assuming that he was inert in the first place. And now we see no need to invoke a concept of motives to explain the directions that his actions take; the fact that he lives in anticipation automatically takes care of that. Result: no catalogue of motives to clutter up our system and, we hope, a much more coherent psychological theory about living man.

Footnotes

At this point our discourse substantially concludes itself. What we have left to offer are essentially footnotes that are intended to be either defensive or provocative, perhaps both. Questions naturally arise the moment one begins to pursue the implications of this kind of theorizing. One can scarcely take more than a few steps before one begins to stumble over a lot of ancient landmarks that remain to serve no purpose except to get in the way. Perhaps it is only fair that we spotlight some of these relics in the hope of sparing our listeners some barked intellectual shins.

Is this a dynamic theory? This is the kind

of question our clinical colleagues are likely to ask. We are tempted to give a flat "No" to that question. No, this is not what is ordinarily called a dynamic theory; it intentionally parts company with psychoanalysis, for example—respectfully, but nonetheless intentionally. However, if what is meant by a "dynamic theory" is a theory that envisions man as active rather than inert, then this is an all-out dynamic theory. It is so dynamic that it does not need any special system of dynamics to keep it running! What must be made clear, or our whole discourse falls flat on its face, is that we do not envision the behavior of man in terms of the external forces bearing upon him; that is a view we are quite ready to leave to the dialectic materialists and to some of their unwitting allies who keep chattering about scientific determinism and other subject-predicate forms of nonsense.

Is this rationalism revisited? We anticipated this question at the beginning of our discussion. We are tempted to answer now by claiming that it is one of the few genuine departures from rationalism, perhaps the first in the field of psychology. But here is a tricky question, because it is not often clear whether one is referring to extrapsychological rationalism or to an essential-psychological rationalism that is often imperfect when judged by classical standards and often branded as "irrationality," or whether the question refers simply to any verbalized structure applied to the behavior of man in an effort to understand him.

Certainly ours is not an extrapsychological rationalism. Instead, it frankly attempts to deal with the essential rationalism that is actually demonstrated in the thinking of man. In doing so it deals with what is sometimes called the world of the irrational and nonrational.

But, in another sense, our interpretation, in its own right and quite apart from its subject matter, is a psychologist's rationale designed to help him understand how man comes to believe and act the way he does. Such a rationale approaches its task the way it does, not because it believes that logic has to be as it is because there is no other way for it to be,

not because it believes that man behaves the way he does because there is no other way for him to react to external determining forces, nor even because the rationale's own construction of man provides him with no alternatives, but, rather, because we have the hunch that the way to understand all things, even the ramblings of a regressed schizophrenic client, is to construe them so that they will be made predictable. To some persons this approach spells rationalism, pure and simple, probably because they are firmly convinced that the nether world of man's motives is so hopelessly irrational that anyone who tries to understand that world sensibly must surely be avoiding contact with man as he really is.

Finally, there is the most important question of all; how does the system work? That is a topic to be postponed to another time and occasion. Of course, we think it does work. We use it in psychotherapy and in psychodiagnostic planning for psychotherapy. We also find a place for it in dealing with many of the affairs of everyday life. But there is no place here for the recitation of such details. We hope only that, so far as we have gone, we have been reasonably clear, and a mite provocative, for only by being both clear and provocative can we give our listeners something they can set their teeth into.

Addendum

The invitation to prepare this paper was accompanied by a list of nine issues upon which, it was presumed, would hinge the major differences to be found among any group of motivational theorists. On the face of it such a list seems altogether fair. But one can scarcely pose even one such question, much less nine of them, without exacting hostages to his own theoretical loyalties. And if a correspondent answers in the terminology of the questions posed, he in turn immediately bases his discourse on the assumptions of an alien theory. Once he has done that he will, sooner or later, have to talk as if the differences he seeks to emphasize are merely semantical.

Yet the nine questions need to be met, if not head on, at least candidly enough to be disposed of.

How important are conscious as opposed to unconscious motives in understanding human behavior? We do not use the conscious-unconscious dichotomy, but we do recognize that some of the personal constructs a person seeks to subsume within his system prove to be fleeting or elusive. Sometimes this is because they are loose rather than tight, as in the first phase of the creative cycle. Sometimes it is because they are not bound by the symbolisms of words or other acts. But of this we are sure, if they are important in a person's life, it is a mistake to say they are unconscious or that he is unaware of them. Every day he experiences them, often all too poignantly; the point is that he cannot put his finger on them or tell for sure whether they are at the spot the therapist has probed for them.

When does a person fall back upon such loosened thinking? Or when does he depend upon constructs that are not easily subsumed? Ordinarily when one is confronted with confusion (anxiety) the first tendency is to tighten up; but beyond some breaking point there is a tendency to discard tight constructions and fall back upon constructs that are loose or which have no convenient symbolizations. It is in the human crises that it becomes most important to understand the nature of a person's secondary lines of defense.

What is the relative importance of direct as opposed to indirect techniques for assessing human motives? Let us change the word "motives" to "constructs." They are not equivalent, of course, but "motives" play no part in our system, whereas "constructs" do. If we ask a person to express his constructs in words, and we take his words literally, then we may say, perhaps, that we are assessing his constructs "directly." If we assume that his words and acts have less patent meanings and that we must construe him in terms of a background understanding of his construct system, shall we say that we have used a more "indirect" technique? But is anything more

direct than this? Perhaps the method that takes literal meanings for granted is actually more indirect, for it lets the dictionary intervene between the client and the psychologist. If time permits, we vote for seeking to understand the person in the light of his personal construct system.

Is it essential in assessing motives to provide some appraisal of the ego processes, directive mechanisms, or cognitive controls that intervene between the motive and its expression? "Ego" is a psychoanalytic term; we still don't know what it means. "Cognitive" is a classical term that implies a natural cleavage between psychological processes, a cleavage that confuses everything and clarifies nothing; let's forget it. The notion of a "motive," on the one hand, and "its expression," on the other, commits one to the view that what is expressed is not the person but the motivational gremlins that have possessed him. Finally, if the term "directive mechanisms" is taken in a generic sense, then we can say that we see these as in the form of constructs formulated by the person himself and in terms of which he casts his alternatives. What we need to assess are these personal constructs, if we wish to understand what a person is up to.

In assessing human motives how important is it to specify the situational context within which the motives operate? Each of a client's constructs has a limited range of convenience in helping him deal with his circumstances. Beyond that range the construct is irrelevant as far as he is concerned. This is the point that was so long obscured by the law of the excluded middle. Knowledge, therefore, of the range of convenience of any personal construct formulated by a client is essential to an understanding of the behavior he structures by that construct.

How necessary is knowledge of the past in the assessment of contemporary motivation? It is not absolutely necessary but it is often convenient. Events of the past may disclose the kind of constructions that the client has used; presumably he may use them again. Events of the past, taken in conjunction with the anticipations they confirmed at the time, may indicate what has been proved to his satisfaction. Again, events of the past may indicate what the client has had to make sense out of, and thus enable us to surmise what constructions he may have had to formulate in order to cope with his circumstances. Finally, since some clients insist on playing the part of martyrs to their biographical destinies, therapy cannot be concluded successfully until their therapists have conducted them on a grand tour of childhood recollections.

At this time is the area of motivation more in need of developing precise and highly objective measures of known motives or identifying significant new motivational variables? Neither.

In attempting to understand human motivation is it advisable at present to focus upon one or a small number of motivational variables, or should an effort be made to appraise a wide array of variables? Human impetus should be assumed as a principle rather than treated as a variable or group of variables.

What is the relative importance of detailed studies of individual cases as compared to carefully controlled experimental research and large-scale investigations? All three have their place in the course of developing psychological understanding. The detailed case studies provide excellent grounds for generating constructs. Experimental research, in turn, permits us to test out constructs in artificial isolation. Large-scale investigations help us put constructs into a demographic framework.

Is there a unique and important contribution to the understanding of human motives that can be made at present through the medium of comparative or lower-animal studies that cannot be duplicated by means of investigations utilizing human subjects? No.

References

Kelly, G. A. *The psychology of personal constructs.* New York: Norton, 1955.

McDougall, W. *Physiological psychology.* London: Dent, 1905.

Mowrer, O. H. *Learning theory and personality dynamics.* New York: Ronald, 1950.

Cognitive Complexity – Simplicity and Predictive Behavior

James Bieri

A common focus of problems in current research has been concerned with what is variously called social perception (Gage, 1953; Scodel and Mussen, 1953), interpersonal perception (Bieri, 1953b; Lundy and Bieri, 1952), understanding others (Cronbach, 1954), empathy (Dymond, 1949), or social sensitivity (Bender and Hastorf, 1933). In these studies, social perceptions often are defined operationally as responses on a questionnaire or rating scale which represent the *predictions* of how the subject (*S*) felt some other individual responded to the questionnaire or scale. By comparing these predictions with *S*'s own responses and with the other's own responses, certain hypotheses about the accuracy of the perceptions are tested. The multiplicity of findings in this area have been reviewed and discussed elsewhere (Bruner and Tagiuri, 1954). The purpose of this paper is to present a tentative theoretical framework into which these diverse empirical findings can be placed. From this framework, several predictions will be evolved, and empirical evidence relative to these predictions will be presented.

It is suggested that what is involved in the studies cited above is primarily the *predictive accuracy* of an individual's behavior. That is, one perceives another accurately to the extent that his predictions of the other's behavior are accurate. The position taken here is that predictive behavior, and its accuracy or inaccuracy, may be fruitfully viewed as a function of certain behavioral variables within a conception of personality structure. In this sense, predictive behavior is akin to expectancy

behavior, as postulated in certain theories of learning and personality (Rotter, 1954).

In the present discussion, those aspects of personality functioning which set the necessary conditions for predictive behavior are construed within a general perceptual or cognitive framework. Following the theoretical orientation developed by G. A. Kelly (1955), it is assumed that a basic characteristic of human behavior is its movement in the direction of greater predictability of an individual's interpersonal environment. It is further assumed that each individual possesses a system of constructs for perceiving his social world. These constructs are invoked and form the basis for making predictions. The constructs composing the system are the characteristic modes of perceiving persons in the individual's environment. Thus, under the supposition that person X is perceived as "hostile" (construct), an individual may make one kind of prediction about his behavior, while if he were perceived as "friendly," another kind of prediction might be made. The relative success or failure of these predictions are postulated as affecting the constructs upon which they are based. Thus, unsuccessful predictions are presumed to cause greater changes in the construct system than successful predictions. Research results to date have generally substantiated these notions concerning construct change (Bieri, 1953a; Poch, 1952).

Assuming these constructs or modes of perceiving persons are fundamental in predictive behavior, the problem arises of determining the predictive efficiency of the individual's system of constructs. A partial answer to this problem should lie in the versatility of the individual's construct system. Inasmuch as constructs represent differential perceptions

From J. Bieri, "Cognitive Complexity-Simplicity and Predictive Behavior," *Journal of Abnormal and Social Psychology*, 1955, **51**, 263-268. Reprinted by permission of the American Psychological Association.

or discriminations of the environment, it would be expected that the greater the degree of differentiation among the constructs, the greater will be the predictive power of the individual. In other words, there should be a positive relationship between how well an individual's system of constructs differentiates people in the environment and how well the individual can predict the behavior of these people. For our present purposes, we have designated the degree of differentiation of the construct system as reflecting its *cognitive complexity-simplicity*. A system of constructs which differentiates highly among persons is considered to be cognitively complex. A construct system which provides poor differentiation among persons is considered to be cognitively simple in structure.

The first general hypothesis would be: Among a group of *S*s, there should be a significant positive relationship between degree of cognitive complexity and accuracy of predictive behavior.

In analyzing predictive behavior, a comparison may be made between the similarity of the predictor's own responses and his predictions of another individual. This similarity has been referred to as a tendency to perceive others as similar to oneself (Bieri, 1953b), as projection (Bender and Hastorf, 1953), and as assumed similarity (Fiedler, 1954). In the attempt to incorporate predictive behavior into the broader realm of personality functioning, it would seem wise to apply more specific terminology to this projective process. Cameron's concept of *assimilative projection* would appear to approximate the type of projection occurring here. That is, the individual assumes others are the same as oneself, often on the basis of insufficient evidence. In reference to persons prone to indulge in assimilative projection, Cameron states (1947, p. 167): "The less practiced a person is in the social techniques of sharing the perspectives of others, the less opportunity he will have of finding out how different from himself other ordinary people can be. The less his opportunities for finding out and sharing in such individual differences, the more likely is he to extend assimilative

projection farther than the actual conditions warrant." Thus, the individual who has not made finer discriminations among his perceptions of other individuals is posited as having a greater tendency to engage in assimilative projection in reference to his perception of other individuals.

This forms the basis for the second general hypothesis: Among a group of *S*s, there should be a significant negative relationship between degree of cognitive complexity and the tendency to engage in assimilative projection in one's predictive behavior.

Method

Subjects

The *S*s in this study were a group of 22 female and 12 male university undergraduates. This group was composed of College of Education sophomores and juniors whose vocational interests centered around primary and secondary teaching.

Cognitive Complexity

A technique for measuring the degree of cognitive complexity among one's perceptions of others is afforded by the Role Construct Repertory Test (RCRT) developed by Kelly. A detailed description of this test can be found elsewhere (Kelly, 1955). Briefly, it consists of a matrix or grid across the top of which *S* lists a certain number of persons in his social environment. The *S* is asked successively to consider three of these persons at a time and to decide in what important personal way two of them are alike and different from the third. In this manner, a series of constructs or modes of perceiving others is formed which is assumed to be relatively characteristic of him as an individual. Each time a construct is formed, check marks are placed in the grid under the names of the persons perceived as similar in some way and the name of the construct entered next to the grid. After all these sorts have been completed, and a certain number of constructs established, the individual is asked to go through each construct row again and check all the other persons in that row, in addition to the two already checked, whom he considers that particular construct applies to most. No limits are placed upon how many others in each construct row the subject may check. This procedure yields a matrix of check patterns which represents how S perceives and differentiates a group of persons relative to his personal constructs. By considering how similar each construct row is to every other construct row in the matrix, in terms of similarity of check patterns, one can objectively ascertain the degree of differentiation the constructs have for the persons in the matrix. That is, if two construct rows have identical check patterns, then these two constructs are presumed to be functionally equivalent, regardless of the verbal labels given the constructs by S. Should many of the construct rows have identical or highly similar check patterns, then the person would be said to have low cognitive complexity (i.e., cognitive simplicity) in his perceptions of others. At the opposite extreme, if an individual's construct rows have check patterns which are all quite dissimilar to one another, then he is considered as having high cognitive complexity in his perceptions of others.

The actual scores of cognitive complexity-simplicity in this study were derived in the following way. Each time a construct check pattern was repeated in its identical form in the matrix, it was given a score of -2. Each time a construct check pattern was repeated save for a difference of *one* check mark, it was given a score of -1. The summation of these scores for the entire matrix yielded the individual's cognitive complexity score. The lower the algebraic score, the lower was the cognitive complexity. Although the use of the -2 and -1 scores was somewhat arbitrary, it had its basis in several considerations. First, a 12 X 12 grid or matrix was employed in the study. That is, there were 12 persons being perceived according to 12 possible constructs. Practical time considerations in the experimental situation were primary in determining the use of this number of constructs. The cognitive complexity scores obtained ranged from 0 (one case) to -22 (one case)

and approximately a normal distribution. Determining the reliability of these scores posed certain problems due to the nature of the construct formation task. Thus, it would be tenuous to assume the equivalence of items for either a split-half or odd-even procedure. However, as part of a larger research project (Bieri, 1953a), retest data on these 34 Ss were available. The time interval between administrations was short, the check pattern data having been collected at the beginning and at the end of the same experimental session. However, as part of the experimental procedure, a set was produced in each S for changes to be made on the second matrix which conceivably would lower the reliability. A test-retest reliability coefficient of .78 was obtained under these conditions. Thus, even with a set to change, Ss were highly consistent in their cognitive complexity scores over this short period of time. Further evidence is available indicating a high degree of consistency in constructs formed by Ss over longer periods of time (Hunt, 1951).

Predictive Instrument

The predictive instrument employed was a Situations Questionnaire consisting of 12 items depicting social situations in which four reasonable behavioral alternatives were presented. A representative item is listed below:

You are working intently to finish a paper in the library when two people sit down across from you and distract you with their continual loud talking. Would you most likely:

    a. Move to another seat
    b. Let them know how you feel by your facial expression
    c. Try to finish up in spite of their talking
    d. Ask them to stop talking

Each S completed this questionnaire by selecting one of the four alternative responses and in addition predicted the responses of two of his classmates who had previously taken the questionnaire. Thus, a total of 24 predictions were made by each S. These two classmates were also used in the construct sortings on the RCRT. The degree of familiarity with a person would conceivably affect one's predictive ability of his behavior. An attempt was made to control this variable by collecting the data early in the quarter while the students were still developing their class acquaintanceships. Each *S* was asked to list six classmates and then rank them one through six in terms of how well he felt he knew them. In every case, two classmates with the intermediate ranks were used in making the predictions (i.e., ranks 3 and 4). Each *S* was encouraged to use his filled-in construct matrix to assist him in making his predictions.

Scores

Three types of data from the questionnaire are used in deriving the scores of predictive behavior. These are (a) the responses which *S* himself gave to the questionnaire, (b) the responses the other person being predicted (*O*) gave to the questionnaire, and (c) the predictions made by *S* of *O*'s responses on the questionnaire. By considering the relation between these responses, three major scores can be derived, i.e., predictive accuracy, assimilative projection, and actual similarity.

Predictive accuracy scores were obtained by summing the correct number of predictions made by each *S* on both *O*s, the criterion for accuracy being the agreement of *S*'s prediction with the responses given by *O*. *Assimilative projection* scores were obtained by totaling the number of accurate and inaccurate predictions made by an *S* which were identical to the responses given by *S* himself. The scores of predictive accuracy and assimilative projection were used in testing Hypotheses I and II, respectively.

Each of these three scores can be broken down into component scores, some of which are shared by the major scores. Analysis of the predictive accuracy score indicates it is composed of two components: (a) those accurate predictions representing responses identical to those *S* made himself (*accurate projections*) and (b) those accurate predic-

tions which are different from the responses given by *S* (*accurate perceived differences*). Similarly, the assimilative projection score contains the accurate projection component plus an *inaccurate projection* component (i.e., *S* and *O* gave different responses but *S* predicted that *O* gave a similar response). If we consider the *actual similarity* between *S*'s own responses and *O*'s responses, we find this score to be composed of the accurate projection component plus those *inaccurate* predictions which are different from the responses given by *S* (*inaccurate perceived differences*). In this latter case, *S* and *O* have identical responses but *S* predicts a difference. We may schematize these scores and their components as indicated below:

Predictive accuracy = accurate projection + accurate perceived differences.
Assimilative projection = accurate projection + inaccurate projection.
Actual similarity = accurate projection + inaccurate perceived differences.

For purposes of this study, three component scores were utilized, namely accurate projection, inaccurate projection, and accurate perceived differences. The relationships of these scores to the cognitive complexity measure will be discussed relative to the experimental hypotheses.

Results

Using the Pearson product-moment coefficient, the various scores discussed above relative to predictive behavior were correlated with the cognitive complexity measure. Inasmuch as directional predictions were made, one-tailed significance tests were employed in assessing results for Hypotheses I and II. Hypothesis I states that a significant positive relationship exists between cognitive complexity and predictive accuracy. From Table 1, it is observed that the relationship is significant at the .05 level. Considering the two component scores subsumed under predictive accuracy, it is apparent that accurate projection shows no relationship ($r = .02$) to cognitive complexity. However, the correlation between accurate perceived differences and cognitive complexity ($r = .35$) is significant at the .05 level (two-tailed test). Thus, it appears that the cognitive behavior measured here relates more directly to the accurate prediction of *differences* between self and others than to the accurate prediction of similarities between self and others.

Hypothesis II states that a significant negative relationship will exist between degree of cognitive complexity and the tendency to engage in assimilative projection in one's predictions. Reference to Table 1 suggests that this is the case. The assimilative projection score correlates negatively ($r = -.32$) with the cognitive complexity score ($p < .05$). It will be noted that the correlations of the two component scores of assimilative projection, namely accurate projection and inaccurate projection, with cognitive discrimination are .02 and $-.40$ respectively. The latter significant negative correlation implies that the tendency for cognitively simple Ss to engage in assimilative projection is largely a function of their tendency to perceive unwarranted or inaccurate similarities between themselves and others.

Table 1. Correlations of cognitive complexity with measures of predictive behavior ($N = 34$).

Predictive Behavior	Cognitive Complexity
Predictive accuracy	.29
Assimilative projection	–.32
Accurate projection	.02
Accurate perceived differences	.35
Inaccurate projection	–.40
Actual similarity	.20

Note: One-tailed p values: 1% = .40, 5% = .29.
Two-tailed p values: 1% = .44, 5% = .34.

The correlation between cognitive complexity and actual similarity yields a positive but insignificant correlation ($r = .20$). This suggests there was some tendency for cognitively complex Ss to predict persons who were relatively more similar to themselves in terms of questionnaire responses. However, the accurate projection component of this score contains the only predictive accuracy measure for actual similarity. Since this component correlates only .02 with cognitive

complexity, we may infer that actual similarity played no significant role in producing greater predictive accuracy for cognitively complex Ss.

It may reasonably be asked what relationship general intelligence may have to these measures, particularly cognitive complexity. For 28 of the 34 Ss, it was possible to obtain total scores on the Ohio State Psychological Examination (OSPE), which is considered to be primarily a measure of verbal intelligence. The correlations between OSPE scores and the various scores in Table 1, including cognitive complexity, were insignificant and low, ranging from .01 to .12.

Discussion

The above results are construed as offering tentative evidence as to the interrelationship of three forms of behavior: (a) the degree of complexity in one's perceptions and differentiations of other persons, (b) the degree of accuracy with which one can predict the behavior of these other persons and (c) the degree to which assimilative projection is invoked in one's predictive behavior. The underlying formulation has been that making adequate differentiations in one's perceptions of others is basic to an optimum predictability of their behavior. Although the relationships posited in the experimental hypotheses are supported at a statistically significant level by the empirical results, the magnitude of the correlations obtained suggests that additional factors must be operating.

Let us consider the relationship between cognitive complexity and predictive accuracy. In this study, our primary concern has been to explain predictive behavior in terms of organismic variables to the partial exclusion of the external behavioral realm to be predicted. Cronbach (1954) and others have pointed out that the complexity of the behavioral situation to be predicted may affect accuracy of prediction. Thus, bringing complex differentiations into a simple situation may lead to lower accuracy than would be the case if simple differentiations were invoked. Undoubtedly, there are many situations in which a response based upon a simple yes-no, this-or-that discrimination would be preferable to responses based upon more elaborate cognitive differentiations. We must not infer, however, that the capacity to make complex differentiations in situations is necessarily equivalent to invoking complex behavior in dealing with the situation. Developmentally, we may assume that complex differentiations arise from more simple ones, and that the presence of the former implies the presence of the latter. Thus, the cognitively complex individual has versatility in both simple and complex behavioral realms, so to speak, while the cognitively simple individual is versatile in only one realm. In addition to these situational factors, it is evident that *qualitative* differences are important in terms of the adequacy of interpersonal differentiations. When the paranoid reacts to an insignificant gesture with an elaborate delusional structure, his complex reaction is considered inappropriate to the objectively simple gesture. Something in addition to degree of cognitive complexity is involved in determining the adequacy of this response. In line with these considerations, the effect of differing modes of adjustment upon both the adequacy and degree of cognitive differentiations is currently being studied.

The results of this study cast light upon the importance of assimilative projection in predictive behavior. When we consider the components of assimilative projection, we find no apparent relationship between accurate projection and degree of cognitive complexity. The significant relationship exists between inaccurate projection and cognitive simplicity. These findings reinforce the belief that the condition of cognitive simplicity reflects an incomplete differentiation of the boundaries between self and the external world, leading to unwarranted assumptions of similarity between self and others. Here again, the implicit role of adjustment and developmental factors would appear to warrant further study.

The similarity between the conceptual framework underlying the present study and related research in the area of *meaning*

should be noted. Osgood's semantic differential (1952) contains certain characteristics of the personal construct. Thus, it is a bipolar dimension ranging from a characteristic to its opposite (e.g., hard to soft) upon which Ss are asked to perceive other individuals. The essential difference between the two approaches rests upon the *source* of the dimensions invoked in perceiving others. Personal constructs represent the individual's own dimensions for differentiating his world, while Osgood, Cronbach, and others use standard, nomothetically derived dimensions. For purposes of conceptual integration into the broader framework of personality functioning, using the person's own perceptions may offer more utility.

Summary

A theoretical approach which conceives predictive behavior to be a function of one's perceptions of others is presented as a means of unifying certain empirical data ordinarily subsumed under the labels of social perception, empathy, or social sensitivity. The viewpoint taken is that all these forms of behavior rest operationally upon the predictive behavior of the individual. Further, this predictive behavior is assumed to be dependent upon the interpersonal discriminations or constructs which the individual invokes in making his predictions. The complexity of an individual's cognitive system relative to the degree of differentiation among his perceptions of others should thus affect his predictive behavior. Two major hypotheses were derived: (a) There should be a significant positive relationship between degree of cognitive complexity and predictive accuracy, and (b) there should be a significant negative relationship between cognitive complexity and assimilative projection. These hypotheses were tested on a sample of 34 Ss, each of whom predicted the behavior of two classmates on a Situations Questionnaire. Both of the hypotheses were supported by the data. By considering the component scores of predictive accuracy and assimilative projection, these relationships were further explored.

Thus, cognitive complexity relates especially to the tendency to predict accurately the differences between oneself and others. Similarly, the tendency to engage in inaccurate projections concerning the similarity between self and others relates significantly to cognitive simplicity. It is concluded that the complexity of one's cognitive system for perceiving others is effectively related to one's ability to predict accurately the behavior of others and to one's tendency to engage in assimilative projection in such behavior. Certain suggestions for further investigation are discussed.

References

Bender, I. E., and Hastorf, A. H. On measuring generalized empathic ability (social sensitivity). *J. abnorm. soc. Psychol.,* 1953, **48,** 503-506.

Bieri, J. A study of the generalization of changes within the personal construct system. Unpublished doctor's dissertation, Ohio State Univ., 1953a.

Bieri, J. Changes in interpersonal perceptions following social interaction. *J. abnorm. soc. Psychol.,* 1953b, **48,** 61-66.

Bruner, J. S., and Tagiuri, R. The perception of people. In G. Lindzey (Ed.), *Handbook of social psychology.* Cambridge, Mass. Addison-Wesley, 1954. Pp. 634-654.

Cameron, N. *The psychology of behavior disorders.* Boston: Houghton Mifflin, 1947.

Cronbach, L. J. Processes affecting "understanding of others" and "assumed similarity." *Tech. Rep. No. 10, Group Effectiveness Research Laboratory* (Contract N6ori-07135). Urbana: Univ. of Illinois, 1954. (Mimeograph)

Dymond, Rosalind F. A scale for the measurement of empathic ability. *J. consult. Psychol.,* 1949, **13,** 127-133.

Fiedler, F. E. Assumed similarity measures as predictors of team effectiveness. *J. abnorm. soc. Psychol.,* 1954, **49,** 381-388.

Gage, N. L. Accuracy of social perception and effectiveness in interpersonal relationships. *J. Pers.,* 1953, **22,** 128-141.

Hunt, D. E. Studies in role concept repertory: Conceptual consistency. Unpublished master's thesis, Ohio State Univ., 1951.

Kelly, G. A. *The psychology of personal constructs.* New York: Norton, 1955. 2 vols.

Lundy, R. M., and Bieri, J. Changes in interpersonal perceptions associated with group interaction. *Amer. Psychologist,* 1952, **7,** 306. (Abstract)

Osgood, C. E. The nature and measurement of meaning. *Psychol. Bull.,* 1952, **49,** 197-237.

Poch, Susanne M. A study of changes in personal constructs as related to interpersonal prediction and its outcomes. Unpublished doctor's dissertation, Ohio State Univ., 1952.

Rotter, J. B. *Social learning and clinical psychology.* New York: Prentice-Hall, 1954.

Scodel, A., and Mussen, P. Social perceptions of authoritarians and nonauthoritarians. *J. abnorm. soc. Psychol.,* 1953, **48,** 181-184.

Two Critical Comments on Kelly's *Psychology of Personal Constructs*

Jerome S. Bruner and Carl R. Rogers

A Cognitive Theory of Personality

These excellent, original, and infuriatingly prolix two volumes easily nominate themselves for the distinction of being the single greatest contribution of the past decade to the theory of personality functioning. Professor Kelly has written a major work.

The book is an effort to construct a theory of personality from a theory of knowledge: how people came to know the world by binding its diverse appearances into organized construct systems which vary not only in organization but in their goodness of fit to the bricks and mortar of reality. The point of view that dominates the work—the author labels it "constructive alternativism"—is one that the author applies both to himself as a science-maker and to his troubled clients. In a deep sense, the book reflects the climate of a generation of nominalistic thinking in the philosophy of science.

Let me summarize the major theoretical elements of the work—a task made somewhat easier than usual by the author's admirable use of a Fundamental Postulate and a set of elaborating corollaries. The Fundamental Postulate is that "A person's processes are psychologically channelized by the ways in which he anticipates events." In short, man's effort is to gain prediction and control over his environment—much as a scientist. Does not man "have his theories, test his hypotheses, and weigh his experimental evidence"—and each in his own way? The

author contrasts this point of view with one that he feels is prevalent among personality theorists: "I, being a *psychologist* and therefore a *scientist,* am performing this experiment in order to improve the prediction and control of certain human phenomena; but my subject, being merely a human organism, is obviously propelled by inexorable drives welling up within him." If it was Freud's genius to cut through the rationalistic cant of nineteenth-century Appolonianism, George Kelly's talent is to outstare the fashionable Dionysianism of the twentieth.

The Eleven Corollaries provide ways of describing or chronicling the vicissitudes of man's fumbling efforts at predicting and controlling his world. The first, or Construction Corollary, has to do with the process of cognitive working-through: "A person anticipates events by construing their replications." It is not from experience but from its reconstruing that we learn. The next two corollaries deal with the idiosyncratic nature of each man's construct world and man's construing acts.

The next corollary leads to some highly original and striking ideas about psychodiagnostic testing. It is the notion of dichotomization that has proved so fruitful in communication theory and in modern structural linguistics. "A person's construction system is composed of a finite number of dichotomous constructs." The dichotomized construct is inferred from triadic judgments. That is to say, given events A, B, and C, A and B are judged similar to each other in the same respect in which C is in contrast to both of them. A construct is not understood unless one grasps the two construct poles that form it, one of which may often be unrecognized by the construing person.

From J. S. Bruner, "A Cognitive Theory of Personality," and C. R. Rogers, "Intellectualized Psychotherapy," reviews of George A. Kelly's *Psychology of Personal Constructs* in *Contemporary Psychology*, 1956, **1**, 355-358. Reprinted by permission of the American Psychological Association.

The Choice Corollary gets the author, I think, into a conceptual trap. "A person chooses for himself that alternative in a dichotomized construct through which he anticipates the greater possibility for extension and definition of his system." That is to say, an event is construed or "placed" at one or the other alternative poles of a construct ("good" or "bad," "healthy" or "hostile," or whatever) depending upon "which seems to provide the best basis for anticipating the ensuing events." One object of categorizing the world in terms of a construct system is to minimize the disruptive surprises that it can wreak on us. This, I think, is the principal doctrine of "motivation" in the book—an implicit one, but one stamped on every page. It is the author's counterproposal to the Law of Effect, to the Pleasure Principle, to the watered-down hedonisms and tension reductions of such various Yale thinkers as Neal Miller, John Dollard, and David McClelland.

But must event-construing or categorizing always be guided by the need to extend cognitive control over one's environment? Need man be viewed *either* as the pig that reinforcement theory makes of him *or* the professor that Kelly implies as a model? I think not: in categorizing events, there is more to be maximized than predictiveness. Here is an example of the folly. "No matter how obvious it may be that a person would be better off if he avoided a fight . . . , such a course of action would seem to him personally to limit the definition and extension of his system as a whole." I rather suspect that when some people get angry or inspired or in love, they couldn't care less about their "system as a whole." One gets the impression that the author is, in his personality theory, over-reacting against a generation of irrationalism.

The next four corollaries have to do with what might be called the dynamics of construct utilization and change. Any given construct anticipates only a finite range of events, and effective action depends upon recognizing this "range of convenience." Construct systems change with time, experience, and the reconstruing of replicates, and they vary in their permeability to the influence of new

events. As he goes through life, a person may develop a construct system with high or low degrees of integration, fragmentation, or incompatibility.

So much, then, for the axiomatic apparatus in terms of which Professor Kelly construes the world. What does he make of it?

For one thing, and a very considerable thing, I believe, he has found a way of ungluing the eye of psychology from the keyhole of projective techniques. His REP test (Role Construct Repertory Test) is a simple and elegant way of determining the manner in which significant figures in the person's life are fitted into a construct system. Take a list of the significant kinds of people with whom a person interacts: parents, boy friends, teachers, sweethearts, bosses, "a person who dislikes you," etc. The client thinks of specific people who fill these roles in his life. He is then given triads of these and asked to indicate which two are most alike, in what respects, and how the third differs from these: the method of getting at the dichotomized contrast poles of the construct. The constructs that emerge from the sorting of the triads are then reduced mathematically and intuitively to get at the nature of general constructs used, the range they comprise, their degree of preemptiveness, etc.

The author then sets forth a subtle and interesting set of dimensions for describing the constructs of patients: looseness-tightness, constriction-dilation, level of cognitive awareness, and then proceeds to redefine some classic concepts in terms of these. He redefines *anxiety* as awareness that events to be coped with lie outside the range of convenience of one's construct system, and *hostility* as an effort to extort validational evidence for an anticipatory prediction already recognized as failing.

I have said nothing about Professor Kelly's approaches to therapy, nor am I particularly qualified to do so. One point I must make, however, for it is at the core of his theoretical approach. The effort in therapy is not to give the patient "insight" which, according to the author, too often means getting the patient's construct system to conform to that of the therapist. Rather the process of therapy is considered as an occasion for learning—for testing the fit of one's own (not the therapist's) construct system to the world. To do this, a kind of role-playing approach is employed, much in the spirit of characters in a Pirandello or O'Neill play who learn of themselves partly through the experience of contrasting or confusing (or both) what they are with the mask they are wearing in different life situations.

Where does the book succeed and where fall down? Who are the ancestors? What is portended by the appearance of this extraordinary and original work? The book succeeds, I think, in raising to a proper level of dignity and importance the press that man feels toward cognitive control of the world. It succeeds too in recognizing the individuality and "alternatives" of the routes to mental health. It succeeds in providing a diagnostic device strikingly in keeping with its presuppositions.

The book fails signally, I think, in dealing convincingly with the human passions. There was a strategy in Freud's choice of Moses or Michelangelo or Little Hans. If it is true that Freud was too often the victim of the dramatic instance, it is also true that with the same coin he paid his way to an understanding of the depths and heights of *la condition humaine.* By comparison, the young men and women of Professor Kelly's clinical examples are worried about their dates, their studies, and their conformity. If Freud's clinical world is a grotesque of *fin de siècle* Vienna, Kelly's is a gloss on the post-adolescent peer groups of Columbus, Ohio, who are indeed in the process of constructing their worlds. Which is more "real"? I have no idea. I wish Professor Kelly would treat more "most religious men in their most religious moments," or even just Nijinsky or Gabriel d'Annunzio.

With respect to ancestry, Professor Kelly seems to care little for it. One misses reference to such works as Piaget's *The Child's Construction of Reality,* the early work of Werner, and the writings of Harry Stack Sullivan, Lewin, and Allport—all of whom are on his side and good allies to boot.

The book is a theory of cognition extrapolated into a theory of personality—a genuine new departure and a spirited contribution to the psychology of personality.

Intellectualized Psychotherapy

This is a man's life work. In this enormous outpouring of 1200 pages (broken into two volumes only because of its bulk) George Kelly has endeavored to express the thinking which has grown out of twenty years of clinical experience, teaching, and supervision of research. Here is his philosophical base, the theory of personality which has emerged in his thinking, a new diagnostic instrument he has developed, a new therapeutic method, plus his extended views on all phases of psychodiagnosis and psychotherapy. In these half-million words he is saying "Here I am." It is a good solid figure which emerges, even if the question grows ever stronger as one reads on, whether any man has 1200 pages to express at one time.

In Kelly's view the framework of the book is provided by his theory of personality and behavior, largely presented in the first three chapters. To this reviewer these 183 pages were much the freshest, most original, most valuable. Kelly takes off from no current theory, but solely from the distillation of his own informed experience with individuals. He attempts to build a theoretical system which looks forward, not backward—which sees behavior as anticipatory, not reactive. He is attempting to hold persons as processes, not objects. He emphasizes phenomenological information, but his theory superimposes normative thinking upon the phenomenological data.

His basic concept is that the individual's behavior is channelized by the way he anticipates events, and that the individual anticipates events by the constructions (interpretations, meanings) he has placed upon his experience. The careful, rigorous logic with which Kelly works out the way in which these constructs are formed, the implications which flow from their mode of organization, and the ways in which they may change, make stimulating and thought-provoking reading. There emerges a picture of man as being not "a victim of his past, only the victim of his construction of it." This view, in Kelly's opinion, allows for the "determinism" which is a part of science, yet permits a concept of "constructive alternativism," or choice, in the way in which the individual construes his world.

It is gratifying to learn that this carefully formulated theory, presented in terms which can be given operational definition, is already being tested in small ways by a very considerable number of doctoral researches at Ohio State University (most of them unfortunately unpublished).

Since the space limits of this review severely restrict the reviewer, he must omit many areas of the book to comment on Kelly's views on psychotherapy.

It is in his chapter on *Fixed-Role Therapy* that the author becomes most personally expressive. It is clear that in this new method he has found an approach congenial to his personality, which is perhaps the basic aim of every therapist. Essentially, a diagnosis is made of the client's psychological constructs as they operate in his most significant interpersonal relationships. Then a number of clinicians (to avoid the bias of any one) develop a sketch of a new person, one that this client might become if his constructs were altered constructively. The aim is to get him to "play-act" this role for several weeks, without any notion that it represents a goal for him. The hope is that by shaking loose the organization of his psychological constructs, by giving him a new role, he will be more able to choose a role for himself built around an altered set of personal hypotheses, which will be confirmed or disconfirmed in his continuing experience.

Kelly shows real zest in his description of the way the client is kept from knowing the purpose of this "play-acting," and the enthusiastic manner in which he coaches the client in his new role, playing the parts, one after another, of the individuals with whom the client will interact. Kelly's statement that the therapist needs "a great deal of enthusiastic

momentum" and "some measure of verbal fluency and acting skill" to succeed in this effort seems a decided understatement, but it is clear that Kelly enjoys it. He describes his clinical experience with the use of this method both in individual and in group therapy (where a role sketch is devised for each person), but there are as yet no research studies of its effectiveness. One point which is unmentioned by Kelly is that this method could not be used with any client who had read about it or heard about it, since it is very important that the client regard the new role initially as simply an exercise, not in any sense as a possible pattern for his personality.

There are many other chapters, including the last five of Volume II, which deal with Kelly's psychotherapeutic observations. It is impossible to do more than indicate briefly some reactions to them.

An overwhelming impression is that for Kelly therapy is seen as almost entirely an intellectual function, a view which should be comforting to many psychologists. He is continually thinking about the client, and about his own procedures, in ways so complex that there seems no time or room for entering into an emotional relationship with the client. One small example. There are ten types of weeping to be differentiated. In dealing with one of them or with some other problem the client is expressing, there are nine techniques for reducing anxiety, twelve techniques (in addition to role playing) for encouraging the client to move or experiment in therapy, fifteen criteria to consider regarding the client's readiness to explore new areas, etc., etc. One has the impression of an incredibly "busy" therapist. This reviewer cannot help but wonder about the relation between "busyness" and effectiveness in therapy.

This approach to therapy is also highly eclectic. The therapist in appropriate situations manipulates the transference, prescribes activities, gives interpretations, uses "non-directive reflecting," confrontation, the discussion of dreams, the playing back of previous recorded interviews, etc. What the effect will be of setting this enormous cookbook of therapy before students who are preparing to undertake therapy is problematical. Certainly they will find almost every problem of therapy mentioned in its pages, but what a student should do about a particular problem with a particular client will depend upon whether he construes the difficulty as "controlling guilt feelings" or "loosening constructs." The recipes are very different. Kelly believes that his views on therapy are given unity by his initial theory, but such unity consists largely in the fact that anything done to the client affects his psychological constructs in some way.

In the beginning of the theoretical presentation Kelly pays tribute to the strength of each individual as a private "scientist" who tests out hypotheses in his own behavior. In the chapters on therapy, however, the wisdom all lies in the mind of the therapist. Since the client's perceptions of therapy and therapist are mostly false, therapy can only reach its proper goal if the therapist carefully chooses the role which should be played with this client at this time and appropriately manipulates the multitudinous aspects of the therapeutic process as suggested above. Confidence in the client as the "scientist" of his own life does not here find much operational expression.

Another disappointing element in this clinician, who has undoubtedly been of help to many individuals, is the lack of any sense of depth in his discussions of therapy. The chapters on theory clearly show an author who has thought deeply about his experience. The chapters on therapy seem to present meager evidence that he has lived deeply with his clients, and the bulk of the anecdotal examples seem to describe but superficial change. This reviewer had the feeling that perhaps Kelly was not doing justice to this phase of his experience. Actually the work might have a stronger impact if much of the last section were omitted.

However any one reader may see their strengths and weaknesses, these two volumes are clearly the measure of a man. They are written with modesty, with occasional humor, with brilliance in the theoretical sections, with earnestness and essential open-mindedness in the diagnostic and therapeutic sections. In spite of being too wordy, they show a person who is not afraid to launch out on his own in the development of theory, who looks to his experience rather than to authority for the source and the confirmation of his ideas. They show a man who believes deeply in the scientific method and who expects his views to be changed by research findings. Psychologists, perhaps especially young ones, will profit greatly from reading these chapters because they will find their own psychological constructs loosened by the experience. And, while any reader will find a great many pages which seem to him of dubious value, that still leaves many pages, ample enough to constitute highly rewarding reading.

10   Leon Festinger

Leon Festinger's (1919-) theory of cognitive dissonance, while not intended as a formal personality theory, is nonetheless an attempt to clarify the various roles that cognitions and motivations play in the psychological resolution of conflict following the occurrence of an emotionally significant event. Central to Festinger's theory are the clusters of opinions, attitudes, and bits of knowledge that compose an individual's cognitive system. When any of these cognitive elements are inconsistent (dissonant) with one another, the psychological system may—depending upon the proximity and strength of the conflicting elements—be thrown into a state of disequilibrium. Since this state of imbalance is presumably an uncomfortable, tension-creating experience, the individual, predictably, will seek to reduce the tension by attempting to resolve the apparent contradiction with which he is faced. This capsule statement suggests the deceptive simplicity of Festinger's theory, which has been applied to explain a wide variety of complex social and individual behavioral phenomena.

The research paper by Dana Bramel is an attempt to explain the psychoanalytic defense mechanism of projection by means of the experimental application of cognitive dissonance theory. According to Bramel's hypothesis, when an individual is exposed to undesirable information about himself, the more incompatible with his perceived level of self-esteem this information is, the greater his tendency to use projection as a defense. Bramel offers an additional hypothesis: that reduction of dissonance will occur when undesirable traits attributed to oneself are projected onto respected, favorably evaluated persons.

In the first part of Bramel's study, subjects were given fraudulent, favorable self-esteem information in one group and unfavorable self-esteem information in another. Then both the favorable and unfavorable groups were exposed to equally undesirable information suggesting the presence of homosexual tendencies. This set was ingeniously reinforced through the use of falsified galvanic skin response feedback during the presentation of pictures of nearly nude men. In this phase of the experiment, all subjects were arranged in pairs; each subject was asked to simultaneously estimate his partner's galvanic skin response to the pictures of men that were being projected on a screen before them. Thus, each subject received false galvanic skin response feedback about himself and was at the same time required to judge his partner's response to the same stimuli.

The chief measure of the attribution of homosexual tendencies to the partner was the numerical difference between the subject's galvanic skin response score (determined by the experimenter and personally recorded by the subject) and his estimation of his partner's galvanic skin response score. Additional rating scales were administered to test the subject's judgement of the masculinity of his partner, his own masculinity, and his own self-esteem.

The results tended to confirm both of the experimenter's expectations. Projection was greatest when the information presented to the subject was most dissonant with his self-concept. Thus subjects in the favorable self-concept set attributed higher reactions to the threatening stimuli to their partners than did subjects in the undesirable self-concept set. The data also revealed that the high dissonance group (favorable self-concept set) only projected when the target was an individual who had been previously evaluated favorably.

The final paper in this chapter, by Natalia P. Chapanis and Alphonse Chapanis, is a careful and thorough review of a sample of cognitive dissonance experiments. The authors critically evaluate the theoretical foundation on which the studies are based, the research designs and statistical procedures used to test the theoretical issues, and the theoretial explanations arising from the experimental data. Their conclusion is that, despite prolific research, the theory has not yielded sufficient convincing evidence to make it an adequate theoretical model for the understanding of complex social behavior.

Suggestions
for Further Reading

A Theory of Cognitive Dissonance, published by Stanford University Press in 1957, is Festinger's classic work. A further elaboration of theory and research can be found in Brehm and Cohen, *Explanations in Cognitive Dissonance*, published by Wiley in 1962, and in Festinger, *Conflict, Decision, and Dissonance,* published by Stanford University Press in 1964.

The Theory of Cognitive Dissonance

Leon Festinger

It has frequently been implied, and sometimes even pointed out, that the individual strives toward consistency within himself. His opinions and attitudes, for example, tend to exist in clusters that are internally consistent. Certainly one may find exceptions. A person may think Negroes are just as good as whites but would not want any living in his neighborhood; or someone may think little children should be quiet and unobtrusive and yet may be quite proud when his child aggressively captures the attention of his adult guests. When such inconsistencies are found to exist, they may be quite dramatic, but they capture our interest primarily because they stand out in sharp contrast against a background of consistency. It is still overwhelmingly true that related opinions or attitudes are consistent with one another. Study after study reports such consistency among one person's political attitudes, social attitudes, and many others.

There is the same kind of consistency between what a person knows or believes and what he does. A person who believes a college education is a good thing will very likely encourage his children to go to college; a child who knows he will be severely punished for some misdemeanor will not commit it or at least will try not to be caught doing it. This is not surprising, of course; it is so much the rule that we take it for granted. Again what captures our attention are the exceptions to otherwise consistent behavior. A person may know that smoking is bad for him and yet continue to smoke; many persons commit crimes even though they know the high probability of being caught and the punishment that awaits them.

Reprinted from *A Theory of Cognitive Dissonance* by Leon Festinger with the permission of the publishers, Stanford University Press. © 1957 by Leon Festinger. Pp. 1-31.

Granting that consistency is the usual thing, perhaps overwhelmingly so, what about these exceptions which come to mind so readily? Only rarely, if ever, are they accepted psychologically *as inconsistencies* by the person involved. Usually more or less successful attempts are made to rationalize them. Thus, the person who continues to smoke, knowing that it is bad for his health, may also feel (a) he enjoys smoking so much it is worth it; (b) the chances of his health suffering are not as serious as some would make out; (c) he can't always avoid every possible dangerous contingency and still live; and (d) perhaps even if he stopped smoking he would put on weight which is equally bad for his health. So continuing to smoke is, after all, consistent with his ideas about smoking.

But persons are not always successful in explaining away or in rationalizing inconsistencies to themselves. For one reason or another, attempts to achieve consistency may fail. The inconsistency then simply continues to exist. Under such circumstances—that is, in the presence of an inconsistency—there is psychological discomfort.

The basic hypotheses, the ramifications and implications of which will be explored in the remainder of this book, can now be stated. First, I will replace the word "inconsistency" with a term which has less of a logical connotation, namely, *dissonance*. I will likewise replace the word "consistency" with a more neutral term, namely, *consonance*. A more formal definition of these terms will be given shortly; for the moment, let us try to get along with the implicit meaning they have acquired as a result of the preceding discussion.

The basic hypotheses I wish to state are as follows:

1. The existence of dissonance, being psychologically uncomfortable, will motivate the person to try to reduce the dissonance and achieve consonance.
2. When dissonance is present, in addition to trying to reduce it, the person will actively avoid situations and information which would likely increase the dissonance.

Before proceeding to develop this theory of dissonance and the pressures to reduce it, it would be well to clarify the nature of dissonance, what kind of a concept it is, and where the theory concerning it will lead. The two hypotheses stated above provide a good starting point for this clarification. While they refer here specifically to dissonance, they are in fact very general hypotheses. In the place of "dissonance" one can substitute other notions similar in nature, such as "hunger," "frustration," or "disequilibrium," and the hypotheses would still make perfectly good sense.

In short, I am proposing that dissonance, that is, the existence of nonfitting relations among cognitions, is a motivating factor in its own right. By the term *cognition* I mean any knowledge, opinion, or belief about the environment, about oneself, or about one's behavior. Cognitive dissonance can be seen as an antecedent condition which leads to activity oriented toward dissonance reduction just as hunger leads to activity oriented toward hunger reduction. It is a very different motivation from what psychologists are used to dealing with but, as we shall see, nonetheless powerful.

The Occurrence and Persistence of Dissonance

Why and how does dissonance ever arise? How does it happen that persons sometimes find themselves doing things that do not fit with what they know, or having opinions that do not fit with other opinions they hold? An answer to this question may be found in discussing two of the more common situations in which dissonance may occur.

1. New events may happen or new information may become known to a person, creating at least a momentary dissonance with existing knowledge, opinion, or cognition concerning behavior. Since a person does not have complete and perfect control over the information that reaches him and over events that can happen in his environment, such dissonances may easily arise. Thus, for example, a person may plan to go on a picnic with complete confidence that the weather will be warm and sunny. Nevertheless, just before he is due to start, it may begin to rain. The knowledge that it is now raining is dissonant with his confidence in a sunny day and with his planning to go to a picnic. Or, as another example, a person who is quite certain in his knowledge that automatic transmissions on automobiles are inefficient may accidentally come across an article praising automatic transmissions. Again, at least a momentary dissonance is created.

2. Even in the absence of new, unforeseen events or information, the existence of dissonance is undoubtedly an everyday condition. Very few things are all black or all white; very few situations are clear-cut enough so that opinions or behaviors are not to some extent a mixture of contradictions. Thus, a midwestern farmer who is a Republican may be opposed to his party's position on farm price supports; a person buying a new car may prefer the economy of one model but the design of another; a person deciding on how to invest his money may know that the outcome of his investment depends upon economic conditions beyond his control. Where an opinion must be formed or a decision taken, some dissonance is almost unavoidably created between the cognition of the action taken and those opinions or knowledges which tend to point to a different action.

There is, then, a fairly wide variety of situations in which dissonance is nearly unavoidable. But it remains for us to examine the circumstances under which dissonance, once arisen, persists. That is, under what conditions is dissonance not simply a momentary affair? If the hypotheses stated above are correct, then as soon as dissonance occurs there will be pressures to reduce it. To answer this question it is necessary first to have a brief look at the possible ways in which dissonance may be reduced.

Since there will be a more formal discussion of this point later on in this chapter, let us now examine how dissonance may be reduced, using as an illustration the example of the habitual cigarette smoker who has learned that smoking is bad for his health. He may have acquired this information from a newspaper or magazine, from friends, or even from some physician. This knowledge is certainly dissonant with cognition that he continues to smoke. If the hypothesis that there will be pressures to reduce this dissonance is correct, what would the person involved be expected to do?

1. He might simply change his cognition about his behavior by changing his actions; that is, he might stop smoking. If he no longer smokes, then his cognition of what he does will be consonant with the knowledge that smoking is bad for his health.

2. He might change his "knowledge" about the effects of smoking. This sounds like a peculiar way to put it, but it expresses well what must happen. He might simply end up believing that smoking does not have any deleterious effects, or he might acquire so much "knowledge" pointing to the good effects it has that the harmful aspects become negligible. If he can manage to change his knowledge in either of these ways, he will have reduced, or even eliminated, the dissonance between what he does and what he knows.

But in the above illustration it seems clear that the person may encounter difficulties in trying to change either his behavior or his knowledge. And this, of course, is precisely the reason that dissonance, once created, may persist. There is no guarantee that the person will be able to reduce or remove the dissonance. The hypothetical smoker may find that the process of giving up smoking is too painful for him to endure. He might try to find facts and opinions of others to support the view that smoking is not harmful, but these attempts might fail. He might then remain in the situation where he continues to smoke and continues to know that smoking is harmful. If this turns out to be the case, how-

ever, his efforts to reduce the dissonance will not cease.

Indeed, there are some areas of cognition where the existence of major dissonance is customary. This may occur when two or more established beliefs or values, all relevant to the area of cognition in question, are inconsistent. That is, no opinion can be held, and no behavior engaged in, that will not be dissonant with at least one of these established beliefs. Myrdal (1944), in the appendix of his classic book, states this quite well in connection with attitudes and behavior toward Negroes. In discussing the simultaneous existence of opinions and values concerning human beings in general, Negroes in general, specific groups of Negroes, and so on, Myrdal states:

A need will be felt by the person or group, whose inconsistencies in valuations are publicly exposed, to find a means of reconciling the inconsistencies. . . . The feeling of need for logical consistency within the hierarchy of moral valuations . . . is, in its modern intensity, a rather new phenomenon. With less mobility, less intellectual communication, and less public discussion, there was in previous generations less exposure of one another's valuation conflicts (pp. 1029, 1030).

While I find myself in disagreement with Myrdal in the importance he places on the public exposure of the dissonance, I feel it is a good statement of some of the reasons why strong dissonance exists in this area.

The notions introduced thus far are not entirely new; many similar ones have been suggested. It may be of value to mention two whose formulation is closest to my own. Heider (1958) discusses the relationships among people and among sentiments. He states:

Summarizing this preliminary discussion of balanced, or harmonious, states, we can say that they are states characterized by two or more relations which fit together. If no balanced state exists, then forces toward the [balanced] state will arise. Either there will be a tendency to change the sentiments involved, or the unit relations will be changed through action or cognitive reorganization. If a change is not possible, the state of imbalance will produce tension, and the balanced states will be preferred over the states of imbalance.

If one replaces the word "balanced" with "consonant" and "imbalance" with "dissonance," this statement by Heider can be seen to indicate the same process with which our discussion up to now has dealt.

Osgood and Tannenbaum (1955) published a paper in which they also formulated and documented a similar idea with respect to changes in opinions and attitudes. In discussing the "principle of congruity," as they call it, they state: "Changes in evaluation are always in the direction of increased congruity with the existing frame of reference" (p. 43). The particular kind of "incongruity" or cognitive dissonance with which they deal in their study is produced by the knowledge that a person or other source of information which a subject regards positively (or negatively) supports an opinion which the subject regards negatively (or positively). They proceed to show that under such circumstances there is a marked tendency to change either the evaluation of the opinion involved or the evaluation of the source in a direction which would reduce the dissonance. Thus, if the source were positively evaluated and the opinion negatively evaluated, the person might end up reacting less positively to the source or more positively to the issue. It is also clear from their data that the particular outcome depends on whether the evaluation of the source or of the issue is initially more firmly rooted in the person's cognition. If his attitude toward the source is highly "polarized," then the opinion is more likely to change, and vice versa. Indeed, by careful initial measurement of the attitudes toward the sources and toward the opinions before the dissonance is introduced, and by careful measurement of how resistant each of these is to change, the authors are able to predict quite nicely the direction, and in some instances the amount, of change in evaluation.

The important point to remember is that there is pressure to produce consonant relations among cognitions and to avoid and reduce dissonance. Many other writers have recognized this, although few have stated it as concretely and as succinctly as the authors we have mentioned. The task which we are attempting in this book is to formulate the theory of dissonance in a precise yet generally applicable form, to draw out its implications to a variety of contexts, and to present data relevant to the theory.

Definitions of Dissonance and Consonance

Most of the remainder of this chapter will deal with a more formal exposition of the theory of dissonance. I will attempt to state the theory in as precise and unambiguous terms as possible. But since the ideas which constitute this theory are by no means yet in a completely precise form, some vagueness is unavoidable.

The terms "dissonance" and "consonance" refer to relations which exist between pairs of "elements." It is consequently necessary, before proceeding to define these relations, to define the elements themselves as well as we can.

These elements refer to what has been called cognition, that is, the things a person knows about himself, about his behavior, and about his surroundings. These elements, then, are "knowledges," if I may coin the plural form of the word. Some of these elements represent knowledge about oneself: what one does, what one feels, what one wants or desires, what one is, and the like. Other elements of knowledge concern the world in which one lives: what is where, what leads to what, what things are satisfying or painful or inconsequential or important, etc.

It is clear that the term "knowledge" has been used to include things to which the word does not ordinarily refer—for example, opinions. A person does not hold an opinion unless he thinks it is correct, and so, psychologically, it is not different from a "knowledge." The same is true of beliefs, values, or attitudes, which function as "knowledges" for our purposes. This is not to imply that there are no important distinctions to be made among these various terms. Indeed, some such distinctions will be made later on. But for the definitions here, these are all "elements of cognition," and relations of consonance and dissonance can hold between pairs of these elements.

There are further questions of definition one would like to be able to answer. For example, when is an "element of cognition" *one* element, or a group of elements? Is the knowledge, "the winter in Minneapolis is very cold" an element, or should this be considered a cluster of elements made up of more specific knowledge? This is, at present, an unanswerable question. Indeed it may be a question which does not need answering. As will be seen in those chapters where data are presented and discussed, this unanswered question does not present a problem in connection with measurement.

Another important question concerning these elements is, how are they formed and what determines their content? At this point we want to emphasize the single most important determinant of the content of these elements, namely, *reality*. These elements of cognition are responsive to reality. By and large they mirror, or map, reality. This reality may be physical or social or psychological, but in any case the cognition more or less maps it. This is, of course, not surprising. It would be unlikely that an organism could live and survive if the elements of cognition were not to a large extent a veridical map of reality. Indeed, when someone is "out of touch with reality," it becomes very noticeable.

In other words, elements of cognition correspond for the most part with what the person actually does or feels or with what actually exists in the environment. In the case of opinions, beliefs, and values, the reality may be what others think or do; in other instances the reality may be what is encountered experientially or what others have told him.

But let us here object and say that persons frequently have cognitive elements which deviate markedly from reality, at least as we see it. Consequently, the major point to be made is that *the reality which impinges on a person will exert pressures in the direction of bringing the appropriate cognitive elements into correspondence with that reality*. This does not mean that the existing cognitive elements will *always* correspond. Indeed, one of the important consequences of the theory of dissonance is that it will help us understand some circumstances where the cognitive elements do not correspond with reality. But it does mean that if the cognitive elements do not correspond with a certain reality which impinges, certain pressures must exist. We should therefore be able to observe some manifestations of these pressures. This hypothesized relation between the cognitive elements and reality is important in enabling measurement of dissonance, and we will refer to it again in considering data.

It is now possible to proceed to a discussion of the relations which may exist between pairs of elements. There are three such relations, namely, irrelevance, dissonance, and consonance. They will be discussed in that order.

Irrelevant Relations

Two elements may simply have nothing to do with one another. That is, under such circumstances where one cognitive element implies nothing at all concerning some other element, these two elements are irrelevant to one another. For example, let us imagine a person who knows that it sometimes takes as long as two weeks for a letter to go from New York to Paris by regular boat mail and who also knows that a dry, hot July is good for the corn crop in Iowa. These two elements of cognition have nothing to do with one another; they exist in an irrelevant relation to each other. There is not, of course, much to say about such irrelevant relations except to point to their existence. Of primary concern will be those pairs of elements between which relations of consonance or dissonance can exist.

In many instances, however, it becomes quite a problem to decide a priori whether or not two elements are irrelevant. It is often impossible to decide this without reference to other cognitions of the person involved. Sometimes situations will exist where, because of the behavior of the person involved, previously irrelevant elements become relevant to one another. This could even be the case in the example of irrelevant cognitive elements which we gave above. If a person living in Paris was speculating on the corn crop in the United States, he would want information concerning weather predictions for Iowa but would not depend upon boat mail for getting his information.

Before proceeding to the definitions and discussion of the relations of consonance and dissonance which exist if the elements are relevant, it may be well to stress again the special nature certain cognitive elements have—usually those cognitive elements which correspond to behavior. Such a "behavioral" element, by being relevant to each of two irrelevant cognitive elements, may make them in fact relevant to each other.

Relevant Relations: Dissonance and Consonance

We have already acquired some intuitive notion of the meaning of dissonance. Two elements are dissonant if, for one reason or another, they do not fit together. They may be inconsistent or contradictory, culture or group standards may dictate that they do not fit, and so on. It is appropriate now to attempt a more formal conceptual definition.

Let us consider two elements which exist in a person's cognition and which are relevant to one another. The definition of dissonance will disregard the existence of all the other cognitive elements that are relevant to either or both of the two under consideration and simply deal with these two alone. *These two elements are in a dissonant relation if, considering these two alone, the obverse of one element would follow from the other.* To state it a bit more formally, x and y are dissonant if not-x follows from y. Thus, for example, if a person knew there were only friends in his vicinity and also felt afraid, there would be a dissonant relation between these two cognitive elements. Or, for another example, if a person were already in debt and also purchased a new car, the corresponding cognitive elements would be dissonant with one another. The dissonance might exist because of

what the person has learned or come to expect, because of what is considered appropriate or usual, or for any of a number of other reasons.

Motivations and desired consequences may also be factors in determining whether or not two elements are dissonant. For example, a person in a card game might continue playing and losing money while knowing that the others in the game are professional gamblers. This latter knowledge would be dissonant with his cognition about his behavior, namely, continuing to play. But it should be clear that to specify the relation as dissonant is to assume (plausibly enough) that the person involved wants to win. If for some strange reason this person wants to lose, this relation would be consonant.

It may be helpful to give a series of examples where dissonance between two cognitive elements stems from different sources, that is, where the two elements are dissonant because of different meanings of the phrase "follow from" in the definition of dissonance given above.

1. Dissonance could arise from logical inconsistency. If a person believed that man will reach the moon in the near future and also believed that man will not be able to build a device that can leave the atmosphere of the earth, these two cognitions are dissonant with one another. The obverse of one follows from the other on logical grounds in the person's own thinking processes.

2. Dissonance could arise because of cultural mores. If a person at a formal dinner uses his hands to pick up a recalcitrant chicken bone, the knowledge of what he is doing is dissonant with the knowledge of formal dinner etiquette. The dissonance exists simply because the culture defines what is consonant and what is not. In some other culture these two cognitions might not be dissonant at all.

3. Dissonance may arise because one specific opinion is sometimes included, by definition, in a more general opinion. Thus, if a person is a Democrat but in a given election prefers the Republican candidate, the cognitive elements corresponding to these two sets

of opinions are dissonant with each other because "being a Democrat" includes, as part of the concept, favoring Democratic candidates.

4. Dissonance may arise because of past experience. If a person were standing in the rain and yet could see no evidence that he was getting wet, these two cognitions would be dissonant with one another because he knows from experience that getting wet follows from being out in the rain. If one can imagine a person who had never had any experience with rain, these two cognitions would probably not be dissonant.

These various examples are probably sufficient to illustrate how the conceptual definition of dissonance, together with some specific meaning of the phrase "follow from," would be used empirically to decide whether two cognitive elements are dissonant or consonant. It is clear, of course, that in any of these situations, there might exist many other elements of cognition that are consonant with either of the two elements under consideration. Nevertheless, the relation between the two elements is dissonant if, disregarding the others, the one does not, or would not be expected to, follow from the other.

While we have been defining and discussing dissonance, the relations of consonance and irrelevance have, of course, also been defined by implication. If, considering a pair of elements, either one *does* follow from the other, then the relation between them is consonant. If neither the existing element nor its obverse follows from the other element of the pair, then the relation between them is irrelevant.

The conceptual definitions of dissonance and consonance present some serious measurement difficulties. If the theory of dissonance is to have relevance for empirical data, one must be able to identify dissonances and consonances unequivocally. But it is clearly hopeless to attempt to obtain a complete listing of cognitive elements, and even were such a listing available, in some cases it would be difficult or impossible to say, a priori, which of the three relationships holds. In many cases, however, the a priori determination of dissonance is clear and easy. (Remember also

that two cognitive elements may be dissonant for a person living in one culture and not for a person living in another, or for a person with one set of experiences and not for a person with another.) Needless to say, it will be necessary to cope with this problem of measurement in detail in those chapters where empirical data are presented and discussed.

The Magnitude of Dissonance

All dissonant relations, of course, are not of equal magnitude. It is necessary to distinguish degrees of dissonance and to specify what determines how strong a given dissonant relation is. We will briefly discuss some determinants of the magnitude of dissonance between two elements and then turn to a consideration of the total amount of dissonance which may exist between two clusters of elements.

One obvious determinant of the magnitude of dissonance lies in the characteristics of the elements between which the relation of dissonance holds. *If two elements are dissonant with one another, the magnitude of the dissonance will be a function of the importance of the elements.* The more these elements are important to, or valued by, the person, the greater will be the magnitude of a dissonant relation between them. Thus, for example, if a person gives ten cents to a beggar, knowing full well that the beggar is not really in need, the dissonance which exists between these two elements is rather weak. Neither of the two cognitive elements involved is very important or very consequential to the person. A much greater dissonance is involved, for example, if a student does not study for a very important examination, knowing that his present fund of information is probably inadequate for the examination. In this case the elements that are dissonant with each other are more important to the person, and the magnitude of dissonance will be correspondingly greater.

It is probably safe to assume that it is rare for no dissonance at all to exist within any cluster of cognitive elements. For almost any action a person might take, for almost any feeling he might have, there will most likely be at least one cognitive element dissonant with this "behavioral" element. Even perfectly trivial cognitions like knowing one is taking a walk on a Sunday afternoon would likely have some elements dissonant with it. The person who is out for a walk might also know that there are things around the house requiring his attention, or he might know that rain was likely, and so on. In short, there are generally so many other cognitive elements relevant to any given element that some dissonance is the usual state of affairs.

Let us consider now the total context of dissonances and consonances in relation to one particular element. Assuming momentarily, for the sake of definition, that all the elements relevant to the one in question are equally important, *the total amount of dissonance between this element and the remainder of the person's cognition will depend on the proportion of relevant elements that are dissonant with the one in question.* Thus, if the overwhelming majority of relevant elements are consonant with, say, a behavioral element, then the dissonance with this behavioral element is slight. If in relation to the number of elements consonant with the behavioral element the number of dissonant elements is large, the total dissonance will be of appreciable magnitude. Of course, the magnitude of the total dissonance will also depend on the importance or value of those relevant elements which exist in consonant or dissonant relations with the one being considered.

The above statement can of course be easily generalized to deal with the magnitude of dissonance which exists between two clusters of cognitive elements. This magnitude would depend on the proportion of the relevant relations between elements in the two clusters that were dissonant and, of course, on the importance of the elements.

Since the magnitude of dissonance is an important variable in determining the pressure to reduce dissonance, and since we will deal with measures of the magnitude of dissonance repeatedly in considering data, it may be well to summarize our discussion concerning the magnitude of dissonance.

1. If two cognitive elements are relevant, the relation between them is either dissonant or consonant.

2. The magnitude of the dissonance (or consonance) increases as the importance or value of the elements increases.

3. The total amount of dissonance that exists between two clusters of cognitive elements is a function of the weighted proportion of all relevant relations between the two clusters that are dissonant. The term "weighted proportion" is used because each relevant relation would be weighted according to the importance of the elements involved in that relation.

The Reduction of Dissonance

The presence of dissonance gives rise to pressures to reduce or eliminate the dissonance. The strength of the pressures to reduce the dissonance is a function of the magnitude of the dissonance. In other words, dissonance acts in the same way as a state of drive or need or tension. The presence of dissonance leads to action to reduce it just as, for example, the presence of hunger leads to action to reduce the hunger. Also, similar to the action of a drive, the greater the dissonance, the greater will be the intensity of the action to reduce the dissonance and the greater the avoidance of situations that would increase the dissonance.

In order to be specific about how the pressure to reduce dissonance would manifest itself, it is necessary to examine the possible ways in which existing dissonance can be reduced or eliminated. In general, if dissonance exists between two elements, this dissonance can be eliminated by changing one of those elements. The important thing is how these changes may be brought about. There are various possible ways in which this can be accomplished, depending upon the type of cognitive elements involved and upon the total cognitive context.

Changing a Behavioral Cognitive Element

When the dissonance under consideration is between an element corresponding to some knowledge concerning environment (environmental element) and a behavioral element, the dissonance can, of course, be eliminated by changing the behavioral cognitive element in such a way that it is consonant with the environmental element. The simplest and easiest way in which this may be accomplished is to change the action or feeling which the behavioral element represents. Given that a cognition is responsive to "reality" (as we have seen), if the behavior of the organism changes, the cognitive element or elements corresponding to this behavior will likewise change. This method of reducing or eliminating dissonance is a very frequent occurrence. Our behavior and feelings are frequently modified in accordance with new information. If a person starts out on a picnic and notices that it has begun to rain, he may very well turn around and go home. There are many persons who do stop smoking if and when they discover it is bad for their health.

It may not always be possible, however, to eliminate dissonance or even to reduce it materially by changing one's action or feeling. The difficulty of changing the behavior may be too great, or the change, while eliminating some dissonances, may create a whole host of new ones. These questions will be discussed in more detail below.

Changing an Environmental Cognitive Element

Just as it is possible to change a behavioral cognitive element by changing the behavior which this element mirrors, it is sometimes possible to change an *environmental* cognitive element by changing the situation to which that element corresponds. This, of course, is much more difficult than changing one's behavior, for one must have a sufficient degree of control over one's environment—a relatively rare occurrence.

Changing the environment itself in order to reduce dissonance is more feasible when the social environment is in question than when the physical environment is involved. In order to illustrate rather dramatically the kind of thing that would be involved, I will give a rather facetious hypothetical example. Let us imagine a person who is given to pacing up and down in his living room at home. Let us further imagine that for some unknown reason he always jumps over one particular spot on the floor. The cognitive element corresponding to his jumping over that spot is undoubtedly dissonant with his knowledge that the floor at that spot is level, strong, and in no way different from any other part of the floor. If, some evening when his wife is away from home, he breaks a hole in the floor at that exact spot, he would completely eliminate the dissonance. The cognition that there is a hole in the floor would be quite consonant with the knowledge that he jumps over the place where the hole exists. In short, he would have changed a cognitive element by actually changing the environment, thus eliminating a dissonance.

Whenever there is sufficient control over the environment, this method of reducing dissonance may be employed. For example, a person who is habitually very hostile toward other people may surround himself with persons who provoke hostility. His cognitions about the persons with whom he associates are then consonant with the cognitions corresponding to his hostile behavior. The possibilities of manipulating the environment are limited, however, and most endeavors to change a cognitive element will follow other lines.

If a cognitive element that is responsive to reality is to be changed without changing the corresponding reality, some means of ignoring or counteracting the real situation must be used. This is sometimes well-nigh impossible, except in extreme cases which might be called psychotic. If a person is standing in the rain and rapidly getting soaked, he will almost certainly continue to have the cognition that it is raining no matter how strong the psychological pressures are to eliminate that cognition. In other instances it is relatively easy to change a cognitive element although the reality remains the same. For example, a person might be able to change his opinion about a political officeholder even though the behavior of that officeholder, and the political situation generally, remain unchanged. Usually, for this to occur, the person would have to be able to find others who would agree with and support his new opinion. In general, establishing a social reality by gaining the agreement and support of other people is one of the major ways in which a cognition can be changed when the pressures to change it are present. It can readily be seen that where such social support is necessary, the presence of dissonance and the consequent pressures to change some cognitive element will lead to a variety of social processes.

Adding New Cognitive Elements

It is clear that in order to eliminate a dissonance completely, some cognitive element must be changed. It is also clear that this is not always possible. But even if it is impossible to eliminate a dissonance, it is possible to reduce the total magnitude of dissonance by adding new cognitive elements. Thus, for example, if dissonance existed between some cognitive elements concerning the effects of smoking and cognition concerning the behavior of continuing to smoke, the total dissonance could be reduced by adding new cognitive elements that are consonant with the fact of smoking. In the presence of such dissonance, then, a person might be expected to actively seek new information that would reduce the total dissonance and, at the same time, to avoid new information that might increase the existing dissonance. Thus, to pursue the example, the person might seek out and avidly read any material critical of the research which purported to show that smoking was bad for one's health. At the same time he would avoid reading material that praised this research. (If he unavoidably came in contact with the latter type of material, his reading would be critical indeed.)

Actually, the possibilities for adding new elements which would reduce the existing dis-

sonances are broad. Our smoker, for example, could find out all about accidents and death rates in automobiles. Having then added the cognition that the danger from smoking is negligible compared to the danger he runs driving a car, his dissonance would also have been somewhat reduced. Here the total dissonance is reduced by reducing the *importance* of the existing dissonance.

The above discussion has pointed to the possibility of reducing the total dissonance with some element by reducing the proportion of dissonant as compared with consonant relations involving that element. It is also possible to add a new cognitive element which, in a sense, "reconciles" two elements that are dissonant. Let us consider an example from the literature to illustrate this. Spiro (1953) gives an account of certain aspects of the belief system of the Ifaluk, a nonliterate society. The relevant points for our purposes here are as follows:

1. In this culture there is a firm belief that people are *good*. This belief is not only that they should be good but that they *are* good.

2. For one reason or another, young children in this culture go through a period of particularly strong overt aggression, hostility, and destructiveness.

It seems clear that the belief about the nature of people is dissonant with the knowledge of the behavior of the children in this culture. It would have been possible to reduce this dissonance in any number of ways. They might have changed their belief about the nature of people or have modified it so that people are wholly good only at maturity. Or they might have changed their ideas about what is and what is not "good" so that overt aggression in young children would be considered good. Actually, the manner of reducing the dissonance was different. A third belief was added which effectively reduced the dissonance by "reconciliation." Specifically, they also believe in the existence of malevolent ghosts which enter into persons and cause them to do bad things.

As a result of this third belief, the knowledge of the aggressive behavior of children is no longer dissonant with the belief that people are good. It is not the children who behave aggressively—it's the malevolent ghosts. Psychologically, this is a highly satisfactory means of reducing the dissonance, as one might expect when such beliefs are institutionalized at a cultural level. Unsatisfactory solutions would not be as successful in becoming widely accepted.

Before moving on, it is worth while to emphasize again that the presence of pressures to reduce dissonance, or even activity directed toward such reduction, does not guarantee that the dissonance will be reduced. A person may not be able to find the social support needed to change a cognitive element, or he may not be able to find new elements which reduce the total dissonance. In fact, it is quite conceivable that in the process of trying to reduce dissonance, it might even be increased. This will depend upon what the person encounters while attempting to reduce the dissonance. The important point to be made so far is that in the presence of a dissonance, one will be able to observe the *attempts* to reduce it. If attempts to reduce dissonance fail, one should be able to observe symptoms of psychological discomfort, provided the dissonance is appreciable enough so that the discomfort is clearly and overtly manifested.

Resistance to Reduction of Dissonance

If dissonance is to be reduced or eliminated by changing one or more cognitive elements, it is necessary to consider how resistant these cognitive elements are to change. Whether or not any of them change, and if so, which ones, will certainly be determined in part by the magnitude of resistance to change which they possess. It is, of course, clear that if the various cognitive elements involved had no resistance to change whatsoever, there would never be any lasting dissonances. Momentary dissonance might occur, but if the cognitive elements involved had no resistance to change, the dissonance would immediately be eliminated. Let us, then, look at the major

sources of resistance to change of a cognitive element.

Just as the reduction of dissonance presented somewhat different problems depending upon whether the element to be changed was a behavioral or an environmental one, so the major sources of resistance to change are different for these two classes of cognitive elements.

Resistance to Change of Behavioral Cognitive Elements

The first and foremost source of resistance to change for *any* cognitive element is the responsiveness of such elements to reality. If one sees that the grass is green, it is very difficult to think it is not so. If a person is walking down the street, it is difficult for his cognition not to contain an element corresponding to this. Given this strong and sometimes overwhelming responsiveness to reality, the problem of changing a behavioral cognitive element becomes the problem of changing the behavior which is being mapped by the element. Consequently, the resistance to change of the cognitive element is identical with the resistance to change of the behavior reflected by that element, assuming that the person maintains contact with reality.

Certainly much behavior has little or no resistance to change. We continually modify many of our actions and feelings in accordance with changes in the situation. If a street which we ordinarily use when we drive to work is being repaired, there is usually little difficulty in altering our behavior and using a different route. What, then, are the circumstances that make it difficult for the person to change his actions?

1. The change may be painful or involve loss. A person may, for example, have spent a lot of money to purchase a house. If for any reason he now wants to change, that is, live in a different house or different neighborhood, he must endure the discomforts of moving and the possible financial loss involved in selling the house. A person who might desire to give up smoking must endure the discomfort and pain of the cessation in order to accom-

plish the change. Clearly, in such circumstances there will be a certain resistance to change. The magnitude of this resistance to change will be determined by the extent of pain or loss which must be endured.

2. The present behavior may be otherwise satisfying. A person might continue to have lunch at a certain restaurant even though they served poor food if, for example, his friends always ate there. Or a person who is very domineering and harsh toward his children might not easily be able to give up the satisfactions of being able to boss someone, even if on various grounds he desired to change. In such instances, of course, the resistance to change would be a function of the satisfaction obtained from the present behavior.

3. Making the change may simply not be possible. It would be a mistake to imagine that a person could consummate any change in his behavior if he wanted to badly enough. It may not be possible to change for a variety of reasons. Some behavior, especially emotional reactions, may not be under the voluntary control of the person. For example, a person might have a strong reaction of fear which he can do nothing about. Also, it might not be possible to consummate a change simply because the new behavior may not be in the behavior repertory of the person. A father might not be able to change the way he behaves toward his children simply because he doesn't know any other way to behave. A third circumstance which could make it impossible to change is the irrevocable nature of certain actions. If, for example, a person has sold his house and then decides he wants it back, there is nothing that can be done if the new owner refuses to sell it. The action has been taken and is not reversible. But under circumstances where the behavior simply cannot change at all, it is not correct to say that the resistance to change of the corresponding cognitive element is infinite. The resistance to change which the cognitive element possesses can, of course, not be greater than the pressure to respond to reality.

Resistance to Change of Environmental Cognitive Elements

Here again, as with behavioral cognitive elements, the major source of resistance to change lies in the responsiveness of these elements to reality. The result of this, as far as behavioral elements go, is to tie the resistance to change of the cognitive element to the resistance to change of the reality, namely, the behavior itself. The situation is somewhat different with regard to environmental elements. When there is a clear and unequivocal reality corresponding to some cognitive element, the possibilities of change are almost nil. If one desired, for example, to change one's cognition about the location of some building which one saw every day, this would indeed be difficult to accomplish.

In many instances, however, the reality corresponding to the cognitive element is by no means so clear and unambiguous. When the reality is basically a social one, that is, when it is established by agreement with other people, the resistance to change would be determined by the difficulty of finding persons to support the new cognition.

There is another source of resistance to change of both behavioral and environmental cognitive elements. We have postponed discussion of it until now, however, because it is a more important source of resistance to change for environmental elements than for others. This source of resistance to change lies in the fact that an element is in relationship with a number of other elements. To the extent that the element is consonant with a large number of other elements and to the extent that changing it would replace these consonances by dissonances, the element will be resistant to change.

The above discussion is not meant to be an exhaustive analysis of resistance to change or a listing of conceptually different sources. Rather, it is a discussion which attempts to make distinctions that will help operationally rather than conceptually. In considering any dissonance and the resistance to change of the elements involved, the important factor in the attempt to eliminate the dissonance by changing an element is the total amount of resistance to change; the source of the resistance is immaterial.

Limits of the Magnitude of Dissonance

The maximum dissonance that can possibly exist between any two elements is equal to the total resistance to change of the less resistant element. The magnitude of dissonance cannot exceed this amount because, at this point of maximum possible dissonance, the less resistant element would change, thus eliminating the dissonance.

This does not mean that the magnitude of dissonance will frequently even approach this maximum possible value. When there exists a strong dissonance that is less than the resistance to change of any of the elements involved, this dissonance can perhaps still be reduced for the total cognitive system by adding new cognitive elements. In this way, even in the presence of very strong resistances to change, the total dissonance in the system could be kept at rather low levels.

Let us consider an example of a person who spends what for him is a very large sum of money for a new car of an expensive type. Let us also imagine that after purchasing it he finds that some things go wrong with it and that repairs are very expensive. It is also more expensive to operate than other cars, and what is more, he finds that his friends think the car is ugly. If the dissonance becomes great enough, that is, equal to the resistance to change of the less resistant element, which in this situation would probably be the behavioral element, he might sell the car and suffer whatever inconvenience and financial loss is involved Thus the dissonance could not exceed the resistance the person has to changing his behavior, that is, selling the car.

Now let us consider the situation where the dissonance for the person who bought a new car was appreciable but less than the maximum possible dissonance, that is, less than the resistance to change of the less resistant

cognitive element. None of the existing cognitive elements would then be changed, but he could keep the total dissonance low by adding more and more cognitions that are consonant with his ownership of the car. He begins to feel that power and riding qualities are more important than economy and looks. He begins to drive faster than he used to and becomes quite convinced that it is important for a car to be able to travel at high speed. With these cognitions and others, he might succeed in rendering the dissonance negligible.

It is also possible, however, that his attempts to add new consonant cognitive elements would prove unsuccessful and that his financial situation is such that he could not sell the car. It would still be possible to reduce the dissonance by what also amounts to adding a new cognitive element, but of a different kind. He can admit to himself, and to others, that he was wrong to purchase the car and that if he had it to do over again, he would buy a different kind. This process of divorcing himself psychologically from the action can and does materially reduce the dissonance. Sometimes, however, the resistances against this are quite strong. The maximum dissonance which could exist would, in such circumstances, be determined by the resistance to admitting that he had been wrong or foolish.

Avoidance of Dissonance

The discussion thus far has focused on the tendencies to reduce or eliminate dissonance and the problems involved in achieving such reduction. Under certain circumstances there are also strong and important tendencies to avoid increases of dissonance or to avoid the occurrence of dissonance altogether. Let us now turn our attention to a consideration of these circumstances and the manifestations of the avoidance tendencies which we might expect to observe.

The avoidance of an increase in dissonance comes about, of course, as a result of the existence of dissonance. This avoidance is especially important where, in the process of attempting to reduce dissonance, support is sought for a new cognitive element to replace an existing one or where new cognitive elements are to be added. In both these circumstances, the seeking of support and the seeking of new information must be done in a highly selective manner. A person would initiate discussion with someone he thought would agree with the new cognitive element but would avoid discussion with someone who might agree with the element that he was trying to change. A person would expose himself to sources of information which he expected would add new elements which would increase consonance but would certainly avoid sources which would increase dissonance.

If there is little or no dissonance existing, we would not expect the same kind of selectivity in exposure to sources of support or sources of information. In fact, where no dissonance exists there should be a relative absense of motivation to seek support or new information at all. This will be true in general, but there are important exceptions. Past experience may lead a person to fear, and hence to avoid, the initial occurrence of dissonance. Where this is true, one might expect circumspect behavior with regard to new information even when little or no dissonance is present to start with.

The operation of a fear of dissonance may also lead to a reluctance to commit oneself behaviorally. There is a large class of actions that, once taken, are difficult to change. Hence, it is possible for dissonances to arise and to mount in intensity. A fear of dissonance would lead to a reluctance to take action—a reluctance to commit oneself. Where decision and action cannot be indefinitely delayed, the taking of action may be accompanied by a cognitive negation of the action. Thus, for example, a person who buys a new car and is very afraid of dissonance

may, immediately following the purchase, announce his conviction that he did the wrong thing. Such strong fear of dissonance is probably relatively rare, but it does occur. Personality differences with respect to fear of dissonance and the effectiveness with which one is able to reduce dissonance are undoubtedly important in determining whether or not such avoidance of dissonance is likely to happen. The operational problem would be to independently identify situations and persons where this kind of a priori self-protective behavior occurs.

Summary

The core of the theory of dissonance which we have stated is rather simple. It holds that:

1. There may exist dissonant or "nonfitting" relations among cognitive elements.

2. The existence of dissonance gives rise to pressures to reduce the dissonance and to avoid increases in dissonance.

3. Manifestations of the operation of these pressures include behavior changes, changes of cognition, and circumspect exposure to new information and new opinions.

Although the core of the theory is simple, it has rather wide implications and applications to a variety of situations which on the surface look very different.

References

Heider, F. *The psychology of interpersonal relations.* New York: Wiley, 1958.

Myrdal, G. *An American dilemma.* New York: Harper, 1944.

Osgood, C. E., and Tannenbaum, P. The principle of congruity and prediction of attitude change. *Psychol. Rev.,* 1955, **62**, 42-55.

Spiro, M. Ghosts: An anthropological inquiry into learning and perception. *J. abnorm. soc. Psychol.,* 1953, **48**, 376-382.

A Dissonance Theory Approach to Defensive Projection

Dana Bramel

Ego defensive processes, as discussed in psychoanalytic theory, often seem to bear some resemblance to the cognitive changes dealt with in Festinger's (1957) dissonance theory. This observation has led to a comparison of the two theories and to consideration of the possibility that certain of the Freudian defense mechanisms might occur in response to dissonance. Especially interesting from the point of view of social psychology is the concept of projection, since it clearly has implications for interpersonal relations.

Consider those situations, described in psychoanalytic theory, in which the individual's perception of some aspect of himself is contrary to his internalized standards of right and wrong (the superego). According to the theory, the perception of this information arouses fear of punishment, perhaps especially a fear of painful guilt feelings (Fenichel, 1945). In order to avoid further anxiety and guilt feelings, the ego is said to initiate defensive measures.

In order to determine the relevance of dissonance theory to this phenomenon, one must ask whether dissonant relations would be expected to exist among the cognitions involved. Imagine, for example, a person who considers homosexuality a bad and digusting thing; on some occasion he is suddenly exposed to information strongly implying that he has homosexual tendencies. According to classical psychoanalytic theory, the crucial relation is the conflict between the information or impulse and demands of the superego. Is the new cognition—that one has homosexual tendencies—necessarily dissonant with

From D. Bramel, "A Dissonance Theory Approach to Defensive Projection," *Journal of Abnormal and Social Psychology*, 1962, **64**, 121-129. Reprinted by permission of the American Psychological Association.

one's belief that such tendencies are bad and that one should not have them? The answer is no. People who conceive of themselves as possessing a mixture of good and bad traits, or a preponderance of bad traits, would not generally expect that new information would be favorable to themselves or consistent with superego standards. It follows that a discrepancy between the new information and superego standards, although threatening in the psychoanalytic sense, would not necessarily be dissonant.

This is not to say, however, that dissonance would be completely absent from the cognition of the person who recognizes that he is not perfect. For example, when he discovers he has homosexual tendencies, this knowledge may be dissonant with his specific belief that he is really quite masculine, even though it is not dissonant with his conviction that homosexuality is a bad thing.

The point can be clarified by a hypothetical example. Imagine two people, A and B. Both consider homosexuality a very bad thing, and both believe they are quite lacking in such motivation. A believes he is an extremely fine person in general; B sees himself as possessing almost no favorable characteristics. Both are then confronted with information that they have strong homosexual tendencies. For both, this information is contrary to superego standards and dissonant with their belief that they are not homosexual. However, for A, the information is also strongly dissonant with his belief that he is a nearly perfect person. For B, on the other hand, the information is quite consonant with his belief that he is a failure. The new information produces more dissonance for the person with high self-esteem, even though the conflict with the superego is substantially the same for the two people. This emphasis upon the actual self-concept in the dissonance theory approach reveals a difference in focus of the two theories.

Can dissonance involving the self-concept be reduced by projecting the offending trait onto other people? Perhaps the most effective mode of dissonance reduction would be to deny the implications of the information. Let us assume, however, that the information is so unambiguous that successful denial is not possible for the person. He is compelled to ascribe the undesirable trait to himself. Under these circumstances, attributing the trait to other persons might reduce dissonance in several ways. By attributing it to respected people, the projector may enable himself to re-evaluate the trait. If respected persons possess it, then perhaps it is not so bad a thing after all. Then possession of the trait would not be contradictory to a favorable level of self-esteem. Another possibility is that the person may attribute the trait to members of his reference or comparison group (Festinger, 1954). In this way he could convince himself that he does not deviate from the persons with whom he ordinarily compares himself. If he is only average in his possession of the trait, then subjectively his favorable level of self-esteem is not so strongly negated.

These possibilities suggest that indeed projection may be used as a means of reducing dissonance. There are several studies in the literature (for example, Murstein, 1956; Wright, 1942) which are specifically relevant and show positive results, but all leave certain important issues unresolved. Consequently, the experiment reported here was conducted to test whether projection occurs in response to dissonance and to throw some light on the particular ways in which this attribution may reduce dissonance.

The hypotheses to be tested were these:

1. If a person is exposed to information strongly implying that he possesses an undesirable characteristic, he is more likely to attribute the trait to others if the information is dissonant with his level of self-esteem; the greater the dissonance, the more likely it is that projection will occur.

2. If a person is compelled to ascribe an undesirable and dissonant characteristic to himself, he will be motivated to attribute the characteristic to favorably evaluated persons and/or to persons with whom he ordinarily compares himself.

Method

Overview

Subjects in the Favorable condition received falsified personality test results aimed at temporarily increasing their general level of self-esteem; subjects in the Unfavorable condition received parallel information intended to lower their general self-esteem. Subsequently, all subjects were privately exposed to further falsified information of an undesirable nature about themselves. It was hypothesized that this information, being more dissonant with the self-concept of subjects in the Favorable condition, would lead to more projection in that condition. Attribution was measured by asking each subject to rate another subject with whom he was paired.

First Session

Each subject who signed up for the experiment appeared individually for the first session. He was told that the first part of the experiment was designed to discover what kinds of people had insight into themselves. He was asked to take a number of personality tests, which, he was told, would be carefully and confidentially analyzed by three members of the clinical psychology staff. He was informed that, after the tests were scored, he would learn the results in an interview, during which time his self-insight was to be measured. Among the tests included were the Taylor Manifest Anxiety scale, the *F, K,* and *L* scales from the MMPI, and an adjective checklist self-concept measure.

At the end of the hour, the subject was told that the second session would also include a measure of his ability to judge the personality of another person on the basis of a first impression.

Second Session

On the basis of the self-concept measure subjects were paired for the second session by matching their level of self-esteem and their concept of their own masculinity.

At the beginning of the second session the two unacquainted subjects scheduled for the hour were introduced to each other. In order to aid subjects in forming an impression of each other, the experimenter asked each in turn (in the presence of the other) a set of questions about himself and his attitudes toward certain current events. At the conclusion of this meeting the subjects were separated and interviewed privately regarding the results of their personality tests.

Unknown to the subject, the "results" which he received had been prepared with no reference whatsoever to his actual test performance. There were only two test reports used in the experiment, one very favorable, the the other very unfavorable. The reports covered the personality "dimensions" of creativity, hostility, egocentricity, and overall maturity. Each section of the report gave a rather detailed discussion of the test results bearing upon the particular dimension. The tone was objective and the general favorability was very consistent throughout the report. The two reports were very similar in form, but the specific contents were directly opposite in implication.

After having been assigned randomly to his experimental condition, the subject was read the report in private by the experimenter, and its discrepancies from the subject's present self-concept were explicitly pointed out by the experimenter. The report was finished in approximately 20 minutes. In each pair of subjects, one was assigned to the Favorable condition, one to the Unfavorable condition. Two interviewers were used for this part of the experiment, alternating between the two conditions.

Following the test report, the two subjects were brought together in another room, where they expected to make some personality judgments about each other. Each was then given a questionnaire consisting of 11 polar adjective seven-point scales to be used

to rate the other person. An over-all favorability score could be computed across the scales. Examples were masculine-feminine, friendly-hostile, competent-incompetent, and mature-immature. A self-concept measure followed, consisting of 16 polar adjective scales similar to those included in the prior rating of the other person. These were selected partially to tap dimensions covered in the personality reports and to serve as a check on the manipulation of self-esteem. As in the previous set, they included the item masculine-feminine, and could be summated to provide a general favorability score. Emphasis was placed upon the anonymity of the questionnaires and upon the earnest request that the subject respond "as *you* see yourself, from your own point of view at the present time."

Introducing the Undesirable Cognition

It was expected that informing a male undergraduate that he has homosexual tendencies would be sufficiently dissonant under certain conditions to provoke defensive behavior. Care was taken to ensure that the degree of threat was not extreme and that no damaging effects would remain at the end of the experiment. These precautions will be discussed in more detail below.

At this point in the experiment, while making ratings of partner and self, the two subjects were seated along one side of a long table, separated by about 4 feet, both facing a projection screen 6 feet in front of them. On the table in front of each subject was a small plywood box containing a galvanometer dial facing him. Issuing from the box were two wires with electrodes on the ends. Each box, with its dial, was completely shielded from the other persons in the room. Thus, each subject perceived his apparatus immediately in front of him and could not see the other subject's apparatus.

Next, the experimenter read a set of instructions to set the stage for the undesirable cognitions about homosexuality. These instructions were largely of a deceptive nature. It was explained that this part of the experiment would be concerned with the perception of sexual arousal. An elaborate explanation of the physiology of sexual arousal and the sensitive techniques for its measurement followed. Care was taken to distinguish the galvanometer response to sexual arousal from that commonly associated with anxiety reactions by pointing out the unmistakable signs of the former. Considerable emphasis was placed on the unconscious nature of sexual arousal and the impossibility of exerting conscious control over its expression in the "psychogalvanic skin response." It was further explained that the experimenter was investigating the perception of homosexual rather than heterosexual arousal. The task set for the subject was to observe his own sexual arousal response on his galvanometer for each of a series of photographs of men which would be projected onto the screen. He was to record this figure on a page of a small anonymous booklet. After he had recorded his own arousal level for the particular picture on the screen, he was to make an estimate of the needle indication of the other subject's apparatus for the same photograph. All subjects were explicitly told that movements of the dial would indicate homosexual arousal to the photographs. As a precaution against excessive threat, they were told that persons with very strong homosexual tendencies would consistently "go off the scale." Further, the anonymity and privacy of the situation were carefully spelled out, with the intention of convincing the subject that no one but he would know what his own responses had been.

Unknown to the subject, the supposed "psychogalvanic skin response apparatus" was not actually responding to changes in his own level of sexual arousal to the pictures. Rather, the galvanometers in each of the two boxes were controlled remotely by the experimenter. Concealed wires led from the galvanometers, in a direct current series circuit, to a calibrated variable resister. Thus, the experimenter exerted complete control over the movements of the needles, which were identical for the two subjects. Each photograph had been direcned an "appropriate" needle reading in advance, so that those de-

picting handsome men in states of undress received more current than did those depicting unattractive and fully clothed men. Both subjects were, thus, led to believe that they were sexually aroused by certain pictures and not by others, according to a consistent pattern. Both subjects were confronted with exactly the same stimulus input at this point of the experiment.[1]

It was expected that the instructions would be so impressive to the subject that denial of the fact that homosexual arousal was being indicated would be very difficult. By closing off certain alternative avenues of dissonance reduction, such as the cognition that the apparatus was untrustworthy, it was intended that the situation would be conducive to the appearance of defensive projection. According to the hypothesis, subjects in the Favorable condition should experience considerable dissonance when observing their needle jump in response to photographs of attractive males. For subjects in the Unfavorable condition there would be many cognitions consonant with the new information concerning homosexuality, and not so many dissonant cognitions. For most subjects there would, no doubt, be some dissonance due to their prior belief that they are not homosexual, but the two conditions would not differ in this respect. Since the test reports contained no material concerning sexuality, subjects in the two conditions were not expected to differ in their concepts of their own masculinity or in their superego standards.

Fifteen photographs of men were used. Many of the men were almost entirely nude and had physiques somewhat more delicate and posed than those typically found in physical culture magazines. These photographs were chosen on the assumption that subjects might perceive them as being the type toward which homosexuals would be attracted.

Measuring Attribution

It seemed that the most meaningful measure for testing the hypotheses would be a

---

[1]A similar experimental technique was independently devised by Harold Gerard (cf. Gerard, 1959; Gerard and Rabbie, 1960).

score representing the difference between the subject's own recorded score and his estimate of his partner's galvanic skin response. This should most accurately reflect the subject's comparison between himself and his partner. Therefore, a total score was computed for each subject, taking the algebraic sum of the differences between own and attributed scores across the 15 photographs. This summary score (P score) would be positive if the subject attributed (on the average) higher needle indications to his partner than to himself (i.e., attributed greater homosexual arousal). It would be zero if on the average there was no difference between own and attributed scores. It would be negative if the subject attributed lower needle indications to the other subject than to himself.

Following the threatening material, the subject responded to anonymous questions about his own and his partner's degree of possession of homosexual tendencies, and about his attitude toward the "psychogalvanic skin response" as a measure of such tendencies.

A considerable amount of time at the end of the experiment was allocated to explaining the true nature of the study and demonstrating in detail that the personality reports and the apparatus were incapable of giving a correct evaluation of a person. The expression of relief which often followed the unveiling of the deceptions indicated that the manipulations had been effective. The necessity for the deceptions used in the experimental analysis of such delicate processes was carefully explained, and all questions were answered. Not until the subjects seemed quite restored and satisfied was the session ended. All available evidence indicates that the subjects considered the experiment interesting and worthy of their participation.

Subjects

All subjects in the experiment were undergraduate men registered in the introductory psychology course. Not all of those who took part in the first session were selected to finish the experiment. Those who scored very high on the Taylor Manifest Anxiety scale and at the same time very low on the defensiveness scale of the MMPI were excluded from the second session, since there was the possibility that the manipulations might be too threatening for them. Of the 98 subjects who participated in both sessions of the experiment, 14 were excluded from the analysis—8 for suspicion regarding the procedure, 3 for excessive age (over 30), and 3 for failure to obey the instructions. Of those excluded, 7 were in the Favorable and 7 in the Unfavorable condition.

Results

Adequacy of Experimental Operations

The major independent variable was the level of self-esteem, or the number of favorable self-referent cognitions. A checklist measure of self-esteem administered before the manipulations revealed no initial difference between the groups. The effectiveness of the personality reports was determined by comparing the Favorable and Unfavorable groups on self-esteem as measured by adjective scales shortly after the manipulation. Mean favorability scores could range from a low of 1 to a high of 7. The results are shown in Table 1. The mean for the Favorable group was significantly higher than for the Unfavorable group ($t = 8.35$, $p < .001$).[2] We may infer, therefore, that the desired difference in self-esteem was successfully created by the fraudulent test reports.

Another important problem of experimental control had to do with the favorability of the subjects' ratings of each other prior to introduction of the cognitions concerning homosexuality. A score was calculated for each subject, taking the mean of his ratings of his partner (scored for favorability) across 10 polar adjective scales, excluding the item masculine-feminine (considered separately below). The first half vs. second half reliability of the score was .57. Possible scores could range from 1 (very unfavorable) to 7 (very favorable). As shown in Table 1, there was no significant difference between the two conditions in favorability of rating of partner.

[2]All reported significance levels are based upon two-tailed tests.

Table 1. Means and standard deviations of variables measured prior to introduction of the undesirable cognition.

Variable	Favorable (n = 42)	Unfavorable (n = 42)
Before self-esteem manipulation Initial self-esteem (checklist)		
M	14.5	15.1
SD	3.6	3.3
After self-esteem manipulation Self-esteem (seven-point scales)		
M	5.52	4.20
SD	.54	.86
Favorability of rating of partner		
M	4.79	4.90
SD	.69	.68
Rating of masculinity of partner		
M	5.39	5.30
SD	1.11	1.32
Rating of own masculinity		
M	5.87	5.56
SD	1.00	1.02

On the masculine-feminine scale, 1 indicated "very feminine" and 7 indicated "very masculine." Mean scores of the two groups did not differ on this scale, as shown in Table 1. Further, the groups did not differ significantly in their rating of their own "masculinity-femininity."

On the basis of these comparisons, it seems justifiable to conclude that the Favorable and Unfavorable groups did not differ regarding these possible artifactual effects of the self-esteem manipulations.

Self-Esteem and Projection

Before comparing the two experimental conditions on the attribution of homosexual arousal, let us check the reliability of the measure, the *P* score. For the first 23 subjects used in the experiment, the series of 15 photographs was repeated, yielding a set of 30 judgment situations for each subject. The discrepancies between his own recorded dial readings and his estimates of his partner's dial were summed separately for the first 15 and the second 15 exposures of the photographs. The correlation between these two sums (*P* scores) was .95. For subsequent analyses, only the *P* score for the first 15 photographs was used.

Subjects in the two conditions did not differ, on the average, in their own recorded scores. That is, they were equal in the accuracy with which they recorded their own needle indications. Therefore, the *P* scores, which were partially derived from the subjects' own recorded dial readings, could not differ between the two groups simply as a function of differences in own recorded scores.

For evidence concerning the relation between dissonance and projection, let us look first at the gross differences between the experimental conditions. As shown in Table 2, the mean *P* score for the Favorable condition was —2.95; the mean for the Unfavorable

Table 2. Means and standard deviations of attribution measured after manipulation of self-esteem.

Attribution	Favorable (n = 42)	Unfavorable (n = 42)
Raw *P* score		
M	-2.95	-11.45
SD	25.52	27.96
P score adjusted for prethreat judgment of masculinity of partner		
M	+4.65	-4.76
SD	24.28	23.99

condition was —11.45. Thus, subjects in the high dissonance condition tended to say that their partner's arousal level was about the same as their own, while those in the low dissonance condition tended to say their partner's arousal was somewhat less than their own. Attributing one's own characteristic to others was therefore more frequent in the high dissonance, or Favorable, group. The difference between the means yielded a *t* (for correlated means, due to matching) of 1.52, which is at the .13 level of significance. In order to arrive at a more firm conclusion regarding the outcome of this comparison, let us look at another source of variance which can be taken out of the gross variance in the *P* scores.

It has been anticipated that part of the variance in *P* scores would be due to the impression of masculinity created by the partner prior to the introduction of the undesirable cognition. If the subject rated his partner as very masculine on the masculine-feminine scale, then he would be likely to make somewhat lower (less homosexual) needle estimates for his partner than if he had rated him as very feminine. Correlations were therefore calculated between perceived masculinity of the partner (prethreat) and attribution of homosexual arousal to the photographs (*P* score). Within the Favorable group the resulting product-moment correlation was —.32 (*p* < .05); in the Unfavorable group the correlation was —.52 (*p* < .01). It will be remembered that the two groups did not differ in their mean (prethreat) rating of the masculinity of the partner (as measured by the masculine-feminine scale); in addition, the distributions of these ratings were very similar in the two groups. Therefore, it was decided that the rather similar within-groups correlations would justify combining the groups, calculating the correlation between the two variables in the total sample, and computing adjusted *P* scores as deviations from the regression line. By means of this procedure the variance associated with how masculine the partner appeared (*prior* to the threat) could be partialed out. Within the total sample (*N* = 84) the correlation between "masculinity" (prethreat) and *P* score was —.42. Each subject's *P* score deviation from the regression line was calculated, and the resulting scores were then interpreted as reflecting differences in attribution due to factors other than the initial perceived masculinity of the partner. The adjusted means for the

groups are shown in Table 2. A *t* test for correlated means yielded a *t* of 2.04 (*df* = 40), significant beyond the .05 level. On the basis of these results one may conclude that the groups differed in attribution in the direction predicted by the hypothesis relating dissonance and projection.

In all subsequent comparisons, the original, unadjusted *P* scores were used. The use of the simpler score should make interpretations clearer and more direct, especially in the case of within-conditions analyses.

It is of interest to look at the relation between self-esteem and attribution of arousal within the two experimental conditions. The product-moment correlation within the Favorable group was +.29 (*p* < .07); within the Unfavorable group the correlation was + .10 (*p* < .55). The relations are presented graphically in Figure 1, showing the mean

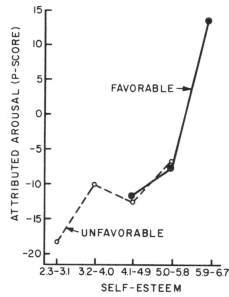

Figure 1. Mean attribution of homosexuality as a function of level of self-esteem.

raw *P* scores within each condition as a function of increasing self-esteem. The lack of correlation in the Unfavorable condition suggests that projection as a means of reducing dissonance occurred only when the amount of dissonance was quite high. From the point of view of the theory, this is not surprising. For the person with low self-esteem the undesirable information is actually consonant with his general self-evaluation (although dissonant with his specific cognitions about his adequate masculinity). Only for the person who believes he is consistently good will the undesirable information be strongly dissonant with his general self-esteem.

In Figure 1 it can be seen that the two groups show considerable continuity where they overlap in level of measured self-esteem. This fact is important because it implies that the self-esteem manipulations did not have strong opposed artifactual effects upon the amount of attribution of homosexual arousal. If the personality test report interviews had had effects on attribution in ways other than through the self-esteem variable, then differences between conditions might have appeared when considering subjects in the two groups with equivalent levels of self-esteem. Judging from Figure 1, persons in the two groups who had equivalent measured self-esteem levels apparently reacted similarly to the undesirable cognition.

Projection and Attitude toward Available Social Objects

There is a well known judgmental tendency which leads a person to perceive others as possessing traits consistent with his general evaluation of those others (a halo effect). On the basis of the halo effect alone, one would expect a tendency to attribute homosexuality (an unfavorable trait) to persons who are evaluated in general relatively negatively. However, the presence of dissonance resulting from self-ascription of homosexuality should introduce a contrary tendency. To the extent that projection, of the type defined in this report, occurs, it should be aimed primarily at persons who are relatively favorably evaluated. Since in this experiment projection was expected to occur to a greater extent in the Favorable group, it follows that the empirical pattern of attribution in that condition should be some compromise between the projection pattern and the halo pattern, since one may expect both forces to be operating. In the Unfavorable condition, on the other hand, one would expect to find a pattern more closely resembling the pure

halo pattern, due to the absence of large amounts of dissonance.

In Figure 2 the results are shown separately for the two conditions. Mean *P* scores are shown as a function of increasingly favorable evaluation of the partner, as measured independently and prior to the introduction of the

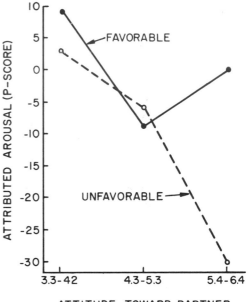

Figure 2. Mean attribution of homosexuality as a function of favorability of attitude toward partner.

cognitions regarding homosexuality. It can be seen that the results are consistent with the hypothesis. For relatively negative and moderate levels of evaluation of the partner, subjects in the Favorable and Unfavorable conditions attributed homosexual arousal consistent with a halo effect. The less favorably they rated the other subject, the more homosexuality they attributed to him. However, when the partner had been evaluated very favorably, subjects in the two experimental conditions reacted in quite different ways. The Unfavorable group continued to follow the halo pattern, attributing very low homosexuality to the partner. The Favorable group, in contrast, exhibited no decrease in attribution when confronted with favorably evaluated objects. In fact, there was a slight but insignificant increase. The difference between the mean *P* scores of the Favorable ($n = 9$) and Unfavorable ($n = 12$)

groups at the high respect point (5.4 to 6.4 in Figure 2) was significant beyond the .05 level by the *t* test. Since the subject's respect for his partner was not experimentally manipulated, it is possible that via self-selection other variables may be contriubting to the observed difference. It should be pointed out, for example, that the measured self-esteem level of subjects in the Favorable group (with respect-ed partner) was slightly higher than that of other subjects in the Favorable group, so that some of the tendency of these particular subjects to project may be traceable to their higher self-esteem rather than to their attitude toward their partner. Unfortunately, the number of cases is too small to allow an internal analysis to throw light on this question. All things considered, one can be fairly confident that the difference between the conditions does reflect a tendency for projection to be directed toward favorably evaluated persons under these circumstances.

Discussion

The results provided good support for the central hypothesis, that projection can be a response to dissonance involving the self-concept. Subjects in the Favorable condition, for whom the undesirable information about homosexuality was more dissonant with the self-concept, attributed more arousal to other persons. It is very unlikely that this difference was due to differences between conditions in severity of superego standards concerning homosexuality. In designing the experimental manipulations, care was taken to avoid any implications about the good or bad aspects of homosexuality. Since subjects were assigned randomly to conditions, it appears safe to assume that the groups did not differ on the average in their moral evaluation of homosexuality as such. The experiment was therefore capable of demonstrating the role of dissonance in projection while controlling the superego variable.

The finding that projection resulting from dissonance was aimed primarily at respected persons supported the second hypothesis. A number of defensive projection processes have been summoned in order to explain phenomena of prejudice toward out-groups (for example, Ackerman and Jahoda, 1950; Adorno, Frenkel-Brunswik, Levinson, and Sanford, 1950). It is important to note that in most cases projection is said to be aimed at persons and groups who are disliked and considered incomparable and inferior to the projector. This is, of course, quite different from the kind of projection revealed in the present experiment.

Let us consider possible alternative explanations for the results shown in Figure 2. Perhaps the dissonance introduced by the undesirable information in the Favorable condition led directly to a re-evaluation of homosexuality. That is, perhaps these subjects were able to change their attitude toward the trait without the intermediate step of associating it with favorably evaluated persons. This re-evaluation prior to attribution might then affect the pattern of attribution in such a way as to give the appearance, deceptively, of projection. Once the undesirability of the trait was reduced, there would be less tendency to attribute it differentially to disliked persons (halo effect). The effect of such a process would be to attenuate the halo pattern in the Favorable condition, and might be revealed in part as a greater tendency to attribute homosexuality to respected persons, as compared with subjects in the Unfavorable condition. Is this hypothesis capable of explaining the results of the experiment without resort to the hypothesis of defensive projection?

The data show that subjects in the Favorable condition did tend to follow the halo pattern when the partner was evaluated unfavorably or moderate in favorability. In Figure 2, the difference between the unfavorable ($n = 9$) and moderate ($n = 24$) points within the Favorable group was significant beyond the .10 level by the *t* test, and was at least as striking as the pattern for the Unfavorable group. If in fact the high dissonance in the Favorable condition had led directly to re-evaluation of homosexuality (without projection), then the halo effect would have been attenuated in this condition at all points in

Figure 2. There is no apparent reason for supposing that re-evaluation of the trait (without defensive projection) would have occurred among Favorable subjects confronted with respected partners more so than among other subjects in the Favorable group.

Consider another alternative explanation of the results. Perhaps the personality test report led subjects in the Favorable condition to conclude that they were generally better than other people, while those in the Unfavorable condition concluded they were worse than other people. Both groups of subjects then were given information that they possessed some degree of homosexual arousal. If subjects in the Favorable condition believed they were generally superior people, they might then have deduced that their partner was likely to be less worthy than themselves. This could result in rating the partner as possessing a greater amount of homosexual motivation. Persons in the Unfavorable condition would, by similar reasoning, conclude that their partner possessed a smaller amount of homosexual arousal. Such nondefensive processes could account for the overall difference in attribution between the two experimental conditions.

The data, as presented in Figure 2, cast doubt upon this alternative explanation. If the over-all difference between conditions were due to nondefensive deductions from the personality test reports, one would expect to find differences between the Favorable and Unfavorable conditions at all points along the attitude-toward-partner dimension. It is apparent, on the contrary, that the difference between conditions occurred only when the partner had been rated favorably.

It is interesting to speculate about the conditions under which dissonance with the self-concept will lead to projection onto favorably evaluated persons. In this experiment the dissonance-producing information was probably quite striking and unambiguous to the subjects. With great care the experimenter had explained that movement of the needle in response to looking at the photographs was a clear and indisputable sign of homosexual arousal. The situation was such that outright denial of the meaning of the needle movements would have been quite difficult for persons in reasonable touch with reality. It is very likely that these subjects were forced to accept the information as implying some degree of homosexual arousal in themselves. Under these circumstances of self-ascription, a good way to reduce the dissonance remaining was to try to get desirable people "into the same boat."

However, if the subjects had been able to deny the direct implications of the galvanic skin response, then a different pattern of attribution might have been observed. If the information were sufficiently ambiguous, so that partial denial occurred, then it would no longer be so comforting to attribute the undesirable trait to persons with whom the subject ordinarily classes himself. That is, when one is attempting to avoid self-ascription, it probably does not help to ascribe the trait to others who are seen as generally similar to one's self. Whether, when denial is possible, projection tends to be directed toward undesirable persons or out-groups, is an interesting question for further experimental exploration.

Summary

A laboratory experiment was conducted to investigate some of the conditions affecting the occurrence of defensive projection. It was hypothesized that such projection is a positive function of the amount of cognitive dissonance resulting from the introduction of a self-referent cognition of negative valence. Further, it was hypothesized that certain types of defensive projection are likely to be selectively aimed at persons who are favorably evaluated by the threatened individual. Two groups of normal subjects were prepared in such a way that different amounts of dissonance would result from their exposure to the same undesirable information about themselves. All subjects received fraudulent information to the effect that they possessed homosexual tendencies. During the presentation of the disturbing material, each subject made estimates of the degree of homosexual arousal of another subject with whom he was paired, and whom he had met only rather briefly just prior to this part of the experiment.

The results supported the hypotheses. On the average, subjects in the high dissonance condition attributed to their partner about the same degree of arousal as they themselves appeared to be having. Those in the low dissonance condition in general attributed to their partner a level of arousal less than their own. The evidence suggested that the high dissonance group projected only when confronted with a partner whom they had previously evaluated quite favorably on adjective rating scales.

The relation between the psychoanalytic and dissonance theory approaches to defensive processes was discussed. It was proposed that study of the selection of objects should throw light upon the possible existence of distinct varieties of defensive projection.

References

Ackerman, N. W., and Jahoda, Marie. *Anti-Semitism and emotional disorder.* New York: Harper, 1950.

Adorno, T. W., Frenkel-Brunswik, Else, Levinson, D. J., and Sanford, R. N. *The authoritarian personality.* New York: Harper, 1950.

Fenichel, O. *The psychoanalytic theory of neurosis.* New York: Norton, 1945.

Festinger, L. A theory of social comparison processes. *Hum. Relat.*, 1954, **7**, 117-140.

Festinger, L. *A theory of cognitive dissonance.* Stanford, Calif.: Stanford Univ. Press, 1957.

Gerard, H. B. A specific study: Conflict and conformity. *Amer. Psychologist*, 1959, **14**, 413. (Abstract)

Gerard, H. B., and Rabbie, J. M. Fear, affiliation, and social comparison. *Amer. Psychologist*, 1960, **15**, 409. (Abstract)

Murstein, B. I. The projection of hostility on the Rorschach and as a result of ego-threat. *J. proj. Tech.*, 1956, **20**, 418-428.

Wright, Beatrice A. Altruism in children and the perceived conduct of others. *J. abnorm. soc. Psychol.*, 1942, **37**, 218-233.

A Critique of the Theory of Cognitive Dissonance

Natalia P. Chapanis and Alphonse Chapanis

This article reviews critically the experimental evidence in support of cognitive dissonance theory as applied to complex social events. The criticisms which can be made of this literature fall into 2 main classes. First, the experimental manipulations are usually so complex and the crucial variable so confounded that no valid conclusions can be drawn from the data. Second, a number of fundamental methodological inadequacies in the analysis of results—as, e.g., rejection of cases and faulty statistical analysis of the data—vitiate the findings. As a result, one can only say that the evidence adduced for cognitive dissonance theory is inconclusive. Suggestions are offered for the methodological improvement of studies in this area. The review concludes with the thesis that the most attractive feature of cognitive dissonance theory, its simplicity, is in actual fact a self-defeating limitation.

Social psychologists have been trying for many years to predict the conditions under which attitudes and opinions are changed. In general their attempts have not been conspicuously successful. One of the first major breakthroughs in this area came when Leon Festinger (1957) published his book *A Theory of Cognitive Dissonance*. In this book the author presented a simple conceptual scheme by which he could predict with precision the outcomes of certain social situations. To support his theory, Festinger marshaled data from an impressive variety of field and experimental studies. In addition, he and other workers have since then conducted a number of studies designed to test specific derivations of the theory. What can we say about all this literature?

Cognitive dissonance theory has already been reviewed by Bruner (1957), Asch (1958), Osgood (1960), and Zajonc (1960). These writers, however, have been primarily concerned with a critical evaluation of the conceptual system employed in dissonance theory. And, whatever they might think of the theory, most workers (except perhaps Asch) have been impressed by the scope, relevance, and ingenuity of the experimental evidence gathered in its support.

There is an engaging simplicity about Festinger's dissonance formulations. No matter how complex the social situation, Festinger assumes that it is possible to represent the meaning which the situation has for an individual by a series of elementary *cognitions*—statements that an individual might make describing his "knowledge, opinions or beliefs" (Festinger, 1957, p. 3). Moreover, a simple inventory of a group of related cognitions is sufficient to reveal whether or not they are consistent. The theory assumes further that people prefer consistency among their cognitions and that they will initiate change in order to preserve this consistency. So far these ideas are not new. They had been promulgated as early as 1946 by Heider with his concept of balance and imbalance. The magic of Festinger's theory, however, seems to lie in the ease with which imponderably complex social situations are reduced to simple statements, most often just two such statements. This having been done, a simple inspection for rational consistency is enough to predict whether or not change will occur. Such uncomplicated rationality seems especially welcome after having been told for years that our attitudes and resulting behavior are strongly dependent on motivational, emotional, affective, and perceptual processes (e.g., Krech and Crutchfield, 1948; Rosenberg, 1960).

Five years have now elapsed since the publication of Festinger's book, and this seems to

From N. P. Chapanis and A. Chapanis, "Cognitive Dissonance: Five Years Later," *Psychological Bulletin*, 1964, **61**, 1-22. Reprinted by permission of the American Psychological Association.

be an appropriate time to pause for a close look at the evidence in support of the theory. For no matter how appealing a theory might be, in the final analysis it is the evidence that counts. This paper, therefore, will be concerned with a review of experiments on cognitive dissonance in humans from two points of view. First we shall consider whether an experimenter really did what he said he did. Then later we shall consider whether the experimenter really got the results he said he did.

Controversial Experimental Manipulations

As we all know, good experimental work always involves manipulating conditions in such a way that we may ascribe changes we observe in our dependent variables to the manipulations we carried out on the independent variables. In actual practice we rarely define these manipulations in careful operational terms. When a pellet drops into a cup in front of a hungry rat we call it a reward or reinforcement; when a wire transmits an electric shock to a person we call it punishment or stress; and so on. Moreover, we do not, in general, quarrel with our fellow experimenter's interpretation of the situation. After all, he was there; he ought to know what it was about. However, when we deal with experiments on cognitive dissonance we have a very special problem on our hands.

Experimental Dissonance

Simply stated, cognitive dissonance theory is concerned with what happens when the cognitions of a person are discrepant. The basic premise is that discrepant cognitions create tension which the individual strives to reduce by making his cognitions more consistent. This tension is called cognitive dissonance, and the drive towards consistency, dissonance reduction. "When two or more cognitive elements are psychologically inconsistent, dissonance is created. Dissonance is defined as psychological tension having drive characteristics" so that when dissonance arises the individual attempts to reduce it (Zimbardo, 1960, p. 86).

For our purposes at the moment the most important thing to note about the theory is that dissonance is an intervening variable whose antecedents are the private internal cognitions of a person. To test a theory like this, it is up to the experimenter to create various degrees of dissonance by introducing various discrepant cognitions within an individual. Whenever contradictory statements or syllogisms or opinions are used, there is not likely to be much controversy about the fact that they must lead to discrepant internal cognitions, and so, by definition, to dissonance. Indeed, studies on cognitive dissonance of this type have yielded results which are well-established, clear-cut, and consistent. But for the experiments under review here, the situation is rarely as simple as this. The Festinger group is primarily concerned with applying their dissonance formulation to predict complex social events. In order to do this experimentally, they use elaborate instructions and intricate relationships between experimenter and S to introduce discrepant cognitions and therefore to produce dissonance. Under such conditions, how can we be sure that the experimental situation has been successful in creating dissonance and dissonance alone?

In the face of such difficulties, it is always a good policy to ask the S himself about the situation, either directly or indirectly. It should be possible, for instance, to find out how the Ss perceived each of the experimental manipulations. One could also determine whether Ss perceived the situation as conflictful and, if so, to what extent. This kind of information is crucial to the theory of cognitive dissonance because all its predictions are based on the assumption that a state of differing, incompatible cognitions has been produced within the S. Unfortunately, evidence of this kind from the Ss themselves is not always available in the studies under review here. As a result, it is up to the reader to decide whether the experimental manipulations had the effect which the authors claim.

The other side of the coin, equally important, is that we must also assure ourselves that the experimental manipulations did not at the same time produce other internal states or cognitions within the S which could contaminate or even account for the findings. In fact, certain "nonobvious" derivations of some of these experiments may perhaps become a little more obvious when the experiments are reinterpreted to take other factors into consideration.

It is worthwhile spending a few moments on these nonobvious derivations. If we disregard the intermediate steps and simply consider the independent and dependent variables, it is possible to describe the essential aspects of some of these derivations by saying that they follow a *pain principle*. Reduced to essentials, some of Festinger's derivations say that the more rewarding a situation, the more negative is the effect; and contrariwise, the more painful a situation, the more positive is the effect. This is clearly illustrated by the following quotation from Festinger (1961): "Rats and people come to love the things for which they have suffered." However, if we carefully examine the kinds of experiments which are supposed to test these derivations, we find that, in general, the situation contains both painful and rewarding conditions, but that the manipulation is interpreted in terms of only one of these. It should be apparent that if a situation is both rewarding *and* painful, and the dependent variable shows a positive effect, it is not legitimate to attribute it solely to the painful variable, or vice versa. To use a statistician's terminology, the variables are confounded.

Our most general criticism, then, is that some dissonance experiments have been designed in such a way that it is impossible to draw any definite conclusions from them.

Examples

The best way of illustrating these points is to describe an experimental procedure and then to analyse it from two points of view: Did the experimenter really produce the discrepant cognitions he said he did? Did the experimental manipulations produce other

cognitions that could contaminate or account for his findings?

Relief or Dissonance? Let us take this experiment: College women volunteered to participate in a series of group discussions on the psychology of sex. They were seen individually by the experimenter before being allowed to join an "on-going group." Some of the girls were told they would have to pass an embarrassment test to see if they were tough enough to stand the group discussion. They were free to withdraw at this point, and one S did so. Girls in the severe embarrassment group had to read out loud in the presence of the male experimenter some vivid descriptions of sexual activity and a list of obscene sex words. Another group of girls— the mild embarrassment group—read some mild sexual material. All of these girls were told that they were successful in passing the embarrassment test. Each S then listened as a silent member to a simulated, supposedly ongoing group discussion, which was actually a standard tape recording of a rather dull and banal discussion about the sexual behavior of animals. A control group listened only to the simulated group discussion. All groups then made ratings about this discussion, its participants, and their own interest in future discussions. The ratings made by the severe embarrassment group were, on the average, somewhat more favorable than those made by the other two groups.

What was this experiment about? Was it to demonstrate the effect of feelings of relief when people discover that a task (the group discussion) is not as painfully embarrassing as the embarrassment test led them to believe? No. Was it to demonstrate the effect of success in a difficult test (passing the embarrassment test) on task evaluation? No. Was it to demonstrate the displacement of vicarious sexual pleasure from a discomfiting, but sexually arousing, situation to a more socially acceptable one? No. The experimenters called it "The Effect of Severity of Initiation on Liking for a Group" (Aronson and Mills, 1959); that is, the more painful the initiation, the more the Ss like the group.

Chapanis and Chapanis   **349**

They predict the outcome for the severe embarrassment group in the following way: In successfully passing the embarrassment test these girls "held the cognition that they had undergone a painful experience" in order to join a group; the discussion, however, was so dull and uninteresting that they realized the unpleasant initiation procedure was not worth it. This produced dissonance since "negative cognitions about the discussion ... were dissonant with the cognition that they had undergone a painful experience." One of the ways they could reduce this dissonance was by reevaluating the group discussion as more interesting than it really was.

All this may be so, but in order to accept the authors' explanation we must be sure the girls really did hold these discrepant cognitions, and no others. We have to be sure, for instance, that they felt no relief when they found the group discussion banal instead of embarrassing, that success in passing a difficult test (the embarrassment test) did not alter their evaluation of the task, that the sexual material did not evoke any vicarious pleasure or expectation of pleasure in the future, and that the group discussion was so dull that the girls would have regretted participating. There is no way of checking directly on the first three conditions, although other experimental evidence suggests that their effect is not negligible. However, to check on the fourth factor we have the data from the control group showing that the group discussion was, in fact, more interesting than not (it received an average rating of 10 on a 0-15 scale). It is, therefore, difficult to believe that the girls regretted participating. To sum up, since the design of this experiment does not exclude the possibility that pleasurable cognitions were introduced by the sequence of events, and since, in addition, the existence of "painful" cognitions was not demonstrated, we cannot accept the authors' interpretation without serious reservations.

It is interesting to speculate what would have happened if the girls had been "initiated" into the group by the use of a more generally accepted painful procedure, such as using electric shock. Somehow it seems doubtful

that this group would appreciate the group discussion more than the control group, unless—and here is the crucial point—the conditions were so manipulated that Ss experienced a feeling of successful accomplishment in overcoming the painful obstacle. It seems to us that if there is anything to the relationship between severity of initiation and liking for the group, it lies in this feeling of successful accomplishment. The more severe the test, the stronger is the pleasurable feeling of success in overcoming the obstacle. There is no need to postulate a drive due to dissonance if a *pleasure principle* can account for the results quite successfully.

The same feeling of successful accomplishment may, incidentally, be the relevant variable involved in some of the "effort" experiments done by the Festinger group (e.g., Cohen, 1959). It seems reasonable to expect that in such experiments the higher the degree of perceived effort, the greater the feeling of successful accomplishment in performing a task. Thus, *effort* would be confounded with *feeling of success*. Note, however, that success is pleasant, whereas effort is painful. Here is a situation which could be both rewarding and painful, but dissonance workers see it only as painful. (Two other effort experiments will be analyzed in greater detail later in this section.)

Reward or Incredulity? Let us look at another experiment, this time by Festinger and Carlsmith (1959): Out of several possibilities, Ss chose to take part in a 2-hour experiment falsely labeled as an experiment on "measures of performance." The Ss were tested individually and were given a "very boring" and repetitive task for about 1 hour. At the end of the hour each S was given a false explanation about the purpose of the experiment. He was told that it was an experiment to test the effect of expectation on task performance. Some Ss were then asked if they would mind acting in a deception for the next couple of minutes since the person regularly employed for this was away. The Ss of one group were hired for $1.00 each, those of another group for $20.00 each, to tell the next incoming S how enjoyable and interesting the experiment had been (ostensibly the expectation variable). Each S was also told he might be called on to do this again. Some Ss refused to be hired. A control group of Ss was not asked to take part in any deception. Subsequently, all Ss (control and hired Ss) were seen by a neutral interviewer, supposedly as part of the psychology department's program of evaluating experiments. During the interview, Ss were asked to rate the experiment along four dimensions. The only significant difference between the three groups was in terms of enjoyment. The control group rated the experiment as just a little on the dull side, the $1.00 group thought it was somewhat enjoyable, and the $20.00 group was neutral. The mean ratings for the control and $20.00 groups were not significantly different from each other nor from the neutral point.

What was this experiment about? The authors call it "Cognitive Consequences of Forced Compliance." They make the prediction that "the larger the reward given to the S" the smaller the dissonance and therefore "the smaller the subsequent opinion change," and "furthermore . . . the observed opinion change should be greatest when the pressure used to elicit the overt behavior is just sufficient to do it." As an aside we should point out that, inasmuch as these statements clearly refer to a maximum and so by inference to some sort of a curvilinear or nonmonotonic relationship, it would have been better if more reward categories had been used. In addition, two more control groups—a *deception-but-no-reward* group, and a *reward-but-no-deception* group—should have been included to separate out the effects of reward and deception. However, our primary concern at the moment is not with such technical matters of experimental design.

Let us examine instead the meaning of the descriptive term "forced compliance." According to Festinger (1957), it means "public compliance without private acceptance" (p. 87). The reward Ss, it is true, complied publicly with the instructions in that they

described a boring task as enjoyable to another S. Notice, however, that even the control group rated the task as only slightly boring. This suggests that the false explanation placed the task in a wider context and may have led to "private acceptance" of the whole situation by both control and reward Ss. We could also question the choice of the word "forced." Forced implies a lack of freedom, but it is extremely difficult to predict how an S perceives his freedom of choice even when this variable is experimentally manipulated (e.g., Brehm and Cohen, 1959a). All we can say is that the term "forced compliance" is not a good description of the events in this experiment.

What seems to be even more important, however, is that the experiment could be more appropriately entitled "The Effect of a Plausible and Implausible Reward on Task Evaluation." As far as we can tell, Ss were not asked to describe their reactions to the size of the reward. Nevertheless, $20.00 is a lot of money for an undergraduate even when it represents a whole day's work. When it is offered for something that must be much less than 30 minutes work, it is difficult to imagine a student accepting the money without becoming wary and alert to possible tricks. In fact, more than 16% of the original Ss in the $20.00 group had to be discarded because they voiced suspicions, or refused to be hired. Under such circumstances, it seems likely that those who were retained might have hedged or been evasive about their evaluation of the experiment. The mean rating for the $20.00 group was $-.05$ on a scale that ranged from -5.00 (dislike) to 5.00 (like); that is, the mean rating was at the neutral point. As other workers (e.g., Edwards, 1946) have suggested, a rating at the zero or neutral point may be ambiguous, ambivalent, or indifferent in meaning and may simply represent an evasion. The authors' data, unfortunately, do not permit us to determine whether individual Ss did in fact respond this way. In any event, if we assume that $1.00 is a plausible, but $20.00 an implausible, reward, then the results fall neatly into the pattern of all previous and more extensive experiments on the effect of credulity on pressures to conformity (Fisher and Lubin, 1958).

To sum up, the design of this experiment does not allow us (a) to check whether discrepant cognitions were in fact produced, and (b) to rule out alternative explanations.

Incidentally, the authors of other related studies (Brehm, 1960; Brehm and Lipsher, 1959; Cohen, Terry, and Jones, 1959) have difficulty in accounting for all of their results according to dissonance theory predictions. These difficulties disappear if we use a plausibility explanation. The argument would proceed along these lines: If an individual is subjected to many pressures towards change from a number of different sources, (a) each pressure will act on the individual, and (b) their effect will be cumulative. For instance, we may increase pressure on an individual by limiting his freedom of choice, by giving him acceptable rewards, by presenting him with statements that strongly support a position discrepant to his own, by increasing the size of the discrepancy, and so on. Each of these alone will produce a greater and greater opinion change until—and this is the critical part of the argument—the situation becomes implausible, at which point the *S* will ignore the pressures and show no change. It also seems reasonable to suppose that a combination of *any* of these factors will act cumulatively to produce the implausible effect.

We can express this situation in statistical terminology. For example, if we have a two-factor experiment with two levels of pressure towards opinion change in each variable, we would expect to find that the two main effects are significant. Moreover, we would predict that the interaction would also be significant primarily because the combination of both "high pressures" would be implausible and so produce the least opinion change. In general, this is the pattern of results obtained by the dissonance workers in experiments of this type.

Mealtime Troubles. Another example of an untested interpretation occurs in the Brehm (1959) experiment on the effect of a *fait accompli* in which boys were offered a prize if they ate a portion of a disliked vegetable. While eating it, some *S*s were casually told that a letter would be sent to their parents informing them of their participation in the experiment and of the vegetable they ate. Those boys who indicated they had trouble about eating the vegetable at home (i.e., it was more often served than eaten) subsequently changed their rating of the disliked vegetable towards a more favorable one. What did the letter mean to these boys? According to the author it meant that "the Ss would have to eat more" of the vegetable at home. But this is a guess, not based on any evidence in the experiment. Furthermore, in an extension of the same procedure at the same school with equivalent *S*s from the same classes, direct manipulation of the commitment to further eating "failed to produce an overall effect on liking" (Brehm, 1960, p. 382). Under the circumstances, we find it difficult to accept the author's contention that the *fait accompli* increased cognitive dissonance by increasing the commitment to eating. There is little doubt that mentioning the letter changed the ratings, but only for boys who had mealtime troubles. The key to the problem most likely lies in the expectation these boys had about the effect of the letter on their parents and on themselves. However, the design of the experiment does not allow us to find out what this expectation was.

Confounded Effort. In a recent experiment, Aronson (1961) tried to separate the effects of secondary reinforcement from dissonance in a rewarding situation.

Reinforcement theory suggests that stimuli associated with reward gain in attractiveness; dissonance theory suggests that stimuli associated with "no reward" gain in attractiveness . . . if a person has expended effort in an attempt to attain the reward (p. 375).

Aronson argues that since the effect of secondary reinforcement is constant, nonrewarded objects should become more attractive as the effort to obtain them increases.

In order to test this hypothesis, Ss fished for cans to obtain a reward ($.25) inside one third of the cans. The rewarded cans were of one color, the nonrewarded ones of another, but the Ss could not determine which they had snared until the cans had actually been pulled out. One group of Ss—the low-effort group—was told that their task was not tedious. They had the relatively easy task of fishing out a can with a magnet, a task which took them, on the average, only 14 seconds per can. Another group of Ss—the high-effort group—was told that their task was extremely tedious. They had the relatively difficult task of fishing out a can with a hook, which took them, on the average, 52 seconds per can. All Ss continued fishing for the reward money until 16 unrewarded cans had been pulled out. The Ss rated the relative attractiveness of the two colors before and after carrying out the task. The results show that in the low-effort condition, the attractiveness of the color on the rewarded cans increased (a secondary reinforcement effect), but in the high-effort condition no change was observed. All of this was interpreted as substantiating the cognitive dissonance predictions.

Aronson explains the lack of change in the high-effort condition by saying that the effects of dissonance and secondary reinforcement are equal but opposite in direction, and so cancel each other. However, if we look more carefully at the experimental manipulation of effort, we see that the low-effort condition is actually a reward rate of $.25 about every 42 seconds, and the high-effort condition is actually a reward rate of $.25 about every 156 seconds. In other words, the low-effort group is, at the same time, a high-reward-rate group, and the high-effort group, a low-reward-rate group. The difference obtained between the two groups could then be simply the result of the difference in reward rates, and the lack of change in the high-effort group the result of their low reward rate.

To summarize, Aronson tried to demonstrate the effect of effort in a rewarding situation. However, the design of the experiment confounds effort with reward rate. As a result, no unambiguous conclusions can be drawn as to the effect of effort.

There is yet another experiment on effort in which confounding occurs. Yaryan and Festinger (1961) tried to show the effect of "preparatory effort" on belief in a future event. The Ss volunteered to participate in an experiment labeled "Techniques of Study" which was supposed to investigate the techniques, hunches, and hypotheses that students use to study for exams. The Ss were told that only half of them would take part in the complete experiment, which involved taking an IQ test. All Ss were given an information sheet on which there were definitions essential to this supposed IQ test. In the high-effort condition, Ss were told to study the sheet and memorize the definitions briefly. The latter were also told that they would have access to the sheet later if they were to take the IQ test. Each S was then asked to express his estimate of the probability that he would take the IQ test. The results show that Ss in the high-effort group thought it was more probable that they would take the test.

The authors (Yaryan and Festinger, 1961) explain the results in the following way: Exerting "a great deal of effort" is inconsistent with the cognition that one may not take the test, so Ss in the high-effort group should believe "more strongly in the likelihood of the occurrence of the event" (p. 606). This might very well be the case, but in this experiment the variable of effort is confounded with the presence of other predictors for the event. All Ss had been told that this was an experiment on the techniques of study, but the only group which *did* any studying was the high-effort group. In addition, the studying that was done was highly relevant for the IQ test. Under the circumstances, it does not seem at all surprising that Ss in this group took these additional cues to mean that they were assigned to the complete experiment and to the IQ test. As it stands now, the Yaryan and Festinger experiment does not separate the effect of effort from that of additional cues.

Reliability Is Not Validity. As we have

seen, most cognitive dissonance formulations are concerned with what happens after a person makes a decision. One of the earliest experiments designed specifically to investigate this problem was the gambling experiment described by Festinger (1957, p. 164) and successfully replicated by Cohen, Brehm, and Latané (1959) with minor variations in procedure. The agreement between these two studies has done much to enhance the belief in the validity of cognitive dissonance formulations (e.g., Riecken, 1960, p. 489).

The experimental procedure in these two studies was relatively simple. Each *S* played a card game with the experimenter for variable money stakes. Before beginning the game each *S* was informed of the rules of the game, and on the basis of this information chose one of two sides on which to play. He was told that he could change sides once during the game, but that it would cost him money. He was led to expect that he would play 30 games. At the end of 12 games, play was interrupted and *S* was given a probability graph to study. The graph, a different one for each side, gave the (false) information that the chosen side was the losing one. The dependent variables were the time spent in studying the graph and the number of people who changed sides. Results were analyzed in terms of a weighted average of the amount of money won or lost. The pattern of results obtained is very complex and would require at least a fourth-order parabola to describe it. Nevertheless, the various ups-and-downs were interpreted as supporting the dissonance theory predictions for postdecision, information-seeking processes.

Two things strike us about the dissonance theory interpretation of this experiment. First, Festinger is not consistent in his dissonance formulations. Let us look at the way in which the results are interpreted. The money winners spent a moderate amount of time studying the graph. Festinger considers this the result of dissonance produced by the information in the graph which purported to show that these winners were actually on the losing side. If we accept this line of reasoning, it should follow that the losers would have no

such dissonance (the graph confirmed their losses), and would therefore spend little time on the graph. This was not so. Festinger (1957), however, has three other dissonance explanations to account for the complex behavior of the losers. He argues, first of all, that loss of money is itself dissonance producing and the bigger the loss, the bigger the dissonance. The small losers spent as much time as they did in the "hope that the graph would tell them they were actually on the correct side" (p. 171). If this explanation is correct, the bigger losers should have spent an even longer time searching the graph—but they did not. Festinger explains this away by saying that the bigger losers would avoid the graph "if the graph were perceived as yielding information which would probably increase the dissonance which already existed" (p. 172). If this explanation is correct, the biggest losers should have spent the least amount of time on the graph—but they did not. To explain this behavior Festinger postulates yet another hypothesis. For the biggest losers, "the easiest way to eliminate the dissonance would be to increase it temporarily to a point when it was greater than the resistance to change of the behavior," that is, they would study the graph, then switch sides. If this explanation is true, then we would expect that all of the biggest losers, and only the biggest losers, would switch sides—but this was not so. It should be noted that these four dissonance hypotheses are inconsistent with each other, since they predict effects in different directions. Moreover, there is no a priori way of determining the degree to which each particular hypothesis applies to the groups. This whole matter can be summarized in another way: If the pattern of results had been exactly the reverse, these same explanations would apply just as well.

This brings us to the second point. The most important criticism of this gambling experiment is that it is not so much an experiment on the dissonance-reducing effects of information in postdecision processes as it is an experiment on "information seeking in predecision processes" (suggested by F. E. Emery). The *S*s had been told they could change sides, and they were actually given an opportunity to do so when they were handed the graph. Festinger (1957) and Cohen et al. (1959) reported that many *S*s, both winners and losers, announced their decision to switch sides at this time. What was not reported, however, was the number of *S*s who looked at the graph in order to reach a decision whether or not it would be more profitable to change sides. In other words, *S*s looked at the graph not to reduce dissonance, but to look for information to help them decide whether they should change sides. With this interpretation, the pattern of results becomes more obvious and reasonable. For example, in one of the two conditions of the Cohen et al. replication those *S*s who neither won nor lost any money spent the most time looking at the graph. This finding is entirely inexplicable in dissonance terms, even with an imaginative use of all four of Festinger's hypotheses. However, if we consider this experiment to be concerned with predecision processes, then we see that these *S*s had gained the least amount of information from the actual play of the game and were, therefore, trying to extract as much information as possible from the graph before reaching a decision.

Taking all of these factors into consideration, we are forced to conclude that Festinger's interpretations, however ingenious, are unnecessarily elaborate and unjustified. Moreover, the successful replication of the experiment suggests—not that the cognitive dissonance formulations are valid—but only that the results of experiments of this type are reproducible.

Subsequent experiments on selected aspects of information seeking in postdecision processes have done nothing to clarify the situation. Adams (1961) and Maccoby, Maccoby, Romney, and Adams (1961) showed that people tend to seek information which agrees with their viewpoint, but Rosen (1961) obtained results which show that people tend to seek information which disagrees with their viewpoint. It seems more likely to us that, in general, people will often seek new information whether it be consonant or contrary. Indeed, this is apparently the kind of result that Feather (1962) obtained. To be sure, when prejudice or some other highly motivated state is involved, people are selective in their perceptions and avoid contrary material. But under these conditions it is the motive itself, and not dissonance, that seems to be crucial.

Interpretation of Manipulations

Perhaps the illustrations cited above will suffice to show that the experiments adduced to support the theory of cognitive dissonance involve highly complex manipulations. The effects of these manipulations are open to alternative explanations which have generally not been dealt with adequately by the authors. We can diagram this in the following way: Let us suppose that the complex experimental manipulations produce the Cognitions 1, 2, 3, 4 ... *n* in the *S*, as illustrated on the left side of Figure 1. Two of these cognitions (Cognitions 1 and 2) are chosen by the experimenter as being the relevant discrepant

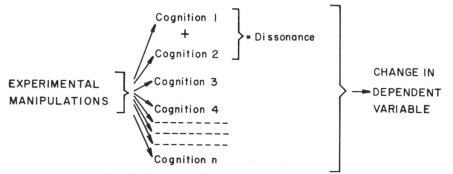

Figure 1. The type of confounding frequently found in experiments on cognitive dissonance.

cognitions producing dissonance. Any observed change in the dependent variable is then attributed to that dissonance. But, as we see by examining the whole of Figure 1, this may not necessarily be the case. Any one cognition, or any combination of cognitions, could have been responsible for the change in the dependent variable. There is no way of ascertaining which, because the effects of all these cognitions have been confounded.

It is possible to design experiments so that these effects are not confounded. As a step in this direction we recommend first of all that the experimental manipulations be simplified. It is difficult to agree about differences in cognitions when the instructions, task, and procedure differ in many ways for control and experimental groups. Our second recommendation is that additional control groups be included in the design of these experiments to deal with the irreducible differences in experimental manipulation. Our third recommendation is that a little more attention be given to discovering the possible cognitions that an *S* might have about the situation, particularly those which might be contrary to dissonance theory. Only under such carefully controlled conditions can we begin to talk about unequivocal evidence in support of cognitive dissonance theory.

Controversial Treatments of the Data

So much for experimental manipulations. Now to see if the experimenter really got the results he says he did. Our most serious criticisms of the experiments cited in support of dissonance theory fall under the heading of methodological inadequacies in the analyses of results. Of these inadequacies the most important is the rejection of cases, not only because it is so fundamental a flaw, but also because the supporters of dissonance theory so often do it.

Rejection of Cases

If an experimenter is interested in the performance of only a certain group of *S*s, it is legitimate for him to select these *S*s before beginning the experiment, or sometimes even

after the experiment, before the results are analyzed. However, when *S*s are selectively discarded after the data of an experiment have been collected, tabulated, and sometimes even analyzed, it leaves the reader with a feeling of uneasiness. The uneasy feeling grows if the *S*s are discarded because their results are said to be "unreliable," or if the experimenter gives inconsistent reasons—or no reasons at all—for their rejection. But let us look at the experiments themselves.

Unreliable Ss.

Brehm and Cohen (1959b) asked sixth-grade children to indicate how much they liked several different toys before and after they had chosen one for themselves. The choice of the gift and the postchoice rating were made a week after the prechoice rating. The authors hypothesized that there would be an increase in the evaluation of the chosen article, and a decrease in the evaluation of the nonchosen article, the greater the dissimilarity among the toys, and the greater the number of alternatives from which to choose. In general these predictions were upheld. But of the original sample of 203 children *only 72* were used in the analysis. In the authors' (Brehm and Cohen, 1959b) words, the reasons for the reduction were as follows:

First, the choice alternatives for each *S* had to be liked, but not so much that an increase in liking would be impossible. Second, one alternative had to be initially more liked than any other so that its choice could be expected. Increased ratings of the chosen item are thus not likely to be simply a result of normal (and random) changes in actual liking from the first questionnaire to the second. *In addition, Ss who failed to choose the alternative initially marked as most liked, were excluded because they gave unreliable or invalid ratings.* Finally, in order to ensure that initially less liked alternatives were seriously considered as possible, initial ratings of these alternatives could not be much lower than the most liked alternative (p. 375; italics added).

Note first that the exact limits of all these requirements were determined only after inspection of the data, despite the fact that each *S* had been given a prearranged choice based on his initial ratings. However, let us look more carefully at the italicized item—the exclusion of *S*s because of unreliability. If *S*s give unreliable results, it is usual to assume that the measuring instrument itself is unreliable; indeed, the authors themselves admit this when they mention "the low reliability of our measure of liking." However, discarding selected *S*s does nothing to improve the reliability of an instrument.

Discarding *S*s who did not choose the alternative initially marked as most liked may in fact falsely reduce the computed error variance, change the mean values, and so enhance the possibility of obtaining a significant difference in rating. To illustrate, the upper half of Figure 2 shows the ratings for

that no random change occurs from just before the choice to just after it. If, as Brehm and Cohen did, we discard all those *S*s who chose Y rather than X, this means that we eliminate from the shaded area in the bottom half of Figure 2 all those cases in which $Y' > X'$. Such a process can only reduce the variance of both distributions of differences in ratings (that is, $X' - X$ and $Y' - Y$) and automatically increase the mean difference between them. Moreover, this selection procedure will automatically produce precisely the effect which the authors predicted, namely, that the mean rating for the chosen toy increases while the rating for the nonchosen toy decreases. Furthermore, these effects

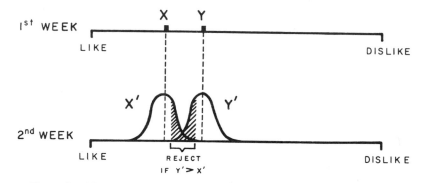

Figure 2. This illustration shows how the rejection of *S*s from the shaded area may have introduced a statistical artifact into the experiment by Brehm and Cohen (1959).

two toys, X and Y, which satisfy the conditions specified by Brehm and Cohen: they are both liked, one is liked more than the other, but the difference is not great. Now let us assume that the ratings are subject to errors of measurement and that they vary randomly from time to time. Let us further assume that the expressed rating, the liking, at any one moment in time, is perfectly correlated with choice.

The situation a week later is shown in the bottom half of Figure 2. The ratings for X are now distributed as X', the ratings for Y as Y'. Now the *S*s are asked to make a choice. Let us assume the null hypothesis, that is, the actual process of choosing a gift does not alter the liking or rating of a toy. Since the choice and the postchoice rating occur so close together in time, we can also assume

will be greatest in the group from which most such *S*s were discarded. Most of these discards came from the "four alternatives condition,"[1] and the change in rating is actually greatest for this condition.

In a footnote (p. 376) the authors (Brehm and Cohen, 1959b) state they carried out similar computations on their "unselected population," that is, on the entire sample of 203 *S*s. Although the sensitivity of the statistical test is now nearly twice as great (because of the increase in *N* from 72 to 203), they find no effect due to the number of alternatives (one of the two predictions made). Tests of the other prediction "yield support" for the "dissimilarity hypothesis." It is not clear, however, whether the authors mean by this a sta-

[1] J. Brehm, personal communication, 1961.

tistically significant difference or simply a nonsignificant trend. To sum up, it seems reasonable to conclude that the significant results obtained in this and similar experiments may very well be statistical artifacts.

Contradictory Reasons

Sometimes it is difficult to reconcile the reasons given for the rejection of cases with other statements by the same author. For example, in the experiment on "Attitude Change and Justification for Compliance" (Cohen, Brehm, and Fleming, 1958), the initial analysis showed no significant difference between the two justification groups. The authors then eliminated more than half of the *S*s (47 out of 92), carried out a second analysis on the remainder, and concluded that "the difference in amount of change is significant by one-tailed *t* test at .07 level." Relatively more *S*s whose opinion did not change were eliminated from the low-justification condition (35 out of 63). Not surprisingly, the new mean for the low-justification condition turned out to be greater than for the high-justification condition.

Part of the reasoning for this selection of cases was as follows (Cohen et al., 1958): "since extremity of position inhibits attitude change . . . it seems reasonable to eliminate the extremes" (p. 277). A year later, however, Cohen (1959) made this statement: "If the individual . . . engages in some behavior with regard to the contrary communication . . . then the greater the discrepancy [extremity of position], the greater the opinion change" (p. 387).

In their original article, Cohen et al. state that their results should be interpreted cautiously, but, unfortunately, they do not follow their own advice. Whenever these authors refer to their findings in later articles (e.g., Brehm, 1960; Cohen, 1960), they quote their results as substantiating cognitive dissonance theory without any of these cautionary reminders.

What Is Going On? An example of sample reduction for obscure reasons occurs in an experiment on the readership of "own car" and "other car" advertisements by new and old car owners (Ehrlich, Guttman, Schonbach, and Mills, 1957). A group of 65 new car owners was randomly chosen from a list of recent auto registrants. The car advertisements read by this group were compared with those read by a group of 60 old car owners chosen from a telephone directory. The raw data for these analyses were the percentages of car advertisements noticed and read in a selection of magazines and newspapers which the owners had previously indicated they read regularly. The cognitive dissonance theory predictions were that new car owners would most often read advertisements about their own make of car and avoid reading those of competing makes. In general, these predictions were upheld for the data presented.

The principal difficulty with this experiment is that cases were successively rejected in various stages of the analysis so that when one finally arrives at the critical statistical test it is virtually impossible to determine what the remaining data mean. Let us see if we can trace the authors' steps in this process. The authors first present a table showing the mean percentage of advertisements noticed and mean percentage of advertisements read of those noticed for each of the categories "own," "considered," and "other car." They (Ehrlich et al., 1957) state in a note accompanying the table that:

The *N*s are reduced because in some cases no advertisements of a particular kind appeared in the issues shown or none of those which appeared were noticed. They are further reduced because not all respondents named cars as "seriously considered" (p. 99).

The first and third reasons impose a limit on the number of *S*s whose results could be used. The largest reduction due to these two limitations was in the category "considered car" for old car owners, where the *N* of 60 was reduced to 31.

The second reason given in the quotation above means that an owner who did not notice any advertisement in a particular category was discarded from the table of "advertisements read" for that category. For example, if an owner noticed (or noticed and read) an ad about another car, but did not notice any advertisements about his own car, he was included under the category of "other car" but excluded from the category of "own car" in computing the mean percentage of "advertisements read of those noticed." Up to one third of the remaining cases were eliminated from the various categories for this reason.

The next point at which still more cases are rejected is in the computation of several sign tests of significance. We are told that the *N*s are reduced because not all comparisons were possible. What this means is that significance tests were computed only on those owners who *noticed at least one advertisement in each of the pairs of categories compared.* Finally, those owners who read an equal percentage of advertisements in each of the two categories were also discarded.

Taking all of the above factors into account we find that as much as 82% of the original sample was discarded in certain categories!

The sign tests mentioned above were used only for making certain pairs of comparisons. For overall tests of their hypotheses the authors resorted to chi square and give terminal chi square values, with their associated probabilities, alongside the tables for the sign tests. The article itself does not say upon what *N*s, or what groupings, the chi squares were computed, but correspondence[2] reveals that the chi square tests were made on the same *S*s as were used in computing the sign tests.

At best, this entire situation may be described as unclear. In the first place, it is difficult to know how to interpret significance tests based on such highly selected data. Furthermore, in computing chi squares for the same *S*s as were used in the sign tests, it appears that the authors discarded some data (the ties) which should properly have been included. If we have been able to thread our way correctly through the authors' manipulations of the data we find that the chi squares, computed for all the relevant data, are less

significant than reported by the authors, and, in two of three cases, change a nominally significant value to a nonsignificant one. In any event, there can be no doubt that the authors' (Ehrlich et al., 1957) summary statement "It was found that new car owners read advertisements of their own car more often than . . ." needs considerable qualification. With so much selection of *S*s and with such intricate manipulations of the data, some of it never fully explained, one can hardly describe the results as *public*, or the findings as necessarily significant.

Manipulation Not Successful. Still another type of rejection we find in these studies is the elimination of entire groups of *S*s. If one variant of the manipulation fails to show an effect, it is not legitimate to discard all the *S*s in that group from the analysis. The analysis should properly be carried out on all the data and the interpretations should be based on the complete analysis. Brehm (1960), for example, used reports on the vitamin and mineral content of vegetables to try to influence the attitudes of *S*s after they had eaten a disliked vegetable. One group of *S*s received the vitamin report, the other group the mineral report. Since the mineral report "failed to affect" the dependent variable "the results for these subjects [were] omitted from this report" (Brehm, 1960, footnote, p. 380). One consequence of rejecting an entire group is that we do not know if there is a significant interaction between type of report and the other variables. Until this is established, it is misleading to consider a segment of the results as significant. In addition, the author nowhere states that his findings are specific to one type of report only. His summary is in terms of "communications about food value."

Reallocation Instead of Rejection. An interesting variant of the rejection of *S*s occurs in the Raven and Fishbein (1961) study on the effect of "Acceptance of Punishment and Change in Belief." Groups of *S*s were run under two conditions, "shock" and "no-shock." There were 13 females and 13 males

[2] J. Mills, personal communication, 1962.

in each of these two conditions. The results show that there was no overall difference between the shock and no-shock groups. However, when the results were tabulated separately for the two sexes, it appeared that the female *S*s in the shock group changed in the predicted direction but that the male *S*s did not. Here is how the authors (Raven and Fishbein, 1961) dealt with the situation:

Overall analysis of variance and interaction was not significant. Assuming that male shock *S*s were part of a common population with the no-shock subjects with respect to dissonance, an analysis of variance was conducted which showed the female shock subjects to be significantly different from the others (p. 415).

In other words the authors disposed of the *S*s who did not conform to their prediction, not by rejecting them, but by reallocating them to another group, the no-shock group. If females in the shock group really are significantly different from all the others, this should show up in a significant interaction. It does not.

Rejection of cases is poor procedure, but reallocation of *S*s from experimental to control group, across the independent variable, violates the whole concept of controlled experimentation.

*Danger of Rejecting S*s. A theme common to many of these rejections is that the unselected sample "does not permit of an adequate test" of the dissonance hypothesis. We are told:

In a social influence situation there are a number of potential channels of dissonance reduction, such as changing one's own opinion, changing the opinion of the communicator, making the communicator noncomparable to oneself, seeking further support for one's position, dissociating the source from the content of the communication, and distorting the meaning of the communication (dissonance theory position ably summarized by Zimbardo, 1960, p. 86).

Such a theoretical formulation is indeed all-encompassing and it provides a rationale which certain other dissonance theory workers have used for rejecting cases. The reasoning goes like this: If some *S*s do not follow the

specific predictions in a particular experiment (for instance, if they fail to show any opinion change) then those *S*s are probably reducing their dissonance through some other channel or else they had little dissonance to begin with. If either of these conditions holds it is legitimate to exclude these *S*s from the analysis since they could not possibly be used to test the particular hypothesis in the experiment. An inspection of results is considered sufficient to determine whether *S*s are, or are not, to be excluded. Unfortunately, this line of reasoning contains one fundamental flaw: *it does not allow the possibility that the null hypothesis may be correct.* The experimenter, in effect, is asserting that his dissonance prediction is correct and that *S*s who do not conform to the prediction should be excluded from the analysis. This is a foolproof method of guaranteeing positive results.

Some people may feel that no matter how questionable the selection procedure, it must still mean something if it leads to significant results. This point of view, however, cannot be reconciled with the following fact of life: it is always possible to obtain a significant difference between two columns of figures in a table of random numbers provided we use the appropriate scheme for rejecting certain of those numbers. For all we know, selecting *S*s so as "to permit an adequate test of the hypothesis" may have had precisely this effect. A significance test on selected *S*s may therefore be completely worthless.

We strongly recommend that *S*s not be discarded from the sample *after* data collection and inspection of the results. Nor is it methodologically sound to reject *S*s whose results do not conform to the prediction on the grounds that they have no dissonance, or that they must be reducing it some other way. If there are any theoretical grounds for suspecting that some *S*s will not show the predicted dissonance-reduction effect, the characteristics of such *S*s, or the conditions, should be specifiable in advance. It should then be possible to do an analysis on all *S*s by dividing them into two groups, those predicted to show dissonance reduction, and those predicted not to show it. If such a thing as dissonance reduction exists, it is theoretically and practically important to know the precise conditions under which it does and does not occur.

A summary of experiments in which Ss are rejected is given in Table 1.

This statement follows hard on the heels of "the more negative the person is toward a communication or communicator, the more he can be expected to change his attitudes in the direction of communication or communicator." These are indeed sweeping generali-

Table 1. List of experiments from which Ss were discarded after data collection.

Experiment	Total N	Discarded (%)	Reasons given
Brehm (1956)	225	35	To permit adequate test of hypothesis 1. Unreliable Ss 2. Conditions not fulfilled
Brehm (1960)	85*	38*	One manipulated condition not significant
Brehm and Cohen (1959b)	203	65	To permit adequate test of hypothesis 1. Ceiling effect for high scorers 2. Adequate separation of choice points for dissonance to occur 3. Unreliable Ss
Brehm and Lipsher (1959)	114	10-14	None
Cohen, Brehm, and Fleming (1958)	92	51	To permit adequate test of hypothesis 1. Extremity of attitude inhibits attitude change
Ehrlich et al. (1957)	125	17-82	1. Material missing 2. Advertisements not noticed 3. Not all comparisons possible 4. Ties
Mills (1958)	643	30	To permit adequate test of hypothesis 1. Ceiling effect for high scorers 2. Honest improvers have no dissonance

* Estimated.

Refusals

The previous section has been concerned with sampling bias due to the deliberate rejection of cases by the experimenter. There is another type of sampling bias, equally important but much more subtle, that occurs when Ss reject themselves from the study by refusing to participate.

In a recent review of cognitive dissonance experiments, Cohen (1960) concluded with what he considered was a "depressing" and "Orwellian" statement:

It could be said that when the individual feels that he has most freedom of choice, when his volition and responsibility are most engaged, he is then most vulnerable to the effects of persuasive communications and to all sorts of controlled inducements from the world at large (p. 318).

zations, particularly since they are based on the results of experiments in which from 4% (Cohen, Terry, and Jones, 1959) to as many as 46% (Rabbie, Brehm, and Cohen, 1959) of the total number of Ss refused to participate. Moreover, there is evidence in these studies that the Ss who refused to participate were actually those who had both the greatest freedom of choice and the strongest (most negative) views on the attitude in question. What actually appears to have happened is that those Ss with the strongest (most negative) views were so *in*vulnerable to the effects of persuasive communications that they exercised their freedom of choice by walking out on the experimenter or refusing to comply in other ways. To take the results of the remaining more vulnerable Ss and extrapolate from them to the population in general seems unjustified.

Inadequate Design and Analysis

It is rare to find in this area a study that has been adequately designed and analyzed. In fact, it is almost as though dissonance theorists have a bias against neat, factorial designs with adequate *N*s, capable of thorough analysis either parametrically or nonparametrically. The majority of their experiments are some variant of the 2 X 2 factorial with unequal, nonproportional, and generally small *N*s in each cell. These restrictions make it impossible for the authors to carry out ordinary analyses of variance. Instead we find them making use of a hodgepodge of *t* tests and a statistic which they refer to as an "interaction *t*" (Walker and Lev, 1953, pp. 159-160).

Making a number of ordinary *t* tests on the same set of data, without a prior overall test of the null hypothesis, can be misleading. The principal difficulty is that in making such multiple comparisons the experimenter is allowing himself a number of opportunities to find an event (significance) which normally occurs infrequently. As a result, the usual *t* tables underestimate the true probabilities, that is, the probabilities obtained suggest a level of significance which is higher than warranted. Another way of saying it is that if, out of several subgroups, one finds one or two *t*'s significant, he is, in effect, capitalizing on chance (e.g., Sakoda, Cohen, and Beall, 1954). A further complication arises if the interaction is significant, since this introduces the usual difficulties about interpreting the main effects (e.g., Lindquist, 1953, p. 209). Some of the special statistical problems involved in the "postmortem" testing of comparisons were, of course, being discussed in the psychological literature well before dissonance theory appeared on the scene (e.g., McHugh and Ellis, 1955); but, for an excellent discussion of the basic issues involved in making multiple comparisons, see the article by Ryan (1959). None of these problems is ever faced squarely by the writers

in this field. As a result, the authors sometimes reach conclusions that are not really warranted.

We can illustrate these remarks by referring to an analysis carried out by Brehm (1960) on two treatment variables, commitment and communication. There are three levels of commitment—control, low-eating, and high-eating—and, in addition, two types of communication—support and no support. Since the *N*s for these six groups are different (they vary from 7 to 11), it is not possible to carry out an ordinary analysis of variance. With such data at least 15 *t* tests and 3 interaction *t*'s are possible. Brehm gives the results of 7 such *t* tests (4 are nominally significant) and 2 such interaction *t*'s (both nominally significant). How do we interpret the results? Frankly, it is impossible. Taken at its face value, the analysis is not only useless, it is misleading.

An allied set of criticisms can be leveled at the analysis carried out by Brehm and Cohen in their study of the effects of choice and chance in cognitive dissonance (1959a). The design involved two types of relative deprivation, high and low. Five sections of an introductory psychology course were used as *S*s. The low- and high-deprivation conditions were experimentally manipulated and perceived as such by the *S*s. The low- and high-choice conditions were, however, determined separately for each section on the basis of their medians on the perceived-choice rating scale. Separate interaction *t*'s were calculated for each of the five sections. The *N*s in each cell were very small, ranging between 3 and 10 with an average of about 7. The probability values for these 5 interaction *t*'s showed that one was significant, two tended to significance, and two were nonsignificant (one was actually a reversal). Here again the authors' failure to compute and report the results of an overall test make it exceedingly difficult for readers to interpret their findings. Moreover, there seems to be little justification for using a different value for the cutoff point between high- and low-choice for each section. In fact, such a procedure might in itself lead to statistically significant median differences between the sections. There may indeed be a significant interaction between choice and deprivation, but the evidence for it is, at best, questionable.

In dissonance experiments there is often a marked change between the pre- and posttest measures for both control and experimental groups. This is in itself an interesting phenomenon and should be thoroughly evaluated. An analysis should be complete—large main effects should not be ignored just because dissonance theory predicts only an interaction, or vice versa.

It is not impossible to apply a rigorous methodology to this area. Dissonance theorists would have done well to emulate the example set by Kelman as far back as 1953 (a study which, incidentally, anticipates and predates most of the areas of interest for cognitive dissonance workers). All of the problems that beset research in this area, such as unequal Ns, class differences, and so on, were handled expertly by Kelman. More recently, such eclectic workers as Rosenbaum and Franc (1960) and McGuire (1960) have also been working in this area and have been using rigorous and comprehensive methods of analysis. In short, there appears to be no reason why methodology in this area cannot be sharpened.

A summary of experiments in which the analyses and statistical interpretations are doubtful is given in Table 2.

Straining for Significance

The final feature of the analyses that is apt to be misleading is the fact that authors tend to present results as significant and as supporting the dissonance theory prediction when the probabilities are greater than the usually accepted value of .05. Probability values between .06 and .15 (once even .50!) do not constitute striking support for any theory, particularly if it is preceded by a selection of Ss and poor analysis. It is also extremely disconcerting to find these statistically nonsignificant trends quoted authoritatively in subsequent reports and later reviews as substantiating the theory, without any qualifying statements.

Overall Evaluation

Having now reviewed much of the experimental work supporting cognitive dissonance theory, we conclude that, as a body of literature, it is downright disappointing. Too many studies have failed to stand up to close scrutiny. Yet it is also obvious that the dissonance framework has a seductive allure for many social scientists, an allure not possessed by the rather similar, but symbolically more complex, interpretations by Heider (1958), Osgood and Tannenbaum (1955), or Newcomb (1953).

The magical appeal of Festinger's theory

Table 2. Summary of some experiments with inadequate design and analysis.

Study	Criticism of design and analysis
Allyn and Festinger (1961)	No control group (repeat attitude test, no talk); interaction significance not presented
Aronson and Mills (1959)	Overall significance not presented
Brehm (1956)	Maximum $N = 225$, but regression equation based on $N = 557$ and $N = 534$
Brehm (1960)	Overall significance not presented
Brehm and Cohen (1959a)	Overall significance not presented
Cohen (1959)	No control group (repeat attitude test, no counterinformation); groups not equated on initial attitude
Cohen, Terry, and Jones (1959)	No control group (repeat attitude test, no new information); groups not equated on initial attitude
Ehrlich et al. (1957)	No control group (predecision car ad reading)
Festinger and Carlsmith (1959)	Overall significance not presented
Mills (1958)	Overall significance not presented
Mills, Aronson, and Robinson (1959)	No control group (preferences, but no decision); overall significance not presented
Rosen (1961)	No control group (preferences, but no decision)

arises from its extreme simplicity both in formulation and in application. But in our review we have seen that this simplicity was generally deceptive; in point of fact if often concealed a large number of confounded variables. Clearly much can be done to untangle this confounding of variables by careful experimental design. Nonetheless, there may still remain another problem more fundamental than this. In general, a cognitive dissonance interpretation of a social situation means that the relevant social factors can be condensed into two simple statements. To be sure, Festinger does not say formally that a dissonance theory interpretation works only for two discrepant statements; but it is precisely because in practice he does so limit it that the theory has had so much acceptance. Which brings us now to the crux of the matter: *is it really possible to reduce the essentials of a complex social situation to just two phrases?* Reluctantly we must say "No." To condense most complex social situations into two, and only two, simple dissonant statements represents so great a level of abstraction that the model no longer bears any reasonable resemblance to reality. Indeed, the experimenter is left thereby with such emasculated predictors that he must perforce resort to a multiplicity of ad hoc hypotheses to account for unexpected findings. We see then that the most attractive feature of cognitive dissonance theory, its simplicity, is in actual fact a self-defeating limitation.

In conclusion, all of the considerations detailed above lead us to concur with Asch's (1958) evaluation of the evidence for cognitive dissonance theory, and return once more a verdict of NOT PROVEN.

References

Adams, J. S. Reduction of cognitive dissonance by seeking consonant information. *J. abnorm. soc. Psychol.*, 1961, **62**, 74-78.

Allyn, Jane, and Festinger, L. The effectiveness of unanticipated persuasive communications. *J. abnorm. soc. Psychol.*, 1961 **62**, 35-40.

Aronson, E. The effect of effort on the attractiveness of rewarded and unrewarded stimuli. *J. abnorm. soc. Psychol.*, 1961, **63**, 375-380.

Aronson, E., and Mills, J. The effect of severity of initiation on liking for a group. *J. abnorm. soc. Psychol.*, 1959, **59**, 177-181.

Asch, S. E. Review of L. Festinger, *A theory of cognitive dissonance. Contemp. Psychol.*, 1958, **3**, 194-195.

Brehm, J. W. Postdecision changes in the desirability of alternatives. *J. abnorm. soc. Psychol.*, 1956, **52**, 384-389.

Brehm, J. W. Increasing cognitive dissonance by a *fait accompli. J. abnorm. soc. Psychol.*, 1959, **58**, 379-382.

Brehm, J. W. Attitudinal consequences of commitment to unpleasant behavior. *J. abnorm. soc. Psychol.*, 1960, **60**, 379-383.

Brehm, J. W., and Cohen, A. R. Choice and chance relative deprivation as determinants of cognitive dissonance. *J. abnorm. soc. Psychol.*, 1959a, **58**, 383-387.

Brehm, J. W., and Cohen, A. R. Re-evaluation of choice alternatives as a function of their number and qualitative similarity. *J. abnorm. soc. Psychol.*, 1959b, **58**, 373-378.

Brehm, J. W., and Lipsher, D. Communicator-communicatee discrepancy and perceived communicator trustworthiness. *J. Pers.*, 1959, **27**, 352-361.

Bruner, J. Discussion of Leon Festinger: The relation between behavior and cognition. In J. S. Bruner, E. Brunswik, L. Festinger, F. Heider, K. F. Muenzinger, C. E. Osgood, and D. Rapaport, *Contemporary approaches to cognition: A symposium held at the University of Colorado.* Cambridge: Harvard Univ. Press, 1957. Pp. 151-156.

Cohen, A. R. Communication discrepancy and attitude change: A dissonance theory approach. *J. Pers.*, 1959, **27**, 386-396.

Cohen, A. R. Attitudinal consequences of induced discrepancies between cognitions and behavior. *Publ. Opin. Quart.*, 1960, **24**, 297-318.

Cohen, A. R., Brehm, J. W., and Fleming, W. H. Attitude change and justification for compliance. *J. abnorm. soc. Psychol.*, 1958, **56**, 276-278.

Cohen, A. R., Brehm, J. W., and Latane, B. Choice of stragegy and voluntary exposure to information under public and private conditions. *J. Pers.*, 1959, **27**, 63-73.

Cohen, A. R., Terry, H. I., and Jones, C. B. Attitudinal effects of choice in exposure to counterpropaganda. *J. abnorm. soc. Psychol.*, 1959, **58**, 388-391.

Edwards, A. L. A critique of "neutral" items in attitude scales constructed by the method of equal appearing intervals. *Psychol. Rev.*, 1946, **53**, 159-169.

Ehrlich, D., Guttman, I., Schonbach, P., and Mills, J. Postdecision exposure to relevant information. *J. abnorm. soc. Psychol.*, 1957, **54**, 98-102.

Feather, N. T. Cigarette smoking and lung cancer: A study of cognitive dissonance. *Aust. J. Psychol.*, 1962, **14**, 55-64.

Festinger, L. *A theory of cognitive dissonance.* Stanford, Calif.: Stanford Univ. Press, 1957.

Festinger, L. The psychological effects of insufficient rewards. *Amer. Psychologist*, 1961, **16**, 1-11.

Festinger, L., and Carlsmith, J. M. Cognitive consequences of forced compliance. *J. abnorm. soc. Psychol.*, 1959, **58**, 203-210.

Fisher, S., and Lubin, A. Distance as a determinant of influence in a two-person serial interaction situation. *J. abnorm. soc. Psychol.*, 1958, **56**, 230-238.

Heider, F. Attitudes and cognitive organization. *J. Psychol.*, 1946, **21**, 107-112.

Heider, F. *The psychology of interpersonal relations.* New York: Wiley, 1958.

Kelman, H. C. Attitude change as a function of response restriction. *Hum. Relat.*, 1953, **6**, 185-214.

Krech, D., and Crutchfield, R. S. *Theory and problems of social psychology.* New York: McGraw-Hill, 1948.

Lindquist, E. F. *Design and analysis of experiments in psychology and education.* Boston: Houghton Mifflin, 1953.

Maccoby, Eleanor E., Maccoby, N., Romney, A. K., and Adams, J. S. Social reinforcement in attitude change. *J. abnorm. soc. Psychol.*, 1961, **63**, 109-115.

McGuire, W. J. Cognitive consistency and attitude change. *J. abnorm. soc. Psychol.*, 1960, **60**, 345-353.

McHugh, R. B., and Ellis, D. S. The "postmortem" testing of experimental comparisons. *Psychol. Bull.*, 1955, **52**, 425-428.

Mills, J. Changes in moral attitudes following temptation. *J. Pers.*, 1958, **26**, 517-531.

Mills, J., Aronson, E., and Robinson, H. Selectivity in exposure to information. *J. abnorm. soc. Psychol.*, 1959, **59**, 250-253.

Newcomb, T. M. An approach to the study of communicative acts. *Psychol. Rev.*, 1953, **60**, 393-404.

Osgood, C. E. Cognitive dynamics in the conduct of human affairs. *Publ. Opin. Quart.*, 1960, **24**, 341-365.

Osgood, C. E., and Tannenbaum, P. H. The principle of congruity in the prediction of attitude change. *Psychol. Rev.*, 1955, **62**, 42-55.

Rabbie, J. M., Brehm, J. W., and Cohen, A. R. Verbalization and reactions to cognitive dissonance. *J. Pers.*, 1959, **27**, 407-417.

Raven, B. H., and Fishbein, M. Acceptance of punishment and change in belief. *J. abnorm. soc. Psychol.*, 1961, **63**, 411-416.

Riecken, H. W. Social psychology. *Ann. Rev. Psychol.*, 1960, **11**, 479-510.

Rosen, S. Postdecision affinity for incompatible information. *J. abnorm. soc. Psychol.*, 1961, **63**, 188-190.

Rosenbaum, M. E., and Franc, D. E. Opinion change as a function of external commitment and amount of discrepancy from the opinion of another. *J. abnorm. soc. Psychol.*, 1960, **61**, 15-20.

Rosenberg, M. J. An analysis of affective-cognitive consistency. In M. J. Rosenberg, C. I. Hovland, W. J. McGuire, R. P. Abelson, and J. W. Brehm, *Attitude organization and change.* New Haven: Yale Univ. Press, 1960. Pp. 15-64.

Ryan, T. A. Multiple comparisons in psychological research. *Psychol. Bull.*, 1959, **56**, 26-47.

Sakoda, J. M., Cohen, B. H., and Beall, G. Test of significance for a series of statistical tests. *Psychol. Bull.*, 1954, **51**, 172-175.

Walker, Helen M., and Lev, J. *Statistical inference.* New York: Holt, 1953.

Yaryan, Ruby B., and Festinger, L. Preparatory action and belief in the probable occurrence of future events. *J. abnorm. soc. Psychol.*, 1961, **63**, 603-606.

Zajonc, R. B. The concepts of balance, congruity, and disssonance. *Publ. Opin. Quart.*, 1960, **24**, 280-296.

Zimbardo, P. G. Involvement and communication discrepancy as determinants of opinion conformity. *J. abnorm. soc. Psychol.*, 1960, **60**, 86-94.

Part Six

Achievement Motivation Theory

11   David C. McClelland

In a strict sense the theory of achievement motivation is not a theory of personality. Yet to ignore the work of David C. McClelland (1917-) and his associates would deprive the student of knowledge about an extensive area of theory and research on human behavior that is germane to the psychology of personality. The work on achievement motivation represents a fruitful combination of clinical theory and experimental methodology, and the discoveries made by its scholars have serious implications for the eventual development of a comprehensive theory of human behavior.

The roots of achievement motivation can be traced back to the 1930's when Henry A. Murray, a psychologist at Harvard University, became interested in how human needs (including a need for achievement) influence a person's imaginal processes. One outcome of Murray's work was the development of the *Thematic Apperception Test* (TAT), a series of pictures of persons in situations of various sorts. Murray felt that stories told by subjects about these pictures could be analyzed in such a way that the subject's unconscious needs could be determined. The TAT immediately became popular with clinical psychologists and psychiatrists, was given the status

of a *projective test*, and since then has been used to diagnose the personality disturbances of the mentally ill. It is interesting to note that Murray had intended the TAT to be used to study normal personality.

The assumption that a person's motivational state influences his fantasy productions, such as making up stories about TAT pictures, was never put to careful empirical test until the late 1940's, when McClelland and his colleagues began to search for a method to reliably and validly measure human motivation. They developed a scoring system for the TAT which has proved to be acceptable, and over the years literally volumes of research have been published on the achievement motive. Although McClelland's interest in achievement motivation has recently moved in a sociological direction, his work still has great import for personality theory. John W. Atkinson, McClelland's associate in the early work on the achievement motive, has retained a more psychological interest in the topic and has restricted his work to the development of a quantitative theory of achievement motivation.

In the first selection in this chapter, McClelland discusses the achievement motive in the context of "motive acquisition." The exis-

367

tence of achievement motivation is assumed, and for McClelland it only remains to demonstrate how one can go about increasing motive strength in adults and in so doing test some general theoretical propositions about motive acquisition. The discussion of theory and research in this paper reflects McClelland's interest in complex, socially relevant human behavior as well as his propensity for testing hypotheses in "real-life" naturalistic situations.

The research study by Michael Argyle and Peter Robinson investigates the influence of the parent-child relationship on the development of achievement motivation in children. Based on results of previous research, the investigators first hypothesize (*the introjection hypothesis*) that when parents set standards of achievement for their children, and when these standards are applied by the child to himself (introjected), then the acquisition of the achievement motive is more likely to be realized. Secondly they hypothesize that, of children who identify with their parents, those children whose parents manifest high achievement motivation will also be high on the achievement motive.

These *hypotheses* are then translated into *predictions* which can be tested empirically by *correlational analysis*. For the present discussion, we will only consider the first hypothesis. It would be predicted that a measure of achievement motive strength in children will correlate not only with measured parental demands for achievement but also with the amount of the child's introjected parental demands for achievement ("super-ego demands"). To test these predictions, three basic measures are necessary. The strength of *achievement motivation* in the children was measured by using the TAT method developed by McClelland and Atkinson. The method is described in the article, so it need not be repeated here except to note that this method yields, in addition to an achievement motive value, a score for "hope of success" and a score for "fear of failure." (A questionnaire measure of achievement motivation was also used. In addition, several measuring instruments were employed in

quantifying other variables. To simplify our present discussion, we will only consider single measures on each variable.)

Parental demand for achievement was measured by using a method called the *semantic differential*. The total scale used by the investigators is reproduced in Appendix II of the article. Note that the total scale contains fifteen seven-point scales and that three of the scales relate to achievement (hardworking—easy-going; stupid—clever; bottom of the class—top of the class). The children were instructed to place a mark at one of the seven points on each of the fifteen scales in response to statements such as "The kind of person my father is." The average rating on the scales constituted the parental demand measure.

Introjected parental demand for achievement was measured by the administration of a *Q* sort developed by the investigators. The *Q* sort is reproduced as Appendix III of the article. The children were instructed to rate ten attributes (the columns in Appendix III) with respect to seven conditions (the top row in Appendix III). Two of ten attributes that were rated referred to achievement, and the ratings on these attributes constituted the introjected parental demand measure.

To test the predictions derived from their introjection hypothesis, the investigators statistically correlated the children's scores on the measures of achievement motivation, parental demand for achievement, and introjected parental demand for achievement. In general the correlations were as predicted, thus confirming the hypothesis.

Eric Klinger, in the third selection of this chapter, critically examines the empirical evidence presumed to support the assumption of achievement motivation theory that arousal of *achievement fantasy* is dependent upon arousal of the *achievement motive*. In particular, he questions the legitimacy of labeling the theory "motivational." He goes on to show that a substantial part of the research results on the achievement motive can be more readily accounted for by nonmotivational interpretations.

After showing that only about half of the

studies on achievement motivation support the theory, Klinger goes on to present a non-motivational model from which he generates several hypotheses. He then tests these hypotheses by using the research results already available and finds that his view provides a better fit to the data than the achievement motive view.

Suggestions for Further Reading

There are three major books on the theory of achievement motivation that can be consulted for an in-depth study of the topic. *The Achievement Motive*, by McClelland, Atkinson, and Clark, was published by Appleton-Century-Crofts in 1953. In 1958, J. W. Atkinson edited a collection of research reports on the achievement motive entitled *Motives in Fantasy, Action, and Society*, published by Van Nostrand. This was followed in 1966 by another volume, co-edited by Atkinson and N. T. Feather, entitled *A Theory of Achievement Motivation* (published by Wiley).

McClelland's major work, *The Achieving Society*, was published in 1961 by Van Nostrand. The book relates the achievement motive to economic development and should be read for an appreciation of McClelland's sociological bent and his skill at subjecting his theory to quantitative testing in naturalistic settings.

For a general introduction to the topic of motivation the student should read J. W. Atkinson's text, *An Introduction to Motivation*, published in 1964 by Van Nostrand. The book presents an excellent treatment of the historical development of the concept of motivation, culminating in a presentation of Atkinson's *Theory of Achievement Motivation*. Another excellent treatment of the topic of motivation is the little paperback, *Motivation: A Study of Action*, by David Birch and Joseph Veroff, published by Brooks/Cole in 1966.

A Theory of Motive Acquisition

David C. McClelland

Too little is known about the processes of personality change at relatively complex levels. The empirical study of the problem has been hampered by both practical and theoretical difficulties.[1] On the practical side it is very expensive both in time and effort to set up systematically controlled educational programs designed to develop some complex personality characteristic like a motive, and to follow the effects of the education over a number of years. It also presents ethical problems since it is not always clear that it is as proper to teach a person a new motive as it is a new skill like learning to play the piano. For both reasons, most of what we know about personality change has come from studying psychotherapy where both ethical and practical difficulties are overcome by the pressing need to help someone in real trouble. Yet, this source of information leaves much to be desired: It has so far proven difficult to identify and systematically vary the "inputs" in psychotherapy and to measure their specific effects on subsequent behavior, except in very general ways (cf. Rogers & Dymond, 1954).

On the theoretical side, the dominant views of personality formation suggest anyway that acquisition or change of any complex characteristic like a motive in adulthood would be extremely difficult. Both behavior theory and psychoanalysis agree that stable personality characteristics like motives are laid down in childhood. Behavior theory arrives at this conclusion by arguing that social motives are learned by close association with reduction in certain basic biological drives like hunger, thirst, and physical discomfort which loom much larger in childhood than adulthood. Psychoanalysis, for its part, pictures adult motives as stable resolutions of basic conflicts occurring in early childhood. Neither theory would provide much support for the notion that motives could be developed in adulthood without somehow recreating the childhood conditions under which they were originally formed. Furthermore, psychologists have been hard put to it to find objective evidence that even prolonged, serious, and expensive attempts to introduce personality change through psychotherapy have really proven successful (Eysenck, 1952). What hope is there that a program to introduce personality change would end up producing a big enough effect to study?

Despite these difficulties a program of research has been under way for some time which is attempting to develop the achievement motive in adults. It was undertaken in an attempt to fill some of the gaps in our knowledge about personality change or the acquisition of complex human characteristics. Working with n Achievement has proved to have some important advantages for this type of research: The practical and ethical problems do not loom especially large because previous research (McClelland, 1961) has demonstrated the importance of high n Achievement for entrepreneurial behavior and it is easy to find businessmen, particularly in underdeveloped countries, who are interested in trying any means of improving their entrepreneurial performance. Furthermore, a great deal is known about the origins

From D. C. McClelland, "Toward a Theory of Motive Acquisition," *American Psychologist*, 1965, **20**, 321-333. Reprinted by permission of the American Psychological Association.

[1] I am greatly indebted to the Carnegie Corporation of New York for its financial support of the research on which this paper is based, and to my collaborators who have helped plan and run the courses designed to develop the achievement motive—chiefly George Litwin, Elliott Danzig, David Kolb, Winthrop Adkins, David Winter, and John Andrews. The statements made and views expressed are solely the responsibility of the author.

of n Achievement in childhood and its specific effects on behavior so that educational programs can be systematically planned and their effects evaluated in terms of this knowledge. Pilot attempts to develop n Achievement have gradually led to the formulation of some theoretical notions of what motive acquisition involves and how it can be effectively promoted in adults. These notions have been summarized in the form of 12 propositions which it is the ultimate purpose of the research program to test. The propositions are anchored so far as possible in experiences with pilot courses, in supporting research findings from other studies, and in theory.

Before the propositions are presented, it is necessary to explain more of the theoretical and practical background on which they are based. To begin with, some basis for believing that motives could be acquired in adulthood had to be found in view of the widespread pessimism on the subject among theoretically oriented psychologists. Oddly enough we were encouraged by the successful efforts of two quite different groups of "change agents" —operant conditioners and missionaries. Both groups have been "naive" in the sense of being unimpressed by or ignorant of the state of psychological knowledge in the field. The operant conditioners have not been encumbered by any elaborate theoretical apparatus; they do not believe motives exist anyway, and continue demonstrating vigorously that if you want a person to make a response, all you have to do is elicit it and reward it (cf. Bandura & Walters, 1963, pp. 238 ff.). They retain a simple faith in the infinite plasticity of human behavior in which one response is just like any other and any one can be "shaped up" (strengthened by reward)—presumably even an "achievement" response as produced by a subject in a fantasy test. In fact, it was the naive optimism of one such researcher (Burris, 1958) that had a lot to do with getting the present research under way. He undertook a conseling program in which an attempt to elicit and reinforce achievement-related fantasies proved to be successful in motivating college students to get better grades.

Like operant conditioners, the missionaries have gone ahead changing people because they have believed it possible. While the evidence is not scientifically impeccable, common-sense observation yields dozens of cases of adults whose motivational structure has seemed to be quite radically and permanently altered by the educational efforts of Communist Party, Mormon, or other devout missionaries.

A man from Mars might be led to observe that personality change appears to be very difficult for those who think it is very difficult, if not impossible, and much easier for those who think it can be done. He would certainly be oversimplifying the picture, but at the very least his observation suggests that some theoretical revision is desirable in the prevailing views of social motives which link them so decisively to early childhood. Such a revision has been attempted in connection with the research on n Achievement (McClelland, Atkinson, Clark, & Lowell, 1953) and while it has not been widely accepted (cf. Berelson & Steiner, 1964), it needs to be briefly summarized here to provide a theoretical underpinning for the attempts at motive change to be described. It starts with the proposition that all motives are learned, that not even biological discomforts (as from hunger) or pleasures (as from sexual stimulation) are "urges" or "drives" until they are linked to cues that can signify their presence or absence. In time clusters of expectancies or associations grow up around affective experiences, not all of which are connected by any means with biological needs (McClelland et al., 1953, Ch. 2), which we label motives. More formally, motives are "affectively toned associative networks" arranged in a hierarchy of strength or importance within a given individual. Obviously, the definition fits closely the operations used to measure a motive: "an affectively toned associative cluster" is exactly what is coded in a subject's fantasies to obtain an n Achievement score. The strength of the motive (its position in the individual's hierarchy of motives) is measured essentially by counting the number of associations belonging to this cluster as compared to others that an individual produces in a given number of opportunities. If one thinks of a motive as an associative network, it is easier to imagine how one might go about changing it: The problem becomes one of moving its position up on the hierarchy by increasing its salience compared to other clusters. It should be possible to accomplish this end by such tactics as: (*a*) setting up the network—discovering what associations, for example, exist in the achievement area and then extending, strengthening, or otherwise "improving" the network they form; (*b*) conceptualizing the network—forming a clear and conscious construct that labels the network; (*c*) tying the network to as many cues as possible in everyday life, especially those preceding and following action, to insure that the network will be regularly rearoused once formed; and (*d*) working out the relation of the network to superordinate associative clusters, like the self-concept, so that these dominant schemata do not block the train of achievement thoughts—for example, through a chain of interfering associations (e.g., "I am not really the achieving type").

This very brief summary is not intended as a full exposition of the theoretical viewpoint underlying the research, but it should suffice to give a rough idea of how the motive was conceived that we set out to change. This concept helped define the goals of the techniques of change, such as reducing the effects of associative interference from superordinate associate clusters. But what about the techniques themselves? What could we do that would produce effective learning of this sort? Broadly speaking, there are four types of empirical information to draw on. From the animal learning experiments, we know that such factors as repetition, optimal time intervals between stimulus, response, and reward, and the schedule of rewards are very important for effective learning. From human learning experiments, we know that such factors as distribution of practice, repetitions, meaningfulness, and recitation are important. From experiences with psychotherapy (cf. Rogers, 1961), we learn that warmth, honesty, nondirectiveness, and the ability to recode associations in line with psychoanalytic or other personality theories are important. And, from the attitude-change research literature, we learn that such variables as presenting one side or two, using reason or prestige to support an argument, or affiliating with a new reference group are crucial for developing new attitudes (cf. Hovland, Janis, & Kelley, 1953). Despite the fact that many of these variables seem limited in application to the learning situation in which they were studied, we have tried to make use of information from all these sources in designing our "motive acquisition" program and in finding support for the general propositions that have emerged from our study so far. For our purpose has been above all to produce an effect large enough to be measured. Thus we have tried to profit by all that is known about how to facilitate learning or produce personality or attitude change. For, if we could not obtain a substantial effect with all factors working to produce it, there would be no point to studying the effects of each factor taken one at a time. Such a strategy also has the practical advantage that we are in the position of doing our best to "deliver the goods" to our course participants since they were giving us their time and attention to take part in a largely untried educational experience.[2]

Our overall research strategy, therefore, is "subtractive" rather than "additive." After we have demonstrated a substantial effect with some 10-12 factors working to produce it, our plan is to subtract that part of the program that deals with each of the factors to discover if there is a significant decline in the effect. It should also be possible to omit several factors in various combinations to get at interactional effects. This will obviously require giving a fairly large number of courses in a standard institutional setting for the same kinds of businessmen with follow-up

---

[2]Parenthetically, we have found several times that our stated desire to evaluate the effectiveness of our course created doubts in the minds of our sponsors that they did not feel about many popular courses for managers that no one has ever evaluated or plans to evaluate. An attitude of inquiry is not always an asset in education. It suggests one is not sure of his ground.

evaluation of their performance extending over a number of years. So obviously it will be some time before each of the factors incorporated into the propositions which follow can be properly evaluated so far as its effect on producing motive change is concerned.

The overall research strategy also determined the way the attempts to develop the achievement motive have been organized. That is to say, in order to process enough subjects to permit testing the effectiveness of various "inputs" in a reasonable number of years, the training had to be both of *short duration* (lasting 1-3 weeks) and *designed for groups* rather than for individuals as in person-to-person counseling. Fortunately these requirements coincide with normal practice in providing short courses for business executives. To conform further with that practice, the training has usually also been *residential* and *voluntary*. The design problems introduced by the last characteristic we have tried to handle in the usual ways by putting half the volunteers on a waiting list or giving them a different, technique-oriented course, etc. So far we have given the course to develop n Achievement in some form or another some eight times to over 140 managers or teachers of management in groups of 9-25 in the United States, Mexico, and India. For the most part the course has been offered by a group of 2-4 consultant psychologists either to executives in a single company as a company training program, or to executives from several different companies as a self improvement program, or as part of the program of an institute or school devoted to training managers. The theoretical propositions which follow have evolved gradually from these pilot attempts to be effective in developing n Achievement among businessmen of various cultural backgrounds.

The first step in a motive development program is to create confidence that it will work. Our initial efforts in this area were dictated by the simple practical consideration that we had to "sell" our course or nobody would take it. We were not in the position of an animal psychologist who can order a dozen rats, or an academic psychologist who has captive subjects in his classes, or even a psychotherapist who has sick people knocking at his door every day. So we explained to all who would listen that we had every reason to believe from previous research that high n Achievement is related to effective entrepreneurship and that therefore business executives could expect to profit from taking a course designed to understand and develop this important human characteristic. What started as a necessity led to the first proposition dealing with how to bring about motive change.

Proposition 1. The more reasons an individual has in advance to believe that he can, will, or should develop a motive, the more educational attempts designed to develop that motive are likely to succeed. The empirical support for this proposition from other studies is quite impressive. It consists of (a) the prestige-suggestion studies showing that people will believe or do what prestigeful sources suggest (cf. Hovland et al., 1953); (b) the so-called "Hawthorne effect" showing that people who feel they are especially selected to show an effect will tend to show it (Roethlisberger & Dickson, 1947); (c) the "Hello-Goodbye" effect in psychotherapy showing that patients who merely have contact with a prestigeful medical authority improve significantly over waiting list controls and almost as much as those who get prolonged therapy (Frank, 1961); (d) the "experimenter bias" studies which show that subjects will often do what an experimenter wants them to do, even though neither he nor they know he is trying to influence them (Rosenthal, 1963); (e) the goal-setting studies which show that setting goals for a person particularly in the name of prestigeful authorities like "science" or "research" improves performance (Kausler, 1959; Mierke, 1955); (f) the parent-child interaction studies which show that parents who set higher standards of excellence for their sons are more likely to have sons with high n Achievement (Rosen & D'Andrade, 1959). The common factor in all these studies seems to be that goals are being set for the individual by sources he respects—goals which imply that his behavior should change for a variety of reasons and that it *can* change. In common-sense terms, belief in the possibility and desirability of change are tremendously influential in changing a person.

So we have used a variety of means to create this belief: the authority of research findings on the relationship of n Achievement to entrepreneurial success, the suggestive power of membership in an experimental group designed to show an effect, the prestige of a great university, our own genuine enthusiasm for the course and our conviction that it would work, as expressed privately and in public speeches. In short, we were trying to make every use possible of what is sometimes regarded as an "error" in such research—namely, the Hawthorne effect, experimenter bias, etc., because we believe it to be one of the most powerful sources of change.

Why? What is the effect on the person, theoretically speaking, of all this goal setting for him? Its primary function is probably to arouse what exists of an associative network in the achievement area for each person affected. That is, many studies have shown that talk of achievement or affiliation or power tends to increase the frequency with which individuals think about achievement or affiliation or power (cf. Atkinson, 1958). And the stronger the talk, the more the relevant associative networks are aroused (McClelland et al., 1953). Such an arousal has several possible effects which would facilitate learning: (*a*) It elicits what exists in the person of a "response" thus making it easier to strengthen that response in subsequent learning. (*b*) It creates a discrepancy between a goal (a "Soll-lage" in Heckhausen's—1963—theory of motivation) and a present state ("Ist-lage") which represents a cognitive dissonance the person tries to reduce (cf. Festinger, 1957); in common-sense terms he has an image clearly presented to him of something he is not but should be. (*c*) It tends to block out by simple interference other associations which would inhibit change—such as, "I'm too old to learn," "I never learned much from going to school anyway," "What do these academics know about everyday life?" or "I hope they don't get personal about all this."

After the course has been "sold" sufficiently to get a group together for training, the first step in the course itself is to present the research findings in some detail on exactly how n Achievement is related to certain types of successful entrepreneurial performance. That is, the argument of *The Achieving Society* (McClelland, 1961) is presented carefully with tables, charts, and diagrams, usually in lecture form at the outset and with the help of an educational TV film entitled the *Need to Achieve*. This is followed by discussion to clear up any ambiguities that remain in their minds as far as the central argument is concerned. It is especially necessary to stress that not all high achievement is caused by high n Achievement—that we have no evidence that high n Achievement is an essential ingredient in success as a research scientist, professional, accountant, office or personnel manager, etc.; that, on the contrary, it seems rather narrowly related to entrepreneurial, sales, or promotional success, and therefore should be of particular interest to them because they hold jobs which either have or could have an entrepreneurial component. We rationalize this activity in terms of the following proposition.

Proposition 2. The more an individual perceives that developing a motive is consistent with the demands of reality (and reason), the more educational attempts designed to develop that motive are likely to succeed. In a century in which psychologists and social theorists have been impressed by the power of unreason, it is well to remember that research has shown that rational arguments do sway opinions, particularly among the doubtful or uncommitted (cf. Hovland et al., 1953). Reality in the form of legal, military, or housing rules does modify white prejudice against Negroes (cf. Berelson & Steiner, 1964, p. 512). In being surprised at Asch's discovery that many people will go along with a group in calling a shorter line longer than it is, we sometimes forget that under most conditions their judgments conform with reality. The associative network which organizes "reality"—which places the person correctly in time, place, space, family, job, etc.—is one of the most dominant in the personality. It is the last to go in psychosis. It should be of great assistance to tie any proposed change in an associative network in with this dominant schema in such a way as to make the change consistent with reality demands or *"reasonable"* extensions of them. The word "reasonable" here simply means extensions arrived at by the thought processes of proof, logic, etc., which in adults have achieved a certain dominance of their own.

The next step in the course is to teach the participants the n Achievement coding system. By this time, they are a little confused anyway as to exactly what we mean by the term. So we tell them they can find out for themselves by learning to code stories written by others or by themselves. They take the test for n Achievement before this session and then find out what their own score is by scoring this record. However, we point out that if they think their score is too low, that can be easily remedied, since we teach them how to code and how to write stories saturated with n Achievement; in fact, that is one of the basic purposes of the course: to teach them to think constantly in n Achievement terms. Another aspect of the learning is discriminating achievement thinking from thinking in terms of power or affiliation. So usually the elements of these other two coding schemes are also taught.

Proposition 3. The more thoroughly an individual develops and clearly conceptualizes the associative network defining the motive, the more likely he is to develop the motive. The original empirical support for this proposition came from the radical behaviorist Skinnerian viewpoint: If the associative responses are the motive (by definition), to strengthen them one should elicit them and reinforce them, as one would shape up any response by reinforcement (cf. Skinner, 1953).

But, support for this proposition also derives from other sources, particularly the "set" experiments. For decades laboratory psychologists have known that one of the easiest and most effective ways to change behavior is to change the subject's set. If he is responding to stimulus words with the names of animals,

tell him to respond with the names of vegetables, or with words meaning the opposite, and he changes his behavior immediately and efficiently without a mistake. At a more complex level Orne (1962) had pointed out how powerful a set like "This is an experiment" can be. He points out that if you were to go up to a stranger and say something like "Lie down!" he would in all probability either laugh or escape as soon as possible. But if you say "This is an experiment! Lie down!" more often than not, if there are other supporting cues, the person will do so. Orne has demonstrated how subjects will perform nonsensical and fatiguing tasks for very long periods of time under the set that "This is an experiment." At an even more complex level, sociologists have demonstrated often how quickly a person will change his behavior as he adopts a new role set (as a parent, a teacher, a public official, etc.). In all cases an associative network exists usually with a label conveniently attached which we call set and which, when it is aroused or becomes salient, proceeds to control behavior very effectively. The purpose of this part of our course is to give the subjects a set or a carefully worked out associative network with appropriate words or labels to describe all its various aspects (the coding labels for part of the n Achievement scoring system like Ga^+, I^+, etc.; cf. Atkinson, 1958). The power of words on controlling behavior has also been well documented (cf. Brown, 1958).

It is important to stress that it is not just the label (n Achievement) which is taught. The person must be able to produce easily and often the new associative network itself. It is here that our research comes closest to traditional therapy which could be understood as the prolonged and laborious formation of new associative networks to replace anxiety-laden ones. That is, the person over time comes to form a new associative network covering his relations, for example, to his father and mother, which still later he may label as "unresolved Oedipus complex." When cues arise that formerly would have produced anxiety-laden associations, they now evoke this new complex instead, blocking out the "bad" associations by associative interference. But all therapists, whether Freudian or Rogerian, insist that the person must learn to produce these associations in their new form, that teaching the label is not enough. In fact, this is probably why so-called directive therapy is ineffective: It tries to substitute new constructs ("You should become an achiever") for old neurotic or ineffective ones ("rather than being such a slob") without changing the associative networks which underlie these surface labels. A change in set such as "Respond with names of vegetables" will not work unless the person has a whole associative network which defines the meaning of the set. The relation of this argument is obvious both to Kelly's (1955) insistence on the importance of personal constructs and to the general semanticists' complaints about the neurotic effects of mislabeling or overabstraction (Korzybsky, 1941).

But, theoretically speaking, why should a change in set as an associative network be so influential in controlling thought and action? The explanation lies in part in its symbolic character. Learned acts have limited influence because they often depend on reality supports (as in typewriting), but learned thoughts (symbolic acts) can occur any time, any place, in any connection, and be applied to whatever the person is doing. They are more generalizable. Acts can also be inhibited more easily than thoughts. Isak Dinesen tells the story of the oracle who told the king he would get his wish so long as he never thought of the left eye of a camel. Needless to say, the king did not get his wish, but he could easily have obeyed her prohibition if it had been to avoid *looking* at the left eye of a camel. Thoughts once acquired gain more control over thoughts and actions than acquired acts do because they are harder to inhibit. But why do they gain control over actions? Are not thoughts substitutes for actions? Cannot a man learn to think achievement thoughts and still not act like an achiever in any way? The question is taken up again under the next proposition, but it is well to remember here that thoughts are symbolic acts and that practice of symbolic

acts facilitates performing the real acts (cf. Hovland, 1951, p. 644).

The next step in the course is to tie thought to action. Research has shown that individuals high in n Achievement tend to act in certain ways. For example, they prefer work situations where there is a challenge (moderate risk), concrete feedback on how well they are doing, and opportunity to take personal responsibility for achieving the work goals. The participants in the course are therefore introduced to a "work" situation in the form of a business game in which they will have an opportunity to show these characteristics in action or more specifically to develop them through practice and through observing others play it. The game is designed to mimic real life: They must order parts to make certain objects (e.g., a Tinker Toy model bridge) after having estimated how many they think they can construct in the time allotted. They have a real chance to take over, plan the whole game, learn from how well they are doing (use of feedback), and show a paper profit or loss at the end. While they are surprised often that they should have to display their real action characteristics in this way in public, they usually get emotionally involved in observing how they behave under pressure of a more or less "real" work situation.

Proposition 4. The more an individual can link the newly developed network to related actions, the more the change in both thought and action is likely to occur and endure. The evidence for the importance of action for producing change consists of such diverse findings as (a) the importance of recitation for human learning, (b) the repeated finding that overt commitment and participation in action changes attitudes effectively (cf. Berelson & Steiner, 1964, p. 576), and (c) early studies by Carr (cf. McGeoch & Irion, 1952) showing that simply to expose an organism to what is to be learned (e.g., trundling a rat through a maze) is nowhere near as effective as letting him explore it for himself in action.

Theoretically, the action is represented in the associative network by what associations precede, accompany, and follow it. So including the acts in what is learned *enlarges* the associative network or the achievement construct to include action. Thus, the number of cues likely to trip off the n Achievement network is increased. In common-sense terms, whenever he works he now evaluates what he is doing in achievement terms, and whenever he thinks about achievement he tends to think of its action consequences.

So far the course instruction has remained fairly abstract and removed from the everyday experiences of businessmen. So, the next step is to apply what has been learned to everyday business activities through the medium of the well-known case-study method popularized by the Harvard Business School. Actual examples of the development of the careers or firms of business leaders or entrepreneurs are written up in disguised form and assigned for discussion to the participants. Ordinarily, the instructor is not interested in illustrating "good" or "bad" managerial behavior—that is left to participants to discuss—but in our use of the material, we do try to label the various types of behavior as illustrating either n Achievement and various aspects of the achievement sequence (instrumental activity, blocks, etc.), or n Power, n Affiliation, etc. The participants are also encouraged to bring in examples of managerial behavior from their own experience to evaluate in motivational terms.

Proposition 5. The more an individual can link the newly conceptualized association-action complex (or motive) to events in his everyday life, the more likely the motive complex is to influence his thoughts and actions in situations outside the training experience. The transfer-of-training research literature is not very explicit on this point, though it seems self-evident. Certainly, this is the proposition that underlies the practice of most therapy when it involves working through or clarifying, usually in terms of a new, partially formed construct system, old memories, events from the last 24 hours, dreams, and hopes of the future. Again, theoretically, this should serve to enlarge and clarify the associative network and increase the number of cues in everyday life which will

rearouse it. The principle of symbolic practice can also be invoked to support its effectiveness in promoting transfer outside the learning experience.

For some time most course participants have been wondering what all this has to do with them personally. That is to say, the material is introduced originally on a "take it or leave it" objective basis as something that ought to be of interest to them. But, sooner or later, they must confront the issue as to what meaning n Achievement has in their own personal lives. We do not force this choice on them nor do we think we are brain-washing them to believe in n Achievement. We believe and we tell them we believe in the "obstinate audience" (cf. Bauer, 1964), in the ultimate capacity of people to resist persuasion or to do in the end what they really want to do. In fact, we had one case in an early session of a man who at this point decided he was not an achievement-minded person and did not want to become one. He subsequently retired and became a chicken farmer to the relief of the business in which he had been an ineffective manager. We respected that decision and mention it in the course as a good example of honest self-evaluation. Nevertheless, we do provide them with all kinds of information as to their own achievement-related behavior in the fantasy tests, in the business game, in occasional group dynamics session—and ample opportunity and encouragement to think through what this information implies so far as their self-concept is concerned and their responsibilities to their jobs. Various devices such as the "Who am I?" test, silent group meditation, or individual counseling have been introduced to facilitate this self-confrontation.

Proposition 6. The more an individual can perceive and experience the newly conceptualized motive as an improvement in the self-image, the more the motive is likely to influence his future thoughts and actions. Evidence on the importance of the ego or self-image on controlling behavior has been summarized by Allport (1943). In recent years, Rogers and his group (Rogers, 1961; Rogers & Dymond, 1954) have measured improvement in psychotherapy largely in terms of improvement of the self-concept in relation to the ideal self. Indirect evidence of the importance of the self-schema comes from the discussion over whether a person can be made to do things under hypnosis that are inconsistent with his self-concept or values. All investigators agree that the hypnotist can be most successful in getting the subject to do what might normally be a disapproved action if he makes the subject perceive the action as consistent with his self-image or values (cf. Berelson & Steiner, 1963, p. 124).

The same logic supports this proposition. It seems unlikely that a newly formed associative network like n Achievement could persist and influence behavior much unless it had somehow "come to terms" with the pervasive superordinate network of associations defining the self. The logic is the same as for Proposition 2 dealing with the reality construct system. The n Achievement associations must come to be experienced as related to or consistent with the ideal self-image; otherwise associations from the self-system will constantly block thoughts of achievement. The person might be thinking, for example: "I am not that kind of person; achievement means judging people in terms of how well they perform and I don't like to hurt people's feelings."

Closely allied to the self-system is a whole series of networks only half conscious (i.e., correctly labeled) summarizing the values by which the person lives which derive from his culture and social milieu. These values can also interfere if they are inconsistent with n Achievement as a newly acquired way of thinking. Therefore, it has been customary at this point in the course to introduce a value analysis of the participants' culture based on an analysis of children's stories, myths, popular religion, comparative attitude surveys, customs, etc., more or less in line with traditional, cultural anthropological practice (cf. Benedict, 1946; McClelland, 1964). For example, in America we have to work through the problem of how being achievement oriented seems to interfere with being popular or liked by others which is highly valued by Americans. In Mexico a central issue is the highly valued "male dominance" pattern reflected in the patriarchal family and in the *macho* complex (being extremely masculine). Since data show that dominant fathers have sons with low n Achievement and authoritarian bosses do not encourage n Achievement in their top executives (Andrews, 1965), there is obviously a problem here to be worked through if n Achievement is to survive among thoughts centered on dominance. The problem is not only rationally discussed. It is acted out in role-playing sessions where Mexicans try, and often to their own surprise fail, to act like the democratic father with high standards in the classic Rosen and D'-Andrade (1959) study on parental behavior which develops high n Achievement. Any technique is used which will serve to draw attention to possible conflicts between n Achievement and popular or traditional cultural values. In the end it may come to discussing parts of the *Bhagavad Gita* in India, or the *Koran* in Arab countries, that seem to oppose achievement striving or entrepreneurial behavior.

Proposition 7. The more an individual can perceive and experience the newly conceptualized motive as an improvement on prevailing cultural values, the more the motive is likely to influence his future thoughts and actions. The cultural anthropologists for years have argued how important it is to understand one's own cultural values to overcome prejudices, adopt more flexible attitudes, etc., but there is little hard evidence that doing so changes a person's behavior. What exists comes indirectly from studies that show prejudice can be decreased a little by information about ethnic groups (Berelson & Steiner, 1963, p. 517), or that repeatedly show an unconscious link between attitudes and the reference group (or subculture to which one belongs—a link which presumably can be broken more easily by full information about it, especially when coupled with role-playing new attitudes (cf. Berelson & Steiner, 1963, pp. 566 ff.).

The theoretical explanation of this presumed effect is the same as for Propositions 2 and 6. The newly learned associative complex to influence thought and action effectively must somehow be adjusted to three superordinate networks that may set off regularly interfering associations—namely, the networks associated with reality, the self, and the social reference group or subculture.

The course normally ends with each participant preparing a written document outlining his goals and life plans for the next 2 years. These plans may or may not include references to the achievement motive; they can be very tentative, but they are supposed to be quite specific and realistic; that is to say, they should represent moderate levels of aspiration following the practice established in learning about n Achievement of choosing the moderately risky or challenging alternative. The purpose of this document is in part to formulate for oneself the practical implications of the course before leaving it, but even more to provide a basis for the evaluation of their progress in the months after the course. For it is explained to the participants that they are to regard themselves as "in training" for the next 2 years, that 10-14 days is obviously too short a time to do more than conceive a new way of life: It represents the residential portion of the training only. Our role over the next 2 years will be to remind them every 6 months of the tasks they have set themselves by sending them a questionnaire to fill out which will serve to rearouse many of the issues discussed in the course and to give them information on how far they have progressed toward achieving their goals.

Proposition 8. The more an individual commits himself to achieving concrete goals in life related to the newly formed motive, the more the motive is likely to influence his future thoughts and actions.

Proposition 9. The more an individual keeps a record of his progress toward achieving goals to which he is committed, the more the newly formed motive is likely to influence his future thoughts and actions. These propositions are both related to what was called "pacing" in early studies of the psychology of work. That is, committing oneself to a specific goal and then comparing one's perform-

ance to that goal has been found to facilitate learning (cf. Kausler, 1959), though most studies of levels of aspiration have dealt with goal setting as a result rather than as a "cause" of performance. At any rate, the beneficial effect of concrete feedback on learning has been amply demonstrated by psychologists from Thorndike to Skinner. Among humans the feedback on performance is especially effective if they have high n Achievement (French, 1958), a fact which makes the relevance of our request for feedback obvious to the course participants.

The theoretical justification for these propositions is that in this way we are managing to keep the newly acquired associative network salient over the next 2 years. We are providing cues that will regularly rearouse it since he knows he is still part of an experimental training group which is supposed to show a certain type of behavior (Proposition 1 again). If the complex is rearoused sufficiently often back in the real world, we believe it is more likely to influence thought and action than if it is not aroused.

As described so far the course appears to be devoted almost wholly to cognitive learning. Yet this is only part of the story. The "teachers" are all clinically oriented psychologists who also try to practice whatever has been learned about the type of human relationship that most facilitates emotional learning. Both for practical and theoretical reasons this relationship is structured as warm, honest, and nonevaluative, somewhat in the manner described by Rogers (1961) and recommended by distinguished therapists from St. Ignatius[3] to Freud. That is to say, we insist that the only kind of change that can last or mean anything is what the person decides on and works out by himself, that we are there not to criticize his past

[3] In his famous spiritual exercises which have played a key role in producing and sustaining personality change in the Jesuit Order, St. Ignatius states: "The director of the Exercizes ought not to urge the exercitant more to poverty or any promise than to the contrary, nor to one state of life or way of living more than another . . . [while it is proper to urge people outside the Exercizes] the director of the Exercizes . . . without leaning to one side or the other, should permit the Creator to deal directly with the creature, and the creature directly with his Creator and Lord."

behavior or direct his future choices, but to provide him with all sorts of information and emotional support that will help him in his self-confrontation. Since we recognize that self-study may be quite difficult and unsettling, we try to create an optimistic relaxed atmosphere in which the person is warmly encouraged in his efforts and given the opportunity for personal counseling if he asks for it.

Proposition 10. Changes in motives are more likely to occur in an interpersonal atmosphere in which the individual feels warmly but honestly supported and respected by others as a person capable of guiding and directing his own future behavior. Despite the widespread belief in this proposition among therapists (except for operant conditioners), one of the few studies that directly supports it has been conducted by Ends and Page (1957) who found that an objective learning-theory approach was less successful in treating chronic alcoholics than a person-oriented, client-centered approach. Rogers (1961) also summarizes other evidence that therapists who are warmer, more empathic, and genuine are more successful in their work. Hovland et al. (1953) report that the less manipulative the intent of a communicator, the greater the tendency to accept his conclusions. There is also the direct evidence that parents of boys with high n Achievement are warmer, more encouraging and less directive (fathers only) than parents of boys with low n Achievement (Rosen & D'Andrade, 1959). We tried to model ourselves after those parents on the theory that what is associated with high n Achievement in children might be most likely to encourage its development in adulthood. This does not mean permissiveness or promiscuous reinforcement of all kinds of behavior; it also means setting high standards as the parents of the boys with high n Achievement did but having the relaxed faith that the participants can achieve them.

The theoretical justification for this proposition can take two lines: Either one argues that this degree of challenge to the self-schema produces anxiety which needs to be reduced by warm support of the person for effective learning to take place, or one interprets the warmth as a form of direct reinforcement for change following the operant-conditioning model. Perhaps both factors are operating. Certainly there is ample evidence to support the view that anxiety interferes with learning (cf. Sarason, 1960) and that reward shapes behavior (cf. Bandura & Walters, 1963, pp. 283 ff.).

One other characteristic of the course leads to two further propositions. Efforts are made so far as possible to define it as an "experience apart," "an opportunity for self-study," or even a "spiritual retreat" (though that term can be used more acceptably in India than in the United States). So far as possible it is held in an isolated resort hotel or a hostel where there will be a few distractions from the outside world and few other guests. This permits an atmosphere of total concentration on the objectives of the course including much informal talk outside the sessions about $Ga^+, Ga^-, I^+,$ and other categories in the coding definition. It still comes as a surprise to us to hear these terms suddenly in an informal group of participants talking away in Spanish or Telugu. The effect of this retreat from everyday life into a special and specially labeled experience appears to be twofold: It dramatizes or increases the salience of the new associative network and it tends to create a new reference group.

Proposition 11. Changes in motives are more likely to occur the more the setting dramatizes the importance of self-study and lifts it out of the routine of everyday life. So far as we know there is no scientific evidence to support this proposition, though again if one regards Jesuits as successful examples of personality change, the Order has frequently followed the advice of St. Ignatius to the effect that "the progress made in the Exercizes will be greater, the more the exercitant withdraws from all friends and acquaintances, and from all worldly cares." Theory supports the proposition in two respects: Removing the person from everyday routine (*a*) should decrease interfering associations (to say nothing of interfering appointments and social obligations), and (*b*) should heighten the salience of the experience by contrast with everyday life and make it harder to handle with the usual defenses ("just one more course," etc.). That is to say, the network of achievement-related associations can be more strongly and distinctly aroused in contrast to everyday life, making cognitive dissonance greater and therefore more in need of reduction by new learning. By the same token we have found that the dramatic quality of the experience cannot be sustained very long in a 12-18-hour-a-day schedule without a new routine attitude developing. Thus, we have found that a period somewhere between 6 to 14 days is optimal for this kind of "spiritual retreat." St. Ignatius sets an outside limit of 30 days, but this is when the schedule is less intensive (as ours has sometimes been), consisting of only a few hours a day over a longer period.

Proposition 12. Changes in motives are more likely to occur and persist if the new motive is a sign of membership in a new reference group. No principle of change has stronger empirical or historical support than this one. Endless studies have shown that people's opinions, attitudes, and beliefs are a function of their reference group and that different attitudes are likely to arise and be sustained primarily when the person moves into or affiliates with a new reference group (cf. Berelson & Steiner, 1963, pp. 580 ff.). Many theorists argue that the success of groups like Alcoholics Anonymous depends on the effectiveness with which the group is organized so that each person demonstrates his membership in it by "saving" another alcoholic. Political experience has demonstrated that membership in small groups like Communist or Nazi Party cells is one of the most effective ways to sustain changed attitudes and behavior.

Our course attempts to achieve this result (a) by the group experience in isolation—creating the feeling of alumni who all went through it together; (b) by certain signs of identification with the group, particularly the language of the coding system, but also including a certificate of membership; and (c) by arranging where possible to have partici-

pants come from the same community so that they can form a "cell" when they return that will serve as an immediate reference group to prevent gradual undermining of the new network by other pressures.

In theoretical terms a reference group should be effective because its members constantly provide cues to each other to rearouse the associative network, because they will also reward each other for achievement-related thoughts and acts, and because this constant mutual stimulation, and reinforcement, plus the labeling of the group, will prevent assimilation of the network to bigger, older, and stronger networks (such as those associated with traditional cultural values).

In summary, we have described an influence process which may be conceived in terms of "input," "intervening," and "output" variables as in Table 1. The propositions relate variables in Column A via their effect on the intervening variables in Column B to as yet loosely specified behavior in Column C, which may be taken as evidence that "development" of n Achievement has "really" taken place. The problems involved in evaluation of effects are as great and as complicated as those involved in designing the treatment, but they cannot be spelled out here, partly for lack of space, partly because we are in an even earlier stage of examining and classifying the effects of our training 1 and 2 years later preparatory to conceptualizing more clearly what happens. It will have to suffice to point out that we plan extensive comparisons over a 2-year period of the behaviors of our trained subjects compared with matched controls along the lines suggested in Column C.

What the table does is to give a brief overall view of how we conceptualize the educational or treatment process. What is particularly important is that the propositions refer to *operationally defined* and *separable* treatment variables. Thus, after having demonstrated hopefully a large effect of the total program, we can subtract a variable and see how much that decreases the impact of the course. That is to say, the course is designed so that it could go ahead perfectly reasonably

Table 1. Variables conceived as entering into the motive change process.

A Input or independent variables	B Intervening variables	C Output or dependent variables
1. Goal setting for the person (P1, P11) 2. Acquisition of n Achievement associative network (P2, P3, P4, P5) 3. Relating new network to super-ordinate networks reality (P2) the self (P6) cultural values (P7) 4. Personal goal setting (P8) 5. Knowledge of progress (P3, P4, P9) 6. Personal warmth and support (P10) 7. Support of reference group (P11, P12)	Arousal of associative network (salience) Experiencing and labeling the associative network Variety of cues to which network is linked Interfering associations assimilated or bypassed by reproductive inter-ference Positive affect associated with net-work	Duration and/or extensiveness of changes in: 1. n Achievement associative network 2. Related actions: use of feedback, moderate risk tak-ing, etc. 3. Innovations (job improve-ments) 4. Use of time and money 5. Entrepreneurial success as defined by nature of job held and its rewards

Note.–P1, P11, etc., refer to the numbered propositions in the text.

with very little advanced goal setting (P1), with an objective rather than a warm person-al atmosphere (P11), without the business game tying thought to action (P9), without learning to code n Achievement and write achievement-related stories (P3), without cul-tural value analysis (P7), or an isolated resi-dential setting (P1, P11, P12). The study units are designed in a way that they can be omitted without destroying the viability of the treatment which has never been true of other studies of the psychotherapeutic pro-cess (cf. Rogers & Dymond, 1954).

But is there any basis for thinking the pro-gram works in practice? As yet, not enough time has elapsed to enable us to collect much data on long-term changes in personality and business activity. However, we do know that businessmen can learn to write stories scoring high in n Achievement, that they retain this skill over 1 year or 2, and that they like the course—but the same kinds of things can be said about many unevaluated management training courses. In two instances we have more objective data. Three courses were given to some 34 men from the Bombay area in early 1963. It proved possible to develop a crude but objective and reliable coding sys-tem to record whether each one had shown *unusual* entrepreneurial activity in the 2 years prior to the course or in the 2 years after

course. "Unusual" here means essentially an unusual promotion or salary raise or starting a new business venture of some kind. Of the 30 on whom information was available in 1965, 27% had been unusually active before the course, 67% after the course ($X^2 = 11.2, p < .01$). In a control group chosen at random from those who applied for the course in 1963, out of 11 on whom information has so far been obtained, 18% were active before 1963, 27% since 1963.

In a second case, four courses were given throughout 1964 to a total of 52 small busi-nessmen from the small city of Kakinada in Andhra Pradesh, India. Of these men, 25% had been unusually active in the 2-year period before the course, and 65% were unusually active immediately afterwards ($X^2 = 17.1, p < .01$). More control data and more refined measures are needed, but it looks very much as if, in India at least, we will be dealing with a spontaneous "activation" rate of only 25% =35% among entrepreneurs. Thus we have a distinct advantage over psychotherapists who are trying to demonstrate an improvement over a two-thirds spontaneous recovery rate. Our own data suggest that we will be unlikely to get an improvement or "activa-tion" rate much above the two-thirds level commonly reported in therapy studies. That is, about one-third of the people in our courses have remained relatively unaffected. Nevertheless the two-thirds activated after the course represent a doubling of the normal rate of unusual entrepreneurial activity—no mean achievement in the light of the current pessimism among psychologists as to their ability to induce lasting personality change among adults.

One case will illustrate how the course seems to affect people in practice. A short time after participating in one of our courses in India, a 47-year-old businessman rather suddenly and dramatically decided to quit his excellent job and go into the construction business on his own in a big way. A man with some means of his own, he had had a very successful career as employee-relations manager for a large oil firm. His job involved adjusting management-employee difficulties, negotiating union contracts, etc. He was well-to-do, well thought of in his company, and admired in the community, but he was restless because he found his job increasingly boring. At the time of the course his original n Achievement score was not very high and he was thinking of retiring and living in England where his son was studying. In an interview, 8 months later, he said the course had served not so much to "motivate" him but to "crystallize" a lot of ideas he had vaguely or half consciously picked up about work and achievement all through his life. It provided him with a new language (he still talked in terms of standards of excellence, blocks, moderate risk, goal anticipation, etc.), a new construct which served to organize those ideas and explain to him why he was bored with his job, despite his obvious success. He decided he wanted to be an n-Achievement-oriented person, that he would be unhappy in retirement, and that he should take a risk, quit his job, and start in business on his own. He acted on his decision and in 6 months had drawn plans and raised over $1,000,000 to build the tallest building in his large city to be called the "Everest Apartments." He is extremely happy in his new activity because it means selling, promoting, trying to wangle scarce materials, etc. His first building is partway up and he is planning two more.

Even a case as dramatic as this one does not prove that the course produced the effect, despite his repeated use of the constructs he had learned, but what is especially interesting about it is that he described what had happened to him in exactly the terms the theory requires. He spoke not about a new motive force but about how existing ideas had been crystallized into a new associative network, and it is this new network which *is* the new "motivating" force according to the theory.

How generalizable are the propositions? They have purposely been stated generally so that some term like "attitude" or "personality characteristic" could be substituted for the term "motive" throughout, because we believe the propositions will hold for other personality variables. In fact, most of the supporting experimental evidence cited comes from attempts to change other characteristics. Nevertheless, the propositions should hold best more narrowly for motives and especially the achievement motive. One of the biggest difficulties in the way of testing them more generally is that not nearly as much is known about other human characteristics or their specific relevance for success in a certain type of work. For example, next to nothing is known about the need for power, its relation to success, let us say, in politics or bargaining situations, and its origins and course of development in the life history of individuals. It is precisely the knowledge we have about such matters for the achievement motive that puts us in a position to shape it for limited, socially and individually desirable ends. In the future, it seems to us, research in psychotherapy ought to follow a similar course. That is to say, rather than developing "all purpose" treatments, good for any person and any purpose, it should aim to develop specific treatments or educational programs built on laboriously accumulated detailed knowledge of the characterisitic to be changed. It is in this spirit that the present research program in motive acquisition has been designed and is being tested out.

References

Allport, G. W. The ego in contemporary psychology. *Psychological Review*, 1943, **50**, 451-478.

Andrews, J. D. W. The achievement motive in two types of organizations. *Journal of Personality and Social Psychology*, 1965.

Atkinson, J. W. (Ed.) *Motives in fantasy, action and society.* Princeton, N. J.: Van Nostrand, 1958.

Bandura, A., & Walters, R. H. *Social learning and personality development.* New York: Holt, Rinehart & Winston, 1963.

Bauer, R. A. The obstinate audience: The influence process from the point of view of social communication. *American Psychologist*, **19**, 319-329.

Benedict, Ruth. *The chrysanthemum and the sword.* Boston: Houghton Mifflin, 1946.

Berelson, B., & Steiner, G. A. *Human behavior: An inventory of scientific findings.* New York: Harcourt, Brace, 1964.

Brown, R. W. *Words and things.* Glencoe, Ill.: Free Press, 1958.

Burris, R. W. The effect of counseling on achievement motivation. Unpublished doctoral dissertation, University of Indiana, 1958.

Ends, E. J., & Page, C. W. A study of three types of group psychotherapy with hospitalized male inebriates. *Quarterly Journal on Alcohol*, 1957, **18**, 263-277.

Eysenck, H. J. The effects of psychotherapy: An evaluation. *Journal of Consulting Psychology*, 1952, **16**, 319-324.

Festinger, L. *A theory of cognitive dissonance.* Stanford, Calif.: Stanford Univ. Press, 1957.

Frank, J. *Persuasion and healing.* Baltimore: Johns Hopkins Press, 1961.

French, E. G. Effects of the interaction of motivation and feedback on task performance. In J. W. Atkinson (Ed.), *Motives in fantasy, action and society.* Princeton, N. J.: Van Nostrand, 1958. Pp. 400-408.

Heckhausen, H. Eine Rahmentheorie der Motivation in zehn Thesen. *Zeitschrift für experimentelle und angewandte Psychologie*, 1963, **X/4**, 604-626.

Hovland, C. I. Human learning and retention. In S. S. Stevens (Ed.), *Handbook of experimental psychology.* New York: Wiley, 1951.

Hovland, C. I., Janis, I. L., & Kelley, H. H. *Communication and persuasion: Psychological studies of opinion change.* New Haven: Yale Univer. Press, 1953.

Kausler, D. H. Aspiration level as a determinant of performance. *Journal of Personality*, 1959, **27**, 346-351.

Kelley, G. A. *The psychology of personal constructs.* New York: Norton, 1955.

Korzybski, A. *Science and sanity.* Lancaster, Pa.: Science Press, 1941.

McClelland, D. C. *The achieving society.* Princeton, N. J.: Van Nostrand, 1961.

McClelland, D. C. *The roots of consciousness.* Princeton, N. J.: Van Nostrand, 1964.

McClelland, D. C., Atkinson, J. W., Clark, R. A., & Lowell, E. L. *The achievement motive.* New York: Appleton-Century, 1953.

McGeoch, J. A., & Irion, A. L. *The psychology of human learning.* (2nd ed.) New York: Longmans, Green, 1952.

Mierke, K. *Wille und Leistung.* Göttingen: Verlag für Psychologie, 1955.

Orne, M. On the social psychology of the psychological experiment: With particular reference to demand characteristics and their implications. *American Psychologist*, 1962, **17**, 776-783.

Roethlisberger, F. J., & Dickson, W. J. *Management and the worker.* Cambridge: Harvard Univer. Press, 1947.

Rogers, C. R. *On becoming a person.* Boston: Houghton Mifflin, 1961.

Rogers, C. R., & Dymond, R. F. (Eds.) *Psychotherapy and personality change.* Chicago: Univer. Chicago Press, 1954.

Rosen, B. C., & D'Andrade, R. G. The psychosocial origins of achievement motivation. *Sociometry*, 1959, **22**, 185-218.

Rosenthal, R. On the social psychology of the psychological experiment: The experimenter's hypothesis as unintended determinant of experimental results. *American Scientist*, 1963, **51**, 268-283.

Sarason, I. Empirical findings and theoretical problems in the use of anxiety scales. *Psychological Bulletin*, 1960, **57**, 403-415.

Skinner, B. F. *Science and human behavior.* New York: Macmillan, 1953.

Origins of Achievement Motivation

Michael Argyle and Peter Robinson

A review of previous investigations shows that achievement motivation can be produced by rewards and punishment in childhood only under special conditions not usually encountered. It is postulated that two other types of learning may also occur (*a*) the introjection of parental exhortation and standards, (*b*) indentification with achievement-oriented parents and others. These hypotheses were tested in a correlational study of five hundred grammar school and other children. Achievement motivation was measured both by the content analysis of imaginative stories and by a questionnaire; relations with parents were obtained from a modified version of the semantic differential. Both hypotheses were confirmed, though both processes were found to work only when there was sufficient identification with parents. An additional finding was that achievement motivation was found to be correlated with various measures of self-aggression and guilt.

1. Introduction

A great deal of research has been carried out in connection with the achievement motive. This seems to have two basic aspects "motive to achieve"—an approach motive, and "motive to avoid failure"—an avoidance motive. Most of the research has been conducted with a measure (*n*Ach) which seems to be primarily an index of "motive to achieve." This research suggests that the achievement motive is a drive which can be aroused experimentally, varies between people and is acquired (McClelland *et al.*, 1953; Atkinson, 1958). It is generally assumed that the two aspects of this drive are acquired through processes of reward and punishment.

From M. Argyle and P. Robinson, "Two Origins of Achievement Motivation," *British Journal of Social and Clinical Psychology*, 1962, **1**, 107-120. Reprinted by permission of the publisher and the authors.

The Effects of Reward and Punishment on n*A*ch

Winterbottom (1953) studied 29 eight- to ten-year-old boys and their mothers. Achievement motivation was measured by the content analysis of imaginative stories, and mothers were interviewed concerning their socialization techniques. The use of verbal and material rewards for fulfilling demands for achievement was unrelated to *n*Ach scores, but physical rewards (kissing and hugging) were so related ($p < 0.05$). None of the three types of punishment considered bore any relation to *n*Ach. Crandell, Preston & Rabson (1960) studied 30 three- to five-year-olds and their mothers. Achievement motivation was assessed not by the projective method but by ratings of achievement efforts at school; material rewards for achievement were rated in the home. A correlation of 0.42 ($p < 0.01$) was found between the two variables. This study differs from the others reported in that achievement motivation was measured from ratings, and in that the subjects were so young. Child, Storm & Veroff (1958) carried out a cross-cultural study of 52 societies. Achievement motivation was assessed from a content analysis of 12 randomly chosen folk-tales from each society, treating the stories as TAT protocols. Various aspects of socialization were rated on 7-point scales by judges using the available ethnographic materials. It was found that a combination of reward for achievement and punishment for absence of achievement-oriented behaviour correlated 0.34 with *n*Ach ($p < 0.06$). However if societies using rigid or compulsive child-rearing are considered separately, this correlation rises to 0.57 ($n = 9$), and *n*Ach is also correlated with punishment for presence of achievement ($r = 0.68$, $p < 0.05$), and conflictful handling of achievement ($r = 0.44$). However, for the 10 societies which do not use rigid methods of socialization, these correlations are insignificant or negative. Similarly, punishment for absence of achievement is very effective in societies low in general indulgence ($r = 0.80$, $p < 0.01$), but not in societies high in indulgence ($r = 0.08$). This important study suggests that reward, and particularly punishment, can produce *n*Ach only in a rigid and non-indulgent setting. Achievement motivation was found to be higher in societies where training was non-rigid ($r = 0.56$) and indulgent ($r = 0.29$), so the question arises, what are the origins in these other societies?

There is, however, some evidence that success at specific tasks does result in greater efforts being made to perform the tasks. Keister (1938) found that nursery school-children came to show more persistence at tasks as a result of success and praise for performance at progressively more difficult tasks. P. S. Sears (1940) found that the level of aspiration increases as a function of success in previous tasks.

It has been found by Robinson (1961) and others that *n*Ach is correlated with I.Q. at about 0.40. This is consistent with the idea that academic success leads to greater achievement motivation. Robinson also found that British school-children who had been selected for grammar school at 11+ had a higher *n*Ach than children of the same I.Q. who were not selected. This confirmed his hypothesis that success would increase *n*Ach.

To summarize, emotional rewards for achievement, punishment for non-achievement in a rigid non-indulgent setting, and experience of success at tasks, may all contribute to the development of *n*Ach.

The Influence of Exhortation on n*Ach*

It was thought at one time that training for independence and self-reliance produced achievement motivation. McClelland & Friedman (1952) in a cross-cultural study of 8 American Indian societies found that *n*Ach as measured from folk-tales was correlated with earliness and severity of independence training; however, Child, Storm & Veroff (*op. cit.*) found no such relation with self-reliance training in their study of 52 societies, nor in a re-analysis of the McClelland & Friedman data. Rosen & d'Andrade (1959) point out that encouragement of independence in general must be distinguished from encouragement of independent achievement in particular.

Winterbottom (*op. cit.*) found that the mothers of boys higher on *n*Ach had made demands for independence and mastery at an earlier age: only the achievement-related demands showed a significant difference. Rosen and d'Andrade (1959) studied 40 nine- to eleven-year-old boys and their parents by setting up experimental tasks in the home and observing parental reactions. Boys high in *n*Ach had parents who set high standards for them and expected them to do well; their mothers, but not their fathers, showed a type of interaction corresponding to a combination of warmth and rejection. Kagan & Moss (1959) found that maternal concern with achievement was significantly higher for high *n*Ach girls; they found no such relation for boys. Wolf (1938) found that persistence at tasks in children was correlated with a high level of demands by adults which were reasonable in the light of the child's ability.

Whereas it has usually been supposed that *n*Ach is acquired by rewards and punishments which occur *after* the achievement-behaviour (or lack of it) has taken place, we now have evidence that exhortations and setting of standards *before* the behaviour may also be effective. We shall postulate that when there are appropriate relations between parent and child—warmth and dependency probably—then these exhortations will become "introjected," i.e. applied by the child to himself and experienced as an "ought." It is quite likely that this process can ultimately be reduced to more familiar principles of learning: for instance the child may have been rewarded for carrying out parental exhortations on previous occasions and thus acquired a learning set to obey all such demands.

It is proposed to test this hypothesis in the current investigation. It is predicted that *n*Ach will be correlated with (i) the strength of parental demands for achievement, and (ii) the reported strength of super-ego demands for achievement.

Identification with Achievement-Oriented Parents as a Source of nAch

It is postulated that children often identify with their parents, and that when their parents are hard-working and successful they will wish to be like their parents and thus acquire a high *n*Ach. This is a second type of learning which is not easily reducible to familiar learning processes. Again it is possible that identification and imitation is rewarded by parents, e.g. mother may praise a boy for being like his father, and thus create a learning set to imitate. Alternatively it could be due to a desire to acquire status in fantasy, or to clarify the self-concept.

Two predictions follow:—*n*Ach should correlate with (i) the reported achievement orientation of the parents, and (ii) identification with parents.

2. Method

Subjects

Five hundred and one subjects were used in all, 236 girls and 265 boys, the results being computed separately for groups varying between 39 and 106 in size. Most of the subjects were grammar school children aged between thirteen and seventeen; there were also two groups of students.

Design and Procedure

Data were collected in the classroom, in the absence of the regular teacher, and were completed within a single period in most cases. The design was correlational; for each homogeneous sample correlations were computed between the relevant variables.

Measurement of Variables—Projective Measure of Achievement Motivation (nAch)

The McClelland-Atkinson method of measurement was used. Three of the follow-ing four pictures were used—boy at desk, operation scene, men with machine, man at drawing board (Atkinson, 1958, p. 488, pictures 8, 7, 2, 28). These were reproduced on cardboard, size 2 ft. $\times$ 1 ft.6 in. and shown for 15 seconds each. The four questions were written on the blackboard as a guide to the stories (1. What is happening? Who are these people? 2. What has led up to this situation? 3. What is being thought or wanted? By whom? 4. What will happen next?). Subjects were given 4 minutes to write each story, with the exception of the 59 grammar school boys, who were given 12 minutes and who produced rather more achievement imagery. The initial instructions were as follows, and were designed to produce a relaxed condition:

You are going to see a series of pictures, and your task is to write a story that is suggested to you by each picture. Try to imagine what is going on in each picture. Then tell what the situation is, what led up to the situation, what the people are thinking and feeling, and what they will do. The questions on the board are to guide you.

In other words, write as complete a story as you can—a story with plot and characters.

You will have four minutes for each story. Write your first impressions and work rapidly. I will keep time.

There are no right or wrong stories or kinds of stories, so you may feel free to write whatever story is suggested to you when you look at a picture. Spelling, punctuation, and grammar are not important. What is important is to write out as fully and as quickly as possible the story that comes to your mind as you imagine what is going on in each picture. Are there any questions?

The reliability of scoring obtained was not as high as that reported by some previous investigators, and was in the area of 0.50. Subsequently we used the scores of the scorer (Robinson) who agreed most closely with the practice manual provided by Atkinson (1958). Test-retest reliability over an interval of two years was obtained for one group, and yielded a reliability of 0.44 ($n = 59$). However, examination of the stories produced by different administrators suggests that the contents are extremely sensitive to minor variations of the testing situation and relations with the tester.

Separate scores were obtained for the hope of success (*n*Ach+) and the fear of failure (*n*Ach-), as distinguished by Clark, Teevan & Ricciuti (1956).

Measurement—The Questionnaire Measure of Achievement Motivation (Q-ach)

Previous investigations by Robinson (1961) had led to the construction of a questionnaire. This consisted of two sets of questions corresponding to a hope of success factor and a fear of failure factor. Scores on the two sub-tests correlated with scores on *n*Ach+ and *n*Ach— respectively. The scale is given in Appendix I. It will be referred to as *Q*-ach, while the projective measure will be called *n*Ach.

Measurement—Uses of the Semantic Differential and Q-sort

In order to measure *strength of parental achievement tendencies, strength of parental achievement demands*, etc., the semantic differential was used (cf. Osgood *et al.*, 1957). Since the original semantic differential does not contain any scales dealing with achievement, a number of such scales were inserted. Out of the six scales introduced, only three were significantly inter-correlated, and these were retained. They are: hardworking—easy going, top-of-the-class—bottom-of-the-class, and clever—stupid. Average ratings on the 7-point scales were used to obtain scores on these variables. The total scale is given in Appendix II.

Several sets of semantic scales were completed by each subject, including (*a*) THE KIND OF PERSON MY FATHER IS, (*b*) THE KIND OF PERSON MY FATHER THINKS I OUGHT TO BE. It was found that when there was an "ought" or similar instruction, subjects tended to use the categories showing maximum achievement, so that there was little variation between subjects. To meet this difficulty a miniature *Q*-sort was constructed (see Appendix III), in which 2 out of 10 attributes to be ranked refer to achievement. The reciprocal of the average rank of these two attributes is taken as the achievement score.

Measurement—Identification

Three methods of measurement were employed:

(1) The similarity of scoring THE KIND OF PERSON I WOULD MOST LIKE TO BE and MY FATHER (etc.) on the Semantic Differential and *Q*-sort. In the case of the *Q*-sort, the similarity was measured by the rank-order correlation between the two sets of rankings. For the semantic differential, various measures of semantic distance were compared and finally the easiest to compute was used—the mean difference of scale ratings—since this correlated highly with more complex measures.

This measure of identification was used since it is closest to our conceptualization of this variable. There might be some advantage in using an independent measure of the attributes of the other person; on the other hand this measure shows how far a subject wants to be like his perception of the other.

(2) An alternative measure used was similar to the first, but based only on the scoring of the achievement scales of the modified semantic differential. It seemed possible that a subject could identify with some attributes of another person, but not with all of them.

(3) Finally, a direct measure was used, consisting of a number of items such as "I would like to do the sort of work that my father does," "My father is the best person to go to for advice," with a 5-point scale of agreement.

Measurement—Guilt and Self-Aggression

In connection with certain unexpected results obtained, which are presented in this paper, it is necessary to describe the relevant measuring instruments. Guilt was measured by means of a scale developed in another study and purified by means of factor analysis. It is given in Appendix IV. Self-aggression was measured by means of a modified version of one of the aggression scales devised by Sears (1961). The new version has higher correlations between the items than the original one had: the average correlation between items and the total score is now 0.50. Use was also made of a set of inter-correlated intro-punitive jokes being compiled by the first author. Subjects indicate how funny they find the jokes: the scores are averaged and are taken as a measure of self-aggression.

3. Results

*Introductory Note on
Selection of Data to Be Used*

Although 501 subjects were tested altogether, not all of the tests were given to all the subjects. Several samples of subjects were discarded because the projection test for *n*Ach did not produce enough achievement related imagery (the reasons for this were discussed above). Other groups of subjects were discarded because the semantic measure of parental demands did not have enough variance (this was replaced by a *Q*-sort measure as described above).

*Relations between the
Different Measures of
Achievement Motivation*

Total *n*Ach scores correlated with total *Q*-ach scores at 0.22 ($p < 0.01$). The subscores for *n*Ach+ and *Q*-ach+ had a small correlation of about 0.10, while *n*Ach— and *Q*-ach— correlated at 0.17 ($p < 0.05$). The approach and avoidance scores for each measure had correlations that were either zero or slightly negative. There is little evidence here that the projective and questionnaire measures were measuring the same variable. Further evidence on this question will be obtained from the correlations of each measure with other variables.

*Achievement Motivation in
Relation to the Introjection
of Parental Demands*

The most direct evidence on this hypothesis consists of the correlations between achievement motivation and reported parental demands for achievement. The relevant correlations are given in Table 1.

Although only one correlation is significant at the 5 per cent level, several more are significant at the 10 per cent level, and nearly all the *n*Ach correlations are positive. There is no confirmation of a relation between parental demands and *Q*-ach, however. The *n*Ach correlations are higher if the upper half of subjects on parental identification are considered separately, in the case of mother-son relations.

Since parental demands are assumed to operate via their introjection, it would be expected that super-ego demands for achievement would correlate with achievement motivation. Unfortunately SE (ach) as measured on the semantic differential has a very small variance—most subjects ascribe maximum achievement demands to the super-ego. A better test of this hypothesis is provided by the samples for whom a *Q*-sort measure was used. The only such sample available consisted of 40 female students. The findings are shown in Table 2.

*Achievement Motivation
and Parental Achievement*

The correlations between achievement motivation and reported parental achievement orientation are given in Table 3. The latter variable consists of average ratings on the inter-correlated semantic scales of hard-working (v. easy-going), top-of-the-class (v. bottom-of-the-class) and clever (v. stupid).

It can be seen that most of the correlations are in the expected direction, two of them being significant. The strongest relations are between *Q*-ach+ and father's achievement for boys, and *n*Ach+ and mother's achievement for girls. However, the correlations are in general higher for father than for mother. Thus the weakest relation is the mother-son one.

*Relations between
Achievement Motivation
and Identification with Parents*

The correlations between achievement motivation and several measures of identification are given in Table 4.

The correlations increase with the directness of the measures of identification used. In

Table 1. Correlations between achievement motivation and the reported strength of parental demands for achievement.

		nAch +	nAch –	Q-ach +	Q-ach –
Father's	(boys)	*0.23* (n = 59)	*0.25*	–0.18 (n = 44)	0.17
	(girls)	0.07 (n = 39)	0.31*	0.10 (n = 79)	–0.09
Mother's	(boys)	*0.23* (n = 59)	*0.25*	–0.16 (n = 44)	0.10
	(girls)	–0.01 (n = 39)	0.07	–0.09 (n = 79)	0.13

In Tables 1-5 * indicates *p* < .05, ** *p* < .01, *** *p* < .001, italics *p* < .10, using a one-tailed test where applicable.

Table 2. Correlations between achievement motivation and SE(ach).

	nAch +	nAch –	Q-ach +	Q-ach –
SE(ach)	0.03 (n = 40)	0.30 (p < 0.025)	0.13 (n = 84)	– 0.21 (p < 0.025)

Table 3. Correlations between achievement motivation and reported parental achievement tendencies.

		nAch +	nAch –	Q-ach +	Q-ach –
Father	(boys)	0.13 (n = 59)	0.10	0.31* (n = 112)	0.07
Father	(girls)	0.20 (n = 39)	0.04	0.16 (n = 130)	0.12
Mother	(boys)	–0.03 (n = 59)	0.14	–0.03 (n = 112)	0.11
Mother	(girls)	0.32*(n = 39)	0.22	0.06 (n = 130)	–0.05

Table 4. Correlations between achievement motivation and identification.

		nAch +	nAch –	Q-ach +		Q-ach –
Father (boys)	EI/F (Sem. Diff.)	0.05 (n = 59)	–0.03	0.05	(n = 112)	0.13
	EI/F(ach)	0.17	0.20			
	Ident. (Quest.)			0.37***	(n = 86)	0.22*
Father (girls)	EI/F	0.10 (n = 39)	0.19	0.01	(n = 130)	0.07
	Ident.			0.24*	(n = 102)	0.31**
Mother (boys)	EI/M	–0.03 (n = 59)	0.06	0.18*	(n = 112)	0.12
	EI/M(ach)	0.19	0.20*			
	Ident.			0.36***	(n = 86)	0.52***
Mother (girls)	EI/M	0.02 (n = 39)	0.15	0.05	(n = 130)	0.10
	Ident.			0.20*	(n = 102)	0.42***

addition the correlations are in general higher for *Q*-ach than for *n*Ach, if the results for the same populations are compared (not shown in this table).

Combined Influence of Parental Achievement and Identification with Parents on Achievement Motivation

There are two possible ways of studying the joint influence of these two variables. One way is simply to calculate multiple correlations for particular samples, the other to find the correlation of achievement motivation with variable A when only those high on variable B are considered.

The multiple correlations can be inferred from Tables 3 and 4; since all of the correlations are positive, the multiple correlations are in general higher than those shown here, and correspondingly significant at a higher level.

Various analyses have been made by dividing samples at the mid-point on one variable to find the correlation of the upper half on a second variable. This was carried out for the most reliable sample for which *n*Ach was measured—the 59 High School boys. The correlation of total *n*Ach and mother's achievement orientation rose from 0.10 to 0.22 if the upper half on maternal identification is considered; the same does not apply to father. The mother-son correlation is the weakest, but is apparently strengthened when only those high in maternal identification are considered. This provides an explanation of the weak mother-son relation—this is the lowest of the four identifications.

Achievement Motivation in Relation to Guilt and Self-Aggression

An unexpected pattern of findings was obtained with measure of guilt and self-aggression, which were administered to the subjects

their relations with other variables measured. The relations between the two measures are positive, but low. Between nAch+ and Q-ach+, $r = 0.10$ ($n = 200$); between nAch— and Q-ach—, $r = 0.17$ ($p < 0.05$). Turning to the correlations with other variables, we find that the predictions about identification are best confirmed for Q-ach, as compared with nAch. On the other hand, the introjection predictions are best confirmed for nAch—. This suggests that there may be different elements within achievement motivation, which have different socialization origins and ways of functioning.

Table 5. Correlations between achievement motivation, guilt, and self-aggression.

	nAch +	nAch −	Q-ach +		Q-ach −
Guilt (boys)	0.29* ($n = 59$)	− 0.11	0.11	($n = 198$)	0.25***
(girls)	0.27 ($n = 39$)	− 0.28	0.17	($n = 197$)	0.19*
Self-aggression (boys)			0.40***	($n = 86$)	0.35**
(girls)			0.42***	($n = 106$)	0.49***
Intropunitive jokes (boys)			0.11	($n = 42$)	0.18

for quite different purposes. Table 5 shows the correlations in question.

4. Discussion

Validity of Measures of Achievement Motivation

The projective measure of nAch has previously been shown to be valid in the sense that scores can be increased by experimental arousal of the drive (McClelland *et al.*, 1949). On the other hand, studies of the association between nAch and external measures, e.g. of performance at tasks or academic achievement with I.Q. held constant, have not consistently confirmed the validity of this measure. Another questionnaire measure—the achievement scales of the California Personality Inventory (Gough, 1957)—was found to be a successful predictor of over-achievement in school and college, with I.Q. held constant.

Further light on the validity of these two kinds of measure can be provided by studying the relation between them and by examining

The Introjection Hypothesis

The hypothesis is generally confirmed by the positive correlations with reported parental demands (Table 1), especially with nAch, though these are not at a high level of significance. The hypothesis is also supported by the correlation of 0.30 between nAch— and super-ego demands. As mentioned above, the best results here in terms of satisfactory measures obtained, were found from students and it is possible that younger subjects would give better correlations. It is understandable that nAch— should be acquired by means of this mechanism. Super-ego demands are commonly of a negative character, so it would follow that an avoidance drive would result. These demands are generally unconscious, and this explains why the drive should appear in nAch but not in Q-ach.

We also find that this mechanism is dependent on sufficient identification with or closeness to the parents: the correlations are higher if only those subjects who identify most with their parents are considered.

The Identification Hypothesis

Reported parental achievement has a generally positive relation with achievement motivation; this is particularly true of the same-sex parent, and in the case of boys and fathers, for Q-ach+. The results for parental identification are better for the most direct measures of identification, but the results are consistently positive for all measures and for most parent-child combinations. While the mother-son relation is weakest on the parental achievement relation, this is strengthened if only those high in maternal identification are considered. This confirms the idea that parental achievement is only effective if there is sufficient identification with the parent.

Achievement and Self-Aggression

The correlation consistently found with guilt and self-aggression was not predicted, so it remains to consider the explanation of this finding.

(*a*) Self-aggression may produce self-rejection and low self-evaluation, and lead to enhanced achievement efforts. If this were so, there should be a negative correlation between nAch and self-estimates of achievement. This however is not found. Similarly we should expect more self/ego-ideal conflict to go with high nAch. Such a relation was found by Martire (1956) for subjects producing high nAch stories under both the aroused and relaxed conditions; we used only the relaxed condition and found no consistent relation here.

(*b*) If nAch— is due to punishment for failure, and if guilt feelings are also due to punishment, it would be expected that nAch— and guilt would be correlated. However, as Table 5 shows, it is nAch+ which has the higher correlation with guilt: this could conceivably be due to punishment for the *absence* of achievement producing both nAch+ and guilt.

(*c*) Guilt and self-aggression could be in part the result of low actual achievement in combination with a high nAch. We have seen that guilt is correlated with nAch; is it also correlated with low self-estimates of achievement? Our results show that it is consistently correlated in this way, in one sample reading -0.36 ($p < 0.01$). It looks as if this is the most likely of the three explanations offered.

Problems about the Direction of Causation

Our results all take the form of correlations between pairs of measures, where both measures were taken from the same subjects. Several distinct problems of interpretation arise. In the first place, the correlation may arise out of a shared "response set," e.g. acquiescent subjects may tend to agree more strongly with all the items. This could not affect the projection test results, and it is difficult to see how the Q-ach scores could be affected by the same response set as the Semantic Differentials. Secondly there may be contamination between measures, i.e. one measure may affect the results on another, e.g. through a desire to appear consistent or via the arousal of some drive state. The projection test was always given first in order to avoid any inter-test influences on this very sensitive measure. However it is possible that people who really have a high nAch tend to ascribe high achievement tendencies or demands to their parents as a further projective manifestation of the drive. McClelland *et al.* (1953, p. 276 f.) found that the correlations between parental attitudes and nAch were the same when the former were estimated by the children or by a psychiatrist; however, no reports on achievement were included here.

A third possibility is that the correlations found are due to a different causal process from that hypothesized. For instance, children with high nAch are thereby likely to have more successful parents. While this is obviously unlikely, it is possible that nAch leads to greater parental identification when parents are themselves successful.

5. Conclusion

Five hundred grammar school children and others were given projective and questionnaire measures of achievement motivation as well as semantic differential or Q-sort tests to assess their relations with parents.[1] Achievement motivation, especially as measured by projective test, was correlated with reported strength of parental achievement demands; the fear of failure component also correlated with reported super-ego demands for achievement.

Achievement motivation, especially as measured by questionnaire, was found to be correlated with the reported achievement tendencies of the same-sexed parent, and with identification with parents. Both processes were dependent on there being sufficient identification with parents.

Achievement motivation correlated with measures of guilt and self-aggression; since the latter also correlated with low self-ratings of achievement it was suggested that the guilt is produced by high motivation and low achievement in this sphere.

APPENDIX I

Underline the Appropriate Alternative

1. In how many activities do you wish to do your very best?
   as many as possible | many | some | few | very few

2. Would you hesitate to undertake something that might lead to your failing?
   nearly always | frequently | about half the time | seldom | hardly ever

3. In how many areas are you personally concerned about how well you do?
   most | many | some | few | very few

4. Success brings relief or further determination and not just pleasant feelings. Do you agree?
   strong agreement | agreement | neutral | disagreement | strong disagreement

5. How much effort do you use to reach the goals you set yourself?
   almost 0% | 25% | 50% | 75% | 100%

6. How often do you lack confidence when you have to compete against others?
   hardly ever | seldom | about half the time | frequently | nearly always

7. How hard do you feel you have to try in seemingly trivial tasks?
   not at all | not very | medium | fairly | very

8. How strong is your desire to avoid competitive situations?
   very | fairly | medium | not very | none

9. How true is it to say that your efforts are directed towards avoiding failure?
   quite untrue | not very true | unsure | fairly true | quite true

10. In how many spheres do you think you will succeed in doing as well as you can?
    most | many | some | few | very few

11. How far do you agree that effort rather than success is what is important?
    strong agreement | agreement | neutral | disagreement | strong disagreement

12. How often do you seek opportunities to excel?
    hardly ever | seldom | about half the time | frequently | most of the time

13. How many situations do you avoid in which you may be exposed to evaluation?
    very few | few | some | many | most

14. Do you ever do better if you are worried about failing?
    hardly ever | seldom | about half the time | frequently | most of the time

15. The stronger the chance of failing the more determined you are to succeed. Do you agree?
    strong disagreement | disagreement | neutral | agreement | strong agreement

[1]We are grateful to Adrienne Dunn, Helen Ross, Dr. Richard Lynn, Ken Hignett, and David Moseley for assistance in the administration of tests, and to the teachers and children of the City of Oxford High School, Didcot Girls Grammar School, Wallingford Grammar School, Banbury Grammar School, Bromsgrove County High School, Witney Secondary Modern School, and Headington Secondary School.

APPENDIX II

happy	.... : .... : .... : .... : .... : .... : .... :	sad
calm	.... : .... : .... : .... : .... : .... : .... :	excitable
strong	.... : .... : .... : .... : .... : .... : .... :	weak
ordinary	.... : .... : .... : .... : .... : .... : .... :	unusual
hard-working	.... : .... : .... : .... : .... : .... : .... :	easy-going
dishonest	.... : .... : .... : .... : .... : .... : .... :	honest
active	.... : .... : .... : .... : .... : .... : .... :	passive
stupid	.... : .... : .... : .... : .... : .... : .... :	clever
small	.... : .... : .... : .... : .... : .... : .... :	large
striking	.... : .... : .... : .... : .... : .... : .... :	plain.
cruel	.... : .... : .... : .... : .... : .... : .... :	kind
impulsive	.... : .... : .... : .... : .... : .... : .... :	placid
soft	.... : .... : .... : .... : .... : .... : .... :	hard
colourful	.... : .... : .... : .... : .... : .... : .... :	dull
bottom of the class	.... : .... : .... : .... : .... : .... : .... :	top of the class

APPENDIX III

Number the words in each column from 1 to 10, putting "1" against the word which applies most, and so on.

Myself as I actually am	*Myself as I ought to be*	*Myself as I would like to be*	*My Father as he is*	*My Mother as she is*	*What my Father thinks I ought to be*	*What my Mother thinks I ought to be*
Friendly	Friendly	Friendly	Friendly	Friendly	Friendly	Friendly .....
Interesting	Interesting	Interesting	Interesting	Interesting	Interesting	Interesting .....
Good at games	Good at games	Good at games	Good at games	Good at games	Good at games	Good at games .....
Reliable	Reliable	Reliable	Reliable	Reliable	Reliable	Reliable .....
Intelligent	Intelligent	Intelligent	Intelligent	Intelligent	Intelligent	Intelligent .....
Brave	Brave	Brave	Brave	Brave	Brave	Brave .....
Happy	Happy	Happy	Happy	Happy	Happy	Happy .....
Hard working	Hard working	Hard working	Hard working	Hard working	Hard working	Hard working .....
Confident	Confident	Confident	Confident	Confident	Confident	Confident .....
Generous	Generous	Generous	Generous	Generous	Generous	Generous .....

APPENDIX IV

Survey of Moral Attitudes

Indicate to what extent you feel worry or guilt about behaviour in the areas listed.

Use this scale

0	1	2	3	4
Not at all	very slight	slight guilt	moderate	considerable guilt

1. Untidiness ....
2. Wasting money ....
3. Greed ....
4. Laziness ....
5. Being unkind ....
6. Not telling the truth ....
7. Cheating ....
8. Not being punctual ....
9. Selfishness ....
10. Cowardice ....
11. Not going to church ....
12. Disobedience ....
13. Not working hard enough ....
14. Bad temper ....
15. Causing suffering ....
16. Not keeping promises ....
17. Stinginess ....
18. Lack of persistence ....
19. Not washing ....
20. Boasting ....

References

Atkinson, J. W. (ed.) (1958). *Motives in Fantasy, Action, and Society.* Princeton: Van Nostrand.

Child, I. L., Storm, T. & Veroff, J. (1958). Achievement themes in folk tales related to socialization practice. Chap. 34 in Atkinson (1958).

Clark, R. A., Teevan, R. & Ricciuti, H. N. (1956). Hope of success and fear of failure as aspects of need for achievement. *J. abnorm. soc. Psychol.*, **53**, 182-6 and Chap. 41 in Atkinson (1958).

Crandall, V. J., Preston, A. & Rabson, A. (1960). Maternal reactions and the development of independence and achievement behavior in young children. *Child Developm.*, **31**, 243-51.

Gough, H. (1957). *Manual of the California Personality Inventory.* Palo Alto: Consulting Psychologists Press.

Kagan, J. & Moss, H. A. (1959). Stability and validity of achievement fantasy. *J. abnorm. soc. Psychol.*, **58**, 357-64.

Keister, M. E. (1938). The behavior of young children in failure: an experimental attempt to discover and to modify undesirable responses of preschool children to failure. *Univ. Ia. Stud. Child Welf.*, **14**, 27-82.

Martire, J. G. (1956). Relationships between the self concept and differences in the strength and generality of achievement motivation. *J. Pers.*, **24**, 364-75 and Chap. 27 in Atkinson (1958).

McClelland, D. C. *et al.* (1953). *The Achievement Motive.* New York: Appleton-Century-Crofts.

McClelland, D. C. & Friedman, G. A. (1952). A cross-cultural study of the relationship between child-training practices and achievement motivation appearing in folk tales. In *Readings in Social Psychology* (eds. G. E. Swanson, T. M. Newcomb & E. L. Hartley). New York: Holt.

Osgood, C. E. *et al.* (1957). *The Measurement of Meaning.* University of Illinois Press.

Robinson, P. (1961). The Measurement of Achievement Motivation. Unpublished Oxford D.Phil. thesis.

Rosen, B. C. & d'Andrade, R. (1959). The psychosocial origins of achievement motivation. *Sociometry*, **22**, 185-218.

Sears, P. S. (1940). Levels of aspiration in academically successful and unsuccessful children. *J. abnorm. soc. Psychol.*, **35**, 498-536.

Sears, R. R. (1961). Relation of early socialization experiences to aggression in middle childhood. Roneo'd.

Winterbottom, M. R. (1958). The relation of need for achievement to learning experiences in independence and mastery. Chap. 33 in Atkinson (1958).

Wolf, T. H. (1938). The effect of praise and competition on the persistent behavior of kindergarten children. *Inst. Child Welf. Monogr.*, No. 15. Univ. of Minnesota Press.

Need Achievement As a Motivational Construct: A Critique

Eric Klinger

The McClelland-Atkinson theory that arousal of achievement fantasy depends upon arousal of the achievement motive is examined critically in light of accrued empirical evidence. The effects of achievement-arousal conditions on fantasy n Ach are shown to be probably nonmotivational. n Ach scores are shown to be correlated with performance measures in about half of the studies reported, but the pattern of hypothesis confirmation presents the theory with difficulties. The addition of perceptual and cognitive situational and developmental variables appears to render the empirical evidence theoretically more tractable. It is argued that motivation influences fantasy by processes more complex and less direct than originally thought.[1,2]

McClelland, Clark, Roby, and Atkinson (1949) set in motion a major research effort characterized by the measurement of motivation, particularly achievement motivation, through scoring of fantasy elicited in story form by TAT and TAT-like stimuli. Their earlier work (McClelland, Atkinson, Clark, & Lowell, 1953) consisted of studying experimentally the effects of presumably motive-arousing antecedent conditions on certain categories of story response. Scores based on those response categories which were affected by conditions were then presumed to constitute measures of the motivation that the experimenter had set out to arouse. When the results had been established as replicable and generalizable to a small class of several kinds of antecedent conditions, the focus of the research shifted to studies that used fantasy scores of motivation as organismic variables in the study of nonfantasy achievement (e.g., Atkinson, 1953, 1957; Atkinson & Litwin, 1960; Atkinson & Reitman, 1960).

One of the issues left unsettled by the shift in focus is whether fantasy achievement scores measure chiefly motivation or whether they measure chiefly other possible processes (Ritchie, 1954). McClelland, Atkinson, Clark, and Lowell (1953, p. 196) described three kinds of determinants of need achievement (n Ach) scores:

1. Cues in the everyday environment and cues in relatively autonomous thought processes of the individual.
2. Specific experimentally introduced cues.
3. Controllable cues in a particular picture.

Although McClelland et al. never excluded the possibility that these cues determine n Ach without motivational arousal, they appear to have theorized chiefly in terms of cues arousing motives which then influence the content of subjects' imaginative stories. Each of the three classes of cues is considered with reference to its effect on the level of achievement motivation, which is then presumed to determine the level of achievement imagery. This orientation was further elaborated by Atkinson (1954). His formulation is distinguished by its espousal of an "expectancy theory" of motivation, in which motives are equated with goal expectancies, and by its explicit analysis of the determinants of achievement imagery in associational terms. The difficulties inherent in continuing to regard the McClelland-Atkinson theory as motivational have been pointed out by Farber (1954) and Brown (1961). However, since McClelland et al. specified that motivational

From E. Klinger, "Fantasy Need Achievement As a Motivational Construct," *Psychological Bulletin*, 1966, **66**, 291-308. Reprinted by permission of the American Psychological Association.

[1]The writing of the present paper was partially supported by Grant No. GS-458 of the National Science Foundation.

[2]Conversations and correspondence with Robert C. Birney that contributed at many points to the development of the argument of this paper are gratefully acknowledged.

arousal in their sense involves affective arousal, rather than purely cognitive tuning, it is clear that they retained a motive arousal mechanism mediating between stimuli and fantasy behavior. Thus, Atkinson stated,

the arousal of a motive is equivalent to the arousal of a family of perceptual and instrumental response dispositions whose strength may be accounted for in terms of the principles of associative learning. . . . The arousal of a motive, then, *mediates* the arousal of perceptual and instrumental response dispositions . . . [p. 86].

He stated further,

Thus individual differences in frequency of imaginative responses aroused by the pictures themselves is (sic) a justifiable basis for inferring that subjects would be differentially motivated when actually in real-life situations similar to those portrayed. This does not mean that all of the variance in imaginative response to a particular picture can be attributed to leaning experiences of the sort which produce differences in strength of motive, but it does suggest that an important part of the variance can be explained this way [p. 88].

Subsequent empirical investigations have been guided by the theoretical position that fantasy n Ach reflects achievement motivation, and discrepant results have instigated major theoretical and investigative efforts to reconcile the results with this motivational interpretation, with little consideration of alternative explanations. Nevertheless, although the position that n Ach is a motivational measure generated hypotheses that initially received frequent experimental confirmation, a substantial portion of the evidence that has accumulated is not readily accounted for by existing motivational theory.

An evaluative review that attempts to relate empirical evidence to constructs encounters some serious theoretical and semantic hazards. Judging empirical results in terms of their consistency with a motivational interpretation requires a workable definition of motivation. The variety of theoretical positions concerning motivation in the early 1950s was described by McClelland et al. (1953) themselves in the course of their adding a further position. There has been little evidence of theoretical convergence since.

Since this is not the place to undertake the extensive task of reviewing relevant motivational theories, the remainder of the present section will attempt to delineate theoretical elements that are sufficiently general to fall within current theoretical consensus but nevertheless specific enough to lead to some usable criteria for assessing the motivational status of fantasy n Ach.

With respect to definition, or perhaps one should say description, of the concept, Jones (1955) wrote,

There are certain general problems in the field. . . . Among these are the broad problems of how behavior gets started, is energized, is sustained, is directed, is stopped, and what kind of subjective reaction is present in the organism while all this is going on [p. *vii*].

The area of agreement seems to embrace the idea that motivation must account for goal-striving and is measurable in terms of behavioral consequences. For instance, part of Atkinson's (1964) "recommended use of the term 'motivation'" was in reference to

the behavioral problem identified by the early "purposivists," viz., the tendency for the direction or selectivity of behavior to be governed in some way by its relation to objectively definable consequences, and the tendency of behavior to persist until the end or goal is attained; . . . [p. 274].

There is further general agreement that motive states vary in intensity and that a particular motive state may energize a morphologically varied assortment of instrumental acts.

The present paper will distinguish between motive states (hereafter called simply "motives"), a construct designed to account for segments of activity directed toward a particular goal; and motivational dispositions, which refer to an organism's characteristic motives. Motivational dispositions may be defined either in terms of the frequency with which a particular class of motives is regnant or the typical intensity of the motives when regnant, but the distinction is rarely made. It should be noted that fantasy n Ach scores have been used as measures of all three—motive and motivational disposition defined in terms of either frequency or intensity. Motivational dispositions are assumed to be reflected in behavior only when the corresponding motives have been "aroused" or "engaged" by theoretically specifiable stimuli of either external or internal origin. Once aroused, the motive is thought to energize behavior, both overt motor and covert symbolic behavior, that has been established in the reinforcement history of the organism as instrumental in attaining a relevant goal object. If the motive is aroused in the absence of opportunity to attain a relevant goal, the motive is widely believed to energize symbolic behavior in the form of fantasy. Both the instrumental and symbolic behaviors energized by a motive may be accompanied by affect.

Brown (1961) pointed out that

to avoid circular explanation, . . . one's definition of the intervening variable, [motivation, must be] completely independent of the specific responses that are assumed to be determined by that variable. This requirement can be met by basing the definition upon [organic states, preceding and concurrent experimental conditions, or other responses, p. 37].

Operational definitions for measuring motives have chiefly utilized measures of choice among goal objects, deprivation of goal objects, affective responses, instrumental sequences, and symbolic activity. Nevertheless, for ascertaining the operation of a particular motive as distinct from other processes in the determination of symbolic activity, only the subject's choice among goal objects and the instrumental sequences employed in realizing his choice may be assumed to present relatively unconfounded measures. At the animal level, some deprivation procedures are also probably adequate. Experimental procedures for arousing motives in humans, however, inevitably stimulate some perceptual and associational processes that are at best loosely affected by the motive presumed to be aroused, and the procedures may indeed also arouse unplanned motives. Thus, arousal techniques by themselves fall short of independent measures of motive strength. In view of the foregoing considerations concerning the measurement of motives, empirical evidence regarding the motivational status of

fantasy n Ach will be reviewed in accordance with the following criteria:

1. To preserve the tenability of the hypothesis that arousal procedures affect n Ach scores by achievement-motivational mediation, (a) the procedures must also be capable of affecting other measures of the regnancy of an achievement motive, such as performance instrumental in attaining an achievement goal, in a closely contiguous time period, and (b) the elimination from the procedures of their supposed achievement-motivating elements, such as "ego-involving" versus neutral instructions, must also eliminate the effect on n Ach.

2. To validate n Ach scores as indices of the regnancy of an achievement motive, they must be shown (a) to be accompanied by the choice of an achievement goal, or (b) to be correlated with other measures of the regnancy of the motive, such as performance in a closely contiguous time period, and (c) not to correlate with variables, either internal or external, that are unrelated to other measures of strength of the motive to achieve.

3. To validate n Ach scores as indices of a motivational disposition to strive after achievement goals, they must be shown (a) to be related to the probability of choosing achievement goals and activities, or (b) to be correlated with other measures of motivational dispositions to achieve, such as performance instrumental to the attainment of achievement goals, and (c) not to be correlated with variables, either internal or external, that are unrelated to other measures of motivational disposition to achieve.

Because of the similar empirical operations implied by Criteria 2 and 3, and because of the practical impossibility of ascertaining from the existing literature that a motive operating during the administration of one test has not dissipated by the time of the subsequent test, evidence relevant to Criteria 2 and 3 will be considered together.

Evidence from Motive Arousal Experiments

McClelland et al. (1953) early recognized the need for a measure of achievement motivation independent of subject's symbolic behavior in the process of validating n Ach. Initially, their operational definition of achievement motivation therefore resided in experimental procedures for arousing it, and the motivational status of n Ach was accordingly predicated on the responsiveness of the scores to variations in the experimental procedures. Since published specifications of standard stimulus conditions for "achievement arousing" have usually been rather gross and the salient achievement-arousing variables have never been experimentally isolated from the extraneous features of the prescribed stimulus conditions, experiments that fail to replicate earlier results must pose a serious challenge to the motivational interpretation of the processes involved. Atkinson (1953), Peak (1960), Smith (1961), and Tedeschi and Kian (1962), using the TAT measure, and Herron (1962), using the French Test of Insight, have reported failures to affect n Ach scores by presumably motive-arousing instructions. On the other hand, Smith (1961) reported higher TAT n Ach under conditions of extrinsic motivation—to leave the experiment earlier than other subjects upon task completion—which is unrelated to achievement motivation as conceived by McClelland et al. Thus, it appears likely that the relevant conditions governing "achievement arousal" have been incompletely specified, and may, in fact, be nonmotivational.

Highly pertinent to the motivational status of n Ach scores is a question regarding the effect of experimentally varied achievement-arousing instructions on other indices of achievement motivation, such as performance on paper-and-pencil tasks. Such tasks as anagrams, scrambled words, and arithmetic problems were often interpolated between instructions and projective testing in the early experimental studies. While the original purpose for including tasks was to render the instructions credible to the subjects and results obtained with these tasks were therefore initially not reported, investigators have become interested in performance scores as motivational measures in their own right. Reitman (1960) reported successful manipulation of performance on such tasks with the kind of instructions that have been effective with fantasy n Ach, but French (1955) reported failure to obtain performance differences with such instructions; Burris (1958) failed to find performance differences after experimentally manipulating subjects' counseling experiences, despite success in affecting n Ach scores; and Haber (1957), who administered both challenging and routine tasks and ran pilot studies to improve the experimental instructions, failed to raise performance scores with achievement-arousing instructions, though he reported a significant effect of instructions on TAT n Ach. Murstein (1963) successfully affected TAT n Ach by varying subject's expectancies of task success, but failed to affect scores on a subsequent arithmetic test. Controlling for experimenter characteristics, Birney (1958) obtained no effects on either TAT n Ach or performance from varying motive arousal instructions. Atkinson (1953) found achievement-arousing conditions to interact with intrinsic TAT n Ach in affecting the strength of the Zeigarnik effect, but, interestingly, the TAT n Ach scores were unaffected by the experimental conditions. Thus, data from performance measures in all but two studies fail to confirm that the experimental instructions designed to arouse motives did so, even though most of them obtained effects on fantasy n Ach.

Choice of Goal Objects

The only clear-cut study of choice of goal objects is the study by Crandall, Katkovsky, and Preston (1962) of the choice of achievement-related activities in the free play of children in relation to TAT n Ach. They obtained nonsignificant relationships for both males and females.

Relation of n Ach to Performance

Other evidence pertinent to the motivational status of n Ach scores arises from studies of the correlations between n Ach scores and performance measures. Such evidence is less straightforward than might appear. Performance on laboratory tasks and on more molar developmental tasks such as undergraduate coursework is determined by many factors, of which achievement motivation is only one. One might expect, then, that relationships between n Ach and performance measures should be at most moderate, and perhaps low, even granting the motivational status of n Ach. Then, also, the relationships might be nonlinear, perhaps nonmonotonic. Such an eventuality would further depress the observed association between n Ach and performance in studies which limit their analyses to linear correlation coefficients. On the other hand, a gross positive relationship between n Ach scores and performance measures is not in itself conclusive evidence that n Ach scores reflect achievement motives. Conceivably, for instance, fantasy reflects relatively more fully the dominant models and modes of behavior to which the subject is currently exposed, while his performance reflects a more enduring set of dispositions learned over a long period of reinforcement. Presumably, in that case, a subject who is currently exposed to achievement-oriented models but who grew up in a family whose reward matrix led him to develop a nonachieving set of motives might produce high n Ach fantasy and low performance. Nevertheless, since it is likely that the models to which subjects choose to be exposed will more often than chance be congruent with the subjects' conditioning histories, positive correlations between n Ach and performance might still occur.

Nevertheless, the sorts of data produced by most studies of these relationships can in general be expected to reflect an association if one exists, and large-sample studies can be expected to demonstrate it. Despite the numerous complexities of the relationship between n Ach and performance, an inquiry into the motivational status of n Ach scores must be concerned with it, at least as a starting point.

Evidence concerning the relationship of fantasy n Ach scores and performance can be divided into two classes according to whether the performance variable is relatively molar,

involving the outcomes of relatively long-term behavior patterns, measured by course grades, grade averages, ratings of long-term behavior patterns, and the like; or whether the performance variable is measured by task instruments that involve only brief segments of behavior and are often administered at the same time as the testing of n Ach. The two classes of evidence will be considered separately. The review will encompass studies employing the three most popular projective measures of n Ach: the TAT-like tests (McClelland et al., 1953), the French Test of Insight (French, 1958a), and the Iowa Picture Interpretation Test (IPIT; Hurley, 1955). Studies in which projective test scores are used jointly with other kinds of scores, such as response-limited anxiety test scores, to measure n Ach will be omitted.

The evidence relating n Ach scores to molar performance measures is summarized in Table 1. Overall, about as many reported relationships fail of statistical significance ($p <$ .05) as achieve it. Closer inspection reveals that two variables determine much of the pattern of hypothesis confirmation and disconfirmation. One of these, often noted in earlier discussions, is subjects' sex. Studies employing female subjects overwhelmingly report lack of relationship between fantasy n Ach and molar performance measures. The second variable, not previously noted, is a function of subjects' age. Nine of the 10 relationships involving males of high school age or younger are reported to be significant, while 9 of the 16 relationships involving college-age and other adult males are reported to be nonsignificant. Nothing in the existing theoretical structure of achievement motivation suggests such an age-related difference.

The molar performance studies permit a further analysis relevant to the motivational interpretation of n Ach. Bendig (1958) pointed out that a motivational variable is expected to be more closely correlated with future performance than with past. McClelland (1961) agreed. Among the studies in Table 1 based on college and other adult subjects, those examining the relation of n Ach to past performance reported significance in about

Table 1. Relation of fantasy n Ach to molar performance measures.

Measure of n Ach	Sex of subject	Child and high school subjects		College and other adult subjects	
		Significant relation	Nonsignificant relation	Significant relation	Nonsignificant relation
TAT	Male	Cox (1962)[1,3,8] Crootof (1963)[1,5,9] Kagen et al. (1958)[4,5,8] Morgan (1953)[3,5,9] Muthayya (1964)[1,5] Ricciuti (1954)[3,5,9] Ricciuti & Sadacca (1955)[1,5,9] Rosen (1955)[1,5,9]	Shaw (1961)[1,5,9]	Bendig (1958)[1,5,10] Block (1962)[5,12] Krumboltz & Farquhar (1957)[2,3,10] Marlowe (1959)[16,5,10] McKeachie (1961)[2,5,10,15] Morgan (1952)[1,5,10]	Bendig (1958)[2,5,10] Bendig (1959)[2,5,10] Cole et al. (1962)[1,3,5,10,13] Isaacson (1963)[1,2,5,10] Parrish & Rethlingshafer (1954)[1,5,10] Ricciuti (1954)[3,5,10] Vogel, Baker, & Lazarus (1958)[3,5,10]
	Female or mixed	Kagen et al. (1958)[4,6,8]	Shaw (1961)[1,6,9]	Chabhazi (1956, 1960)[1,3,7,10] McKeachie (1961)[2,6,10,15]	Bendig (1959)[2,6,10] Cole et al. (1962)[1,3,6,10] Isaacson (1963)[1,2,6,10] Krumboltz & Farquhar (1957)[2,6,10] Mitchell (1961)[3,10,6] Sundheim (1962)[1,6,10]
French	Male	Shaw (1961)[1,5,9]		Atkinson & Litwin (1960)[2,5,10]	Herron (1962)[1,5,10]
	Female or mixed		Shaw (1961)[1,6,9]		Herron (1962)[1,6,10] Sundheim (1962)[1,6,10]
IPIT	Male			Mayo & Manning (1961)[2,5,11,14]	Hedlund (1953)[2,5,10]
	Female or mixed				Barnette (1961)[1,7,10] Reiter (1964)[1,7,10]

[1] Cumulative or previous-year grades.
[2] Course grades.
[3] Current term or year grades.
[4] Aptitude and intelligence measures.
[5] Male subjects.
[6] Female subjects.
[7] Both sexes.
[8] Children.
[9] High school age subjects.
[10] College subjects.
[11] Other adult subjects.
[12] The performance variable is supervisor's rating of productivity of industrial workers.
[13] Considering the males only, Cole et al. found a significant inverse relationship between achievement imagery and past scholastic achievement.
[14] With aptitude partialled out, the correlation dropped to nonsignificance.
[15] The relationship was positive only in low-achievement-cue classrooms.
[16] Sociometric ratings of long-term achievement motivation.

the same proportion as those that examined the relation of n Ach to concurrent or future performance. Most of the studies employing child and high school age subjects measured n Ach after the criterion performance.

Several investigators have pointed out that the relation of n Ach to performance must be considered in light of the achievement cues operative in the performance situation. However, there is disagreement regarding the direction of the effect. Thus, Reitman (1960) argued that before achievement motives become operative, they must be engaged by appropriate achievement cues; while Mc-Keachie (1961) suggested that intrinsic achievement motivation makes its differential impact on performance most clearly in situations poorly cued for achievement. Since nearly all of the performance criteria were some form of school grades, and nearly all investigators administered the test of achievement motivation under neutral conditions, the available literature concerning molar performance permits no test of these hypotheses.

The validity of these analyses of the existing literature depends heavily on the reasonableness of using reported statistical significance as a measure of empirical relatedness. Actually, the diversity of statistical tests and of descriptions of data precludes any alternative manner of summarizing the literature. Perhaps the greatest pitfall lies in the dependence of statistical significance on sample size. In this regard, there appears to be no systematic confounding relationship between the sample size of the studies in Table 1 and any of the variables that have been employed in summarizing the various empirical reports.

The second major class of studies of the relationships between n Ach and performance, which employ performance on relatively brief tasks, is summarized in Table 2. Again, approximately half of the studies reported predominantly significant relationships, and half nonsignificant ones, but the pattern of hypothesis confirmation is quite unlike that in Table 1. The studies of task performance suggest that results depend partly on the n Ach instrument, in that the French Test of Insight produced nearly uniformly significant results, whereas both the TAT and IPIT measures of n Ach produced more nonsignificant than significant results. The studies also suggest an interaction of Instrument X Sex of Subject, in that of the studies that used the TAT, a higher proportion of those with male subjects reported significance than those with females, while the reverse was true with the IPIT. Also, unlike the studies of Table 1, subjects' age had no apparent bearing on the significance of the relationship of n Ach and performance. Of the five studies that

employed child or high school age subjects, only one reported significant results. The lone study that reported results for male children yielded nonsignificance. The overall pattern of results can only be described as puzzling. They shed little light on the motivational status of n Ach.

The studies of task performance present a sufficient variety of conditions of administration to permit some comparisons regarding the role of achievement cues in moderating the fantasy-performance relationship. For purposes of this investigation, all of the empirical reports cited in Table 2 were reclassified with respect to the conditions of administration of the projective instrument, either neutral or achievement-aroused, and with respect to the conditions of the task administration, whether neutral, achievement aroused, or motivated by extrinsic or multiple incentives. For purposes of classification, "neutral" was defined as administration using standard instructions for the instruments involved, without communications designed to increase achievement motivation, but including occasional procedures which were designed to produce a "relaxed" atmosphere by deemphasizing or denying the achievement relevance of the situation. The "achievement-aroused" category included those procedures which explicitly stated that performance reflects on the subject's competency or related characteristics, or employed induced failure or evaluative judgments to arouse achievement motivation. Extrinsic incentives include monetary rewards, permission to leave the experiment early, or avoidance of electric shocks. Multiple incentive procedures combine achievement arousal with extrinsic incentives. The studies were further cross-classified according to whether the projective instrument and the task were administered in the same or in separate sessions, and further according to the nature of the projective instrument. Some studies provided data under more than one condition and were tallied more than once accordingly. The total number of tallies was 57.

Of the six possible kinds of arousal condi-

Table 2. Relation of fantasy n Ach to task performance measures.

Measure of n Ach	Sex of subjects	Significant relation	Nonsignificant relation
TAT	Male	Atkinson & Raphelson (1956)[7,8,13]	Atkinson & Reitman (1956)[7,8,13]
		Atkinson & Reitman (1956)[3,8,13]	Birney (1958)[3,7,8,13,20]
		Birney (1958)[3,7,8,13,20]	Clark & McClelland (1956)[1,8,13]
		Burdick (1964)[3,8,13]	Crandall, Katkovsky, & Preston (1962)[3,4,7,8,11]
		Feather (1961)[6,8,13,15]	Haber (1957)[1,3,8,13]
		Lazarus et al. (1957)[7,8,13]	Hills (1960)[3,8,13]
		Lowell (1952)[1,3,8,13]	Reitman (1960)[2,3,7,8,13]
		Marlowe (1959)[4,8,13]	Smith (1961)[3,8,13]
		Pottharst (1956)[7,8,13]	Vogel, Baker, & Lazarus (1958)[7,8,13,18]
		Reitman & Atkinson (1958)[3,8,13]	Wendt (1955)[3,8,13,15]
			Yeager (1957)[1,8,13,16]
	Female or mixed	Wendt (1955)[3,10,12]	Crandall, Katkovsky, & Preston (1962)[3,4,7,9,11]
			Hills (1960)[3,9,13]
			Karolchuck & Worrell (1956)[1,10,11]
			Miller & Worchel (1956)[7,10,13]
			Murstein & Collier (1962)[3,7,10,11]
French	Male	Atkinson, Bastian, Earl, & Litwin (1960)[2,8,13]	
		French (1955)[7,8,14]	
		French (1958b)[1,8,14]	
		French (1958c)[1,8,14]	
		French & Thomas (1958)[1,8,14]	
	Female or mixed	French & Lesser (1964)[1,9,13]	Wrightsman (1962)[1,10,13]
		Sampson (1963)[5,9,13]	
IPIT	Male		Chubb & Barch (1960)[5,8,13]
			Hills (1960)[3,8,13]
			Johnston (1957)[3,8,13]
			Miles (1958)[2,8,13,17]
	Female or mixed	Hurley (1957)[5,10,13]	Hills (1960)[3,9,13]
		Johnston (1955)[5,10,13]	
		Johnston (1957)[3,9,13]	
		Williams (1955)[3,10,13]	

[1] Verbal problem solving tasks, including scrambled words and stories, tests of aptitude, reasoning problems, and anagrams.
[2] Perceptual-motor tasks.
[3] Arithmetic.
[4] Ratings of free activity.
[5] Learning.
[6] Persistence at a "perceptual reasoning" task.
[7] Clerical tasks.
[8] Male subjects.
[9] Female subjects.
[10] Both male and female subjects.
[11] Subjects were children.
[12] Subjects were of high school age.
[13] College student subjects.
[14] Noncollege adult subjects.
[15] N here was only 14, but the data showed a trend toward an inverted "U" curvilinear regression of n Ach on performance.
[16] Median age was 26, suggesting that the subjects may be largely part-time students.
[17] Significant inverse relationship.
[18] No relationship was observed with neutral instructions, and a negative relationship occurred under achievement-arousing conditions.
[19] There was a strong interaction of n Ach with expectancy of success. When the subject was led to expect success, n Ach was directly related to persistence, but when the subject was led to expect failure, the relationship was inverse. In this study, subjects high in n Ach were also selected to be low on test anxiety, and vice versa.
[20] Significant with a student experimenter, but not with a faculty experimenter.

tions, two for the projective instrument times three for the tasks, three combinations accounted for 52 of the 57 tallies—24 neutral for both the projective and the task (neutral-neutral), 13 achievement-aroused for both (aroused-aroused), and 15 neutral for the projective and achievement-aroused for the task (neutral-aroused). Of these 52, 25 produced statistically significant relationships between n Ach and performance. Overall, studies in which the projective was administered in a different session from the task produced more significant results, 15 out of 27, than studies that administered both in one session, which produced 12 significant results out of 30. The difference is probably attributable to the concentration of aroused-aroused studies in the same-session classification. The neutral-neutral conditions produced significance 12 out of 24 times, aroused-aroused only 3 out of 13 times, but neutral-aroused 10 out of 15 times. Insofar as inspection can reveal, these trends are all independent of the projective instrument used, the task instrument, and subject's sex.

Can one reconcile this pattern of hypothesis confirmation with a purely achievement-motivational interpretation of n Ach? The high incidence of significant n Ach-performance relationships in the neutral-aroused combination of activities is entirely consistent with the McClelland-Atkinson theoretical structure. So is the lower incidence of significance under neutral-neutral conditions since it can be argued that in the absence of experimental attempts to arouse achievement motivation, fewer high n Ach subjects will perceive such tasks as arithmetic tests or scrambled words to be particularly relevant to their achievement striving. However, the motivational theory of n Ach unquestionably predicts a respectable incidence of significance under aroused-aroused conditions (Smith, 1961), and this prediction has failed.

The generalization that neutral-aroused conditions favor n Ach-performance relationships and that aroused-aroused conditions vitiate them may account for an ostensibly divergent result. One of the nonsignificant neutral-aroused relationships occured as a portion of Birney's (1958) experiment, using

a faculty experimenter to administer both the TAT cards and the task. In the same experiment, Birney found a significant n Ach-performance relationship when the experimenter was a student. It appears that with the faculty experimenter administering the TAT, the ostensibly neutral-aroused condition more closely resembled an aroused-aroused condition.

The finding that neutral-aroused conditions yield positive n Ach-performance relationships is probably also consistent with McKeachie's (1961) finding of positive n Ach-performance relationships in classes relatively low in achievement cues. Most college classes might be expected to generate achievement arousal at a level comparable to the degree of arousal attained with achievement-arousal instructions in an experimental situation.

Vogel, Baker, and Lazarus (1958) reported a lack of relation between TAT n Ach and McKinney Reporting Test performance under neutral conditions, and an *inverse* relationship under achievement-aroused conditions, but the inverse relationships may well have been somewhat artifactual. In their experiment, the TAT cards were administered after the McKinney test, which "failure-stresses" subjects by repeatedly reporting to them performance norms which they will not have attained. It is possible that since poorly motivated subjects probably experienced a larger gap between their actual performance and the reported norms on the McKinney test, they would have been differentially highly aroused, which might well have resulted in their verbalizing more achievement imagery in the subsequent TAT protocols.

Two other studies reported results that bear on a motivational interpretation of n Ach. Wrightsman (1962), using the French Test of Insight to measure n Ach and the Adaptability Test of intelligence as a performance measure in a predominantly female sample, found no significant relationship under neutral conditions; but under subsequent achievement-arousing conditions, low n Ach subjects performed worse on the performance measure, while high n Ach subjects performed at about the same level as under neutral conditions. The result failed to support an achievement-motivational interpretation of the n Ach scores, but suggests the operation of test anxiety in the low n Ach subjects (Alpert & Haber, 1960). Finally, Karolchuck and Worrell (1956) found no relationship between n Ach and directed learning, but did find n Ach correlated with the amount of incidental learning. While their result suggests that subjects high in n Ach display greater curiosity and more inner direction, it is nevertheless opposite to what one would expect from the operation of a motivational variable.

n Ach and Level of Aspiration

In another line of inquiry relevant to the motivational status of n Ach, achievement scores based on the French Test of Insight have been found related to level-of-aspiration (LOA) measures (Atkinson, Bastian, Earl, & Litwin, 1960; Atkinson & Litwin, 1960); scores based on TAT measures have (Clark, Teevan, & Ricciuti, 1956; Smith, 1961) and have not (Reitman & Williams, 1961). In general, subjects high in n Ach are found to display a moderate, realistic LOA, involving intermediate risks of failure; whereas subjects low in n Ach display LOA that is more frequently extremely high or low, involving extremely high or low risks of failure. Smith obtained the relationship only under relaxed, nonarousal conditions of task administration. Although these studies have frequently been accepted as supporting the motivational status of n Ach, such a relationship may exist without TAT n Ach providing a direct measure of momentary motive state. The motivational theory of goal-setting seems well-established and is not questioned here. However, the relation of n Ach to LOA is probably rather complicated. Both n Ach and LOA are affected by cognitive variables, such as acquaintance with and sophistication about achievement situations, but these cognitive variables themselves undoubtedly reflect in part the subject's motivational history. Thus, a subject who has long been concerned about achievement is likely to think about achievement frequently and to be familiar with his own behavior in achievement situations; and he will therefore more likely tell achievement-related stories to TAT cards than other subjects and be more realistic, and perhaps more careful, in announcing his LOA. The point here is not to exclude achievement motivation as one of the contributing influences on n Ach, but rather to question that n Ach directly and primarily reflects achievement motives.

Stability of n Ach

Findings concerning the stability of n Ach scores and the interrelationships among the various instruments for measuring n Ach also pose difficulties for an interpretation of scores as measures of enduring motivational dispositions. Despite consistently high inter-scorer and score-rescore correlations reported for n Ach scoring systems (Atkinson, 1960; Himelstein & Kimbrough, 1960; McClelland et al., 1953; Sadacca, Ricciuti, & Swanson, 1956), test-retest correlations are generally either low or nonsignificant for both the TAT (Birney, 1959; Feld, 1959; Kagan & Moss, 1959; Krumboltz & Farquhar, 1957; Moss & Kagan, 1961) and the French test (French, 1955; Himelstein & Kimbrough, 1960) measures of n Ach. Morgan's (1953) test-retest correlations of .56 and .64 for a TAT measure seem exceptional. The instability of the scores might contribute to the frequent failure to find n Ach related to long-term nonfantasy indices of performance. However, since inter-scorer reliability is high, and since the replicability of certain effects on n Ach is satisfactory, the fact of instability would seem to reach beyond a problem simply of an undesirable psychometric property of the measuring instruments to a question of validity, of whether n Ach scores are sufficiently independent of extraneous influences to constitute a measure of enduring motivational disposition.

Of course, weakness in measuring long-term intrinsic motivation cannot in itself preclude the possibility that the instrument strongly reflects momentary, situationally induced achievement motive states, but that eventuality is unlikely in view of the fact that n Ach scores frequently bear no relation to scores from other achievement-motivational measures administered immediately preceding or following the fantasy instruments. Other evidence (Himelstein, Eschenbach, & Carp, 1958; Shaw, 1961) indicates that three measures of n Ach—the TAT, French Test of Insight, and a scale from the Edwards Personal Preference Schedule—are all uncorrelated, and so are TAT and IPIT measures of n Ach (Hills, 1960). Alternate forms of the French test are similarly unrelated (Himelstein & Kimbrough, 1960), and n Ach scores on TAT stories beyond the first four produce correlations of only about .30 with scores based on the first four stories (Reitman & Atkinson, 1958). It seems clear that whatever n Ach scores measure is quite ephemeral, capable of registering differently in different fantasy instruments, differently in fantasy as contrasted with cognitive task instruments, and differently at different times in the same experimental session with the same or similar instruments.

Alternative to the Motivational Interpretation of n Ach

In a number of respects, then, empirical studies that have used fantasy measures of achievement motivation have produced results that initially were not or could not be predicted from motivational theory—failure of performance measures to respond to achievement-arousing instructions, more frequent significant n Ach-molar performance relationships with precollege than with older subjects, lack of superiority of prediction over post-diction, the attenuating effect on n Ach-performance correlations of administering the projective under arousal conditions, and the absence of relationship between n Ach and choice of achievement-related activity in free play. As some of these difficulties arose, the theory was extended amid a flurry of generally fruitful research to account for discrepant data while preserving a motivational interpretation of fantasy n Ach. Thus, in two elegant empirical analyses, McKeachie (1961) demonstrated the interaction of n Ach and situational variables in predict-

ing course grades and articulated a theoretical formulation to reconcile the results with motivational theory; and French and Lesser (1964) demonstrated that arousal instructions must be relevant to subjects' personal values in order to arouse achievement fantasy and that the sex of the stimulus figure in the projective instrument moderates the relation of n Ach to performance. Even though they and other investigators have succeeded in integrating these important classes of discrepant data into the motivational framework, the theoretical structure would have to be stretched well beyond the bounds of tolerable parsimony to accommodate the remaining classes.

The question then arises as to alternative theoretical formulations. The position in the following part of this paper will be that (*a*) the difficulties by which the motivational theory of achievement fantasy has been beset arose out of the tendency to limit consideration of the determination of fantasy n Ach to a hypothetical process mediated by motivational arousal, and (*b*) therefore a viable determination of fantasy n Ach including but not limited to achievement motivational determinants. The purpose of the following sections is to reexamine the main classes of empirical evidence regarding fantasy n Ach to inquire whether and to what extent accounting for the occurrence of achievement fantasy requires postulating the mediation of motivational arousal. This strategy is in some respects parallel to Postman's (1953), in his examination of motivational determinants of perception.

The Arousal Experiment

The arousal experiment (McClelland, Clark, Roby, & Atkinson, 1949) consisted of a brief visual and verbal exposure of subjects to an experimenter who attempted to present himself in particular roles and to convey particular sets of expectations. The intent was to arouse in the subjects certain motives which were expected to affect subjects' subsequent responses to TAT cards. However, this intent by no means exhausts the likely means by which the experimenter influenced his subjects. In the somewhat new and strange situation of the psychological experiment, the subject finds himself in the initial stages of a relationship with an experimenter whose personal demeanor constitutes information that is highly relevant for the subject's orientation to the experimenter, and to which the subject might therefore be expected to attend closely. Most experimenters attempt to establish some degree of rapport with their subjects, and most subjects respond with cooperation and the desire to help the experimenter successfully complete his experiment. Meanwhile, the experimenter serves as a potential model for his subjects, and his generally respected status and, occasionally, his power to reward or punish should lead some of his subjects to imitate him. A growing body of experimental studies has demonstrated experimenter effects on self-description, motor imitation, perception, and fantasy. Experiments by Stotland, Zander, and Natsoulas (1961), Burnstein, Stotland, and Zander (1961), Stotland and Patchen (1961), Stotland and Cottrell (1962), and Bandura (1965) have described modeling effects in situations that have a number of interpersonal elements in common with the arousal experiment. Subjects in these studies acquire some of the models' expressive behaviors, values, self-evaluations, and patterns of self-reinforcement in the absence of explicit reinforcement for the imitation. Rosenthal (1963) and Rosenthal, Persinger, Kline, and Mulry (1963) demonstrated that subjects' behavior may sharply reflect the experimenter's hypotheses, and they suggested that the transmission of this "experimenter bias" occurs in the initial minutes of an experimental session and primarily by visual means. In hitherto unpublished experiments to investigate the experimenter effect in achievement-arousal experiments, Klinger (1965) has shown that the arousal of TAT n Ach, as in the studies by McClelland et al. (1949, 1953), is independent of the supposedly motive-arousing instructions. An actor played the part of an achievement-oriented, neutral, and affiliative experimenter, respectively, for three groups of subjects in the course of administering a scrambled words test and four TAT-like

slides. Instructions were varied in accordance with the actor's role, and the TAT protocols yielded the expected differences in n Ach. However, three additional groups of subjects in adjacent rooms, who observed the actor-experimenter deal with the first three groups on television without sound, also produced TAT protocols that differed in n Ach in the same way as the first three groups and as the subjects in the original McClelland-Atkinson experiments. The viewer subjects were completely shielded by the procedures from contact with the real experimenters, and their responses could therefore not be attributed to "experimenter bias" other than that generated by the actor-experimenter on television. Related experiments have exposed subjects to brief televised scenes of other kinds that vary in the achievement activity of the models, such as biologists in a laboratory, persons reading newspapers, a coffee shop conversation, etc., which are shown without sound. These similarly affect subjects' subsequent TAT n Ach scores. There is little reason to suppose that any of these stimuli affected subjects' states of motivation.

Thus, TAT n Ach at least *can* primarily reflect situational factors other than specific motivational arousal. If the arousal experiments influence TAT n Ach through chiefly non-achievement-motivational processes, performance would be expected not to vary in accordance with arousal instructions. This expectation is consistent with results of studies already in the literature, which were described in an earlier section.

n Ach and Performance

Earlier sections noted that about half of the reported investigations of n Ach and performance variables found significant relationships, which in itself constitutes modest support for the motivational interpretation of n Ach, but the pattern of confirmation and disconfirmation is difficult to explain in motivational terms. Can a nonmotivational analysis do better? As in the description of previous investigations, the discussion will be divided into two parts, one concerned with measures of molar, relatively long-term performance, and one with task measures.

As measures of the associational train of which fantasy is a part, n Ach scores are determined by the effects of the subject's experiences, during and prior to testing, on his subsequent associations, as reflected in his thoughts and fantasies. If the conditions of testing are objectively uniform for all subjects, as they typically are in correlational studies of n Ach and molar performance, then the variability of n Ach scores must result from differences in the subjects' fantasy response tendencies in such testing situations. Under some conditions, these response tendencies appear to be correlated with performance measures, and under other conditions, not. The question arises then as to the nature of the necessary conditions under which an experimenter simultaneously arouses achievement imagery in different subjects in such a way that their imagery is correlated with their performance. The answer resides in the determinants of performance as well as of fantasy since correlations between the two depend upon the operation of factors that determine both of them jointly.

Presumably, some important determinants of performance lie deeply embedded in the subject's developmental history, the history of his past successes and failures, of deliberate or unwitting reinforcement regimes, of reliably conditioned emotional responses to achievement situations, and to the attempt to achieve. The history of a person's performance is relatively stable. The best predictor of college performance is performance in high school, which is better than aptitude and even than achievement test scores despite the frequently disjunctive nature of the transition from high school to college. Now, since individuals who usually perform well will have grown up in environments that in fact encouraged good performance, it is likely also that those environments will have been relatively rich in achievement cues, in the vocabulary, ideas, and strategies of achievement, whether explicitly or implicitly. Furthermore, the achieving subject, by virtue of his activities, must end up with a more differentiated life space in the area of achievement than his less achieving peers. Since environ-

mental cues generally, and human models particularly, affect ideation, he may be expected to have experienced more frequent achievement-oriented perceptions, thoughts, and fantasies; and therefore, on a frequency basis, achievement imagery will be more accessible to him, richer in variety and articulation, and more probable. Such a subject is also more likely to respond with achievement imagery in a test situation because, on the basis of perceptual set, he is more likely to perceive the experimenter or examiner as an achieving model, and will have a richer, readier repertory of achievement imagery to draw upon for his test responses.

Thus, achievement fantasy and concern for performance develop interrelatedly in a common milieu and might therefore be expected to exhibit some degree of intercorrelation even without assuming that the fantasy responses directly reflect motivation. On the other hand, the content of fantasy is determined not only developmentally, but also by recent experience and immediate situations; and, judging from their relative stability, n Ach scores seem more markedly subject to situational influences than molar measures of performance. Fantasy might then be expected to be frequently incongruent with performance at particular moments in time, and, certainly, fantasy at a particular moment need have but little correspondence with criteria for long-term realization of achievement goals.

The foregoing argument describes the development of response tendencies for achievement fantasy and performance as two aspects of general cognitive and motivational development, whose intercorrelation results from the support and demands of a particular developmental environment. This view leads to the hypothesis that the correlation between n Ach scores and performance should be greatest with subjects who at the time of testing still live in the environment that gave rise to the correlation. This hypothesis is consistent with the finding (Table 1) that correlations based on precollege age subjects tended generally to be positive. One would also expect that correlations based on college subjects would be more often positive with students who commute from home or frequently return to their parental homes than with students whose connections with their parental homes have become more tenuous. Precise data on this prediction are presently unavailable, but it is interesting to note that both studies in Table 1 performed with males at the University of Minnesota, which has a large commuting population, reported significant relationships, while the three studies performed at small private liberal arts colleges—Clark, Occidental, and Wesleyan— reported nonsignificant relationships.

The nonmotivational view places n Ach in a probabilistic relationship to performance. Correspondence between them would then be easily disrupted by the presence of certain kinds of strong cues in the testing situation. Unfortunately, the literature on n Ach and molar performance contains no basis for testing this hypothesis.

The analysis of the relationship between subjects' fantasy and their task performance necessarily differs from the foregoing analysis of the relationship between fantasy and molar performance. Molar performance reflects determinants that operate relatively consistently for extended periods of time, typically months or years. Task performance, on the other hand, encompasses behavior in a brief segment of time, often just a few minutes, and is therefore less subject to the stabilizing effects of such consistent long-term environmental influences as are imposed by the expectations and support of family, friends, and institutions. Rather, task performance, more than molar performance, must reflect, first, the persistent effects of the subject's developmental reinforcement history in the form of his contemporary response tendencies to particular kinds of achievement situations, and, second, therefore, the properties of the achievement situations themselves. Whereas the environment that produced certain fantasy response tendencies could continue directly to influence the molar performance of subjects who remain in that environment, in the case of task performance any n Ach-performance correlation depends upon the persistence of response tendencies operating in the absence of direct support from the environment that gave rise to the correlation. The consequence should be to weaken the effect of subjects' age and residential status on the correlation. This conclusion is consistent with the absence of such an effect in the studies cited in Table 2.

If fantasy n Ach reflects (*a*) response tendencies to fantasy about achievement and (*b*) situational effects on the subject's train of association, achievement cues in the testing situation should attenuate the n Ach differences between subjects high and low in response tendencies to fantasy about achievement and should therefore attenuate n Ach-performance correlations. When, for instance, TAT cards are administered under neutral conditions, subjects will tend to respond with fantasy that reflects relatively autonomous ideation and the impact of recent stimuli. Therefore, subjects who are frequently concerned with achievement, who recently experienced an emotionally arousing achievement situation, or who were recently exposed to achievement stimuli are likely to respond with fantasy high in n Ach, and such subjects are also more likely than others to perform well on subsequent tasks if the tasks are such that subjects generalize from previously rewarded performance experiences. If, on the other hand, the TAT testing situation contains potent achievement cues, these would, in the present view, be expected to arouse achievement fantasy in subjects who otherwise would have fantasied about something else. Because most subjects, regardless of developmental history, will now be experiencing achievement cues of some kind, external if not internal, n Ach scores should be less able to differentiate among subjects who differ in their predispositions to achievement activity. Thus, correlations with performance variables should be weakened. This account is consistent with the pattern of relationships described in an earlier section between n Ach and task performance, where it was noted that investigators who administered their projective instruments under aroused conditions reported a far lower incidence of positive relationships. The present view thus provides a better fit to the data than the strictly motivational account in a case where the two views clearly differ.

Instability of n Ach

A theoretical position that acknowledges a large number of perceptual and associational determinants of n Ach can readily predict instability of the scores from occasion to occasion. The instability of n Ach during a single occasion poses somewhat more of a challenge. Nevertheless, the phenomenon is consistent with evidence concerning another phenomenon governed largely by perceptual and associational processes, the maintenance of perceptual set. Postman and Crutchfield (1952) presented evidence of the rather rapid demise of initial, experimentally produced perceptual sets. Possibly related both to perceptual sets and n Ach is Rosenthal's (1963) report that the production of experimenter bias occurs primarily in the initial minutes of an experimental session. Thus, in this respect, n Ach behaves like predominantly nonmotivational phenomena, further suggesting the importance of situational and associational factors in the determination of n Ach.

Conclusion

Evidence accumulating during the past 15 years has tended to support the existence of a relationship between fantasy n Ach and some behavioral measures commonly accepted as including a motivational component; but the structure of the evidence casts doubt on the position that n Ach usually provides a direct, immediate reflection of a regnant achievement motive. A theory that links the arousal of achievement imagery directly to the arousal of the achievement motive fails to account for important parts of the empirical evidence, and is perhaps unnecessary to account for the remainder.

The motive-arousing experimental conditions on which the motivational interpretation of n Ach was initially predicated appear to have affected n Ach scores by processes other than arousal of achievement motives. First, they have been unable consistently to affect other indices of motive arousal. With elimination of the presumably motive arousing elements from the arousal conditions, they continue to affect n Ach scores in the same way. A number of investigators have reported failure to influence n Ach with motive arousing instructions, which again suggests that an important part of n Ach arousal operates through nonmotivational variables that tend, however, to be frequently associated with the intended motive arousal procedures. The relevant variables have not at this point been isolated, but they behave like such variables as perceptual set, associational properties of the projective testing situation, and possibly modeling processes.

About half of the studies of the relation of n Ach to performance have obtained significant results, which appears sufficient to establish the existence of some sort of relationship, however tenuous. However, a theory that regards n Ach as a measure of motivational disposition to achieve has difficulty accounting for the more frequent occurrence of a significant relationship between n Ach and performance in child and high school age subjects as compared with college subjects, the lack of superiority of predictive over postdictive relationships, the attenuating effect on the relationship of administering the projective test under achievement arousing conditions, and, in apparently the only study applicable, the failure to find n Ach related to the choice of achievement-related activity in free play.

The n Ach-performance evidence that the motivational interpretation of n Ach handles well, on the other hand, is susceptible to explanation by means of principles of perceptual and cognitive development which, in interaction with the development of motivational characteristics, presumably contributes to the determination of fantasy response tendencies. It appears, then, that achievement motivation indeed influences fantasy, but that adequate accounting for the empirical evidence requires application of broad principles of fantasy determination as well as motivational theory, and explanation of the relationship between fantasy and motivation in terms of the separate principles governing each.

References

Alpert, R., & Haber, R. N. Anxiety in academic achievement situations. *Journal of Abnormal and Social Psychology*, 1960, **61**, 207-215.

Atkinson, J. W. The achievement motive and recall of interrupted and completed tasks. *Journal of Experimental Psychology*, 1953, **46**, 381-390.

Atkinson, J. W. Explorations using imaginative thought to assess the strength of human motives. In M. R. Jones (Ed.), *Nebraska symposium on motivation: 1954*. Lincoln: University of Nebraska Press, 1954, Pp.56-112.

Atkinson, J. W. Motivational determinations of risk-taking behavior. *Psychological Review*, 1957, **64**, 359-372.

Atkinson, J. W. Personality dynamics. *Annual Review of Psychology*, 1960, **11**, 255-290.

Atkinson, J. W. An introduction to motivation. Princeton, N. J.: Van Nostrand, 1964.

Atkinson, J. W., Bastian, J. R., Earl, R. W., & Litwin, G. The achievement motive, goal setting, and probability preferences. *Journal of Abnormal and Social Psychology*, 1960, **60**, 27-36.

Atkinson, J. W., & Litwin, G. H. Achievement motive and test anxiety conceived as motive to approach success and motive to avoid failure. *Journal of Abnormal and Social Psychology*, 1960, **60**, 52-63.

Atkinson, J. W., & Raphelson, A. C. Individual differences in motivation and behavior in particular situations. *Journal of Personality*, 1956, **24**, 349-363.

Atkinson, J. W., & Reitman, W. R. Performance as a function of motive strength and expectancy of goal attainment. *Journal of Abnormal and Social Psychology*, 1956, **53**, 361-366.

Bandura, A. Behavioral modification through modeling procedures. In L. Krasner & L. P. Ullmann (Eds.), *Research in behavior modification*. New York: Holt, Rinehart & Winston, 1965. Pp. 310-340.

Barnette, W. L., Jr. A structured and a semistructured achievement measure applied to a college sample. *Educational and Psychological Measurement*, 1961, **21**, 647-656.

Bendig, A. W. Predictive and postdictive validity of need achievement scores. *Journal of Educational Research*, 1958, **52**, 119-120.

Bendig, A. W. Comparative validity of objective and projective measures of need achievement in introductory psychology. *Journal of General Psychology*, 1959, **60**, 237-243.

Birney, R. C. The achievement motive and task performance: A replication. *Journal of Abnormal and Social Psychology*, 1958, **56**, 133-135.

Birney, R. C. The reliability of the achievement motive. *Journal of Abnormal and Social Psychology*, 1959, **58**, 266-267.

Block, J. R. Motivation, satisfaction and performance of handicapped workers. Unpublished doctoral dissertation, New York University, 1962.

Brown, J. S. *The motivation of behavior*. New York: McGraw-Hill, 1961.

Burdick, H. A. Need for achievement and schedules of variable reinforcement. *Journal of Abnormal and Social Psychology*, 1964, **68**, 302-306.

Burnstein, E., Stotland, E., & Zander, A. Similarity to a model and self-evaluation. *Journal of Abnormal and Social Psychology*, 1961, **62**, 257-264.

Burris, R. W. The effect of counseling on achievement motivation. Unpublished doctoral dissertation, Indiana University, 1958.

Chahbazi, P. Use of projective tests in predicting college achievement. *Education and Psychological Measurement*, 1956, **16**, 538-542.

Chahbazi, P. Use of projective tests in predicting college achievement. *Educational and Psychological Measurement*, 1960, **20**, 839-842.

Chubb, W., & Barch, A. M. Paired-associate learning and achievement imagery. *Psychological Reports*, 1960, **6**, 30.

Clark, R. A., & McClelland, D. C. A factor analytic integration of imaginative and performance measures of the need for achievement. *Journal of General Psychology*, 1956, **55**, 73-83.

Clark, R. A., Teevan, R., & Ricciuti, H. N. Hope of success and fear of failure as aspects of need for achievement. *Journal of Abnormal and Social Psychology*, 1956, **53**, 182-186.

Cole, D., Jacobs, S., Zubok, B., Fagot, B., & Hunter, I. The relation of achievement imagery scores of academic performance. *Journal of Abnormal and Social Psychology*, 1962, **65**, 208-211.

Cox, F. N. An assessment of the achievement behavior system in children. *Child Development*, 1962, **33**, 907-916.

Crandall, V. J., Katkovsky, W., & Preston, A. Motivational and ability determinants of young children's intellectual achievement behaviors. *Child Development*, 1962, **33**, 643-661.

Crootof, C. Bright underachievers' acceptance of self and their need for achievement. Unpublished doctoral dissertation, New York University, 1963.

Farber, I. E. Comments on Professor Atkinson's

paper. In M. R. Jones (Ed.), *Nebraska symposium on motivation: 1954.* Lincoln: University of Nebraska Press, 1954. Pp. 1-45.

Feather, N. T. The relationship of persistence at a task to expectation of success and achievement related motives. *Journal of Abnormal and Social Psychology*, 1961, **63**, 552-561.

Feld, S. Need achievement and test anxiety in children and maternal attitudes and behaviors toward independent accomplishments: A longitudinal study. Paper read at American Psychological Association, Cincinnati, September 1959.

French, E. G. Some characteristics of achievement motivation. *Journal of Experimental Psychology*, 1955, **50**, 232-236.

French, E. G. Development of a measure of complex motivation. In J. W. Atkinson (Ed.), *Motives in fantasy, action, and society.* Princeton, N. J.: Van Nostrand, 1958. Pp. 242-248. (a)

French, E. G. Effects of the interaction of motivation and feedback on task performance. In J. W. Atkinson (Ed.), *Motives in fantasy, action, and society.* Princeton, N. J.: Van Nostrand, 1958. Pp. 400-408. (b)

French, E. G. The interaction of achievement motivation and ability in problem-solving success. *Journal of Abnormal and Social Psychology*, 1958, **57**, 306-309. (c)

French, E. G., & Lesser, G. S. Some characteristics of the achievement motive in women. *Journal of Abnormal and Social Psychology*, 1964, **68**, 119-128.

French, E. G., & Thomas, F. H. The relation of achievement motivation to problem-solving effectiveness. *Journal of Abnormal and Social Psychology*, 1958, **56**, 45-48.

Haber, R. N. The prediction of achievement behavior by an interaction of achievement motivation and achievement stress. Unpublished doctoral dissertation, Stanford University, 1957.

Hedlund, J. L. Construction and evaluation of an objective test of achievement imagery. Unpublished doctoral dissertation, State University of Iowa, 1953.

Herron, W. Intellectual achievement motivation: A study in construct clarification. Unpublished doctoral dissertation, University of Texas, 1962.

Hills, B. B. The effects of need for achievement, achievement imagery and test anxiety on arithmetic performance. Unpublished doctoral dissertation, State University of Iowa, 1960.

Himelstein, P., Eschenbach, A. E., & Carp, A. Interrelationships among three measures of need achievement. *Journal of Consulting Psychology*, 1958, **22**, 451-452.

Himelstein, P., & Kimbrough, W. W., Jr. Reliability of French's "Test of Insight." *Educational and Psychological Measurement*, 1960, **20**, 737-741.

Hurley, J. R. The Iowa Picture Interpretation Test: A multiple choice variation of the TAT. *Journal of Consulting Psychology*, 1955, **19**, 372-376.

Hurley, J. R. Achievement imagery and motivational instructions as determinants of verbal learning. *Journal of Personality*, 1957, **25**, 274-282.

Isaacson, R. L. Need achievement, need affiliation, anxiety, and performance. Paper read at American Psychological Association, Philadelphia, August 1963.

Johnston, R. A. The effects of achievement imagery on maze-learning performance. *Journal of Personality*, 1955, **23**, 145-152.

Johnston, R. A. A methodological analysis of several revised forms of the Iowa Picture Interpretation Test. *Journal of Personality*, 1957, **25**, 283-293.

Jones, M. R. Introduction. In M. R. Jones (Ed.), *Nebraska symposium on motivation: 1955.* Lincoln: University of Nebraska Press, 1955. Pp. vii-x.

Kagan, J., & Moss, H. Stability and validity of achievement fantasy. *Journal of Abnormal and Social Psychology*, 1959, **58**, 357-364.

Kagan, J., Sontag, L., Baker, C., & Nelson, V. Personality and IQ change. *Journal of Abnormal and Social Psychology*, 1958, **56**, 261-266.

Karolchuck, P., & Worrell, L. Achievement motivation and learning. *Journal of Abnormal and Social Psychology*, 1956, **53**, 255-257.

Klinger, E. Nonmotivational arousal of achievement imagery. Morris: University of Minnesota, Department of Psychology, 1965. (Mimeo)

Krumboltz, J. D., & Farquhar, W. W. Reliability and validity of the n-Achievement Test. *Journal of Consulting Psychology*, 1957, **21**, 226-228.

Lazarus, R. S., Baker, R. W., Broverman, D. M., & Mayer, J. Personality and psychological stress. *Journal of Personality*, 1957, **25**, 559-577.

Lowell, E. L. The effect of need for achievement on learning and speed of performance. *Journal of Psychology*, 1952, **33**, 31-40.

Marlowe, D. Relationships among direct and indirect measures of the achievement motive and overt behavior. *Journal of Consulting Psychology*, 1959, **23**, 329-332.

Mayo, G. D., & Manning, W. Motivation measurement. *Educational and Psychological Measurement*, 1961, **21**, 73-83.

McClelland, D. C. *The achieving society.* Princeton, N. J.: Van Nostrand, 1961.

McClelland, D. C., Atkinson, J. W., Clark, R. A., & Lowell, E. L. *The achievement motive.* New York: Appleton-Century-Crofts, 1953.

McClelland, D. C., Clark, R. A., Roby, T., & Atkinson, J. W. The projective expression of needs: IV. The effect of the need for achievement on thematic apperception. *Journal of Experimental Psychology*, 1949, **39**, 242-255.

McKeachie, W. J. Motivation, teaching methods, and college learning. In M. R. Jones (Ed.), *Nebraska symposium on motivation: 1961.* Lincoln: University of Nebraska Press, 1961. Pp. 111-142.

Miles, G. Achievement drive and habitual modes of task approach as factors in skill transfer. *Journal of Experimental Psychology*, 1958, **55**, 156-162.

Miller, K. S., & Worchel, P. The effects of need-achievement and self-ideal discrepancy on performance under stress. *Journal of Personality*, 1956, **25**, 176-190.

Mitchell, J. V., Jr. An analysis of the factorial dimensions of the achievement motivation construct. *Journal of Educational Psychology*, 1961, **52**, 179-187.

Morgan, H. H. A psychometric comparison of achieving and nonachieving college students of high ability. *Journal of Consulting Psychology*, 1952, **16**, 292-298.

Morgan, H. H. Measuring achievement motivation with "picture motivations." *Journal of Consulting Psychology*, 1953, **17**, 289-292.

Moss, H. A., & Kagan, J. Stability of achievement and recognition seeking behaviors from early childhood through adulthood. *Journal of Abnormal and Social Psychology*, 1961, **62**, 504-513.

Murstein, B. I. The relationship of expectancy of reward to achievement performance on an arithmetic and thematic test. *Journal of Consulting Psychology*, 1963, **27**, 394-399.

Murstein, B. I., & Collier, H. L. The role of the TAT in the measurement of achievement as a function of expectancy. *Journal of Projective Techniques and Personality Assessment*, 1962, **26**, 96-101.

Muthayya, B. C. Frustration-reaction and achievement motive of high achievers and low achievers in the scholastic field. *Psychological Studies*, 1964, **9**, 21-25.

Parrish, J., & Rethlingshafer, D. A study of need to achieve in college achievers and non-achievers. *Journal of General Psychology*, 1954, **50**, 209-226.

Peak, H. The effect of aroused motivation on attitudes. *Journal of Abnormal and Social Psychology*, 1960, **61**, 463-468.

Postman, L. J. The experimental analysis of motivational factors in perception. In, *Current theory and research in motivation: A symposium.* Lincoln: University of Nebraska Press, 1953. Pp. 59-108.

Postman, L., & Crutchfield, R. S. The interaction of need, set, and stimulus structure in a cognitive task. *American Journal of Psychology*, 1952, **65**, 196-217.

Pottharst, B. S. The achievement motive and level of aspiration after experimentally induced success and failure. Unpublished doctoral dissertation, University of Michigan, 1956.

Reiter, H. H. Prediction of college success from measures of anxiety, achievement motivation, and scholastic aptitude. *Psychological Reports*, 1964, **15**, 23-26.

Reitman, E. E., & Williams, C. D. Relationships between hope of success and fear of failure, anxiety, and need for achievement. *Journal of Abnormal and Social Psychology*, 1961, **62**, 465-467.

Reitman, W. R. Motivational induction and the behavior correlates of the achievement and affiliation motives. *Journal of Abnormal and Social Psychology*, 1960, **60**, 8-13.

Reitman, W. R., & Atkinson, J. W. Some methodological problems in the use of thematic apperception measures of human motives. In J. W. Atkinson (Ed.), *Motives in fantasy, action, and society.* Princeton, N. J.: Van Nostrand, 1958. Pp. 664-683.

Ricciuti, H. N. *The prediction of academic grades with a projective test of achievement motivation: I. Initial validation studies.* Princeton, N. J.: Educational Testing Service, 1954.

Ricciuti, H. N., & Sadacca, R. The prediction of academic grade with a projective test of achievement motivation: II. Cross-validation at the high school level. Technical report, 1955, Naval Research Contract Nonr-694 (00), Project design NR 151-113.

Ritchie, B. F. Comments on Professor Atkinson's paper. In M. R. Jones (Ed.), *Nebraska symposium on motivation: 1954.* Lincoln: University of Nebraska Press, 1954. Pp. 121-176.

Rosen, B. C. The achievement syndrome. *American Sociological Review*, 1955, **21**, 203-211.

Rosenthal, R. On the social psychology of the psychological experiment. *American Scientist*, 1963, **51**, 268-283.

Rosenthal, R., Persinger, G. W., Kline, L. V., & Mulry, R. C. The role of the research assistant in the mediation of experimenter bias. *Journal of Personality*, 1963, **31**, 313-335.

Sadacca, R., Ricciuti, H. N., & Swanson, E. O. *Content analysis of achievement motivation protocols: A study of scorer agreement.* Princeton, N. J.: Educational Testing Service, 1956.

Sampson, E. E. Achievement in conflict. *Journal of Personality*, 1963, **31**, 510-516.

Shaw, M. C. Need achievement scales as predictors of academic success. *Journal of Educational Psychology*, 1961, **52**, 282-285.

Smith, C. P. Situational determinants of the expression of achievement motivation in thematic apperception. Unpublished doctoral dissertation, University of Michigan, 1961.

Stotland, E., & Cottrell, N. B. Similarity of performance as influenced by interaction, self-esteem, and birth order. *Journal of Abnormal and Social Psychology*, 1962, **64**, 183-191.

Stotland, E., & Patchen, M. Identification and changes in prejudice and in authoritarianism. *Journal of Abnormal and Social Psychology*, 1961, **62**, 265-274.

Stotland, E., Zander, A., & Natsoulas, T. Generalization of interpersonal similarity. *Journal of Abnormal and Social Psychology*, 1961, **62**, 250-256.

Sundheim, B. J. The relationships among "n" achievement, "n" affiliation, sex-role concepts, academic grades, and curricular choice. Unpublished doctoral dissertation, Columbia University, 1962.

Tedeschi, J. T., & Kian, M. Cross-cultural study of the TAT assessment for achievement motivation: Americans and Persians. *Journal of Social Psychology*, 1962, **58**, 227-234.

Vogel, W., Baker, R. W., & Lazarus, R. S. The role of motivation in psychological stress. *Journal of Abnormal and Social Psychology*, 1958, **56**, 105-111.

Wendt, H. W. Motivation, effort, and performance. In D. C. McClelland (Ed.), *Studies in motivation*. New York: Appleton-Century-Crofts, 1955. Pp. 448-459.

Williams, J. E. Mode of failure, interference tendencies, and achievement imagery. *Journal of Abnormal and Social Psychology*, 1955, **51**, 573-580.

Wrightsman, L. S., Jr. The effects of anxiety, achievement motivation, and task importance upon performance on an intelligence test. *Journal of Educational Psychology*, 1962, **53**, 150-156.

Yeager, M. Behavioral correlates of achievement need and achievement value. Unpublished doctoral dissertation, University of Houston, 1957.

Author Index

Subject Index